John L. Puckett and Mark Frazier Lloyd

Becoming **Penn** *The Pragmatic American University, 1950–2000*

PENN

UNIVERSITY OF PENNSYLVANIA PRESS

Philadelphia

Published by
University of Pennsylvania Press
Philadelphia, Pennsylvania 19104-4112
www.upenn.edu/pennpress

Printed in the United States of America on acid-free paper
10 9 8 7 6 5 4 3 2 1

Library of Congress Cataloging-in-Publication Data
Puckett, John L., author.
    Becoming Penn : the pragmatic American university, 1950–2000 /
John L. Puckett and Mark Frazier Lloyd.—1st edition.
        pages cm
    Includes bibliographical references and index.
    ISBN 978-0-8122-4680-3 (hardcover : alk. paper)
  1. University of Pennsylvania—History—20th century.   2. Community
and college—Pennsylvania—Philadelphia—History—20th century.
3. Urban renewal—Pennsylvania—Philadelphia—History—20th century.
I. Lloyd, Mark Frazier, author.   II. Title.
    LD4530.P83 2015
    378.748'11—dc23
                                                    2014040327

Dedicated to the memory of

Lee Benson (1922–2012)

A brave companion

Contents

Preface

Our book stands on the shoulders of Roy Franklin Nichols and Jeannette Paddock Nichols, husband and wife—and distinguished members of the University of Pennsylvania's Department of History—who, in the 1960s, set out to write a social and institutional history of the University. Their book would take as its starting point Edward Potts Cheyney's magisterial *History of the University of Pennsylvania, 1740–1940* (University of Pennsylvania Press, 1940). Recognizing the magnitude of the changes they had witnessed since their arrival at Penn in 1925, the Nicholses planned to cover the three decades between 1940 and 1970. Surveying his more than forty years' experience as a Penn faculty member, Roy Nichols wrote in 1968, "A university amorphous and slow-paced, where so little seemed to happen, had achieved a new vision of itself and created a new image. Strength, vitality, and enterprise were transforming characteristics. These experiences I shared as I had participated in them."[1]

Lacking access to the archival records for the University presidencies of Thomas Sovereign Gates, George W. McClelland, Harold Stassen, and Gaylord P. Harnwell, the couple decided to base their study on oral history interviews they would conduct themselves. Unfortunately, Roy, a Pulitzer Prize-winning historian, a major doyen of the Social Science Research Council and the American Historical Association, and an internationally famous scholar, died in 1973, leaving his undaunted spouse to soldier on with the project. Though Jeannette, who died in 1978, never completed the book or even a manuscript fragment, she left behind some one hundred transcribed interviews for future researchers to mine. A knowledgeable, astute, and sometimes cantankerous observer of University affairs in the postwar era, Jeannette constructed her interviews as colloquies with her informants and felicitously intruded her own informed perspectives into the archival record.

Cheyney's history had no follow-up until 1978, when Penn's president, Martin Meyerson, and Dilys Pegler Winegrad published *Gladly Learn and Gladly Teach: Franklin and His Heirs at the University of Pennsylvania, 1740–1976* (University of Pennsylvania Press, 1978). Their book is arranged chronologically in chapters that are minibiographies of eminent Penn scholars of different eras in the physical and life sciences, law, medicine, anthropology, history, engineering, and architecture. Roy Nichols was one of the stalwarts portrayed by Meyerson and Winegrad. This book is a celebration of the University, written for the nation's bicentennial, though published belatedly.

The next institutional history to appear was George Thomas and David Brownlee's treatise, *Building America's First University: An Historical and Architectural Guide to the University of Pennsylvania* (University of Pennsylvania Press, 2000). Featuring a raft of elegant photographs and precise architectural descriptions, their book sketches the physical development of three Penn campuses since 1751, with a central focus on Penn in West Philadelphia since 1872, and showcases the academic precincts of the modern campus.

Published histories of Penn's schools, the best of which is Steven A. Sass's *The Pragmatic Imagination: A History of the Wharton School, 1881–1981* (University of Pennsylvania Press, 1981), and published memoirs, for example, Judith Rodin's *The University and Urban Revival: Out of the Ivory Tower and into the Streets* (University of Pennsylvania Press, 2007), round out the University's historiography, though leaving appreciable gaps, especially in the formative decades of Penn's modern era. In the spring of 2005, we decided, with more than a grain of modesty, to undertake the kind of history we believed that Roy and Jeannette Nichols would have written had they had but world enough and time. Accordingly, we envisioned a spirited historical account—a study that would be neither hagiographic nor polemical, but rather appropriately critical and balanced in the sense that we would weigh multiple perspectives before forming an interpretation of a key decision, main event, turning point, or, for that matter, a University president and his or her administration. As our primary interest was the development and functioning of the modern campus, we decided to center our research on the second half of the twentieth century, when Penn became one of the world's truly great universities. The question that intrigued us more than any other was how Penn had managed to build and sustain a beautifully landscaped, contiguous, park-like pedestrian enclave in the midst of a poor, deteriorating, and—after the 1950s—increasingly crime-ridden and turbulent urban district. We would keep this question in full view throughout the eight years of research and writing that brought this book to fruition.

■

John Puckett came to this study following a circuitous route. With a background in rural education and economic development in the South, he arrived at Penn in the fall of 1987 as an assistant professor of education. His research interest was the relationship of schools and communities, including the role of community studies in curriculum development. In the fall of 1988, Puckett affiliated himself with two Penn history professors, Lee Benson and Ira Harkavy, social activists who believed that the West Philadelphia public schools were the strategic key to improving the quality of life in the disadvantaged neighborhoods that bordered University City, which was home to Penn, Drexel University, the University City Science Center, two major hospitals, and several strong neighborhood associations. Over the next decade, their concept of academically based community service would slowly take root in the classrooms of the University and the West Philadelphia schools, with undergraduate and graduate students working with schoolteachers and their students to try to solve myriad local problems and issues, some of which are described in this book.

For ten years, Puckett and his wife, Karin Schaller, lived on the tenth floor of an art deco apartment building at 47th and Pine streets, with a view, two blocks north from their living room, to the castle of West Philadelphia High School, a structure that had opened on Walnut Street in 1912 as one of the nation's premier high schools. By the spring of 1988, when Puckett first visited this once elegant Tudor Gothic building—a relic of an era when cities took enormous pride in their school buildings; a structure replete with crenellated towers, Vermont-marble staircases, and two auditoriums with fifty-foot-high ceilings, classical statuary, and, in one auditorium, a Curtis organ (once one of the world's great organs)—the building was in a state of disrepair, the organ, as well as the school's clocks, long since dysfunctional. Seeing broken windows in classrooms on the lower floors, Puckett was struck by the disparity of the deteriorating condition of this once-great American high school and the $1 billion capital campaign under way at the University of Pennsylvania, just seven blocks to the east of the high school.

Over the next decade, with the help of Benson, Harkavy, and other faculty colleagues, he organized academically based community service courses at the Graduate School of Education—and, in the mid-1990s, in the Department of History. From 1989 to 1993, Puckett and a group of energetic teachers built a grant-funded computer lab/publication center and created the West Philadelphia High School Student Research Apprenticeship Program. In this academic-credit program, students published their community studies as a school and neighborhood newsletter—and laid the foundation for a community newspaper that the school's English Department organized after Puckett moved on to other projects, one of which was helping to build the University of Pennsylvania's Center for Community Partnerships (CCP, today's Netter Center), established by President Sheldon Hackney in 1992.

Puckett met Mark Lloyd in the summer of 1988, when he first visited the University Archives, which, at the time, was located under the weight room at Franklin Field. Curious about the state of Penn's community relations, Puckett spent several weeks that summer in the archives, reading back issues of the Penn student newspaper. He returned to the archives several years later to read about the 1969 College Hall sit-in and its impact in West Philadelphia. After this, he was diverted by other projects, not the least of which was a decadelong study of the 120-year history of the uses of public schools as social centers, community centers, and community schools. From 1989, the CCP's governing approach was "university-assisted community schools"— the idea that schools, supported by universities, can be effective centers and catalysts for educational, recreational, cultural, and health and social services for all members of their constituent communities, as well as for community organizing and community development; two books that Puckett coauthored located Penn's strategy in the context of the wider history of America's community schools.

As these books slowly wended their way to publication, Puckett realized that what he had been groping toward for some twenty years was a complete contextual framing of the work of the CCP/Netter Center and the University's social responsibility. He recognized that the next logical piece— perhaps the key element—of this framing, the one that now fully galvanized his interest, was the University context of this work. In the spring of 2005, he returned to the University Archives to discuss this project with Mark Lloyd.

Educated at the University of Chicago and trained as an American historian, Lloyd had been director of archives at Penn since 1984. At the outset of his employment, he was encouraged and supported by faculty in the Department of History, including Richard Dunn, Drew Faust (at this writing, the president of Harvard), Walter Licht, Bruce Kuplick, Robert Engs, and Michael Zuckerman. For a decade or more, his interests centered on the University Archive collections associated with early American history, and he partnered with Dunn, an expert in that field, on various history projects. Over time, Lloyd came to realize that the richest collections entrusted to his care were those dealing with the twentieth century. By the 2000s, his focus had begun to shift to contemporary American history. In 2005, he met Lee Benson, who, with Ira Harkavy, persuaded him to teach an undergraduate seminar entitled Penn and West Philadelphia: From Indifference to Conflict, to Reconciliation, 1870 to the Present. Joining Lloyd as coteachers in the seminar were professors Engs and Licht, who also partnered with him on the development and maintenance of the West Philadelphia Community History Center, an online virtual history museum, which debuted in the spring of 2008. By then, Puckett and Lloyd's research interests were fully aligned and the ideas for the book fully formed.

■

A plentitude of primary sources were available for our study. The University of Pennsylvania Archives and Records Center (UARC), the major repository for Penn's history, contains the administrative, professional, and personal papers of four of Penn's postwar presidents: Harold Stassen, Gaylord P. Harnwell, Martin Meyerson, and Sheldon Hackney. In accordance with the University's standing archival policy—the Protocols for the University Archives and Records Center—the first three collections are fully open to researchers, as are the papers of the first half of the Hackney administration. Also fully available to researchers are the abundant interview transcriptions for the University History Project, which the Nicholses inaugurated forty years ago. Sheldon Hackney generously gave us special access to his personal papers and journals, giving us his vantage point in situ on a tumultuous decade at Penn.

The "twenty-five-year closure rule" imposed by the Protocols keeps the Rodin-era archives unavailable until 2019 and not fully available until 2029. We have perforce relied primarily on published sources for Rodin's presidency: the weekly *Almanac*, Penn's in-house administrative journal; the *Pennsylvania Gazette*, the University's candidly written and vastly informative alumni magazine; and the *Daily Pennsylvanian*, the University's student newspaper, whose reporters and editors followed campus events and controversies with the tenacity of Jack Russell terriers. We also draw on the resources of the Faculty Senate University Governance Oral History Project, our own interviews and conversations with key informants, and assorted documents provided by these individuals.

Other important archival materials are available online. The UARC website hosts a collection of several thousand photographs of Penn at various stages of growth in West Philadelphia. Under the label *Mapping Penn: Land Acquisitions, 1870–2007*, the website also features Geographic Information Systems (GIS) property maps for every parcel, building, and street in Penn's real estate portfolio since 1870, including the property-transfer information on each holding. This extraordinary digitized resource allowed us to circumvent the cumbersome toil of deed searches and, most important, to view, in overlay form, the original parcels and streets on which contemporary buildings stand. The previously mentioned UARC-supported West Philadelphia Community History Center, an online archive of historic maps, papers, and photographs maintained by Penn undergraduates, includes digitized versions of the Bromley *Atlas of West Philadelphia* for 1916 and 1927. UARC's valuable library collection includes Penn's annual reports (including the *Financial Report*), *Minutes of the Trustees*, the *Almanac*, the *Pennsylvania Gazette*, the *Daily Pennsylvanian* (microform), *Benjamin Franklin's Record* (student yearbook), Penn's general institutional and professional-school histories, histories of Philadelphia, and numerous other relevant volumes. Another valuable repository is the Fisher Fine Arts Library, whose city and regional planning collections include publications of the Philadelphia City Planning Commission, annual reports of the City of Philadelphia Redevelopment Authority, and sundry urban renewal documents.

Two other repositories were indispensable. The Philadelphia City Archives houses papers of the City Planning Commission, and the City Archives' website, Phillyhistory.com, contains scores of high-quality photographs of Penn and West Philadelphia in various stages of development after 1950. Urban Archives, at Temple University's Special Collections Research Center, holds the papers of the West Philadelphia Corporation and the indexed clippings and photographs of the *Philadelphia Evening Bulletin*, from 1847 to 1982, a treasure trove for researchers interested in Philadelphia history.

U.S. Census data were vital to our study, affording a portrait of social and economic conditions in West Philadelphia's neighborhoods across the twentieth century. Two years into our research, we discovered Social Explorer.com, a remarkable website that provides digitized census-tract maps, full data compilations, and spreadsheet sorting of key social and economic indicators for every census tract since 1940. Social Explorer does not report census block data; where traditional neighborhood boundaries and census tracts in our study did not coincide, we consulted the census-block hard-copy volumes in the U.S. Census of Housing. For Philadelphia Redevelopment Authority planning units in the 1960s and 1970s, which overlapped census tracts, we conducted manual block-by-block analyses.

Introduction

In the second half of the twentieth century, the University of Pennsylvania became one of the world's most celebrated research universities. This book views Penn's rise to eminence in the multiple historical, social, institutional, moral, and aesthetic contexts that shaped it and, in one form or another, other American research universities in the decades after World War II. Urban renewal in American higher education is a leitmotif of our study—Penn illustrates the role of urban renewal in the postwar redevelopment and expansion of urban universities and the indispensable role these institutions played in the remaking of postwar American cities. We are also interested in student life, campus politics, and faculty affairs—and the social forces and contexts that impinged on these aspects of university life. Born of tensions in the larger society in the long aftermath of the U.S. civil rights movement, racial, ethnic, and gender conflict roiled the campus for a quarter of a century. Penn was by no means exceptional in this regard; contested issues of diversity were problematic for all major public and private universities after the 1960s. The impacts of periodic economic retrenchments, campus labor conflicts, and, more recently, corporatization, are also part of this shared history. Though the particulars vary, controversial issues that spurred student activism and protest at Penn appeared at roughly the same time on other campuses, as they were broadcast by national media, student information networks, and national activist organizations. In this respect, our book limns the broader social history of American higher education since World War II.

Becoming Penn is organized chronologically in four parts, with chapters arranged by topics. We trace the University's development under its four major presidents since World War II: Gaylord Harnwell (1953–70), Martin Meyerson (1970–81), Sheldon Hackney (1981–93), and Judith Rodin (1994–2004). We also include, though briefly, an account of Harold Stassen's presidency (1948–52), and Claire Fagin's one-year interim presidency (1993–94). We are mindful that Penn's present stature as a great American university did not happen on one president's watch. The hallmarks of a great research university evolved over the second half of the last century, with each president building on an inherited foundation, leaving intact, modifying, or, in some cases, transforming an existing component of campus structure, operations, or affairs. Rarely was a major idea, strategic plan, or institutional innovation developed sui generis or out of whole cloth.

The true starting point of this book is the campus master plan proposed in 1948 by the Penn trustees' Committee for the Physical Development of the Campus. Chaired by Sydney Martin, a prominent Philadelphia architect for whom the plan was named, the trustees' committee envisioned street closings, new arterial lines for foot traffic, and strategic landscaping to transform the historic core of the campus into a leafy pedestrian enclave. What the Martin Plan did not, and could not, recognize in 1948 was the sheer volume and complexity of changes that were about to be unleashed by the combined social forces of demography (the postwar baby boom), the Cold War (the burgeoning postwar federal research apparatus), and urban renewal (a federally sponsored change engine). "The plan provides for more open space surrounding the various buildings than exists at the present time," Martin's committee wrote. "In this respect we have gone the limit towards what we believe is possible to achieve with an urban college. It offers much flexibility and room for expansion without upsetting the basic elements."[1]

Penn would far surpass that limit, in large part because its presidents responded with alacrity to the postwar embarrassment of riches the federal government pipelined to research universities and cities.

In the 1950s Penn entered an intense competition for wealth, power, and prestige that the nation's research universities waged aggressively among themselves amid the coalescing social forces we have just mentioned. Whereas before the war Penn was content to rest on its laurels as a "top-twenty" university—and a regional one at that—after the war, with each successive presidency, it aspired more and more to be recognized as a truly great university, a "top-ten"-caliber institution recognized on both a national and international scale—a goal the University would finally realize at the turn of the twenty-first century. Modest by comparison with what came after the 1950s, the original Martin Plan was modified and rolled into far more ambitious and evolving campus development plans that charted Penn's ascent over the course of the past half century into the pantheon of world-class universities.

The University's history in West Philadelphia prior to 1948, when the Martin Plan was released, is not inconsequential for this book. Trends and developments from 1872, when Penn arrived in West Philadelphia, to World War

II form a critical historical backdrop for our study. In the following sections, we limn this framework, giving particular attention to the main decisions, actions, and turning points in this earlier span of time that are touchstones for the post–World War II history we take up as the book's central focus.

■

Penn's founding dates to 1749, when Benjamin Franklin and his associates in Philadelphia organized an academy that became a Colonial college in 1755 and America's first university in 1765. Spanning the Colonial, Revolutionary, Early Republic, National, Civil War, and Postbellum periods, the first half of Penn's 275-year history took place in central-city Philadelphia, within walking distance of the Delaware River. In 1872, to escape the industrial city and a "vile neighborhood, growing viler every day,"[2] the University moved its small campus from 9th and Chestnut streets across the Schuylkill River to 34th and Walnut streets in the district of West Philadelphia, a partially settled, "emerging" suburb of large estates and undeveloped crabgrass tracts, ornate mansions, villas and cottages, middle-class twins and working-class row houses.[3]

"Upon coming to West Philadelphia," remarked Penn's first campus planner, the celebrated Beaux-Arts architect Paul Philippe Cret, "the University entered a semi-rural region traversed by quiet streets and country roads, reached by two car lines of slow-moving horse cars and ideally situated for a community requiring academic quiet and comparative isolation." In 1913, when Cret penned this description, West Philadelphia was no longer a pastoral suburb, but rather "a closely built city," congested with heavy street traffic and "numberless factories," all interfacing with and disrupting the University.[4] The buffering of Penn from the encroachments of the city, the creation of a pedestrian-oriented, residential campus, and the expansion necessary to build a truly great university were not feasible, however, until after World War II, when Penn's leaders gained access to an extraordinary trove of political and capital resources from the federal government, the Commonwealth of Pennsylvania, and the City of Philadelphia.

From the Colonial period to 1930, the University's chief administrative officer was the provost, a title "derived from the traditional title of the heads of certain Colleges at Oxford." Like their Old World predecessors, Penn's provosts, until 1866, were clergymen. Historically the Penn trustees were a parochial body of Episcopalians selected from the city's *Social Register*. As the trustees governed "by committee" rather than centralizing authority, the provost lacked executive authority. Such campus-wide powers as the provost was able to exercise had to be arrogated to his office "through the force of his personality and dedication to his job."[5] As a consequence of this "stultifying committee system of the trustees," Penn was "the only institution of higher learning in America to have had a provost rather than a president at its head throughout most of its long history."[6] Though constrained by their lack of executive authority, three forceful and dedicated provosts of the late nineteenth century moved Penn decisively in the direction of a chief executive officer.

The first of these transformational leaders was Charles Janeway Stillé, who oversaw the relocation of the campus from 9th and Chestnut streets to West Philadelphia. Once the decision was made in the late 1860s to leave the central city, the Penn trustees signed an agreement to sell the 9th Street campus to the federal government at a premium.[7] Then, in 1870, they purchased ten acres in West Philadelphia from the grounds of the Blockley Almshouse, the city's poorhouse, which included, among other buildings, an indigent hospital and an insane department.[8] By selling high in the central city and buying low in West Philadelphia, the trustees netted a tidy profit of more than $400,000, a huge sum at the time, for the new campus. By the end of the 1870s, Stillé had placed four buildings designed by Thomas W. Richards on the almshouse tract—neo-Gothic edifices of green serpentine stone: College Hall (arts and sciences, 1872), Logan Hall (The Medical School, 1874), the Hospital of the University of Pennsylvania (the nation's first university-owned teaching hospital, 1874), and Hare Hall (medical laboratories, 1878). "This began the process by which the University has added 'house to house and field to field,'" Edward Potts Cheyney said in 1940, "nibbling the old almshouse tract and adjoining property, obtaining possession of it on every variety of consideration, till it has now more than a hundred acres, for the most part covered with buildings for purposes not conceived of in 1870."[9]

By the mid-1890s, twenty-five buildings stood on Penn's campus of fifty-two acres. Stillé's successor, Dr. William Pepper, provost from 1881 to 1894, spearheaded this growth. "He found the University a respectable school," Pepper's biographer wrote in 1904. "He transformed it into a real University—created thirteen departments [including the Wharton School of Finance and Economy], erected twenty costly and appropriate buildings for its use, increased the Faculty from a corps of ninety to one of nearly three hundred, and the attendance from eight hundred to above twenty-eight hundred. For the endowment and use of the institution he raised over four million dollars, and added more than forty acres in the heart of the city to its campus."[10] These forty acres were gifted by the city as a quid pro quo for the University's pledge to award fifty full-tuition scholarships in perpetuity to male graduates of the city's public high schools.[11] Himself "a wealthy and well-connected Philadelphian," Pepper was able to tap the wealth of the city's industrial elites, "Proper Philadelphians," and to "[make] support of the University fashionable."[12]

Pepper's hard-driving successor, Charles Custis Harrison, provost from 1894 to 1910 and the second captain of Penn's pre–World War I expansion, oversaw the building at Penn of the modern undergraduate experience. In 1896, he simultaneously constructed Houston Hall, the nation's first student union; twenty-eight houses of "The Quad," the magnificent College Gothic residence halls designed by the celebrated architectural firm of Cope and Stewardson; and Franklin Field, one of the nation's first great arenas for intercollegiate athletics. Harrison also significantly expanded the physical plant for professional education—law, medicine, engineering, and veterinary medicine. Rounding out Harrison's expansion program was the University Museum and the acquisition of sixty more acres of almshouse property from the city, in exchange for an additional seventy-five full-tuition scholarships.[13]

Yet for all the construction, there was no campus plan, no overarching design, no grouping of buildings according to academic purpose. In 1913 the architects' committee of the board of trustees, chaired by Paul Phillipe Cret, complained vigorously that new buildings were being sited haphazardly. "Upon one very serious aspect of present conditions we would lay especial stress, namely, the total disorganization—or lack of organism [*sic*]—of the University's physical growth," the Cret committee declared. "Growth has proceeded without plan and through mere accretion, advancing step by step through marginal enlargements, into an ever-increasing confusion." The upshot was "a vast agglomeration of buildings, without organic arrangement," forestalling the "possibility of proper expansion of departments or of the introduction of new cognate departments in proper relation thereto, unity of architectural character and other advantages of a properly organized plan."[14]

By 1913, University buildings and campus facilities extended south of Woodland Avenue from the west bank of the Schuylkill River to beyond 38th Street. Penn's holdings also included swaths of undeveloped land between the old almshouse, later renamed the Philadelphia General Hospital, and the riverfront. In the future, Penn's academic buildings would be located in precincts designated by disciplinary function or affinity. Some of this limning was under way by 1913: several disciplines—the physical sciences, the medical and biological sciences, law, and veterinary medicine—already had their precincts.[15] The delineation of humanities and social science precincts—the former in the historic campus core, whose preeminent building was College Hall, the latter between Walnut and Spruce from 37th to 38th streets—would have to await the planning frenzy of Penn's Great Expansion after World War II.

Penn's first West Philadelphia expansion, 1881–1910, was emblematic of the competition for wealth, power, and prestige among the elite universities that contemporary historians recognize as the bellwethers of the modern research university. The "imperative to grow large" was a "crucial element" in their institutional behavior.[16] Penn rose from relative obscurity as "a small local institution, with no national reputation throughout most of the nineteenth century," to become "a nationally recognized institution" before World War I.[17]

By 1910 the "university idea" was blooming; Penn was a rising research institution. On several indicators, including founding membership in the prestigious Association of American Universities, production of scholarly publications, and recruitment of eminent scientists, Penn was listed near, if not within, the top tier of American universities.[18] The University merited a chapter in Edwin Slosson's 1910 survey of fourteen "great American universities." Slossen wrote glowingly that "no other university of these fourteen has so many handsome buildings as Pennsylvania. I do not know that all of the rest of them put together can match them." Of the Veterinary Building, he said, "no other comes into consideration. The University of Pennsylvania has better accommodations for its pigs than most universities have for their presidents." The University Museum, he declaimed, rivaled "in some respects" the Louvre and the British Museum.[19]

Penn's Great Expansion in the 1950s and 1960s would ensure that the University, on the basis of periodic national surveys and rankings, would remain near though not in the top tier—the so-called top ten—of American universities. With the advent of *U.S. News and World Report* rankings in the mid-1980s, Penn would push to be recognized as a truly great university, a permanent member of the elite ten. This lofty status, the pitfalls of *U.S News* rankings notwithstanding, would be achieved by President Judith Rodin.

■

Emblematic of the Pepper-Harrison era was the rise of the Wharton School as "a genuine seat of learning and free research in all the social disciplines."[20] The early Wharton School was notably a center of reformist social science. The Industrial Age ironmaster Joseph Wharton bestowed his name to the School of Finance and Economy he endowed in the College in 1881. Committed to the proposition that "research and teaching could benefit from political activity," the economist Edmund James, who headed the Wharton School from 1886 to 1895, transformed Joseph Wharton's benefaction, in ways Wharton had not intended, into "a unique organizational innovation—a school devoted to providing a social scientific response to the problems of industrialization."[21]

James's own social scientific investigations reflected "his commitment to policy-oriented research and research-based reform." In 1886, he presented a seventy-six-page report to the Philadelphia Social Science Association entitled *The Relation of the Modern Municipality to the Gas Supply, with Special Reference to the Gas Question in Philadelphia*. This widely acclaimed report gave James's colleagues in Philadelphia's good government movement the case they needed to force the city to quit its custom of leasing the municipal gas works to private operators—the notorious "Gas Ring." James also introduced courses on municipal government into the Wharton curriculum. In 1893, Wharton undergraduates compiled scholarly research on the city's administrative departments for their baccalaureate theses and then published their findings in a collection of essays called *The City Government of Philadelphia*.[22]

A scholar qua activist and organizing dervish, James was instrumental in putting together Progressive Era reform coalitions such as the Municipal Reform League of Philadelphia and the National Municipal League. Perhaps his most enduring contribution was founding the American Academy of Political and Social Science, the *Annals* of which are still published by the University. Though supported by Joseph Wharton and (now trustee) William Pepper, James drew the ire of Provost Charles Harrison. Resentful of "the independent authority and the huge salary of six thousand dollars that James had extracted from Pepper," Harrison, on his first day as provost, forced James, a future president of both Northwestern University and the University of Illinois, to resign his professorship.[23]

James's successor at the Wharton School was Simon Nelson Patten, hailed by Wharton chronicler Steven Sass as "perhaps the greatest mind in the history of the institution." Continuing James's strong urban emphasis and commitment to "social regeneration," Patten and his faculty protégés introduced a program of "practical," reformist sociology and established the first university school of "social work" (a term Patten is credited with having coined) in the United States. Wharton School professors and graduate students, the latter called "Patten's men," investigated such controversial public issues as rate gouging in utility and transit companies, child labor in the coal and textile industries, and inefficiency in the food distribution system.[24] They were, in Patten's view, "on the firing line of civilization."[25]

Patten and the Wharton School showed that being actively engaged in public affairs could contribute to significant academic success. It was Patten's Wharton School that published W. E. B. DuBois's monumental sociological survey *The Philadelphia Negro*, though not without a great deal of retrospective complaint from DuBois and historians regarding how the University had treated him.[26] But the window of reform opened by the Progressive zeitgeist was about to close. While "Wharton's aggressive program of reform was intellectually exciting," it was also "politically dangerous, exposing the school to the rapidly shifting tides of power in 'progressive' America. The campaign for social regeneration isolated the school from its traditional supporters and alienated it from rising interests. The faculty found itself increasingly vulnerable to external pressures."[27] More and more, Patten and his colleagues raised the hackles of University trustees who had vested interests in unregulated industry and municipal corruption.[28] The New Deal economist and Brain Trust planner Rexford Tugwell, a 1916 Wharton graduate, recalled in his 1982 autobiography that it was "essentially a conservative, even a reactionary, environment in spite of some liberalism among my instructors."[29]

Turning to new sources of income after Harrison retired in 1911, the trustees added to their number "businessmen with lucrative interests in utility companies and upstate coal fields and Republican politicians with access to the state treasury." And they appointed Edgar Fahs Smith, a chemistry professor with strong ties to those same politicians, as Harrison's successor. Smith reportedly accosted several Wharton teachers with the following interrogatory: "Gentlemen, what business have academic people to be meddling in political questions? Suppose, for illustration, that I, as a chemist, should discover that some big slaughtering company was putting formalin in its sausage; now surely that would be none of my business."[30]

This attack on Wharton's progressives came when they were allied with the independent, progressive mayor Rudolph Blankenburg (1912–16). In one of his classes, Patten's protégé Scott Nearing, a vigorous opponent of child labor, ridiculed Edward Townsend Stotesbury, a partner of J. P. Morgan and a Penn trustee, whose stepson happened to be in the class. That may have been the last straw for the trustees, who had many reasons to be rid of Nearing, not least among them the threat he posed to the upstate coal interests that held the purse strings on the University's appropriation in the state legislature. (Penn, a private institution, received some state funds for its School of Education.) Nearing was fired without a hearing in the spring of 1915. And to expunge fully the Wharton apostasy, the trustees, in 1916, denied Patten the University's traditional courtesy of extending a professor's contract beyond the retirement age. Steven Sass, in his astute account of the Wharton School's first century, provides a searing epitaph for these shenanigans: "In the aftermath of the Nearing affair and the disgrace of Patten, a stench lay over the university. The scandal prevented the Wharton School from attracting any first-rate, critical mind to replace Patten, and it raised serious questions about the future of the institution. In 1917, the school lost its intellectual, a man who lived for ideas. Thereafter, it had to make do with professionals who lived off ideas."[31]

By World War I, the urban reformist spirit of the early Wharton School had disappeared at Penn, the faculty's moral-preceptor role vanquished by the priority American research universities assigned, conservatively, to the pursuit of "value-free," objective knowledge; the student-citizen's role displaced by the "collegiate way": the pleasures of dormitory life, fraternities, and self-referential social activities; prideful denigration of scholarship and one's professors; and often delinquent, sometimes deadly, campus rituals.[32] Self-identifying as "scientific" researchers, professors started to downgrade teaching in the undergraduate college. "Faculty in the natural and social sciences tried to establish their primary position in the university as researchers rather than undergraduate teachers," writes the historian Julie Reuben. "Scientists wanted universities to dedicate more facilities and resources to research, to free a larger portion of the faculty's time for research, to specify research as the prime criterion for appointment and promotion, and to create special research professorships and institutes devoted to particular scientific problems."[33]

Changing demographics and widened working-class access to the American high school played favorably to these aspirations. Between 1889–90 and 1919–20, total high school enrollments for the 14–17 age group increased from 5,355,000 to 7,736,000—a gain of 44 percent; in the same thirty-year period, the percentage of high school graduates aged seventeen rose from 3.5 to 16.8.[34] As market forces increased the value of a postsecondary degree in the early twentieth century, more and more young people with high school diplomas entered the nation's colleges. A successful undergraduate college became a sine qua non of the American research university: the college's tuition receipts provided funds for the research apparatus, it served as a repository of future master's and doctoral students, and it inspired loyalty among graduates and benefactors. For American youth, college-going was "fashionable and prestigious," and it also meant having a good time.[35]

As research universities jettisoned reformist courses like those in the pre–World War I Wharton School, they began to slough off curricular responsibility for moral education, which largely defaulted to activities outside the classroom. As Reuben says, "University administrators . . . expected administrative changes and extracurricular activities to solve the problem of undergraduate character development. They hired special administrators to handle 'student life,' instituted programs for student advising, hired special faculty for undergraduate teaching, and created new activities such as 'freshman orientation.' The most important 'moral reform' in those decades was the establishment of the dormitory."[36] Responsibility for moral education, or character development, devolved to organizations such as the Young Men's Christian Association and Young Women's Christian Association.[37] At Penn, the student-controlled Christian Association, founded in 1891 as the University

Branch of the Philadelphia YMCA, sponsored, from the 1900s to the 1960s, not only a coeducational, nondenominational campus ministry but also social settlements in South Philadelphia and racially integrated summer camps for boys and girls.[38] The Christian Association's influence was marginal; the large majority of Penn students in the 1910s and 1920s gravitated to the boisterous rituals and frivolities that marked the "collegiate way" of the pre–Depression Era campus. In these decades, anti-intellectualism was rife on U.S. campuses—students who took their studies seriously were marked as "grinds," their exchanges with professors accompanied by classmates' "smirks, coughing, squeaking chairs, and other reminders that enough was enough."[39]

The rules and regulations that were expected to make dormitory life a moral reform had no traction in the Quad. Here the tradition of the testosterone-fueled "Rowbottom," a term synonymous with Penn student riots, started in 1909 or 1910. The term is attributed to one Joseph T. Rowbottom, a grind whose burning of the midnight oil in Bodine Hall provoked the nightly cry of "Yea Rowbottom" from a classmate across the Quad. One night when the Penn football team took up the chant, mocking the studious Rowbottom, other Quad residents "sought to quell it with a hail of wash bowls, pitchers, garbage cans and anything else handy."[40] Rowbottoms sometimes ratcheted into "full-scale rioting." Philadelphia's finest joined these periodic frays wielding nightsticks, water hoses, and blank cartridges, bludgeoning students and hauling them away in paddy wagons and squad cars.[41] A Rowbottom in March of 1928, one of two student riots that year, was not atypical of the havoc wreaked by these flare-ups, in this case a "wild revelry" that followed the basketball team's victory over Princeton: "A crowd of about 1,000 students set fire to trolley wires, pulled trolley poles from overhead wires, and lit bonfires in front of the Psi Upsilon Fraternity. When firemen arrived, different groups of students carried off the fire hose, made away with a large red Philadelphia Rapid Transit automobile trailer, and changed the workings of the 'automatic traffic semaphore.' Seventeen students were arrested on a charge of inciting a riot."[42]

In the 1930s, the campus quieted, its masculine excesses perhaps moderated by the increased presence of women in campus social life, which was given impetus by the opening of Sergeant Hall, a women's dormitory near the campus, in 1924.[43] The women's residential presence at Penn would be folded into the matrix of a conservative campus by the 1950s, one that was quintessentially "Joe College"/"Betty Co-ed,"[44] a sedate campus disturbed only by an occasional Rowbottom or panty raid, a venue dominated by fraternity life, patriarchal faculty, and in loco parentis.[45] While this quietude would be disrupted by leftist students protesting the University's ties to the Department of Defense in the 1960s, and by campus racial and gender politics in

Rowbottom, 1930. Police drag a University student from a sandwich shop near 37th Street and Woodland Avenue. More than three hundred students were arrested in disorders that resulted when a nervous officer turned in a riot call. Collections of the University Archives and Records Center.

the 1970s and 1980s, Penn faculty, with some few exceptions, would continue to eschew the kind of academically based social activism that marked the early Wharton School. Ivory-tower aloofness would, for reasons discussed in this book, be challenged by a growing number of faculty after the mid-1980s, when the James-Patten-Nearing reformist tradition began to reappear in various schools and departments of the Penn campus.

■

By 1930, Penn was the ninth largest American university and the fourth largest private institution, with a total enrollment of 13,828 (regular full time, 7,252). By 1937, its endowment value stood at $22,323,000, putting it ahead of the leading public universities (California, Illinois, Michigan, Minnesota, Wisconsin) but ahead of only one major private research university, Caltech—and significantly trailing Harvard ($135,032,000) and Yale ($100,448,000), as well as Columbia, Cornell, Chicago, Johns Hopkins, Princeton, Stanford, and MIT. There is no gainsaying that Penn had established itself as a research university, perhaps as early as the 1910s, certainly no later than the 1920s when the provost, Josiah H. Penniman, "took as a major interest developing the research potential of the university," and the trustees established a board of graduate education and research, which received financial support from the

Rockefeller Foundation.[46] It would be an exaggeration, however, to suggest that it was a paragon of *Grosswissenschaft* (financial support for long-term research projects) realistically comparable to such lustrous peers as Harvard, Columbia, Yale, Caltech, and California, institutions that by 1940 "could report that they expected their faculty to devote about half of their time to research."[47]

Though nationally recognized, Penn was in some key respects a parochial, distinctively Philadelphia institution; its student clientele was regional, its campus nonresidential, with the exception of the all-male Quad—hence the moniker "commuter university." The University's governance was inbred in the city's upper class; in 1940, Proper Philadelphians dominated its thirty-member board of trustees. Thomas Sovereign Gates, Penn's first president (1930–44), "was the most influential and respected member of the upper class in Philadelphia in 1940." A graduate of the University and a member of the elite Rittenhouse and Philadelphia clubs, Gates, a financier, had risen to senior partnerships at J. P. Morgan and Drexel and Company.[48] Not until after World War II would the University expand its board's membership to warrant the label of a truly national and international institution.[49]

In the Depression Era, Gates confronted a diminished campus. "The consequences of the economic collapse on the industries that supported the University were drastic," the architectural historian George Thomas writes. "Programs were dropped, faculty positions were eliminated, buildings deteriorated." Campus development was at a virtual standstill: "Between 1929 and 1949 new construction on the campus nearly ceased. From the completion of Irvine Auditorium in 1928 to the end of World War II, the only realized projects were the 1940 Chemistry Building by Paul Cret and two minor projects."[50] To bolster sagging revenues, the University hosted Army and Navy training programs during the war, though it never recouped the maintenance costs for military uses of its buildings.[51]

For all these financial problems, the University under Gates still boasted "outstanding" programs in law, medicine, dentistry, and classical archaeology; the campus also showcased "a superb anthropological museum."[52] Especially in medicine, but also in the physical sciences, a critical mass of leading academic scientists arrived at Penn in the aftermath of the war, many of them veteran researchers from federally funded wartime projects, some returning to their home departments. Among Penn's many postwar luminaries were the founders of Penn's biomedical research empire: the nephrologist Alfred Newton Richards, whose experiments in renal physiology led to the development of the artificial kidney, and I. S. Ravdin, a world-renowned surgical pioneer in cancer treatment and kingmaker of the American College of Physicians and the American Cancer Society, hailed as "a giant in his own time."[53] As vice president in charge of medical affairs after 1939, Richards "established the groundwork for the great explosion in research opportunities with the coming of the National Institutes of Health after the Second World War. . . . The success of medical research kept the University of Pennsylvania among the elite institutions of higher learning in the United States." The postwar return of Penn's future president Gaylord P. Harnwell and Gates's recruitment of Harnwell's Princeton University colleague Louis Ridenour marked a turning point toward a "premier Physics Department" and the beginning of a "new wave of faculty" in the Physics Department.[54] By the end of Gates's presidency, Penn was well positioned to take advantage of the federal government's postwar stance on "academic research [as] a matter of public policy" and tap the flood of federal research dollars in the coming decades:[55] Penn ranked tenth among academic and nonindustrial organizations in the amount of wartime research funds awarded by the federal Office of Scientific Research and Development (OSRD) and eighth in the total number of OSRD contracts. Richards used his position as chair of OSRD's Committee on Medical Research to direct "the most advanced programs of medical research for malaria and the production of penicillin for the war effort. Richard's stature and efforts kept the Penn Medical School at the forefront of biomedical research." Harnwell, director of the Navy's underwater sound laboratory in San Diego, and his colleagues in the Physics Department gained vital experience "in managing and administering government funds and large-scale research efforts."[56]

In one important area of wartime research and development, Penn failed egregiously to take advantage of a golden opportunity on its own doorstep. A tremendously important technological breakthrough developed by two Penn engineers under a wartime contract with the U.S. Army was never exploited by the University or the engineers themselves. J. Presper Eckert and John Mauchly constructed the Electronic Numerical Integrator and Computer (ENIAC), "the first digital, general-purpose, electronic computer," on the dingy first floor of the Moore School of Electrical Engineering.[57] ENIAC's persuasive claim to being "the first true electronic computer," in an era when there were other "plausible" claimants to the title, was based on three "major innovations" in its design: it was "digital, electronic, and programmable." ENIAC, though it was terribly unwieldy, weighing about thirty tons and incorporating eighteen thousand vacuum tubes, "was the wave of the future." Of no mean significance, the women who programmed ENIAC are today regarded as the world's first computer programmers.[58]

Shortsightedly, the University refused to allow Eckert and Mauchly, so long as they were Penn employees, to file patents for the separate innovations that in tandem made ENIAC operable. Five weeks after the first public demonstration of ENIAC in February 1946, Eckert and Mauchly resigned their positions in the Moore School and left the campus to organize the Eckert-Mauchly Computer Corporation. In the years ahead Eckert and Mauchly managed to lose their company to Remington Rand (which was later sold to Sperry/UNISYS) and, following an unfavorable judicial ruling, the ENIAC patent itself—and to become, unjustly, ciphers in the history of computers.[59]

For its part, Penn erred strategically in two ways to forfeit its national leadership role in the postwar field of commercial computing and a potential financial windfall: first, by providing desultory institutional support for ENIAC—University administrators and Moore School faculty believed that the project was chimerical, having no commercial viability; second, by brushing off the geniuses Eckert and Mauchly after ENIAC was fully operational. "Penn might have become the early center of the computer industry," bemoans ENIAC's chronicler, Scott McCartney. "The school had a very important lead on MIT and Harvard, which were both wedded to analog rather than digital methods for years. Philadelphia could have been what Boston became—a technology center with a huge, highly skilled employment base."[60]

From the mid-1960s, Penn would have an opportunity to rectify this mistake in the form of the University City Science Center, a brainchild of Gaylord Harnwell's presidency. Yet the Science Center was to be embroiled in controversy, and, for reasons explained in this book, it would fail to do for Philadelphia what Harvard and MIT did for Boston. This failure of the Science Center to catalyze a city and regional technological revolution notwithstanding, the four presidencies keynoted in this book, each by degrees, would establish Penn as one of the world's foremost scientific-research institutions.

∎

Successfully leveraging funds for federally vetted basic and applied research (the latter including "'programmatic' research defined by the needs of patrons") in the Cold War era required Penn and its competitors "to become larger, more complex, more segmented organizations."[61] From the standpoint of size, complexity, and segmentation, Penn was disadvantaged by being a landlocked urban campus standing in close proximity to the industrial city. The liabilities of Penn's location were manifest as early as the 1890s.

The University of Pennsylvania Museum of Archaeology and Anthropology was, with Franklin Field in the mid-1890s, a bellwether of Penn's expansion toward the river. Situated on almshouse property in the vicinity of the tracks of the Pennsylvania Railroad, northeast of the almshouse hospital, the museum opened in 1899 on "a wretched stretch of land" on which reposed a city dump. According to William Pepper's biographer, when Pepper and the University's archaeological curator, Sara Yorke Stevenson, accompanied the department store magnate Justus C. Strawbridge, a prospective donor, to the South Street Bridge for an inspection of the construction site, "with each passing train a dense black smoke rolled up in sooty masses, enveloping railroad tracks, goats, and refuse in a black mist, whilst blasts of coal gas smothered the lungs of the visitors." Strawbridge confided to Stevenson, "I cannot bear to throw cold water on Dr. Pepper's enthusiasm, but what an extraordinary site for a great museum! Of course, I would like to help him; but what a site!"[62]

In 1913, the trustees' architectural commission warned that the disadvantages of Penn's urban location threatened to outweigh the advantages. "Traffic conditions," Paul Cret and his colleagues averred, "constituted the chief menace to the University's proper development." Not the least of these problems was the thoroughfare of Woodland Avenue, which carried oil-belching automobiles as well as several clanking trolley lines past College Hall. The Cret Report cited "subway construction through the University territory" as a potential, though not optimal, solution, an idea whose time would come more than forty years later. The architects' commission proposed reconfiguring the campus as a pedestrian-oriented enclave of green spaces enclosed by buildings of various sizes, arrayed along a pedestrian mall bordered with "grass plats, shrubbery and trees" and stretching a thousand feet from College Hall to Chestnut Street via a footbridge over Walnut.[63] For lack of funds this plan made no headway; the pedestrian campus would remain a planner's vision until the 1950s. Until then the city would entwine the campus. The economist and New Deal Brain Truster Rexford Tugwell, a 1917 graduate of the College, recalled the aesthetic incongruity of the "romantically vine-covered" campus and the fine Tudor dormitories situated cheek by jowl with the Dickensian industrial city and some neighbors "of doubtful respectability." "There was, for instance, Blockley," he wrote, "the enormous and shamefully crowded insane asylum, just over the fence from the Botanical Gardens [south of Hamilton Walk, behind the Quad], its gloomy pile always visible; and there was a fringe of stockyards, wholesale markets, and factories between us and the river. In this a soccer field made only a small gap—and one, at that, crossed by the Pennsylvania Railroad's tracks. Also there were small hotels down by the Thirty-fourth Street station, favored places of assignation for students who possessed complaisant enamoratas."[64]

By the 1920s, Franklin Field, on the eastern edge of the campus, was framed bleakly by congested rail yards, smokestack industries, and ramshackle buildings—structures that filled the quarter mile of bottomland between the stadium and the river; just below the field, the High Line of the Pennsylvania

Aerial view of Franklin Field and the freight yards of the Pennsylvania Railroad, 1926. Collections of the University Archives and Records Center.

Railroad rose on steel and stone pedestals forty feet above the rail yards, transporting freight around the central city.

In 1940, Martin Meyerson, the future city planner and fifth president of the University, then an undergraduate at Columbia University, visited Penn for the first time. "When we came to the University campus," he recalled decades later, "I very much liked the atmosphere of the University. However, I thought the . . . physical campus was dreary."[65] The definitive element of this dreariness was the raucous thoroughfare of Woodland Avenue, a noisy laceration through the heart of the campus. Of Woodland's perpetual disruptions, a dismayed undergraduate wrote in 1932, "It is somewhat disconcerting to say the least, to listen to a lecture, only to miss an essential phrase or idea because a trolley car is lumbering on its way, or a shriek of automobile horns

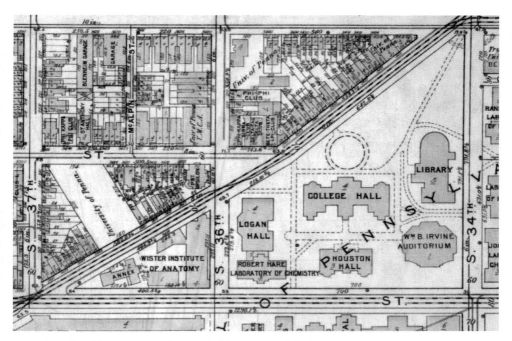

Woodland Avenue trolley lines in the historic core of the Penn campus. *Atlas of The City of Philadelphia*, Wards 24, 27, 34, 40, 44 & 46, West Philadelphia. Collections of the University Archives and Records Center.

assails the ear." This writer spoke of a "crushed sense of beauty" on the Penn campus.[66] In 1937, the student newspaper complained of "the roar and rattle of traffic at all hours of the day," "the repellant parking lot at 37th and Woodland Avenue," and "the shacks which serve as stores along 37th Street."[67] "Dull and depressing," wrote David Goddard, a University provost in the 1960s, of the campus that greeted his arrival in 1946. "The physical facilities were inadequate and their maintenance was poor; little construction had occurred in the last three decades. . . . Trolley cars clattered by so loudly that often lecturers in College and Bennett halls had to pause to wait for the racket to subside. Old factories, hotels, and run-down houses threatened to engulf the neighboring community."[68]

A photograph from around 1950 shows unkempt, mixed commercial-residential brownstones, trolley lines, and unregulated signage at the complicated intersection of Woodland Avenue and 37th and Spruce streets. Along Woodland east of 37th Street, unregulated, low-end development encroached on the area around College Hall. Ironically, "some of the 'blight' was the

Woodland Avenue trolley approaching the intersection of Spruce and 37th streets at the Quad; the service station in the background marks the site of the future Stouffer Triangle, ca. 1950. Collections of the University Archives and Records Center.

result of cheap boardinghouses, restaurants, and bars proliferating around the area to serve Penn's students."[69] Indeed, as University property maps suggest, some of the blight stood on Penn-owned properties.

From the Depression Era to the early 1950s, the Penn trustees adopted, and periodically considered, the Kelly Plan to move the male undergraduate college to a farming estate twenty-two miles from West Philadelphia, in Chester County near Valley Forge: the 175-acre Cresswell Farm, which the University had acquired from an alumnus benefactor in 1924. The farm offered the benefits of education in a pastoral setting. "After the war the Valley Forge possibility continued to provide a tempting alternative," Martin Meyerson and Dilys Pegler Winegrad note in their history of the University, "particularly by the fifties when it became clear that, if the University were to remain in the city, it would have to expand."[70]

Expand the University would. Just months after his election as Penn's third president in 1948, Harold Stassen announced the trustees' approval of "far reaching plans" that would increase the size of the campus from 113 to 148 acres. As proposed by the trustees' architects' committee, chaired by Sydney Martin, "the University ultimately would cover the area bounded on the east by 32d Street; on the west by 40th Street; on the north by Walnut Street. Hamilton Walk, below Spruce Street, would be the southern boundary."[71] The Martin Plan projected the University's westward expansion along the Locust Street axis, in contrast to the 1913 Cret Report's call for northward expansion from College Hall to Chestnut Street. In the spirit of the Cret committee's vision of a pedestrian campus, the Martin team recommended closing Woodland Avenue and moving its trolley lines underground, closing streets on the east-west axis, and widening 38th Street, then a single-lane, one-way thoroughfare, to accommodate the overflow traffic from the Woodland removal. The City Planning Commission incorporated all of these recommendations into the city plan.

Elements of the Martin Plan that were completed or begun during Stassen's five-year tenure included a new building for the Wharton School; a new eight-story hospital wing for the outpatient department, named for the late Thomas Sovereign Gates; and Penn's first experience with urban redevelopment, the clearing of houses to make way for a new physics building (the David Rittenhouse Laboratories). Another priority of the Martin Plan, a capacious new library to replace the cramped Furness Library, the University's main library since 1891, would be deferred until the 1960s. Construction of a tunnel for the Woodland trolley lines began in 1952, with completion targeted for 1955.

To their lasting credit, the trustees ultimately rejected other elements of the Martin Plan—notably several proposals that today seem preposterous. Trained in the Beaux-Arts tradition, Martin and his architectural colleagues extolled the virtues of long axial lines that ended in monumental structures—they loathed Frank Furness's Industrial Age library and had scant regard for Thomas Richard's neo-Gothic College Hall. Memorably, their plan called for "a 30-story limestone-clad skyscraper designed in the setback massing of the RCA tower of Rockefeller Center," which was to stand on the vacated intersection of 36th and Locust streets. The proposed monstrosity would be a "'Cathedral of Learning' like the University of Pittsburgh's 1920s skyscraper . . . a visual sign of Penn's renewed vigor."[72] The long axial line they envisaged ran east and west from the tower. To form a straight line east of the tower to connect Locust and Smith walks via 34th Street, the plan called for the demolition of Furness's masterpiece, an idea the trustees prudently discarded. Another errant idea that soon lost traction was a women's campus planned for the blocks in the quadrant of Spruce and Walnut between 38th and 40th streets—a plan

Aerial photograph of University of Pennsylvania campus, with
Woodland Avenue diagonal, 1948. Collections of the University
Archives and Records Center.

Campus Master Plan rendering, with Woodland Avenue removed, 1948. Proposed thirty-story tower at 36th and Locust streets (upper center). Collections of the University Archives and Records Center.

that would have permanently isolated Penn women from the rest of the campus, evidently to the satisfaction of the all-male architects' committee.

Harold Stassen's successor, Gaylord Harnwell, was the avatar of a more ambitious strategy than the Martin Plan. Harnwell and his planners aimed to build Penn into a world-class research university. Under Harnwell, a gifted academic *qua* entrepreneur, the University was able to marshal a huge volume of federal research dollars. A skilled politician, he took full advantage of—and in part, his administration orchestrated—federal, state, and city legislation to ensure an abundance of urban renewal dollars for Penn's enlargement. The upshot of all this was Penn's Great Expansion, which we take up in part I.

Part I　**The Builder**

1

Rise of the Urban Renewal University

In the spring of 1953 the University of Pennsylvania trustees appointed Gaylord P. Harnwell as the University's fourth president. Since his arrival at Penn in 1936, Harnwell had held appointments as the Mary Amanda Wood Professor of Physics, chair of the Physics Department, and director of the Randal Morgan Laboratories. While on wartime leave from Penn from 1942 to 1946, he directed the University of California Division of War Research at Point Loma, San Diego, where sonar detection devices were developed for the U.S. Navy, with devastating consequences for Japanese submarines. Harnwell was an attractive candidate for the Penn presidency because of his reputation as a leading physicist, his success in strengthening the Physics Department, and his adroitness as a fund-raiser.[1]

From his office in 100 College Hall, Harnwell charted Penn's rise to the status of a truly national university. During his long tenure from 1953 to 1970, he presided over the University's transformation from a "sleepy" commuter campus with a regional orientation to a residential campus with a geographically diverse student body; from an institution landlocked by an increasingly congested urban environment to a tree-lined, pedestrian enclave with closed streets and quadrangles, buffered if not fully protected from the encroaching city.

Under Harnwell, Penn entered a fierce, unprecedented competition for wealth, power, and prestige among the nation's postwar research universities. From the mid-1950s to 1970, U.S. research universities spent furiously and haphazardly on buildings, graduate programs, faculty salaries, and expanded administrative staffs to support their burgeoning research edifices. Bigness was deemed a blessing and a virtue; it was also a point of pride. Universities spent profligately on the strength of a buoyant national economy and the federal government's Cold War commitment to basic and applied research. Flush with federal research dollars, Penn was no exception. The University was a prime beneficiary of the vastly accelerated flow of federal R & D grants in the wake of the Soviet launch of the Sputnik 1 communications satellite in 1957—the federal budget for basic research on the nation's campuses tripled, with federal support rising from 43 percent to 79 percent of university research expenditures by 1964, a period of unprecedented federal largesse that the historian Roger Geiger calls "the golden age of academic science."[2] As the historian Walter McDougall puts it, the post-Sputnik acceleration of federal R & D dollars was "a saltation, an evolutionary leap in the relationship of the state to the creation of new knowledge."[3] Of particular importance to Penn, whose main strength was biomedical research, was the sponsorship of the National Institutes of Health (NIH), which, after 1958, provided both research dollars and infrastructural support for research facilities and PhD training.[4] In 1969, Penn ranked seventeenth among universities and colleges in federally sponsored R & D, and ninth in the amount received from the Department of Health, Education, and Welfare.[5] Harnwell's administration more than tripled the value of the physical plant and quadrupled the University's assets, building the endowment from $39 million to $200 million, increasing research and training contracts from $4 million to $45 million, and expanding total enrollments from fourteen thousand to nineteen thousand and the academic staff from twenty-six hundred to forty-six hundred.[6]

Harnwell's greatest achievement, and his enduring legacy, was the indelible footprint he left on the landscape of West Philadelphia: the modern Penn campus, with manifold new buildings and radical renovations to house the burgeoning faculties and federally sponsored research projects, as well as the geographically diverse cohorts of undergraduates spawned first by the GI Bill, then by the middle-class baby boom. With his eye squarely on the future, Harnwell disentangled the University from the creep of heavily trafficked city streets, clanging trolley lines, and tawdry commercial establishments. He built the present-day West Central and West campuses, expanded the North Campus between 32nd and 38th streets, and established a sphere of influence between Chestnut Street and Lancaster Avenue. A consummate fund-raiser, he spearheaded a capital campaign in the 1960s that raised some $102 million, which helped fund twenty-five new buildings, twenty-eight endowed professorships, and significant growth in scholarships and student aid. Hailed as "the most successful chief executive the University has had since its inception in the eighteenth century,"[7] Harnwell also founded a multi-institutional collaborative, the West Philadelphia Corporation, which sponsored development of an urban industrial park, the University City Science Center, which became a de facto component of Penn's campus expansion in the Cold War era, though not without unintended, long-term consequences for the University's community relations.

There were other contributions. Harnwell was Penn's first president to solicit and organize alumni giving, traveling the world in search of alumni dollars. Under Harnwell, the University consulted with the shah of Iran to help create the American-style Pahlavi University in Shiraz—external development work that poured overseas petroleum money into the campus coffers. Joining other major university presidents, he stood firm against legislative assaults on academics' freedom of speech during the McCarthy era, even though he loathed communism. In the 1960s, with his encouragement, Penn students gained a stronger voice in campus governance through the student-controlled Student Committee on Undergraduate Education (SCUE), whose recommendations prompted a reform of the undergraduate curriculum. Abolishing parietal rules and opening new dormitories

Gaylord P. Harnwell. Collections of the University Archives and Records Center.

as coeducational facilities by the end of the decade, the Harnwell campus largely divested itself of in loco parentis. The political conservatism of the mainstream student body, coupled with the tempered response of Harnwell and the trustees to student protest activity, mitigated the campus impact of the antiwar movement. Penn never experienced anything like the violence at Columbia, Wisconsin, or Berkeley.

When Harnwell took office in 1953, the campus was still in physical disarray, not much improved since Paul Cret wrote his trenchant critique of campus planning in 1913. The diagonal of Woodland Avenue, part of the state highway system, still carried trolleys and automobiles past Logan and College halls. John Boyles's iconic statue of Benjamin Franklin presided over the unpleasant thoroughfare. Locust Street crossed 36th Street just a short distance north of Woodland, contributing to a congested gaggle of people, stoplights, and machines. A foot-traffic analysis of these intersections from November 1946 shows about twenty-seven thousand pedestrian crossings for a three-day period.[8] Student-oriented small businesses, many of them of low quality and shady appearance, stood cheek by jowl with campus buildings along Woodland and 36th and 37th streets. The celebrated urban planner

View of College Hall and Woodland trolley lines, probably early 1950s. This photo shows John Boyles's iconic statue of Benjamin Franklin, which the University acquired in 1939. The trolley lines were replaced by a subway-surface tunnel in 1955. Collections of the University Archives and Records Center.

Martin Meyerson recalled that when he arrived at Penn as an associate professor in the Department of City and Regional Planning in 1952, campus streets "were choked with traffic and crowded with noisily distracting commercial uses. Of course, as perhaps befits a 'streetcar' university, there were but few more buildings than there had been twenty-five years before, and what there were had drifted into obsolescence and even decay."[9] Indeed, between 1930 and 1950 only one new building was constructed: the Chemistry Department's Cret Wing on Spruce Street.

On a trapezoidal block across from College Hall on the north side of Woodland, aged brick and brownstone buildings housed sundry retail services, campus offices, and fraternity houses. Between 1952 and 1955, commensurate with Penn's long-expressed need for a pedestrian-oriented campus and the urban renewal vision of Philadelphia's reformist, pro-growth Democratic leaders and modernist city planners (1951–62), the city removed the trolley lines from Woodland Avenue and rerouted them into a subway tunnel under the Penn campus. In 1957 the City Council removed Woodland Avenue at Penn from the city plan altogether and deeded the roadbed to the University. (Penn would soon build a new library complex on the trapezoidal block opposite College Hall.) With the interior spaces of the historic campus core now fully controlled

View north from the old University Library toward Woodland Avenue and the trapezoidal block between 36th and 34th streets; College Hall at left, 1930. The row of buildings along Woodland marks the future site of the Van Pelt and Dietrich libraries. Collections of the University Archives and Records Center.

by Penn, the University joined hands with the Philadelphia Redevelopment Authority, the Philadelphia City Planning Commission, and the Pennsylvania General State Authority to take advantage of favorable urban renewal legislation and to launch a juggernaut building program that extended the campus west of the historic core to 40th Street and north above Walnut Street, demolishing old brownstones and displacing residents (mostly white) and merchants from 32nd to 40th streets.

The charter plan of the Great Expansion was the 1954–59 Educational Survey—to that time the largest self-study ever undertaken by an American university—which provided the academic rationale for Penn's facilities planning after 1962.[10] To fulfill the vision of the Educational Survey, Penn needed land. This was not "a general demand for space," but rather a demand for "specific adjacent and adjoining areas." Beyond this requirement, Penn, like the University of Chicago and Columbia University, demanded "a surrounding community compatible with the character of the educational institution itself."[11]

Baby-boom cohorts fueled the Great Expansion. The salient demographics are these: 76.4 million babies, accounting for approximately two-fifths of the total U.S. population, were born between 1946 and 1964, with the college-age group counting 24.7 million in 1960.[12] Between 1950 and 1970, the number of students in institutions of higher education soared from 2.66 million to 7.14 million. Driven by the GI Bill, the percentage of college students in the total population increased from 1.19 in 1946 to 1.76 in 1950, then leveled off until the baby boomers started to come of age. Between 1960 and 1970, the decade with the greatest concentration of college-age boomers, the number of higher education matriculates as a percentage of the total population increased from 1.79 to 3.51.[13] Underpinning this extraordinary leap were a flush national economy, parents' increasing recognition of the strong link between a college degree and social mobility, and the competitive growth of higher education institutions after midcentury. Keenly aware of the baby-boom phenomenon, Penn planners projected 41 percent growth in cumulative undergraduate student enrollments for the 1960s and a 65 percent increase for the two decades spanning 1960 to 1980. The University's Integrated Development Plan of 1962 called for, among numerous other building projects, the construction of new dormitories to house the majority of the 7,800 full-time students in the undergraduate colleges and 5,730 graduate and professional students expected by 1970.[14]

With the completion of the Harnwell-era building program in the early 1970s and the occupancy of myriad new academic buildings, research facilities, and high-rise dormitories, America's first university in large part achieved its present size and physical form. "It is true of course that these were years of expansion everywhere," Martin Meyerson would later write, "but at no ranking private institution was the expansion and differentiation as great as at Pennsylvania."[15]

Giving particular attention to developments in the first decade of Harnwell's presidency, this chapter looks closely at the early stages of the Great Expansion, when the University broke out of the historic core and began to build the campus westward and northward. Our primary interest is *how* Penn's enlargement happened. Accordingly, we examine the organizational structure of urban renewal in Philadelphia, the instruments of expansion made available to the University from city, state, and federal governments, and their applications in West Philadelphia. We keynote the close relationships of University administrators and trustees with the city's Democratic mayors, the Greater Philadelphia Movement, the City Planning Commission, and the Redevelopment Authority. And we highlight the critical role of the General State Authority.

◼ The University and Postwar-Philadelphia City Planning

In November 1947, Philadelphia's celebrated urban planner Edmund Bacon, chairman of the Philadelphia City Planning Commission, remarked on the city's self-interest in the redevelopment of the blocks north of the Penn campus, saying, in effect, that what was good for Penn was good for the city. As Bacon saw it, the situation of this area was incompatible with the "dignity" of a university (he had the Drexel Institute of Technology in mind as well). Focusing primarily on "the extremely decadent commercial area" between Walnut and Market streets, he declaimed, "If present deterioration . . . is allowed to spread, the good sections [that is, middle-class blocks] to the west will be cut off from the city center by a band of blight, and their rapid decline may be expected. Conversely, if the area is intelligently redeveloped so as to establish a sound connection with the heart of the city, the desirable areas of West Philadelphia will tend to be stabilized." Furthermore, Bacon argued, "the development which takes place on the north side of Market Street will have a strong effect on the University area and should be considered in connection with it."[16] It would take another two decades for Penn and the city to rectify the structural problems Bacon adumbrated, even as university-style urban renewal contributed new problems and failed to abate the growing urban crisis.

After joining the City Planning Commission in 1946 as a senior land planner, Bacon teamed with the architects Oskar Stonorov and Louis Kahn and

Planning Commission director Robert Mitchell to design the 1947 Better Philadelphia Exhibition, which the Planning Commission displayed publicly with
great fanfare on two floors of Gimbel's Department Store in Center City. The
splendid exhibition marked the "beginnings of comprehensive city planning"
to transform "an unlovely industrial metropolis."[17] "The exhibition's climax
was a model of Center City Philadelphia, 33 feet by 14 feet in size. . . . It was
meticulously crafted with 45,000 buildings, 25,000 cars and buses, 12,000 trees
and cost $50,000. The model showed Philadelphia exactly as it was in 1947.
Then, narrated by a speaker's voice, one section of the model lifted up and rotated until the entire model changed to that of Philadelphia's future in 1980.
Then all-at-once the panels rotated back to the familiar present."[18] "Standing in front of the exhibition," writes the economist Kirk Petshek, "many a
businessman began to think more concretely about what his city could become. . . . To their surprise, Philadelphians realized that their city could be
exciting."[19] Some 385,000 people attended the five-week Better Philadelphia
Exhibition. The exhibition persuaded the Penn trustees that "if we can do it
in Center City, we can do it throughout Philadelphia, and obviously West
Philadelphia is just across the [Schuylkill] river, and in effect part of Center
City or just an extension of it."[20]

The Better Philadelphia Exhibition was the first salvo in a decade of tremendous optimism and urban renewal activity orchestrated by the City Planning Commission, in concert with the Greater Philadelphia Movement, a
coalition of reform-minded business and professional elites that was cofounded
by Robert T. McCracken, an attorney and Penn trustee.[21] In 1951, the Greater
Philadelphia Movement campaigned successfully for a new home rule charter, which "created a strong Mayoral office, overhauled City Council, proposed
a strong merit system for city jobs, and created a number of appointed boards
as well as reorganized several service departments in a rational format."[22] Then
elite Democratic reformers led by the patrician lawyer Joseph "Gentleman Joe"
Sill Clark, Jr., the newly elected mayor, and Clark's fellow aristocrat Richardson Dilworth, the new district attorney, ousted the notoriously corrupt Republican Party machine. Clark, who served as mayor until 1955, when he ran
successfully for the U.S. Senate, was succeeded by Dilworth, who held the
office until his resignation in 1962 to run (unsuccessfully) for governor. The
Edmund Bacon–inspired planning efforts of the Clark-Dilworth era included, controversially, a series of major urban renewal projects in Center
City: Penn Center, which replaced the old Broad Street Station and the
"Chinese Wall" (elevated tracks) of the Pennsylvania Railroad with modernist office towers, plazas, and walkways; Market Street East, which, when
completed in 1984, long after Bacon's tenure at the City Planning Commis-

sion, connected commuter trains originating at Suburban Station with lines running out of the new Market East Station, with direct access to a new shopping mall; Washington Square East/Society Hill, which integrated restored eighteenth-century homes, low-rise townhouses, and residential towers, the latter designed by I. M. Pei—all intended to attract middle-class suburbanites while displacing low-income minority renters.[23] (Unlike Robert Moses, New York City's master builder, Bacon lacked multiagency authority to impose his ideas on other city agencies; while his formidable political skills and adroit social networking compensated for this deficit, he invariably had to compromise on his designs.)[24] Throughout the Clark-Dilworth era, redevelopment—and 45 percent of the city's urban renewal dollars by 1963—was "concentrated on the downtown area," apropos of recommendations from the Redevelopment Authority's Central Urban Renewal Area study of 1956, whose authors included the Penn planning professors Martin Meyerson and G. Holmes Perkins.[25] After 1959, Penn's expansion and the attendant development of University City would be hotly contested focal points of urban renewal activity outside Center City.[26]

The first step in the extended process that led eventually to federally assisted university expansion in West Philadelphia was certification in early 1948 by the City Planning Commission of a planning unit designated the University Redevelopment Area, "an irregularly shaped section of West Philadelphia totaling about eighty blocks," bordered by Market Street on the north to South Street/Spruce Street and Woodland Avenue on the south and southwest, Schuylkill Avenue (beyond the tracks of the Pennsylvania Railroad) on the east, and 42nd Street on the west.[27] The planners delineated the boundaries of Penn's future growth, which, with a few notable exceptions to the north, would be directed westward from the historic core. Perhaps unsurprisingly, given that the chairman of the City Planning Commission from 1943 to 1956 was the Penn trustee and devoted alumnus, Edward Hopkinson, Jr. (a senior partner of the investment firm Drexel and Company and a "very, very distinguished" and "powerful" figure in city affairs),[28] the Planning Commission's plan for the area's growth, published in 1950, aligned with the Martin Plan, the campus development plan proposed in 1948 by the Trustees' Committee for the Physical Development of the University of Pennsylvania. Yet well in advance of the Martin Plan, as early as 1945, the Planning Commission had initiated negotiations with Penn on rerouting trolleys and cars in the campus area. The starting point and enabling catalyst for implementing the resulting joint Planning Commission–University transit plan was the city's decision to complete its project begun in 1930 to put the trains of the Market Street Elevated railway, which ran west of the Schuylkill River, into a subway tunnel.

Market Street Elevated at 32nd Street, 1952. From 31st to 45th Street, the El was replaced by a subway tunnel, which opened in 1955. An extension tunnel, also completed in 1955, left the Market Street line to carry trolleys underground between 33rd and 39th streets. Two stations served Penn, one at 36th and Sansom, the other at 37th and Spruce. Photo courtesy of PhillyHistory.org, a project of the Philadelphia Department of Records.

From the time it opened in March 1907, the Market Street Elevated, "the El," spurred suburban growth and commerce west of the Schuylkill River, conveying commuters to the center of the city in cars manufactured by the J. G. Brill Company. The EL figured enormously in the doubling of West Philadelphia's population by 1930. Crossing the Schuylkill on a railroad bridge, the El connected the trolley terminal at 69th Street (where it joined with trolley lines from Delaware and Montgomery counties) to the railway's central-city extension, and from there to the South Street ferryboats on the Delaware River. While the El was a boon to suburban commuters traveling from the far reaches of West Philadelphia, the decision that "the Market Street Line would be an elevated railway" had long-term harmful effects on the neighborhoods beneath it. "Once completed," writes the historian Margaret Marsh, "this unsightly structure overshadowed its surroundings and became the dominant feature of the environment."[29] Deterioration was built into the very construction of elevated rapid transit.

In 1930, the city announced plans to replace the El with a subway between 23rd Street in the central city and 46th Street in West Philadelphia. Construction of the subway, which included a tunnel under the river, was stymied by the Great Depression and World War II, and was not resumed in earnest until 1948–49.[30] City photographs support the City Planning Commission's finding of "extreme blight" in the Market Street corridor where the University City Science Center would be built in the 1960s. The Planning Commission, the Redevelopment Authority, and the Housing Authority highlighted the "sub-area" between Chestnut and Market streets, which had a high incidence of substandard housing. Summarizing the general conditions north of the Penn campus, the agencies reported, "The mixture of residential [a high percentage of renters] with commercial and industrial land use, one of the first signs of blight, is prevalent in the University Area. There are very few blocks that are strictly residential, and many of the structures throughout the area have dwelling units on upper floors and business units in the basement on the first floor. [sic]" The agencies described tenement conditions in buildings that had been converted to apartments: "In many cases, this conversion has been faulty—no new toilet and bath facilities have been installed, which has resulted in sharing of the original facilities by two or more households; many of the large rooms have been divided into rooms of substandard size, and no new stairway or fire escape has been added so that many of the buildings are fire traps."[31] The 1950 plan for the Market Street area called for "concentrated, intensive commercial centers at specified locations and . . . [development of] the remainder of the abutting property for garden apartments."[32]

After twenty-five years of delays, West Philadelphia's integrated subway system, which included an extension tunnel carrying subway-surface trolleys under the University, finally opened for business in November 1955. The "rumble and clatter of the Elevated" ended in 1956, with the demolition of the old eyesore structure from the Schuylkill to 46th Street, where the main subway tracks emerged through a portal as the new Market Street Elevated, continuing on to 69th Street in Upper Darby. The city brought down the fourteen-block section of the El above the new West Philadelphia tunnel in a six-month period.[33]

■ The Stassen Connection: Launching the Great Expansion

Construction of the subway-extension tunnel and its two stations at Penn began in 1952, when Harold Stassen was president of the University. Stassen, who is accorded a footnote in U.S. history as a former three-term ("boy wonder") governor of Minnesota, a founder of the United Nations, and a seventime candidate for the U.S. presidency, laid the first bricks of the Great Expansion and of Penn's rise as a great research university. His legacy to Penn was diminished "because of his outsider roots, his nonacademic background that led to conflicts with faculty, his relatively short-term status, and later his seemingly perpetual and quixotic pursuit of the U.S. presidency."[34] In 1952, disgruntled faculty established the Faculty Senate in response to Stassen's alleged indifference to the low status of faculty salaries. Jeannette Nichols's interviews for the History of the University Project, 1925–77, turned up lingering resentment among trustees and faculty; Nichols, herself a Penn professor for three decades, deeply resented Stassen.[35]

When the University trustees offered Stassen the presidency, soon after his defeat by New York governor Thomas Dewey at the 1948 National Republican Convention, they gambled that Stassen would remain at Penn for at least seven years, given their calculation that Dewey would capture the U.S. presidency in 1948 and repeat in 1952. (It is doubtful, however, that the trustees viewed Stassen as a likely prospect to succeed Dewey as president.) Of Stassen's motives, the historian John Terino writes, "A position in Philadelphia appealed to him because of the presence of a strong Republican Party in the state, his personal relationship with some of the Trustees, and the freedom the position would give him to campaign and rally support for Republican causes and issues close to him." National politics and government affairs were Stassen's Lorelei. Ever in pursuit of the highest office in the land, he resigned from Penn in December 1952 to accept a high-level appointment in the Eisenhower administration in Washington, D.C., where for several years he directed the Mutual Security Agency, a coordinating agency for foreign aid; after 1955 he served as Ike's disarmament assistant.[36]

In hindsight a much stronger University president than his reputation would suggest, Stassen is properly credited with using his celebrity to drive a $32 million capital campaign; with clearing the land and laying the foundation of the Rittenhouse Laboratories for physics, mathematics, and astronomy at 33rd and Walnut streets; and with building Dietrich Hall, the new home of the Wharton School of Business and Commerce on the 3600 block of Locust Street, and the Thomas Sovereign Gates Memorial Pavilion of the University hospital on the 3400 block of Spruce Street.[37] Stassen persuaded the trustees to give first priority to the Wharton School and the new medical building, both of which were built on properties the University already owned; Dietrich Hall (today's Steinberg/Dietrich Hall) was ready for students in 1952, and the Gates Pavilion opened to patients in 1953, shortly after Stassen's departure. By refinancing the University's mortgage, with the help of his friends in banking and insurance (and without first consulting the trustees), Stassen ensured that funds were available for the new physics building after the $32 million campaign fell short of its target. Because Penn had to acquire the property through the Redevelopment Authority, completion of the building was delayed until 1954. Construction of a new library, a high priority of the 1948 Martin Plan, would have to be deferred until the 1960s.[38]

Two notable people associated with Stassen's presidency contributed significantly to the University's postwar expansion. The first is the Penn alumnus and trustee Edward Hopkinson, Jr., whom Edmund Bacon described as "the magnificent chairman of the City Planning Commission at that time." Hopkinson spearheaded the construction of the West Philadelphia subway extension tube under the Penn campus.[39] The second is the modernist architect G. Holmes Perkins, who arrived at Penn in 1951 to serve as the dean of the School of Fine Arts, having previously chaired Harvard University's Department of Planning. In his remarkable twenty-year tenure as dean, Perkins restructured the formerly Beaux-Arts-oriented school as the Graduate School of Fine Arts, built world-class programs in architecture and urban planning, and established what he called a "triumvirate" of architecture, landscape architecture, and city and regional planning.

A magnet for extraordinary talent, Perkins presided over the "Philadelphia School," a faculty of luminaries that included, among others, Lewis Mumford, Shasa Navitsky, Louis Kahn, Robert Geddes, Robert Venturi, Denise Scott Brown, Romaldo Giurgola, Ian McHarg, Robert Mitchell, Herbert Gans, Robert Geddes, Martin Meyerson, and Edmund Bacon. Perkins also had protean civic interests, and he became an enthusiastic proponent of urban renewal.[40] Perkins followed Hopkinson as chair of the City Planning Commission from 1958 to 1968—a position he wielded to advance the University's expansion plans and, as we will show, managed in ways that feathered his own nest financially and politically. All things considered, especially Penn's future as an elite institution, the appointment of Perkins was Stassen's greatest presidential achievement.

Stassen's authority derived at least in part from his stature as a national political figure, but even more it was grounded in the trustees' recognition that Penn needed strong presidential leadership to remain competitive in the febrile research climate of the first postwar decade and beyond. Stassen effected a clear, formal, and permanent delineation of the role of the president (administration) and the trustees (policymaking), bequeathing to Gaylord Harnwell "the type of presidency Stillé had envisioned eighty years before." Lillian Burns, a reliable observer, said, "The University really came into

(L–R) Louis I. Kahn, G. Holmes Perkins, and Graduate School of Fine Arts students, 1958. Collections of the University Archives and Records Center.

modern times with Stassen."[41] Modern times required a centralized research administration for processing large federal grants. After 1949, when the Soviet Union built an atom bomb and Mao Tse-tung seized China, federally sponsored research became (literally) the coin of the realm and total federal research dollars the hallmark of an elite research university. With a calculated eye to the future, Stassen created the Office of Sponsored Research, which Donald Murray, a Wharton statistics professor, directed for the next two decades.[42]

In the following sections, we consider details of the physical developments that marked the first phase of the Great Expansion, beginning with how Penn overcame the transit problems that made it a congested urban institution. Next, we turn to the nascent role of the Philadelphia Redevelopment Authority (RDA) and federally sponsored urban renewal in Penn's expansion projects.

Then we look at the role of the Commonwealth of Pennsylvania's General State Authority, another source of urban-renewal largesse for the University.

■ **Building the Subway-Surface Tunnel and Closing Woodland Avenue**

Shortly after his arrival at College Hall, Stassen confronted the perennial question on the trustees' docket: whether to leave the city for "a country estate" at Valley Forge. Although the new president opposed leaving the city, he recognized that a busy public thoroughfare in the middle of the campus would jeopardize future development. "We had to get those trolley tracks out of Woodland and get Woodland closed." Decades later, Stassen would recall that Edward Hopkinson, Jr., who was chair of the City Planning Commission, expressed grave doubts that Woodland could be closed. By Stassen's account, the University organized a petition, "mobilized the alumni to come to City Council in great numbers," including "many of the leading people in the community," and made "such a demonstration [at the public hearing] . . . that this was a *real* need and had *real* support" as to sway the Council to authorize the removal. "And Mr. Hopkinson said, 'I never thought you could get that done.'"[43]

Stassen's account misrepresents the pivotal role Hopkinson played in moving the trolleys underground. "It was learned reliably," the *Philadelphia Evening Bulletin* reported in January 1948, "that the extension project originated with the University of Pennsylvania, and was brought into focus by Dr. Thomas S. Gates, chairman of the board, and Edward Hopkinson, chair of the planning commission and a trustee of the University."[44] Endorsed by planners in several city agencies, the tunnel project, which included the closing of Woodland Avenue to unify the campus, was proposed in September 1947, a year before Stassen's arrival at the University, and was on the planners' drawing board as early as 1945.[45] The consummate "Philadelphia Gentleman," Hopkinson served on the boards and executive committees of the city's leading financial, industrial, and civic institutions. Arguably "the most powerful man in Philadelphia in the mid-1940s," Hopkinson was able to leverage formidable political resources to support the project—he was, after all, chairman of the City Planning Commission and chairman of the executive committee of the Philadelphia Transportation Company.[46] "I was quite shocked at this proposal, it seemed to be very daring, and I couldn't imagine where the money would be coming from," recalled Edmund Bacon. "But Mr. Hopkinson was a great man with money. And so, indeed, he was able to make the necessary arrangements, and it moved forward."[47]

36th Street, looking north from the central campus, 1955. The street was closed to traffic as the subway-surface tunnel was being built to replace the old Woodland Avenue line. The stone building on the right was Blanchard Hall, prototype for the cartoonist Charles Addams's Addams Family house, replaced by the Dietrich Graduate wing of Van Pelt Library in 1967. Across Walnut Street stands the West Philadelphia Title and Trust Company office building, purchased by the University in 1977. Collections of the University Archives and Records Center.

The City Council approved the trolley-tube extension in January 1951, and construction was under way by the winter of 1952. The Council, having raised $6 million for the project through a bond issuance, awarded a fifty-year lease to the Philadelphia Transportation Company to operate the two-way connector system.[48] In the spring of 1953, the trolleys on the Penn campus were diverted off Woodland Avenue at 36th Street to temporary tracks that were laid on Locust Street from 36th Street to 40th Street; Woodland between 36th and 37th streets was closed, as digging for both the tunnel and a subway station in the area of the Wharton School (Dietrich Hall) and the Wistar Institute required ground-level work.[49]

The extension tunnel meandering below the campus was completed, on Gaylord Harnwell's presidential watch, in November 1955, realizing one of the city's objectives for the tube-extension project: "to protect pedestrians from possible damage in the confusion of traffic caused by the trolleys."[50] The new subway-surface extension branched off the main tunnel at 32nd Street, continued to Ludlow and 36th Street, ran below 36th Street onto the campus, veered west under Woodland Avenue, and, after several blocks, exited the tunnel through a portal near the intersection of Woodland and 40th Street.

The next step for the University and the city planners was to remove "the rude thrust of Woodland Avenue" in the middle of the campus.[51] (Cross-streets were in the planners' crosshairs as well.) Two government actions enabled the removal of Woodland at Penn. In 1956, the General Assembly, apparently responding to a lobbying campaign mounted by Penn and the city, struck Woodland Avenue between 34th and 37th streets from the state highway system. It remained for the city to make the final disposition of the roadbed. The deal was consummated in the summer of 1957, when the city conveyed title to the University, with the authorization to use the Woodland roadbed "for future development purposes."[52]

"Formal, official closing ceremonies" took place on Founder's Day, 11 January 1958, when a jubilant Gaylord Harnwell and a throng of dignitaries, including Mayor Richardson Dilworth, gathered to speechify and mark the closing of Woodland between 34th and 37th streets by constructing a barricade at the 36th Street end of the cordoned area. "They had come to bury Woodland Avenue, not to praise it," declaimed an observer.

"Dignified, hammer-wielding gentlemen banged away happily at the nails in a spanking-new barricade. Underfoot, damp and slushy from thawing snow, the roughly paved stretch that had for years been a misnomer [*sic*] made the most of its final opportunity to annoy Pennsylvanians. There was much nostalgia, but few kind words for the old avenue."[53] Several days later, workers began the job of laying sod on the former street surface in the shadows of College Hall and Logan Hall.[54]

Closing Woodland at Penn posed a major logistical problem for the city: what to do with the traffic displaced by the avenue's removal. In the mid-1950s, the Planning Commission and the Department of Streets designed a plan that would reroute traffic in a circuit around the Penn campus. An extension of 33rd Street, a campus-boundary street that was stripped of trolley tracks and widened between Walnut and Spruce streets in 1950, was to cross a corner of

(Top) Looking south from Locust Street along 36th Street to the intersection at Woodland Avenue and cars passing Logan Hall, 1951. Photo courtesy of PhillyHistory.org, a project of the Philadelphia Department of Records.

(Bottom) Contemporary view of the former intersections, with Claudia Cohen Hall, formerly Logan Hall, in background. Photograph by Michael M. Koehler. Collections of the University Archives and Records Center.

Ceremony for closing Woodland Avenue between 34th and 37th streets, 11 January 1958, intersection of 36th and Locust streets. Collections of the University Archives and Records Center.

the University Museum's property on the south side of Spruce Street and join 34th Street to form a widened Convention Boulevard (replacing Curie Avenue), which would carry two-way traffic around the Hospital of the University of Pennsylvania (HUP) and Philadelphia General Hospital. (The HUP Nurses' Annex on the east side of 34th Street would be a casualty of the 33rd Street extension.) The plan also included widening 38th Street by thirty feet into a four-lane boulevard, connecting it south of Woodland Avenue to University Avenue and the University Avenue Bridge, and completing the loop around Penn at the intersection of University Avenue and Convention Boulevard, just above the bridge.[55]

The 1948 Martin Plan "provided for the closing of 34th Street in order that the university could expand its facilities within an *Island* area extending from 32nd Street to 40th Street." The University viewed the striking of this corridor from the city plan as a reasonable quid pro quo for transferring part of its museum property to the city for the 33rd Street extension.[56] The city demurred, noting that closing 34th Street was politically indefensible and logistically infeasible: to placate "citizen objection to closing Woodland Avenue" and "to handle today's traffic in this area," 33rd Street and 34th Street would have to be "a paired system," with 33rd for northbound traffic and 34th for southbound. The campus planners had to accede to the city's wishes—after all, the University was holding a very thin reed as to 34th Street when the city was about to give it Woodland Avenue.[57] (See Chapter 2 for more on completing the circuit around Penn.)

■ **The University and the Philadelphia Redevelopment Authority: The Wharton School and the Physics Building Units**

The Redevelopment Authority was established in 1946 as "a body corporate and politic established pursuant to the [Commonwealth of Pennsylvania] Urban Redevelopment Law of May 24, 1945 . . . and Resolution of the Council of the City of Philadelphia approved 21 May 1945 for the purpose of acquiring, replanning and redeveloping blighted areas within the City of Philadelphia."[58] As Edmund Bacon observed, the RDA "preceded any federal law for urban renewal; it was a state law and this state showed remarkable foresight in development of a law before [the Housing Act of 1949]."[59] With the approval of the Court of Common Pleas, the RDA could exercise eminent domain when the price offered for a property could not be settled with the owner; in this case the RDA would confiscate the property and pay the owner an amount set by the Court.[60] The Urban Redevelopment Law of 1945 obligated the RDA to make "adequate provisions . . . to rehouse displaced families, if any, without undue hardship."[61] The Redevelopment Law authorized the RDA to sell the acquired properties to a developer—in Penn's case, the University trustees—who would provide "a guaranty of completion within specified time limits."[62]

The RDA "had final responsibility for detailed planning" in areas certified by the City Planning Commission.[63] Following City Council and mayoral approval of the certification of the University Redevelopment Area on 12 March 1948, and the Planning Commission's release of the University Redevelopment Area Plan in September 1950, the RDA submitted proposals for the development of sites for the Wharton School and the physics building to the Planning Commission, where they were approved and transmitted to the City Council, whose City Planning and Zoning Committee received them on 5 April 1951, and then held public hearings on the merits of the proposal. Next, pursuant to the Zoning Committee's endorsement, the Council approved the Wharton and physics units on 16 May 1951 and authorized the RDA to "execute the redevelopment contracts."[64] An ordinance of 23 May 1952 further authorized the RDA to "strike from the City plan and vacate" Chancellor Street between 32nd and 33rd streets to make way for the new physics building, first called the Benjamin Franklin Center for Physics, later renamed the David Rittenhouse Laboratories.[65] The RDA "was able to assist in acquiring part of the sites needed for the two buildings"—the Wharton School would build its new home, Dietrich Hall, in the 3600 block of Locust Street, west of the historic core (founded in 1881, the school was housed in Logan Hall from 1906 to 1952). No federal or city funds were available for the two sites. "The University compensated the Authority [in full] for the costs involved in acquiring the sites and existing buildings and in carrying out the demolitions, construction and landscaping. Some of the properties involved already were owned by the University and were taken from the school, then resold to the University." For example, the Wharton School benefactor and namesake, the ironmaster Joseph Wharton, deeded half of the Wharton unit block to Penn in 1902; in the late 1940s, it was being used as a tennis court. A total of fifty-two persons were displaced by the two projects.[66] In the physics unit, "little areas," "tiny little pieces" of houses that were "dilapidated," were obtained "property by property."[67] By the mid-1950s, the University was casting a wider net; the acquisition of "tiny little pieces" would no longer suffice for its growth needs.

■ The Hill Field Demolition

The 1948 Martin Plan earmarked white, predominantly middle-class blocks west of 38th Street between Walnut and Spruce streets as the location for a women's campus, which would include a horseshoe-shaped dormitory, a dining room, and athletic/recreational facilities. At the time, two-thirds of Penn women students were commuters; noncommuting women were housed off campus in Sergeant Hall at 34th and Chestnut streets or at scattered sites around Penn. By 1955, University planners had shelved the plan for a women's campus beyond 38th Street and turned their sights toward the blocks bounded by Chestnut, 32nd, Walnut, and 34th streets, a white working-class, mixed commercial-residential neighborhood that the RDA, fortuitously from Penn's perspective, had previously certified as blighted. The University would later foreswear any involvement in the decision that initially targeted the 12.9-acre tract for demolition.[68]

Penn acquired these properties by twists and turns. In 1950, the City Planning Commission recommended redevelopment of these blocks for "garden apartments," with no mention of the University.[69] As of August 1954, Penn still planned to build a women's dormitory in the 38th–40th Street quadrant and showed no interest elsewhere.[70] Over the next several months, the plan changed; in January 1955, the Penn trustees proposed to be the redeveloper for the Walnut-Chestnut blocks, having learned that the American Association of Engineering Societies, the city's top claimant for the blocks east of 34th Street, had decided not to build its headquarters in West Philadelphia.[71] Over the next two years, Gaylord Harnwell ingratiated himself with Mayor Richardson Dilworth and the city reform movement; Dilworth told him, "Never has a city administration had more wholehearted cooperation from, or a more pleasant relationship with the University than has this administration, and this due entirely to your efforts."[72] The appointment of G. Holmes Perkins of Penn's Graduate School of Fine Arts as chairman of the City Planning Commission in 1958—"Mayor Dilworth's personal choice"—further sealed the alliance. Perkins had a close relationship with Edmund Bacon, executive director of the Planning Commission from 1949 to 1970, who taught a class on the History and Theory of Urban Design in Penn's Graduate School of Fine Arts.[73] Harnwell called it "an unmixed blessing that several members of the Commission, including its Chairman, are closely identified with the University and neighboring institutions."[74]

By the spring of 1957, Penn had the city's writ to redevelop the Walnut-Chestnut blocks for women's housing, student activities, and off-street parking.[75] The plan was technically consistent with the "residential" intent of the 1950 University Redevelopment Area plan and the "predominantly residential" requirement of the 1949 Housing Act (more below), "although the residences would be owned by an institution and the technical use would be institutional."[76]

Designated by the RDA as University Redevelopment Area Project A, Units 1 and 2, this section was "a dismal setting," recalled a former Penn planner. In Unit 2, "there was that big hotel over there, and the Lido Restaurant and those car repair shops and things that were on the other side. It was very disreputable, particularly the hotel."[77] A Planning Commission report from 1951 cited "only 11 substantial shops and restaurants" along the entire Woodland diagonal from 32nd Street, which bisected Unit 1, to 37th Street; the report listed only three reputable businesses in the 3300 block of Woodland, the heart of Unit 2.[78]

The RDA listed a total of 139 structures to be acquired in the project area: 101 residential and 38 commercial; and a total of 553 people to be displaced: 539 white (97 percent), fourteen nonwhite (3 percent).[79] In this case, Penn averted the sustained uproar and lingering bitterness that would accompany

View east showing RDA Unit 2, with Woodland Avenue diagonal above Walnut between 34th and 33rd streets, future site of Hill Field; ca. 1957. Collections of the University Archives and Records Center.

large-scale displacement in Unit 3 to make way for the Science Center complex (more on this in chapter 3). Their initial "storm of protest" notwithstanding, most of the owners were placated by the "fair market" amount RDA paid for their properties.[80] For renters and commercial employees, however, it was a very different story: "For example," reported the *Philadelphia Inquirer*, "there is August Gamils, who runs the Socony service station on the northeast corner of 33rd and Walnut, across from the Penn School of Engineering. Gus Gamils has spent 21 years building up his business. His customers mostly are Penn faculty, students and the hospital staff. He rents the station from Socony, and if he is forced out, he will get nothing for his going business. The law forbids payments for goodwill. So Gus will be left with the equipment he owns, and no location. His eight employees will lose their jobs."[81]

In the winter of 1958, demolition began in the two units.[82] By the late autumn of 1958 the RDA "wrecking ball" had converted the entire area into "a rubble-strewn wasteland."[83] After the property titles had been conveyed and the interior streets closed by city ordinances in 1960 (Woodland Avenue in

Hill Hall (center), Zeta Psi fraternity (foreground), and Hill Field;
Woodland Avenue remnant at Drexel Institute (top left), 1961.
Collections of the University Archives and Records Center.

Unit 2 from 32nd to 34th streets; Moravian, Sansom, and Ionic streets in Unit
1 between Walnut and Chestnut streets),[84] the University started construction. In the fall of 1960, the first campus building "constructed expressly as a
women's dormitory" opened in Unit 2, flanking Walnut Street. Designed by
Eero Saarinen,[85] the $4 million dormitory comprised "four adjacent houses
forming a quadrangle around a roofed grand court with a landscaped dining
terrace on the ground level."[86]

The architectural historian George Thomas describes Hill Hall (today's
Hill College House) as "a mighty medieval fortress of crudely formed brick,
surrounded by a moat, entered by a bridge, and crowned by the modern version of a Victorian cornice."[87] A project for a second women's dormitory, scheduled for 1963, failed to materialize, leaving an expansive field (Hill Field) and
a plot of land for surface parking. For the next forty-five years, the only other
structure on the huge block of Hill Hall would be the Zeta Psi fraternity house,
built in 1909 at the northeast corner of 34th and Walnut streets, the only sur-
vivor of the 1957 demolitions.

Across 33rd Street in Unit 1, James Creese, president of the Drexel Institute since 1945, demanded a piece of the redevelopment pie for Drexel on the

Chestnut Street side. The problem had started with City Ordinance 1102, which awarded Unit 1 to Penn. In May 1957, the ordinance stalled in the City Council after Creese wrote Council president James H. J. Tate urging him to postpone the final vote on the bill until Drexel could work out an agreement with Penn on Unit 1.[88] Apparently pressured by Tate, Penn negotiated with Drexel, and the two parties finally agreed to split the unit. Accordingly, Penn received the Walnut Street side of the block (Unit 1A), where it built the Laboratory for Research on the Structure of Matter in 1962 and a "high architecture" parking garage in 1964.[89] On the Chestnut side (Unit 1B), Drexel built the James Creese Student Center.[90] This project was Penn's first involvement in a federally funded endeavor. RDA records show that the net cost of Project A (Unit 1A and 1B, Unit 2) was $2.9 million (about $23 million in 2012 dollars), of which the federal government paid two-thirds and the city and state one-third, commensurate with the terms of the 1949 Housing Act.[91]

In 1975, Edmund Bacon complained bitterly that the University behaved egregiously by leaving Hill Field vacant: "I walked by it today . . . and my resentment was renewed because there it stands . . . an open parking lot and . . . a field without a single soul in it. . . . It was extremely painful to take the brunt of putting people out of their houses. They lived there. They loved their houses." Bacon called it "a capricious and irresponsible utilization of a space after such destruction."[92] Another three decades would pass before the University finally put a second building on the site: the McNeil Center for Early American Studies, which opened in 2005. In 2008, fifty years after the demolitions, President Amy Gutmann announced plans for a new three-building college house on the Hill Field property—a "Quad-like" project with the residence halls framing a copious swath of green space replacing the Frisbee field so detested by Bacon.

■ **The University and the General State Authority: Urban Clearance and New Libraries in the Historic Core**

Standing catercorner to the east wing of College Hall is the Furness Building, of "fiery red brick" construction, "a conflation of towers, chimneys, skylighted rooms, and foundry-like clerestoried halls" reminiscent of a Victorian train station, designed by Philadelphia's famed Industrial Age architect Frank Furness. Since 1891, this extraordinary building had housed the University's main library. By the mid-1950s, the structure was "antiquated" and "disgracefully inadequate" for its main library purpose. "Orange crates and outposts have been pressed into service to house the thousands of books which cannot be accommodated in the main University library," groused the campus newspaper; "every nook and cranny of the University is used for storage purposes," Harnwell complained.[93] Anticipating up to 50 percent growth in student enrollments by 1970, Penn listed a new undergraduate library as its highest construction priority; the goal was to have a completed building by 1959. The targeted site for the new library was the trapezoidal block that fronted the Woodland diagonal from 34th and Walnut to 36th and Locust, opposite College and Logan halls. A large graduate library wing was to be a later addition.

In the 1950s, a hodgepodge of some twenty-one buildings, all University properties, filled the trapezoid, including six fraternities, a Horn and Hardart cafeteria (on the site since 1932),[94] a commercial laundry, a barber shop, a shoe repair shop, a medical and nursing supplier, several academic departments, and various administrative offices. As the University already owned the properties, the redevelopment project did not qualify for RDA assistance.[95]

Penn could not have undertaken the myriad building projects for its great expansion—a new undergraduate library, a graduate library, a new administrative building, and new classroom buildings for the social sciences, education, veterinary medicine, humanities, and fine arts—without the Pennsylvania General State Authority (GSA). Established by the state legislature in 1949, the multipurpose GSA originally included only land-grant colleges in its higher education category; in 1956, however, the General State Authority Act was amended to include "universities receiving State aid," a qualification that Penn met by virtue of its School of Veterinary Medicine, which received Commonwealth funds. The GSA had "the power to acquire, purchase, hold and use property, and to lease as lessee property for a term not to exceed 99 years . . . including the power to acquire property by the exercise of eminent domain." After the stipulated number of years, the property would revert to the lessee institution. The GSA was responsible for developing the site, with contracts to be awarded competitively. Through a quirky statutory machination, the legislature designated the Department of Public Instruction as the intermediary, proxy lessee in GSA leases involving state-aided higher education institutions. "When any such project is leased by the Authority to the Commonwealth of Pennsylvania," according to Senate Bill 517, "the Department of Public Instruction shall have the power and authority with the approval of the Governor to sub-lease such project to the university receiving State aid or school district for which said project has been undertaken upon such terms and conditions as shall be agreed to."[96]

By February 1958, the GSA had agreed to pay $4 million of the estimated $4.5 million required for the library project (the final cost of the project would be $5 million).[97] Fortuitously for Penn, the sublease agreement entailed "the nominal rental of one dollar per year," an arrangement that would hold for all new GSA buildings until 1963.[98] Demolition of the 3400 block of Walnut Street began in the winter of 1957, with the razing of buildings in the 3401 block of Woodland.[99] (In Philadelphia even numbers, for example 3400, denote the south side of east-west streets; odd numbers, for example 3401, denote the north side; odd numbers mark the east side of east-west streets, even numbers the west side. The east-west streets radiating from the Center City grid are named streets, for example, Market, Chestnut, Walnut; the main north-south streets are numbered streets, for example 36th Street, with the numbers increasing to the west.) Two fraternities in the library block whose properties abutted 36th Street—Alpha Chi Rho and Phi Kappa Sigma—were spared the wrecking ball; four fraternities were relocated, including Delta Phi (see below).[100] The Woodland block's shoemaker, Yervant Yegavian, a sixty-one-year-old immigrant from Turkey who lived in a room above his shop, told the *Daily Pennsylvanian* that he bore the University no ill will, though he remarked, "I know no one will hire a man at my age, and the possibility of opening another shop is impractical with such high rents and low demand for shoe repair shops."[101]

The Charles Patterson Van Pelt Library, "the central research collection of the university," opened in 1962, its massive brown-brick façade ornamented by a "giant concrete colonnade," with "small windows punctuating the upper levels" to "denote readers' carrels."[102] Edmund Bacon bristled at Roy Larson, the architect of the new library, for having "repudiated the axis of College Hall and . . . simply put this library as though it had no connections with the history of the great buildings around it." Bacon also complained "that he put all of the service [delivery entrances] on Walnut Street, he ruined Walnut Street!"[103]

Five years later, after demolishing the remaining brownstones on the northwest side of the Woodland trapezoid adjacent to the Van Pelt Library—one of them Blanchard Hall, the Victorian-age model for Penn alumnus Charles Addams's "Addams Family" cartoons—the University built the Dietrich graduate wing of the University Libraries, whose west façade flanks 36th Street. The GSA funded the construction of the Dietrich Library, a $4.9 million project.

From 1962 to 1970, the GSA funded nineteen new buildings on the Penn campus, many of them constructed on properties previously owned by the University: for example, on the periphery of the historic core, Meyerson Hall for the Graduate School of Fine Arts, completed in 1968, and Williams Hall for the humanities, completed in 1972.[104] Financial exigencies that burdened all research universities after 1968 would delay the landscaping of the refurbished central campus for another decade. "Even on College Green," wrote the

(Top) Looking northeast on Woodland Avenue between 36th and 34th streets, late 1950s. Collections of the University Archives and Records Center.

(Bottom) Contemporary view northeast on Woodland Walk: Van Pelt Library (left), viewed through the trees. Photograph by Michael M. Koehler. Collections of the University Archives and Records Center.

(Top) Victorian brownstones adjacent to Van Pelt Library; this view is from the intersection of 36th and Walnut streets, ca. 1961–62. Photo courtesy of PhillyHistory.org, a project of the Philadelphia Department of Records.

(Bottom) Contemporary view, Dietrich Graduate Library. Photograph by Michael M. Koehler. Collections of the University Archives and Records Center.

famous landscape architect Sir Peter Shepheard, "the new buildings simply sit on their platforms, surrounded by a patched-up arrangement of walks and eroded grass, hardly concealing the ghostly curbs and sidewalks of Woodland Avenue." The completion of Shepheard's splendid 1977 landscape design plan and the 1977 dedication of Blanche Levy Park, a distinguished venue "replenished with saplings and edged in granite, walkways of brick and Heidelberg blue stone, small amphitheater and umbrella-covered café tables toward 36th Street (itself incorporated into the park) and numerous benches," all complemented by world-famous sculpture pieces such as Claes Oldenburg's *Split Button* and Alexander Calder's *Jerusalem Stabile*, would bring closure to the Harnwell-era building boom.[105]

■ Building the West Central Campus: The Annenberg School for Communication and Social Science Centers I and II

In 1960, the RDA began its fourth urban renewal project in the University Area, acquiring and leveling thirty properties (2.24 acres total) in the block just west of 36th Street at Walnut to make way for the new Annenberg School for Communication. (This was the second expansion project west of the historic core; the Wharton School's Dietrich Hall was the first.) In 1958, the publishing magnate and Wharton School alumnus Walter Annenberg donated $3 million to establish the Annenberg School.[106] "The School of Communications [*sic*]," the RDA announced, "will be located within the rectangle bounded by 36th, Locust, 37th and Walnut Streets. Plans for improving this block will get underway in the summer of 1960. . . . City Council conducted its hearing on the Authority's plan and proposal on December 1, 1959, and gave its approval on December 17, 1959. The ordinance was signed by the Mayor [Richardson Dilworth] on December 24, 1959. All properties are expected to be vacated by May 1960." The RDA assured owners and renters that the Authority would offer them "every help in finding standard housing that is safe, sanitary and waterproof, with all the standard facilities," with the stipulation that "these dwellings must fall within the family's ability to pay and be convenient for travel to and from work for the head of the household."[107]

South McAlpin Street, a narrow one-way street in the west central sector of the campus, bisected the center of the full block between 36th and 37th streets from Locust to Walnut. The "three-story, whitewashed stone" Faculty Club building fronted South McAlpin at Walnut. From 1957 to 1959, a new five-story Faculty Club (Skinner Hall), today's Charles Addams Hall, was under construction on the corner of 36th and Walnut streets, sited on properties that Penn had held since 1952. The remainder of this racially white block included fraternity and sorority houses, other residential properties, and commercial garages on Walnut Street; census-block data show "only one non-white dwelling unit out of . . . 77 that were occupied."[108] The demolition, which started in 1960, spared several historic buildings in the 3601 block of Locust Street, notably a Second Empire twin house on the corner of 37th and Locust (ca. 1872, today's Women's Center), "a row of brownstone-fronted, mansarded townhouses (ca. 1873)," and the Delta Psi fraternity house (ca. 1907). Another surviving fraternity house, Delta Phi (St. Elmo), had been built in 1959 following relocation of the fraternity from the Van Pelt Library construction site. The Annenberg School for Communication, "a serene limestone building with a vast, glass-face lobby," opened in 1962 with a line of sight south toward Dietrich Hall, its brick entranceway from Locust Street covering the footprint of South McAlpin. In 1964, the Department of Streets closed Locust Street between 36th and 37th streets.[109]

In 1971, the Annenberg Center theater complex, with a plain, brown-brick façade that presents a windowless flank to Walnut Street, arose above a plaza shared with the School for Communication; as George Thomas observes, "The overall severity of the design perhaps unconsciously reiterates the theatrical truth that 'the Play's the Thing.'"[110] Like other Harnwell-era buildings that abutted Walnut—the Graduate School of Education, the Faculty Club, and the Van Pelt and Dietrich libraries—the Annenberg Center turned away from the street. The art historian David Brownlee says, "And the astonishing thing that we should create . . . a public theater, and not place its entrance on the street, is almost unmatched in the annals of planning history."[111]

Expansion of the West Central Campus into the adjacent block bounded by Walnut, 37th, Locust, and 38th streets involved the dispensation of the General State Authority for the eastern half of the block. In 1956 the University requested that the GSA fund a "center for the social sciences." That proposal, which included a spate of other buildings, was approved in 1958.[112] In 1961 and 1962, the GSA acquired eight Walnut frontage properties for the new Graduate School of Education, one of four buildings that would enclose the Social Science Plaza. The project was labeled "Social Science I." The State Authority acquired fifteen properties for the Department of Political Science (Stiteler Hall), three properties for the School of Social Work (Castor Building), and eight properties for the Department of Psychology; the plaza itself and its adjacencies, one of which would be landscaped as a terraced, concrete park, covered at least sixteen properties.[113] Prior to demolition the Social Science I half of the block was densely packed with buildings; a photograph from 1961 displays a row of brownstones, two with front porches, on the site

(Top) Locust Street, view east from 37th Street, Rowbottom in progress, 1962. Photograph by the *Philadelphia Evening Bulletin*, 23 April 1960. Special Collections Research Center, Temple University Libraries, Philadelphia.

(Bottom) Contemporary view: Locust Walk at 37th Street. Photograph by Michael M. Koehler. Collections of the University Archives and Records Center.

Contemporary view of the Social Science Center I quadrangle, looking north from the Graduate School of Education. These reddish-brown brick modernist buildings were designed by General State Authority architects. Photograph by Michael M. Koehler. Collections of the University Archives and Records Center.

of the future Graduate School of Education. The same photograph shows a storefront on the first floor of a row house; storefronts appear in two other photographs, suggesting a crowded residential-commercial block.[114] This block was overwhelmingly white prior to urban renewal: the 1960 Census of Housing showed 346 people residing in 177 housing units, of which only 9 (5.2 percent) were occupied by nonwhite residents.[115] In 1962–63, properties on the 3701 side of Locust Street included apartment rentals, low-end eateries, and a single fraternity, Alpha Epsilon Pi.[116]

Designed in a brown-brick palette with "pilaster like concrete piers," the four GSA-funded social science buildings were completed in 1965 (political science) and 1966 (education, social work, and psychology).

In 1966, the Redevelopment Authority claimed the other half of the block for Penn—a development we take up in our discussion of University Redevelopment Area Unit 4. The Social Science II project consisted of a new building for the departments of sociology and economics (both controlled by the Wharton School) that was sited on properties Penn acquired between 1931 and 1961 in the block bounded by Spruce, 37th, Locust, and 38th streets; that project came to fruition in 1970 as the five-story McNeil Building, another edifice with a brown-brick palette and concrete piers.[117]

■

In the first phase of the Great Expansion, Penn's campus development projects included the West Philadelphia subway-extension and trolley-car tunnel, the closing of the Woodland Avenue diagonal, and the construction of the Gates Pavilion, Dietrich Hall, the David Rittenhouse Laboratories, the Women's Residence Hall (renamed Hill Hall), and the Annenberg School for Communication. By the end of Phase I, planning was under way for Van Pelt Library in the historic core, and Social Science Center I and II in the new West Central Campus. In Phase II, which we take up in the next chapter, Penn, in its largest expansion initiative, RDA Unit 4, would complete the acquisition and building of the modern campus, abetted by Section 112 of the 1959 Housing Act—urban renewal legislation specifically tailored to the growth needs of urban universities.

2

Campus Expansion and Commercial Renewal in Unit 4

In the early 1960s, the Redevelopment Authority staked out three new urban renewal units in the University Redevelopment Area. Unit 4, at Penn, charted the completion of the West Central Campus, the creation of a West Campus beyond 38th Street, and the redevelopment of the Walnut Street commercial zone. Unit 5 accommodated an expansion of the Drexel Institute. Unit 3, established in the area of Market Street, designated the core of urban renewal blocks that would ultimately compose the University City Science Center, the brainchild of the West Philadelphia Corporation, a consortium of University City higher education and medical institutions that was dominated by Penn. The primary focus of this chapter is RDA Unit 4, the centerpiece of the second phase of Penn's Great Expansion, 1962–70. As backdrop for this discussion, we keynote Section 112 of the 1959 Housing Act and its importance to urban universities in the 1960s.

■

In the fall of 1959, the University appointed Harold Taubin, an experienced planner who had studied at the Harvard Graduate School of Design, to direct the first University Planning Office, which Harnwell established close on the heels of the report of the Educational Survey. "Our original mandate," Taubin told Jeannette Nichols, "was to work on the physical plan for the University . . . we were to be acquainted with the educational policies and objectives of the educational survey during the 1950s and translate . . . those conceptions and objectives, etc. into physical plant proposals for consideration by the authoritative bodies to be established by the President."[1] Establishment of the Planning Office also coincided neatly with the passage of the Housing Act of 1959; on the strength of this turning-point legislation, the Planning Office inaugurated the second phase of Penn's postwar expansion.

Harold Taubin, University Planning Office, 1960. Collections of the University Archives and Records Center.

In the first phase, 1948–62, the Philadelphia Redevelopment Authority played the indispensable role. For the new Wharton School and David Rittenhouse Laboratories unit, Penn relied on the RDA for the "piecemeal" acquisition and clearance of residential properties, as opposed to the "whole-block" approach used by the RDA in the removal of residential and commercial properties for the Women's Residence Hall and the additional student housing proposed for the blocks bounded by Walnut, 33rd, Chestnut, and 34th streets—the RDA's federally funded Project A (Unit 1A and 1B, Unit 2).

After the fall of 1959, Penn embarked on a continuous planning process, taking advantage of federal housing legislation to engage with the RDA in federally sponsored urban renewal activities for academic and commercial purposes that had nothing to do with housing. Indeed, the University played an instrumental role in directing the original purpose of the landmark 1949 Housing Act away from housing.

■ The Section 112 Federal Housing Windfall

The pivotal second phase of Penn's Great Expansion, 1962–70, occurred against the backdrop of the 1954 and 1959 revisions of the 1949 Housing Act, which led to Philadelphia's embrace of the University as a full partner in urban renewal. Enacted after four years of congressional debates, the 1949 Housing Act provided a two-pronged strategy for the postwar revitalization of America's cities: public housing and urban redevelopment. The original aim was "a decent home and suitable living environment for every American family." Explicitly "residential" in its orientation, the 1949 legislation allocated $1 billion to cities for slum clearance and blight removal (the "federal bulldozer" approach) and $500 million over six years for "new low-rent public housing units."[2] Of particular future significance for urban renewal, Title I "authorized financial assistance by the Housing and Home Finance Administrator to a local public agency [for example, Philadelphia's RDA] for a project consisting of the assembly, clearance, site-preparation, and sale or lease of land at its fair value for uses specified in a redevelopment plan for the area of the project." Federal grants would reimburse the local public agency in an amount up to two-thirds of the net cost of the project; the net cost was calculated as "the difference between what a city had to pay for acquiring slum or blighted properties, clearing the site and providing the necessary service facilities and street changes for the area when rebuilt and the smaller amount recovered by the city from selling the cleared land to a private redeveloper." The local agency would pay one-third of the net project cost; it was eligible for federal loans to conduct surveys and plans, which would be repaid through the proceeds of land sales and other legislated means.[3]

Concurrent with the new federal legislation, the Commonwealth of Pennsylvania enacted the Housing and Redevelopment Law, which appropriated $15 million to supplement the local grant for projects such as the Women's Residence Hall.[4] The first major revision of the 1949 Housing Act was the Housing Act of 1954, which expanded the Title I program, substituting "urban renewal" for "urban redevelopment."[5] The revision augmented the local public agency's authority by subsidizing not only slum clearance (that is, redevelopment, as in the 1949 Act), but also the implementation of "plans for a program of voluntary repair and rehabilitation of buildings or other improvements in accordance with the urban renewal plan" (that is, conservation in "gray areas"); in other words, redevelopment or conservation, or both in the same project.[6] Significantly, Title III of the 1954 Act introduced an important exception to the residential requirement of the 1949 Act, authorizing federal aid for renewal of an area "which is not predominately residential [that is, 51 percent] in character . . . [but which] contains a substantial number of slum, blighted, deteriorated, or deteriorating dwellings or other living accommodations, the elimination of which would tend to promote the public health in the locality involved and such area is not appropriate for redevelopment for predominately residential uses."[7] This codicil would be of no mean importance to the creation of the University City Science Center.

Critical to Penn's campus expansion in West Philadelphia was the 1959 Housing Act, which opened a wide door for involving higher education institutions in urban renewal projects.[8] Three urban universities, one of them Penn, played instrumental roles in creating the pivotal 1959 legislation. According to Lillian Burns, a former Penn planner, "The University of Pennsylvania, with John Moore as the front man, and the University of Chicago, with Julian Levi, who was president of the South East Chicago Commission, closely related with the University of Chicago, [and] the president of New York University, . . . our three institutions worked very hard to develop a strategy for . . . introducing into the national legislation a section that would be . . .

helpful to university expansion and, after discussing and looking at it, we came up with a proposal for Section 112, which provided for compatible neighborhoods for universities."[9] Moore, Penn's business vice president, joined Levi and NYU vice president and treasurer George Bauman in speaking for the amendment in hearings held by the House Committee on Banking and Currency in the winter of 1959. "Like many other urban universities," Moore told the committee, "the University of Pennsylvania . . . cannot expand unless it is given some instrument to assist it in its endeavors"; Penn required sixty-three acres to remedy its "deficiency in land."[10] At the same hearings, Harnwell's ally Richardson Dilworth testified that Philadelphia required $156 million to complete its urban renewal program, at least $10 million of which he claimed was needed to counter blight in University City.[11]

The draft of Section 112 of the 1959 Housing Act, which amended Title I of the 1949 Housing Act, first appeared as a document accompanying Levi's oral testimony before the Senate Committee on Banking and Currency. The amendment had the backing of the American Association of Universities, under whose auspices the AAU's urban institutions conducted a survey of "their environmental problems."[12] (Lillian Burns recalled, "We had a lot of meetings and we met with representatives of institutions from around the country, developing this and trying to get it organized."[13]) Levi told the committee, "The story over the entire country is that it is virtually impossible for such institutions to assemble usable construction sites through the acquisition of needed land by negotiation." He sketched "an even grimmer" scenario: "environments of slum and blight or near blight" were undermining "the community of scholars" by driving them into the suburbs.[14] (Elsewhere Levi would famously describe urban universities as "collections of scholarly commuters rather than communities of scholars.")[15] John Moore filed a written statement with the Senate committee and also presented oral testimony. The omnibus housing bill with Section 112 easily passed both houses, which were controlled by Democratic majorities. Another Harnwell ally, the Philadelphia reformer Joseph Clark, a member of the Senate Banking and Currency Committee, stood squarely behind the bill, which after some jousting with President Eisenhower was signed into law on 23 September 1959.[16]

Writing in 1963, one expert on urban renewal explained the bountiful license Section 112 gave to urban universities:

Section 112 projects are exempt from the requirement, applicable to other Title I projects, that the urban renewal area be predominately residential in character, and that it be redeveloped for predominantly residential uses. While over the years the Congress has been granting some exceptions to this requirement (the law now provides that 30 percent of the total Title I authorization for urban renewal project grants may be used for nonresidential projects), the increasing interest of cities in redevelopment of blighted commercial areas for nonresidential purposes is resulting in Federal commitments approaching the 30 percent limitation. Since the residential requirement does not apply to Section 112 projects, this limitation does not affect colleges.[17]

Not only did Section 112 give urban universities a formidable writ to use urban renewal to expand their campuses, it also allowed them to redevelop commercial zones in their surrounding blocks. In Unit 4, Section 112 would allow Penn to replace marginal businesses on the boundary streets of the central campus—Walnut Street on the north, Spruce Street on the south—with academic buildings, administrative offices, and upscale retail operations.[18]

Section 112 offered another distinct advantage to urban universities. The local renewal agency would do the hard labor of condemnation, acquisition, and demolition; it would sell the cleared properties to the university at a fair market price for unimproved land, providing a considerable savings to the university, considering what it would have had to pay without urban renewal support, namely, "the capitalized value of the buildings as well as the costs of demolition." Section 112 provided a strong incentive for cities to initiate collaboration with universities in urban renewal projects: the cost of such projects would be credited to the city's one-third share of funding wherever the city chose to spend it.[19] Prior to Section 112, "the direct benefit to the city was not always clear since the land was often removed from the tax rolls after local and federal authorities had paid to acquire and clear the land as well as to relocate the former occupants. . . . The immediate benefits to the city from selling cleared land to the university might not necessarily outweigh the direct costs required by the federal government. . . . . Levi's Section 112 was designed to remove that possibility."[20] The city was eligible to benefit directly from campus urban renewal in the form of federal credits that could be applied as part or all of the city's contribution to a federally funded urban renewal project—credits that could be based on the campus acquisitions before Section 112. Accordingly, Penn's planning office "certified [the properties the University acquired from July 1952 to February 1961] to the City so that they could use that amount of money as part of the City's matching funds to the federal funds for Urban Renewal projects in the city of Philadelphia, not just in Unit 3 or Unit 4."[21]

No university of the urban renewal era, public or private, achieved a greater expansion of its campus core or made more use of urban renewal tools than

Penn. The Great Expansion was in large part synonymous with Unit 4, a ben-eficiary of Section 112. Penn's history as a bellwether of university-based ur-ban renewal illustrates the important role played by major higher education institutions in the redevelopment of the postwar American city. In the 1950s and 1960s, other urban universities confronted the specter of declining neigh-borhoods on their doorsteps, and, like Penn, they required land in their bound-ary areas for campus expansion and private development commensurate with their institutional needs. According to a knowledgeable commentator, "by mid-1962, 34 separate renewal projects involving Section 112 credits from 38 institutions of higher education or from hospitals were in project development. Another 51 projects were being planned or discussed. Section 112 credits for institutional land purchases and relocation expenses were estimated at $32,000,000 for the approved projects and $112,000,000 for the projects in some stage of planning or discussion, a total [allocation] of $144,000,000."[22]

The national phenomenon of university urban renewal is properly described in terms of four types. In the appendix to this book, we profile three of these types—de novo campus development, campus-core expansion, and scattered-

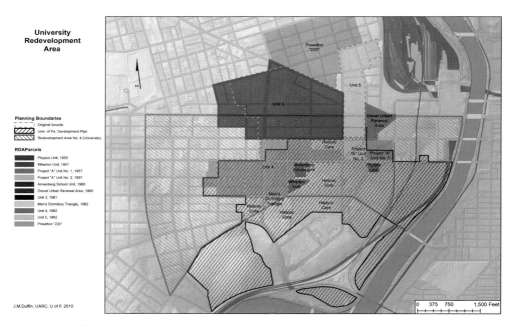

Map of University Redevelopment Area. GIS map by J. M. Duffin, December 2010. Collections of the University Archives and Records Center.

site campus expansion. Our discussion of the fourth type—proxy campus expansion—appears in chapter 3, where we take up Penn's "shadow expansion" in Unit 3 under the aegis of the West Philadelphia Corporation and compare Penn's approach to actions taken at the University of Chicago and Columbia under the aegis of the South East Chicago Commission and Morningside Heights, Inc.

We now turn to Penn in Unit 4. Here the University mobilized the full panoply of federal and state funding instruments at the disposal of urban universities and their cities by the 1960s. Engaged by the City of Philadelphia as a full partner in urban renewal, Penn, along with city planners, mixed and matched funds and bulldozers at various sites in Unit 4. They contributed, controversially, a modernist architectural flair to the campus, including Le Corbusier-style ("towers in the park") residence halls. And they managed, controversially, the complexities of residential and commercial displacements, the legal challenges mounted by recalcitrant property owners and tenants, and the moral and aesthetic thicket of competing visions of the American city.

■ The Great Expansion in Unit 4, 1962–70

Section 112 of the 1959 Housing Act applied to Unit 4, which included about eight large rectangular blocks of redevelopment properties. Here the RDA, the General State Authority (GSA), and the Pennsylvania Higher Education Facilities Authority (PHEFA, established in 1967) worked in tandem to condemn and purchase properties earmarked for University buildings. From the late 1960s to the early 1970s, the three authorities were involved in an array of projects. In some cases, the RDA condemned properties for PHEFA projects.

Completing the West Central Campus: Unit 4 East of 38th Street

In the spring of 1959, Gaylord Harnwell consulted with the University's trustees and responded to a letter from the RDA's executive director, Francis J. Lammer, which recommended "a rather large scale acquisition by the University of Pennsylvania in order to accomplish the redevelopment of a much larger area—'University City.'" Harnwell listed Penn's expansion priorities for a gaggle of blocks roughly bounded by Chestnut and Spruce streets on the north and south and 36th and 40th streets on the east and west; these priorities included undergraduate and graduate dormitories, academic buildings, and local retail and restaurant development. Of particular note were plans to construct dormitories in blocks from Walnut to Spruce between 38th and 40th streets, which would move the campus deeper into West Philadelphia, and the development of the blocks from Walnut to Sansom Street between 34th and 36th streets for University offices and high-end, campus-related retail businesses.[23] Two years later, Harold Taubin's Planning Office produced the first Campus Development Plan, "a general guide for the University's physical development," which was approved by the City Planning Commission as part of the area redevelopment plan for what was now being called University City (more on this appellation below); the Penn trustees agreed that the 1961 plan would be continuously updated to reflect new needs and opportunities. The plan projected an increase in full-time undergraduate and graduate enrollments between 1960 and 1970 from 9,384 to 12,000 students, a 27.8 percent spurt; this projection spawned nine new dormitories in Unit 4.[24] Exceeding projections, the total full-time enrollment was 13,801 by 1967; projected full-time enrollments were 16,100 for 1972–73 and 18,541 for 1976–77.[25]

The 1961 Campus Development Plan covered 240 acres, including the historic Woodlands Cemetery, just southwest of the campus, in operation since 1845. For all the grisliness and potential for controversy, cemetery removals for urban renewal purposes were not uncommon in the 1950s and 1960s.[26] Penn wanted the Woodlands for "athletic open space, expansion of the academic plant after 1970, and housing." Taubin told Harnwell, "The one requirement established by the City Planning Commission, when it approved the [50-acre] tract for inclusion within the University's approved development area, is that the Hamilton Mansion [a Federalist structure] be preserved."[27] An attorney for the dismayed Cemetery Company wrote the University, "There is presently no portion of the Cemetery large enough for any use which Dr. Harnwell suggested the University had in mind without disturbing some graves and therefore the Cemetery Company does not look with favor upon any steps designed even for the remote future to divert any of the Company's land from its present use."[28] Those were fighting words; by the summer of 1963, the University had withdrawn its claim to the cemetery.[29]

The University's overvaulting ambitions, bolstered by the city's staunch commitment to area redevelopment, sparked a planning frenzy at Penn. In May 1962, the trustees approved the Integrated Development Plan, the brainchild of a multicommittee task force of trustees, faculty, and administrators. Drawing from the 1954–59 Educational Survey and subsequent developments, this document specified the University's educational and research goals and embedded them in a set of capital proposals, many of which came to fruition as Unit 4 projects, notably "Superblock" undergraduate and graduate housing.[30] Such was the importance of the 1962 Integrated Development Plan, which incorporated the capital projects of the 1961 Campus Development Plan, that the trustees established a new vice presidency for coordinated planning, naming John Hetherston as the first incumbent of that office. To raise the money that would fund the plan, E. Craig Sweeten, vice president for development, headed the University's $93 million development campaign of 1965–70. The highly successful campaign, which raised $100,103,000 by May 1969, underwrote the capital projects in the Integrated Development Plan, as well as twenty-seven endowed professorships, scholarship and fellowship endowments, and student loan funds.[31]

In 1962, the City Council authorized the RDA's establishment of Unit 4 (Penn) and Unit 5 (Drexel).[32] Consistent with federal policy, Philadelphia's urban renewal process charged the RDA to conduct a prescribed survey of each urban renewal unit and to submit a site plan to the City Planning Commission "for its recommendation to City Council." The plan for Unit 4 was aligned with the Planning Commission's University Area Development Plan (1950) and its periodic updates, which incorporated the University's continuous planning process (see below). Following the public hearing prescribed by law, the City Council approved the proposal, authorizing the RDA to apply for a "contract and grant" from the Housing and Home Finance Administration. Federal authorization and the award of federal urban renewal funds to the RDA (a 2-1 match) gave the Authority its writ to execute the plan.[33]

Unit 4 was a 49.3-acre agglomeration that included four groupings of blocks tortuously configured. The first grouping was 34th-36th-Walnut-Sansom streets (with Moravian Street between Walnut and Sansom) and an undeveloped portion of the Annenberg School block; the second grouping was 36th-38th-Walnut-Chestnut streets (including Sansom Street, between Walnut and Chestnut) and a row of properties on the west side of 38th Street; the third grouping was the blocks of 37th-40th-Spruce-Walnut streets (including Locust and Irving streets, and, in one block, Chancellor Street) and two half blocks on the west side of 40th Street.[34] City planners described Unit 4 as "a predominately residential project. Many structures in the area are deteriorated and obsolete in terms of present usage. A number of streets within the area are inadequate to support present day traffic volume. Off-street parking is virtually non-existent and off-street unloading space is lacking in many of the commercial and industrial establishments." A total of 309 residential buildings and sixty-three nonresidential structures were targeted for clearance.[35] The Survey and Planning Application for Unit 4, completed in January 1962, listed 1,065 families living in the unit, 966 (90.7 percent) of which were white, and only 99 (9.3 percent) black; also listed were 85 individuals and 99 "business concerns."[36]

To accomplish the goals of the 1962 Integrated Development Plan and its periodic updates, the University required "a single zoning designation" for

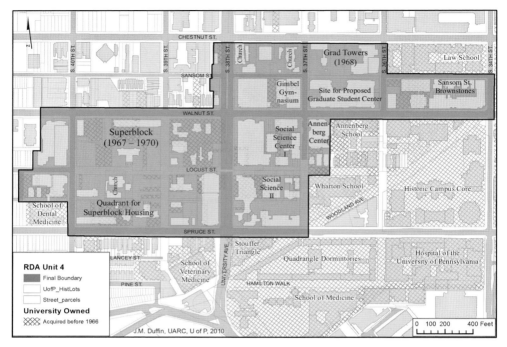

Map of Redevelopment Authority (RDA) Unit 4 in 1966. GIS map
by J. M. Duffin. Collections of the University Archives and Records
Center.

Unit 4. Without an "institutional development zone," the University would
be entangled in "10 different zoning designations," having to appeal to the
Zoning Board of Adjustments each time it needed a variance in any of the categories. The City Council approved the institutional development zone in 1965
after the Zoning Board of Adjustments refused to grant variances to allow
construction of the new fine arts building (later named Martin Meyerson
Hall), which was located near the intersection of Woodland Walk and 34th
and Walnut streets. G. Holmes Perkins, in his dual role as dean of fine arts
and chairman of the City Planning Commission, no doubt influenced this
decision. This was ostensibly a conflict of interest, yet, as an *Evening Bulletin*
editorial declaimed, "Still there is a case for giving Penn most—if not all—of
what it asks. Under institutional zoning, a college or hospital or church can
plan for growth within certain bounds but with freedom from niggling variance requirements. The whole spirit of the institutional district is beneficial
to their growth and appears to be a healthy addition to zoning legislation."[37]

The "niggling variance requirement" of immediate concern to Perkins was the requirement "to provide off-street parking as part of the Fine Arts Building. But the new zoning permits the university to take into account parking within 1,000 feet of new construction. A large parking garage, [at] 32d and Walnut sts., is well within the 1,000-feet limit, permitting construction of the Fine Arts building under 'institutional' zoning without the variance."[38] (That the Graduate School of Fine Arts, with only "a small graduate enrollment," was able to "invade" the humanities core of the central campus testified not only to Perkins's influence on the Planning Commission but also to the bargaining chip his chairmanship gave him in his dealings with Harnwell and the trustees: the new building was their quid for Perkins's quo.)[39] The irony that Meyerson Hall (a GSA-funded project), "one of the worst examples of architecture ever done," would house Penn's Department of Architecture did not elude Edmund Bacon, who castigated Perkins, his erstwhile friend and colleague. No "environmentally sensitive culture," he railed, would have "tolerated a building like that."[40]

■

Thirty-Eighth Street, a north-south street that figured prominently in Unit 4, presented a formidable obstacle to an integrated campus, especially as the city planned to widen the street into a "major boulevard" to accommodate the heavy traffic unleashed by the elimination of Woodland Avenue east of 38th Street. Indeed, as early as 1946 city planners had anticipated the congestive effects of removing the Woodland diagonal through the campus between 38th and Market streets.[41] By the late 1960s, the dangers posed by widening 38th Street in the absence of a pedestrian bridge were evident: pedestrian movement through the intersections of 38th Street and Spruce, Locust, and Walnut Streets was heavy—some twenty thousand daily crossings.[42] The pedestrian bridge was also essential to Harnwell's project of establishing a contiguous campus between 32nd and 40th streets; the bridge would join the newly planned, residential West Campus, the crown jewel of Unit 4 planning, with the West Central Campus and, two blocks further down Locust Walk, with the historic core. Penn's Unit 4 planning priorities for completing the West Central Campus also included closing Locust Street west of 37th Street to 40th Street, extending the redevelopment on the Social Science Center I block to 38th Street, and expanding the domain of the Wharton School.

East of 38th Street, Locust Street was the dividing line for two sets of redevelopment projects. Wrapping the southeast corner of Locust at 38th Street, the eighteen-unit Victoria Apartments occupied parcels that Penn had acquired in a private transaction in 1926; the rear of the apartment buildings

Gaylord Harnwell with Unit 4 model. Collections of the University
Archives and Records Center.

straddled Irving Street, a back street that ran from 37th to 40th Street. In 1968
and 1969, the city closed these four blocks of Irving. Soon thereafter, the University demolished the aging Victoria, clearing the rubble for a surface parking lot that covered the site until 1986, when the University, under President
Sheldon Hackney, built the Wharton School's Steinberg Conference Cen-
ter/Aresty Institute for Executive Education. One block to the east, in the area
of 37th and Spruce streets, the RDA bulldozed a student-friendly commercial district for Vance Hall, the Wharton School's brick-and-glass graduate
building, which opened in 1973, its entrance facing the former roadbed of
Irving Street.

(Top) Locust Street looking west toward 38th, with temporary trolley tracks, photo showing 3732–3734 Locust Street units of Victoria Apartments; the steeple of St. Mary's Episcopal Church is in far background, mid-1950s. Collections of the University Archives and Records Center.

(Bottom) Contemporary view of Locust Walk below 38th Street: Steinberg-Aresty Hall (former site of Victoria Apartments) (left), Class of 1949 Bridge and Hamilton Village high-rise dorms (background). Photograph by Michael M. Koehler. Collections of the University Archives and Records Center.

(Top) Looking south from Locust Street toward the Quad towers, ca. 1967. Irving Street marks the space between the buildings on right. Collections of the University Archives and Records Center.

(Bottom) Contemporary view showing Wharton School's Lauder-Fischer Building and the Quad Towers. The steps (center right) mark the former roadbed of Irving Street. Photograph by Michael M. Koehler. Collections of the University Archives and Records Center.

In 1965, on the north side of Locust Street, the University took steps to acquire the land between Social Science Center I and the east side of 38th Street for new buildings for the Nursing School (projected for the north end of the block) and the School of Allied Medical Professions (projected for the south end), and a new wing of the Graduate School of Education.[43] In 1966, the RDA condemned the properties for clearance and transfer to Penn.[44] The plan, however, was never pursued, and in 1968 the University built a new Nursing Education Building on a property of the Philadelphia General Hospital behind the University hospital.[45] The University opted instead to erect cheaply built, single-story, jury-rigged structures that would serve as temporary quarters for the Penn bookstore and for fourteen retail merchants who were displaced by projects in Unit 4. Dubbed University Plaza, the motley complex, which opened in the fall of 1968, was earmarked as a temporary solution, pending final relocation of the merchants in the new commercial sites arising in Unit 4 and the development of a permanent site plan for the east side of 38th Street below Walnut.[46]

University Plaza, whose rental agent was Hertzfeld & Associates, would feature new chain stores such as the Wawa Food Market and Records Unlimited alongside "oldtimers like Kelly & Cohen's, where corned-beef-on-rye was 15 cents in 1927, and cobbler Mike Mackrides, who is now repairing shoes for grandchildren of his 1918 customers." Bulldozing for the Wharton School's Dietrich Hall in the late 1940s had forced Mackrides to move to the 3701 block of Spruce Street. Twenty years later, Unit 4 bulldozing in the area of 37th Street and the north side of Spruce had Mackrides on the move again. "He has survived recession, depression, inflation and the rise of technology," a sympathetic University news source reported, "and now he faces another challenge: Mike MacKrides has been urban-renewed."[47] Ironically, the University bookstore and some of the same displaced merchants—notably the Pennsylvania Book Center, University Jewelers, and Joseph Anthony Hair Stylists—occupied the "interim location" buildings until the late 1990s, when the site was finally cleared to build the gargantuan Huntsman Hall, which the Wharton School opened in 2002.[48]

The Class of 1949 pedestrian bridge was the last Unit 4 project in the West Central Campus. In order to meet the City's clearance standard of 16.6 feet, construction of a gradually sloping, reinforced-concrete, railed-topped pedestrian ramp over 38th Street required lowering the street eight feet below its present elevation. The accompanying street-widening project was under way in 1970, though not before undergraduates had already settled into new dormitories in the Superblock west of the thoroughfare.[49] Finally completed in

Lowering and widening of 38th Street beside University Plaza. The street was lowered eight feet to accommodate a pedestrian bridge. Photograph from *Poor Richard's Record*, 1972. Collections of the University Archives and Records Center.

1973, "the bridge," declared Harold Taubin, "has enabled the University to create a continuous pedestrian-oriented enclave."[50]

Building the West Campus

The first dormitory in the Superblock of Walnut, 38th, Spruce, and 40th streets was the Harold C. Mayer Residence Hall, a low-rise residence for married Wharton students, located in the 3801 block of Spruce Street and built without RDA assistance. The new dormitory stood on properties Penn had purchased in 1948 and 1952; the site was one of many occupied by fraternities in the targeted dormitory blocks. A "tripartite agreement" between the RDA, the Pennsylvania Higher Education Facilities Authority, and the University governed redevelopment of the Superblock, as well as a block of properties bounded by Chestnut, 36th, Samson, and 37th streets. According to the agreement, the RDA would convey the properties to the PHEFA, which would build and then lease the dormitories to Penn for forty years. The University's obligation was a semiannual rent to amortize the loan; after forty years Penn would own the buildings.[51]

Before redevelopment, the Superblock comprised four crowded residential blocks and streets that featured, among other structures, Victorian houses, four stately mansions (former homes of the Drexel, Fels, and Eisenlohr families) in the northeast quadrant of the site, St. Mary's Episcopal Church on

Looking west on Locust Walk, Class of 1949 Bridge, 1973. Collections of the University Archives and Records Center.

the 3900 block of Locust Street, which dated to 1873, and a branch of the Philadelphia Free Library, a Federalist-style building at the corner of 40th and Walnut streets. According to the 1960 census of housing, 1,220 people lived in 447 dwelling units, 368 of which were renter-occupied; blacks lived in only 18 (4.5 percent) of the units. These blocks were overwhelmingly white.[52] Students lived in boarding houses and fraternities, the latter contributing a nighttime racket to the already congested blocks. "It was horrible," recalled Fran Scott, who lived in the St. Mary's rectory in the early 1960s.[53] The

Construction of Le Corbusier-style high-rise dormitories in the
Superblock complex, 1970; looking east from 40th Street with
St. Mary's Episcopal Church at center. Collections of the University
Archives and Records Center.

mansions of the northeast quadrant, St. Mary's Church and rectory, and the public library were spared the wrecking ball, as were the Victorian houses on the north side of Spruce Street and two splendid relics of the circa 1870s streetcar suburb: "small Gothic villas" standing side by side on Locust Street in the 3801 block: today's Kappa Alpha Society and the Kelly Writers House, formerly the University chaplain's home.[54] The other structures on the four blocks, including thirteen fraternities, were leveled in 1968 and 1969.[55] (Unit 4 urban renewal compelled the relocation of seventeen fraternities, a number of them to the Victorian 3901 block of Spruce Street.)[56] The Streets Department closed four streets in the Superblock: Locust, Chancellor, and Irving in 1968 and 1969; 39th Street in 1971 and 1975.[57]

The Unit 4 plan called for three T-shaped, concrete-and-steel high-rise dormitories of twenty-five stories patterned unimaginatively on the model of Le Corbusier's "tall towers," each to house approximately one thousand students. Three low-rise dormitories—four-story walk-ups to accommodate 550 students—were also planned, as well as a dining commons building and two parking garages.[58] In 1966, the RDA acquired the properties; it conveyed them to the PHEFA in 1969. In his role as dean of the Graduate School of Fine Arts, G. Holmes Perkins spearheaded development of the Superblock complex, which failed on both aesthetic and practical grounds. "Each tower sits in a different position within its block," George Thomas wrote of the functionalist high-rises, which dominate the west side of the campus. "The easternmost [High-Rise East, today's Harnwell House] is pushed toward the west side by the Class of 1920s Commons [on Locust, just above the 38th Street bridge, with an adjoining garage]; the southwest tower [Harrison Hall, today's Harrison House] stands closer to Spruce Street, and the northwest tower [High-Rise North, today's Rodin House] stands with its south-facing stem centered on Locust Walk. Together they are a heroic statement about the belief in technology as a force for progress. Unhappily this Stalinist grouping has proven no more successful for undergraduate dormitories than it did for public housing."[59]

Perkins seems to have feathered his own nest with the Superblock. His architectural firm, Perkins and Romañach, was retained as a consultant for the project, which required the City Planning Commission's authorization. Perkins wielded his power as chair of the commission to pressure the RDA staff to reverse their initial rejection of what was, in effect, *his* proposal. Explaining the staff's decision, Francis J. Lammer, the executive director, said, "It seemed to have a lot of open space and the land wasn't used as densely as it had been before." The *Evening Bulletin* reported what happened next: "When he heard about the rejection of the plans, Perkins said in an

Move-in day, 10 September 1970. Collections of the University
Archives and Records Center.

interview, he telephoned Gustave G. Amsterdam, banker, civic leader, and chairman of the Redevelopment Authority. Shortly after this, the authority's staff backed away from its original decision. Staff personnel reportedly were told by higher authorities that they could not reject the plans." Perkins usurped the Planning Commission's customary process of having a staff member present a proposal to the full commission, intervening to make the presentation himself. "I did know more about this plan than anyone else and this seemed to be the simplest thing to do," he said. When asked by the reporter if this was not a conflict of interest, Perkins said, "I'm always worried about something like this, particularly from the point of view of the city. In this case we were supporting the interests of the city. I think the city was being extraordinarily well served."[60]

The three high-rises were attractively refurbished under President Judith Rodin in the late 1990s, when the splendidly relandscaped Superblock was renamed Hamilton Village; the 1960s low-rises are today's Stouffer House (formerly Mayer Hall, now a partner house with the dormitory in the Stouffer Triangle), DuBois House, and the Class of 1925 House/Gregory House.[61] Speaking twenty years after the high-rises were completed, a penitent Edmund Bacon lamented, "The whole thing could have been done in low rise courts . . . the large open spaces are entirely unnecessary, and a number of the old Victorian houses, many of which were very beautiful, could have been saved."[62] (Apparently calculating that their own costs would outstrip the available state funds, the trustees quashed the low-rises in 1967.)[63] G. Holmes Perkins emphasized that, for better or worse, the height-conformity guidelines for Unit 4 redevelopment, which were established by the Commission and Bacon himself, were followed in the Superblock: "To 38th Street and between Spruce and Walnut, the buildings are all low, and that's part of the plan, that you have to stay low and conform to the old campus. But if you go beyond that on either side, either to the medical area or to the west beyond 38th Street, you can go high."[64] (Completed in 2002, "looming over Walnut Street," and flanking the east side of 38th Street for an entire block, the outsized postmodern edifice of the Wharton School's Huntsman Hall, "the reification of the Wharton hegemony," violates this long-standing Unit 4 design agreement.)[65] The opening of the 1920 Commons and the two-level garage in 1971, and the Class of 1949 Bridge in 1973, marked the completion of the Superblock.

Urban Renewal on the South and West Edges of Unit 4

Just outside Unit 4, also in Penn's path of expansion, stood a triangle of commercial buildings that was bounded by 38th Street (the base), Woodland

Avenue (the hypotenuse), and Spruce Street between 37th and 38th streets. In 1962, the RDA acquired the fourteen properties in this triangle; the University had previously owned half of the properties, one of which was leased to a Sunoco service station at the apex of the triangle. The block also included "an old, dilapidated apartment building" and stores that were "run down and poorly maintained."[66] The RDA's annual report for 1964 earmarked the site for a project called the "Men's Dormitory Triangle." The University's plan called for "a dining hall and residence structure which would include storefronts for merchants in the 3700 block of Spruce Street and enable them to be relocated [from sites in Unit 4] without interruption to their businesses."[67] To create a pedestrian corridor between the triangle and the adjacent Dormitory Quadrangle (the Quad), the University's splendid collegiate-Gothic residential quadrangle (built in stages beginning in 1896), the Woodland Avenue diagonal from 38th Street to Spruce Street was re-

Sunoco service station in triangle opposite the Quad; Woodland Avenue (left), 37th Street (foreground), Spruce Street (right), 1952. Photo courtesy of PhillyHistory.org, a project of the Philadelphia Department of Records.

moved from the city plan in the spring of 1964.[68] The RDA deeded the total package of properties at cost to Penn for $216,373; in this case, the University paid the acquisition and demolition costs.[69] The Stouffer residence hall (later college house) and new Spruce Street retail and restaurant storefronts opened in the 3700 block in 1972.

Also outside Unit 4 across 38th Street, on a triangle originally bounded by that street, Spruce, and Delancey, the General State Authority, in 1963, built a reddish-brown brick and limestone-trimmed veterinary research and instruction facility, the Gladys Hall Rosenthal Building; the new building covered the footprint of Delancey Street, which the city had closed in 1962. On the southwest side of the block, the Rosenthal Building adjoined the "late medieval revival quadrangle" of the School of Veterinary Medicine, completed in 1913.[70] Penn's last GSA building of the Harnwell era, standing just inside Unit 4 on the western periphery, was similarly constructed to upgrade the

Contemporary view: Stouffer Triangle complex: Platt Student Performing Arts Center, Stouffer College House, and retail businesses on Spruce Street. Photograph by Michael M. Koehler. Collections of the University Archives and Records Center.

facilities of a professional school built before World War I: the Thomas W. Evans Museum and Dental Institute (School of Dental Medicine), completed in 1915, for a half century a collegiate Gothic outpost of the University that still fronts Spruce Street and extends along 40th Street. In 1966, the RDA acquired the properties a half block to the north at the corner of 40th and Locust streets, where the GSA funded construction of the Leon Levy Oral Health Sciences Building in 1969. (Described by George Thomas as "a concatenation of brick towers and reinforced concrete piers," the Levy Building is now "screened" by the Shattner Center, completed in 2001, a "light-filled" structure whose "brick and limestone façade" recalls the 1915 Evans Building.)[71]

Across Locust Street, the adjoining commercial block was assigned to Unit 4. Here, in the fall of 1966, the RDA designated the University City Shopping Center Association, a group of five displaced University City merchants, as the redevelopers for the west side of 40th Street between Locust and Walnut, some 1½ acres of properties, which were the only Unit 4 parcels not earmarked for Penn redevelopment. "The block to be redeveloped contains a garage, gasoline station, laundry and rooming houses occupied by University of Pennsylvania students," reported the *Evening Bulletin*. "These buildings will be razed. In their place, the association expects to put up, at a cost of nearly $2 million, one eight-story apartment building with 40 apartments and a one-story building, housing stores."[72] No apartment building would ever rise on 40th Street. Student-oriented businesses and restaurants of variable quality would fill the block for decades; the frontage of 40th Street at Penn would have no high-end anchor businesses until after 1993, the year the University finally acquired the block.[73]

Urban Renewal in the Walnut Street Commercial Corridor and the North Campus Expansion

Unlike on the Superblock, the RDA bulldozers moved haltingly on the north side of Walnut Street from 34th Street to 40th Street, on the blocks from Walnut to Sansom between 34th and 36th streets, and on the block from Chestnut to Sansom between 36th and 37th streets. Some of the redevelopment projects were not challenged by the owners or tenants of condemned buildings; other projects, however, were vigorously contested.

In 1967, the General State Authority completed, without disruption, the University's Franklin Building, "a tough-looking quasi-industrial office building." This administration and general services building and its rear annex stood at the center of the 3401 block of Walnut Street. Its next-door neighbor, the art deco West Philadelphia Title and Trust Company at the corner of 36th and Walnut streets, would be the only pre-urban-renewal building left standing after the Walnut clearances; later renamed the Mellon Bank Building, today it houses a trendy fashion boutique.[74] In 1966, two blocks to the west, the GSA-funded Bernard F. Gimbel Gymnasium (today's David S. Pottruck Health and Fitness Center) arose on the northwest corner of 37th and Walnut streets, a site previously occupied by Kelly and Cohen, a popular restaurant displaced by Unit 4 redevelopment; Gimbel featured a "rough-textured brick façade" and "massive piers," suggestive of a "Greek temple."[75] (GSA structures approved before 1963, including the Franklin and Gimbel buildings, were designated "rent-free"; structures approved after 1963 would pay an "effective interest rate" of 6 percent of the total GSA cost.)[76] In 1968 the RDA acquired and conveyed the properties on the block bounded by Chestnut, 36th, Sansom, and 37th streets to the Higher Education Facilities Authority. The Le Corbusier-style Graduate Towers, described as "throwbacks to the heroic age of modernism, reveling in their height against the surrounding buildings," opened in the northern half of this block in 1970.[77]

For several years, two major property holders were able to forestall demolitions on the Walnut blocks east of 38th Street. Of far greater irritation to the University, a highly educated, litigious group that called itself the Sansom Committee delayed the University's plan for mall development in the 34th-36th-Walnut-Sansom quadrant. Penn planned two projects for the Walnut Street commercial corridor between 34th and 37th streets. One project was a proposed University graduate center and computer center, structures designed to fill the block bounded by Sansom, 36th, Walnut, and 37th streets. The other project was a proposed eleven-story building that would extend a half block along Walnut Street from 34th Street to the Franklin Building and along 34th Street one block north to Moravian Street, with the first four floors earmarked for upscale retail operations and seven floors projected for University offices.[78] The latter plan also called for the renovation of deteriorating brownstones on Sansom Street between 34th and 36th streets as shops, stores, and restaurants. The goal was to "bring to the University the same liveliness that is provided by Harvard Square." Penn's "University Square" would presumably become a destination for fashionable Philadelphians.[79] (Forty years later, that moniker would be attached to Judith Rodin's administration's spectacular redevelopment of the 3601 block of Walnut Street; see Chapter 10 for details on this project.)

As early as 1963, Walnut Street property owners prepared to mount a legal challenge to urban renewal in Unit 4. Lillian Burns of the Planning Office was particularly mindful that the "general deterioration of the neighborhood" was the essential precondition for university-related urban renewal: "The legislation specifies that: a) 50 percent of the structures in an area be so substandard as to warrant clearance, or b) that 20 percent of the structures be so substandard to warrant clearance *and* there be two environmental deficiencies." Among the latter, Burns listed "overcrowding or improper location of structures on the land . . . obsolete building types, such as large residences or other buildings which through lack of use or maintenance have a blighting influence . . . inadequate public utilities or community facilities contributing to unsatisfactory living conditions or economic decline." Burns worried that Louis Weisenthal, who owned at least twenty-eight rental properties (commercial and residential) in Unit 4, including ten in the 3401 block of Walnut, would tie up the University in litigation. Weisenthal's recent improvements to these (in some cases, recently purchased) properties "may make it difficult for us to prove that this is a deteriorated and deteriorating area. Should Mr. Weisenthal, for example, bring suit to force the Redevelopment Authority to prove that urban renewal is necessary here this could develop into a very delicate and difficult situation. It may cost us a great deal of money to straighten all of this out."[80] As events proved, Weisenthal's ploy was to maneuver Penn and the RDA into dealing with him on *his* terms to ensure a profit from selling his land to the RDA.

Weisenthal owned Campus Apartments, University City's largest student-housing business, which he managed from an office at 3601 Walnut Street.[81] The West Philadelphia Corporation regarded Weisenthal as a slumlord and speculator who was jockeying to raise the value of his buildings: "Weisenthal was buying and speculating on his ability to fight the Redevelopment Authority"[82]; "Weisenthal came to Philadelphia from Detroit where he was operating, by his own admission, slum properties. . . . he thought this [Unit 4] was a blighted slum area and he could pick them up cheap and make a pile of dough on students, and he has tried on many occasions to go to the University to unload these properties at extravagantly inflated prices and so on."[83] The *Daily Pennsylvanian* and the president of the University Plaza Merchants Association reported negatively on Weisenthal's properties: "The ceiling literally fell on Jos. A Banks [a clothing store] a month ago, crashing to the floor with three large fluorescent light fixtures in tow, and totally smashing a heavy wooden armchair, besides slicing a three-inch piece out of a wooden clothes rack"; "merchants have complained of hundreds of leaks in the buildings, causing linoleum to break and crack"; "in many places, the floors are cracking and eroding"; "the stores have not been painted in six years, although normal procedure for business establishments is new paint every three years."[84]

At issue in the 3601 block of Walnut were the properties owned by the restaurateur Charles Pagano and his family, which occupied "the major portion of the site allocated for the construction of the computer center."[85] Pagano joined Weisenthal and another litigant to file a preliminary objection with the RDA, challenging the city's claim that Unit 4 was blighted.[86] "Well, as far as I can see, it's firmly blighted," argued Edmund Bacon. "It contains a great many of the elements defined in blight, such as undesirable inter-mixture of land uses and social [*sic*] and economically unproductive subdivision of land, and so forth."[87] To avoid protracted litigation, even though Pagano's case was flimsy, the Authority made a deal that designated him as the redeveloper of the northwest and southwest corners of 38th and Chestnut Streets; at present, the dreary 38th Street frontage of these blocks forms an isolated commercial strip uncongenial to Penn planners, including two student-oriented restaurants and two bars, one of which is a seedy nightclub.

■

An irony of Unit 4 urban renewal was the failure of the University to realize its extravagant plans to build a graduate center and a computer center on the 3601 block of Walnut Street. The completed graduate center would have extended the West Central Campus northward via a pedestrian bridge over Walnut Street, which would have connected the center to the Annenberg School for Communication and the Social Science I quadrangle.[88] Unable to marshal any significant contribution from the General State Authority, in 1972 the University finally decided that the graduate center was too expensive to complete, and it also quashed its plan for the computer center.[89] In 1976 the RDA finally demolished all the buildings on the 3601 block, among them the House of Pagano ("Pizzeria, Restaurant, Cocktails"), Ye Olde Tobacconist, the William Penn Bowling Center, and the Record Mart.[90] The Authority then allowed Penn to use the vacant properties as a large surface parking lot, which, for the next twenty years, was a magnet for nighttime crime.

Another surface parking lot stood adjacent to Gimbel Gym on properties the RDA cleared in 1978; this parking lot replaced the brownstone that housed Smokey Joe's Tavern, "the campus dive" founded in 1933, since 1962 located across Walnut Street from the Graduate School of Education—"you buy a hamburger in the front where the light bulb is, then feel your way to the bar for a pitcher of beer. The high-backed wooden booths are carved with decades of initials." (The original Smokey's stood next to the Hillel Foundation on 36th Street, across from the Alpha Chi Rho fraternity.) Eschewing Penn's offer for space in University Plaza at 38th and Walnut streets, the owner moved his "cave" and booths to 40th Street.[91]

As they did with Pagano, Penn's attorneys and the RDA finally made a deal with Weisenthal, whereby Weisenthal agreed to withdraw his preliminary objections and foreswear further legal action regarding his holdings in the 3401 block of Walnut and in the Graduate Towers area. In the late spring of 1968, the RDA designated Weisenthal the redeveloper for three areas, one of them being the southwest corner of 36th and Chestnut, where retail store-fronts were planned for the first floor of the Graduate Towers; and the Penn trustees agreed to designate Weisenthal as the rental agent for the planned commercial district in the 3401 block of Walnut. The University added $106,000 ($667,000 in constant dollars) to seal the deal.[92]

Redevelopment of the institutional-commercial district on the Walnut block east of the Franklin Building stood at a standstill. By 1971 most of the apartments in the 3401 block stood empty, even as retail operations such as the Pennsylvania Book Center, Jerry's Records, the New Deck Tavern, the Shoe Bazaar, and the Lido Restaurant continued to operate—buildings hous-ing these businesses were finally razed in September 1974. Tenants of the 3400 block of Sansom Street, a street of Second Empire brownstones (dating back to 1870–71) that the RDA had condemned five years earlier, adamantly re-fused to budge. "No one is moving out," reported a chagrined Titus Hewryk of the Office of Planning and Design. "In fact, the Sansom Street tenants have promised to resist all University efforts to change the block."[93]

In April 1970, the savvy, feisty tenants of the 3400 block of Sansom Street organized the Sansom Street Committee, Inc., "primarily to offer an alter-native to the existing means and results of urban renewal." The organizers in-cluded Elliot Cook, owner of La Terrasse Restaurant and ringleader of the organization; Cook's restaurant manager, Judy Wicks, the future proprietor of the famous White Dog Café; Penn architectural student Sam Little; and Robert Engman, a sculptor and professor in the Graduate School of Fine Arts. The Sansom Committee campaigned to preserve the block's unique charac-ter, embodied in its signature physical structures. They aimed to recruit owner-managed restaurants and shops of local origin and bohemian character to the ground floors of the block, leaving the second and third floors as single-family residences. They campaigned to protect their homes and other vested inter-ests in the block—in Cook and Wick's case, La Terrasse.[94]

La Terrasse stood apart from the "basic grunge" places of Walnut Street, the downscale eateries and smoke-filled hangouts where students routinely congregated, "places like Smokey Joe's, Pagano's, Kelly and Cohen, Grand's, and the Penn Luncheonette, better known as the Dirty Drug." In contrast, La Terrasse was "like a Left Bank place." "For the first time in memory, Penn had what could legitimately be called 'fine dining.' The restaurant served re-gional French cuisine and reeked of . . . [a] sophisticated Bohemian atmo-sphere." A former habitué recalled, "It was an escape from time and place. Once you were in there it felt very European—certainly not West Philadelphia."[95]

The Sansom organizers also fought to block Penn's demolition of worn red-brick buildings in the adjacent 3401 block of Walnut Street, arguing vociferously for the renovation of these historic structures.[96] Waging a protracted legal battle in the name of housing conservation and artful redevelopment—a fight they funded themselves—they stymied Penn's plans for a multistory mall and office complex in this section of Unit 4 for another fifteen years. We explore the details of this long-fought litigation and its final resolution in Chapter 9, in our analysis of Sheldon Hackney's conciliatory stance in Penn's community relations. In Chapter 3, we turn to the University's embroilment in Unit 3, a zone of redevelopment in which Penn carried no legal warrant, but was able to control through its domination of the West Philadelphia Corporation.

3
Shadow Expansion in Unit 3

The Redevelopment Authority's annual report of 1960 announced the creation of Unit 3 in West Philadelphia, which ran "roughly from Powelton and Lancaster Avenues south to Chestnut Street, between 34th and 39th Streets." Unit 3 properties would be redeveloped in conjunction with the West Philadelphia Corporation (WPC), an institutional coalition that included the University of Pennsylvania, the Drexel Institute of Technology, the Philadelphia College of Pharmacy and Science, and the Presbyterian and Osteopathic hospitals in West Philadelphia. The RDA heralded Unit 3 as "a major step toward the concept of a great university city extending from the Schuylkill River to 44th Street."[1] The orchestration of Unit 3—the RDA demolitions, the construction of the much ballyhooed University City Science Center, and the permanent removal of the unit's predominantly black population—undermined Penn's community relations in West Philadelphia for decades after the clearances, with aftershocks that are still felt today. This chapter provides a detailed account of Unit 3's history. Our analysis also serves as a cautionary tale for urban universities in their dealings with their neighbors—one that Penn president Judith Rodin took to heart thirty years later when she launched the West Philadelphia Initiatives.

■ North of Market: The African American Diaspora in West Philadelphia

At the outset of the Great Expansion, the University confronted transformations in the demography and economy of the city and West Philadelphia. The burden of these changes fell heaviest on the city's burgeoning African American population. The great migration that was spurred by World War I and continued into the 1920s contributed some 140,000 southern blacks to

Philadelphia's total population, fostering the growth of three sizable black districts in the city: the southern tier of Center City, North Philadelphia, and West Philadelphia (the old 24th Ward, Market Street to Girard Avenue, 32nd to 44th streets). Relegated to the bottom rung of the city's economic ladder, with the exception of a small middle class of African American doctors, lawyers, teachers, and caterers ("Old Philadelphians" like the attorneys Raymond Pace Alexander and his wife, Sadie Tanner Mossell Alexander, who held a Penn PhD in economics as well as a Penn law degree), blacks encountered wretched housing conditions in a rent-profiteering market and entrenched hostility, denigration, harassment, and violence at the hands of Philadelphia's Irish, Italian, and "old-stock" Euro-American groups. African American employment gains during World War I, primarily in the railroad and steel industries, dissipated after the war: "domestic service and unskilled labor" were the only jobs available for the large majority of Philadelphia blacks, many of whom were unemployed. In the city's heavily segregated textile industry, blacks could only find jobs as janitors.[2]

Wretched conditions improved incrementally for Philadelphia blacks with the New Deal and the Democratic Party's courting of northern blacks as a voting bloc. A limited breakthrough came in 1944 when the city's black activists, working with the Roosevelt administration's Fair Employment Practices Commission and leaders of the integrationist Transportation Workers Union, forced the Philadelphia Transportation Company to employ African Americans as drivers and motormen on the city's buses and trolley lines. This was a Pyrrhic victory, however, as it marked a realignment of city politics that would disadvantage Philadelphia blacks in the coming years: many race-conscious Irish and Italian Americans left the party of the New Deal for the Republican Party.[3]

World War II set the stage for a second great migration of black southerners to Philadelphia and other major cities outside the South. "The urgent need for soldiers to fight abroad and for wage-earners to forge an 'arsenal of democracy' at home," as one historian puts it, "convinced a flood of African Americans to leave the South. Mechanized cotton pickers shrunk the need for agrarian labor just as the lure of good jobs in war industries sapped the will to stay in the fields."[4] Between 1940 and 1950, Philadelphia's black population grew by 50 percent, from 250,000 to 375,000.[5] But the economic boom was short lived. Tens of thousands of factory jobs were lost after the war. The closing of Cramp's Shipyard; heavy layoffs at Baldwin Locomotive, Midvale Steel, Sun Ship, and the Frankford Arsenal; and starting in the early 1950s, the movement of the city's textile jobs to nonunion southern cities, signaled the decline of Philadelphia manufacturing, with dire ramifications for blacks and working-class whites with insufficient means to leave their ethnic enclaves.[6]

The southern black influx continued into the 1950s, with in-migration and natural population growth occurring against the backdrop of the city's diminished industrial base and the metropolitan area's transition to a service economy.[7] By 1960, Philadelphia's African American population totaled more than 529,000, a 41 percent increase since 1950, with blacks holding a 26.4 percent share of the city total.[8] In the 1950s, white out-migration to the suburbs accounted for a loss of 69,000, or 3 percent, in the general population, a diminution that was never recouped.[9]

In the postwar decades, the suburbs supplanted the city in population and economic growth.[10] Much of the job outflow was to new landscaped factory sites and industrial parks in the city's northeast tier, and in Montgomery and Bucks counties.[11] The city's long-term losses were staggering: 115,000 manufacturing jobs disappeared over four decades, with textiles and apparel accounting for 79 percent of the attrition. Forty-two thousand jobs, "mostly in manufacturing," disappeared in one eighteen-month period amid the national "stagflation" of the early 1970s.[12]

Discriminatory hiring practices at the new suburban plants combined with segregation in suburban housing markets served to ghettoize blacks in Philadelphia, where they were excluded from the city's dwindling industrial base. While blacks gained substantial representation in the municipal sector through the "non-partisan, merit-based civil service system" enacted by the 1951 city charter, their jobs were in the low-wage categories. A growing increment of the African American population was poor, marginally employed, and living in segregated neighborhoods abandoned by white ethnics. In 1959, 43 percent of unemployed Philadelphians were black; in 1960, the nonwhite unemployment rate stood at 10.7 percent, compared to the white rate of 5 percent. Segregation in the city's crafts and building trades unions ensured that blacks in these trades earned about one-third less than their white coworkers.[13]

Housing and public education were also structured to disadvantage blacks. Compounding racial isolation, public housing, such as it was (only fourteen thousand units were built between 1937 and 1963), was segregated.[14] Redlining by lenders contributed to the deterioration of black neighborhoods, and racially motivated school board decisions on site selection and design of new schools relegated black children to the city's oldest and worst public schools.[15]

■

West Philadelphia's census tracts recorded expansive growth in African American settlement, from 18.8 percent of the district's total in 1940 to 52.8 percent by 1960. North of Market Street, the figure for "nonwhite" was 58 percent (compared to 27 percent for the city).[16] Mantua, a racially segmented neighborhood about ten blocks (one mile) north of Penn, comprised two of these tracts. Between 1940 and 1950, blacks increased their share of Mantua's population from 45.7 percent to 78.2 percent. By 1960, they accounted for 94.7 percent of 16,886 residents; by 1970, 97.2 percent of 12,044. Between 1950 and 1960, a tipping effect apparently occurred with a precipitous exodus of whites in Mantua, from 4,208 to 862.

In 1960, 10.8 percent of Mantua's black labor force was unemployed, compared to 2.6 percent of white workers. Among "nonwhites" counted as employed in 1960, only 1.6 percent was in the category of "professional, technical, and kindred workers," compared to 5.8 percent of whites. That 79.5 percent of household incomes fell below $39,018 (constant 2011 dollars) suggests a community that was struggling economically (a poverty index was not reported in the 1960 census). Reported in the 1970 census, Mantua's poverty rate was 37.2 percent, compared to the city rate of 11.2 percent. That 43.6 percent of Mantua's families were headed by females with no husband present, compared to 18.9 percent for the city, suggests a breakdown of the neighborhood's social fabric in the 1960s.[17]

The largest part of Unit 3 was assigned to two census tracts that wrapped around the blocks between 31st and 40th Street, from Market to Spring Garden, Mantua's southern boundary. Tract 24I included the area between 36th and 40th streets. At the start of the decade, blacks dominated tract 24I—though not to the same extent as in Mantua and adjacent neighborhoods to the west—accounting for 78.8 percent of the tract's population. Many of these people experienced grinding poverty: a third of black households earned less than $15,607 (2011 constant dollars). The small white minority fared even worse, with 46.7 percent of households earning less than $15,607.[18] On its eastern flank, Unit 3 extended about two blocks east and three blocks north into tract 24F—Market to Spring Garden between 31st and 36th streets. (Tract 24F included the Drexel Institute and RDA Unit 5, a zone of higher-education-based urban renewal in the East Powelton neighborhood.)[19] Nearer the Penn campus, Unit 3 included a swath of blocks in census tracts 27A and 27B, south from Market to the north side of Chestnut between 34th and 40th streets. The University City Science Center, the raison d'être of Unit 3 and the bête noire of poor and working-class African Americans in these blocks, would extend one block deep along both sides of Market Street between 34th and 38th streets. The new University City High School, another controversial Unit 3 development, would claim several blocks just northwest of the Science Center complex.

The West Philadelphia Corporation and the University City Science Center

The proximate cause for establishing the West Philadelphia Corporation was a single incident of mayhem. On the rainy night of April 25, 1958, a twenty-six-year-old South Korean graduate student at the University of Pennsylvania was brutally murdered in Powelton Village. In-Ho Oh rented an apartment at 3610 Hamilton Street, a block south of Spring Garden Street, the historical boundary between Powelton and Mantua. Oh had just posted a letter at the mailbox across the street at the corner of 36th and Hamilton streets. As he was about to return to his apartment, he was set upon by eleven black youths. According to one account, "Suddenly they swarmed over him, flailing him with fists, a Blackjack, a piece of pipe, a soda bottle. When he was down they stomped on him in an outburst of savagery."[20] The *Evening Bulletin* reported, "He was horribly beaten about the face and head. A broken bottle lay nearby. It was apparently one of the weapons. There were also indications that a blackjack had been used. Oh's glasses lay closer to the corner, making it appear that it was there that he had been first hit and that he tried to run from his assailants."[21] The motive for the killing, which sent shock waves across the city, was never conclusively determined, though speculation was rife that the youths were on the prowl for ticket money to a dance at a nearby church that evening.

Media reports on the crime and its perpetrators, though accurate as to some of the details of the murder, were sensationalist and prejudicial toward African Americans: descriptions such as "a barbarous killing executed with jungle-like ferocity," "outburst of savagery," and "uncivilized, and bound to be a menace to society" speak for themselves.[22] Describing the youthful suspects as "cowardly savages," a *Philadelphia Inquirer* editorial declaimed that "University of Pennsylvania and Drexel Institute of Technology authorities are understandably concerned because of the continuing wave of hold-ups and attacks in the area near the schools and student residences." Indeed, eight of the eleven youths indicted for the murder listed home addresses in Mantua or just north of that neighborhood; all of them had prior arrest records.[23] The founding of the West Philadelphia Corporation followed the In-Ho Oh tragedy in short order.

The initial recommendation for the creation of such an entity had come from the urban planner Martin Meyerson in 1956, when he was a professor in the School of Fine Arts. Drawing on his experience with the South East Chicago Commission, an entity of the University of Chicago working to stabilize and upgrade the university's boundary community of Hyde Park-Kenwood, Meyerson warned that Penn, like Chicago, could "create a desirable neighborhood, or . . . stand by and see develop a 'sea of residential slums with commercial and institutional islands.'" He called for a "West Philadelphia planning and development corporation led by U.P. [and other local higher education institutions and hospitals]." Meyerson believed that Penn could not create a "community of scholars" without the prerequisite of an attractive neighborhood that included "decent housing, open space, good schools, shopping, safe streets, [and] absence of blight." Citing Columbia University's Morningside Heights, Inc., and the South East Chicago Commission as precedents, he prefigured the West Philadelphia Corporation's adoption of an area-wide strategy.[24]

Here it is relevant to consider the aims, programs, and long-term impacts of these precedents. As at Penn, changing racial demographics were a major factor in urban renewal at both Columbia and the University of Chicago. In both cases, a university-dominated coalition of nonprofit institutions transformed the urban landscape.[25]

■

To cope with postwar demographic changes affecting neighborhoods northeast and south-southeast of Morningside Heights in Manhattan, and "to promulgate physical change benefitting the middle class constituency of the area's institutional employment group," Columbia University and fourteen other Upper West Side institutions formed Morningside Heights, Inc. (MHI) in 1947.[26] Drawing on urban renewal funds and city and state programs, MHI first built two high-rise housing developments several blocks north of the campus. Morningside Gardens—a middle-income, multitowered, 972-apartment cooperative whose planning dated to 1952—opened in 1960 between LaSalle and West 123rd streets. Built just to the north and east of Morningside Gardens between La Salle and West 125th Street, the 1,950-apartment General Grant Houses—"ten high-rise slabs"—opened to carefully screened low-income residents in 1957. These two projects displaced 1,626 families.[27]

The liberal planners' hope of achieving racial and social class integration within, and between, the neighboring projects was largely vitiated: whites (intellectuals and white-collar workers) constituted 75 percent of the Morningside Gardens residents; low-income African American and Puerto Rican tenants, whose behavior was "monitored and controlled," composed 89 percent of the General Grant Houses residents. The General Grant Houses functioned as a cordon sanitaire that separated the middle-class neighborhoods of Morningside Heights from the poor neighborhoods to the north and northeast in Manhattanville and Harlem.[28]

In his analysis of Columbia and MHI, the historian Michael Carriere traces Columbia's domination of Upper West Side urban renewal to 1957, when Grayson Kirk, Columbia's president, replaced David Rockefeller as president of MHI; Kirk, in turn, appointed Columbia's treasurer William Bloor, an expert in property acquisitions, to direct MHI's urban renewal operations for the benefit of the University; other university officials played operational roles as well, and Kirk controlled the appointment of the nonprofit's executive director. The University's major investment was to convert or demolish the area's low-income, poorly maintained tenant hotels, so-called SROs (single-room-occupancy) hotels that had proliferated in Morningside Heights during the war to house thousands of unmarried defense workers.

The planners viewed the worst SROs as a serious threat to their vision of the Heights as "an American Acropolis." Led by Columbia—with the city's complicity—MHI maneuvered around the Morningside General Neighborhood Renewal Plan (GNRP), the city's federally approved urban renewal plan for the Upper West Side, to exclude SROs from the GNRP. Had the SROs been included in the GNRP, the city would have had to replace them with federally funded public housing—a prospect that was anathema to the University. Accordingly, Columbia enlisted MHI's real estate subsidiary "to buy up as many SRO buildings in the community as possible." Even before the GNRP, Columbia was acquiring SROs, and by 1968, with Columbia as "the key actor," "58 of the 309 residential buildings [34 of which were SROs] were demolished, converted into dormitories, offices, or renovated apartment buildings (for predominately upper-middle class Columbia faculty members, or emptied of tenants)," with a total displacement of as many as 9,500 people.[29] One SRO hotel was converted for the School of Social Work and renamed McVicar Hall; another converted SRO hotel was renamed Armstrong Hall, home of the Goddard Institute of Space Studies.[30] Other buildings were demolished for campus expansion: "Columbia tore down sixteen rowhouses and five apartment buildings for the construction of East Campus, including the law school, School of International Affairs, a residence hall, and a raised platform and bridge over Amsterdam Avenue."[31] (Notoriously unsuccessful was Columbia's ill-advised project in 1968 to build an off-campus gymnasium in Morningside Park, a debacle we take up in Chapter 4 in our comparison of student protest at Penn and Columbia.)

■

Led by a coalition of Hyde Park professionals and businessmen who hoped to forge an integrated neighborhood suitable for "professional-class" residents,[32] the University of Chicago/South East Chicago Commission (SECC) launched a major planning effort for housing conservation and demolition/replacement housing in Hyde Park-Kenwood, an 856-acre urban renewal area where the nonwhite population grew from 6.1 percent in 1950 to 36.7 percent in 1956— an increase of 23,162—and the white population declined by 19,989 (the percentage decline was not reported). This initiative had grudging support from the liberal Hyde Park-Kenwood Community Conference, founded in 1949.[33] Created in 1952, the SECC was the mediating structure for the University's "overwhelming presence" in Hyde Park-Kenwood urban renewal. Nominally a coalition of six area-wide agencies, the SECC was in fact "a university creation," one that was "generally regarded as an appendage" of the University. The accelerating in-migration from Chicago's South Side "Black Belt" in no small way motivated the creation of the SECC and the University's urban renewal plan for Hyde Park-Kentwood, the goals of which were "a predominately white and economically upgraded community."[34] Approved by city and federal agencies, the 1958 urban renewal plan, the brainchild of the SECC and its director Julian Levi, forecast the demolition of 21 percent of the area's buildings and 21 percent of the total dwelling units; designated 4,087 families (59 percent nonwhite) for relocation; and projected the construction of more than two thousand new dwelling units by private developers.[35] An occasionally ruthless pragmatist, Levi bluntly expressed a sentiment that would inspirit the West Philadelphia Corporation, though without such frank public language:

> If we are really serious about the needs of our institution, then our problem is not one of compromise; it is rather the establishment of priorities. If we are really serious about the next generation of teachers and scholars, lawyers and doctors, physicists and chemists, then we have got to worry about the adequate housing of the graduate student; about the clearing of land for a new laboratory; about the closing of streets to divert traffic from campuses; about the development of a "compatible environment" including substantial slum clearance. . . . We cannot have it both ways. We are either going to have graduate students, who produce leadership for the next generation . . . or we are not going to achieve these results because we are unwilling to disturb existing owners and populations.[36]

The largest redevelopment initiative spearheaded by the University of Chicago and SECC tandem was labeled "Hyde Park A and B," which proposed to clear and redevelop a swath of "residential and commercial properties along 55th Street and the Illinois Central tracks."[37] The project area of 47.3 acres featured Hyde Park's largest concentration of substandard buildings. The plan received the necessary city and federal approvals, and the demolitions were under way by the spring of 1955. By the 1960s, the renewed project area, once home to twenty-two bars and taverns, boasted a new shopping district, with expensive new townhouses and moderately priced apartment buildings, the latter especially attractive to University faculty and staff. The social costs included the relocation of more than twelve hundred families and 150 businesses.[38]

While Morningside Heights, Inc. was a precedent for the West Philadelphia Corporation, it was probably only a talking point at Penn. By contrast, the South East Chicago Commission provided an explicit model for organizing the West Philadelphia Corporation.

Rise of the WPC

From the planners' perspective, the murder of In-Ho Oh lent immediate urgency to establishing something like the South East Chicago Commission in West Philadelphia[39]—an idea that Martin Meyerson had broached in 1956. At a meeting on 10 June 1958, the representatives of the five private institutions stated their intent to establish the West Philadelphia Corporation. "While [the situation of] our overall area is perhaps not now so critical as that of institutions in other cities," the collective statement read, "nevertheless we face the potential of an ever increasing and encroaching area of residential slums surrounding our colleges and our hospitals." More cryptically, the representatives stated, "Also we face the alternatives of ignoring the succession of land uses and population changes in this vicinity and suffering from the effects of these or assuming leadership in creating and maintaining a desirable neighborhood in which our institutions can flourish."[40]

Planning for the WPC proceeded throughout the summer and fall of 1958, involving consultation with Julian Levi and Jack Meltzer of the South East Chicago Commission. Penn business vice president John Moore underscored the Commission's contribution: "The [bylaws] committee met with Jack Meltzer for two days and these by-laws and the statement of purposes included in them were drafted with his advice. We have followed very closely the framework of the South East Chicago Commission"; indeed, at this point the institutional planners called their corporate entity the West Philadelphia Commission.[41] The West Philadelphia Corporation was publicly announced on 22 April 1959, and hailed by Mayor Richardson Dilworth as "a splendid step toward improving and rehabilitating a key area of our City"; it was, Dilworth proclaimed, a bulwark "against the inroads of deterioration." On

10 July 1959 the Court of Common Pleas approved the articles of incorporation of the West Philadelphia Corporation.[42]

The historian Margaret Pugh O'Mara aptly observes that a mix of economic
and racial considerations played a role in Penn's construction of a "city of
knowledge" in West Philadelphia, whose catalyst was the West Philadelphia
Corporation. The planners associated blacks, who "because of market conditions and discrimination" were increasingly poor, with blight.[43] For example,
a WPC report ca. 1959 listed five "signs of deterioration," one of which was
"the accelerated in-migration of non-academic lower-income families settling
in concentrated groups,"[44] in other words, blacks. As O'Mara notes, "one irony
of the Penn community's distress about a changing West Philadelphia was
that some of the 'blight' was the result of cheap boarding houses, restaurants,
and bars proliferating around the area to serve Penn students."[45]

Ample evidence exists to support O'Mara's claim that the WPC "was, for
all intents and purposes, a Penn-dominated group."[46] For example, the general plan appeared in Martin Meyerson's memorandum at the Graduate School
of Fine Arts in 1956. John Moore organized the meetings that planned the
WPC, and Harnwell was appointed president and director of the executive
board, primus inter pares, in deference to Penn's stature; Harnwell served as
board chair of the Corporation until 1977.[47] Penn's annual financing of the
WPC was more than the total amount paid by the other four institutions.[48]
(At $26,400,000, Penn's total payroll was more than six times that of Drexel,
the second largest institutional partner.)

Drawn up by John Moore's committee, the WPC bylaws gave voting rights
to the presidents of the five institutions—designated "active members"—and
a board of twenty-one directors, sixteen of whom were officials of the institutions. "Associate members," for example, representatives of local community associations or other stakeholder groups, did not have voting rights—a
glaring omission of democratic process that was not rectified until 1983, when
Penn president Sheldon Hackney reorganized the WPC as the West Philadelphia Partnership and put the community associations on an equal foot-
ing with the institutions (see Chapter 9 for further discussion).[49]

As perhaps its signature legacy, the WPC established the boundaries of
an artificial neighborhood that the city and the "higher eds and meds" in the
City Planning Commission's University Area advertised as "University City,"
which, "unlike other West Philadelphia neighborhood titles that emerged
more organically . . . was a brand name . . . dreamed up by city planners."[50]
Gaylord Harnwell attributed the name's provenance to Francis Lammer, executive director of the RDA, calling it "a kind of common law designation"
for an "aging neighborhood" marked by "decay, neglect, and misuse."[51] The

boundaries of the proposed "West Philadelphia Corporation Market Area," which enveloped University City, were Haverford Avenue on the north, the Schuylkill River on the east, the Media line of the Pennsylvania Railroad on the south, and 52nd Street on the west. In 1960 the total population of the market area was 101,362, two-thirds of which was "nonwhite." The borders of University City were Powelton Avenue on the north, 44th Street on the west, and the river and the Media line on the east and south.[52] The WPC aimed to develop "a community which holds and attracts institutional cultural facilities, compatible industrial and commercial uses, standard and marketable residential areas served by adequate schools, parks, churches and shopping, thus providing a supply and range of housing which will appeal to large numbers of the population not now attracted to the area."[53] The *Philadelphia Inquirer* rhapsodized, "University City will transform this area, sprinkled now with dilapidated commercial structures and substandard housing, into a park-like panorama of college campuses, educational and medical buildings, research centers—plus appropriately designed and attractively landscaped business and residential communities. . . . It is a new kind of approach to urban redevelopment whereby the established institutions of higher learning seek to fulfill important roles of good citizenship and civic duty."[54]

Put differently, the goal of "Brainsville" (the press moniker for University City) was "to attract as many campus-type families back to the area as possible."[55] O'Mara interprets this approach skeptically as a self-conscious effort to build a "new city of knowledge" populated by a "White, professional community of scholars," and "to replace the disorderly urban landscape with an idealized community of scientific production." Certainly, the fact that "campus-type families" would be overwhelmingly white by virtue of the racial demographics of higher education and the learned professions of the 1960s could not have eluded the planners. Yet it may be speculative overreach for O'Mara, lacking further evidence (which we haven't found either), to assert that the WPC, through the construction of the Science Center, deliberately imposed "a physical barrier between the White, professional community of scholars and working-class, Black West Philadelphia."[56] That said, there is plenty of evidence of hubris and elitism (O'Mara's terms) and insensitivity on the part of the planners. Whether intended or not, one fact remains unaltered: Unit 3 redevelopment effectively formed a cordon sanitaire between Penn and the neighborhoods north of Market Street.

From Stanford to West Philadelphia: The Concept of the Science Center

The WPC planners envisaged the University City Science Center as the catalyst for the economic, cultural, and scholarly efflorescence of University City.

The City Planning Commission hailed the Science Center project as "a substantial research development" involving "a concentration of government- and industry-sponsored basic research that benefits by being able to take advantage of the staff and facilities at the University of Pennsylvania and Drexel Institute of Technology. This group of buildings, together with the existing research facilities at these institutions, will create a major basic research center for the metropolitan area."[57] As recruitment magnets for the Science Center and the "community of scholars," the WPC institutions dedicated dollars and human capital to school-improvement initiatives (Universities-Related Schools—the Lea, Powel, and Drew Schools, the West Philadelphia Free School, the West Philadelphia High School Motivation Program); housing initiatives (demonstration houses and residential planning with five community associations, housing conservation in the 3900–3901 block of Pine Street, condominium developments at 45th and Spruce streets and 44th and Osage, and a guaranteed mortgage plan for Penn faculty and staff); historical preservation (the University City Historical Society); arts and culture (the University City Arts League); beautification (the University City Beautification Committee) and recreation (the University City Swim Club); and retail and restaurant development (Unit 4).[58]

The first mention of a WPC-related research park appears in a letter from Harnwell to John Moore, dated 15 June 1959:

> Alfred Williams [chairman of the Penn trustees] called me this morning in regard to an idea which he had over the weekend. This is that in our plans for the West Philadelphia area, we might profitably consider the inviting in of certain desirable neighbors such as corporations desirous of setting up research establishments which would find proximity to University personnel, libraries, and laboratories particularly congenial. He is going to give a little further thought to this matter, but I wanted to keep you informed of the suggestion. There may indeed be groups within the city government with whom the West Philadelphia Corporation should eventually get in touch who are charged with attracting desirable industrial activities to the city. No one seems to have any particular research activity in mind, but it is an interesting idea.[59]

By September 1959, the WPC institutions, the Chamber of Commerce of Greater Philadelphia, and the quasi-public Philadelphia Industrial Development Corporation (PIDC) were abuzz with interest in the potential of a research center or "park" that would attract industries to a central R & D site for their labs. Lest there were any doubt about the appropriate location for such an entity, Allen T. Bonnell, Drexel's vice president, proclaimed, "I should like to place on record our interest in relating any Philadelphia Research Center, both geographically and organizationally, to the West Philadelphia institutions now represented in the Corporation. . . . A Research Center located in West Philadelphia would both benefit from and complement the current research activities, graduate programs, and staffing of these two universities and the other institutions." Championing a site near the campuses, Gaylord Harnwell avowed that "the educational opportunities such institutions offer can be a major inducement to firms employing young scientists. The relatively depressed real estate values in the area can also be an incentive to the location of research laboratories in our neighborhood."[60] Harnwell may well have been mindful that a major R & D center, designed in large part by his leadership team, would offset the stigma of Penn's having forfeited any claim, following the ENIAC debacle, to a leadership role in digital computing.

In January 1960, the WPC hired as its executive vice president Leo Molinaro, a planning consultant with the James Rouse Company, which spearheaded high-profile, avant-garde projects, such as the Fanueil Hall "festival marketplace" in Boston, the Harborplace in Baltimore, and the New Town of Columbia, Maryland. Molinaro had organized 109 metropolitan affiliates of the American Council to Improve Our Neighborhoods (ACTION), whose president was James Rouse. The savvy, ebullient, and highly influential Molinaro cultivated a close personal relationship with Harnwell and the Penn planner Harold Taubin.[61] The protean Martin Meyerson, a colleague of Molinaro's at ACTION, likely had a hand in his hiring, which was the most important WPC appointment of the Harnwell era.

At the outset, the Unit 3 planners had in mind two research complexes, one inside and one outside Unit 3. The latter project appeared on the drawing board first. The plan called for a research tower in the bottomland adjacent to Walnut and 31st streets. Molinaro attributed the idea of the research tower to the PIDC, whose president Richard Graves was enamored with Stanford University's industrial research park, the nucleus of the future Silicon Valley. While the PIDC recognized that Stanford had five thousand acres of rural/suburban property at its disposal for regional economic development, and the pastoral nature of the property factored heavily in the park's success, the organization nonetheless called for a thirty-three-story research tower for densely urban West Philadelphia, a mammoth structure that would accommodate five thousand researchers.[62] Perhaps because they finally realized that two R & D centers in University City were simply not feasible, Molinaro and the PIDC moved the tower plan to a ten-acre site in Unit 3, in the quadrant of Market Street and Lancaster Avenue between 34th and 36th streets. But the research tower had no traction with the WPC board of directors, who reported in January 1963: "The best evidence would indicate that to compete with suburban locations it would not be advisable to build a tower but to plan several five to six-story buildings with about 10,000 square feet per floor."[63] This board meeting marked the genesis of the University City Science Center (UCSC), in which "both high-tech firms and quasi-independent research departments of Penn and its medical affiliates would have a home . . . it was to be a place where scientific innovation literally existed next door to the commercial application of technology."[64]

Was the Stanford Industrial Park, established in 1951, a model for the UCSC? Molinaro recalls that Stanford was not a model, but rather "a good talking point." "This is an *urban* center," he notes, and unlike the Stanford Industrial Park, which had a single university sponsor, the UCSC started with five institutional sponsors—the WPC members. While the WPC planners did not discount the extraordinary advantage that swaths of pastoral landscape conveyed to Stanford (whose wildly successful R & D partners included, among others, Hewlett-Packard, General Electric, and Lockheed) and to the Research Triangle Park in North Carolina, the University City planners gambled that Penn's brand and the promise of University City amenities would convey a distinctive urban advantage for recruiting high-tech industries.[65]

In the late fall of 1963, the Court of Common Pleas approved articles of incorporation for the University City Science Center and the University City Science Institute (UCSI).[66] The UCSC was the real estate developer for the Science Center complex, designated for that purpose by the RDA with the charge to create "a scientific enclave which will contain in close juxtaposition a compatible arrangement of buildings, open spaces, streets and walkways which will provide a unique environment conducive to scientific creativity in its broadest concept."[67] The purpose of the Science Institute, the Science Center Corporation's "wholly owned non-profit subsidiary," was to recruit scientists, industrial research teams, and technicians; broker "mutually beneficial and stimulating relationships" between these professionals and the faculty of the member institutions; and publish research results and market patented research products. In sum, "the UCSC would acquire land and construct buildings in which the UCSI would enable researchers to develop and sell their ideas."[68] More than the Stanford Industrial Park, the Stanford Research Institute, founded in 1946 as "a locus on campus for research of direct interest to industrial patrons,"[69] provided a repository of ideas for the UCSI. Penn trustee Robert Trescher visited Stanford in the late spring of 1963 to collect information and advice for developing a Philadelphia version of the Institute; the language of Trescher's in-house memorandum hints at Penn's control of the Science Center; for example, "again it was recommended that Pennsylvania [Penn's moniker at the time] not consider erecting a building until a large volume of contract research is developed."[70] Unlike Stanford's approach, the WPC integrated (and did so in the articles of incorporation) the UCSI as a component of the Science Center—on paper, at least, *not* a component of the University of Pennsylvania.

The University City Science Center was a "regional" conception, "in that the stock subscriptions to the Center Corporation [UCSC] are all held by non-profit institutions of higher learning, hospitals, and medical schools in Pennsylvania, Delaware, and New Jersey."[71] The Penn trustees made the University's participation in the Science Center contingent on their holding "no less than 51 percent of the stock." Harnwell assured a contentious William Hagerty, president of the Drexel Institute (James Creese's successor), that Penn "would not build any of its own academic buildings north of Market Street or otherwise in the area designated for the Science Center."[72] Hagerty was obviously mindful that Penn not only controlled 51 percent of the stock but also held a vastly disproportionate share vis-à-vis any of the other shareholders, including Drexel; for example, by the spring of 1967, Penn held two thousand shares versus one hundred shares for each of eighteen other Delaware Valley "higher eds and meds" in the Science Center.[73]

The president of the Science Center was the Penn trustee Paul J. Cupp. Of the nine officers of the Center Corporation, Penn members held four of the appointments; and Leo Molinaro, the vice president for continuing education at UCSC and the executive vice president of the WPC, was a watchdog of Penn's interests. Exemplifying the interlocking directorate that advanced Penn's interests in West Philadelphia, Gustave Amsterdam, chairman of the RDA, and a future Penn trustee, adjured Penn trustee Paul Cupp, "The Redevelopment Authority is very anxious to see the University City Science Center become a physical reality. . . . the Authority and the various City Departments concerned hope to see the development of a unique Science Center which will be a success both aesthetically and in the rate of construction."[74]

In the fall of 1964, the Science Center directors hired Jean Paul Mather, former president of the University of Massachusetts, as executive vice president, "the key administrative officer charged with the institution's development." In light of the parlous times ahead for the Science Center, when black activists and student dissidents from Penn and across the Delaware Valley took up cudgels against Penn and the Science Center on behalf of displaced residents, Mather's appointment would prove to be fateful and, from Harnwell's perspective, regrettable.

■ Turmoil in Unit 3

A WPC memorandum from 1963 describes Unit 3 as an 82.3-acre site, with a total population of 3,432 people and 1,203 dwelling units, of which only 241 were owner-occupied; 987 families, of which 444 were white, 543 nonwhite; and 122 businesses. The planning for Unit 3 as an urban renewal site and WPC-related project provoked a groundswell of protest from African American residents who accused Penn and the RDA of conspiring to destroy a viable community. Leo Molinaro angrily denied this charge: "This area has never had any 'neighborhood' identification, or organization. It was from the beginning, marginal in use and occupancy. All of the land from which protests have come (34th to 38th Streets; Market Street to Lancaster Avenue) is currently zoned for industrial and commercial uses. None of it is zoned for residential use. In other words, this is not a fine neighborhood which has been neglected and can now be restored." Molinaro further noted that RDA-commissioned

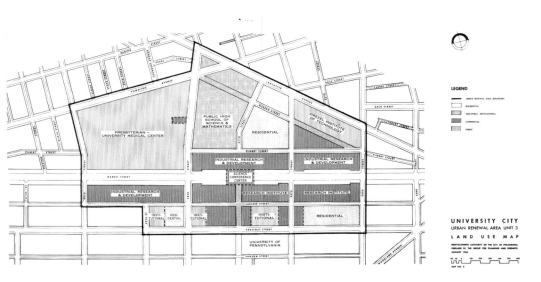

University City Urban Renewal Area Unit 3, Land Use Map (January 1964). GIS map by J. M Duffin. Collections of the University Archives and Records Center.

studies of Unit 3 "revealed that only 127 of 628 structures had any possibilities for rehabilitation. All homeowners were carefully interviewed. It was found that only a few had the means to undertake the needed repairs and rehabilitation. In other words, if these structures are allowed to remain in the hands of present owners, they can only continue to slide into worse neglect. The more likely possibility is that speculators will buy them on the open market and hold them for later resale at inflated prices."[75]

The civil rights activist, youth educator, and Penn adjunct professor Walter Palmer, who grew up in this neighborhood from around 1941 to 1955, sharply disputes Molinaro's claim that this was not an organic community. He recalls his neighborhood as a place where doors and windows were left open, and "anybody could walk in any time they wanted. . . . You could walk on the street [at] 2 o'clock, 3 o'clock in the morning. My mother tells a story of how people would see her coming from Aunt Bea's speakeasy walking home, the guys on the corner hiding their cigarettes, tipping their hat, and saying 'Good evening, Mrs. Palmer,' and [she knew] she was safe." Palmer, whose extended family of twelve children and two adults lived in two rented rooms in the back of a beauty shop at 3645 Market Street, recalls a "spirit" that bound the residents of the neighborhood communally, especially in the blocks from Market to Lancaster between 34th and 40th streets. Simultaneously, however, Palmer suggests that he was raised in a community governed, in part at least, by fear and violence. "This was a culture—the gangs . . . protected you when you went to school. Nobody messed with anybody from the Black Bottom. You went to any school in West Philadelphia you wanted to, and [if] they knew you came from the Black Bottom, you were protected, you were safe. Nobody messed with you if you went to prison [or] jail, juvenile or adult, if they knew you were from the Black Bottom. That's how notorious this history was, how strong the history was, how strongly connected they were."[76] This notoriety dominated outsiders' perception of the neighborhood.

Palmer does not contest that some form of blight existed in the area he recalls as the Black Bottom. His own use of the term "tenements" to describe the Market Street dwellings behind or above the businesses on that corridor makes that point. Photographs of dilapidated houses, junk dealerships, and service loading zones on arterial streets in Unit 3 are also revealing.[77] According to 1960 census block data, 44 percent of the area's housing stock was "deteriorating" or "dilapidated"; only 55 percent was reported "sound."[78] And according to the RDA's 1964 application for a federal loan and grant, "of a total of 807 structures in the Clearance Section, 378 or 47% are structurally substandard to a point warranting clearance and 181 or 22% warrant clearance to remove . . . blighting influences."[79] Ironically, one of these "blighting influences" was the construction of the Market Street subway tunnel, which rattled houses and threw up debris from 1948 to 1955. "That construction helped to make it look like it was run-down," says Palmer. "You can imagine what that would do to houses and to properties, great big holes in the middle of the street . . . tons of brick and mortar all over the place."[80]

Palmer and other members of the Black Bottom Association, a cross-generational group he helped found in 1976, were embittered by the Unit 3 planners' assumption that "this neighborhood never had any identification" and by Penn's motives in Unit 3; the continuing hue and cry for reparations—admissions and scholarships for the grandchildren and great-grandchildren of the displaced residents—has always been directed at Penn, not Drexel or any other Science Center partner from the 1960s. In a similar vein, Michael Zuckerman, a Penn history professor and an observer of the 1969 College Hall sit-in (described in Chapter 4), calls Penn's role in Unit 3 "the invincible rallying point."

> That is what really sticks in the craw; that is the thing that's usable as a weapon against Penn forever. And no matter how much it recedes into ancient history, it is what stokes the fire of skepticism about Penn and its intentions, certainty that Penn looks after Penn and anything else is window-dressing at best. I think that there is an inevitably wary relationship between Penn and the neighborhood.[81]

In 1974, Walt Palmer organized the first Black Bottom reunion. The first Black Bottom picnic was held in Fairmount Park in 1976, and it has been annual event ever since; according to Palmer, it is "the oldest and largest neighborhood community picnic in the history of Philadelphia."[82] In Philadelphia newspapers' reports on the annual picnic, former residents recall the "neighborliness" that Palmer describes:

> They talk about the Liberty Baptist Church on 37th Street, the place to hear the best gospel music—the Dixie Hummingbirds, the Four Blind Boys. The club Zal-Mar on Market Street was the best nightspot in the neighborhood, and it provided uniforms for the baseball team. On Sundays the neighborhood kids parked cars for fans going to the Eagles games at Franklin Field. On Tuesday free meals were available at Father Divine's Mission on Mantua Avenue. . . . 'You didn't have to leave [the neighborhood] for nothing. We had three barbers, Jack Goldstein's grocery store at 37th and Warren. We had a poolroom, the Fans movie theater on Market Street.[83]

Sensationalist newspaper accounts, not to mention the "halo-effect" dia-logue of an oral history play produced on the Black Bottom of the 1940s and 1950s, give the impression of highly selective memories that mute the harsher aspects of that world. The painful memory of displacement and the bitter-ness these former residents harbor is no doubt part, and perhaps the primary component, of their identification with the community they recall as the Black Bottom. The absence of any mention of this term in any existing West Phila-delphia Corporation or Penn planning document or student newspaper ac-count of the 1950s and 1960s, and only one mention of it in the *Evening Bulletin* (an allusion to the "Black Bottom Gang"), prior to the clearances suggests one of two possibilities: that the concept of the "Black Bottom" was an African American cultural construction to which white elites, prior to the clearances, were not privy, *or* that the concept acquired inflated significance after the re-movals as an identifier and rallying point for Unit 3's black diaspora.[84]

There is no denying the psychological harm that "Negro removal" inflicted on many of these displaced people. Mike Roepel, an African American pen-sioner who had spent his career at the City Planning Commission, relates a case in point. Roepel recalls that his grandmother Hattie Hunter was a pil-lar of the blocks around 36th and Market streets. Hattie owned her own three-story house on 36th Street between Market and Filbert streets, which she and her late husband had received as a gift, in 1936, from Quakers who employed her as a housekeeper. To make ends meet, Hattie sold corn liquor to her neigh-bors, hooch that was smuggled in from her hometown of Edenton, North Car-olina, on Albemarle Sound. Mike lived in Hattie's house from 1948, his birth year, to 1960. Then Mike's brother, Joe Hunter, nineteen years older, took Mike to live with him in the Cobbs Creek neighborhood at 58th and Hazel streets. "The Bottom was getting kind of rough," Roepel says. "People started getting locked up." Penn students walking between Powelton Village and the campus were targets for robberies. The murder of In-Ho Oh in 1958 "was the beginning of . . . opportunity crimes." In fact, Roepel recalls a time when "half of my Boy Scout troop was in the Youth Study Center for snatching pocketbooks."

Hattie sold her house to the RDA in the mid-1960s, and moved to 53rd Street and Pentridge Street, in Southwest Philadelphia. "Thirty-sixth and Market reconstituted itself in that whole area," a four- or five-block swath south of Baltimore Avenue around 54th Street and Florence Avenue, in the Kingsessing neighborhood, about two miles from Unit 3. Hattie kept her old status as a wise community leader at her new address on Pentridge. But other displaced residents lost their roles in the shakeup. Says Roepel, "I can remember where some older folks deteriorated quicker because that's what kept them alive . . . because they were *it*, as you say."[85] Such were the markers of an authentic communal life that planners like Molinaro and his colleagues failed to understand.

From the planners' perspective, there was nothing salvageable about such businesses as Club Zal-Mar, Walker's Billiards, Bucket of Blood Tavern, or the tenements Palmer describes. It was "rock bottom in many ways," Molinaro avers. Palmer does not deny that the neighborhood was "rough and tough," or that an underground economy—a numbers racket and speakeasies, for example—thrived on the blocks; indeed, these are points of pride for him. Palmer himself was a gang leader; he told Matthew Countryman, the author of *Up South*, that "his first arrest came at the age of twelve for burglary of a University of Pennsylvania dormitory. During frequent run-ins with rival gangs as well as the police, Palmer survived a couple of stabbings, one gunshot wound, and repeated arrests."[86]

University City High School Gone Awry

Embracing a Cold War trend of national interest in science education,[87] the WPC proposed a new "science high school" for University City in 1963, with the Bronx High School of Science and the Baltimore Polytechnic Institute considered as models.[88] Gaylord Harnwell envisaged the proposed "Public High School for Science and Technology" as a logical extension of the Science Center's operations that would provide "an opportunity to create a most productive relationship among secondary education, higher education, and practicing scientists in research and development industries."[89] Integrationists on the West Philadelphia Schools Committee, however, feared that such a high school "would channel many of the White students around University City into it and therefore would narrow the possibility of integration *and quality education* in other West Philadelphia high schools" (original emphasis).[90] The WPC advocated building the science high school in the blocks from Filbert (one block north of Market) to Lancaster between 36th and 37th streets—in the immediate area of the Science Center complex in Unit 3.

The WPC planners claimed that their aim was a "planning partnership" to redevelop Unit 3, asserting in their 1961 annual report, for example, that "citizen participation will be sought at every step of the process"; this report cited fifty previous meetings "with citizen organizations and their representatives."[91] The fact that Unit 3 redevelopment on the WPC's terms was in large part a fait accompli, however, belied the rhetoric of citizen participation. While the residents who would be displaced by urban renewal were given the opportunity to receive information, ask questions, and vent frustration at community meetings on Unit 3 redevelopment, they were excluded from the decisions that determined the fate of their homes. In February 1962, some three

Community meeting held by the RDA on Unit 3 redevelopment, at Drew School, Warren and DeKalb streets. Photograph by the *Philadelphia Evening Bulletin*, n.d. Special Collections Research Center, Temple University Libraries, Philadelphia.

hundred residents turned out at the Drew School, at Warren and DeKalb streets, for a meeting with Richard Watson, the RDA's director of public relations. Here an outraged resident spoke for herself and her neighbors: "We have a lot of widowed women here. What will happen when they are displaced? Are you going to stack us up like cattle? Before you tear down our homes build us some new ones. We don't want any project houses." Another participant told the *Evening Bulletin*, "It seems like one race always gets uprooted by redevelopment."[92]

Ironically, a black-controlled citizen's initiative for housing conservation in Unit 3 thwarted itself, though not without delaying the Unit 3 removals for several years. In May 1963, John H. Clay, a black attorney qua developer in West Philadelphia, and fourteen members of a group called the Citizens'

Committee of University City Unit 3, inserted themselves physically in the Unit 3 planning process, staging a sit-in outside Mayor James Tate's office at which they demanded to be recognized by the city as "consultants for Unit 3," a designation the Redevelopment Authority was willing to make.[93] Problematically for the WPC, the Citizens' Committee wanted housing conservation in the same blocks that Harnwell and Molinaro were targeting for the new science high school. Ostensibly to avoid a charge of racism—Clay was "the only Negro speculator in West Philadelphia"—Mayor Tate, Gustave Amsterdam of the RDA, and G. Holmes Perkins of the Planning Commission acceded to the Clay group's demands for housing conservation, notwithstanding these officials' conviction that "there wasn't the economic capacity to pay for the rehabilitation."[94] Perhaps they were also persuaded that "efforts to retain sound housing would permit some of the present residents to share in the planning and development of the renewal area."[95] In any event, Clay organized the nonprofit University City Citizen's Development Corporation (UCCDC), with himself as executive director, to negotiate housing conservation with the RDA, which designated the UCCDC as the redeveloper for 6.8 acres in the earmarked blocks. The contract with the UCCDC, which was effective until June 1965, required that the nonprofit submit "a plan to include rehabilitation of about of about 78 homes and construction of new houses."[96]

An observer of the events that led John Clay down the road to repudiation by the RDA and the Planning Commission wrote, "He hired a Baltimore architect to come up with a restoration plan for the section of Unit 3 under his trusteeship. Using a dressy model, Clay showed the Redevelopment Authority that he would build a few high rises and some town houses. When pressed about the original commitment to the about-to-be-evicted residents, Clay admitted few of them could afford his dream."[97]

Presented in May 1965 to the RDA, Clay's so-called restoration plan undermined his group's claim to represent Unit 3 residents. "Much to everyone's surprise, all pretense at rehabilitation was abandoned," Leo Molinaro reported. "Instead, the proposal called for total clearance and all new construction—two ten story buildings, 75 garden apartment units and 50 townhouses. The Redevelopment Authority told Clay that this was completely inconsistent with the plan for rehabilitation which his group approved fourteen months before."[98] "[Clay] is dead wrong when he says the Redevelopment Authority wants demolition of the area," Molinaro wrote. "*He* wants it and the Authority is telling him to rehabilitate or get out of the picture."[99] An RDA informant told the *Philadelphia Inquirer*, "[The UCCDC] has presented to the authority a plan calling for total clearance and construction of high-rise apartments and town houses. This would result in dislocation of everyone in the area. In presenting this new concept, Mr. Clay insisted [the] costs of rehabilitating present homes makes the course impossible."[100]

Clay explained that he could find no willing lenders for rehabilitation who would not "require the expenditure of at least $10,000 on each particular house," an amount "not affordable by current residents even with federal help." He claimed that his new plan, with rent subsidies, would be affordable, and the project would be "a planned integrated community." Clay vowed that the Citizens' Committee of University City Unit 3 would continue the fight for citizen-controlled redevelopment, citing pledges of support from the National Association for the Advancement of Colored People (NAACP), the Congress of Racial Equality (CORE), and the 400 Ministers Association: "The Redevelopment Authority of the City of Philadelphia now wants to go into total demolition in this area and the Negro people in this particular community are absolutely tired and sick of being pushed out of the proposed new communities only to wind up in another slum area."[101]

In September 1965, having granted the Clay group a ninety-day extension to present an acceptable plan and hearing nothing by the deadline, the RDA withdrew its contract with the UCCDC, and the City Planning Commission reauthorized inclusion of the seven-acre tract in the proposed high school site. Firing off a vitriolic letter to Mayor Tate and copying President Lyndon Johnson, Franny Robinson of the UCCDC charged the Unit 3 planners with racism. "We know that the land is a valuable piece of land and that the institutions want this for the wives of professors and other business people; we know that the White people feel that this land is too valuable for Negroes to live on," she wrote. "You, Mr. Mayor, the Redevelopment Authority, the West Philadelphia Corporation never intended to let the Negroes live in this area. The Redevelopment Authority . . . lied time after time hoping we would leave." Alluding to the lethal race riot in the Watts neighborhood of Los Angeles, the previous month, Robinson declared, "If we do not hear from you, and there has been no action on no ones [sic] part, we will call people together to determine what action should be taken. We would not like this to be another Los Angeles."[102]

In high dudgeon, Leo Molinaro replied to Robinson. "It is totally inaccurate and unfair for you to accuse me and our program of any racial discrimination," he wrote. "The seven acres in the area you are concerned with are by your admission substandard. We believe the area is better suited for public school buildings which will benefit thousands of children, Negro and White, rather than a handful of residents. We stand ready to demonstrate our good faith by helping to find better housing within University City for all persons who are being displaced by public action." In a letter to the Housing and Home Finance Agency, Molinaro declared the WPC's goal of a racially integrated high school: "University City is one of the few areas left in the city where a new school can hope to have an integrated enrollment. Our Corporation supports the Board of Public Education in this proposal, and we pledge ourselves to take every step necessary to make certain the enrollment is integrated."[103]

In November 1965, the UCCDC filed a civil rights lawsuit against the RDA, City Planning Commission, and WPC, among other defendants, with Clay charging that "the only basis the [RDA] had to cancel the agreement was that it wanted to get rid of all the present Negro residents in the area . . . to make way for White professors from Penn, Drexel, and the Science Center and their wives."[104] In July 1966, the same month the School District announced its claim to the disputed seven-acre tract, the U.S. District Court in Philadelphia dismissed Clay's lawsuit—a decision that drew the ire of civil rights organizations. Raising the specter of racial violence in Unit 3, representatives of CORE, the NAACP, and the Student Nonviolent Coordinating Committee (SNCC) persuaded the Department of Housing and Urban Development to suspend the $12.8 million allocated to the RDA for Unit 3 redevelopment, pending an equitable settlement of the conflict. After the RDA finally promised to set aside 7.6 acres in Unit 3 for rehousing displaced residents, HUD reactivated the funding in the late fall of 1966.[105] (Perhaps currying favor, Penn had awarded Robert C. Weaver, secretary of HUD, an honorary doctor of laws [LLD] degree the previous spring; Weaver was also the 1966 commencement speaker.)[106] Molinaro lamented bitterly "a total of two full years of delays and frustrations . . . caused by Mr. Clay and a handful of associates as they tried to impose their plans upon the residents, the City, and the federal government."[107] The two years of delay seem less significant when considering that it took more than fifteen years for the promise of low-income housing to be fulfilled. In the 1980s, townhouses were finally built on reclaimed Science Center land on the south side of Market west of 39th Street.

■

Racial politics formed a citywide backdrop for the struggle over University City High School. A "war" for control of the city's public schools pitted a reform-minded school board led by Richardson Dilworth, who was the board's president after 1963, and Mark Shedd, the district's reform-minded superintendent, against a powerful antireform coalition that included the city's demagogic police commissioner, Frank Rizzo. In 1967, Rizzo infamously turned a nonviolent, "festive" march on the school board building by thirty-five hundred black high school students into a police riot—and then spurred a "white backlash against Black Power" that would lead to Rizzo's election as mayor in 1971 and the end of the Dilworth-Shedd reform era.[108]

Aerial view south, 1968, showing RDA Unit 3 demolition sites for the Science Center (along Market Street) and University City High School (bounded by the trapezoidal fence in foreground), with the University Quad in the background. Photograph by the *Philadelphia Evening Bulletin*, 18 August 1968. Special Collections Research Center, Temple University Libraries, Philadelphia.

Construction began on what was now a fourteen-acre high school site in the fall of 1968. Another four years would pass before the beleaguered edifice would finally open, by which time the conception of a Bronx Science-style high school was off the drawing board. In 1969, a burgeoning fiscal crisis in the school district, paralleled by Penn's own mounting financial instability and institutional fatigue, boded poorly for continued support from any quarter for a specialized high school. Reasoned speculation suggests two reasons for Penn's dissociation from the high school project. First, the WPC's proposal for a science high school was viewed by West Philadelphia blacks and their liberal white supporters as privileging the neighborhoods of University City, leaving the University open to "charges of unfairness and racial bias," a political problem that was aggravated by Penn's role in the Science Center. Second, Harnwell's leadership team worried that the school district's financial problems would leave the University holding the bag at a time when Penn's own resources were diminished. With Jessica Oliff, who wrote a scholarly paper on University City High School, we would also conjecture that the University's role in the West Philadelphia Free School presented an honorable and relatively inexpensive way out of this dilemma. A radically innovative public high school housed

(Top) View north from Filbert Street to a Unit 3 site leveled for the University City High School. Two groups of houses stand in the 3600 block of Filbert Street, pending the relocation of two families. "Family Can't Find New Home, Stays in University City Rubble," says the accompanying headline for this photo. Photograph by the *Philadelphia Evening Bulletin*, 5 May 1968. Special Collections Research Center, Temple University Libraries, Philadelphia.

(Bottom) Contemporary view shows a Science Center parking lot facing the 3600 block of Filbert, with the brick-and-mortar fortress of University City High School in the background. Parking lots west of 36th Street dominated the north side of Market Street into the 2000s. Photograph by Michael M. Koehler. Collections of the University Archives and Records Center.

at scattered sites around University City, the Free School opened in the fall of 1970 with a $60,000 contribution from Penn and the promise of relieving overcrowding at West Philadelphia High School. The Free School "required substantially less capital and did not require major cooperation with the school district. For this reason perhaps Penn felt the Free School offered a 'safe' way to fulfill its responsibilities to the community and education, without forcing the University to expend huge amounts of its own money."[109]

The opening of University City High School in the fall of 1972 as a predominantly African American, comprehensive high school coincided with the mayoral election of Rizzo and, in the aftermath of Rizzo's victory, the resignation of Superintendent Shedd, the firing of school board president Dilworth, and the school district's abandonment of progressive education reform. Located some three hundred yards from the University City Science Center, the new high school arose as an immense, monolithic brick-and-mortar fortress. George Thomas writes sardonically that the building "took the form of a giant square surrounding a roofed-over interior courtyard—itself a telling image of an outside world that had lost its bearings. Like a Renaissance palazzo or John Haviland's Eastern State Penitentiary, it appeared to be designed to defy urban insurrection. When the education staffers added grilles over the windows, the building looked even more prison-like. There was much of the urban prison in its internal demeanor of cinder-block corridors with metal doors as well."[110] Within a year of opening, University City High School was torn apart by gang violence and assaults on teachers—violence made easy by the building's Minoan labyrinth of interior and exterior hallways[111]—an irony in light of the WPC's vision of a magnet high school that would attract University City's white middle class.

Unit 3 Farewell

In January 1965, the UCSC purchased a headquarters building for the Science Center, formerly the home of the Stephen Greene Company, a printing firm, at 3401 Market Street. The die was cast: the city proceeded apace with preparations for Unit 3 removals. In April 1965, the RDA reported that the Authority's property acquisitions in Unit 3 would displace an estimated total of 574 families, of whom 107 were white and 467 nonwhite; 353 nonwhite families (more than three-fourths) were listed as tenants, 114 as owners; 83 white families (71 percent) were listed as tenants, 24 as owners. Suggesting a high rate of black poverty, 329 (more than 70 percent) of a total of 467 black families in Unit 3 were eligible for federally subsidized public housing.[112]

In 1967, the WPC announced that all the city and federal approvals had finally been granted to allow the completion of urban renewal in University

Demolition of a building near the southwest corner of 34th and Market streets, 1967. In background, the Science Center headquarters building on the north side of Market. In January 1965 the Science Center Corporation acquired the building from the Stephen Greene Company, a printing firm. Collections of the University Archives and Records Center.

City: "After five years of planning sessions and public hearings, involving at least a thousand participants, University City Urban Renewal Units #3, #4, and #5 were accorded final approval by the City Planning Commission, the Redevelopment Authority, City Council and the U.S. Department of Housing and Urban Development."[113] The RDA's use of eminent domain, which involved a total of *seven* developers in Unit 3 (the Science Center, the School District, and the Presbyterian-University Medical Center[114] were the unit's major developers), was completed by the fall of 1968.[115] Citing data confirmed by Jean Paul Mather of the Science Center and Charles Kuper of the RDA, Karen Gaines of the Penn News Bureau reported that 2,653 people were "known to have been displaced" in Unit 3. Of this number roughly 2,070 were black—here the calculation is imprecise, as "the exact breakdown by race" of 580 single people was not available; Gaines reported a conservative estimate of 290 single African Americans. For the twenty-six acres of the Science Center complex, Gaines reported 115 families and 137 single individuals; calculating "an average of 4.6 members per family (based on the totals given earlier

(*Top*) Before urban renewal: the Market Street corrider in Unit 3. The view is east from 38th Street toward Center City, ca. 1965. Courtesy of Charles Dilks, University City Science Center.

(*Bottom*) Urban renewal: University City Science Center along Market Street. The view is east from 38th Street, ca. 1980. Courtesy of Charles Dilks, University City Science Center.

for the overall Unit)," she concluded that the total number of individuals displaced by the Science Center complex was 666. Including the 806 people calculated from census block data as living on the University City High School site in 1960, as many as or perhaps more than 1,472 residents were displaced by the Penn/WPC "science city" strategy.[116]

Few data exist on the final disposition of the Unit 3 residents. Some Unit 3 African American families and individuals, as noted previously, moved to Southwest Philadelphia; others moved further west into Wynnefield, formerly a Jewish neighborhood.[117] A 1968 survey of about 15 percent of the displaced people conducted by the Volunteer Community Resources Council, an affiliate of the Tabernacle Church in Unit 3, reported that fourteen of the sample families had moved to Mantua.[118] Census block data show that Unit 3 lost 3,934 people in the 1960s: the population fell from 4,603 in 1960 to 654 in 1970. All of the ten remaining owner-occupied buildings in Unit 3 in 1970 were on one block, from Warren to Lancaster between 36th and 37th streets, across the street from the rising fortress of University City High School; eight of the ten, the only conserved houses in Unit 3, were "Negro-owned."[119] Renewal Housing, Inc., a black nonprofit redeveloper in Unit 3, rehabilitated the Warren Street houses.[120]

By the fall of 1968, with the Unit 3 removals a fait accompli, the Science Center was under siege as student demonstrations protested the insensitivities of urban renewal and the Science Center's alleged role in chemical-biological warfare. Although it was a largely rearguard action with respect to the fate of Unit 3, this protest activity, which culminated in February 1969 with the demonstrators' seizure of College Hall, set the terms for future incursions by Penn in West Philadelphia.

4

Student Protest and the End of the Great Expansion

"By the standards of a true radical, the University sit-in this week was one of the dullest in history," declared the *Evening Bulletin* reporter Rose DeWolf in her account of the peaceful student occupation of College Hall in February 1969.[1] A spontaneous occurrence, with abundant confusion at the outset about its purpose, this relatively quiet yet deeply thoughtful protest action was to gain coherence after a group of pragmatic, moderate leftists wrested control of it from a cadre of utopian radicals—and steered it away from confrontational protest toward deliberation with the trustees. The College Hall sit-in of 1969 remains an iconic event in the University's postwar history, often invoked by liberals as the signal expression of this conservative university's better self, one of the "good" skeletons in Penn's closet for administrators to rattle in public from time to time. The sit-in marked a turning point in Penn's community relations for two reasons. First, the compromise that came from the demonstration obligated the University in perpetuity to render transparent what had formerly been opaque, to repudiate the kind of unilateral, hierarchical decision making that made institutional expansion in Unit 3 a fait accompli before homeowners, renters, and merchants were brought into the process. Second, the sit-in showcased the organizing brilliance of student leader Ira Harkavy, who, since the early 1980s, has been a driving force behind an evolving reconciliation between the University and West Philadelphia's African American communities.

In the first section of this chapter, we look at student and faculty activism at Penn in the 1960s, the 1969 College Hall sit-in, and the role that campus activists played in guaranteeing that any future plans for University expansion would follow deliberative consultation with West Philadelphia community leaders and residents who lived in the zone of the proposed expansion. We consider why campus protest took a conciliatory turn at Penn at a troubled time when other universities were in turmoil. In the second section, we provide a dénouement for the Great Expansion, probing the failure of the University City Science Center in light of the espoused public purposes that justified its establishment.

■ The 1969 Sit-In and the Quadripartite Commission

The civil decorum and constructive outcome of the College Hall sit-in invite comparison with the violent demonstrations, prolonged upheaval, and lingering bitterness that roiled Columbia University in April and May 1968, and beyond. For all the differences in the style of protest between Penn and Columbia, the activists on both campuses targeted similar institutional arrangements. Like their counterparts at Penn, Columbia's protest leaders fixated on a "symbolic shorthand" for the university's "huge network of complicity with the [Vietnam] war."[2] At Columbia, the symbol was the Institute for Defense Analysis; at Penn it was the University City Science Center. Two other issues gave impetus to the student eruption at Columbia: the university's project to build a gym in Morningside Park, "which symbolized the shortcomings of Columbia's attitude toward her black neighbors"; and the administration's decision to discipline five Students for a Democratic Society (SDS) leaders while denying them a public hearing.[3] From the standpoint of the Penn students and their faculty allies the Science Center raised two problematic issues: it was the agent of the University's shadow expansion in West Philadelphia and the symbol of the University's support for war-related research. While at Columbia radical students famously trespassed and seized buildings and administrative offices (and even rifled President Grayson Kirk's records while they smoked his cigars), Penn demonstrators negotiated amicably though firmly with University officials and trustees. Penn had no media lightning rod like Columbia's militant protest leader, Mark Rudd.

A reasonable starting point for any inquiry into the College Hall sit-in is Harnwell's decision to establish the Institute for Cooperative Research (ICR) in 1954. After 1950, concerned that the Soviet Union was experimenting with biological weapons, the Department of Defense authorized the military to conduct extensive R & D on chemical-biological warfare. Jockeying to become an elite national institution, in the fall of 1951 Penn accepted a secret contract from the Air Force with the code name of "Big Ben." Previously, the University had eschewed classified research, accepting only contracts that allowed unfettered publication of findings. University officials now recognized that "Big Ben could serve as a magnet for more federally sponsored research and greater academic prestige," even as they rationalized their participation as

The bobby-socks generation of Penn students, ca. 1955. Collections of the University Archives and Records Center.

providing a necessary countermeasure to a dire Soviet threat.[4] In 1954, Harnwell asked the ICR to administer the University's classified research, including its chemical-biological warfare (CBW) projects; accordingly, Big Ben was assigned to the new institute. "Big Ben," writes Jonathan Goldstein, the author of an authoritative paper, "made Penn a center for Cold War-oriented CBW research and development."[5]

Research and development of chemical and biological warfare projects played out against the backdrop of a conservative, overwhelmingly white Ivy League campus in the 1950s and early 1960s.

The sardonic description provided by the actress Candace Bergen (who flunked out of Penn in her sophomore year) aptly portrays the campus ethos of that era: "In a layout in Holiday magazine on Ivy League universities, I found what I was looking for," Bergen, states in her memoir. (Already a celebrity when she entered the University in fall 1964, Bergen was elected homecoming queen within two months of her arrival.) She writes:

At the old and distinguished University of Pennsylvania, three-quarters of the student body were men and one-quarter were women. Students were shown picnicking in boaters and blazers on checkered tablecloths on the grassy banks of the Schuylkill; preppy young men and women in madras passed through the school quad—built of brick in the nineteenth century—and ivy was everywhere. . . . In the early Sixties, college campuses were not yet hotbeds of political activity but raucous last gasps of irresponsibility. Berkeley led the political pack, as always, but if the answer, my friend, was blowin' in the wind, it had bypassed Penn. It was a passive, conservative campus; the students of its famous school of business were more concerned with *mastering* capitalism than with overthrowing it.[6]

Paul Lyons, a historian of Philadelphia's New Left, writes in a similar vein: "The campus seemed to be dominated by Greeks, jocks, and the utilitarian pursuit of careers. One *Daily Pennsylvanian* editorial bemoaned the 'intellectual ennui' driven by the fraternities, which corralled 45 percent of undergraduates and 'comprised the most unenlightened, unstimulating large unit in the University,' mostly concerned with sports, partying, and drinking . . . the election of Candace 'Cappy' Bergen, the beautiful daughter of Edgar, as

Skimmer Day, 1961, the annual rite of spring marking the junior class's stepping up to the senior year. In the 1950s and early 1960s, the times definitely weren't a changin'. Collections of the University Archives and Records Center.

Miss University seemed to ignite the campus more than civil rights or peace activism."[7] (More than thirty years after leaving Penn on less than cordial terms, Bergen received an honorary doctorate from the University.)

Not surprisingly in this climate dominated by Greeks and jocks (the so-called Red and Blue faction), CBW was not an object of student unrest, nor would it be until the fall of 1965, after President Lyndon Johnson ordered combat troops into South Vietnam and unleashed Operation Rolling Thunder, the bombing of North Vietnam. The first protest action at Penn started in the spring of 1964, with an environmental focus—a series of orderly marches and peaceful gatherings organized by concerned students who contested the removal of open space and elm trees near the southwest corner of Walnut and 34th streets to make way for a new building for the Graduate School of Fine Arts. "Along with others," Bergen relates, "I took my turn carrying a sign that read, simply, S.O.S. (Save Open Spaces), marching all afternoon around the giant elms."[8] The administration countered, truthfully, that the new building would buffer the College Hall area from the din of Walnut Street traffic; moreover, "open spaces will remain at either end of the building, which will be set back a little from the street to save a row of old elms." Working the system, the SOS leaders persuaded the Zoning Board to halt the project, which they correctly observed violated an existing zoning ordinance that mandated "accessory off-street parking" for new buildings.[9] As we have seen, the Planning Commission chairman G. Holmes Perkins, who was also the Graduate School of Fine Arts dean, used his leverage with City Council to get an Institutional Development Zone designation for the University, which gave a green light to the fine arts building by allowing parking within one thousand feet of new construction. Over the 1965 Christmas holiday, the administration outflanked the students by clearing the fine arts site and erecting a wooden fence.[10] SOS collapsed, as ecology failed to galvanize student sentiment for direct action against the project.

SOS was one of three indicators of a campus experiencing a degree of liberalization by the mid-1960s. Another was the dismantling of in loco parentis, whose foundation cracked when the men's Student Government Association and the Women's Student Government Association merged in November 1966 and a woman, Barbara Berger, was elected the first president of the University of Pennsylvania student government. Within the next two years, parietal rules became a dead letter as the administration gave the student government purview of campus social rules; by 1970, following a national trend, Penn's dormitories were coeducational.[11] A third indicator that augured well for reform rather than revolution was the rise of the Student Committee on Undergraduate Education (SCUE) in 1965. On its own initiative, SCUE

Save Open Spaces campaign. Students protesting the location and design of the new Graduate School of Fine Arts building, November 1964—Penn's first campus-wide protest of the 1960s. Collections of the University Archives and Records Center.

carried out an extensive survey of the undergraduate educational experience at Penn, which showed, alarmingly, among other findings, that only 14 percent of students thought the University afforded an intellectual environment. The SCUE staffers took one of Harnwell's declamations to heart: "the campuses of the nation must be forums for serious debate, rather than for formal demonstrations or emotional harangues."[12] And the administration reciprocated by implementing SCUE recommendations for such reforms as a pass-fail option, a Free University, and the termination of in loco parentis.[13] More than any other factor, the level-headed willingness of both administrators and trustees, however grudgingly, to accede to reasonable student demands modulated the intensity of student unrest as the U.S. involvement in the Vietnam War escalated for the remainder of the decade. "The University accepts the proposition that student proposals for reform, carefully and properly presented, are legitimate bases for change," wrote Robert Gross, a *Daily Pennsylvanian* (*DP*) news editor, in the spring of 1966. "Students have recognized the University framework for reform; and thus their proposals normally proceed to the conference table rather than to the picket line." Gross concluded presciently, "With this attitude, and with continued student diversity, the administration can expect to avoid a Berkeley-like uprising on the campus."[14]

Over a twenty-month period, from 1965 to 1967, campus dissent with a wider base of support than SOS arose to challenge the University's "complicity" in the war. With editorial support from the *DP*, student activists targeted two Department of Defense chemical and biological warfare research projects, code-named Summit and Spicerack, which were housed in the ICR offices on the southeast corner of 37th and Walnut streets (the future site of the Annenberg Center theater complex). The activists charged that the ICR projects serviced the production and dispersal of chemical defoliants in Vietnam—

Summit-Spicerack demonstration, 1967; protesting research on germ warfare at Penn. Collections of the University Archives and Records Center.

UPI Telephoto

'Rights of Spring'

a charge that neither Harnwell nor the ICR director, Knut Krieger, ever persuasively denied.[15] The accusation has never been proven as the details of both projects are still classified.

Seeking to disarm further protest after several hundred demonstrators mobilized by the Philadelphia Area Committee to End the War in Vietnam picketed the ICR, Harnwell took steps to transfer the two projects to the Science Center, where Penn was a 53-percent shareholder. Harnwell's ill-considered machinations only further infuriated the demonstrators, who demanded the University's full and unequivocal divestment of the projects. To get that result, they organized STOP (Students Opposed to Germ Warfare Research) and staged a two-day sit-in in Harnwell's office in April 1967. With Harnwell dithering on quashing Summit and Spicerack, the University trustees, faced with more picketing and mounting faculty dissension, "returned both contracts, incomplete, to the Department of Defense," which farmed them out to a Chicago firm. While they prudently reduced Penn's majority holdings in the Science Center to a plurality of the stock, the trustees did not disavow classified research at the Science Center, leaving an open wound to fester on the campus. For his part, Jean Paul Mather, the Science Center's stiff, uncompromising president, resented the Penn trustees for their behavior in the Summit/Spicerack affair almost as much as he loathed the local chapter of Students for a Democratic Society for stirring the pot.[16]

The relative quiescence of the mainstream student body is suggested by the low rate of student participation in the huge antiwar demonstration staged in New York City in April 1967. Only two hundred Penn demonstrators boarded a bus for the ninety-mile trip.[17] In November 1967, some eighty demonstrators staged a peaceful sit-in at Logan Hall (now Cohen Hall), the classroom building next to College Hall, to block access to rooms where recruiters from Dow Chemical Company, the manufacturer of napalm, and the Central Intelligence Agency were scheduled to conduct interviews. The *Daily Pennsylvanian* reported, "The protest was aimed at the University's 'complicity' by allowing certain organizations to recruit on campus."[18] The demonstrators, whose action was opposed by the campus student government, were able to block only four of twenty-six interviews, and only twenty protesters returned the following day to continue the sit-in—hardly a significant disruption.[19] This is not to say that they weren't victorious. Undoubtedly mindful of how easily a peaceful demonstration by "door blockers" could, if mismanaged by a campus administration and local constabulary, escalate into a riot of baton-wielding cops, flying tear gas canisters, and rock-throwing dissidents—the violent eruption at the Dow protest at Wisconsin in October 1967 provided a pointed example of the ugly consequences of administrative

Student sit-in to disrupt recruitment by the Dow Chemical Company, the manufacturer of napalm, in Logan Hall, November 1967. Unlike at Columbia, Berkeley, and Wisconsin, 1960s protest at Penn was calm and respectful—a reflection of the University's moderately conservative ethos and President Harnwell's temperate response to the demonstrators. Collections of the University Archives and Records Center.

ineptitude in the face of peaceful student protest—Harnwell's staff persuaded Dow to cancel its campus recruitment event the following year.[20]

A few months after the Dow protest, Harnwell informed readers of the *Pennsylvania Gazette*, the campus alumni magazine, that "two forms of protest . . . the one noisy and overt—the other quiet and unnoticed" were making the rounds at the University. He averred, probably correctly, that only about 1 percent of Penn's seven thousand undergraduates were involved in protest actions. Harnwell praised the 8 percent of the student body that participated in the service-oriented Community Involvement Council in West Philadelphia, the counterpart of the liberal Citizenship Council at Columbia, an organization described by the former Columbia radical Mark Rudd as "a do-gooder way of participating in the most important social movement of our time, the civil-rights movement."[21]

By the winter of 1969, urban renewal and classified research were moral issues galvanizing a core of moderate New Left activists who belonged to Penn's small chapter of SDS. The most salient issue for them was urban renewal in Unit 3, for which they held the University, through the actions of the Science Center, accountable. The rally these students led at a Science Center construction site escalated into the sit-in at College Hall, a six-day affair that was supported by students from area colleges and universities as well as local black activists. At the sit-in, Penn SDS and their liberal allies would face radical extremists in the Labor Committee, formerly a Marxist-Leninist faction within the national SDS, which had dissolved into splinter groups in the aftermath of the organization's self-destructive national convention in Chicago in June 1968. The chapters that composed the moderate rump of the national organization, among them Penn's, claimed the name SDS for themselves.

The SDS-led rally at the Science Center started in the frigid early afternoon of Tuesday, February 18, with the absurdist high jinks of a guerrilla theater ensemble that farcically bracketed two issues: Unit 3 and military research. The journalist Judith Fowler described the seriocomic "direct action" event as follows:

> Accompanied by hisses and an accordion rendition of "Home on the Range," a cloaked villain (UCSC) wearing ski goggles and mask evicted a small dog (community resident) from a small cardboard house and drew a circled cross (condemned symbol) on the door. Two construction workers (Redevelopment Authority) leveled the house, replacing it with a box representing the Center. A white-coated "scientist" doing pantomime research was approached and offered a scroll of paper (classified military research) by the villain. The scientist refused, then accepted when offered money. "Discovering" a secret poison, he administered it to a hapless bystander who fell dead in the rubble. Demonstrators rushed in to trample the box as actors went among the crowd drawing condemned marks in chalk on several persons."[22]

Soon after the demonstrators returned to campus, their rally, spontaneously it seems, reorganized itself as a sit-in on the second floor of College Hall, where a steering committee representing an uneasy coalition of moderates and radicals from Penn, Temple, Swarthmore, Bryn Mawr, and Villanova agreed to issue a call for a plenary meeting of all interested parties in Room 200, "the high-ceilinged, Gothic-windowed room" that had formerly served as the campus chapel. On the first evening of the sit-in, with some thousand students, faculty, and community members present, the plenary assemblage voted to abide by open expression guidelines that had been recommended the previous spring by a University-wide committee of faculty, administrators, and students chaired by Prof. Robert Mundheim, though not yet adopted by the University Council, the highest-level advisory group to the president. As its primary focus, the plenary approved three demands that would frame the sit-in: (1) transfer of UCSC land to Renewal Housing, Inc., an African American nonprofit, which would build low-income housing in Unit 3; (2) development of a fund for low-income housing by the trustees; (3) revision of the UCSC charter to ban classified military research.[23] Significantly, the plenary accepted the Science Center as a fait accompli: "The students, then, have not asked for the science center to be torn down and replaced with low-cost housing (despite the popular slogan: 'Housing for People, Not profits for Penn.') but only that the center or Penn or somebody put up some low cost housing for some low income people."[24]

Coincidentally for the fate of the sit-in, nine members of the trustees' student affairs committee, including the trustee chair, William Day, were on campus the following evening for a scheduled dinner meeting with the Society for African and Afro-American Students. Showing their support of the demonstrators, Society members canceled their meeting to allow the trustees to meet with a team of negotiators elected by the plenary of the sit-in. Held at the Christian Association, with Harnwell in attendance, the deliberative debate at this meeting marked the starting point of a peacefully negotiated settlement. Several faculty members, some working behind the scenes, played an important role in pushing both sides toward a moderate resolution: among others, the Faculty Senate president Charles Price, the communications professor Sol Worth, the biochemists Robert Rutman and Robert Davies, the city planner Lawrence Goldfarb, the sociologist Philip Pochoda, and the historians Al Rieber, Michael Zuckerman, and Lee Benson. Of the Faculty Senate members who deliberated with students in the fray, Lillian Burns recalled, "All these people worked very hard, and they would come and sit, talk to them all night long trying to keep a lid on the situation, which they did."[25] The Rev. John Scott, the chaplain of St. Mary's Episcopal Church and a counselor at the Christian Association, and Jack Russell, Harnwell's even-handed vice provost, were also "conciliatory forces" in the negotiations. Of critical importance was the endorsement the demonstrators received from the City-Wide Black Community Council and a number of black community activists, including Herman Wrice of the Young Great Society, Andrew Jenkins of Mantua Community Planners, the Rev. Edward Sims of the Volunteer Community Resources Council, and Forrest Adams of the Mantua Mini School. Their aims, which included democratic consultation and participation in future campus expansion plans, were incorporated into the students' demands. And their participation undermined the radical position of the Labor Committee, which espoused a crude form of Marxism-Leninism.[26]

The Labor Committee was a self-proclaimed agent of working-class revolution organized by "Columbia radicals" under the sway of the former Trotskyite Lyn Marcus (née Lyndon LaRouche), who made a brief appearance at the College Hall sit-in. From their home base within Columbia SDS, the Labor Committee fanned out to form cells around the country; one of their founders, Steve Fraser, a student at Temple, organized a Philadelphia cell that attracted radicalized students from Temple, Penn, and Swarthmore.[27] At Penn's College Hall sit-in, the Philadelphia Labor Committee introduced an imposter posing as a local Black Panther to attack any agenda that failed to endorse socialist revolution as its goal. Representing the displaced residents and merchants of Unit 3, the civil-rights activist Walter Palmer formed an alliance with Ira Harkavy, the Community Involvement Council's cochair, whom Mantua's black leaders trusted, to keep the sit-in focused on Penn and the Science Center. Indeed, Palmer brought in Reggie Shell, the leader of the Philadelphia Black Panther Party, who exposed the faux Panther.[28]

Arrogantly styling themselves avatars of scientific socialism, the Labor Committee roiled the Friday evening plenary with their call for a confiscatory tax on corporations as a preparatory step for a Third World–style revolution. Harkavy, who had emerged as the centrists' leader and represented the plenary's dominant position, issued a scathing rejoinder to the radical Steve Fraser, the Temple student who spoke for the Labor Committee's plank: "We came into this building with relevant ideas and proposals and we have a chance to work within the system to achieve real need [*sic*] for real people now. Don't declare socialism now 'cause it ain't happening." The plenary voted with Harkavy to endorse federal funding as a politically acceptable means for funding low-income housing. As Fowler put it, "the vast majority, demonstrators and community alike, felt the immediate scope of the College Hall movement coincided with West Philadelphia's borders." The pragmatically minded plenary would have nothing to do with the delusionary utopianism of the far—very far—left wing of the New Left. Such was the consensus to expunge the Labor Committee that "if the possibility of violence ever existed during the six days, it existed then as pent-up emotions surfaced and tempers soared." Fortunately, the Labor Committee left the sit-in before any fighting broke out.[29]

In the end, the College Hall sit-in was more than nonviolent; it was also rational and respectful. The *Evening Bulletin* put it this way: "Conducted with the university's permission, and within university guidelines, the sojourn in the administration building was peaceful, tidy, injured no one, damaged nothing, kept no administrator from his desk, barred no student from his classes. The demonstrators did not hold a gun at the university's head, and if they did make any threat it was the one implicit in the fact that their conduct might focus public attention on their demands. If what the young people did is Philadelphia's nearest approach to the Columbia University sit-in, then the difference is clear: Columbia's demonstrators were trespassers; those at the U. of P. were not."[30] Consistent with the open expression guidelines, the demonstrators also policed themselves: "To keep order, give emergency instructions and first aid, run errands, take care of clean-up crews and perform organizational tasks, 37 marshals were designated. Green plastic garbage can liners and blue cloth were torn in strips for armbands symbolizing their authority."[31]

This nationally publicized demonstration, in the end controlled by Penn's moderate student leaders, concluded with an agreement between the "community of demonstrators" and the Penn trustees, whereby the latter established a "Quadripartite Commission" of students, faculty, administrators, and West Philadelphia blacks as a watchdog nonprofit to guarantee fair play in the University's future land dealings west and north of the campus.[32] In the wake of the sit-in, heavy pressure from students and faculty compelled the Science Center board of directors to foreswear "contracts whose purpose is the destruction of human life."[33] In most respects a conservative campus with trustees and campus administrators who were conciliatory and willing to negotiate with demonstrators, Penn averted the kind of violent eruptions that military research fueled at Columbia University and the University of Wisconsin.[34]

The reason Penn students rejected radicals' call for "one, two, three, many Columbias" was not that they were "less adventuresome" than their counterparts at radicalized institutions.[35] Nor does the influence of Philadelphia's Quaker tradition provide a satisfactory explanation.[36] The answer seems to lie in the relative openness of Penn administrators and a group of trustees to student participation, if not voting privileges, in University governance. Examples of this liberalizing climate prior to February 1969 included Harnwell and provost David Goddard's recognition of SCUE, the curriculum-reform organization of students' making (it is still a major campus presence at this writing); trustees' "very close contact" with students to hear them out on campus issues; and student representation on the Mundheim Commission, which drew up the open expression guidelines for campus demonstrations (they are still in force at this writing).[37] In any event, an amalgam of pragmatist voices—

Sociology lecturer Phillip Pochoda (left) and student leader Ira Harkavy (right) during the College Hall sit-in, 1969. Collections of the University Archives and Records Center.

administrators and trustees who kept their cool in the face of student demonstrators and bothered to *listen* to the grievances (undoubtedly the firing of William Sewall at Wisconsin and the resignation of Grayson Kirk at Columbia lit their way); a core of influential faculty members dedicated to democratic deliberation and the preservation of civility; and a group of black activists from Mantua and the city, also dedicated to civility, who seized on the sit-in as an opportunity to get resource commitments from the University—came together to forge the terms that concluded the demonstration.[38]

Bleary-eyed and ebullient, Ira Harkavy, the plenary's spokesperson for pragmatic centrism, declared the sit-in an unprecedented triumph: "We unanimously and enthusiastically feel we have won more than any other college movement in history. We changed the decision-making processes and priorities at this institution. Nothing was destroyed, but we built a hell of a lot."[39] SDS leader Joe Mikuliak, Harkavy's ally at the sit-in, called the event a "most amazing and positive occurrence," given that no more than 150 people had shown up at any previous rally, and then only to be harassed by the Red and Blue faction. Mikuliak, who leaned further left politically than Harkavy, hailed it as "one of the greatest victories for a radical movement at an American university." Unfortunately for Mikuliak, not to mention the antiwar movement, the national SDS was a bygone organization, the torch having (literally) passed to the Weathermen and other revolutionary types.[40]

The efforts of Harnwell, the trustees, Harkavy, and their supporting casts averted the rubber truncheons, teargas canisters, and paddy wagons of Police Commissioner Frank Rizzo's cops and saved Penn from the agony of Columbia, of which a former provost of that institution has written: "Some brilliant faculty members subsequently left the university. Columbia lost its sense of purpose, and its financial health declined. All told, it took Columbia more than two decades to recover from the casualties of the conflicts among faculty and students tied to those events."[41]

According to the sit-in agreement of 23 February 1969, the Quadripartite Commission (QPC) was to be composed of "five community members designated by Renewal Housing, Inc., five University of Pennsylvania students designated by the community of demonstrators, five faculty designated by the University of Pennsylvania Faculty Senate, all but one of whom must be resident in West Philadelphia, and five Trustees or their representatives." The agreement "empowered" the Commission "to review and approve all existing plans involving future land acquisition or development of currently owned land contiguous to existing residential neighborhoods, and shall be informed of the initiation of all such future plans and studies." In the event of any future demolition of housing units for University expansion, Penn would provide "an equivalent number of housing units at equitable prices and rentals." The trustees also agreed to use their connections with "corporations, businesses, institutions and agencies" to help create a community development fund of $10 million ($61,800,000 in 2011 dollars). And they pledged to provide office space and $75,000 per annum to staff the Commission.[42]

Founded in 1967, Renewal Housing, Inc., in consultation with the Young Great Society (Mantua), the Mantua Community Planners, and the Volunteer Community Resources Council, among others, appointed three of its own leaders—Lorenzo Graham, Herman Wrice, and Andrew Jenkins—and two other black activists to the QPC.[43] From the outset, the Commission was torn by dissension; for example, Russell Ackoff, a white Penn faculty member who sponsored Wharton School projects in Mantua, reproached the disaffected Andy Jenkins of the Mantua Community Planners for "treating your friends as enemies"; moreover, Ackoff told Jenkins, "your attendance at the meetings of the Commission, its committees and subcommittees of which you are a part, has been close to the worst, if not the worst."[44] Lorenzo Graham, president of Renewal Housing, Inc., stormed off the QPC, alleging that the Penn trustees had reneged on their pledge to "use their connections and their ex-pertise" to raise the community development fund; the trustees claimed to have meant they "would secure the co-operation of financial institutions to participate in housing programs to the tune of $10,000,000 worth of *loans for construction*" (emphasis added).[45]

In the winter of 1970, a year after the sit-in, Francis Betts, Harnwell's as-sistant for external affairs, wrote that the QPC was in trouble. Betts noted "the general feeling of [community] antipathy toward the Commission—West Philadelphia black leaders viewed the QPC as the domain of the University, as three-fourths of the members were "Penn people" (students, faculty, trust-ees), and the Commission was totally dependent on Penn for its funding.[46] By the fall of 1970, Betts would write, "The Commission has been continu-ally plagued by personal and philosophical differences between its constitu-ent groups." A "schism" had opened over the lack of progress toward establishing the community development fund and a "democratic mechanism for the elec-tion or designation of representatives to the Commission from the commu-nity."[47] Russell Ackoff lamented the lack of any *institutional* commitment at Penn to low-income housing, "a potent symbol for the community." Confront-ing one of the most serious financial crises in the University's history, trustee chairman William Day wanted to reduce Penn's financial obligations in West Philadelphia; he recommended that Francis Betts's Office of External Rela-tions take over the role and responsibilities of the QPC. Noting that the com-munity representatives no longer attended the meetings, trustee John Eckman, a frustrated Commission member, railed against the student participants who "have conducted an endless dialogue of 'new left' rhetoric that has success-fully hampered any real progress and has understandably created faculty and trustee apathy when it did not excite outright antagonism."[48] In October, the QPC suspended its activity while the members awaited a renewed commit-ment from the University to community development; when a firm commit-ment was not forthcoming, the QPC formally disbanded in February 1971. Some months later, the *DP* published a trenchant postmortem: "The Com-mission, internally torn and disenchanted by its uselessness and ineffectual-ity, despairingly committed suicide."[49]

During the months the QPC existed, the Penn campus experienced mi-nor shock waves as the Nixon administration pursued its calamitous strategy of "peace with honor" in Vietnam. Harnwell and Provost Goddard acceded to the requests of students to lower the American flag on College Green to half-mast on Moratorium Day (15 October 1969), even as they announced uni-laterally that the flag lowering was "an expression of sorrow," not a symbol of protest. Days later, when students upped the ante by demanding that the flag remain at half-mast for as long as the Vietnam War lasted, vice provost Jack Russell removed it from the Green altogether, igniting what the *Evening Bulletin* described as "the great Flag flap." The fifteen-day controversy, which featured, on the one hand, a pestering student vigil outside Harnwell's office and, on the other hand, denunciations of the University by the American Legion and Pennsylvania governor Raymond Shafer, was resolved by a gathering of cool heads not unlike the one that had prevailed in the College Hall sit-in ten months earlier. But for this clever, peaceable resolution, described as "an effort among a group of students, together with members of the faculty in Fine Arts, to establish some appropriate memorial symbolizing a commitment to peace and a feeling of sorrow at the tragic loss of life in Vietnam, including the deaths of university alumni," the flag flap itself would have no enduring significance. In the twilight of 28 January 1970, with a light snow falling, some six hundred students and faculty members dedicated the beautifully sculpted Peace Symbol, "a 15-foot tall iron circle holding the three-pointed bomber silhouette," in the west lee of the entrance staircase to Van Pelt Library, opposite College Hall, where it has stood for more than forty years.[50]

A spring of political discontent followed the Peace Symbol compromise, with student antiwar protest centering by May 1970 on Nixon's expansion of the war into Cambodia and the shooting of students by Ohio National Guardsmen at Kent State University. (The University of Pennsylvania itself was no longer a target of antiwar protest.) Skipping final exams, Penn students joined peers at fourteen area colleges and universities to "strike" against the war, this strike taking the form of a boycott of classes to free up time for political activities, the largest of which was a march of fifteen hundred protestors from College Hall to City Hall and back. Happily for the striking students—and a big reason the campus remained open and relatively calm—the majority of the faculty allowed the students to reschedule their exams.[51] This is not to say that Penn experienced no spasms of violence in the final spring of Harnwell's presidency; to the contrary: as described in Chapter 5, arson and vandalism unrelated to the war broke out on the campus in April 1970.

What did the 1969 College Hall sit-in accomplish in terms of the demonstrators' primary goal of a fair deal for community members? The answer is less than hoped, but *something.* Though conflicting interpretations of the trustees' pledge to support housing programs in West Philadelphia were never reconciled and the QPC broke apart over the controversy, the trustees had committed Penn, unambiguously, to deliberate democratically with local community representatives regarding future campus acquisitions and plans that would have impacts in West Philadelphia neighborhoods. Of course, this assurance was cold comfort for the displaced families and individuals of Unit 3 who

Antiwar protestors on College Green after Nixon's announcement of the U.S. incursion in Cambodia, 4 May 1970. The Peace Symbol sculpture is next to Van Pelt Library. Collections of the University Archives and Records Center.

would pass their bitterness on to their children and grandchildren. Not until the 1980s and Sheldon Hackney's presidency did Penn slowly begin to redress the anger and mistrust provoked by its role in the Unit 3 removals.

■ The End of Expansion

By the time of Harnwell's retirement in September 1970, the heyday of the West Philadelphia Corporation was over, its financial base too heavily dependent on Penn, which by this time was mired in a financial crisis. The WPC's education projects withered in the 1970s, notably the Universities-Related Schools programs, which for a number of years had infused academic expertise and resources into the public schools of University City. Some of the WPC's contributions were durable: University City and the University City Science Center, and neighborhood enhancements such as the University City Arts League and the University City Swim Club.

The history of the Science Center raises a hard question: Did it realize the stated mission that justified its creation? In our judgment, the answer is *no*. Having opened its first new building in November 1969, the Science Center recruited the Monell Chemical Senses Center, whose own building was completed in April 1971 and continues to operate. Yet the corporation was unable to match its R & D coup with Monell elsewhere on Market Street. For example, the federal Food and Drug Administration announced with fanfare, and then withdrew, its plans for a laboratory building. The General Services Administration put up a fifteen-story office building on the corner of 36th and Market streets to house local units of four federal agencies—the departments of Labor; Housing and Urban Development; and Health, Education, and Welfare; and the Office of Economic Opportunity—a purpose that had nothing to do with research. The plan for a hotel and conference complex never materialized, though it remained on the drawing board as late as the 1990s, and its failure doomed the much ballyhooed World Forum for Science and Human Affairs.[52]

Outraged by what he considered to be a disgraceful capitulation to student radicals in the wake of the College Hall sit-in and contemptuous of his own board's repudiation of military-related research, the contrarian Jean Paul Mather resigned the presidency of the Science Center in August 1969. In the wake of Mather's resignation, Gaylord Harnwell said publicly, "Clearly we made the wrong choice of director. . . . He had been the president of the University of Massachusetts, he had been an outspoken fellow. He gave the impression to many people here, including myself, that he would be sufficiently adaptable to live with the population of Philadelphia. He was not. Every conference he had set their teeth on edge. . . . He beavered away and he did a lot for the Science Center on every front but his public relations, his human image in this community."[53]

In February 1970, Randall Whaley, former director of the Center for the Application of Science and Technology at Wayne State University, Detroit, was appointed president of the Science Center. As his signal contribution, Whaley redirected the Science Center's focus from the recruitment of R & D groups and industrial research divisions to the incubation of small businesses pioneering applications of new knowledge and technologies; in fact, Whaley restructured the Science Center as the nation's first small business incubator. Contrary to the earlier vision of Science Center national research

University City Science Center viewed from intersection of 36th and
Market streets, contemporary. Photograph by Michael M. Koehler.
Collections of the University Archives and Records Center.

laboratories occupying single buildings, the emphasis evolved toward "start-up ventures in an incubator environment offering lots of interaction and a host of business support services" housed in multitenant buildings.[54] By 1984, the Science Center had launched forty-four small businesses.[55]

Whaley inherited a financially beleaguered operation that was losing $30,000 per month. Under his leadership, UCSC achieved financial stability, reporting its first operating surplus in 1972. By 1988, 105 organizations maintained offices at UCSC, employing over six thousand people; the total capital investment was over $90 million; the Science Center generated over $68 million in cumulative city wage and real estate taxes; and twenty-eight colleges, universities, and hospitals were shareholders.[56] Yet Whaley and his board were stymied by a lack of funds to complete the research park; indeed, the area from 36th to 38th streets between Market and Filbert streets remained a wasteland of surface parking lots and after-hours danger until the late 1990s–early 2000s, when three new buildings were completed, one of them a parking garage. And the Science Center never became the "gauntlet of research and research-serving facilities along Market Street" that Harnwell and Molinaro envisioned.[57] Building units and office space were often leased or sold to organizations with operations having little or nothing to do with scientific research.[58]

Margaret Pugh O'Mara notes "a tax and regulatory environment" in Philadelphia that was "highly unfriendly to new companies," including the imposition of "an ever increasing wage tax" and other financial disincentives; this and the deteriorating condition of the area's public schools and accelerating incidents of violent crime in the 1970s militated strongly against the Science Center.[59] While O'Mara does not dismiss University City and UCSC as "total failures," she writes that the WPC's "success paled in comparison to that of Stanford and Silicon Valley. The university [Penn] also fell short in its mission to turn West Philadelphia into a vibrant college-town-within-a-city and to lure large numbers of professionals and young families back from the suburbs."[60] It was "an opportunity lost," says a long-time observer of the Science Center. "That in the generation of high-tech explosion with Silicon Valley and Route 128 and Long Island, and the Washington corridor and all of those places, this was Philadelphia's and what a fizzle! This was the best we could do—and obviously it's not the best we could do; what happened out King of Prussia way and the 202 corridor and all the rest is a success story. But I think this was the one that was touted, this is the one that got public resources from the city and state, this is the one that had the University pushing hard and this was never what it was cracked up to be."[61] As an instrument of urban renewal, the Science Center had marginal economic impact in West Philadelphia, as most of its jobs were tailored to individuals with "a great deal of education or training."[62] Finally, the Science Center was an aesthetic flop, a visual failure of urban renewal described by one journalist at the turn of the millennium as "a combination of cold, sterile-looking laboratory buildings and vast stretches of parking lots, which give the area a desolate industrial steppe feeling."[63]

The completion of Unit 4 and Unit 3 marked the end of the University of Pennsylvania's Great Expansion. For the next three decades, Penn maintained a relatively low profile in West Philadelphia, recommitting significant resources to the area only after Penn president Judith Rodin recognized in the mid-1990s that a crescendo of violent crime, rampant drug dealing, failing schools, and intolerable litter jeopardized the University's future. Fortunately, Rodin's planners took to heart some hard lessons from Penn's 1960s debacle in Unit 3 about the ethical and practical necessities of transparency and community consultation in University development projects. Starting with Sheldon Hackney's administration in the 1980s, the University has gradually improved its relations with West Philadelphia. That alienation and drift marked Penn's community relations in the 1970s is not surprising. Martin Meyerson had his hands full just to keep the University afloat and on an even keel in the face of severe budget deficits; strained racial, gender, and labor relations; a national zeitgeist of political apathy on college campuses; and an urban crisis that evoked great fear on the campus. As will be shown in part II, to which we now turn, Meyerson left a legacy of significant and enduring, though somewhat contradictory, contributions to the University.

Part II **The Visionary**

5

Martin Meyerson's Dream of One University

Martin Meyerson made a number of significant contributions to the University of Pennsylvania as Penn's president from 1970 to 1981. His contributions included the splendid landscape design of the modern campus; the completion of the expansive building program that had begun in the 1950s; the development of a transformative budgetary system that kept the University on an even keel through the tight economic straits of the 1970s and still governs the institution's finances; and the creation of the Faculty of Arts and Sciences. Meyerson's most enduring and significant contribution, however, was not a completed building program, campus plan, or other structural contribution, but an idea. His dream of One University projected an intellectually integrated and respectfully diverse research university.

In 1970, when he donned the mantle of Penn's presidency, Meyerson found the University at a critical juncture. The era of Penn's Great Expansion was over; yet while physical growth had been successfully accomplished, there was little integration of the departmental, disciplinary, and student activities housed in the new or renovated buildings, and the historic core of the campus remained without a landscape design. Meyerson's embrace of One University promised to remedy such academic fragmentation and factionalism, which in his judgment impeded Penn's advance into the pantheon of the world's leading research universities. Yet in the 1970s, One University was an endangered idea, threatened not only by the inertia of traditional academic behavior but also by a severe financial crisis and unprecedented social tensions on the campus. In this chapter, we look at the reality behind the rhetoric of Meyerson's vision, centering on his formidable efforts to steer the University through hard times and his struggle to unify the campus physically and administratively. In the following chapter, we take up the social turmoil and interest-group politics that roiled the Penn campus in the 1970s and dealt an injurious blow to Meyerson's hope for a respectfully diverse campus. We also

Martin Meyerson, with a map of the University Development Plan,
ca. 1975. Collections of the University Archives and Records Center.

consider Meyerson's legacy to Penn and the enduring strengths and limitations of his dream of One University.

∎

At Penn, as at other major universities, the fast-and-fallow 1970s were a far cry from the halcyon, free-spending days of the 1950s and 1960s. Meyerson inherited a severe financial crisis from his predecessor, one that Harnwell's financial officers claimed they had forecast even though they had not prepared for the coming storm. In his report for fiscal year 1969, Harold Manley, Penn's vice president for business and financial affairs, extolled the University's healthy financial condition, reporting a huge leap in the operating budget from $48.6 million in 1960 to $151.6 million in 1969, and a more than doubling of the value of the physical plant, from $151 million to $338 million in the same period. Yet Manley had to eat crow in his report for FY 1970. "The University of Pennsylvania is one of those [universities] in financial difficulty," he wrote sparingly; indeed, by July 1969, the University had a deficit of more than $5 million in the operating budget.[1] In his annual report for 1969–70, Harnwell declaimed:

> The financial situation at Pennsylvania is not unique. The gravity of
> the physical crisis everywhere is jeopardizing the maintenance of the

quality of teaching and research programs as well as the capability of extending adequate financial aid to students. . . . Institutions large and small, gift and tax-supported, find themselves in the same bind due to the combination of inflation, economic recession, declining investments, government cut-backs, and in some instances, a decline in philanthropic contributions. . . . Gone are the euphoric years when universities were riding a wave of unlimited public enthusiasm, which coincided happily with a rising stock market. Back of us, too, is the excitement aroused by the campaign for Pennsylvania's Development Program of the Sixties, which stimulated both capital and current giving to unaccustomed heights.[2]

Harnwell left the presidential stage as the crisis was deepening, leaving the reckoning to Meyerson, without comment on "how the day-to-day activities of major research universities conspired to produce these results."[3]

■ Meyerson's Plan for One University: Premises and First Steps

The Penn Board of Trustees hailed Meyerson as a "fitting choice" to be the University's sixth president. "At this particular juncture in the University of Pennsylvania's history," trustee chairperson William Day proclaimed on 28 January 1970, "Martin Meyerson comes to us endowed by temperament and experience to deal sensitively and innovatively with the academic, governance, and community problems affecting the character of this independent urban university in a time of dramatic change."[4] Though Meyerson had not been the trustees' first choice—that honor was accorded Derek Bok, the former dean of the Harvard Law School, who declined further consideration by Penn and accepted the presidency of Harvard—Meyerson stood at the top of the short list in December 1969.[5]

By the age of forty-seven, Meyerson had established a brilliant career as an urban planning scholar, his resume a litany of impressive academic appointments: University of Chicago (assistant professor, 1947–51), Penn (associate professor, 1951–57), Harvard (Frank Backus Williams Professor of City Planning and Urban Research, 1957–63; and founding director of the MIT-Harvard Joint Center for Urban Studies, 1958–63); Berkeley (dean of the College of Environment Design, 1963–66).[6] As we detail in Chapter 3, it was Meyerson's 1956 memorandum, written during his first tenure at Penn, that helped to spur Gaylord Harnwell to organize the West Philadelphia Corporation, the Penn-dominated, multi-institutional planning coalition in University City.

Meyerson made his most significant contributions to the theory and practice of urban planning at the MIT-Harvard Joint Center for Urban Studies. The planning historian Eugenie L. Birch writes that Meyerson and his MIT colleague Lloyd Rodwin made the Joint Center "the nation's preeminent source of urban scholarship." Among the ten books published under Meyerson's direction—all eminent, some hotly controversial—were Kevin Lynch's *Image of the City* (1960) and Nathan Glazer and Daniel Patrick Moynihan's *Beyond the Melting Pot* (1963). Meyerson and Rodwin put the Joint Center on the global stage with their plan for the design of the Venezuelan new town of Cuidad Guyana, built on the Orinoco River, today a city of one million. "As guided by Meyerson and Rodwin," says Birch, "this project would stimulate scholarly assessments of regional economic development and new town design that form the foundation of today's thinking on these topics."[7]

Not only was Meyerson one of the world's leading urbanists, he had held the top administrative post at two state universities, serving first as interim chancellor of Berkeley in 1965, in the aftermath of the Free Speech Movement and the mass (largely peaceful) demonstrations that fueled it; and then as president of the State University of New York (SUNY) at Buffalo from 1966 to 1970. No doubt the Penn trustees were impressed by Meyerson's success in restoring a semblance of trust between faculty and students during his interim chancellorship. They would also have noted his experience directing an early phase of SUNY Buffalo's transition from a private regional campus, the University of Buffalo, which had emphasized engineering and medical education, to its reincarnation as the SUNY system's flagship university, with world-class arts and sciences faculty and research programs. Meyerson made research across the disciplines SUNY Buffalo's top priority, recruited renowned senior scholars from other universities, and introduced an innovative system of undergraduate colleges.[8]

What the Penn trustees apparently discounted was Meyerson's failure at SUNY Buffalo to calm violent antiwar demonstrations and head-bashing police actions, the like of which he had not encountered at Berkeley in the mid-1960s. (Campus politics at Berkeley would take a radical, violent turn after Meyerson's departure.) Meyerson's project to make Buffalo "the Berkeley of the East" included raising undergraduate admissions standards to the level of the Ivy League. According to the historian Kenneth J. Heinemann, this policy outraged the city's lower-middle and working classes—predominately Catholics of Italian and Polish descent—whose children, formerly the campus's primary constituency, were unable to meet the new standards. The admission of numerous New York City Jewish applicants stoked the ethnic fires of community resentment, and antisemitism likely played a role in the fervor of Buffalo police assaults on SUNY demonstrators.[9]

Meyerson was beleaguered on both ends of the political spectrum. As a compromise with conservative faculty, he grudgingly allowed the University to accept a $1.2 million Department of Defense grant for Project Themis, a submarine-refueling experiment. By doing so, Meyerson, whom Heinemann describes as "a Great Society liberal," gave SDS and other New Left militants, including a core of radical faculty, a casus belli for violent campus protests and acts of vandalism that would include the ransacking of campus offices of the Reserve Officer Training Corps (ROTC). His own antiwar sentiments notwithstanding, Meyerson upheld what he believed to be academic freedom by allowing Dow Chemical recruiters on campus in the fall of 1967; some five hundred fighting-mad students clad in khaki-green guerrilla pants chased the terrified Dow recruiters off campus, notes Heinemann. Soon after the Dow debacle, Meyerson succumbed to mounting conservative pressures within his administration and announced a new policy to suspend or expel miscreant students.[10]

Campus protests spilled over into the city, where police officers wielded blackjacks at antidraft and anti-Nixon demonstrations. Heinemann describes the violent police action that occurred in August 1968 at a downtown Unitarian church where SUNY draft resisters had sought sanctuary. The high-profile trial of the so-called Buffalo Nine—the group of radicals arrested at the church and indicted on federal charges of refusing military induction—focused an unwanted national spotlight on the campus and Meyerson's administration. In the fall of 1969, with destructive vandalism on the upswing, directed first at Project Themis, then at the ROTC, the harried Meyerson took a leave of absence, preparatory to resigning his presidency. As a fitting epitaph for Meyerson's tenure at SUNY Buffalo, Heinemann writes that "Martin Meyerson thought that he could reason with protestors. Tragically, most of his rebellious students, and some of his faculty, were not reasonable."[11]

■

After a thirteen-year hiatus from the University, Meyerson returned to Penn in September 1970. By the winter of 1971, he had a clear understanding of the limitations of Harnwell's massive building program and the gravity of Penn's other ailments. He later wrote, "Growth is the vitalizer, and the revitalization of Pennsylvania was begun under Harnwell. But not the transformation. That would remain unfinished business; more precisely business beyond what he had attempted."[12] The challenge henceforth was consolidation and coherence, including the creation of a school of arts and sciences to consolidate an array of scattered departments, programs, and courses taught in five different schools and colleges. Meyerson also recognized that Penn was habitually dependent on "current educational funds," that is, nonendowment revenue such as research grants and student tuition, in which the University was awash in the 1960s, but which in the next five years would diminish as a result of spiraling inflation and the impact of declining birth cohorts since the mid-1950s. A major capital campaign was essential to build the endowment, reduce Penn's dependence on current dollars, and continue the momentum of the Harnwell era.[13]

To achieve coherence and consolidation, Meyerson adopted the idea of One University, the theme of the January 1973 report of the ad hoc University Development Commission, which conducted a yearlong institutional self-study. Meyerson appointed the commission in 1972 "to review his proposals, which included the reallocation of existing funds and the planning of future growth using the concept of 'selective excellence' to strengthen undergraduate education and to promote particularly strong graduate fields to national rank."[14] The One University report recognized the great advantages of a single contiguous campus, even as it glossed over Harnwell's contributions to establishing a coherent physical plan—Harnwell had sited new buildings within precincts according to function, though without a landscape design plan. A new medical research library and office building bridged the Penn medical school and the biology research complex, itself boasting two grand new buildings by the great modernist architect Louis I. Kahn, creating a vibrant life-sciences precinct. Harnwell also constructed a social sciences complex west of the historic core between Locust Walk and Walnut Street, near the Wharton School and the new Annenberg School for Communication. And a complement of new buildings, including Van Pelt and Dietrich libraries, the Graduate School of Fine Arts, and the soon-to-rise Williams Hall for the humanities, rounded out the historic core of the campus. Still, there is no denying that intellectual fragmentation, the upshot of departmentalization and specialization, belied such physical integration.

The commission report called for "increased interaction between research and training for the professions on the one hand, and research and training in the arts and sciences on the other."[15] Meyerson described the goal as "the establishment of needed linkages among disciplines and professions, departments and schools, and between the theoretical and the applied in both teaching and research."[16] In theory, Penn had a foundation on which to build this kind of integration—"interdisciplinary graduate groups, centers and institutes, and special programs that cut across departments and schools."[17] Presumably, the best new theoretical knowledge would be produced at the intersection of the disciplines, the new frontier of research; the production of integrated theoretical knowledge itself would constitute a public good, as hitherto unimagined applications might come of it: to wit, "[the University] cannot expect to change the world, but it can expect to train people and generate ideas that will change the world." (As we show later, such rhetorical statements would prove too vague and remote from real-world contingencies to galvanize faculty sentiment around "One University.")[18]

In Meyerson's pragmatic view, One University would uniquely define Penn, giving it a competitive advantage vis-à-vis Harvard, Princeton, and Stanford, among other elite peer institutions. A precondition of One University was the cultivation of research excellence in every academic unit. Any school or department that failed to do research or to do it well would be terminated or restructured; hence, Meyerson's strategy of "selective excellence." It is important to note also that One University, as the report of the University Development Commission said, would include a diverse student body, interdisciplinary curricula, and residential, thematically focused college houses. But the main thing was research, and that was the criterion Meyerson and his second provost, Eliot Stellar, applied in their careful scrutiny of the Graduate School of Education and the School of Allied Medical Professions.

Established as the School of Education in 1914 and reestablished as the Graduate School of Education (GSE) in 1962, the "ed school" was a perennially low-status institution on the Penn campus, associated with the low-status field of classroom teaching. Arguably, its low status was merited. In the fall of 1973, Neal Gross, dean of the GSE, wrote a confidential and caustic letter to the University's budget director, complaining bitterly of the tenured faculty at the GSE, whom he described as "generally of mediocre quality" and the "Achilles Heel" of the school. "When they do publish," he lamented, "they publish on 'pedestrian issues.'" Fair or not, this negative appraisal by the school's own dean undoubtedly fueled Meyerson and Stellar's decision to do something about the GSE, whose thirty-two "regular" full-time faculty members managed a total of eighteen specializations that could not be maintained without substantial university funds. Following Gross's abrupt resignation as dean, Meyerson and Stellar commissioned an external evaluation of the school. Written by the prominent education evaluator Ralph Tyler, the report called for a faculty of no more than twenty and implied that the present tenured faculty was not up to the task of building a distinguished school of education.[19] In February 1975, at a meeting with the GSE faculty, the president and provost outlined two options for the school's future: exercise selective excellence in cutting programs; or close the school and redistribute the faculty "where possible" and "perhaps [transfer] high-quality programs." Minutes of the meeting suggest that Meyerson wanted to close the school.[20] Faced with the "threat of extinction," GSE faculty closed ranks with the American Association of University Professors, challenging the "threatened actions" as "arbitrary and capricious," and raising the specter of a backlash by faculty across campus, as well as a negative reaction from state legislators who held the purse-strings of Penn's annual Commonwealth appropriation.[21] These considerations, buttressed by an outpouring of support for the school by "students, alumni, and others," forced the president and provost into a corner;[22] the "eventual decision" was "to contract [the school] to the strongest programs," and reduce the number of faculty "by attrition from 32 to 26."[23] The new GSE dean appointed in the aftermath of the 1975 troubles was not an education scholar, but rather a renowned anthropologist and sociolinguist in Penn's newly established Faculty of Arts and Sciences (see below). The GSE was "saved," though it would take another fifteen years for the school to establish a national reputation as a leading research institution.

The School of Allied Medical Professions (SAMP) suffered a harsher fate under the policy of selective excellence than the GSE: it was closed. Unlike the GSE, which did poor quality research, the SAMP, which offered undergraduate programs in physical therapy, occupational therapy, and medical technology, virtually eschewed research altogether. In other words, the SAMP, with only four tenured faculty members, was considered a vocational or trade school.[24] Meyerson and Stellar's decision to terminate the SAMP raised a storm of protest, with eighty-five student organizations supporting the school and some four hundred students participating in a demonstration at College Hall, not to mention an outpouring of vitriol from many of the SAMP's twenty-five hundred alumni, whose protest letters fill nine folders in the Penn archives.[25] The University Council, the highest faculty-student-staff advisory committee to the president, and the Faculty Senate, each voted for strengthening, not phasing out, the SAMP.[26] A former dean recounted, "Students, faculty, and minority groups . . . pointed out that . . . an aging America needed the services of such a school to provide competent professionals for health care, auxiliary services, physical therapy, etc. The decision to close the SAMP created a great deal of ill will toward the provost and the president. There were votes of no confidence, student organizing, and national appeals to reverse the decision."[27] The SAMP's termination date was June 1981.

Among other things, selective excellence meant highlighting and strengthening the arts and sciences at Penn. In an era of economic downturn and accumulated budget deficits, it was no mean feat to establish a unified Faculty of Arts and Sciences (FAS) from the fragmented disciplinary programs and courses offered in several of Penn's colleges and schools. To organize and direct this consolidation as the first FAS dean, in 1974, Meyerson appointed Vartan Gregorian, the University's Tarzian Professor of Armenian and Caucasian History. The new FAS comprised the Graduate School of Arts and Sciences; the College (of Men); the College of Liberal Arts for Women; the social sciences—sociology, economics, political science, and regional studies—formerly housed in the Wharton School; and the College of General Studies, which offered continuing education and master's degree programs to commuters outside the normal University workday. Clearly Meyerson's finest structural achievement, "the faculty of Arts and Sciences (FAS) brought together twenty-eight departments, thirty-three graduate groups, eight special programs and offices, 528 faculty members, some 5,500 undergraduates, and 2,500 graduate students. It formed the largest single component of the university, consisting of one-third of the standing faculty [tenured or tenure-track appointments] (and if one includes the biomedical faculty affiliated with the Faculty of Arts and Sciences, then FAS constituted almost 50 percent of the standing faculty), and an original budget of approximately $42 million [$199 million in 2013 dollars]."[28]

Meyerson and Gregorian had to overcome considerable faculty resistance and turf wars to forge the new FAS, which, as Meyerson commented, "in terms of consultation and time [was] the most difficult single non-fund raising task of my presidency."[29] With a $25 million target, "the same as the medical school's," Gregorian made FAS an integral part of the University's ambitious $255 million capital campaign, the Campaign for the Eighties, which Meyerson boldly launched with the trustees' enthusiastic support, not "to cover the university's budget deficits but rather to advance new ideas, challenges, research, and excellence."[30] The establishment and financing of FAS was the centerpiece of his One University project:

> In the fall of 1975, for the first time, men and women entered the University in the arts and sciences under a common set of requirements. Freshman and senior seminars and thematic studies became a regular part of the Faculty of Arts and Sciences undergraduate experience. General Honors was expanded and tied to the then new Benjamin Franklin Scholars Program. Undergraduate academic advising was improved. The College of General Studies and the Summer School were brought under the Faculty of Arts and Sciences with the aim of creating a curriculum staffed increasingly by our regular faculty. More money was raised (from the Program for the Eighties) specifically for the arts and sciences than in the entire prior history of the University; arts and sciences was a major beneficiary of . . . 43 new named professorships. With

the solving of the administrative problems inevitably associated with merger of previously separated departments, Dean Gregorian and his able successor, Robert Dyson, increasingly were able to create an integrated arts and sciences organization. Procedures and rules were reconciled across the newly associated departments, an integral advising service was instituted, [and] admissions and alumni activities were taken on.[31]

Another coherence task, certainly Meyerson's most *visible* structural legacy, was landscaping the Penn campus, an achievement that bore the imprint of Paul Cret and the 1913 architects' plan (see Introduction). Sir Peter Shepheard, dean of the Graduate School of Fine Arts and the lead architect of the University's 1977 landscape development plan, wrote critically of the Harnwell-era "building boom," with explicit reference to Cret:

Instead of following Paul Cret's "fixed principle" of creating "open spaces enclosed by buildings and not employed to surround them" these buildings sit in isolation as on a chessboard; moreover though the buildings themselves were expensive enough, no money was spent on renewing the old spaces *between* them. Even on College Green, the new buildings simply sit on their platforms, surrounded by a patched-up arrangement of walks and eroded grass, hardly concealing the ghostly curbs and sidewalks of Woodland Avenue. Such landscapes are impossible to maintain: paths in the wrong places cause grass to be trampled; undrained paths cause it to wash away. Much effort is annually wasted in the attempt to keep up the present bedraggled appearance of College Hall Green.[32]

(The only landscaped venues of the Harnwell era were Locust Walk and a sequestered stone-terraced park built by the architect Ian McHarg to cover the footprint of Woodland Avenue above 36th Street.[33]) Funded by the University's capital campaign, Blanche Levy Park, as the College Green precinct was now called, was dedicated in 1979. Bounded by three hallowed structures—the green serpentine, neo-Gothic edifice of College Hall; Boyle's statue of Benjamin Franklin; and the "fiery-red-brick" Fine Arts Library designed by the Industrial Age architect Frank Furness—the park was "replenished with saplings and edged in granite, walkways of brick and Heidelberg blue stone, a small amphitheater and umbrella-covered café tables toward 36th Street (itself incorporated into the park) and numerous benches."[34]

Contemporary southwest view of Blanche Levy Park, completed
1981; Claes Oldenburg's *Split Button* in foreground. Photograph by
James R. Mann, Facilities and Real Estate Services, University of
Pennsylvania.

The Campaign for the Eighties started just as Penn's operating budget was moving toward the black, though the accumulated deficit would remain problematic, reaching a high-water mark of $12.4 million in fiscal year 1976.[35] The international oil crisis, coupled with double-digit inflation, had taken a heavy toll. "During fiscal year 1973–74," a campus financial officer wrote, "the University of Pennsylvania experienced along with the nation one of the worst inflationary periods in modern history, and suffered from substantial increases in its costs of operation, particularly in the cost of energy";[36] the latter expenditure rose from under $3 million in 1970 to $15 million by 1979.[37] Finally in 1976, Penn turned the corner, reporting an operating surplus of over $100,000, attributable to "tight budgeting and control" and "new campus-wide efficiencies."[38]

The principal means that Meyerson used to help Penn survive the 1970s was "responsibility center budgeting"—today called "responsibility center management," or simply RCM. This was Meyerson's third major structural decision to have a lasting impact on the University, though this decision would jeopardize his One University project. Jon Strauss, Meyerson's chief budget officer and a national authority on university finance, credits Meyerson as the architect of RCM, which today is operational in numerous public and private higher education institutions.[39] Vartan Gregorian has written, "The idea was imported from Harvard and commonly referred to as 'each tub on its own bottom.' It envisaged that each school would be charged to match, as nearly as possible, its expenses to its income."[40] Meyerson briefly explained the mechanics of RCM to the Board of Trustees in his "State of the University" report of January 1973: "To each responsibility center (principally the schools) would be credited the tuition income 'earned' through teaching, and all other income brought in from restricted endowments, gifts, and research contracts. Each center must then cover its direct costs, such as faculty and staff salaries, plus all 'directly attributable' costs, plus some share of indirect costs (central administration, student services, insurance, etc.) from its 'own' income plus a subvention from general University income."[41]

To impose fiscal control on the University in hard times, Meyerson seemed willing to risk what Gregorian calls "the danger of organizing the university around the schools and departments with saleable skills, each competing to maximize tuition and grant income."[42] "It's much [in the various responsibility centers'] interest to teach students from other schools, but it is *not* in their interest to have their students *take* courses in other schools," observed a knowledgeable faculty member in the pre-FAS Graduate School of Arts and Sciences. "The central administration, having gone the responsibility center route, must now develop a series of restraints to prevent schools from so gerrymandering their curricula that the students do not feel free to actually participate in 'one' University."[43] After several years of RCM, by then an "integral part" of the University with "wide support," the deans of the various schools also voiced this concern to a greater or lesser degree, one in particular venting, "I am disturbed by the trend of schools duplicating other schools' courses simply to increase their incomes. This does not sound like a One-University perspective to me."[44] For all the efficiencies imposed by RCM, the policy militated against the One University idea. More than twenty years later, the problem was deeply entrenched. Complaining about RCM, a Faculty Senate subcommittee said in 1996: "Current budgetary procedures, for example, have led to strict limits on the number of course units that may be taken outside a student's home school, thus restricting the student's explorations and discouraging the creation of cross-school courses and programs."[45]

■

Thus far, we have seen that Meyerson made enduring contributions to Penn, including the landscape design of the modern campus, the School of Arts and Sciences, RCM, his advancement of the University's research trajectory (a considerable achievement in tough economic times), and his idea of One University. Yet Meyerson's presidency had an Achilles' heel as well: his inability to deal effectively with the sources of intense conflict that rived the Penn campus in the 1970s. Quite simply, the demands of the time outstripped Meyerson's capacity to deal with them, his dazzling intellect notwithstanding. We turn in the next chapter to the difficulties that undermined his presidency.

6

Identity Politics in the Arena

In the 1970s, social forces and interest-group agendas further fragmented the University of Pennsylvania and stymied the One University idea. It was a turbulent decade at Penn—a prelude to even greater campus agitation in the 1980s. Following a national trend, student activism at Penn splintered from a more or less unified focus on participatory democracy and attacks on U.S. foreign policy and the global inequities of corporate capitalism ("imperialism," with which Penn was associated) into identity politics and the advancement of agendas for progressive programmatic changes on the Penn campus— for example, a women's center and a women's studies program; a department of black studies and an African American college house. Campus-wide protest also took a self-referential turn as otherwise politically somnolent Penn students mobilized en masse against tuition increases and budget cuts in extracurricular programs. This mainstream unrest was linked to the University's escalating budget crisis and, more broadly, to the dire state of the nation's economy, which obtruded in sundry ways on Penn and every other American research university. Hostile labor relations also inflamed campus politics and embroiled the University in a dispute with Pennsylvania state legislators.

■

Though his administration made strong and concerted efforts to strengthen the "black presence" (Penn's term) and the overall diversity of the campus, these efforts were insufficient to satisfy the University's African American constituents, who were inspired and unified by the civil rights movement's turn to Black Power. The emergence of "identity politics" introduced a critical campus tension between blacks' uncontroversial demand for recognition and inclusion in University life and their controversial demand for a degree of separation and self-determination. A second source of tension was the Penn women's movement, which centered militantly on the establishment of a women's center—a mobilization whose proximate cause was an outbreak of sexual assaults on Penn women by West Philadelphia youths. A third tension was raised in labor disputes incited by the administration's attempt to impose new efficiencies in facilities management by reducing the labor force; striking and strike-supportive Penn workers, black and white, roiled the campus for a number of years. And campus-wide student demonstrations further stirred this volatile pot, born of post-1960s generational priorities and highlighting such egoistic concerns as annual tuition increases and the administration's proposed diminution of student activities.

The Black Presence and Its Discontents

Robert Rhoads has described the "acquiescence of the 1970s," when "student social and political issues fell into a kind of slumber as the pursuit of more individualistic goals took precedence for the vast majority."[1] Trends documented in *The American Freshman* study of the Higher Education Research Institute, a treasure trove of annually reported longitudinal data on "the changing nature of students' characteristics, aspirations, values, attitudes, expectations, and behaviors,"[2] sustain these often taken-for-granted conclusions about the 1970s. A few examples of student values must suffice to illustrate the general point: "having a meaningful philosophy of life" declined from 85.8 percent of all freshmen in 1967 to 60.3 percent in 1979; "keeping up to date with political affairs" declined from 60.3 percent in 1966 to 41 percent in 1975; and "being well off financially" declined from 42.2 percent in 1966 to 36.2 percent in 1972, then rose by leaps and bounds to 58.5 percent by 1979.[3] At Penn in the 1970s, student social and political issues were largely restricted to two group agendas that marked the emergence of identity politics on the campus. Beyond the demonstrations of these two organized activist groups—African Americans and (mostly white) feminists—the campus remained largely quiescent on social and political issues, aroused in the main only when administrative actions threatened students' pocketbooks or denied them a voice in budgetary decisions.

The primary mover and shaker in African American politics at Penn was the Society of African and Afro-American Students (SAAS; after 1971 called the Black Student League, or BSL), an activist organization that held a "Black Power perspective."[4] Emergent Black Power at Penn fueled charges of "separatism," whereas the real goal, as the historian Wayne Glasker argues persuasively, was "group self-determination not segregation." In other words, blacks would organize themselves as a "self-conscious [ethnic] interest group" to claim an equal slice of the American pie in competition with other ethnic groups.

Struggle for a black residence hall, resolved with the establishment of DuBois House in Low-Rise East (Superblock) as a college house for students interested in African American culture, ca. 1972. Collections of the University Archives and Records Center.

African American students at Penn "initiated a pattern of 'dual organization,' with parallel black organizations alongside 'white' (nominally desegregated) campus organizations," the goal being "pluralism," or "biculturalism." The issue of separatism would be contested on the campus in 1969–70, bequeathing to Meyerson's presidency a very troubled institution.[5]

Troubled race relations preceded Meyerson's arrival in College Hall. Succumbing to real and imagined threats of violence from West Philadelphia African American activists who were perhaps galvanized by the College Hall sit-in, Penn admissions officers accepted thirty-one applicants from racially segregated West Philadelphia High School (nine blocks west of the campus) for matriculation in the fall of 1969, twenty-one of them admitted grudgingly, ten others without reservation.[6] The issue of an infrastructure of institutional support for these and Penn's other black students became a cause célèbre for SAAS, which demanded and got, though not without heated controversy, an "all black social center," the House of the Family, an independent, nonprofit corporation that, in conjunction with SAAS, leased the University-owned parish house of St. Mary's Episcopal Church on Locust Walk. "The House of the Family became a center for efforts to build and empower the black community," Glasker writes, "and became better known simply as the 'Black House.'"[7] Dissatisfied with the University's summer preparatory program for entering black freshmen labeled academically deficient, SAAS demanded an advising program that embraced the theme of black nationalism. The ensuing conflict over this ideological program "escalated into the most serious and destructive clash between black students and the Penn administration in the decade of the 1970s."[8]

Viewed in hindsight, the events of April 1970 seem almost surreal. On April 13, the black associate dean of students resigned in protest over the provost and dean of admissions' refusal to fund the proposed black advising program, which they regarded as ideological and separatist. On April 16, as many as one hundred black students marched into College Hall and issued a militant press release charging the University with institutional racism.[9] On the night of April 22, the campus was shaken by four fires and vandalism at the University bookstore, with Philadelphia police suspicions focused on the House of the Family. On April 25, shortly after midnight, a Molotov cocktail exploded in Houston Hall; soon thereafter, city police swarmed the campus, made one arrest, and raided the House of the Family, looking for "paraphernalia or other ingredients used in the manufacture of Molotov cocktails or other explosives or incendiary devices," which they did not find.[10] In a bizarre twist, the suspect who was arrested and charged with "arson, malicious mischief, and conspiracy" was none other than the former associate dean who had resigned his position in protest two weeks earlier—he was acquitted at trial of all charges in the firebombing incident.[11]

Assuming the presidency in the fall of 1970, Meyerson inherited the upside of black anger, racially motivated campus violence having dissipated since the events of the previous spring. Over the summer, negotiations had resulted in a pre- and postfreshman summer advising program divested of "nationalist" ideology and representing multiple perspectives. When Meyerson took charge that fall, the faculty was considering a plan to establish an African American studies program, which had been originally proposed as a department, next as a school, then as a program, an option that was finally approved though grudgingly accepted as a last best hope by the black activists. "Eventually in the 1970s, a recognized major in Afro-American studies was established," writes Glasker. "African American studies at Penn, however, remained an academic program and an interdisciplinary major led by a committee of faculty that reported to the provost until the 1990s." To restate the point: "it was an interdisciplinary program, but not a department."[12] (Forty years would pass before the Department of Africana Studies was finally created by a vote of the trustees in 2012.)

By 1972, a heated controversy swirled around a proposal to establish a residential college house program for blacks, as critics, including the NAACP, conjured the dual specters of "reverse discrimination" and "separatism."[13] In some respects, this plan aligned with a campus housing trend of the Meyerson era: at least seven residential college houses (an idea first discussed at Penn in the 1960s) appeared on the campus in the 1970s, the first being Van Pelt College House, which opened in a Superblock low-rise dormitory in the fall of 1971.[14] Integral to President Meyerson's emerging conception of One University, college houses provided a "living-learning" experience that featured informal academic and cultural programs, forums, and social networking in the context of residential life. The "granddaddy" of Penn college houses, the Van Pelt program originated as a response to what the historian Alan Kors, a founder of the original program, calls the "atomization" of the University: "[Undergraduate] students, graduate students, and faculty rarely interacted on an informal basis, scientists and poets rarely met, the engineers and string quartets rarely met, and seniors and freshmen rarely met." Mixing some sixty undergraduates, two faculty masters, and twelve resident faculty and graduate fellows, Van Pelt was touted by Penn administrators as "the" model for the living-learning concept.[15]

The original proposal for a black residential house, however, differed from the Van Pelt concept in one fundamental (indeed self-evident) respect: it was to be a *blacks-only* living-learning center, with "Black residence counselors and academic advisors."[16] Notwithstanding assurances from the students and the newly established Committee of Black Faculty and Administrators that "all cultural and academic affairs" at the black college house would be open to the wider campus, Provost Curtis Reitz (who held that position until 1972), and the Faculty Senate, after a furious debate, rejected the original proposal. Finally, all parties agreed to an uneasy compromise whereby the new college house would open in the fall of 1972 on a nonexclusionary basis to freshmen and sophomores "who have a particular interest in and commitment to black culture, and a particular need for the educational opportunities and services which the Center and its environment will provide."[17] That compact would be the long-term basis for the residential college house, which for a decade bore the nondescript label "Low Rise North" until it was dedicated as W. E. B. DuBois House in 1982. At this writing, DuBois House, long since racially integrated, has stood for more than four decades as a center of black cultural and academic affairs.

African American students at Penn, 1974. Collections of the
University Archives and Records Center.

Fully in step with the times, when college and university campuses, especially
in the Ivy League, were changing their notions of merit and seeking to diversify
undergraduate admissions and to restrict the proportion of students admitted
solely on the basis of performance on "objective" predictors of academic success
(SAT, GPA, for instance),[18] Meyerson, himself the first Jewish president of an
Ivy League institution, took to heart the challenge of strengthening campus
diversity, in particular Penn's black presence. The University Development
Commission's report of 1973, *Pennsylvania: "One University,"* echoed that commitment, noting the substantial progress made in black student recruitment,
even as the authors sharply criticized the paucity of black professors at Penn (for
example, only three with full-time appointments in the College and Wharton
School, of a total of 627).[19] From 1970–71 to 1975–76, the University's average
yearly matriculation rate for black freshmen stood at 8 percent (or 168) of total
matriculations, with a high-water mark of 9.1 percent in 1972–73, followed by a
three-year decline that was pervasive in the Ivy League.[20] For the four-year
1972–75 cohort, the Office of Undergraduate Admissions reported a total of
620 black undergraduate students at Penn, 7.6 percent of the total.[21]

Notwithstanding the implementation of Penn's first affirmative action plan and ramped-up minority recruitment efforts, the University showed only slight progress in hiring African American faculty, prompting accusations from Penn's black constituents that the University was foot-dragging. By 1978, Penn had only twenty-six African Americans in its "standing faculty" of some seventeen hundred, about 1.5 percent of the total, compared to a total of thirteen faculty positions in 1972; only six held the rank of full professor, compared to four in 1972, and only thirteen held tenure.[22]

Future progress toward increasing the number of black faculty would be painfully slow. A major University report from 1992 shows only fifty black professors among some nineteen hundred standing faculty, about 2.6 percent (and only twenty-four "Hispanic" professors, 1.3 percent). The same report shows a tremendous growth in undergraduate "minority" freshman matriculations from a total of 13.4 percent in 1980 to 31.3 percent in 1991, largely explained, however, by a more than quadrupling of "Asian" representation—blacks represented 4.8 percent of the class; Hispanics, 4.7 percent; Native Americans, 0.17 percent; and Asians, 21.6 percent.[23] Interracial conflict would persist into and beyond the 1980s; among other problems, Penn blacks would endure bomb threats at DuBois House, racist graffiti in the dormitories, white harassment from the high-rise rooftops, and the taunts of white fraternity brothers along Locust Walk.

■ The Campus Women's Movement: The Nexus of Penn Feminism and Violent Crime in West Philadelphia

From the late 1950s to the mid-1970s, rapidly accelerating violent crime, in particular rape, was a pressing issue at Penn, to the extent that a climate of fear and suspicion of West Philadelphia blacks prevailed on the campus. The nation's large cities experienced a decadelong rise in so-called index crimes—rape, robbery, aggravated assault, burglary, grand larceny, and auto theft. Philadelphia was no exception: in the first six months of 1970, the city reported twenty-one thousand index crimes, compared with 17,400 for all of 1960.[24] Security concerns were rife on the Penn campus. "One does not wish to cause alarm unduly," wrote the associate dean of the College, "but the state of security on the campus is not good, and there is growing erosion of morale among female employees doing secretarial work who have begun to fear for their safety."[25] The chair of the Political Science Department complained of rampant theft and vandalism in an underground parking garage: "To my personal knowledge since last Thursday alone . . . six cars have been broken into and rifled (mine, too, has been victimized twice in the recent past) and nine had their windshields smashed—eight of these en masse at 8:oo p.m. last Thursday evening! Moreover, car owners who must enter the garage late at night have come to fear for their personal safety."[26]

The *Philadelphia Evening Bulletin* reported eight rapes on the Penn campus between September 1971 and May 1972.[27] A series of sexual assaults on Penn women in March 1973 finally provoked a feminist revolt that was led by Women for Equal Opportunity at the University of Pennsylvania (WEOUP). Their demands included strengthened and expanded security measures, a women's center and coordinator, medical and psychological counseling services, and free women's self-defense classes. "The issue of rape is crucial to the women's movement," declaimed Carol Tracy, president of WEOUP, who clarified that "protecting women does not mean violating the rights of black male students or men in the community."[28] After a four-day sit-in involving some two hundred women, the administration agreed to the demonstrators' security demands and the establishment of a women's center that would be "designed to serve as the focal point for development and implementation of a program for medical, psychological, and legal support of assault victims, of training and information programs concerning personal safety, and of other academic and non-academic University functions and services pertaining to women."[29]

Decades later, Tracy, who directed the Women's Center from 1978 to 1984, recalled the obstacles that confronted the city's rape victims in the early 1970s: "There were no services for rape victims," she recounted. "The police didn't investigate, the district attorney's office paid no attention to what was the second most serious crime, [and] even medical institutions were hostile to victims. It was a radical act to have an advocate in the hospital—and Philadelphia was the first to formalize the relationship of advocates in the emergency room, at the old PGH [Philadelphia General Hospital]." Fear more than activism galvanized Penn feminists until the male campus security director callously advised them "not to wear provocative clothing," kicking them into action; one accosted him directly: "I can walk down this campus buck naked, and your job is to protect me."[30]

By 1979, the Public Safety Department, now with forty-nine full-time uniformed police and bolstered by the hiring of a veteran Philadelphia policewoman as a crime-prevention specialist, had taken substantial measures to improve security, though campus and adjacent-area crime would continue to be a serious problem for the next twenty years.[31] Emblematic of Penn's expanded security apparatus by the end of Meyerson's presidency were a plethora of high-intensity lights and blue-light emergency phones, twenty-four-hour campus guards in the high-rises, and an escort service; there was even talk of a centralized, electronic-card security system, though this high-tech development would take another two decades to install.

Another gender tension was faculty hiring. In the spring of 1971, an ad hoc committee on the status of women reported dismally low percentages of women in the three ranks of the standing faculty (tenured or tenure-track appointments): full professors, 2.5 percent; associate professors, 7.0 percent; assistant professors, 12.7 percent; and total faculty positions, 7.0 percent; there were no women full professors in either the men's or women's undergraduate (premerger) colleges.[32] Two years later, the percentages for faculty women in the three ranks were only 3.6 percent, 8.7 percent, and 14.5 percent, respectively.[33] In 1978 and 1979, Meyerson reported better progress on this front: an increase of women in the standing faculty from seventy-seven in 1970 to more than 175 in 1978, and a doubling of their total representation, now at 14 percent.[34] (By 1982, two hundred and fifty-three women represented 14.8 percent of the standing faculty and 9.8 percent of the tenured faculty, compared to 12.9 percent and 8.6 percent, respectively, in 1973; by 1989 the figures were roughly 17 percent and 11.5 percent, respectively.)[35]

■ The Revolt of Penn Labor: Housekeepers, Teamsters, and the Commonwealth of Pennsylvania

One very successful response to Penn's economic crisis in the 1970s was "tight budgeting and control," achieved through "new campus wide-efficiencies," such as energy conservation and responsibility center management, the budgetary strategy that proved irresistible to Meyerson and his administrative team, even as it contradicted the One University idea.[36] While the national economy remained inflationary and, as previously noted, Penn's energy costs soared (quadrupling between 1973 and 1979), the University under Meyerson was able to whittle down the accumulated deficit after 1974.[37] Replacing what Meyerson called "an antiquated budget system and comptroller system," RCM kicked into high gear in FY 1975, producing balanced budgets throughout the second half of Meyerson's presidency. That in itself was a remarkable achievement, and it was complemented by Penn's strengthening its national research profile, with total external grant and contract dollars flowing ahead of inflation, from $34 million in FY 1970 ($72.2 million in 1980 dollars) to $111.5 million in FY 1980.[38]

These gains notwithstanding, other efforts at fiscal control were controversial, and they hurt Meyerson's reputation. Under selective excellence, as we previously pointed out, Meyerson and the trustees terminated the School of

Picket line during housekeepers' strike to protest the contracting out
of their services, University of Pennsylvania, 1977. Collections of the
University Archives and Records Center.

Allied Medical Professions and shrank the Graduate School of Education—
broadsides that signaled research as the University's highest priority, even as
they provoked widespread resentment toward Meyerson and Provost Stellar.
Annual tuition increases, as well as budget cuts in extracurricular activities,
outraged students, who periodically besieged College Hall. Quieting a particularly voluble demonstration in 1978, Meyerson's blanket accession to student demands without the advice and consent of faculty irretrievably damaged
his presidency (more on this below). An earlier blow to Meyerson's prestige
was his administration's widely publicized failed attempt to cut costs by downsizing or outsourcing key components of Penn's organized labor force, a corporate management strategy too far ahead of its time that backfired and
jeopardized the University's annual Commonwealth appropriation.

Mobilized in the summer of 1977, the most consequential union strike in Penn's history played out against a background of labor dissension that had been escalating since the early 1970s. In the spring of 1971, Penn's unionized cafeteria workers struck successfully for higher wages and a first-time benefits package; they were joined by a sympathy strike of Penn library workers and supportive students on the picket lines.[39] In the fall of 1975, three inflation-pinched union locals—operating engineers, building-maintenance workers, and animal lab workers—struck for higher wages and improved benefits, with the cafeteria and library workers joining them in the work stoppage, a total of one thousand union members off the job. The strikers' primary tactic was to block campus deliveries (food, oil, linens) and trash disposal; fisticuffs, vandalism, reeking garbage, and the howls of inconvenienced students, who by this time were no longer ardent labor sympathizers, kept the campus in an uproar for the duration of the six-week strike, whose final resolution was small contractual gains for the disaffected unions.[40]

The housekeepers' strike of 1977 could not have been more badly timed from the administration's perspective, for it coincided with debates (and ensuing doubts) in the Pennsylvania legislature regarding Penn's annual state appropriation, with $17.7 million ($68.2 million in 2013 dollars) at stake. This strike was occasioned by an administrative decision authorized by Meyerson to contract out Penn's housekeeping operations—cleaning, custodial, and trash-removal services, a total of 343 employees—to off-campus maintenance contractors.[41] Meyerson and his management and finance team contended that they resorted to outside contractors only when negotiations with Local 1202 of the independent United Building Service and Maintenance Employees had stalemated and were not resumed by the International Brotherhood of Teamsters Local 115, the housekeepers' successor union as of June 1977.[42]

Amid vitriolic charges and countercharges of unfair labor practices, among them the accusation that Penn was "union busting," the housekeepers' contract expired in August and all of them were given pink slips.[43] As the laid-off housekeepers picketed the campus, Penn contracted out their services.[44] Meyerson faced a major crisis when the state senate, under "intense Teamster pressure," denied Penn its annual appropriation—an action that "interjected the legislative process . . . into labor relations," and, according to Meyerson, threatened the University's "survival in anything like its present form."[45] Applying pressure locally, the Teamsters logjammed traffic on Walnut Street, staging several raucous conveys with air horns blasting.[46] Cutting his losses by "going to Canossa," Meyerson prudently dropped the outsourcing plan. Following the University's offer to reinstate the fired housekeepers and to recognize Local 115 as their collective bargaining agent, a mutual resolution of the formal complaints registered with the National Labor Relations Board, and the promise of a new contract favorable to the 311 housekeepers who chose to return to their jobs, the state senate overwhelmingly approved Penn's appropriation.[47]

Forging the Self-Referential Campus: Penn Students and the Retreat from Civic Engagement

While the 1970s was indisputably a turbulent decade at Penn, a decade that saw more campus-wide turmoil than even the late 1960s, it was marked by the pronounced civic and political disengagement of Penn students from West Philadelphia, another factor of no mean consequence to the University's community relations. Deprived of its galvanizing antiwar component, campus activism turned away from the non-self-selected "larger public" of West Philadelphia and the vision of participatory democracy that had galvanized the College Hall activists of 1969 and the Quadripartite Commission to the "little publics"[48] of self-selected interest groups such as the BSL or the WEOUP; or, far more egoistically and more widespread, to sit-ins against tuition hikes and the University's decision to scrap the hockey team and other small sports.

The attitudes of Penn undergraduates, in the main, reflected the central tendency of civic and political quiescence and careerism that marked the 1970s generation of American college students.[49] Newspaper accounts and University reports of the 1970s reveal this shift in student attitudes from ideology and global issues to self-referential concerns. Leftist student activism was largely restricted to the separate agendas of two reference groups (blacks and feminists), and such activism lacked a superordinate goal that might have bridged and bonded these groups with labor and the wider campus.

Perhaps more than any other indicator, the fate of the Penn People's Park in the superblock west of 38th Street signaled the demise of participatory democracy and hopes for cooperative activism at Penn. Organized in the spring of 1971 by a coalition of students, faculty, and West Philadelphia residents, the People's Park Coalition emulated the motley assortment of environmentally minded student and countercultural groups that had gathered in May 1969 to establish a community park on an urban-renewal site owned by the University of California, Berkeley, and earmarked for a dormitory. As is well known, this California happening, which was peaceful until the University egregiously fenced in the site, led to a fatal police riot, the city's occupation by National Guardsmen, and the helicopter tear-gassing of the Berkeley campus.[50] Meyerson, formerly an acting chancellor of Berkeley (1965–66), sagely

Park advocates landscaping a squatted site in the Superblock adjacent to the West Philadelphia Free Library (left rear), 1974. Collections of the University Archives and Records Center.

acceded to the West Philadelphia coalition's proposal for the peaceful development of a community park on a parcel of land between High Rise North and the Free Library at 40th and Walnut streets—vacant land that was being used as a surface parking lot. An architectural volunteer designed an elegant plan for the space that featured a "sunken amphitheater," "tree-shaded plaza," and "enclosed sculpture garden," and the coalition raised preliminary funds to start the landscaping.[51] Yet the park was never completed, as costs for the various components continuously ran far ahead of revenue, some of which the University provided to no avail. The *Daily Pennsylvanian* published an epitaph for the People's Park in 1981: "Ten years of unrealized efforts to create 'a haven for all people' on the University's campus ended this spring. . . . [Of the ambitious original design] what stands . . . is a small brick plaza with benches, flowers, and decorative urns" gathered from "Victorian buildings that once stood on the land." By then there were no Penn students "to take up the issue"—the times had indeed changed.[52]

In the 1970s, the primary locus of student disquietude and disruption, as on other campuses, was "the immediate educational and financial well-being of University students."[53] The spring of 1978 was especially volatile. The University proposed to raise tuition and fees to $4,825, an 8.4 percent increase over the previous year—$17,283 in 2013 dollars (compared with the $45,890 charged Penn students in 2013–14). Even more disturbing to students was the administrative decision to terminate hockey, gymnastics, golf, badminton, and the Annenberg professional theater program. Chanting "Input now!" twelve hundred of them stormed onto College Green to reclaim the threatened programs and demand a significant voice in University budget decisions as they affected students. Next, they moved into College Hall for four days of "singing, talking, and snacking," according to the *Philadelphia Inquirer*.[54]

Vacationing in Barbados that week, Meyerson made perhaps the biggest mistake of his presidency by choosing to return to the campus and negotiate directly with the demonstrators, whose ranks had swollen to about twenty-five hundred, rather than delegating that responsibility to a team of administrators and faculty. (According to Vartan Gregorian, Meyerson's "subordinates" had panicked when confronted with the list of student demands.) Without consulting the Faculty Senate, Meyerson and Stellar agreed to the following demands: "more voice in University governance," "continuation of a professional theater series at Annenberg," "reinstatement of badminton, golf, and gymnastics programs," and "formation of the United Minorities Council," the latter attached to the College Hall list by a coalition of Penn minority groups led by the BSL; also approved was a "third world center" (the Albert Greenfield Intercultural Center would open under President Sheldon Hackney in 1982).[55]

■ Valedictory

Meyerson and Stellar's unilateral decision-making without faculty consultation and their appeasement of students in the March 1978 sit-in provoked a faculty uprising. The chairman of the Faculty Senate charged that the president and provost had subverted faculty governance under "mob pressures."[56] Other Senate members viewed the sit-in settlement as yet another example of an imperious presidency; they harbored resentments over Meyerson and Stellar's termination of the SAMP, their treatment of the GSE, and their recent peremptory decision to award graduate fellowships "on the basis of merit through a University-wide competition."[57] Perhaps fearing repercussions for the Campaign for the Eighties, however, the voting faculty (some six hundred at a special meeting of the Senate) rejected a motion to censure the president, though they voted unanimously to register their "serious concerns" with trustees and to establish a faculty review panel to negotiate collegial governance with the administration and to attempt to restore "an atmosphere of confidence throughout the University."[58] Amid the spring furor, Stellar wearily submitted his resignation as provost, effective December 1978, having, in his words, forfeited his "political stock" with the faculty. Grudgingly, in September 1978, Meyerson announced his own retirement, to be effective sometime in FY 1981 following completion of the Campaign for the Eighties. In its report of September 1978, the Faculty Panel on the Administrative Functioning of the University cited "a wide range of incidents, attitudes, procedures, practices and policies that seemed to point to malfunctioning of the administrative processes." The roles of the provost and president had blurred, with the provost being cast inappropriately as the president's "chief of staff" and "alter ego"; the solution was to reinstitute a traditional demarcation of roles: the president as chief executive officer, the provost as chief academic officer, the latter to maintain transparency and to consult with the faculty.[59]

As Stellar's replacement, Meyerson appointed Vartan Gregorian, the flamboyant dean of FAS and an immensely popular figure with faculty and students, who became provost in January 1979. That Paul Miller was the trustees' chairman, having succeeded Donald Regan[60] in that role in 1978, did not bode well for the feverish bid Gregorian was about to make for the Penn presidency. The campus's attention was soon riveted on the charismatic Gregorian's public courtship by Berkeley to be that university's next chancellor, a position he claims he turned down in favor of Penn, where he was accounted the "odds-on favorite" to be the president. But as the drama of the seven-month search unfolded at Penn—making Meyerson a conspicuous lame duck—a breach opened between Gregorian and Miller, with the majority of trustees lining up behind Miller. An ethnic Armenian, Gregorian believed that the conservative trustees were affronted by his "accent and hair and ethnicity," not to mention his flamboyance, which they associated with a lack of "social graces." He writes, "I assumed that after Martin Meyerson, they did not want another 'ethnic' president for Penn. They wanted somebody from central casting."[61]

Adding salt to a festering wound, the trustees announced their selection of Tulane University's president Sheldon Hackney as Penn's president-designee without having given Gregorian, as he had requested, sufficient notice to withdraw from the search "with dignity." "Humiliated, betrayed, depressed," Gregorian immediately resigned as provost, effective 24 October 1980. His future was hardly bleak: after Penn, he achieved international renown as the savior of the New York City Public Library, president of Brown University, and president of the Carnegie Corporation.[62]

■ Meyerson's Legacy: One University in Contemporary Perspective

Having successfully concluded the Campaign for the Eighties, Martin Meyerson left College Hall in January 1981 to return to academic life as University Professor of Public Policy Analysis and City and Regional Planning. As president emeritus, he was extraordinarily active on numerous fronts, serving not only as an éminence grise at Penn for more than twenty-five years, but also ubiquitously as an international consultant in West Africa, Spain, and Japan; as a director or member of numerous international councils and worldwide university, institute, and foundation boards; and as an advisor to humanitarian and economic development initiatives in Indonesia, South Asia, and Yugoslavia. Meyerson's legacy to Penn includes the School of Arts and Sciences and the splendid landscape design of the present campus. Through responsibility center management and selective excellence, his administration kept Penn solvent in the 1970s, even accelerating the University's research growth and building a stronger endowment—and these principles still govern the University's financial and academic policies. Under Meyerson, the University established its Women's Center and the DuBois College House. The School of Design, formerly the Graduate School of Fine Arts, was dedicated as Meyerson Hall in 1983; the Meyerson Professorship of Urbanism honors both the emeritus professor and his wife, Margy Ellin Meyerson, herself a noted urban planner.[63]

Meyerson's most enduring legacy is his idea of One University, which resonates with the strategic orientation of the University under President Amy Gutmann. In her 2004 inaugural address, Penn's ninth president unveiled the Penn Compact, a statement of "our boldest aspirations for higher education," which she enumerated as follows: "to increase access, to integrate knowledge, to engage locally and globally." A sine qua non for solving the incredibly complex problems of our global era is interdisciplinary research and teaching; in President Gutmann's words, "We cannot understand the AIDS epidemic, for

Martin Meyerson, in retirement, ca. 1985. Collections of the University
Archives and Records Center.

example, without joining the perspectives of medicine, nursing, and finance
with those of biochemistry, psychology, sociology, politics, history, and literature."[64] The Penn Compact calls on the University not only to view complex social problems as having (inextricably) both local and global dimensions
but also to conceptualize Penn's work in West Philadelphia as part of a comprehensive effort to solve universal problems (for example, poverty, inadequate
health care, failing public schools) as those problems are manifested locally.[65]

A broadly based One University approach that galvanizes faculty support
while honoring Meyerson's legacy and the local-global service charge of the
Penn Compact is the University's program of "academically based community service" and its pedagogy of "problem-solving learning," an emerging hallmark of Penn undergraduate, and to some extent graduate, education. Where

Martin Meyerson and his colleagues never specified a *unifying* means for realizing One University, a focus on concrete, real-world problems in Penn's local environment of West Philadelphia—problems that by their very nature require an interdisciplinary approach if they are to be solved—may well provide such a means and contribute to transforming One University from an aspiration into Penn's most powerful organizational and intellectual attribute. Embodying this approach, problem-focused, academically based community service courses and related community-based research projects target the improvement of public education, health, and general well-being in West Philadelphia, as well as develop replicable, strategic initiatives, most notably through university-assisted community schools[66] that Penn has helped develop with other partners.

A recent example is the school-based Community Health Promotion and Disease Prevention Program at West Philadelphia's Sayre High School, led by the School of Medicine and supported by some twenty faculty members, an array of academically based community service courses, and "literally hundreds of students" from medicine, dentistry, social work, and arts and sciences. Program activities are embedded in the high school curriculum and integrated with a school-based, community primary-care and dental clinic, in conjunction with a community advisory board. Sponsored by the University's Netter Center for Community Partnerships, this activity "resurrects" and translates the One University idea into a workable "action program."[67]

It is a short analytic leap from Martin Meyerson's idea of One University to Amy Gutmann's Penn Compact. By encouraging a unifying practical means to integrate knowledge for local and global problem solving, the Penn Compact helps rectify a critical shortfall of Meyerson's original concept.

In part III of this book, among other topics, we look at the foundation of academically based community service in Sheldon Hackney's conciliatory actions in West Philadelphia and his relationship with Ira Harkavy, who led the 1969 College Hall sit-in. The 1980s was perhaps the most turbulent decade in Penn's history, and Hackney's management of that turbulence, for better and worse, has shaped his legacy. In Chapter 7, we turn to the single most disruptive factor of Hackney's presidency—a campus climate of hostile race relations. As we show in subsequent chapters, racial issues were embedded in other campus controversies, and they roiled the waters of Penn's community relations at a time when West Philadelphia's street life turned lethal.

Part III **The Conciliator**

7

A Decade of Racial Discord

At age forty-seven, Sheldon Hackney, an American historian, a former provost of Princeton University, and the president of Tulane University since 1975, assumed the mantle of Penn's presidency on 2 February 1981. Hackney's tenure in College Hall is properly described as tumultuous. Conflicts over race relations and gender issues, many rooted in a campus fraternity culture gone badly awry in the 1980s, vexed Hackney and his staff from the day he took office until the day he left it. Related issues of free speech and academic freedom compounded these problems. Other issues kept Hackney and his staff distracted, notably escalating crime and violence in the neighborhoods around the University, a consequence of the near collapse of the city's manufacturing base, middle-class flight, and the outflow of tax dollars; the concentration of poverty and anomie in many African American blocks of West Philadelphia; the area's persistently failing public schools; and, not least, murderous crack-cocaine trafficking and simmering rage against whites and "the system," all of which spilled over onto the Penn campus. The fallout from these enormous problems diminished public and even faculty awareness of Hackney's genuine contributions.

Among Hackney's significant contributions was a policy of reconciliation to overcome the burden of Penn's troubled community relations—the burden we described in part I of this book as the collateral damage of University-based urban renewal in the 1950s and 1960s. Hackney viewed reconciliation as a mutually beneficial process for the University and its community. For the University, the process was constructed to serve the institution's historic mission of creating and transmitting knowledge. Hackney established a mediating structure, the Center for Community Partnerships (today's Netter Center), which linked Penn's teaching and research to the needs of West Philadelphia residents, organizations, and institutions, in particular the public schools. The university-community partnerships built under Hackney were building blocks for Judith Rodin's spectacular West Philadelphia Initiatives and Amy Gutmann's recent agenda for Penn's campus expansion east to the Schuylkill River. And the Netter Center's core strategy of "academically based community service" has become a unifying practical means, if not yet a prairie fire, toward realizing Meyerson's dream of One University.

A southern moderate liberal and racial integrationist who held a PhD in American history from Yale University, Hackney had married Lucy Durr, daughter of the Montgomery, Alabama, civil rights activists Virginia and Clifford Durr (Clifford was Rosa Parks's pro-bono attorney in Montgomery), in her own right an attorney and activist for mentally disabled children, the founding president of Pennsylvania Partnerships for Children, and a board member of the Children's Defense Fund. Centered on politics and race relations in the postbellum South, Hackney's scholarship was inspired by his Alabama background and the mentorship of Yale's eminent New South historian C. Vann Woodward. From 1965 to 1972, Hackney was a professor in the History Department at Princeton, where he helped found the Afro-American studies program and served as acting director of the program for a time. Under Princeton president William Bowen, he served as the university's provost for three years before assuming the Tulane presidency in 1975, an appointment he held for five years until an offer from the Penn trustees drew him back to the Ivy League.[1] When Hackney arrived as Penn's new president in February 1981, he faced the controversy stirring around Vartan Gregorian. This difficulty was compounded by the fact that Hackney was the first true outsider to be named as president.

Beyond entrenched hostility to the flamboyant Gregorian, why did the trustees elect Hackney? The *New York Times* reported that "Dr. Hackney's most widely praised quality, and by most accounts the key to his selection, was his energy and skill as a fund raiser."[2] The *Times* noted that Hackney had given Tulane its first balanced budget in twenty-five years—an accomplishment that obviously appealed to the Penn overseers. For all his management acumen, Hackney was also regarded as a "student's president."[3] Paul Miller, who was chairman of the board of trustees at the time, has written, "The combination of Sheldon and Lucy, I thought to myself, ought to satisfy the most crusading of liberals. And there were plenty of them on the Penn campus."[4]

A source of immediate vexation for Hackney was the long shadow cast by Gregorian. In his failed bid for the Penn presidency, Gregorian had the resounding support of most of the deans, the Faculty Senate, and the Undergraduate Assembly. And popular sentiment held that Hackney was usurping

Sheldon Hackney. Collections of the University Archives and Records Center.

Gregorian's rightful inheritance. "Obviously, he came in under an immense cloud," recounts the Penn historian Michael Zuckerman, "because so many of us were in love with Vartan, . . . so many of us thought that Vartan would take hold of this university in dramatic ways that would be wondrous to behold. From the day he arrived and through the early months and years of his arrival, it was clear that Hackney was no Gregorian. It was clear . . . that he was not going to rock boats that Vartan might have rocked. . . . Most of us among my friends took for granted that that was part of why Vartan wasn't made president—that he could have stood up to the trustees and that Hackney could not. So there was a real sourness . . . a real sense that this was an opportunity lost that would never come again, and that Hackney was nobody who was going to bring any sort of transformative experience or vision to the University."[5]

For students it was a matter of Hackney's personal style: Gregorian's ebullient charisma versus Hackney's understated, dignified self-presentation and genteel reticence. The *Daily Pennsylvanian* was pointedly unkind: Hackney's "youthful looks and easy-going manner" and his self-effacing "low-key style" paled beside Gregorian's "flamboyant style and ever-present brilliance."[6] A former Undergraduate Assembly chair told the *DP*, "Hackney came into a very volatile environment. He was clearly at a disadvantage because so many of the students and the faculty had wanted and expected Greg to be named president."[7] Leftist activists portrayed Hackney as the antithesis of the magnanimous, gregarious Gregorian: "conservative and managerial," "the oppressive representative of corporate America."[8] Understandably, Hackney was annoyed by such comparisons and the disruption Gregorian left in his wake. He vented his frustration in a journal entry: "VG, I have decided after hearing all the stories, was a charmer who made everyone feel good. One of the reasons is that he seldom said no, and we have discovered commitments that he could not possibly have kept."[9]

Yet Hackney faced problems far weightier than Gregorian's vast popularity. Throughout his presidency, the Penn campus was roiled by the urban crisis and bitter racial, gender, and free speech controversies—it is not an exaggeration to say that crisis followed crisis. Some were tempests in teapots, while others cast a negative national spotlight on the University. Penn's campus volatility reflected turbulence in the higher education youth culture of 1980s America, where overt acts of racism, sexism, and homophobia were unfortunately a sign of the times—campus incivilities foreshadowed the wider society's culture wars of the 1990s. Some of Hackney's decisions in the heat of these controversies provoked articulate critics of both liberal and conservative persuasion to lampoon the University.

Here we offer a fresh appraisal of Hackney's presidency—one that takes account of, but also looks beyond, the harsh exposés that have caricatured his tenure. We recognize that Hackney governed Penn in a particularly difficult time. Even more than in the 1960s, the University was driven by turbulent social forces in the 1980s. Our analysis shows the magnitude and complexity of the problems his administration had to deal with, starting with the rampant crime in the University area.

■ The Urban Crisis on Penn's Doorstep

When Hackney arrived at Penn, the crisis of the city was deepening. As two historians of the city aptly summarize:

> By almost every measure, the 1970s had been a disaster. In that single decade the population dropped 260,000. The employment base seemed to be collapsing, as manufacturing jobs fell 40 percent. The resulting erosion of the tax base left the city with a chronic fiscal crisis. In 1976 alone, local property taxes rose by one-third. Under the administration of Mayor Frank Rizzo (1972–80), violent crime jumped, despite his trademark swagger and tough talk. Racial animosities ran deep—in City Council chambers and in the neighborhoods. In impoverished districts, especially in lower North Philadelphia, landlords simply abandoned their properties, which became derelict fire hazards and havens for drug addicts and gangs. The schools struggled to teach amid the social chaos. Homeless people were sleeping on the sidewalks. In January 1982, after 134 years, the *Philadelphia Evening Bulletin*, long the leading newspaper, ceased publication. It was an ominous sign.[10]

Crime perpetrated against Penn students, faculty, and staff persisted throughout the 1980s.[11] The urban crisis had calamitous effects on the campus and haunted Hackney's presidency. A major site of mayhem was the area around 40th and Walnut streets, just two blocks west of the president's Eisenlohr mansion. Numerous other blocks and venues were menaced as well by teen marauders ("wolf packs"), drug dealers, junkies, muggers, car thieves, burglars, vandals, and con artists. For more than a decade after the mid-1980s, a crack-cocaine epidemic virtually paralyzed the largely African American blocks north, west, and southwest of Penn and manifested horrifically in the blocks closer to the campus, with drug-related shootings, arson, muggings, beatings, and the like. Hackney bolstered campus security and, to his great credit, pursued other institutional means to ameliorate the crisis and recast the University's role in West Philadelphia.[12]

The troubled year of 1980, when black teenagers murdered a Wharton student in West Philadelphia, witnessed seventy-one armed robberies and 328 burglaries on the Penn campus, increases of fifty-five and eighty, respectively, from the previous year. (Following a national trend, citywide crime escalated that year.) The streets were poorly lit, and the campus subways were dangerous. In the face of these problems, the University maintained a campus police force of fifty, posted guards at dormitory reception desks, and provided outside emergency phone lines, an escort service, and a campus bus; in March 1981, it opened the Office of Off-Campus Living to help students "obtain safe, adequate housing." But high-tech security devices that are de rigueur on urban campuses in the 2010s were nonexistent at Penn when Hackney took office—no twenty-four-hour identification card system coupled with a computerized monitoring system.[13] To head "a patrol and supervisory force" of sixty-four officers, Hackney appointed Capt. John Logan director of public safety in the spring of 1983. Logan had twenty-eight years of experience with the Philadelphia Police Department, where he headed the department's civil affairs bureau.[14] By 1987, the campus Department of Public Safety had a budget of $3.6 million.

In two books, *Streetwise* and *Code of the Streets*, the sociologist Elijah Anderson writes about the high levels of social dysfunction and violence in West and Southwest Philadelphia's poor African American neighborhoods in the 1980s, where the crack-cocaine epidemic spread unabated until the mid-1990s. Concentrated poverty, intertwined with high rates of school failure, teenage pregnancy, housing abandonment, physical and mental health disorders, anomie, and despair, provided a fertile soil for the drug epidemic and the decadelong crime wave it spawned. Hierarchically organized drug dealing became business as usual in neighborhoods like Mantua, where the "code of the street" challenged norms of decency and civility. Drug dealers replaced "old heads" as figures of respect and inspiration for young people, and "top dogs," the ruthless, thirty-something entrepreneurs who controlled the area's drug corners and the flow of drugs, engaged young boys as their sellers.[15] Drug traffickers sold their wares with impunity from automobiles.

Violence, or the threat of it, was integral to the code (it still is, though today it and other drug-related crime are much less pervasive.) "Its basic requirement is the display of a certain predisposition to violence," writes Anderson. "A person's public bearing must send the unmistakable, if sometimes subtle, message that one is capable of violence, and possibly mayhem, when the situation requires it, that one can take care of oneself." Black youths in particular gravitated to "staging areas" such as centers of public transit, "multiplex theaters, sporting events, and concerts," areas where crowds tended to congregate. "There are often enough young people in the staging area to provide the critical mass of negative energy necessary to spark violence, not just against people like themselves but also against others present in the staging area, creating a flashpoint for violence."[16] By the late 1980s, the intersection of 40th and Walnut streets was such a staging area for criminal activity, literally a stone's throw from the campus.

The *Daily Pennsylvanian* reported twenty-two serious incidents near the troublesome intersection from the fall of 1987 to the spring of 1989, nine of which involved Penn students, one almost fatally. A popular McDonald's franchise on the northeast corner of 40th and Walnut, a University parking lot on the northwest corner, a Burger King franchise on the southwest corner, and an AMC multiplex cinema and video arcade in the middle of the 3901 block of Walnut were magnets for late-night mischief. Headlines trumpeted the crisis: "Crime Wave Hits Area Surrounding 40th and Walnut," "40th Street Has Violent History," "Under the Golden Arches: Murder, Robbery, Stabbings," "3 Students Stabbed; 1 Critically Wounded," "Four Robbed at Gunpoint off 40th Street"; "U. Student Shot on 40th Street"; "Student Beaten in AMC on 3900 Block of Walnut."[17] That two "anchor" stores on these blocks were all-night fast-food franchises exacerbated the situation.[18] The worst incident occurred on the night of 1 September 1990, an event Hackney recorded stoically in his journal: "Last Saturday four black teenagers were gunned down as they sat in their car at midnight at 40th & Sansom, near the busy corner of 40th & Walnut where Lucy and I were just minutes after the shooting. Two died & two are in the hospital."[19]

"Stickups" involving one or more assailants and one or more victims were a prevalent mode of criminal activity throughout the campus area, easily accomplished given the paucity of foot traffic after dark, poor lighting, and police shortages. Lacking "street smarts," Penn students were especially vulnerable in these potentially lethal situations, as they were not attuned to what Anderson calls the "etiquette of the stickup," which required a display of deference on the victim's part: "At issue is a core tenet of the code of the street: respect."[20] According to the 18th Police District, the large majority of these muggings were drug related. Nine of them happened in a single week in September 1989 in the blocks around 40th and Spruce streets.[21] Fortunately, more often than not the victims of stickups emerged unscathed for no other reason than being scared witless.

So-called wolf packs, roving gangs of black youths, attacked Penn students. One of their staging areas was the Civic Center, a venue for professional wrestling and concerts on 33rd Street near the hospital and medical complex. In September 1988, the *Daily Pennsylvanian* reported "a string of post-wrestling assaults on University students over the past 18 months," the latest occurring on 10 September, involving "a rampaging group of approximately 40 youths."[22]

In October 1989, a gang of some twenty black youths and adults, following a late-evening concert at the Civic Center, "rampaged" along the 3400 block of Walnut, "looting a clothing store, vandalizing cars and harassing students."[23] Some wolf-pack attacks were racially motivated. One of them, apparently unprovoked, occurred in April 1989 at a late-night hour on 40th between Chestnut and Market, when a group of black youths beat up and injured (one seriously) six Penn freshmen who were trying to get to the subway station at 40th and Market. The students were an easy mark, white and "kind of preppy," according to a police officer.[24] The worst attack on a Penn student occurred on the evening of 8 October 1988 in Clark Park at 43rd Street and Baltimore Avenue, where three West Philadelphia youths robbed and beat comatose, with a tree branch, Cyril Seung Leung, a Penn graduate student from Hong Kong, who died several weeks after the attack.[25]

Not surprisingly in this climate, the University had serious problems with on-campus security, the inadequacy of which was shockingly revealed on 2 December 1985, the Monday following the Thanksgiving holiday, when Meera Ananthakrishnan, a physics graduate student, was found bound, gagged, and stabbed to death in a Nichols House dormitory room in the Graduate Towers. That the killer, a non-West Philadelphia resident whose apparent motive was robbery, was able to enter the dormitory without detection disquieted the campus, although it would take another violent incident two years later to prompt major campus-wide improvements in dormitory security.[26] Following the multiple rape of a female visitor in the Quad by an intruder and a rising level of anxiety in the residence halls, the University hired a consultant and subsequently invested more than $1.5 million to strengthen dormitory security, contracting with a private security firm for a twenty-four-hour guard service in the University residence halls, installing ID card readers and turnstiles, and issuing a "PennCard" with a magnetic stripe to faculty, staff, and students. These measures were in place by the spring of 1987, though not without glitches such as malfunctioning turnstiles and guards sleeping on duty. To preserve a modicum of student freedom and aesthetics, the administration refused to install barbed wire on the Quad fences.[27]

By the late fall of 1990, a measurably strengthened campus security system was in operation. The Department of Public Safety, under a newly appointed police commissioner, counted seventy-six employees, including sixty-nine commissioned police personnel (thirteen in management positions) and seven support staff. Each police officer received training at the city's police academy, participated in a six-week orientation at the University, and served for six months in a probationary status before joining the campus force. The department included two plainclothes teams and five patrol cars. The campus purchasing department provided twenty-nine campus security guards from private firms holding contracts with Penn. The Penn police shared information with the Philadelphia Police Department and reported all crimes to the Pennsylvania State Police. The security apparatus included 250 automatic-dial emergency telephones and a computerized 511 phone system, including the following procedure for entry to the residence halls: "Anyone without a PennCard, the University's identification, is a 'visitor' to a residence. This includes the University members without their cards and all guests. Visitors must go to a building desk receptionist, show identification, and wait while the receptionist obtains approval from a resident host. The resident host must be with the visitor or telephoned by the receptionist. Each approved visitor completes a pass with the receptionist and turns it in at an ID checkpoint." Other measures were instituted: "All residences are locked or monitored by a security guard. All student rooms are equipped with a dead bolt or card-proof lock. Windows less than seven feet from the ground have bars or security screens. Most other higher windows have window stops or screens."[28] While these measures protected the residents from outside assailants, they were ineffectual against other forms of violence, such as acquaintance rape.[29]

Off-campus security, as we have seen, was a persistent dilemma, compounded by Penn students' tendency "to be at a time in their life where they feel pretty invincible," for example, frequenting off-campus ATM machines after midnight. Penn and the Philadelphia police stepped up surveillance and foot patrols in the corridors between 40th and 44th streets.[30] The most visible and ubiquitous off-campus security measure of the Hackney era, in operation since the fall of 1990, was the upgraded escort service, which offered "a free door-to-door van service to neighboring off-campus addresses every night."[31] White vans bearing Penn logos started picking up riders every fifteen minutes at selected campus venues in the late afternoon, and they remained on the streets until the early morning hours. While University officials reasoned that the van service was essential in the face of the persistent crime wave, they failed to foresee its unintended consequences. Indeed, the escort vans soon created an irrepressible demand and became in effect a free taxi service. Though a boon to Penn riders, the service actually jeopardized the area's safety by removing foot traffic from local streets.[32]

All of these safety and security measures were defensive, not proactive. The University had neither a plan nor the funds to implement a long-range solution. ID cards, more campus police, emergency phones, and a continuous stream of nighttime vans into University City did not get at the heart of Penn's security problems. A multipronged development strategy for University City and the money to implement it would have to wait until Judith Rodin and the boom years of the Clinton-era economy, the abatement of the crack-cocaine epidemic, and the playing out of Penn's culture wars. The trustees' top priority in the 1980s was one of the largest capital campaigns in the history of American higher education up until that time, which by 1994 had raised $1.4 billion, more than $200 million beyond its goal, to strengthen faculty development, research facilities, undergraduate education, minority recruitment, and campus, cultural, and outreach programs. Hackney and his senior administrators had their hands full, not only with the capital campaign and campus safety but also with myriad internal social crises and rampant incivilities, which were by no means peculiar to Penn. Of the latter perturbations, the ones involving hostile race relations were perhaps the most volatile.

■ The Persistent Dilemma of Race

In the 1980s Penn experienced the continuing discontent of black students, a spate of Black Power protest actions, and a protracted controversy over the University's investments in companies doing business in apartheid South Africa. And not the least of Hackney's worries, the black presence at Penn provoked a backlash from racist whites on campus, some of whom were identified with fraternities along Locust Walk. In the Hackney era, the University was an institution at war with itself.

Penn's African American students issued a vigorous complaint to Hackney on the very day of his gala inauguration as the University's sixth president, 23 October 1981. Following their picketing of the inauguration in Irvine Auditorium, black demonstrators confronted Hackney at the statue of Benjamin Franklin in front of College Hall:

> The two student leaders addressed Hackney, who was accompanied by [Provost Thomas] Ehrlich. Dwayne E. Everett . . . president of the Black Student League, charged the University with "institutional racism," evidenced, he said, "by declining enrollment of Black and Hispanic students and discriminatory hiring and promotional practices of the University toward Black and other minority employees on all levels." He also accused the University of a "projection of racist attitudes onto the broader community, exemplified in Penn's physical expansion [into] the West Philadelphia community without sufficient reciprocation to the community." And finally, he spoke of "the University's continued investment in the oppressive government of South Africa" and the "University's tolerance, and thus benign neglect of pervasive individ-

ual acts of racism" on campus. "We therefore feel it necessary," he said, "to display our total dissatisfaction with the intolerable conditions that we face here as well as the half-hearted attempts of the institution to effect change." He went on to say he hoped that the protest "will strongly move the new administration to working more directly, closely, and expeditiously" with Black leaders.[33]

In the week following Hackney's inauguration, the campus was beset by a "rash of racial incidents," including numerous "racist phone calls," bomb threats against DuBois College House, and even a death threat against a visiting professor residing in that building.[34] On 30 October, Janis Somerville, the holdover vice provost for university life from Meyerson's presidency, organized an antiracism demonstration. At "the rally against racism," between fifteen hundred and two thousand people, exhorted to action by Provost Ehrlich, marched arm in arm from College Hall to DuBois House, where they formed "a protective circle around the House, holding hands and singing 'We Shall Overcome.'"[35] Within the next two weeks, the University withdrew recognition from the Kappa Sigma fraternity, a denizen of the Locust Walk fraternity row since 1924, for showing "a continuous pattern of serious disciplinary problems," including racial slurs. Charging the entire fraternity with "collective responsibility" for the bad apples in the group—one had shouted racial slurs at schoolgirls in the fraternity's back yard; another wore a Ku Klux Klan costume to a Halloween party and, with other Kappa Sigma brothers, "became abusive" when black students showed up to protest the behavior; yet others accosted a black judicial inquiry officer, accused him of a bike theft, and threatened him with a crutch ("retaliatory intimidation," decreed the judicial inquiry officer on the case)—Somerville cited the fraternity, which had been on probation for some of these behaviors since the spring of 1980 yet apparently had learned nothing, for "personal threats and physical assaults, instances such as racial and antisemitic harassment, unauthorized possession and misuse of BB and air gun firearms as well as other disruptive behavior."[36] (According to the alumni magazine, "some members of Kappa Sigma kissed [the fraternity house] goodbye by breaking windows, strewing trash and furniture in the yard, removing doors from their hinges, and writing on the walls.")[37] Together, the bomb threats at DuBois House and the Kappa Sigma fraternity incidents signaled "a rising level of intolerance" on the campus.[38]

In 1981–82, a century after James Brister became the first African American to receive a degree from Penn (from the dental school in 1881), blacks were still underrepresented in the undergraduate population: 115 in the freshman class, 5.6 percent of the total.[39] Women for Equal Opportunity at the University of Pennsylvania (WEOUP) charged the University with institutional racism given the paltry number—only thirteen—of tenured black faculty members. By WEOUP's lights the prevalence of the N-word on the campus and a firestorm in the law school over the tenure and promotion of Ralph Smith, a controversial black assistant professor, gave added weight to the charge.[40] (Denied tenure in 1981, Smith finally gained it in 1982 following a favorable second review prompted by criticism of the law faculty's initial handling of the case and Smith's own surge in publication activity in the intervening year.)[41]

In race matters, the University made progress on one front—undergraduate admissions—while it dithered on another—South Africa divestment. In September 1982, the admissions office reported the matriculation of 137 blacks (6.4 percent) in the Class of 1986 and an increase in "racial minority groups" among freshmen from 13.3 percent in 1981 to 16.7 percent in 1982.[42] After a downturn in 1983, the number of black matriculates rose to 151 in 1984 (6.9 percent of 2,190 enrolled); "minorities" accounted for 18 percent of the Class of 1988, the largest proportion of which was Asian (7.9 percent of total students).[43] In his 1985 annual report, Hackney described Penn's student body as "national" and noted 450 "minority" students in the freshman class. He also expressed his and Ehrlich's "deep commitment" to "increasing the number of women and minorities among the University's faculty."[44]

The South Africa Divestment Controversy

As the admissions front quieted, the divestment front heated up. In June 1981, the University's investment portfolio included twenty-nine companies doing business in South Africa, six of which repudiated the Sullivan Principles, which, since 1977 had been the informal international guidelines for ethical business practices in that country, and to which Penn had subscribed in 1978. Following a national trend among higher education institutions, campus protests against the University's investments started in earnest on the frigid afternoon of 22 January 1982, when some three hundred students organized by the Penn Coalition for Divestment boisterously picketed outside and inside the Fine Arts Library, where the trustees were meeting. Impatient with the University's "policy of selective divestment" (written by the Trustees' Committee on University Responsibility, adopted by the full board in 1980, and bolstered by new resolutions in 1981), the students clamored, to no avail, for full divestment. The trustees voted to consider divestment on a case by case basis rather than adopt "an all encompassing institutional position." Gloria Twine Chisum, an African American psychologist on the board, proffered a moral rationale for this decision: "Divestment seems to me to be withdrawal of the voice of conscience of the world from any influence in South Africa."[45]

By June 1985 Penn's total endowment stood at $359 million, with $209.7 million held in equities, $83.8 million of which was invested in companies doing business in South Africa. The latter figure constituted about 40 percent of the equity portfolio. Obviously, more than the "voice of conscience" was involved in the University's policy of selective divestment: the University stood to lose a great deal of money if it followed Columbia University's lead in full divestment. This is not to say that the trustees stood pat. In 1982, they had sold off $817,000 in the stocks of two companies that refused to comply with the Sullivan Principles. And in 1984, they announced that the University would divest its stocks in any South Africa-related company that took on significant new business in the country, expanded operations, or sold goods to the South African police or military.[46]

In the early fall of 1985, trustee chair Paul Miller presented divestment as a two-edged sword that jeopardized the University's interests:

> As a shareholder, Penn has a long tradition of wanting the companies in which it holds stock to pursue high standards of conduct even if the society in which they are operating is politically organized and/ or controlled in a morally repugnant way. It is only through ownership that we can urge corporations to create or maintain such standards. The Trustees have found the Rev. Leon Sullivan's principles on the rights of black South African workers employed by American companies to be appropriate standards for corporate practice for companies held in the University portfolio. If we sell our holdings for non-investment reasons, we then have no influence and no assurance that the new holder to whom we sell will be as concerned with these matters as we are.

Then Miller turned to the quandary of divestment for the University's "educational mission": "As fiduciaries," he observed, "the Trustees have a duty to earn the maximum return consistent with reasonable risk on the endowment assets entrusted to them. Achieving the highest possible earnings on endowment is a principal requirement for achieving our educational mission. To do so requires the broadest possible range of choice among investments available in the financial markets. To severely restrict the universe of securities available for investment, as would be the case if we were to shun companies with South African operations, almost certainly would serve to reduce the long-term return of the portfolio."[47]

Hackney appears to have accepted the trustees' position. He urged "reflection and discussion" of the issues, cited "the abhorrence with which the Penn community views apartheid and the moral urgency of the deteriorating situation in South Africa," and joined nineteen other college and university presidents who petitioned congressional leaders to impose economic sanctions against South Africa. Testifying before the Senate Committee on Banking, Housing, and Urban Affairs, Hackney recommended sanctions on loans to South Africa that did not involve social services. On 14 January 1986, Desmond Tutu, the Anglican bishop of Johannesburg (later the archbishop of Cape Town), winner of the 1984 Nobel Peace Prize, delivered the keynote address for Penn's weeklong celebration of the life of Martin Luther King, Jr.; Bishop Tutu's talk inaugurated Hackney's President's Forum for 1986–87, a series of colloquia entitled Colorlines: The Enduring Significance of Race.[48]

To the chagrin of the trustees, the majority of the University Council was not buying any form of selective divestment, viewing the policy as waffling on a profound moral issue. It made little difference to divestment advocates that none of these companies had more than 1.2 percent of their operations in South Africa, or that Penn held no investments in South African-owned businesses.[49] Rallies, resolutions, and informational sessions raised a hue and cry for complete divestment. *Daily Pennsylvanian* headlines in the spring and fall of 1985 captured the agitation: "400 Join Campus Rally Against Racism, Apartheid" (5 April); "300 Attend Rally to Urge U. to Divest, End Racism" (14 October); "250 Rally for Divestment Outside Trustee Meeting (28 October). Hedging again to mollify the students, the majority of the trustees resolved at their winter meeting, held in the relative quietude of the spacious Wistar Institute, to "divest stock" if the South African government did not show "substantive progress" toward dismantling apartheid by 30 June 1987, about eighteen months from the date of the resolution, 17 January 1986.[50] Once again the anti-apartheid coalition stood its ground, organizing a "round-the-clock" sit-in at College Hall that started on 22 January and lasted for twenty days, with the demonstrators camping out in the front hallway. The protest action was civil, even genteel (College Hall offices provided free coffee to the demonstrators); the only violation of the open expression guidelines occurred when a contingent of fired-up students, among them Mayor Wilson Goode's son, illegally (though peacefully) occupied Hackney's office for a twelve-hour stint on the first day.[51] Following another national trend, the anti-apartheid coalition constructed a replica wood-and-cardboard shantytown on College Green and erected thirteen crosses to "commemorate the eleven children murdered by South African forces, March 26, 1986" (a similar protest at Berkeley the previous week had resulted in more than ninety

Student protest against apartheid, to encourage the Penn trustees
to divest from companies doing business in South Africa, ca. 1985.
Collections of the University Archives and Records Center.

arrests).[52] For all these tensions, a relieved Hackney was able to write at year's
end, "We read in the newspaper through the spring stories of demonstrations
and confrontations and arrests on one college campus after another: Cornell,
Berkeley, Dartmouth, Yale. We came close to a disaster a couple of times, but
we avoided the head-line making bash."[53]

By 30 June 1987, the trustees' deadline for "substantive progress," the South African government had taken no steps to dismantle apartheid. In any event, the deadline was virtually a moot point: the trustees were nearly off the hook, with "only three companies in the University's endowment which still are doing business in South Africa"—Tenneco, Caterpillar, and Boeing. Projecting moral rectitude, the Committee on University Responsibility resolved, "If a company refuses to withdraw or fails to withdraw from South Africa within a reasonable period of time, which period shall not extend beyond June 30, 1988 unless a company satisfies the Committee that extraordinary circumstances require an additional period, the committee will recommend that the University divest its holdings in that company."[54] Later that year, after seven years of controversy, the University finally divested its stocks and bonds in South Africa-related companies.[55] Five years later, in 1994, the Trustees' Committee on University Responsibility would reopen its portfolio to South African investments following the repeal of apartheid laws and the opening of biracial participation in the country's governance.[56]

Several years after the divestment controversy was settled, the University was involved in another racially charged political imbroglio, this time with the City of Philadelphia. This was a legal dispute rooted in the contested language of a 1977 city ordinance that spelled out new though vaguely worded terms for the University's obligation to the city, standing since the nineteenth century, to admit and provide scholarships to deserving Philadelphia public school students. Beginning in 1990 and raging through 1992, the question of how many scholarships were to be awarded each year was not only litigated but also ratcheted into a racial controversy.

The Mayor's Scholarship Program Dispute

When city officials deeded forty-seven acres of Blockley Almshouse property to Penn in 1882, they attached a city ordinance that obligated the University, as a quid pro quo for the property transfer, to provide "at least 50 free scholarships" to Philadelphia public school students "from time to time," no less than $7,500 annually. The scholarship winners were designated by the Board of Education. An ordinance of 1910 governing another conveyance of land added seventy-five new scholarships, these to be awarded by the mayor, and granted eligibility to graduates of "all the schools of Philadelphia."[57] The institution's obligation to provide Mayor's Scholarships endured through "reenactments" of these ordinances in 1931, 1950, and 1954, when additional conveyances were made. In 1958, the annual value of the seventy-five Mayor's Scholarships was $75,000 ($1,000 tuition). In 1977, Mayor Frank Rizzo combined the Board of Education Scholarships with the Mayor's Scholarships to create a total of 125 four-year, full-tuition Mayor's Scholarships. The ambiguous wording of the city ordinance that effected this consolidation sparked a heated controversy in 1991; black leaders fought for a legal ruling that would, in effect, compel Penn to offer scholarships to more black graduates of the city high schools.[58]

The following language in the 1977 ordinance was contested: "The University shall agree to establish and forever maintain at least one hundred twenty-five, four-year, full tuition scholarships or their equivalent, in any of the Departments of the University, to be awarded annually by the Mayor of the City of Philadelphia to deserving students from all of the schools of the City."[59] (In practice, the mayor's role was to ratify the University's designees.) On 28 October 1991, the Public Interest Law Center of Philadelphia (PILCOP) filed a class-action suit against the University on behalf of twelve organizations, including, among others, the Philadelphia teachers union, the Parents Union for Philadelphia Public Schools, and three University organizations—the Black Student League, the Asociación Cultural de Estudiantes Latinoamericanos , and the African American Association (Penn black faculty, administrators, and support staff). Citing the 1977 ordinance, the plaintiffs charged that the University had reneged on its contractual obligation to provide 125 four-year, full-tuition scholarships *annually* "to deserving students from all of the schools of the city." In other words, a total of five hundred scholarships should be active every year. The University vigorously objected to PILCOP's interpretation, arguing that its obligation was 125 scholarships "at any time," an opinion supported by the acting city solicitor. The city's African American press charged that by any interpretation Penn was not honoring its obligation—the *Philadelphia Tribune* complained that of 104 black freshmen in 1990, only five were from Philadelphia. Black leaders bristled when Mayor Ed Rendell recommended that the City Council excise the word "annually" from the 1977 ordinance. They demanded a payback for the city's sponsorship of Penn-based urban renewal in the 1950s and 1960s, and they wanted "needy" students to be the recipients. Representative Dwight Evans of Philadelphia, chair of the House Appropriations Committee, led a contingent of powerful black state legislators who admonished Hackney and trustee chair Alvin Shoemaker to offer 125 scholarships yearly or risk losing the University's annual state appropriation ($41.2 million).[60]

Penn's financial woes in the 1970s lay at the root of the dispute. In 1976 Penn sought to refinance a $12 million mortgage held by the Equitable Life Assurance Society of the United States, payable over twenty-five years. Strapped for cash when the Equitable mortgage came due, the University turned to the Prudential Life Insurance Company to refinance the loan at 9.25 percent over fifteen years. Included in Prudential's mortgage package were six tracts of land that composed the forty-seven acres conveyed to Penn by the City in 1882, including the grounds of the University Hospital, the University Museum, and the River Fields. As the 1882 conveyances prohibited Penn from "alienating" (selling or mortgaging) these properties, Martin Meyerson's financial officers had to cut a deal with the city to allow the Prudential loan to proceed. In exchange for the freedom to mortgage the forty-seven acres, Penn financial officers agreed to Mayor Frank Rizzo's terms in consolidating the Board of Education and Mayor's scholarships into one scholarship pool. Incredibly, these same Penn officials stood by as the City Council inserted ambiguous language into the 1977 ordinance, leaving the University in a legal quandary when PILCOP discovered the ambiguity in 1992 and tried to wrench an interpretation of five hundred scholarships from the ordinance.[61] For its part, Prudential held a first lien on forty-two Penn buildings and a total of seventy-four acres.[62]

In February 1993, Penn (and the city as a codefendant) won the PILCOP lawsuit in the Court of Common Pleas. Citing historical documents, the University's attorneys argued persuasively that Penn and the City had consistently awarded about a quarter of the total scholarships annually.[63] Hackney recognized, however, that this was a Pyrrhic victory that attracted negative media coverage and ruffled feelings in the African American community, not to mention having cost Penn exorbitant legal fees. In the waning months of his presidency Hackney sought to repair the damage by publicly committing the University to a ramped-up Mayor's Scholarship program, including bolstered funding for Philadelphia-wide recruitment. "Our real challenge has not been winning a lawsuit, but raising awareness of our commitment to Philadelphia," he told the press. "This is why we have in recent months moved aggressively to strengthen our implementation of the Mayor's Scholarship Program and intensify our recruitment of students from the local community. We view this as our civic and social obligation, part of our long-standing commitment to Philadelphia, and we welcome the opportunity to have more Philadelphians attending the University of Pennsylvania."[64] In June 1993 the University reported 164 Mayor's Scholars, receiving a total of $2 million, a number in excess of the 125 scholarships obligated under the 1977 city ordinance.[65] Hackney could also point to Penn's numerous contributions to the city and to his policy of reconciliation with the University's West Philadelphia neighbors—matters we take up in Chapter 9.

The relative civility of the divestiture protests and the absence of any significant campus opposition to Hackney's position on the Mayor's Scholarships belied the profound racial disharmonies of campus life in the 1980s. Penn, like other higher education institutions in the 1980s, was a cauldron of social discord, and troubled race relations were a critical ingredient in this volatile mix of issues. The University's climate of racial discord stemmed from racial incidents and misunderstandings.

The Climate of Racial Discord

Though Penn student activists, participants in a wider social movement, played an important role in speaking for human rights and steering the trustees toward divestment, theirs was only a small-minority voice on the campus, one that made only a tiny dent in the rampant boorishness and incivility, racism, sexism, homophobia, and criminality of undergraduate behavior that stalked the Penn campus in the 1980s. At a time when the nation's colleges were reporting "worsening racial tensions" and "a growing pattern of bigotry and animosity toward minority students,"[66] race relations at the University reached a nadir in the postwar history of the institution; the tensions flaring by mid-decade would not abate until the mid-1990s. African American students were targets of abusive behavior perpetrated by white male fraternities; they were subjected to anonymous acts of vandalism and threatened or symbolic violence; and on one well-publicized occasion, they were insulted if not harassed by a white professor. Right-wing white students defended racist slurs and innuendoes as free speech, decrying administrative efforts to prevent such behavior as "political correctness." Understandably, black students occasionally took the bait, sometimes projecting their own stereotypes onto whites, sometimes venting their anger in counterproductive ways. To the consternation of Jewish students, the Black Student League endorsed Louis Farrakhan and the Nation of Islam, and the *Daily Pennsylvanian* became a battleground of contentious letters to the editor from Jews and blacks alike. All of this made Penn a racially tense, hotly contested, unpleasantly confrontational institution—the quintessential noncommunity; "segregated diversity" was the campus norm.

On 13 February 1985, more than one hundred members of the Black Student League entered a business law class taught by Murray Dolfman, a Wharton senior lecturer, first to charge Dolfman with "harassing and haranguing black students in [his] classroom," then to conduct a silent sit-in. The protest action was precipitated belatedly by an incident in Dolfman's class the previous November in which "he referred to five black students as 'ex-slaves' and asked them to recite from memory the Thirteenth and the Fourteenth Amendments to the Constitution, which outline civil rights." The BSL used the incident to voice their outrage at pervasive institutional racism on the Penn campus.[67]

A week later, a large contingent of BSL members staged a one-hour sit-in in Hackney's office, charging the administration with "inaction" given that Dolfman was not dismissed from the faculty. "The statements of . . . Murray Dolfman, though best seen as the latest in an unrelenting series of assaults on the self-esteem of black students, are a particularly clear indication of the climate which exists here," according to a BSL proclamation presented to Hackney, who was quoted as saying, "I don't have the power to do some things. I told the BSL yesterday that I would not promise to do more than I could."[68] Several days after the sit-in, the BSL mobilized as many as three hundred demonstrators (accounts vary as to the number), among them two city politicians and black professors Ralph Smith and Houston Baker, for an eight-hour vigil at Eisenlohr, the president's mansion on Walnut Street, at the edge of the campus. "Hour after hour," reported the *DP*, the speakers incited the crowd, calling on them "to support the [black] students in their struggle for dignity, for justice and for humanity."[69]

For their part, Hackney and Ehrlich promised a "strong" University policy on racial harassment and affirmative action, racism awareness workshops (though not mandatory ones), support for racial diversity (the 1986–87 *Colorline* colloquia would be a case in point), targets for minority faculty recruitment (the appointment of Valarie Swain Cade as executive assistant to the provost and Marion Oliver as associate dean in the Wharton School would support that commitment), and review of Dolfman's case by the Wharton Committee on Academic Freedom and Responsibility.[70] Following the review, Wharton dean Russell Palmer notified Hackney and Ehrlich: "The school has concluded that certain comments and actions by Mr. Dolfman in class were not acceptable." To the satisfaction of the BSL and its supporters, Dolfman would not be allowed to teach in the coming fall, his reinstatement on the faculty would be contingent on his attendance at "sensitivity and racial awareness sessions," and the Legal Studies Department would monitor his teaching for an "adequate" probationary period. Noting that the overall faculty reaction to the decision was "mixed," the *DP* flagged the concern of perhaps many faculty members that Dolfman's academic freedom was violated by the sensitivity workshop provision of Palmer's ruling.[71] Years later, Hackney put it another way: "The accusation was that treating [Dolfman] in this way was political correctness gone mad."[72] The charge would be repeated with devastating effect in the book *The Shadow University*, a withering critique alleging the reign of political correctness in the Hackney era, authored by Alan Kors, Hackney's libertarian nemesis in Penn's History Department.[73] In any event, Dolfman resumed his teaching contract with the Wharton School in September 1986, without further disruption.[74]

Among "the usual number of disasters, stresses and strains" facing his presidency in 1985, Hackney counted the "Murray Dolfman incident" as "the chief energy absorber." With considerable satisfaction, he celebrated the resolution of that crisis: "Tom E. and I spent a large amount of time between Jan 30 and late April managing that crisis and negotiating with the leaders of the Black Student League. We did that successfully, ending with an agreement that commits us to do various things to enhance the black presence, things we actually *can* do and that will be good to do." Exuding a sense of relief, he also noted that the Dolfman affair distracted the BSL from the divestment controversy: "because the black community was so thoroughly absorbed in the crisis, we were mostly spared the sorts of disruptive demonstrations on South African divestments that exploded at Columbia, Cornell, Princeton, Berkeley and lots of other places."[75]

In the fall of 1986, the focus of campus racial tensions shifted to the Black Student League's selection of the Black Muslim leader Louis Farrakhan as the keynote speaker for the organization's National Black Student Unity Conference, which began on 30 October 1986, with Farrakhan's speech scheduled two days later for Saturday evening in Irvine Auditorium; other speakers included Jesse Jackson (at the time a presidential candidate) and Kwame Ture (formerly Stokely Carmichael). The decision to invite Farrakhan was guided by Conrad Muhammed (formerly Conrad Tillard), the controversial BSL chairman who belonged to the Nation of Islam. (Tillard's election to the post and the BSL's refusal to admit the white applicant Sydney Thornburgh as a full voting member branded the organization as black separatist.)[76] Outraged by Farrakhan's famously vitriolic antisemitism and the BSL's decision to invite him to the campus, Jewish students organized a rally against the speech, in alliance with the militant Jewish Defense Organization (JDO), based in New York City. (JDO leader Mordechai Levy allegedly described Farrakhan as a "candidate for assassination.") Farrakhan canceled his speech after Penn's security director, John Logan, beyond offering to provide forty-eight uniformed officers for the event, refused to allow the metal detectors or body searches Farrakhan's bodyguard, the Fruit of Islam, demanded as a precondition for his appearance. "We don't search people here at the University of Pennsylvania," Logan said. "We don't think it's necessary."[77]

In the wake of Farrakhan's cancellation, noisy altercations described as "tense shouting matches" took place that Saturday between Black Student Unity Conference participants and anti-Farrakhan protesters, the latter including Mordechai Levy and his JDO contingent. The "verbal battle," which was monitored by ten public safety officers, did not escalate to violence; according to the *DP*, "many among the crowd termed the verbal sparring a useful airing of grievances."[78] Charging that the Penn administration's refusal to comply with Farrakhan's demand for weapons checks was "racist," Conrad Muhammed declared: "We have not given up bringing him here, and after this right has been wronged, we expect to bring him here at the expense of the University." "On the basis of all the information that we had," Hackney replied, "it was determined that we could provide adequate security without altering our normal procedures in this case." After all, weapons checks had not been used at campus speeches by President Gerald Ford, General William Westmoreland, and Rev. Jerry Falwell.[79]

Several months later, Nation of Islam representative Abdul Khalid Muhammed addressed a racially mixed audience of some 450 at the University Museum. While security was "tight," there were no metal detectors or body searches. According to the *DP*, "The spokesman for the Nation of Islam leader Louis Farrakhan spoke in a loud, brash style that occasionally overwhelmed the amplification equipment. Throughout the three-hour speech, he was surrounded by a platoon of private security guards known as the Fruit of Islam." Arguing that Farrakhan had been misunderstood, that he was not anti-Semitic, Khalid Muhammed avoided saying anything to disparage Jews or provoke a wider breach in black-Jewish relations on the campus. His speech, however, failed to mollify the JDO.[80]

In the spring of 1988, Conrad Tillard finally succeeded in luring Louis Farrakhan to the University. To Farrakhan's satisfaction, the University finally agreed to provide handheld metal detectors. On the day of the talk, 14 April 1988, an ad signed by more than six hundred "people of conscience" appeared in the *DP* to "protest the abuse of speech [by Farrakhan] to incite hostility, prejudice, and violence." Farrakhan finally spoke for two and a half hours to a predominantly black audience of sixteen hundred to eighteen hundred at Irvine Auditorium, with hundreds more milling around outside looking for scalped tickets. "In a thundering oratory, the Nation of Islam leader ignited an overflow crowd with fiery rhetoric and prophecies of apocalypse," said the *DP*. "Each time the speech rose to a crescendo, the audience shouted in agreement, jumping up with frequent standing ovations. . . . Farrakhan lived up to his description as an apocalyptic minister with his frequent vague predictions of doom for white-dominated society which drew cries of support from many blacks, but little outward response from whites in the crowd." Though Farrakhan made multiple references to Jews, he avoided making an incendiary statement: "I did not come here to incite violence." The *Pennsylvania Gazette* reported, "If there was a central theme, it was the need to uplift the black race socially, economically, and spiritually."[81]

An estimated 450 demonstrators, many of them enlisted by the Penn chapter of Hillel, some of them wielding signs brandishing slogans such as "Farrakhan is a Racist" and "Farrakhan Promotes Hatred," had gathered peacefully at the chemical laboratories opposite Irvine at 34th and Spruce streets to listen to anti-Farrakhan speakers. Though there was no evidence of malice, the irony of scheduling Farrakhan's speech on Yom Hashoah, Holocaust Remembrance Day, was not lost on the Hillel organizers. That evening, after the doors closed for Farrakhan's speech, Farrakhan supporters without tickets clashed verbally with Jewish students at the same intersection. Their ire evidently drawn by a sign that suggested Farrakhan's approval of Hitler and the Holocaust, blacks retorted with such barbs as "Death to Zionism." In any event, violence was averted, perhaps by the presence of more than one hundred police, eight of whom were on horseback, perhaps because nobody wanted fisticuffs.[82] The *New York Times* reported: "Blacks and whites alike on the campus said today [April 14] that in coming through the difficult trial successfully and with dignity, the University had opened the way to a new and more constructive period of race relations."[83]

Unhappily for Hackney and the University this "unity" would not cohere. In the fall of 1988, racist graffiti marred campus buildings: a racial obscenity and swastika at Hill College House, a swastika in the basement of the law school and one in the high-rises. In November, several hundred students, led by BSL leader Melissa S. Moody, marched in silent protest. "Things are not as they should be," Hackney told a special session of the University Council.[84] As will be shown in Chapter 8, one of these errant "things" was the egregious behavior of fraternities on Locust Walk.

8
Throes of Diversity

Diminished "campus community" in Penn's undergraduate social life mirrored disturbing central tendencies of American higher education in the Age of Reagan, when economic, demographic, and political changes in the larger society played out in microcosm on the nation's campuses, provoking a similar pattern of problems across the institutions.[1] The 1980s and early 1990s witnessed a national epidemic of "overt bigotry," racial assaults, acquaintance rape, alcohol and drug abuse, and other malefactions on college campuses.[2] Young people enrolled on college campuses where affirmative action for minorities and women was de rigueur and codified. Deconstructionist, poststructuralist, and feminist modes of scholarship, whose rationale was "to expose power and oppression," were also a sign of the times. Academics of the postmodern persuasion, in English and the social sciences, valorized the "particularistic claims" of women and blacks, Latinos, Native Americans, and gays and lesbians; derided traditional scholarship and curricula as products of white-male privilege; and excoriated conservatism of any stripe.[3] A national trend that privileged the claims of historically subordinate groups was, no doubt, threatening to ego-deficient, conservative white males, who felt as if they were under siege. A black activist at Penn put it this way: "These white males who have been socialized to believe that the world was theirs—and they didn't have to compete with black men and women and white women—now feel the tensions of that competition."[4] Epitomizing a national trend, the upshot of these tensions on the Penn campus was a decade of culture wars that were not resolved until the mid-1990s.

This chapter centers on the wide range of diversity issues in the Hackney years. In addition to the racial matters discussed in Chapter 7, these issues included fraternity "bad boy" behavior and feminist challenges to the fraternities' domination of Locust Walk, as well as free speech controversies. We focus in particular on two incidents, the alleged Alpha Tau Omega (ATO) fraternity gang rape of 1983 and the "Water Buffalo" free-speech controversy of 1993, which stained, perhaps indelibly, Hackney's presidency and created a great deal of doubt about his managerial effectiveness.

■ Fraternity Matters: Bad Boys and Gender Issues on Locust Walk

Writing in the early 1970s, Penn administrators noted a downward trend in the fraternity presence. While in 1953 more than 70 percent of freshmen pledged a fraternity, that figure soon leveled off to about 50 percent per year until 1969, at which point it dropped precipitously to 30 percent, then in 1970–71, to 21 percent; a similar decline was noted in sorority pledges. Fraternities, the "Red and Blue" faction at Penn, with strongholds in the business and engineering schools, dominated the student government until 1963. A strong profraternity bias was prevalent among alumni, faculty, and administrators in the office of student affairs until the mid-1960s. Bitter feelings existed between Christian and Jewish fraternities, between fraternity and nonfraternity members; "institutional intolerance" and anti-Semitism were endemic in the Penn fraternity culture. By the late 1960s, in the wake of New Left and counterculture uprisings, the climate of opinion on the nation's campuses had turned against the fraternities. Penn was no exception. Professor and former provost David Goddard and assistant ombudsman Linda Koons, staunch critics of the fraternity culture, applauded the change in the campus ethos: "Gone are the days when Penn students were more concerned about Saturday night dates, beer blasts, and which fraternity to pledge, when they involved themselves in Rowbottoms, a Pennsylvania way of blowing off steam (sometimes developing into panty raids), or Skimmer, the annual crew race on the Schuylkill which became an excuse for excessive drinking and such high jinks as overturning trolleys, setting cars on fire, and dunking people into the river. Rowbottoms have nearly disappeared, and one celebrates Skimmer these days by attending a rock concert. Even fraternities have almost disappeared."[5]

The revival of Greek life at colleges and universities was a national phenomenon in the 1980s. At mid-decade, the *Nation* reported on the resurgence at the University of Michigan and other institutions:

> From the late 1960s to the early 1970s at the University of California, Berkeley, the number of women rushing sororities had dwindled to about 150 per year; now it's five times that. On campuses where chartered sororities never existed—Yale, Princeton, the University of Chicago—new chapters have been "colonized," an interesting choice

of verb by a group almost entirely of white Protestants. Even at Amherst College, where fraternities were abolished in 1984, they continue to thrive unofficially off campus. In the past ten years, fraternity membership has doubled—even though the full-time undergraduate population has increased only by 20 percent, from 5 million to 6 million. And undergraduate sorority membership has grown by about 30 percent, from 180,000 in 1975 to 240,000 in 1985.[6]

Penn did not experience a Greek revival per se. In the 1980s, fraternities and sororities still counted as members a relatively small minority of undergraduates, just 16 percent of the total in 1983, even smaller than the proportion reported by Goddard and Koons a decade earlier.[7] The concentration of thirteen of Penn's twenty-seven fraternities on or near Locust Walk, the spine of the University, gave them disproportionate visibility and influence in campus social affairs.[8]

In 1983 and 1984, fraternity gang rape became a bitter cause célèbre and embarrassment for the University.[9] Penn was not alone. Accompanying the national Greek revival was the disturbing phenomenon of widespread fraternity gang rape, highlighted in a 1985 publication of the Association of American Colleges.[10] No other university, however, experienced such heated controversy about wayward frat boys as Penn. The center of this campus storm was Alpha Tau Omega.

The Alpha Tau Omega Scandal

An article written by Mark Bowden, a journalist for the *Philadelphia Inquirer Magazine*, 11 September 1983, opened a Pandora's box into what was already a nightmare for Hackney and Provost Tom Ehrlich, airing previously unavailable details of an alleged gang rape committed by six to eight brothers at the ATO fraternity house at 39th Street and Locust Walk. "A troubled young woman came to the ATO party at Penn that night, tripping on acid and drinking beer," Bowden wrote as his lead. "In the early morning, she was taken upstairs, where she had sex with a succession of men, in what must have seemed like the realization of some male pornographic fantasy. But to the woman, and others, it was rape."[11]

Peggy Reeves Sanday, an anthropologist and prominent feminist at the University, published a book on the episode of serial sex that took place at the ATO house on the night of 17–18 February 1983.[12] Sanday stipulated that the legal case against the fraternity was weak. The assistant district attorney for sex crimes, who was certain that the brothers were guilty of rape, "pointed out that a charge of rape has to be proved beyond a reasonable doubt. If the brothers had a good reputation, that would be grounds to acquit because of reasonable doubt. The case was also tough because of the problem of proof. If Laurel [Sanday's pseudonym for the alleged victim] consented to sex with anybody during the course of the evening, there is always room for reasonable doubt as to whether she consented to all sexual activity, making it virtually impossible to convict in the case of party gang rapes." As the legal system was unlikely to be responsive, the moral burden of the case shifted to the University. That a young woman who was intoxicated, drugged, and disoriented was singled out for sex with the brothers was not in dispute; the men admitted as much, though they contended adamantly that the sex was consensual. According to Sanday, "the university, of course, does not have to prove a rape occurred, only that some specifically defined rule was violated. The university can decide . . . that ganging up sexually on a woman, regardless of her state, is behavior that will not be tolerated. The line between consent and rape need not be specified for the university to take vigorous action. In fact, a university can say that a fraternity that creates an environment that fosters ambiguity about determining whether a rape has occurred can be expelled."[13] Laurel filed an official complaint, and after a month of administrative dithering the case was referred to the University student judiciary system. At issue were the culpability of the fraternity members as individuals and the collective responsibility of the fraternity for the conduct of its members.

To the dismay of many campus observers, including members of the Faculty Senate, a lenient, undisclosed punishment was negotiated with the men charged with misconduct. "In our judgment," Hackney and Ehrlich explained, "the settlements reached with the Fraternity members were in keeping with the University's basic educational purposes, recognizing also the limits of our judicial system in handling this case. By the terms of the settlements made under the Charter of the Fraternity Student Judiciary System, public disclosure is not permitted."[14]

The Faculty Senate Executive Committee appointed an ad hoc committee to investigate the administration's handling of the matter. "Although the terms are secret," the historian Michael Katz, who chaired the ad hoc committee, noted, "it is known that the settlements required the men to undergo a process of reeducation through reading, essay writing, discussion and community service. Because settlements reached under the university's judicial charter preclude expulsion or suspension as sentences, these sanctions were not available."[15] Reporting in December 1983, the Katz committee concluded that the University's existing judicial procedures, the centerpiece of which was the student panel hearing, were "wholly inadequate" for complaints that involved "personal violence, serious sexual misconduct, or possible felonies." The ad hoc committee stated that Hackney and Ehrlich should have closed the loophole of individual settlements and assigned the case to a faculty hearing board. Regarding behavior that they believed mocked "the idea of a civilized community," the committee declaimed: "The respondents deserved serious and public punishment. . . . We are concerned that the apparent leniency of the sanctions has undermined the purpose and effect of the effort to remove ATO from the campus and the Administration's statements on sexual harassment." The committee also criticized Hackney for failing to provide medical or financial assistance to Laurel, who was anguished by the decision not to disclose the punishments.[16] June Axinn, chair of the Faculty Senate, which commissioned the report, told the *Inquirer*: "The entire case, since February, has seemed to indicate to many faculty members that ineptness, bungling, or even a cover-up might be involved. . . . We saw grossly inadequate sanctions—a negotiated settlement with the fraternity brothers to read several books about women's rights and perform community service equivalent to a part-time job. Frankly, the Faculty Senate and virtually all faculty members were shocked and upset by the disparity between the seriousness of the charge of rape and the trivial nature of the sanctions."[17] In his journal, Hackney complained of the "officious and self-righteous manner" of the Senate investigation. "My worst fears were realized when we got copies of the Katz Committee Report last Monday. It was a devastating and unrelieved and undiscriminating eleven pages of criticism." Hackney believed that the Senate's explosive reaction was fueled, in part at least, by lingering resentment over Gregorian's ouster: "There is no doubt that some of the revolt is motivated by the old pro-Gregorian and anti-trustee faction, the kamikaze left."[18]

Why did Hackney and Ehrlich not intervene to impose a faculty hearing panel to adjudicate the students involved? The answer most probably lies in what they saw as the limits of Hackney's presidential authority. Though he recognized "the constraints imposed by the existing Student Judicial Charter,"[19] Hackney worried—as he would worry a decade later in the Water Buffalo incident (see below)—that he might precipitate a governance crisis by contravening the procedures of an existing judicial charter that had been approved by the University Council.

Next was the question of the fraternity's collective responsibility, in the first instance a matter for inquiry by the University's Fraternity and Sorority Advisory Board, which included alumni, faculty, and students. Did ATO violate the University's recognition policy, which specified a code of conduct for campus fraternities? Yes, according to the Advisory Board, which "recommended that the chapter be suspended immediately and remain suspended until 31 January 1984." On the strength of this and other recommendations,

Viewed from 39th Street is Alpha Tau Omega (left), site of an alleged fraternity gang rape in 1983; Harnwell College House (right) faces Locust Walk in the Superblock. Photograph by Michael M. Koehler. Collections of the University Archives and Records Center.

on March 23, 1983, the acting vice provost for university life issued his ruling. The fraternity would be suspended immediately, though he extended the reinstatement date until September 1984. Citing "excessive drinking and hazardous social activities," he took a hammer to the organization: for the chapter's reinstatement the national fraternity would have to present a restructuring plan for the University's approval, and "no present member (or pledge)" would be allowed membership in the reconstituted fraternity.[20]

For the next year, the University was tied up in a lawsuit over this ruling. The ATO members complained that they had not received a fair hearing. For a number of months their litigation was embroiled in the question of whether the case was actionable in a state court. Once this issue was resolved in favor of the fraternity, Judge Lois Forer of the Court of Common Pleas remanded the case to the University for a hearing "before an impartial tribunal or hearing officer," with guidelines for the hearing agreed upon between Forer and the attorneys for the University and the fraternity.[21] The University designated Leo Levin, a Penn law professor, to conduct the hearing, the outcome of which was disappointing to everyone. On 14 February 1984, Levin issued his ruling, which was binding on both parties by their mutual consent. Constrained by Laurel's inability or unwillingness to testify (by all accounts she was traumatized), Levin found that "the University has, in effect, charged rape. Forcible rape has not been proved. Moreover, the credible evidence disproves any such charge." That noted, he ruled that ATO had violated the University's recognition policy by fostering an environment that encouraged or tolerated acts of seriatim sex, involving probably six of the brothers "pulling train" (fraternity argot for the comradely act) with Laurel. Levin also said that "nowhere in the record is there an unequivocal statement that today the fraternity considers such an event improper, to be condemned rather than condoned." He ordered the fraternity's suspension to remain in effect until September 1984 and the chapter to vacate the house by February 29. Levin said he would allow the present members (and pledges) to continue in the chapter following reinstatement of the fraternity, though none of them could serve as officers.[22] This decision angered Hackney and Ehrlich, who wanted a stiffer punishment for ATO.[23]

Disgusted by Levin's ruling, which he called a "slap on the hands," the city's assistant district attorney for sex crimes fulminated: "I would have closed the house, thrown out the boys, and that would have been the end of it."[24] A *Daily News* editorial pilloried the ATO brothers, calling them "overprivileged monsters," "louts," and "Ivy League crumbs."[25] Carol Tracy, who resigned after eight years as director of the Women's Center in April 1984, remarked, "I personally remain very disappointed that the boys involved went virtually unpunished, that the woman suffered so extremely from it including spending three months in an institution. . . . And I'm tired. I'm tired of picking up the pieces of the victims. I'm tired of people coming in who have been hassled on Locust Walk. I'm tired of the people who have been bothered at parties."[26]

Hackney consoled himself that the individual respondents and the collective membership had been punished, however lightly. In the early spring of 1984, looking back on the case, he told a correspondent:

> The offense of rape is a criminal charge and should have been pursued by the District Attorney if he felt that he had a reasonable case. He investigated and decided not to prosecute. At none of the University's disciplinary hearings was the charge of rape proven. That is the explicit finding of the final review officer, Professor Leo Levin. I agree with your sentiments about the abhorrence of rape, but that is not the offense that is being punished in the instance of the ATO case at Penn. The thing being punished is a different kind of irresponsible behavior. I believe that one of the accomplishments of the Penn judicial process, even in this confused case, was that we sustained the power and the willingness of the University to discipline students for behavior that does not amount to a criminal offense. In other words, we made it clear that the University's standards of conduct for its own students and faculty and staff are considerably higher than the standards set by criminal statutes. The other remarkable outcome of the situation at Penn was that we achieved a "conviction" even when the young woman involved did not testify.[27]

In any event, with Hackney's support, the University Council revised the Student Judicial Charter in September 1984. Thereafter, all undergraduate cases were submitted to a hearing board panel of two undergraduates and three faculty members, or, if the complainant and respondent agreed, to the vice provost for university life for a hearing. Special settlements by the judicial inquiry officer for individual respondents were now off the table.[28]

Locust Walk: Diversification by Fraternity Attrition

The fraternities of the Locust Walk environs shaped and reflected a general climate of incivility, a problem Hackney noted "that's sort of shot through the community, in a way." An example was the misbehavior of members of Kappa Sigma, since 1923 a fraternity housed in a neo-Georgian edifice on the Walk at 37th Street. Citing "a continuing pattern of serious disciplinary problems despite formal administrative intervention," Janis Somerville, the vice provost for university life, suspended the fraternity's charter for three years, 1981 to 1984.[29]

At least one complaint of egregious racial indiscretion appears in the archival record of Kappa Sigma's misdeeds, described in a letter to Hackney from an employee in the Sociology Department, and later confirmed by Hackney:

> Last Thursday afternoon, three young girls wearing Catholic elementary school uniforms were walking across the back lawn of the Kappa Sig fraternity house, presumably on their way home from school, when a man shouted at them from one of the frat's windows, calling them "niggers" and demanding that they get off the property.
>
> One of my co-workers in the Sociology office, Jennifer Spann, heard the shouting and, watching from her office window, saw the girls run across the lawn and then stop across the road near Vance Hall, to worry about a jacket one of them had dropped—apparently too frightened to go back for it. Soon a young boy offered to get the jacket for them, and entering the yard, suffered the same verbal abuse—this time from *two* men at separate windows, one of whom announced the building to be the "official house of the Ku Klux Klan."[30]

In the fall of 1987, a campus forum, "Civility Under Siege," was organized to address "nasty remarks and other signs of rudeness, harassment, and disorderly behavior—nothing specific but a noticeable accumulation of campus incidents of varying degrees of severity."[31] Later in the academic year, the University suspended the Zeta Beta Tau (ZBT) fraternity for eighteen months for "staging sexually and racially offensive activities during its fall rush." The fraternity hired two African American female strippers with whom the members and their guests cavorted in "sexually degrading" ways. "Before being reinstated," the *Pennsylvania Gazette* reported, "ZBT must produce a written plan of action to eliminate racist and sexist behavior among members; and each member must complete 25 hours of community service."[32] "Striptease Frat Shut by Penn," trumpeted a *Daily News* banner headline.[33] Shortly after the ZBT ruling, the University suspended the Alpha Chi Rho fraternity for hiring a stripper to perform at a party, though the event had none of the "lewd stuff" or racial overtones of the ZBT incident.[34]

Recognizing that alcohol fueled behavior of this sort, Hackney and his new provost Michael Aiken (Thomas Ehrlich had left the University to become president of Indiana University) summarily ordered a ban on beer kegs in the fraternity houses and dormitories, an action greeted with howls of protest from undergraduates. One *Daily Pennsylvanian* editorial forecast "tragic consequences not just for undergraduates but for the University, which as an institution would lose one of its most valuable assets: the best campus nightlife in the Ivy League." Others said the policy was "repressive and unnecessary," the administration was trying to "stifle campus social life." One writer said, "The center of traditional campus nightlife has been the fraternity party. And the center of the party has traditionally been the beer keg."[35] In one demonstration more than seventy fraternity men barricaded Locust Walk with twenty-one empty beer kegs, chanted slogans, and held up foot traffic. After demonstrators deposited the kegs in College Hall, enterprising administrators returned them to the distributor, collected $900, and donated the proceeds to the campus alcohol and resources education program.[36] Shortly thereafter, the administration lifted the ban with the proviso that the fraternities and other groups present an "established plan," in advance of any parties, to circumvent illegal drinking.[37]

In February 1990, the Philadelphia police filed criminal charges against a Psi Upsilon fraternity brother and a pledge for allegedly kidnapping and assaulting a member of Delta Psi, a rival fraternity. (Psi Upsilon, also called "The Castle," with its crenellated white-stone towers and neo-Gothic entrance archway facing College Green, had occupied the southwest corner of 36th and Locust streets since 1897.)[38] The judicial inquiry office and the national fraternity were involved in the campus investigation of Psi Upsilon. After a seven-week investigation, the judicial inquiry office found Psi Upsilon collectively responsible for the incident; the office issued its finding of collective responsibility to the Fraternity and Sorority Advisory Board, which reviewed the judicial inquiry office's finding and recommended sanctions to Kim Morrisson, the vice provost for university life.

The Psi Upsilon caper offered a bizarrely different scenario of fraternity misconduct from what critics of the Locust Walk scene had come to expect: Psi Upsilon was racially integrated, and the accused perpetrators were black.[39] William O'Flanagan of Delta Psi was kidnapped on the evening of January 20 by "masked Psi Upsilon members"; he was "blindfolded and bound at the hands and feet, tethered to a metal pole and taunted with racially charged rhetoric, including tapes of Malcolm X. . . . During the abduction, which lasted 2½ hours, O'Flanagan was subjected to a mock trial in which he was accused of being racist and anti-Semitic. His abductors also taunted him with a knife. . . . But the target was actually another Delta Psi member, suspected of being a racist, and O'Flanagan was taken by mistake."[40]

Completing her review in early May, Morrisson suspended the fraternity for at least three years with "no automatic right of return." As Penn owned the property (years before, the national fraternity had sold it to the University, with the fraternity holding a reversionary interest),[41] the vice provost for university life incorporated the building into the campus system of residential college houses. By August, ten Psi Upsilon brothers faced charges in the city's criminal case. The district attorney's office agreed not to try the students with the proviso that they "enter a program for defendants with no previous criminal record. If the students do not get arrested for a year, the charges will be dropped." In 1991, Psi Upsilon reportedly paid a court settlement of $145,000 to O'Flanagan.[42]

Against this backdrop, a student and faculty campaign against offending fraternities started in the spring of 1990. On the night of April 11, some fifty demonstrators, among them two highly respected biology professors, Helen Davies and her spouse Robert Davies, marched under the banner of the Progressive Student Alliance against Phi Kappa Sigma, which was on Locust at 36th Street just above the Van Pelt Library. The marchers were outraged by

> an incident in March, during the annual Gay Jeans Day, when members of the University community are encouraged to wear jeans to support the rights of gays. Some brothers in the Phi Kappa Sigma house near a rally for gay rights blasted from their windows what was characterized (accurately) by the Lesbian, Gay, and Bisexual Alliance as homophobic music: specifically, a hate-filled song by the rock group Guns n' Roses called "One in a Million." When people at the rally protested, they were at first rebuffed: the music played on. A few days later, however, the president of Phi Kappa Sigma issued an apology. Subsequently, the Lesbian, Gay, and Bisexual Alliance filed a complaint against Phi Kappa Sigma with the Committee on Open Expression.[43]

Having announced in the spring that "the current mix of student residences along Locust Walk must change," Hackney appointed an ad-hoc committee, the Committee to Diversify Locust Walk, in the fall and charged it to "consider [the Walk's] physical as well as social character. . . . What would it take to make Locust Walk one of the country's premier residential walkways? . . . There are options that hold the promise both of substantially diversifying our campus's central pedestrian precinct and of increasing the density of student activity within it." Hackney deftly deflected the oft-heard charge that he was hostile to fraternities by saying, "Given considerations of fairness, we therefore intend to accomplish our goals without requiring the relocation of any fraternities currently located along the Walk."[44] Considerations of fairness did not include Theta Xi at 3643 Locust Street, whose charter was lifted by the fraternity's national organization after a riotous party that left the house with eighteen broken windows, the latest in a string of incidents.[45] Here it is tempting to conclude that the administration, unwilling to diversify the Walk by fiat, adopted a strategy of attrition by which rotten apples would be removed by the campus judicial process or the national fraternity.

Shortly after the Committee to Diversify Locust Walk took up its charge, the President's Committee on University Life, which was chaired by Drew Faust, a future president of Harvard University, tendered its report. The committee wrote:

> Built over more than a century, Penn's physical spaces provide some serious impediments to the enhancement of community life we seek. While we recognize that we cannot start entirely anew in this area, nevertheless, it is important to acknowledge the symbolic and interactional significance of these spaces. . . . Spaces make statements as eloquent as any emanating from administrators in College Hall. The current arrangement of the campus, with white male fraternities lining its central artery, Locust Walk, is more appropriate to Penn of the 1950s than to what Penn hopes to be in the 1990s. Again and again the issue of Locust Walk was voiced to us by concerned students, staff and faculty who saw it as a site of racial and sexual exclusivity, and, too often, verbal and physical harassment.[46]

The Committee to Diversify Locust Walk worked for a year compiling information from many sources, including an architectural study of the Walk by the prestigious firm of Venturi, Scott Brown and Associates. Its final report noted "substantial support within the committee and within the University for a Locust Walk without fraternities." As Hackney had already precluded that option, the committee could only urge "those chapters now on the Walk to work with their alumni to evaluate their needs and to give careful consideration to how those needs might be met in other locations, and . . . recommend that the University facilitate potential relocations that grow out of these discussions." Within the next several years, as several fraternities permanently forfeited their houses on the Walk, one of the committee's recommendations bore fruit, namely, "several types of spaces and programs, some permanent and some informal, to attract more non-residents to the Walk and to increase their sense of comfort."[47] Consistent with this recommendation, during Judith Rodin's presidency the Women's Center, the Graduate Student Center, and the Penn Humanities Forum took up their abodes in converted fraternities on the Walk. Yet diversifying the Walk did not solve the larger problem of diminished "campus community."

As if to punctuate that point, Hackney recalls his harrowing experience with black student outrage on the night of 29 April 1992, in the wake of the acquittal of the Los Angeles police officers who were charged with criminal abuse in the arrest of Rodney King, an African American. As King's bludgeoning had been videotaped and witnessed by millions of television viewers, the "not guilty verdict" announced in the Ventura County courthouse unleashed riots in heavily black and poor South Central Los Angeles. Hackney worried that the violence in California would reprise on the Penn campus. "As the news of the verdict spread on the campus that day," he says, "feelings of both anger and dismay were palpable immediately." Shortly after 11 p.m., a crowd of about five hundred mostly black, "restless and angry" demonstrators marched from DuBois college house down the 3900 block of Walnut Street to Eisenlohr, Hackney's residence. With the block cordoned off by police, the demonstrators massed in Walnut Street, facing the front gate of the president's house. Standing with his wife at the top of the steps, Hackney collected himself to address the crowd. Hackney later reflected on the experience:

> I was scared. I always tried to appear calm and unworried, and I think I managed that well enough. . . . As I started talking, the crowd grew quiet. I said that I understood their frustration and agreed with their sense of outrage at the verdict (which was true). I also spoke of the long way we had come as a society since the 1950s, and how much progress Penn in particular had made. Even though the Rodney King verdict dramatized how much was left to be done, we could be much more effective in fighting racism if we worked together in positive ways rather than lashing out in destructive ways. I promised to meet with Penn student leaders the next day to identify things we could actually do. I was not Demosthenes, but they listened.

As the crowd was mollified by Hackney's remarks, "the leaders decided to march off in the direction of City Hall, twenty-four blocks away. They left shouting slogans, with the police protecting their flanks and getting the traffic out of the way. No injuries and minimal damage resulted. My meeting with the black students the next day went very well."[48]

The Rodney King demonstration happened a year before Water Buffalo exploded in the national press on the eve of Hackney's Senate confirmation hearings (more below).

■ Water Buffalo: Contexts and Consequences

On 13 January 1993, a Penn freshman, Eden Jacobowitz, studying in his room in the high-rise dormitory complex west of 38th Street, responded to

a late-night clamor outside his window by shouting down to a group of reveling African American sorority members, "Shut up, you water buffalo! If
you want a party, there's a zoo a mile from here." Jacobowitz was one of
many dorm residents yelling down at the revelers, a few of them bandying
racial epithets like "black bitches" and "black asses." When the campus police investigated the incident, Jacobowitz, alone among all the students
who participated in the verbal flogging, confessed to his insult, though he
disavowed any racial intent or content in his action. Indignant at what they
interpreted as a racial insult, five of the women filed a racial harassment
complaint with the Office of University Life. A few weeks later, Jacobowitz
stood accused by a judicial inquiry officer of a violation of the campus
speech code, which proscribed "any verbal or symbolic behavior" that was
intentionally demeaning and directed toward "an identifiable person or
persons" on the basis of race, color, ethnicity, or national origin. When Jacobowitz staunchly refused to accept the settlement offered by the judicial
inquiry office, which would have ended the affair with several minor though
humiliating in-house punishments, his case was forwarded, according to
the established protocol, to a judicial hearing board. Here the stakes were
much higher for Jacobowitz, including the very real possibility of expulsion
from the University.[49]

Continuing to insist that his use of the epithet "water buffalo" had no racial content or motive, Jacobowitz enlisted Alan Kors, a prominent Penn history professor and noted libertarian, to represent him in navigating Penn's
judicial process. As attested by experts in linguistics, folklore, and other disciplines, Jacobowitz "was using an insult frequently used among Orthodox
Jews like himself, derived from the Hebrew word *behamah*. It figuratively
means fool or thoughtless person and also translates as beast or buffalo."[50] Jacobowitz's advocates, including a legal team from the Pennsylvania American Civil Liberties Union, claimed that the University speech code and the
judicial process it invoked banned speech protected by the First Amendment.[51]
Though the University, as a private institution, was not bound by the First
Amendment, its reputation as Benjamin Franklin's University was based in
no small way on its avowed commitment to the disinterested pursuit of knowledge and its pragmatic openness to diverse ideas. Water Buffalo posed a huge
potential embarrassment for Penn.

Penn's judicial administrator refused to reschedule Jacobowitz's hearing,
which was set for April 26, when Kors had to be off campus. Convinced that
a fair hearing was off the table, Kors notified Hackney that Jacobowitz would
appeal to "the deeper court of public opinion."[52] Portraying Jacobowitz as
the victim of political correctness run amok, the *Wall Street Journal* turned

Jacobowitz's quandary into a cause célèbre. Other newspapers picked up the story, and conservative columnists voiced their outrage.

Unfortunately for Hackney, national media reports conflated Water Buffalo with another free speech imbroglio that arose from the theft of more than fourteen thousand issues of the *Daily Pennsylvanian* on 15 April. Hackney had a major crisis on his hands, drawing heated criticism for his apparent indecisiveness in both incidents. The early morning removal of the *DP* from campus distribution sites was a protest action staged by a group of black students who called themselves "the Black Community." They were outraged that the *DP* had published the racially charged fulminations of Greg Pavlik, a conservative columnist for the paper whom Hackney likened to "a garden variety bigot with a good vocabulary,"[53] and whose continuous fulminations Claire Fagin, the interim president who succeeded Hackney, scathingly called "racist' and "unbelievably ugly."[54] Black students took matters into their own hands after the Office of University Life declined to discipline Pavlik, citing his First Amendment rights.

A week later, on April 20, Hackney published a statement about the *DP* fracas in the *Almanac*—one that drew a charge of "equivocation" from Kors. Hackney was deeply ambivalent about how to respond to what he called a "protest action." Significantly, he did not call it a "theft"; rather, it was a "removal." "This is an instance," he said, "in which two groups important to the University community, valued members of Penn's minority community and students exercising their rights to freedom of expression, and two important University values, diversity and open expression, seem to be in conflict." Several paragraphs later he reiterated the point: "As I indicated above two important University values now stand in conflict. There can be no compromise regarding the First Amendment right of an independent publication to express whatever views it chooses. At the same time, *there can be no ignoring the pain that expression may cause*" (emphasis added). In another statement on the same page, as if to have it both ways, he asserted: "Though I understand that those involved in last week's protest against the *DP* may have thought they were exercising their own rights of free expression, I want to make it clear that neither I nor the University of Pennsylvania condone the confiscation of issues of the *Daily Pennsylvanian*. I would like to remind all members of the University community of the policy I promulgated several years ago (*Almanac* 7/18/89), reprinted below specifically banning such actions. Any violations of this policy will be pursued through the University judicial system as chartered by the schools of the University."[55] Whereas previously Hackney had unequivocally championed free speech and free artistic expression, however repugnant to him personally—his list included, among others, Louis Farrakhan; Robert Mapplethorpe, whose "sexually explicit, homoerotic, and sadomasochistic pictures" were displayed at Penn's Institute of Contemporary Art; and Andres Serrano, whose notorious "Piss Christ" displayed a plastic crucifix standing in a vial (putatively) of Serrano's urine[56]— in the rifled-newspapers controversy, he stopped short of declaring free speech an absolute value. Indeed, in his "two values in conflict" statement, Hackney leaned toward a sentiment espoused by a black law professor: "The right to protest injustice and oppression deserves no less protection than the right to publish."[57] Kors, an absolutist on free speech, detected this ambivalence on Hackney's part and excoriated him for it.

For several months, "the worst period of my life," Hackney suffered the slings and arrows of outraged journalists who scorned him with epithets like "the Pope of political correctness," "Mr. Wimp," and "bozo." Penn was variously depicted as "a collegiate Star Chamber," "the cutting edge of lunacy," "theater of the absurd," and "Kafkaesque."[58] Fueling these salvos was Bill Clinton's nomination of Hackney as chair of the National Endowment for the Humanities (NEH). At his Senate confirmation hearings in late June, Hackney calmly fielded abrasive questions about Water Buffalo and the *DP* removal, which he now called a theft. Regarding his refusal to intervene in the University judicial process, he told Senator Nancy Kassebaum:

> As awful as the spring was, I still think it was not appropriate for me to intervene in the judicial procedure. There is no provision for the President or for any officer of the University to intervene. To have intervened would have called into question the legitimacy of the entire system that handles dozens of cases every year, denied to the complainants their right to have their complaint adjudicated by a faculty-student hearing panel, and thrown the campus into an even more divisive crisis than the one through which it actually lived. Had the system worked properly, and a hearing panel heard the case, I believe that justice would have prevailed [that is, the exoneration of Jacobowitz]. As it turned out, the case came to a close when the complainants withdrew their charges [on 24 May 1993, claiming they could not get a fair hearing in light of all the media hoopla].[59]

As for his *Almanac* statement on the newspaper theft, which Senator Orrin Hatch called "mushy," Hackney writes, "I admitted that if I could do it over again, I would craft my statement to be more clear in its commitment to free speech and less amenable to distortion." Hackney also says, "I wish I had thought to point out then, or at some time during the whole horror show, that the correct question to ask was not whether that particular statement was clear enough in its defense of free speech, but whether I had left anyone at Penn in doubt about the theft of newspapers being a violation of University regulations."[60] In the end, the Senate confirmed Hackney's appointment.[61] He served in the Clinton administration for four years, after which he returned to Penn to a professorship in the History Department, where he and his erstwhile nemesis Kors taught in uneasy proximity.

Another of Hackney's colleagues in the History Department, Michael Zuckerman, who found Kors's "strident self-righteousness" unconscionable, nevertheless blamed Hackney for the lion's share of the debacle: "Obviously Hackney handled it atrociously. And obviously he barely survived the aftermath of it, which was the NEH hearings and all the rest. It seems to me that you could expect trouble on the national political scene, that's a different audience. But he should never have been in the trouble that he got into within the University community, and that was just maladroit management."[62] "There are several things about that period that just drive me nuts," says Linda Koons, who at the time was the executive assistant to the provost. "One of them was that Sheldon didn't intervene. And, of course, according to our judicial process, he's not allowed to intervene. Probably we should have made an exception."[63]

Hackney's reputation suffered even more when Kors published *The Shadow University* in 1997, which cited Penn under Hackney as Exhibit A in a meticulously researched indictment of political correctness on the nation's campuses.[64] Kors painted a persuasive and devastating portrait of truculent "in loco parentis ideologues" in the Judicial Inquiry Office, the Office of Residential Life, and the Women's Center. He blamed Hackney for not cleaning out the nest of vipers before things got out of hand. For many observers, Water Buffalo seemed to confirm the image of Hackney as a president who was out of his depth. Zuckerman says, "I think it really cast Hackney in a way which was emblematic of the way a lot of people saw his presidency more generally, that it was wonderfully well-intentioned, all the right social sympathies, but that it was just ineffectual in accomplishing what it wanted to do in the way of implementing those social sympathies."[65] Dismayingly, Penn's "drowning in racial problems" and the furor over Water Buffalo also served to mask Hackney's many substantial contributions to the University. "At the end of Sheldon's tenth year, he was a hero," recalls Claire Fagin. "But those last two years, something happened. The place sort of . . . lost its spirit."[66]

Judith Rodin would add insult to injury by ignoring Hackney. Unlike Martin Meyerson, Hackney was not accorded the status of éminence grise after he returned to Penn from NEH in 1997. Indeed, Rodin portrays herself in a recent book as the new sheriff in town. In *The University and Urban Revival*, her triumphant account of her administration's West Philadelphia Initiatives, she gives only scant attention to the foundation for urban revival that she inherited from Hackney—the path of reconciliation that Hackney charted to redress the harmful effects of the Great Expansion in the 1960s and the stagnation of Penn's community relations in the 1970s.

9

Penn and the City
Inextricably Intertwined

In 1992, Sheldon Hackney, then in the midst of the Mayor's Scholarship controversy, could point with pride to Penn's financial and service contributions to Philadelphia. The University admitted more than twenty-three hundred Philadelphia students between 1978 and 1991, matriculating about 60 percent of them. By 1992 more than fifty-eight hundred of the University's roughly 12,360 employees claimed West Philadelphia as their home. Penn's 1990 employee wage taxes to the city totaled $23.5 million. In 1990, when Philadelphia faced bankruptcy, Penn prepaid $10 million in wage taxes to help keep the city solvent.[1] A Coopers & Lybrand study for FY 1990 reported that Penn's direct contributions and "multiplier effects" amounted to a total contribution of at least $2.5 billion to the Commonwealth.[2] Of no mean consequence, the University boasted the region's largest medical center: the gargantuan Hospital of the University of Pennsylvania (HUP), the Penn medical school, and the University's clinical practices.[3] Penn, under Hackney, was also engaged in restructuring the University's uneasy relationship with West Philadelphia—a restructuring based on the proposition of mutual benefit. What Hackney initially saw as Penn's moral responsibility to West Philadelphia, he would also later regard as enlightened self-interest: Penn would contribute to West Philadelphia's revival in ways that strengthened the University's historic missions of research, teaching, and service; a revitalized West Philadelphia would be Penn's best guarantee of an open, secure, and beautiful campus.[4]

Mindful of the structural causes of the urban crisis, the Christian Association's assistant director, Rev. Florence Gelo, spoke prophetically in 1988, when she said, "While in the short term, greater security might be a response to this issue, it will not in the long term create the kind of society and the kind of relationships between the University and the community that will foster the necessary environment for long-term safety. Our vision of a safe and just community depends on these improved relationships."[5] Toward this goal,

Hackney declared in 1988 that Penn's social responsibility to the city included service initiatives in West Philadelphia commensurate with the University's historic mission of producing and transmitting knowledge. Penn and Philadelphia, Hackney said, "stand on common ground, our futures very much intertwined."[6] Several years later, he established a permanent center whose main purpose was to build an infrastructure for teaching and research within the University focused on solving problems in West Philadelphia. "Though Hackney was a student of the rural South and Meyerson of the cities," says Michael Zuckerman, "I think it's clear that the University did more with the city under Hackney than it had done under Meyerson, and that Hackney's heart was in that."[7]

This chapter centers on Hackney's contributions toward a reconciliation with West Philadelphia. Undeniably, his actions reversed the alienation and drift that had severely damaged the University's community relations in previous decades. In particular, we look at Hackney's creation of the Center for Community Partnerships (a milestone development in American higher education), his reconstruction of the West Philadelphia Corporation as the West Philadelphia Partnership, and his resolution of the twenty-year-long Sansom Street imbroglio. Underscoring the considerable inheritance his administration bequeathed to his successor, Judith Rodin, we also enumerate his contributions toward establishing Penn as a top-tier university. Segueing to the Rodin era, we conclude the chapter with a brief discussion of the not-inconsequential interregnum of Claire Fagin, Penn's interim president from 1993 to 1994.

■ The Center for Community Partnerships: A Mediating Structure for Penn and West Philadelphia

The Center for Community Partnerships (CCP) originated in the Office of Community-Oriented Policy Studies (OCOPS) in the School of Arts and Sciences in 1983. Ira Harkavy, the former student leader of the 1969 College Hall sit-in and member of the Quadripartite Commission, now with a PhD in American history, directed OCOPS and cotaught an undergraduate seminar on University-community relations with two other Penn historians, Lee Benson[8] and Hackney. Hackney recalled:

> One day Ira and Lee Benson came to see me. They said, "We're interested in West Philadelphia and we teach a course on West Philadelphia— a seminar in which students are supposed to go get some kind of internship in West Philadelphia and . . . we do the theory in class, they

go out and do their thing, and they write a paper on how the theory and practice relate to each other. And we want you to teach with us." This was very shrewd. . . . I guess it appealed to me because I was then increasingly active in West Philadelphia, and it made sense, so I said, "Sure," and I did. They didn't overwork me. I did a couple of sessions during the semester and would sit in at other times; [I] enjoyed it, I learned a lot. I came to admire both of them—very different people.[9]

In the summer of 1985, the students in the Benson-Harkavy-Hackney seminar responded to the devastation of the infamous MOVE fire by organizing a youth corps, the West Philadelphia Improvement Corps (WEPIC), and acquiring a U.S. Department of Labor grant to employ West Philadelphia high school students to work on school and neighborhood beautification projects in the area of the fire. (The fire was ignited by a satchel bomb dropped from a helicopter during a shootout between Philadelphia police and MOVE, a militant, back-to-nature African American cult; the melee resulted in the deaths of eleven MOVE members and the destruction of two full blocks of middle-class row houses in West Philadelphia's Cobb's Creek neighborhood.)[10] The first project site was the Bryant Elementary School, just a few blocks from the MOVE site. Such was the enthusiastic reception for this initiative from city and local leaders that by 1989, WEPIC was able to expand to other West Philadelphia schools, notably the John P. Turner Middle School and West Philadelphia High School, where WEPIC, now with a full-time staff and an assortment of state, federal, and local grants, sponsored evening and weekend cultural, educational, vocational, and recreational workshops and programs for students, their families, and local residents. The myriad WEPIC activities ranged from pipe-organ restoration to carpentry, to ceramics and calligraphy, to African American storytelling, to basketball and swimming. These programs were the vanguard of a Penn-West Philadelphia joint initiative—one that involved Penn faculty, staff, and students in collaboration with teachers, school administrators, local politicians, and neighborhood cultural affairs leaders—to establish "university-assisted community schools" in West Philadelphia. Since 1989, the participants in this initiative have acted on their core proposition that the neighborhood school can effectively serve as the core neighborhood institution and catalyst for urban community development—an institution that both provides primary health and social services, and galvanizes other community institutions and groups to support education- and community-improvement initiatives. Extensive research by Penn faculty on the history, theory, and pedagogy of community schools supports the viability of this proposition.[11]

Observing the growing interest in this work among faculty and students, the School of Arts and Sciences established the Penn Program for Public Service, an expansion of OCOPS, with Harkavy as director. Believing that WEPIC projects warranted the University's institutional imprimatur, Hackney appointed a task force that included Harkavy, John Gould (Hackney's chief of staff), Francis Johnston of the Anthropology Department, Jane Lowe of the School of Social Work, and John Puckett of the Graduate School of Education to write a proposal to establish a University center for WEPIC project development; the task force completed its work at a Campus Compact retreat on service-learning at Stanford University in the summer of 1991. A signature component of the proposal was the concept of "academically based community service" (ABCS), that is, service rooted in academic study that centers on a real-world social problem. Having approved the proposal, in 1992 Hackney established the Center for Community Partnerships on the fifth floor of the University-owned office building at 36th and Walnut streets, with Harkavy appointed as the founding director. Of Hackney's role in cultivating Harkavy's formidable organizing skills for turning around Penn's community relations, Zuckerman observes, "I think what was going on from the day that Ira arrived as an administrator at Penn, from the day he decided not to go looking for a teaching job when he finished his PhD but to make his career trying to do community relations for Penn, that Ira has been a genius, extending himself, finagling for himself, extending the reach of the community relations operation at Penn. And I would certainly credit Hackney with creating the institutional structure that augmented Ira's operation."[12]

After more than twenty years, the CCP (as of 2007, renamed the Netter Center for Community Partnerships) is a national model of both service-learning and higher education civic engagement in urban community affairs. Unlike many other centers at Penn, which are fully dependent on external resources, the CCP, since its inception, has been institutionalized within the University's formal administrative structure, and its director and administrative staff are funded by College Hall. The Netter Center's permanence is properly attributed to its fidelity to the University's academic mission; in fact, its hallmark is academically based community service courses offered by the University's professoriate in several different schools and departments.

The academic centering of ABCS courses distinguishes them from conventional service-learning, which typically detaches the service component from academic study. Approximately 150 ABCS courses and seminars have been developed de novo, or have involved the redesign of existing courses, in education, social work, history, English, mathematics, engineering, fine arts (landscape architecture, city and regional planning), urban studies, business, communications, medicine, anthropology, sociology, linguistics, classics, environmental studies, and biology. A WEPIC national replication project at other universities evolved through several iterations with foundation support. The Center has developed a substantial body of theoretical and empirically grounded literature to advance its agenda on a national stage.[13] Research is also a component of CCP work, though the oft-stated goal of "communal participatory action research"[14] has been slower to develop than the ABCS component. CCP-sponsored or affiliated work at ten schools has included curricular and cocurricular programs that bring disciplinary perspectives to schoolchildren's studies in nutrition and disease detection/prevention, urban environmental issues (lead toxicity, brownfields, submerged urban floodplains, urban gardening and landscaping, for example), social-base mapping, vest-pocket park design, transit-oriented development, and African American culture and history in West Philadelphia.

Research projects at the sites have developed programmatic components that contribute directly to teaching and learning. For example, a study of reading difficulties among African American children at the Wilson Elementary School, directed by William Labov, a world-renowned professor of linguistics, led to the development of a reading improvement program that was tested at this and other WEPIC sites—and in the Oakland, California, schools as well.[15] The Urban Nutrition Initiative, headed by Francis Johnston, one of the world's foremost physical anthropologists, translated research findings from nutrition studies of West Philadelphia schoolchildren into curricular materials for use at several West Philadelphia schools.[16] And a study of the Mill Creek submerged floodplain in West Philadelphia, directed by Ann Spirn, a leading historian of urban landscape design, resulted in the development of imaginative curricular activities at the Sulzberger Middle School related to the beautification and potential uses of abandoned property in the floodplain.[17] Healthcare-pipeline programs from local high schools to the Penn Health System and the Penn-assisted Community Health Promotion and Disease Prevention Program at West Philadelphia's Sayre High School, which involves faculty and students in the medical, dental, and nursing schools, as well as social work and departments in the School of Arts and Sciences, represent a One University approach.[18]

■ The West Philadelphia Partnership

A reconstituted West Philadelphia Corporation (WPC), renamed the West Philadelphia Partnership in 1983, played a key support role in the growth of the CCP, providing an office for the WEPIC component, as well as the imprimatur of University City's community associations and African American leaders in a wider swath of neighborhoods in West Philadelphia. Changes Hackney introduced as chairman of the WPC marked a critical turning point in Penn's community relations after two decades of mutual distrust.

For a quarter of a century, the WPC represented the interests of the universities and hospitals in University City. As noted previously, the Corporation was established in 1959 as a de facto operation of the University of Pennsylvania, with Penn positioned as the dominant shareholder and senior partner. Leo Molinaro, the first executive director of the WPC, was Gaylord Harnwell's agent in University City. Drexel and the other institutions were willing to stand in Penn's shadow, as they stood to benefit from the University's leveraging of resources to improve University City. While the neighborhood associations were kept abreast of developments and allowed input at WPC board meetings, they had no vote. The most substantial development was the University City Science Center, the much ballyhooed Market Street project that arose in the bulldozed landscape of Unit 3. It was, and fifty years later remains, controversial. For the displaced black residents of Unit 3, the removals became a rallying cry and symbol of the University's callous disregard of poor and working-class African Americans in West Philadelphia. Even today the mistrust lingers, as old-timers see Penn-sponsored gentrification encroaching as far west as 52nd Street, even as the University moves its campus development eastward to fill in unoccupied land between 32nd and 36th streets and the Schuylkill River.

Under Hackney, the West Philadelphia Corporation took a first step toward redressing the long-standing public relations disaster wrought by Unit 3 displacements and demolitions. He learned about the West Philadelphia Corporation when he was appointed, pro forma, the chairman of the organization. Anthony Marks, one of Hackney's assistants (later a president of Amherst College and chief executive officer of the New York City Public Library) who became the president's eyes and ears in the surrounding neighborhoods, helped him reorganize the WPC. "It quickly became apparent to me that this was not organized right," Hackney recalled. "This was an organization that allowed [the major institutions] to coordinate their activities in West Philadelphia . . . but there were no West Philadelphia people in it. So we reorganized it. I did the talking to the other institutions in getting it together. . . . This is something I'm actually pleased about and proud of: we got everybody together and changed the name of the organization to the West Philadelphia Partnership."

A revision of WPC bylaws in March 1983 gave an equal vote on the board of directors to the neighborhood associations: Mantua Community Planners,

Powelton Village Civic Association, Spruce Hill Community Association, Walnut Hill Association, Garden Court Civic Association, and Cedar Park Neighbors. And civic and business leaders were given the opportunity to participate in ways that had real clout.[19] African American leadership became increasingly prominent in the Partnership, beginning with the appointment of George Brown as executive director in 1985. Hackney would later hail the Partnership as "a true tripartite organization that is composed of the major institutions in University City, the organized neighborhoods of West Philadelphia, and civic spirited individuals who are active in West Philadelphia."[20]

As a show of good faith to the Partnership, Hackney instituted a "Buy West Philadelphia" policy. Whereas before 1985, Penn's contracts with West Philadelphia vendors "amounted only to a couple of hundred thousand dollars," by FY 1990 the total was $5 million. By FY 1993, the total was $10 million, of which $2.7 million was directed to black-owned businesses.[21] Hackney's major local impact, however, was on public education. Under Partnership auspices, Penn implemented numerous public school improvement initiatives. Starting in the fall of 1987, for example, the Graduate School of Education, under Dean Marvin Lazerson, sponsored Say Yes to Education, a program funded by wealthy Penn donors George and Diane Weiss, who pledged full college scholarships to 112 sixth graders at the Belmont Elementary School, with the proviso that they graduate from high school and gain admission to a college or university; the GSE and the Weiss family provided sustained guidance and mentoring to keep the youngsters in school and on track to college. The Wharton School's West Philadelphia Project included, among other programs, Young Entrepreneurs at Wharton, which helped local high school entrepreneurs to start their own businesses. The most widespread, long-standing, and impactful program in Penn's outreach portfolio was the aforementioned WEPIC, the Penn–West Philadelphia coalition that grew out of Ira Harkavy and Lee Benson's undergraduate seminar in 1985 and evolved into the Netter Center for Community Partnerships.[22]

■ Sansom Street Dénouement

Among the community problems Hackney inherited from his predecessors was the Sansom Street imbroglio. As previously noted, it was a battle waged by the Sansom Street Committee over the University's plans for Unit 4 commercial redevelopment in the block from Walnut to Sansom Street between 34th Street and the imaginary line of 35th Street. In 1966, the RDA, with authorization from the Department of Housing and Urban Development, had condemned the 3401 Walnut Street properties for graduate classrooms. But in the spring of 1971, the University signed a "nominee agreement" with the firm of Fox and Posel to develop the area not for institutional use but for a commercial high-rise. Now the University's plan, which was once again authorized by HUD, was to "buy the parcel of land from the Redevelopment Authority and lease the land to the private developers, at a rate sufficient to amortize the University's investment in the area. The lease to the private developers [would] be for a term of 50 years with two 20-year renewal options. The private developers [would] plan and construct, subject to the University's approval, such University-related facilities as commercial stores, office space, and research, apartment, hotel, and parking facilities all of which were recommended by studies conducted in 1963 by the Baltimore based firm of Hammer and Company Associates and became the basis of the approved urban renewal plan."[23] It appears that the new plan initially called for the demolition of the Sansom Street houses and construction of an eleven-story complex of retail enterprises and offices that would wrap around the 34th Street corners of Walnut and Sansom streets. In the late fall of 1971, the plan was revised to renovate the houses for "commercial use": "The character of Sansom Street will be much the same as at present, though the houses will be remodeled into a variety of shops and restaurants. An arcade will be created on Moravian Street [a cul-de-sac between Walnut and Sansom], with a transparent roof on a space frame." There was no mention of any residential use of the houses or their historic character.[24] In June 1973, the Sansom Committee filed a suit in federal district court against the RDA and HUD for having authorized a diversion of the 1966 plan without an environmental impact study or a City Council hearing. (HUD subsequently agreed to do the study.) "We don't object to the university tearing down buildings for academic facilities," Elliot Cook of the Sansom Committee said. "We do object to the university destroying the neighborhood to turn it over to a private developer to build a non-university commercial high-rise."[25]

Whereas the Sansom Street Committee insisted that the deteriorating Walnut houses could be effectively conserved, Martin Meyerson, ever the city planner, scoffed at the idea and told HUD that they were "slum buildings . . . dangerous to their few occupants and to others as well," and lacking "any architectural, aesthetic, historical or other significant value which would make them worth rehabilitating." In July 1974, a federal district judge, Clarence C. Newcomer, ruled that the demolition of the 3401 Walnut properties could proceed, as "it would pose an unjustified threat to the public welfare if the hazards

GARY PALMA

RESIDENTS AND MERCHANTS of the 3400 block of Sansom Street have threatened to sue the University if it does not meet certain redevelopment stipulations. Planning officials are now negotiating with developers for the construction of an office building on the corner of 34th and Walnut.

The *Daily Pennsylvanian* reported faithfully on the decades-long struggle to save the Sansom Street houses from Penn's redevelopment schemes. Photo dated 17 November 1971. Collections of the University Archives and Records Center.

created by these properties were allowed to continue until the impact statement was prepared and its sufficiency litigated, a process that might take years."[26]

Soon after Newcomer's decision, a bulldozer appeared on narrow Moravian Street behind the condemned Walnut Street buildings. "I heard this rumble coming up the back alley," Judy Wicks, a former Samson Committee member, recalls. "It was a bulldozer, and [it] was systematically ramming into the backs of each of the houses on Walnut Street. And I figured out later what he was trying to do was to just irreparably damage [the houses] before we could do anything." While Wicks "lay down in front of the bulldozer," Elliot Cook called the Sansom Committee's lawyer to get a restraining order from the Emergency Court of Appeals for the Third Circuit. "We got the restraining order," Wicks says. "And we kept them from tearing down the houses for I don't know how many more months."[27] But the restraining order was only a temporary stoppage.

HUD dithered for a few weeks, first ordering RDA not to demolish the buildings, then, under pressure from Meyerson, rescinding its order to halt the demolition: "There is no barrier to their demolition and the Redevelopment Authority of Philadelphia may proceed without any further delay," a HUD official told Meyerson.[28] The evictions and demolitions proceeded in August 1974. The building that housed Cy's Penn Luncheonette (the Dirty Drug) was the first Walnut structure to fall. Anticipating his eviction notice, Cy Braverman had left 3401 Walnut temporarily and then returned to open Cy's Place in the middle of the block, assured by Elliot Cook that the Sansom Committee would win its legal battle against Penn and the RDA.

Potter Hall, a University-owned building that stood next to the townhouses on the southwest corner of Sansom and 34th streets, was flattened at the same time as the Dirty Drug—the Sansom Committee, which tried to save Potter Hall, put up a sign in the new parking lot on the site, "Martin Meyerson Memorial Parking Lot." (Wicks claims that John Hetherston, Meyerson's vice president for operational services, kept a brick from the Potter Hall demolition on his desk, vowing to collect a brick from every building the RDA flattened.)[29] Wrecking crews leveled the remaining Walnut Street buildings, beginning on September 17. Cook lamented, "I felt as though I had let Cy and the others down. I talked them into staying and then we lost."[30]

By the end of 1974, Meyerson stood firmly behind plans to wrap the corner of 3401 Walnut with a large L-shaped building no taller than the Franklin Building that he vowed would be for mixed commercial and office use. Regarding the Sansom Committee's grievance, Meyerson acknowledged the value of the old brownstones: "Recognizing the shortage of restaurants, small book shops, and other ancillary services to provide the required amenities for the University's residential population, the plans call for the retention of Sansom Street, the bringing of those buildings up to code standards for the continuance of small restaurants, boutiques, and other enterprises on the lower levels and the development of flats on the upper levels."[31] He refused, however, to consider a full-block rehabilitation, which would have conserved the brick row houses on Walnut as well as the Sansom brownstones. In 1977, the City Planning

(Top) Red-brick houses with commercial facades, 3401 block of Walnut Street, before RDA Unit 4 demolition. Collections of the University Archives and Records Center.

(Bottom) Contemporary view of the Shops at Penn, 3401 block of Walnut Street. Photograph by Michael M. Koehler. Collections of the University Archives and Records Center.

Commission approved a developer's proposal for the project when the University promised to build a parking garage on 34th Street above Chestnut.[32]

The Walnut Street demolitions, which Elliot Cook called a "nightmare," left a grassed-over lot that stood empty for a decade.[33] Judy Wicks had two small children whose playground in the early 1980s was the Walnut vacant lot. Following the demolitions, the Penn-Sansom Committee dispute flared in and out of court—it was a bitter and protracted struggle. In January 1981, the two parties grudgingly signed a consent decree. Wicks recalls that "Newcomer decided to cut the baby in half," giving Walnut Street to Penn and Sansom Street to the Sansom Committee. Jane Jacobs, author of *The Death and Life of Great American Cities*, was the Sansom Committee's mentor, says Wicks. "She really believed in living above the shop and the ballet of the city sidewalk . . . which [was] certainly the case on [Sansom Street], with all the characters that lived here." Wicks and her associates had two plans, both of which envisioned Walnut and Sansom as residences on the second and third floors, with restaurants and shops on the first floors. One plan had the commercial operations fronting Moravian, which would be an interior corridor for retail and restaurant activity, and had the residences facing Walnut and Sansom. The other plan located the commercial toward the thoroughfares and the residential toward Moravian. Walnut Street was integral to both plans. "It was the *whole* block that we looked at," says Wicks. "So we were really upset when Newcomer decided to give Penn Walnut Street because we didn't feel that one block was enough to make a difference on the campus. And we wanted to have a Georgetown feel or a Cambridge feel. And if we were just left with half of a block, we wouldn't be able to have the impact that we were looking [for] in terms of really transforming the feeling of the Penn campus. So that was a huge blow."[34]

The consent decree of 1981 established that the designated redeveloper of both parcels at issue—Parcel IA (3401 Walnut); Parcel IB (3400 Sansom)—would be the University of Pennsylvania. According to the consent decree, "the Sansom Committee or its designees as *nominees of the University* shall purchase and rehabilitate [Parcel IB]."[35] In a 1982 consent decree, the University acceded to a "sunlight clause" that prohibited the envelope of Parcel IA redevelopment from blocking winter sunlight into "greenhouse style dining rooms" on the southern side of Sansom Street on the shortest day of the year—more concretely the clause restricted the height of the proposed Walnut Street complex to five stories.[36] Two years later, the Sansom Committee refused to budge when offered $100,000 to allow the University to raise the height of the building.[37] In the spring of 1984, worried that Sansom Street might become "a street-long strip of bars that will adversely affect the University

Contemporary view west on the 3400 block of Sansom Street. These elegant Victorian brownstones compose a thriving restaurant venue. Photograph by Michael M. Koehler. Collections of the University Archives and Records Center.

community,"[38] overzealous Penn administrators moved to block a liquor license for Wicks's new White Dog Café. That summer, Wicks, who was a board member of the West Philadelphia Partnership and chair of the Economic Development Committee, exposed the absurdity of such reasoning. She told the Partnership:

For the past fourteen years, our community organization, the Sansom Committee, has worked to purchase, restore and develop the 3400 block of Sansom and Walnut streets, providing needed quality businesses on the first floors of owner occupied housing. It is our goal to establish an exciting commercial center for the campus with the atmosphere and vitality of a Harvard Square. Sansom Committee members are currently in the process of buying and renovating the Sansom Street houses. LaTerrasse will be expanding into a fourth house; LeBus has developed the house on the other end of the block as a gourmet cafeteria; the White Dog Café occupies two houses in the center; and other members of the group are planning a newspaper shop (carrying papers from around the world), a handcrafted jewelry store, an Irish restaurant, a quality clothes store, and more. The development of Sansom Street properties is strictly controlled to insure quality commercial development and proper renovation of the historically significant buildings. The completion of our project will result in a lovely row of Victorian brownstone houses, providing quality services to the University community.[39]

When some Sansom Street designees withdrew their proposals in 1983, the University filed a motion in Judge Newcomer's court on "the question of whether the Sansom Committee may designate new parties to replace any of the parties . . . who decided to withdraw from development." The University claimed the right to purchase those properties under the terms of the 1982 consent decree. Newcomer ruled against the University, stating that the consent decree did not limit "the power of the Sansom Committee to designate designees." In the fall of 1984, the University's appeal reached the U.S. Supreme Court, which refused to hear the case, letting stand the 3rd Circuit Court of Appeals denial of the University's appeal.[40] In an agreement signed 28 November 1984, the University finally agreed to the liquor licenses, and both parties reaffirmed the terms of the 1982 consent decree.[41]

For all the aggravation she experienced with the Office of Operational Services, Wicks found a sympathetic ear in Sheldon Hackney, who inherited what he described wearily as an altercation "so prolonged and confused."[42] "First of all, he moved onto the block," Wicks recounts. "He lived here while they were fixing up the presidential mansion. So he and Lucy and their old black lab . . . lived in [G. Holmes] Perkins's house [at 3414 Sansom]. And they loved it here. So I think he was trying to figure out what [was] going on, and he was very diplomatic, I mean he didn't want to come in and step on toes or whatever. I think he was just trying to figure out what

(Top) Cy's Penn Luncheonette ("Dirty Drug"), 3401 Walnut Street, 1971. Collections of the University Archives and Records Center.

(Bottom) Contemporary view of the northwest corner of 34th and Walnut streets. Starbucks Coffee marks the former site of Cy's Penn Luncheonette. Photograph by Michael M. Koehler. Collections of the University Archives and Records Center.

was happening. Overall, he was a good guy."[43] The battle-scarred Wicks wanted to "wrap this up" with Hackney. "I do believe in your personal good intentions," she told him. "I admire the attention you are giving to public education and economic development and the encouragement you have given the entire University to become more involved in the real issues of the community. . . . You and I seem to share many values. We should be able to work out an agreement which protects our mutual concerns, and which can show that an institution and a community can work together for the best interests of all."[44]

After the mid-1980s, as Wicks predicted, the block thrived as a mixed commercial-residential venue. Years after the Dirty Drug's removal, Cy Braverman joined his son David at LeBus, the bistro/bakery that the younger Braverman had opened in 1984 in a Sansom brownstone. True to the pioneering spirit of the Sansom block, David Braverman launched LeBus in the winter of 1977–78 in a converted school bus that he parked across the street from the brownstones. By the mid-1980s, the block claimed four restaurants that far surpassed the likes of the erstwhile Pagano's and Grand's on Walnut: LeBus, La Terrasse (originally named the Moravian), New Deck Tavern, and Wicks's White Dog Café, the jewel in the crown, a restaurant that became nationally famous in the 1990s. The café's moniker honored the block's colorful history: "The White Dog got its name from a 19th-century mystic and founder of the Theosophical Society named Madame Helena Blavatsky, who once resided in the Sansom Street building and claimed to have been cured of a serious illness by having a white dog lie on her." Wicks later opened the Black Cat Boutique in an adjoining brownstone, with a passageway connecting the two businesses. After Wicks opened the White Dog, Cook left Philadelphia and La Terrasse closed in 1986. LaTerrasse reopened at the same site under new ownership in 1997.[45] In the winter of 1988, more than twenty years after the RDA's condemnation of the block, Penn opened the $21 million, five-story, L-shaped retail mall and office complex on Walnut Street, called the Shoppes at Penn, "an ugly monstrosity" replete with ground-floor fast-food chains such as Philly Steak & Gyro, Cosimo's Pizza, Bain's Deli, Bassett's Original Turkey, and Everything Yogurt. (At this writing, Starbucks Coffee occupies the corner spot that was once the Dirty Drug; Dunkin' Donuts is a few doors up the street.) "There almost couldn't be a worse-looking building than the one they built back here. I mean, it's just horrible," laments Wicks, who argues that the brick houses on Walnut were salvageable. "They were actually much nicer than these [Sansom Street] houses. These were kind of the working class houses. They were grander houses. They had parquet floors and marble bathrooms. I mean, they needed a lot of work—granted—a tremendous amount of work to restore those houses. There were all these tacky facades put on the front, really horrible, sloppy stuff. . . . But that would have been the first choice . . . to restore those grand houses that were facing Walnut."[46]

■ Keeping Franklin's Promise: Other Contributions of the Hackney Era

Though Hackney was not a transformative president, he wrought incremental changes that moved the University "in directions that would be . . . both economically and intellectually profitable for Penn."[47] "Sheldon did a good, solid job as president," says Paul Miller, who was the trustee chairman for five years of Hackney's term and served on the board until 1996. "His strongest suit was his ability to choose very good people as managers under him. He was never shy about being upstaged and even seemed to encourage it and was always ready to give others full credit rather than claiming it for himself. There were certainly times when I wished he would be more forceful and more of an A-type personality, but I believe he was right for the time."[48]

One reason—perhaps the key factor—the Penn trustees hired Hackney was his proven ability as a fund-raiser. Keeping Franklin's Promise, an "over-the-top" capital campaign from 1989 through 1994, which raised $1.4 billion, an astounding sum at the time, is properly credited to Hackney's adroit social networking and affable persuasiveness as a fund-raiser. The primary beneficiary of this largess was the School of Arts and Sciences. Recalling Gaylord Harnwell's orchestration of the Educational Survey of 1954–59, Hackney summoned five-year strategic plans from each school—a process that provided the rationale and impetus for the capital campaign. His administration produced an ambitious campus master plan in 1988, which forecast many of Judith Rodin's campus initiatives in the flush economic years of the Clinton administration. Hackney instituted measures for strengthening undergraduate education, raising scholarship funds, sponsoring the standing faculty's development and teaching of undergraduate seminars, and establishing the Provost's Council on Undergraduate Education as a central planning unit. On Hackney's watch the University quadrupled its endowment, which stood at roughly $1.73 billion when he left office.[49] And his administration oversaw the introduction of the digital revolution at Penn, the upshot of which was PennNET, the University's first campus-wide network of personal computers, and an enormous proliferation of computerized library, research, and data-management services, visible "in all corners of the campus, all complemented by an ever-growing network of technical support for schools and departments.[50]

Establishment of the Medical Center

Of no mean consequence, Hackney consolidated the formerly separate operations of the University Hospital, Medical School, and Clinical Practices into a single administrative unit called the Medical Center, headed by an executive vice president, a "CEO-type." Hackney's appointment of William Kelley of the University of Michigan as both dean of the Medical School and executive vice president of the Medical Center in 1989 marked a turning point that lifted Penn into the top tier of the world's leading medical research institutions. Although Kelley, a notoriously undiplomatic mover and shaker, would preside over huge financial losses in the Health System (which comprised the Medical Center, three additional hospitals, and Clinical Associates) after the mid-1990s and be fired by Judith Rodin, his accomplishments were formidable. As John Kastor attests in his account of this period:

> The University of Pennsylvania appointed Dr. William N. Kelley dean of its school of medicine and leader of its medical center on August 2, 1989, and discharged him from these responsibilities on February 16, 2000. During the intervening ten and a half years, the Kelley administration formed a health system; bought three hospitals and the practices of 270 primary care physicians; constructed two medical school research buildings and one new hospital building; equipped several suburban practice facilities; renovated one million square feet of space in the medical school and the principal teaching hospital; appointed new chairs for each basic science department (one twice) and all but three of the clinical departments (one twice); created twelve institutes and centers; revised the curriculum for medical students; and helped recruit so many productive investigators that the research conducted by the medical faculty won a level of support from the National Institutes of Health (NIH) surpassed only by the medical enterprises at Harvard and Johns Hopkins universities.[51]

Hackney-Era Buildings

The University constructed nine new buildings on Hackney's watch: the Wharton School's Steinberg/Aresty Conference Center, at 38th and Spruce Street, replacing a parking lot (formerly the Victoria Apartments) on that site; Lauder-Fisher Hall, also of the Wharton School, at 37th and Locust streets; the Founders Pavilion of HUP in the Medical Education Quadrangle on

Hamilton Walk; the Clinical Research Building—Penn's first building in the new Philadelphia Center for Health Sciences, on the former grounds of the Philadelphia General Hospital at Curie Boulevard and Osler Circle; the Stellar-Chance Laboratories on Curie Boulevard, also in the Health Sciences Center; the Mudd Biological Research Laboratory on 38th Street below Hamilton Walk; Tannenbaum Hall, a new wing of the Law School and home of the Biddle Library, on the 3401 block of Sansom Street; and the Institute of Contemporary Art on the northwest corner of 36th and Sansom. The entrances to the three new Wharton buildings faced the newly landscaped park of the Shearson Lehman Hutton Quadrangle, in the former roadbed of Irving Street.[52] Under Hackney, Penn's design review committee oversaw the early stages of the restoration of College Hall and the exterior refurbishment of Logan Hall (both completed under Judith Rodin in 1996 and 1997, respectively); the renovation of the Quadrangle dormitories; and the centenary restoration of the historic, Furness-designed Fine Arts Library to its Victorian elegance.[53]

In 1989, Penn purchased a thirteen-story Beaux-Arts building on 44th Street in New York City between Fifth and Sixth avenues for the Penn Club. Located on the same block as four other Ivy League clubhouses, Penn's social club, after a major building renovation, opened to alumni, faculty, staff, and students in 1994.[54] Six other major projects were in various stages of development when Hackney left College Hall, all of them completed under Judith Rodin: the Institute for Advanced Science and Technology on 34th Street in the physical sciences precinct; the Rhoads Pavilion of HUP; a biomedical research facility in the Philadelphia Center for Health Sciences; a new clinical and research building for the School of Dental Medicine; and a six-hundred-car parking garage and air conditioning facility at the corner of 38th and Walnut streets.

Advancing Research and Teaching

From the standpoint of federally sponsored research and research productivity, Hackney bequeathed to Judith Rodin a strong, first-rate institution. For the 1980–90 decade, the University ranked seventh in total federal R & D funding for Research 1 private institutions and eleventh for Research 1 public and private institutions; in 1986, Penn's social sciences departments ranked sixth overall in federal R & D support in that category; in 1990 the medical school ranked tenth overall in NIH research awards; for the period 1986–88, Penn ranked seventh among Research 1 private institutions in per-capita publications and ninth among Research 1 public and private institutions in that category.[55]

In 1989, *U.S. News & World Report* introduced a multi-indicator, quantitative procedure for ranking the quality of undergraduate colleges in different categories of institutions (national universities, regional universities, liberal arts colleges). Before 1983, when *U.S. News* asked college and university presidents to rank the undergraduate colleges, reputational surveys had focused exclusively on the quality of the nation's graduate schools. These rankings remained remarkably stable across a period of eighty years. As Clark Kerr put it, "A reputation once attained usually keeps on drawing faculty members and resources that sustain that reputation. A reputation, once established, is an institution's single greatest asset." Penn was no exception: ranked eleventh among the nation's research universities in 1906, it stood at fourteenth in 1982, with an average rank of thirteen for the eighty-year period.[56] Yet being perennially listed below the likes of Harvard, Yale, Princeton, and Columbia, says Robert Zemsky, gave the University an image problem—"an internal sense of not being quite as good as its competition." Despite Penn's considerable strengths, this inferiority complex would not be fully purged until Rodin's presidency. Rodin would make *U.S. News* "the president's business" and charge her deans to achieve a "top-ten ranking" for each school, with "spectacular results," according to Zemsky.[57]

As Zemsky notes, "15th is about where Penn consistently placed in the *U.S. News* rankings prior to Rodin." This is not a criticism of Hackney; *U.S. News* does not measure "good teaching, engaged faculty, and industrious students," [58] substantive qualities of particular concern to Hackney, who assigned a high priority to strengthening undergraduate education. He called for, among other improvements, greater involvement of students in faculty research, more teaching of undergraduate courses by standing faculty, and a stronger interface between the College (Arts and Sciences) and the three undergraduate professional programs (Wharton, Engineering, and Nursing). In *Six Working Papers for Strategic Planning* (January 1982), the Academic Planning and Budget Committee pledged fealty to One University, even as they acknowledged the continuing barrier of responsibility center management: "We reaffirm that concept with enthusiasm. The current budgeting system, however, may encourage some schools and departments to build fences around their resources and to dissuade their students from taking courses elsewhere."[59]

In *Choosing Penn's Future* (January 1983), Hackney reaffirmed his administration's commitment to undergraduate education, now listing it as one of the University's top three priorities, calling for an increased number of standing faculty teaching undergraduates, as opposed to fobbing that responsibility onto graduate students. He cited four undergraduate majors—the design of the environment, urban studies, management and technology, and the biological basis of behavior—as models for programs involving "mixed faculties," and he called for the expansion of such programs. Hackney asserted "research excellence" and "student aid and financial assistance" as the University's other strategic planning priorities. Writing against the backdrop of the economic recession of the early 1980s ("an adverse economic situation," he called it) and the fiscal conservatism of the Reagan administration, he worried about "the threatened shifts in federal policy—particularly with respect to research support and student aid—that, together with the precarious budgetary situation of the Commonwealth, presage unequal levels of government support."[60] When he presented the plan to the trustees, Hackney adjured them, "Even though the times are stringent and we are facing challenges, we can still be masters of our fate if we take action deliberately and thoughtfully and very forcefully."[61]

Hackney announced the formation of a new Faculty Council for Undergraduate Education, which he charged to "recommend a set of curricular options and instructional mechanisms for University undergraduates that draw on the strengths, experiences, and academic perspective of faculty from the liberal arts and the professions."[62] Over the next several years, this faculty council, which issued periodic recommendations, evolved into "a number of cross-School committees" that were coordinated by a new Provost's Council on Undergraduate Education, in conjunction with the Council of Undergraduate Deans and curriculum committees of the four undergraduate schools.[63] In 1986, a $10 million Undergraduate Education Fund was established to fund, among other initiatives, faculty development of freshmen seminars, Writing Across the University (a cross-school program sponsored by the English Department), an enhanced General Honors program, and undergraduate research. By 1987, each undergraduate school had concluded a five-year planning process that included "major commitments to undergraduate education in the years ahead."[64]

In the summer of 1981, Hackney and his provost, Thomas Ehrlich, mandated the aforementioned five-year plans from each school. Not since the Educational Survey of 1954–59 had University-wide five-year plans been required of the deans. The first drafts were completed in April 1984. Though Hackney and Ehrlich acknowledged that these drafts were "developmental prospectuses," they were concerned that some of the plans were quixotic—a number of the schools proposed to increase the size of the faculty even when the budgetary and enrollment projections failed to justify these expenditures. "If a choice must be made between maintaining academic quality and reducing scale, the former is our first priority," said Ehrlich. "In short, we must at all costs ensure adequate resources for the faculty we have, in terms of compensation, research assistance, and other support."[65] Put differently, "selective excellence" would be applied to schools and departments that had shortfalls in their five-year balance sheets. The revised five-year plans were published in May 1985.[66]

Breakthrough Capital Campaign

Nearly two years later, Hackney and Ehrlich reported to faculty and administrators that they were planning a "breakthrough campaign," the basis of which were the academic needs fleshed out in the schools' five-year plans. The "first priority" of the capital campaign would be to strengthen the quality of the faculty through endowed chairs (a minimum of one hundred) for retention and recruitment of distinguished faculty, with special attention to Arts and Sciences, "currently the School with the greatest need for sustained external investment."[67] Hackney acknowledges that when he put a price tag of $1 billion on the campaign at the October 1987 meeting of the trustees, they were "visibly nervous"; they told him, in effect, "If you announce this campaign goal and it fails, it's going to have a depressing effect on the psychology of the University and it will be a terrible thing." In any event, the trustees agreed to the amount Hackney wanted and undertook a "quiet campaign" to raise $250 million over the next two years—the amount they agreed would be necessary to make it likely that, when the five-year campaign was announced publicly, it would have a good chance of succeeding (the rule of thumb in capital campaigns is to raise one-quarter to one-third of the goal before the public phase starts). Spurred by a $25 million contribution from the publishing mogul and former ambassador to Great Britain Walter Annenberg and his wife, Lee, the quiet campaign raised $344 million.[68] In October 1989, the trustees announced the Campaign for Penn: Keeping Franklin's Promise. The campaign started as a $1 billion development drive and concluded in December 1994 with $1.47 billion added to Penn's coffers—for a brief period the largest amount ever raised by an American university in a five-year campaign. The capstone donation was $120 million from the Annenbergs to endow the Annenberg School and to establish the Annenberg Public Policy Center, to be directed by the Annenberg School's dean, Kathleen Hall Jamison.[69]

"With nearly half the total earmarked for the Arts and Sciences," reported the *Almanac*, "the drive is described as a people-and-programs campaign with only six building projects in view and with 150 endowed professors targeted."[70] Student financial aid, a casualty of the first Reagan administration, was a campaign priority. In the wake of federal cuts in the early 1980s, college and university outlays nationally for student aid rose from $904 million to $3 billion. Between 1979–80 and 1984–85, federal Pell Grants, which did not require repayment by grantees, were cut by 41.6 percent in constant dollars.[71] Responding to Hackney's call for bolstered student support, the campaign raised

$50 million for undergraduate scholarships and another $96 million for PhD fellowships and other graduate and professional support—a total of $149 million. And the campaign raised another $35 million to support Penn's minority presence (fellowships, professorships, recruitment/retention of faculty and students), "the most ever raised by any institution for this purpose."[72]

New Campus Master Plan

The Hackney presidency bequeathed to Judith Rodin the largest of the capital campaign and the vision of the 1988 Campus Master Plan, which was developed by the Center for Environmental Design and Planning of the Graduate School of Fine Arts. The Master Plan provided a bold conceptual framework that Rodin's presidency, taking advantage of a surging stock market and open-pocket donors, brought to practical fruition. The Master Plan, for example, underscored the centrality of Walnut Street to Penn's future: "As Locust Walk was the thematic element of the master plans of the 1960s, the central theme of the Campus Master Plan for the next 25 years will be the development of the Walnut Street corridor. . . . As the prime westbound connection between the city and the Campus, it is undeniably a part of the campus of the 1990s and beyond." The Master Plan called for reorienting campus buildings along Walnut and Spruce toward the street in community- and pedestrian-friendly ways and for improvements "in the character and quality of these streets as important public spaces." Significantly for the future expansion of the campus, the Master Plan envisioned that the University would purchase the 19.2-acre Civic Center properties, opposite HUP on Convention Boulevard, for expanding the Health System—as the city was building a new Convention Center in Center City, the old Civic Center had become a white elephant. Other major sites the Graduate School of Fine Arts planners earmarked for purchase and redevelopment were the huge U.S. Post Office on Market Street opposite 30th Street Station, and the Postal Lands in the Schuylkill River flats between Walnut Street and Penn's River Fields. The Postal Lands were an empty wasteland south of Walnut that was used for post office parking and maintenance. Here the planners envisaged "a major gateway to University City and the University," a mecca for "new housing, parking, recreation, retail, and research facilities."[73]

These proposals and others, such as "a strong reaffirmation of the Woodland Diagonal" on Hill Field, which was a well-traveled footpath by the 1980s, and completion of the 1977 landscape development plan on 38th Street between Walnut and Spruce, were implemented in spectacular fashion by Rodin and her executive vice president, John Fry. Rodin and Fry put their particular stamp on these projects, incorporating in lively ways the red-brick palette of several nineteenth-century campus buildings in the redevelopment of the 3601–3801 (north side) blocks of Walnut Street—blocks on the edge of the academic core of the campus—and opting for bold retro-futuristic designs for new commercial buildings in the 3901, 4000, and 4001 blocks of Walnut— blocks on the periphery of the Superblock residence hall complex. It does not detract from Hackney's contributions to say that implementation of the elements of the 1988 Master Plan required a president of a less modest demeanor than his—indeed, a president of Judith Rodin's vaulting ambition, hubristic temperament, and damn-the-torpedoes fortitude, a charismatic president who was able to galvanize the trustees behind her goal of kicking Penn into the very top tier of the nation's research universities.

■ Valedictory: Toward Campus Reconciliation

Hackney's resignation from Penn, effective 30 June 1993, left three critical issues to be resolved by his interim successor, Claire Fagin, the former dean of Penn's School of Nursing. The first thorny issue was how to resolve the case of black students' removal of fourteen thousand copies of the *Daily Pennsylvanian* as a protest action. The second issue was how to change Penn's student judicial code to soften its adversarial orientation. The third issue, an even larger problem of the campus ethos, was how to strengthen the campus community to prevent such incidents as Water Buffalo. Prior to leaving College Hall, Hackney appointed a Panel to Reform Judicial Procedures and a Commission on Strengthening the Community, the latter to be chaired by Penn African American trustee Gloria Twine Chisum.[74]

Fagin's most pressing concern on her arrival at College Hall was the *DP* theft case, which the vice provost for university life referred to social work professor Harold Arnold, a special judicial inquiry officer appointed to investigate the complaint filed against nine of about sixty students involved in the newspaper seizures. Acknowledging that the accused students, members of the Black Student League, had violated University policy by removing the papers from the distribution sites, Arnold reported that he saw "no need for further judicial or disciplinary action"—he declared the matter "resolved," ostensibly because the protestors were probably unaware of the University's confiscation policy. Arnold himself stood squarely with the students, viewing their behavior as an opportunity for education on the harmful effects of institutional racism. Accepting Arnold's recommendation, Fagin and interim provost Marvin Lazerson declared that "the confiscation of any publication on campus is wrong and will not be tolerated," that henceforth "individuals who engage in such actions will be subject to the full range of judicial sanctions." As the confiscation policy would appear in new editions of the student handbook, "there can be no further doubt or confusion as to the policy's significance or the seriousness with which the University will respond to its violation." Issuing "a rare dissent," the trustees reproached Fagin and Lazerson for a decision they considered pusillanimous.[75] Perhaps, but it was also a fair and prudent decision, removing any doubt that a real or imagined racial or ethnic insult would be treated by the University as an allowable justification for newspaper theft. And it had the effect of quelling racial tensions that were still roiling in the aftermath of the Water Buffalo spring.

The Commission on Strengthening the Community began its work in September 1993 and issued its final report on 5 April 1994. Its recommendations included, among many others, disestablishing the student racial speech code. Henceforth the content of student speech would not be subject to disciplinary action, although this protection would not apply to threats of physical harm, bomb threats, and the like. Commission members argued that offensive speech should be considered a subject for education, not a cause for discipline. They called for the University faculty to articulate "clear norms of civility, honesty, academic integrity, and responsibility for being an effective member of the community . . . to students during orientation, and regularly and consistently thereafter." They called on the president and provost to strengthen community service programs "both inside and outside the established curriculum." They advocated implementation of "the University of Pennsylvania version of a College House system as soon as possible," expanding the existing program to create "virtual colleges" that included every undergraduate dormitory. And they gave a ringing endorsement to "The Report of the Committee to Diversify Locust Walk."[76] Within the following month, Fagin abolished the student speech code, echoing the Commission's recommendation: "student speech, as such, should not be the basis of disciplinary action."[77]

Following her first semester as Penn's new president, Judith Rodin, in January 1995, reaffirmed in writing that the speech code was a dead letter:

> Hearing the hateful is the only way to identify and educate the hater. Seeing the offensive is a necessary step to understanding and rejecting the perspective from which it comes. Seriously considering even the most distasteful idea is the absolute precondition to arguing effectively against it. . . . Only conduct that violates the law or interferes with the educational mission of the University merits punishment. . . . The words of hatred and bigotry, insult and ignorance, destroy dialogue and community and must be answered. I hope the day will come when no one

in our community will use such words or inflict pain on others with intent. But until then, when we are faced with words of offense and awfulness, we must draw those who use them into the dialogue of ideas. That is the essential precondition of the dynamics of change. That is why we must *censure* speech, but never *censor* speakers.[78]

Among other flaws in Penn's judicial process, Water Buffalo exposed the absence of a mediation clause, which might have allowed an amicable settlement behind closed doors. "It should have been handled by Penn informally through mediation," Hackney wrote ruefully in his memoirs, "bringing the involved parties together so that they might learn from each other why tempers had flared up, and why words that had been used stung so much."[79] In January 1995, the Code of Student Conduct was amended to include a clause for informal mediation—"a voluntary discussion and agreement for resolution of a dispute or allegation between the respondent and the complainant, facilitated by a trained mediator. The University is not a party to such agreements and assumes no responsibility for their enforcement." The judicial inquiry office and a hearing board could be involved in mediated cases only if the disputants failed to reach an agreement.[80] In 1996, the University transferred the judicial inquiry office's responsibilities to the newly established Office of Student Conduct, which included a Student Dispute Resolution Center.[81]

By the mid-1990s, progress toward conciliation was evident on another diversity front—Penn's lesbian, gay, bisexual, and transgender (LGBT) community. Outraged by the military's policy of discrimination against homosexuals, LGBT people had lobbied the University in the 1980s to ban military recruitment at Penn, an administrative action that might have jeopardized the University's relationship with the federal government. In 1983, Hackney tiptoed pragmatically around the issue. As the military's policy of "limiting employment" on the basis of sexual preference was "not illegal in Philadelphia or elsewhere," Hackney said, the University would continue to allow the services to recruit on campus. "At the same time, in order to promote maximum opportunity for Penn students, I will continue to urge that the armed forces review their restrictive employment policies, including those concerning enlistment and retention of homosexuals."[82] Hackney issued a similar response in 1991 when the University Council voted to recommend the removal of ROTC: he set aside the recommendation with the assurance that he would once again lobby the Department of Defense to change its policy.[83] Penn opened other doors to LGBT people. In 1992, the vice provost for university life extended family housing to gay and lesbian couples, as well as unmarried heterosexual partners.[84] And in 1993, the trustees approved the same benefits package—"all health, retirement, and tuition benefits"—for gay and lesbian couples that were "currently extended to spouses and children of married employees," with the proviso that these couples present "evidence of a committed relationship and of mutual financial responsibility."[85] Though there were occasional expressions of antigay sentiments, a general climate of tolerance and support prevailed after the mid-1990s. And in 2002 the Rodin administration renovated the Carriage House in Hamilton Village (the renamed Superblock) to house the new LGBT Center.[86] The ROTC issue was finally laid to rest in 1996 when Provost Stanley Chodorow announced that ROTC would remain at Penn and further negotiations with the military would not be pursued.[87]

■

The year following Hackney's retirement marked a shift in campus firestorms from internal racial matters to issues of security and aesthetics on the University's periphery. "Crime, poverty, trash, homelessness, panhandling, and decline of the built environment"—these were still unresolved crises in Penn's boundary areas. Though Penn under Hackney made a good start toward improving conditions in the boundary areas through a strengthened police presence and educational and economic supports for West Philadelphia, these initiatives were insufficient in the face of the continuing crack cocaine epidemic and the attendant, often deadly, crime wave. A sizable, well-organized, politically savvy group calling itself Penn Faculty and Staff for Neighborhood Issues (PFSNI) mobilized in 1992 to pressure the University to ratchet up efforts to stave off decline in the neighborhoods west and north of the campus. PFSNI included an eleven-member steering committee and eight named committees, with scores of participants and some five hundred faculty and staff signatories to PFSNI's petition to the University. While the group applauded Hackney's outreach efforts, they were adamant that the urban crisis on Penn's doorstep demanded a full-hearted, multipronged initiative from the University. Only a concerted effort to preserve "the well being of the communities surrounding the University" would suffice for the continued viability of the institution, the steering committee announced.[88]

PFSNI's proposed "action steps" for urban revival in University City harkened back to the multifaceted programs initiated by the West Philadelphia Corporation thirty years earlier. The Penn-dominated WPC was forced to curtail its programs in the face of the University's severe economic crisis in the 1970s and the upswing of crime in University City. PFSNI called for Penn to upgrade two of the area's public schools, to recruit University faculty and staff to University City through an enhanced mortgage program, to invest in the local housing stock (especially in declining neighborhoods), and to promote "retail and entrepreneurial enterprises" on Baltimore Avenue, between 45th and 50th streets, and a "University atmosphere" in the blocks around 40th and Locust streets, bustling with restaurants, pubs, bookstores, and cinemas. PFSNI's public safety committee struck an urgent chord, calling for Penn to hire more campus police officers, expand the area of Penn police patrols west of 43rd Street, south of Baltimore and north of Walnut, install twenty new blue-light emergency telephones, and provide matching funds for homeowners to install streetlights. PFSNI also recommended the demolition or redevelopment of the Walnut Mall, a low-end, small shopping area owned by Penn in the 3901 block of Walnut. Perhaps most important, in a recommendation that prefigured the University City District organized by Judith Rodin, the group called for "formal collaboration with other major institutions in the area, including the College of Pharmacy, Drexel, and the major hospitals, to officially designate the communities west of campus as being of 'special interest' to these institutions for security purposes. This area need not have precise boundaries, but it would help everyone concerned if it had a name."[89]

Concomitantly, behind-the-scenes strategic planning at Penn paralleled and supported PFSNI's public advocacy. Trustee chairman Alvin Shoemaker, Ira Harkavy, and John Gould, the acting executive vice president, spearheaded this in-house project. Their "vision thing" was a multipronged West Philadelphia strategy that asserted "the external environment" as "Penn's highest priority over the course of the next decade." Some of their recommendations helped chart the path that Judith Rodin followed in the next decade: the creation of a Penn-assisted public school "for the children of faculty members, graduate students, staff, and community members," and partnerships with the West Philadelphia public schools; the development of the 40th Street corridor from Locust Street north to the south side of Market Street, to include bookstores, jazz clubs, craft stores, bakeries, small shops, and small restaurants; the (unspecified) development of the north side of Walnut Street between 39th and 40th streets; the development of Baltimore Avenue between 48th and 60th streets "as a combined retail, residential avenue"; the purchase and rehabilitation of housing east of 47th Street; and the establishment of "school-based, limited primary care facilities, linked to health education and the training of health professionals" in West Philadelphia schools.[90]

A third plan, sponsored by the Spruce Hill Community Association and released in 1995, was also visionary and emphatic. The neighborhood nearest to the Penn campus, Spruce Hill is bounded by 39th and 46th streets on the east and west, Market Street and Woodland Avenue on the north and south. By the 1990s, this racially, ethnically, economically diverse neighborhood—hailed by the Spruce Hill planners as the area "with the greatest American architecture and urban design of the late nineteenth century"—was threatened by drug-related crime, trash, declining property values, housing deterioration, and housing abandonment—and the neighborhood had no public school. Spruce Hill's white population, which in 1990 accounted for 59 percent of the neighborhood total, had diminished by 11 percent since 1980, while the African American population, with 24 percent of the 1990 total, had increased by 12 percent. Asians, a growing constituency, composed 15 percent of the 1990 total. The rental housing market for one- and two-bedroom apartments was undermined by the flight of graduate students to Center City and an influx of cost-conscious undergraduates who eschewed apartment dwelling in favor of single-family houses owned by absentee landlords, into which they could pack up to ten students, exacerbating noise, litter, and general disorder in the neighborhood (more on this in Chapter 10).[91]

Assisted by a planning team from the Center for Community Partnerships, the Spruce Hill planners offered more specific recommendations than the other proposals we have just reviewed. Saliently, they called for a partnership public school that would be on the grounds of the Penn-owned and -stewarded Divinity School buildings in the quadrant of Locust, Spruce, 42nd, and 43rd streets. Citing a plan recently adopted at Yale University, they also advocated that Penn strengthen its guaranteed mortgage plan to include "direct acquisition subsidies over several years" as "incentives" for faculty and staff to move to Spruce Hill; for Penn homeowners who already resided in Spruce Hill, they called for "a home maintenance and moderate rehabilitation program." Eyeballing the 40th Street corridor, the association planners were disturbed by the presence of "too many low quality businesses, which, to give examples, sell cheap clothes, perfume and electronics, as well as check cashing and notary services." They might have added the presence of dueling hamburger franchises, McDonald's and Burger King, at opposite corners of the intersection of 40th and Walnut streets; or, for that matter, the absence of any high-quality anchor store in the corridor.[92]

In combination, the 1993 PFSNI report, the Shoemaker-Harkavy-Gould in-house project, the Spruce Hill plan, and the 1988 Campus Master Plan proposed many ideas that Judith Rodin implemented, often in novel ways, as the basis of her transformative presidency. Her administration also brought to fruition the incomplete elements of RDA Unit 4, as well as the 1977 campus landscape plan: parking lots and empty streetscapes bequeathed by 1960s urban renewal were transformed into architecturally adventurous buildings and vibrant pedestrian venues. In the next chapter, we view Rodin's West Philadelphia Initiatives in historical perspective, showing the continuities and differences between her decisions and actions and those taken by her predecessors in College Hall.

Part IV **The Implementer**

10

Triumph in University City

On 7 December 1993, the Penn trustees announced their selection of Judith Seitz Rodin as the University's seventh president. At age forty-nine, Rodin would be the first woman inaugurated as president of an Ivy League university, a role for which she was highly qualified. A PhD graduate of Columbia University in psychology, Rodin taught at Yale University from 1972 to 1994, holding joint professorships in psychology, medicine, and psychiatry. A widely published authority on obesity, aging, and the relationship of psychological and biological processes, she also held three major administrative posts at Yale: chair of the Department of Psychology, dean of the School of Arts and Sciences, and provost of the University. Rodin favorably impressed many of the Penn trustees, themselves the chief executive officers of major corporations, as a "determined, controlling, a strong-willed leader" who "emphasized the corporate or executive model" of university governance. Of further appeal to the trustees, Rodin was no stranger to Philadelphia or Penn, having been raised in Southwest Philadelphia and East Mount Airy and educated at the Philadelphia High School for Girls before attending Penn's College of Liberal Arts for Women. At Penn, from which she graduated in 1966 with a BA in psychology and a Phi Beta Kappa key, Rodin played an instrumental role in the merger of the women's and men's student governments.[1]

Rodin's appointment was assured at her first meeting with the presidential search committee, such was the profound impression she made on the committee's chair, Alvin Shoemaker, who also chaired the board of trustees.[2] The former Penn provost Eliot Stellar, a renowned professor of physiological psychology and a professional mentor to Rodin, wrote the first nomination letter to the trustees on her behalf. Because of Stellar's stature and his enthusiastic endorsement, the trustees chose to read his letter to Rodin, who recalls that she was "ecstatic" when offered the presidency of her alma mater. "This is my

Judith Rodin. Collections of the University Archives and Records Center.

native city, all my family is here, this is the school that I loved," she says. "To imagine having the opportunity to come back and lead a place that you love, in a city that you feel passionate about, is really a once in a lifetime opportunity."[3] From the trustees' perspective, this homegrown, tough-skinned, pragmatic, charismatic Ivy League psychologist was exactly who was needed to propel Penn to the level of Harvard, Yale, and Princeton.

In the following chapters, we will show that aspects of Rodin's leadership embodied some of the strengths of her predecessors in College Hall—in a sense, she was a builder, a conciliator, and a visionary. On the one hand, her contributions in each of these domains built on established foundations and moved in directions charted by her predecessors, maintaining the *continuity* in the University's history in the second half of the last century. Many Rodin-era construction and campus redesign projects, for example, were located in the former urban renewal area of Unit 4, which Penn had acquired from the Philadelphia Redevelopment Authority in the Harnwell era. On the other hand, her presidency effected a *transformation* of the Penn campus and its surroundings. By this we mean that Rodin greatly accelerated Penn's evolution to the stature of a top-tier American university. She and her leadership team did this in three ways. First, they reshaped and gave exuberant new expression to campus trends, plans, and projects that were in various stages of completion when Rodin arrived in 1994. Second, they succeeded where the West Philadelphia Corporation (WPC) of the 1960s had failed by implementing, with spectacular results, a multipronged strategy called the West Philadelphia Initiatives, which established, finally, a compatible neighborhood for the University. Third, they created a dynamic synergy that linked components of the West Philadelphia Initiatives in interactive ways to campus physical development and curriculum reform. By no means was Rodin's decade in College Hall free of conflict or dissension: her "corporate style" of management ruffled many feathers, and she had to negotiate some prickly student issues, though nothing like the revolving-door student crises of the Meyerson and Hackney eras.

■ An Echo of In-Ho Oh

Shortly after her arrival in 100 College Hall, Rodin faced the disturbing reality of the urban crisis on Penn's doorstep. On the night of 29 August 1994, Al-Moez Alimohamed, a PhD candidate in the Mathematics Department, was beaten, robbed, and shot to death at a phone booth near the corner of 48th and Pine streets, eight blocks west of the campus. The perpetrators were five African American youths, one of whom wielded a sawed-off shotgun. In the wake of the killing, Penn Faculty and Staff for Neighborhood Issues (PFSNI) importuned Rodin to "do something *now*," "to act immediately on the recommendations PFSNI has been pressing for the past two years." On behalf of the steering committee, the Penn historian Lynn Lees called on the new president "to make the revitalization of West Philadelphia and University City in particular, the highest priority of the University of Pennsylvania." PFSNI called for the creation of a "special services district" and a multipronged initiative:

> Mr. Alimohamed's death illustrates tragically the highly dangerous conditions of the neighborhoods west of 40th Street, conditions that spill onto the Penn campus with alarming regularity and diminish the spirit, confidence, and vitality of the University. More police cars, escort vans, and blue-light telephones—while undeniably necessary—are not the answer to University City's security problems. The solution, we believe, lies in investment—a decisive, strategic financial involvement and engagement of academic resources to assist the revitalization of West Philadelphia. That the West Philadelphia youths who have been charged in the murder of Mr. Alimohamed are residents of an area outside the traditional boundaries of University City underscores, in our judgment, the need for a major community revitalization effort that includes, but extends well beyond, the University's immediate geographic area.[4]

On the night of 12 September, exactly two weeks after the murder, PFSNI sponsored a candlelight march that drew some six hundred participants; the march started at the Peace Symbol at Van Pelt Library, paraded west on Spruce Street with a police escort, and ended on the 4701 block of Pine Street, near the site of the murder. "We've organized this candlelight march to mobilize government, community, and institutional resources to prevent another tragedy like Alimohamed's death," said Lees.[5]

While Rodin marched and then addressed the assemblage from the back of a truck on Pine Street, she did not share PFSNI's sense of dire urgency. In the first two years of her presidency, she implemented a piecemeal strategy: strengthening campus security through additive measures (for example, employing more uniformed police officers—a total of seventy-nine in 1995, compared to fifty-six in 1989) and replacing Hackney's security chief with Tom Seamon, a former deputy commissioner of the Philadelphia Police Department, as the managing director (a new title) of the Division of Public Safety. Strategically placed, though short-lived, security-and-information kiosks, stepped-up bicycle patrols, and more blue-light telephones on the campus periphery were the key changes.[6] Ever the Cassandra, Lees upbraided Rodin in the *Almanac* for not moving simultaneously and aggressively on multiple fronts. "Particularly those of us who live near, as well as work at, Penn," she wrote, "have good cause to be alarmed by the robberies, muggings and murders that have recently taken place in University City and in the Powelton area. But how is safety to be provided? The standard solution—more policemen and retreat from a threatening urban world—seems to me to be not only short-sighted, but ultimately counterproductive. . . . Penn's policies on transportation, on mortgages, on real estate rental, on aid to local schools have far more impact on the public safety issue than does the number of police or blue light phones it puts on local streets."[7]

The nonfatal shooting of Penn senior Patrick Leroy during an armed robbery attempt in the vicinity of 40th and Locust streets in the early hours of 25 September 1996 capped a month of escalating crime in University City that was marked by "approximately *one* robbery a day," a situation Tom Seamon described as "unprecedented."[8] (A citywide analysis for the year ending 31 July 1996 pinpointed University City as a "hot zone" for armed robberies.)[9] Rodin assured frightened students that she would add more tactical patrols and more blue-light telephones. Yet, as if to underscore the horrific truth of PFSNI's jeremiads, Vladimir Sled, a thirty-eight-year-old Russian émigré and research associate in biochemistry and biophysics at Penn, was stabbed to death in a Halloween night robbery on Larchwood Street just west of 43rd. "A Halloween Homicide Jolts a Reeling Penn," declared the *Philadelphia Inquirer* without hyperbole on November 2. Sled's murder and the hue and cry it raised kicked Rodin into action to implement a multipronged neighborhood improvement strategy that was later named the West Philadelphia Initiatives. In *The University and Urban Revival*, her memoir of the Initiatives, she writes, with a dash of melodrama: "Sometimes there is one decisive moment—one seminal incident—that leaves no choice but to seek an entirely new paradigm. With the events of that Halloween night—a random act of violence in a neighborhood that had become increasingly rife with crime—that moment was foisted on me. As President of the University of Pennsylvania, I knew that the time for unprecedented action had arrived."[10] Rodin's declamation brings to mind President Gaylord P. Harnwell's response, forty years earlier, to the brutal murder of In-Ho Oh, a Penn graduate student, in East Powelton—the killing that spurred the creation of the West Philadelphia Corporation.

More than any of her other accomplishments, the West Philadelphia Initiatives marked Rodin's presidency as transformative. The Initiatives, however, were not sui generis. The comprehensive strategy that Rodin and her staff implemented between 1996 and 2004 existed in a broad form in the PFSNI report of February 1994 and in faculty letters to the president in the months before and after Sled's murder.[11] And the idea predated PFSNI by several decades. As we detailed in part I, the West Philadelphia Corporation adopted a holistic strategy in the 1960s, working simultaneously on housing, commercial development, education, beautification, and the arts to create a compatible neighborhood for University City's higher education and medical institutions—an effort that had only modest success for Penn and more than a few failures, and did great damage to Penn's community relations. The West Philadelphia Initiatives, in combination with the University City District, a multi-institutional collaborative led by Penn, provided a contemporary analog to the WPC's holistic strategy of the 1960s and finally realized the WPC's vision of University City as a compatible neighborhood for Penn.

We have seen that Penn lacked the financial resources to sustain the WPC's University City initiatives after 1970. By contrast, money was no obstacle to Rodin's ambitions; she began her tenure at the onset of the flush economy of the Clinton era, inherited the largesse of Hackney's $1.47 billion Keeping Franklin's Promise campaign, and herself was able to raise $3.5 billion for the University, even without a capital campaign. Between 1994 and 1999, marking the first half of her presidency, the endowment grew from $2.22 billion to $3.78 billion—an increase of 51 percent in constant dollars.[12]

With the enthusiastic support of the trustees, the Rodin administration boldly invested millions in the West Philadelphia Initiatives and leveraged millions more from investors and developers. Rodin and John Anderson Fry, Penn's new executive vice president, worked on an unprecedented scale—"at warp speed," in Rodin's words—to transform the neighborhoods surrounding the campus. Rodin took Penn and University City to a new level of functioning as an educational, cultural, and retail hub—a "destination," in the parlance of city planners. The revitalized University City that emerged between the mid-1990s and early 2000s represented the synergy of the various components of the West Philadelphia Initiatives, which were undertaken by Penn in collaboration with Drexel University, the University of the Sciences (formerly the College of Pharmacy and Science), neighborhood associations, and health care, business, and civic organizations in University City. This synergy was integral, indeed indispensable, to Rodin's larger project to propel Penn into the front rank of the world's great universities. Her regal, egoistic, often imperious management style and assertive corporatization of critical aspects of Penn's daily operations and academic affairs were instrumental in achieving this next level of excellence—and she accomplished her goals, though not without conflict, and certainly not without the foundation built by her College Hall forebears since World War II.

In this chapter we introduce Rodin's extraordinary presidency by way of the West Philadelphia Initiatives. Our aims in part IV are to delineate the goals, accomplishments, and controversies of Rodin's tenure; to trace the integration of the West Philadelphia Initiatives with Rodin's fast-paced academic and campus-development agendas; to ascertain the relative strength and impact of external social forces and contexts on Rodin's presidency, and to identify preexisting campus initiatives, infrastructural components, and West Philadelphia-related developments that Rodin and her senior administrators built on.

■ Rodin's West Philadelphia Initiatives Reconsidered

Vladimir Sled's death sounded a tocsin for Rodin and the trustees to implement "a vision, a strategy, and a plan for deploying leadership and resources": "We would strive to rebuild West Philadelphia's social and economic capacity by simultaneously and aggressively acting on five interrelated fronts," says Rodin. "We would make the neighborhood clean and safe with a variety of new interventions. We would stabilize the housing market. We would spur economic development by directing university contracts and purchases to local businesses, many of which we would help to initiate. We would encourage retail development by attracting new shops, restaurants, and cultural venues that were neighborhood friendly. We would improve the public schools. We were committed to a spirit of seeking true partnership." True partnership, Rodin declaimed, would entail openness and consultation with community members on all projects. She also vowed that Penn "would never again expand . . . to the west or to the north into residential neighborhoods. We would only expand to our east, which was made up entirely of abandoned buildings and commercial real estate."[13]

Rodin regarded Sheldon Hackney's restructuring of the West Philadelphia Corporation, his establishment of the Center for Community Partnerships (CCP), and the Buy West Philadelphia program as necessary but insufficient steps toward positive change in the area. "These programs succeeded in terms of breaking down some barriers between town and gown and opening channels of communication," she wrote, "but they failed to halt the decline of the neighborhood. They did not address the inherited problems of housing age and deterioration, as well as racial isolation and ethnic differentials in housing and economic opportunities. And without a sufficient job and tax base, it was not possible to alter the basic trends. Minus a large-scale commitment of money and resources, CCP alone was not able to stem the tide of further decline."[14] Rodin and the trustees would commit "major University funding" to the West Philadelphia Initiatives. Acutely aware of the long-standing bitterness in Penn's community relations, Rodin and her planners repudiated the hierarchical, nonconsultative practices of the architects of Penn's Great Expansion in the 1960s, vowing transparency in the University's dealings with the community: "partnership" was the mantra of her leadership team.

Ironically, for all the differences involved, the West Philadelphia Initiatives stood on the shoulders of 1960s urban renewal. For example, Harnwell's urban renewal project bequeathed to Rodin the 3601 block between Walnut and Sansom streets, used since the mid-1970s as the campus's largest surface parking lot. Rodin's deputies built Sansom Common (later renamed University Square) on the 3601 block as Penn's answer to Harvard Square, a spectacular development that included the Inn at Penn, the new University bookstore (a Barnes & Noble "superstore"), the campus computer store, two avant-garde restaurants and a café, flashy boutiques, and student-friendly clothing stores along 36th Street. (Lacking interested private developers at the outset, Penn had to put up $150 million for construction in Sansom Common.)[15]

Putting new buildings on Unit 4 blocks in the 1990s was a far cry easier than condemning and clearing those sites had been in the 1960s and 1970s; indeed, most of the parcels on which executive vice president John Fry's office built new retail shops and restaurants were in Penn's real estate portfolio prior to 1994. The land on which the postmodernist Fresh Grocer and parking garage opened in the 4001 block of Walnut, for example, was purchased in 1965 and used for decades as a surface parking lot. Across Walnut, wrapping the corner at 40th Street, the ultramodern multiplex Bridge Cinema de Lux (now Rave) and Marathon Grill (now Harvest Seasonal Grill and Wine Bar) replaced a Burger King and formed a new anchor building for 40th Street between Walnut and Locust. This block, which had been shabbily redeveloped in the 1970s by the University Shopping Center Association, a group of expatriate merchants from Unit 4, was purchased by the Hackney administration in 1993, and ultimately stabilized and upgraded by Rodin and Fry as the Hamilton Shops.

The dirty work of urban renewal at Penn was a decades-old fait accompli that gave Rodin's real-estate and financial managers the formidable advantage of not having to enlist the RDA to bulldoze swaths of blocks. And it allowed Rodin to dissociate the West Philadelphia Initiatives from urban renewal in her community relations campaign, even as her deputies built on old urban renewal sites.

Rodin recognized that Penn was the only West Philadelphia institution with sufficient infrastructure to lead the Initiatives. She says, "It boiled down to this: if Penn did not take the lead to revitalize the neighborhood, no one else would." Rodin and her senior administrators set about restructuring Penn's administration and operations to plan and implement the Initiatives, first by establishing a regular reporting line from the President's Office to the newly formed Trustees Standing Committee on Neighborhood Initiatives; second, by effecting a major administrative reorganization that included, among other significant changes, the creation of a new position—vice president for government, public, and community affairs, who reported to the president—and a consolidation of the Division of Real Estate and the Office of Facilities Administration to create the Office of Facilities and Real Estate Services under the executive vice president. Among Rodin's senior administrators, the major operational players in the Initiatives were John Fry, executive vice president, and Omar Blaik, vice president for facilities and real-estate services, who reported to Fry. Blaik carried the symbolic burden of the Initiatives. "His focus was on integrating every element of the built environment across the five neighborhood Initiatives, linked to relevant campus planning and construction activities," says Rodin. "The Initiatives had to find a physical form, in part, to communicate the transformation. In essence, changes in physical space became a central element of the fabric on which the Initiatives were knitted together."[16] Broadly put, the five Initiatives were neighborhood safety and cleanliness, housing stabilization and reclamation, neighborhood retail development, locally targeted campus purchasing, and public education investments.

Neighborhood Safety and Cleanliness

Neighborhood safety and cleanliness were a joint, immediate priority after 1996—the safety priority took its impetus from the slaying of Vladimir Sled that fall; the cleanliness priority was driven by out-of-control littering and daily garbage spills along the campus entryways of Pine, Spruce, and Locust streets,[17] as well as the trash-cluttered neighborhoods west of 43rd Street where annual block cleanups were ineffectual rituals. As the Initiatives progressed, Penn's Division of Public Safety, among other measures, added nineteen new police officers; collaborated with the Philadelphia Police Department to patrol perennial trouble spots such as the area of 40th and Walnut streets, as well as the neighborhoods west of 43rd Street; moved its headquarters to the vicinity of Chestnut and 40th (that is, into the streets); and set up twenty-two closed-circuit television cameras at strategic points for street-level surveillance.[18]

The single most important step toward improved security was the Penn-initiated University City District (UCD), an independent, nonprofit consortium of institutions that was inaugurated on 18 June 1997. According to the *Almanac*, "A special services district (SSD) is an effort by local property owners and other stakeholders to develop and carry out a program of cleaning, security and other services that are specially tailored to their area and its needs and opportunities. An effective SSD works with the City and serves as an advocate for improved City services. SSDs improve areas in terms of attractiveness, livability and development." The eleven institutional partners included, among others, University City's three higher education institutions, Penn, Drexel, and the Philadelphia College of Pharmacy and Science (now the University of the Sciences in Philadelphia), as well as the Penn Health System, the University City Science Center, the U.S. Post Office, Amtrak, and Children's Seashore House. The UCD's boundaries were 30th Street on the east, 48th Street on the west, Spring Garden Street on the north, and Woodland Avenue on the south. Programs were concentrated in three neighborhoods west of Penn—Spruce Hill, Garden Court, and Cedar Park: "those areas where the interrelationships between the institutions and residential and commercial areas were most dense and inter-related." For the first five-years, more than 70 percent of the $4.3 million annual cost of the UCD's professional service program was paid by the institutions, with Penn and its Health System as the lead contributors; businesses, homeowners, nonprofit organizations, civic associations, grants, and other sources made up the rest on a voluntary basis. By 2005, the UCD's budget stood at $5.7 million, with more than 70 percent still provided by the institutions.[19]

A program that marked a major turning point in the security of the neighborhoods west of the University was the UCD Ambassadors, thirty-four trained staff members dressed conspicuously in bright blue-and-yellow uniforms, packing two-way radios. "On foot and on bicycle," these roving safety ambassadors patrolled the neighborhoods day and night, reporting suspicious activity and problems such as potholes and graffiti; John Fry likened them to "a professional Town Watch," "hotel concierges," and "walking billboards for all things we are doing in University City."[20] Augmenting this important service was UC Brite, a UCD-managed program that provided matching funds to homeowners and landlords who agreed to purchase and install sidewalk-level lights on their properties; in the eighteen months of the program's existence, some twelve hundred properties installed such lighting.[21] Benefiting from the dissipation of West Philadelphia's crack-cocaine epidemic in the late 1990s, these programs contributed to a resurgence of evening foot traffic on neighborhood streets that previously were ominously dark and crime-plagued at night. The Division of Public Safety reported a reduction in overall crime in the campus area by 40 percent between 1996 and 2002.[22]

The UCD and UC Green, a separate nonprofit organization, operated or supported programs that dramatically improved the area's cleanliness and attractiveness. Every day, a UCD "public space maintenance team" picked up litter and removed graffiti west of 40th Street. UC Green volunteers, in conjunction with the Pennsylvania Horticultural Society and Philadelphia's Fairmount Park Commission, planted trees, constructed gardens, and did landscaping. In a similar vein, a major coup for local residents was the rehabilitation of crime-plagued Clark Park, West Philadelphia's largest park, which straddles the 4300–4400 blocks of Baltimore and Chester avenues. The UCD collaborated with the Friends of Clark Park, "a volunteer citizen advocacy group" formed in 1973, to raise more than $85,000 from corporations, foundations, and private sources to rrelandscape and refurbish the park. Formerly a haven for drug dealers—and the site of the murder of a Penn graduate student in 1988—the park was transformed into a flourishing venue, an attractive, well-used site for concerts and community events that included state-of-the-art playground equipment (supported by a $100,000 donation from the city) and a bustling biweekly farmer's market.[23]

Housing Stabilization and Reclamation

In the 1960s, the West Philadelphia Corporation tried with only modest success to strengthen the quality of single-family housing in University City. The WPC attracted local developers to build two small condominium complexes in the Spruce Hill neighborhood and to invest in rehabilitating the nineteenth-century townhouses on a block of Pine Street just off the West Campus. The Corporation also sponsored demonstration houses and consulted with the neighborhood associations on housing improvements. Penn offered guaranteed mortgages to faculty and staff members who purchased houses in West Philadelphia *or* across the Schuylkill River in Center City, the latter option eventually thwarting the WPC's aim of University City development, since for the next thirty years urban-dwelling Penn members were more likely to settle in Center City than in West Philadelphia. We have seen that by the late 1950s, University City was already succumbing to what would be a multidecade crime wave, which accelerated after 1985 when crack cocaine appeared on the streets and well-organized drug-dealing operations proliferated.[24] A menacing social climate was hardly conducive to building a strong housing market in University City, and many of the homeowners who were already there were stampeding out by the mid-1990s. Between FY 1989 and FY 1994, the percentage of graduate students living in West Philadelphia declined from 60 percent to 29 percent—a loss of 1,460 students.[25] In fact, so many students chose to live in Center City that local landlords, unable to turn a profit anymore, simply let their properties deteriorate.[26] Drug-related shootings, muggings, burglaries, auto theft, and arson were rampant in the neighborhoods west of Penn and south of Walnut out to 49th Street.

On the housing front of the West Philadelphia Initiatives, Penn worked in three domains. First, Rodin's senior administrators restructured the guaranteed-mortgage program to provide an additional financial incentive for Penn affiliates to purchase homes in University City: as of the spring of 1998, giving Penn-affiliated homebuyers the choice of a $15,000 interest-free loan from the University that could be applied against closing costs as well as the mortgage principal and forgiven after seven years if the same owner remained in the house; *or* $21,000, to be paid out at the rate of $3,000 per year for seven years and forgiven on the same basis as the smaller loan. In 1999, Rodin removed Center City from the list of eligible sites for a Penn-guaranteed mortgage. The enhanced mortgage program in University City was a huge success, with 386 home purchases recorded between 1998 and 2004, when Penn ended the enhanced mortgage.[27]

Second, recognizing that eyesore rental housing contributed to the decline of the area, Penn purchased and rehabilitated five "highly visible, deteriorating or poorly managed" apartment buildings, expensively upgrading a total of 211 units to rent at affordable rates to moderate-income families and individuals. The centerpiece project is the three-building, 116-unit Cornerstone complex, located in Garden Court at 48th and Pine streets, just a stone's throw from where Alimohamed was gunned down in 1994. In several blocks where "one or two houses were lost to fire or became unoccupied and began to deteriorate, threatening decline for the surrounding houses," Penn purchased twenty houses for rehabilitation and resale at prices that ranged from $89,000 to $150,000.[28]

Third, Penn attracted outside developers to invest in new avant-garde apartment buildings on strategic though problematic off-campus properties in its real-estate portfolio. In 1996, some seventeen blocks east of the Cornerstone,

Penn was finally able to purchase the long-vacant, crime-plagued, massive General Electric building in the 3101 block of Walnut Street, which Sheldon Hackney's planners had targeted for redevelopment. Through a long-term ground-lease contract with the University, Carl Dranoff, a Philadelphia developer, converted this historic Art Deco industrial building into the Left Bank, home to 282 luxury apartments, gated indoor parking, a rooftop fitness center, and retail and office space, as well as the Division of Facilities and Real Estate Services and the Penn Children's Center (child care), all of which debuted in 2001.[29]

Three other ground-lease developments opened in the mid-2000s, offering new "flexible residential options" for students, and, like the Left Bank, featuring street-level shops and restaurants. The first of these developments was Domus, a congeries of 290 luxury apartments, built at a cost of $100 million on the site of a parking lot at 3401 Chestnut Street, a 2.6-acre swath of properties the University had obtained in 1965. In the area just north of the West Campus, John Fry's office inaugurated "a process of consultation with community groups" to enhance the commercial attractiveness of several blocks around 40th Street, from Ludlow to just above Chestnut. Supported by a consultative group, the Friends of 40th Street, Penn purchased eleven vacant or dilapidated row houses and several other buildings of marginal quality for conservation or redevelopment through ground-lease arrangements; the signature redevelopment project of this process is the Hub, a funky, multihued bank building converted to apartments and a two-level upscale restaurant at 40th and Chestnut streets. Two blocks south of the Hub is Radian, a retro-futuristic student-housing edifice in the 3901 block of Walnut Street, with an upscale pub and a street-level eatery and café. Radian solved Penn's long-standing problem of finding a viable commercial use for a troublesome property acquired in 1974 and redeveloped as a tiny strip mall, the Walnut Mall; a movie theater in the mall was a frequent crime scene involving West Philadelphia youths.[30]

New student housing options, in combination with Penn's new College House System (see Chapter 11), were strategically designed in part to lure undergraduates who lived in West Philadelphia's converted Victorians and brick row houses back to the campus, with the intent of forcing a downturn in the area's student-housing market and freeing up these rental properties for sale to families. "Undergraduates are terrible in a neighborhood," explains Rodin, matter-of-factly. "They tend to live six or eight in a house, the landlords of such houses are usually quite negligent, students are not good neighbors, they have loud parties, they forget to take out the garbage, and families don't usually want to be their next-door neighbors. So if we really were to revive and reanimate the neighborhood, we needed to get the undergraduates back on campus in greater numbers."[31]

Neighborhood Retail Development

Not without considerable risk to their reputations, Rodin and Fry gambled that the commercial revival of the Walnut Street and 40th Street corridors, coupled with the positive impacts of the other Initiatives and the University City District, would catalyze economic development in Spruce Hill, Garden Court, and Cedar Court. Their bet paid off. Entrepreneurs have flocked to these neighborhoods, converting old apartment buildings to state-of-the-art condominiums; opening new microbrew taverns, cafés, and a mélange of new ethnic restaurants, especially along Baltimore Avenue between 43rd and 50th streets; and stabilizing difficult blocks with solid anchor businesses—the colorful and lively Copacabana replacing Billybob's, a grungy dive at 4000 Spruce, is a case in point. The UCD upgraded the pedestrian streetscape of 40th Street between Walnut and Spruce streets with "new lighting, trees, sidewalk paving, bike racks, and litter baskets," while the Redevelopment Authority made similar improvements on 40th Street between Walnut and Chestnut streets.[32]

Architecturally, these developments differentiate the commercial blocks around the campus core from the blocks around 40th Street. Rodin credits the actor Robert Redford with persuading her leadership team to eschew both Penn's traditional reddish-brown brick palette in the latter blocks in favor of avant-garde designs for the new commercial buildings. Redford's company Sundance Cinemas was Rodin's first choice for a cinema project on the southwest corner of 40th and Walnut; when Sundance's parent company declared bankruptcy in 2000, Penn had to pony up $15 million to complete the building and find a new company to operate the cinema.[33] (Penn's total investment of $30 million in the theater project "required a bit of chutzpah," as Omar Blaik puts it.)[34] Redford's idea of bold avant-gardism took root as Penn engaged the cutting-edge Boston architect Carlos Zapata to design the Fresh Grocer and the six-screen Bridge (now Rave) Cinema, the former opening in 2000, the latter in 2002.[35] According to the University's 2002 "design guidelines and review of campus projects," the "point of departure for new [campus] structures" would be the reddish-brown brick palette, whereas "commercial structures adjacent to the campus may depart from the predominant campus materials, but should be respectful in other ways (program, scale, contribution of life onto streets, etc.) to the campus, and should not overwhelm their residential or commercial neighbors."[36] "Warm woods and expansive glass, jutting angles and curves" characterize the Zapata designs, offering "the sizzle we were looking for," says Rodin.[37]

From the perspective of Rodin and her senior administrators, the approximately one hundred curbside food-truck and food-cart vendors who dispensed inexpensive food on or near the campus were eyesores that vitiated "sizzle" and the boutique-quality ambience the planners strived to create. "Their presence on the streets was detrimental to a quality retail atmosphere, and contributed especially to the lack of restaurants," says Rodin.[38] She and Fry were in a quandary, as the trucks were wildly popular with Penn members. Needing a city ordinance to remove the trucks from the streets that bounded the Sansom Common development site, they drew support from West Philadelphia's Councilwoman Jannie Blackwell and Mayor John Street in persuading the City Council to designate the blocks in University City where street vending would be permitted. Given Penn's economic clout in the city, Walnut, 36th, and 37th streets did not appear on the City Council's list of authorized vending sites in the street-vending ordinance that was approved on 16 April 1998, with an effective date of 22 July. "We have an obligation to the second-largest employer in the City of Philadelphia," declared Street, reflecting the dominant sentiment of city officials.[39] The University removed the vending trucks from Walnut, 36th, and 37th streets, moving many of them to so-called fresh-air plazas, which "provided water, electricity, sanitary refuse removal, and a more attractive and safer environment for the vendors as well as their patrons."[40]

West Philadelphia Purchasing and Hiring

A related local economic development activity that Rodin prioritized as one of the five Initiatives, designating it "economic inclusion," was her expansion of Sheldon Hackney's Buy West Philadelphia initiative. "In fiscal year 1996," she writes, "Penn purchased $20.1 million in goods and services from West Philadelphia suppliers and $24.6 million from minority suppliers, $7.2 million of which was from African American suppliers. In fiscal year 2003, purchases from West Philadelphia suppliers amounted to $61.6 million, with purchases from minority suppliers totaling $41.4 million, $13.1 million from African American suppliers." The University also channeled $134 million in construction projects to minority- and women-owned businesses. Rodin could also point with pride to the three thousand West Philadelphia residents who were employed in the University's offices, service departments, and hospitals, and the hiring of West Philadelphia residents, under Penn's auspices, for jobs at the Inn at Penn, Sheraton University Hotel, and the new Penn bookstore.[41]

Public Education Investments

Investing in local economic development was riskier for the University than implementing the education priority of the Initiatives, which was to improve public education. Yet the plan for public education created greater dissension in West Philadelphia. On 18 June 1998, the University, the School District of Philadelphia, and the Philadelphia Federation of Teachers announced that they would partner to establish a high-quality, Penn-assisted elementary (pre-kindergarten through eighth grade) school that would open in the fall of 2001 in the block bounded by 42nd, 43rd, Locust, and Spruce streets, on the old Philadelphia Divinity School grounds owned by Penn since 1977. Penn would lease the property "at nominal cost" to the school district, which would pay for the construction under a "turnkey" arrangement with Penn and would then own the new building, to be designed by a Penn-selected architect. The Graduate School of Education agreed to organize and mediate community participation in the planning process and help develop the curriculum. To ensure that the school would have relatively small classes, Rodin pledged a subsidy of $700,000 per year for a period of ten years, or $1,000 per student for a total enrollment of 700—this in addition to the school district's annual per pupil expenditure for the school. Granting the new Penn-assisted school the status of a "demonstration school," the Philadelphia Federation of Teachers waived its contractual right to appoint new teachers on the basis of seniority in the Philadelphia schools, giving the University and the School District autonomy to hire the school's faculty in consultation with parents.[42]

While Superintendent David Hornbeck celebrated Penn's role in assisting the new public school, some of Penn's neighbors fretted that a fait accompli in every respect had just been announced. In fairness to Rodin, she and her partners could not devise a consultative process with University City residents until they had first drawn up a memorandum of understanding for the institutional partnership that was required to build a new school in University City. As events proved, each phase and component of the school's development engaged community input and was transparent and consultative. A few weeks after the announcement, Rodin's leadership team for the project addressed an "overflowing and anxious crowd of community residents" at the Penn Faculty Club. "Many of those in attendance expressed a level of frustration with the University administration, specifically with regards to a lack of communication," reported the *Daily Pennsylvanian*. "Some pointed to the fact that they did not learn about the agreement between Penn, the city and the teachers union until newspaper headlines appeared three weeks ago." The Penn administrators explained the memorandum of understanding and gave assurances of a community-wide planning process, though they had no answers to such questions as how enrollment decisions would be made.[43] Several months later, the University City Community Council, which represented the six neighborhood associations, approved a resolution that enumerated their major concerns about the new school: its impact on property values, its effect on other local schools (for example, the Powel School, a racially integrated elementary school in Powelton Village), and the problem of determining a catchment area (attendance zone).[44] The catchment area would be the major bone of contention as the planning moved forward.

A collaborative community-wide process was in place by mid-October 1998, with three planning committees involving a mix of parents, teachers, and residents of University City: a site and facility committee, an educational programming committee, and a community programming committee. Though these groups were racially diverse, they included few if any of the area's low-income parents or residents. A fourth group, the coordinating committee, included Rodin's chief of staff Stephen Schutt, Dean Susan Fuhrman of the Graduate School of Education, and School District chief of staff Germaine Ingram; this group met monthly with the chairs of the three planning committees. Nancy Streim, one of the GSE's associate deans, took charge of organizing and integrating the planning effort—appropriately, the GSE was the University's lead agent in developing the school; Streim also chaired the educational programming committee. The Pew Charitable Trusts supported the four committees with a $325,000 grant, which, according to the Trusts, was "to plan how the school and its educational mission will be developed, and to assure that residents of the West Philadelphia Neighborhood will be involved in this community-based education initiative for many years to come."[45]

Though the planning was completed in the spring of 1999, contentious issues delayed the groundbreaking for two more years. One was the argument of local politicians that Penn should be investing "exclusively" in rehabilitating an existing school, not in building a new one in its own privileged backyard. Penn's counterargument—one that would prove more rhetorical than substantive in the long term—was that a new, architecturally innovative school in the relatively safe, environmentally hospitable, easily manageable precincts of the old Divinity School campus would be better suited as a state-of-the-art "demonstration school" than an existing school in West Philadelphia would be. Penn and the new school's other promoters envisioned the school as a site for demonstrating "best practices" that would be delivered through workshops and site visits to teachers in all of West Philadelphia's schools. Having easy pedestrian access to Penn's cultural and academic resources, such as the University Museum, the Institute of Contemporary Art, the Van Pelt Library, and the University Archives and Records Center, not to mention immediate access to the University City Arts League, just across Spruce Street from the Divinity School property, provided a further justification. That the school would presumably be—at least the rhetoric said as much—a "commu-

The jewel in the crown of Judith Rodin's West Philadelphia Initiatives: the Sadie Tanner Mossell Alexander School, known as the Penn Alexander School. Photograph by Michael M. Koehler. Collections of the University Archives and Records Center.

nity school," in the sense of being a venue for community organizing and offering social, cultural, and recreational programs for the larger West Philadelphia community, made the pill of giving Penn what it wanted easier for the politicians to swallow.[46]

Between 1999 and 2001, Rodin and her partners had to fight off local-neighborhood and citywide efforts to make the Penn-assisted school a magnet school that any Philadelphia child could attend, subject to the outcome of a lottery. In her memoir, Rodin probably understates her idée fixe: "We felt passionately . . . that a strong neighborhood public school would prove to be the most important element in redeveloping the community and building sustainability." Yes, the issue was volatile, she writes:

> Community members found themselves taking sides. Some supported a neighborhood catchment area and others wanted a larger "attendance by lottery" magnet school available to the whole city. No topic was more charged than that of the catchment area, and conversations about it could be overheard everywhere. There were all kinds of meetings, many in private homes with just a small group of residents, some of them held in secrecy. Even the neighborhood associations were pitted against each other over the catchment-area issue. One association, Spruce Hill,

dropped out of the University City Community Council, which was in favor of the lottery plan. Sometimes the educational issues got lost in the clamor, and the conflict occasionally seemed to be more about who would benefit financially from the inevitable rise in property values in the catchment area than about who would benefit educationally.[47]

After "many months of wrangling and negotiation among community groups" and several public hearings on the issue, the school board finally decided to designate a catchment area for the school, perhaps calculating the likelihood of Penn's withdrawal from the project if the magnet option were selected. With several exceptions, the catchment area included the blocks between 40th and 47th streets, from Sansom Street (one block north of Walnut) to Woodland Avenue. The groundbreaking ceremony for the new building, originally named the Penn-Assisted PreK-8 Neighborhood School, took place in March 2001, attended by Penn officials, local dignitaries, and a chorus of hecklers. The school's kindergarten and first grade opened that fall in the former Divinity School's refectory and dormitory, preparatory to the new building's debut in the fall of 2002, with grades K–2, 5–6, and a Head Start program to start. Officially renamed the Sadie Tanner Mossell Alexander University of Pennsylvania Partnership School in 2002, in honor of the Penn graduate who was the nation's first African American to receive a PhD in economics, the $19 million Penn-assisted school had a full complement of grades pre-K–8 by the fall of 2004.[48]

Responding to criticisms from the Walnut Hill Community Association that Penn was neglecting the other schools in its immediate geographic area, Rodin agreed to provide $1.5 million to strengthen the curriculum and the library at the Henry C. Lea elementary school at 47th and Locust streets. In 2002, under pressure from the School District, the University partnered with two other West Philadelphia elementary schools, the William Bryant School and the Alexander Wilson School, to provide "technical assistance and professional development services."[49] The three Penn Partnership Schools echoed the Universities-Related Schools program of the 1960s, which was led by the WPC and the Penn GSE; as well as the West Philadelphia Free School, a Harnwell-GSE initiative that provided seed funding and technical assistance to several vocationally oriented small high schools housed in sundry buildings under the auspices of West Philadelphia High School. In the 1960s, the (at the time) racially integrated Lea School was the centerpiece of Penn's education outreach, with an accelerated curriculum supported by GSE faculty. In the 1960s, Penn and the WPC focused exclusively on improving existing schools, an effort that ultimately failed. By contrast, Rodin and her allies decided to build a new public school, one that stood squarely in Spruce Hill, the neighborhood closest to the campus, a public school in which the University would have a decisive voice. Penn's institutional support for the Lea, Wilson, and Bryant schools (the Bryant arrangement was short lived) was motivated by political pressures and was a secondary priority for the University.

At the same time these other initiatives were rolling out, the University operated a parallel track of school-improvement programs through the Center for Community Partnerships, today's Netter Center. The CCP and its predecessor organization, the Penn Program for Public Service, had more than a decade's worth of experience in the West Philadelphia schools. CCP's cocurricular work in some of the city's toughest schools, especially three racially isolated neighborhood high schools (Sayre, West Philadelphia, and University City), was more challenging than supporting the development of the Penn Alexander School, a de novo, state-of-the-art, architecturally innovative elementary school in a park-like setting (replete with a wetlands component) in a leafy, pedestrian-friendly neighborhood a few blocks from one of the nation's great universities. Rodin, perhaps understandably, favored the GSE and Penn Alexander over the CCP; after all, Penn Alexander was something she could point to and say, "That's mine. I built that." While Rodin's memoir of her presidency speaks highly of the CCP, especially the Center's support of academically based community service seminars, Penn Alexander unquestionably was her first priority, the jewel in her crown of the West Philadelphia Initiatives, in which the CCP played only a secondary role. And while Rodin recognized the important political role Ira Harkavy played in strengthening Penn's image in West Philadelphia, she never acknowledged the enormous debt the West Philadelphia Initiatives owed to the politics of reconciliation that he, Lee Benson, and Sheldon Hackney pursued in West Philadelphia in the 1980s.

Undeniably, the West Philadelphia Initiatives provided "real and significant improvements" to the quality of life in University City, reviving and completing the project Gaylord Harnwell and the WPC had begun in 1959. By the 2000s, University City was an economically diverse, multiethnic, multinational district, much more so than in the Harnwell era. Rodin acknowledges, in her book *The University and Urban Revival*, that "despite the best efforts, the tension between gentrification and affordability has increased, and the issue needs vigilance." One indicator of this tension has been the dramatic increase in the median sale price of houses in the Penn Alexander catchment area, from $94,750 in 1999 to $248,000 in 2003 (tripling in value in just four years), to $410,000 in 2007.[50] The shift in the ethnic diversity of Penn Alexander's enrollments is another indicator: from 57 percent African American, 19 percent Caucasian, 18 percent Asian, 6 percent Latino in 2004, to 39 percent African American, 32 percent Caucasian, 14 percent Asian, and 6 percent

Latino in 2010.[51] An analysis of block-level census data shows that between 2000 and 2010, "the African American population within the Penn Alexander catchment declined by 52 percent in just ten years, even as the white and Asian populations increased by 27 percent and 56 percent, respectively." These findings make it "hard not to conclude that higher property values, fueled in large part by Penn Alexander, have displaced some lower-income African Americans from the catchment."[52]

The health of Penn's larger urban ecology in West Philadelphia also needs continuous vigilance. Rodin issues a caveat in her memoir, saying that "significant needs still exist in an 'outer ring' of blight and instability located outside the original target area."[53] A report to Penn's vice president for government and community affairs in 2006 describes conditions in the outer ring, including one particularly ominous admonition: "The devastation in New Orleans and throughout the Gulf Coast from Hurricane Katrina grimly reminded the nation that issues of race and poverty have not been addressed in this country. Four neighborhoods just north of Market Street and quite proximate to the University (Belmont, Haverford North, Mantua, and Mill Creek) have higher poverty rates (40–43%) than [the] New Orleans Lower Ninth Ward (36%). Both West Philadelphia and New Orleans as a whole have more than one-quarter of their populations living below the federal poverty line; and in both locations the median income is far less than the national median." The subtext here is that West Philadelphia is a New Orleans in the making.[54]

In 2006, following a national trend, violent crime soared once again in Philadelphia, with a total of 406 murders for the year, up 7 percent from 2005. Neighborhoods within a one-to-two-mile radius of the University were devastated by an outbreak of handgun murders. "In southwest Philadelphia, violence and poverty go hand in hand," according to Reuters. "In three local zip codes covered by a recent City of Philadelphia survey, at least 15 percent of adults are unemployed, almost a third of high school students don't graduate, and around four in ten meet federal poverty standards. Many poverty indicators in the neighborhood, where 78 percent of residents are black, exceed those for the city as a whole."[55] Though this rash of homicides was confined to the outer ring, Rodin's successor, Amy Gutmann, responding to pressure from frightened parents after a nonfatal shooting at 38th and Walnut streets, increased the security budget by $5 million in January 2006, adding 20 percent more Penn police officers, 50 percent more security guards, and more lighting, security cameras, and emergency phones; Penn had already added $2 million in supplemental funds for safety and security earlier in the fiscal year, raising the total of new funds in 2005–06 to $7 million.[56] Unsurprisingly, *Security Magazine* ranked Penn "No. 1 for safety in the educational market."[57]

11
Agenda for Excellence

Rodin's presidency marked a throttle-to-the-floor acceleration of Penn's evolution as a top-tier American university. Her charisma, fierce intelligence, and assertive and occasionally combative "corporate" leadership style were well suited for the extraordinarily competitive zeitgeist of American higher education in the 1990s and early 2000s. Indeed, she often portrayed herself as a CEO. "Judy solidified the corporatization of the University," says Phoebe LeBoy, a former chair and thirty-five-year member of the Faculty Senate. "I'm not sure where she got it from. I don't think it was a legacy from her time at Yale. I think it was mostly because of lengthy discussions with members of the board of trustees and the chair of the board. But her idea was that Research I universities were big businesses, we had to start acting like big business, and this was a corporation."[1]

In the previous chapter, we described Penn's wheeling and dealing in commercial buildings, which was one characteristic of Rodin-style corporatization. In this chapter, we examine her internal management of the University as a CEO-directed, hierarchically structured business, emphasizing Rodin's strategic decision making without faculty advice and consent; executive vice president John Fry's outsourcing of facilities management and real estate operations; and Rodin's corporate-style power struggle with William Kelley, the outsized dean of the Medical School and executive vice president of the Medical Center. Next we take up Rodin's Agenda for Excellence, which successfully exerted tremendous pressure on the deans to lead their schools to top-ten rankings. Then we analyze the changes in the undergraduate curriculum that Rodin and the faculty introduced under the banner of the 21st Century Project, attending to their establishment of a college house *system* and their endorsement of academically based community service, both of which meshed with Rodin's commitment to West Philadelphia. We conclude the chapter with a brief discussion of the minority population at Penn in the Rodin era.

■ Penn in the Marketplace

The most consequential administrative appointment of Rodin's tenure was John A. Fry as the University's executive vice president in February 1995. At the time of his appointment, Fry headed the National Higher Education Consulting Services at Coopers and Lybrand, the national accounting firm whose report of January 1995 Rodin regarded as the starting point for "our project of analyzing and restructuring the University's administration."[2] On 17 January, the University released a Coopers and Lybrand report that included a "proposed vision and principles for administrative restructuring." The report, whose senior author was Fry, prefigured the corporate-business ideology and discourse that would guide the administrative governance and operations of the Rodin campus in the sectors of Fry's purview. Specifically, the report called for "a creative and tough-minded approach to improving [Penn's] administrative practices and reducing its administrative costs . . . by $20 to $30 million over the next three to five years, through an aggressive program of reengineering and restructuring." Penn's administration would be "lean, client driven, and market competitive"; the Executive Vice President Center— the responsibility management center in charge of human resources, finance, information systems, facilities management, public safety, and business services—would "be subject on a periodic basis to regular free market comparisons similar to a for-profit client service operation." Like a business, the University would operate according to the principles of "total quality management." Downsizing, in the name of "selective excellence," would be done (in theory at least) compassionately by helping displaced employees find new positions within or outside the University; indeed, Rodin proudly touted "our new Position Discontinuation and Staff Transition (PDST) plan."[3]

Market competition was the driver of restructuring at Penn. Fry, whom the *Chronicle of Higher Education* described as the embodiment of "the new, corporatized Penn,"[4] informed the University Council that "we're in a very competitive market for attracting the best faculty and the best students—and to compete successfully every available dollar needs to be invested in high-impact, mission-relevant areas. . . . In this regard it is important to note what our competitors are doing. They are engaged in similar exercises, as I know from my previous work around the country consulting for Stanford, Chicago,

Yale, Columbia, Harvard, Michigan, California—the list goes on. Everyone is engaged in some form of this activity."[5] Fry was "corporate" in every way. "I remember the first time he addressed a faculty group at a public meeting, and he referred to the faculty as his clients," recalled LeBoy. "It was an accident and he never did it again. But that was what was happening to the University."[6]

Sheldon Hackney had created the administrative domain that John Fry now surveyed as Rodin's executive vice president. Recognizing the need for a highly qualified manager to operate the business side of the campus, Hackney, in September 1981, established the Office of Senior Vice President, to whom six vice presidents—facilities and real estate, finance, human resources, business services, public safety, and government relations—reported; the vice president for development and alumni relations reported directly to the president. That Hackney's first appointment to the new position was Edward Jordan, a former chairman and CEO of Conrail (the Consolidated Rail Corporation), did not reflect a corporate ideology on Hackney's part; he simply wanted the best manager available for the job. "Good managers can manage anything, anytime," he often said. In any case, Jordan's "heavy-handed" corporate style was a "mismatch" with the University, and he left Penn after nine months.[7]

Three subsequent appointments to this position rounded out the next decade of Hackney's presidency, and none of these senior administrators had a corporate background. Helen O'Bannon, who held the position from 1983 to 1988, was a former associate dean of the Carnegie Institute of Technology.[8] Following O'Bannon's death from cancer, Hackney appointed Marna Whittington, the University's dynamic vice president for finance, to the senior post. Before coming to Penn in 1984, Whittington had managed government finance and administrative services for the state of Delaware. The change in Whittington's title to executive vice president in 1991 still did not reflect a corporate turn at the University. Indeed, when Whittington stepped down in September 1992, Hackney appointed Janet Hale, who at the time was an associate director in the federal Office of Management and Budget, as Whittington's replacement. Hackney, apparently unwittingly, created a structure that could be easily converted to corporate-style management; with Fry's appointment, Rodin made that conversion and funded it with a vengeance.

■

Within a year of Fry's arrival, the University had a contract with Barnes & Noble to develop a megabookstore on the Unit 4 urban renewal block of 3601Walnut Street. The company contracted to operate the new University bookstore in a building that would double the bookstore's former size while

(Top) View east along the 3601 block of Walnut Street, with tiny McAlpin Street at left, 1964, and House of Pagano Pizzeria. Collections of the University Archives and Records Center.

(Bottom) Contemporary view of the 3601 block: the Inn at Penn, upscale shops, and the University bookstore—Walnut Street components of University Square. Photograph by Michael M. Koehler. Collections of the University Archives and Records Center.

upgrading its services. According to the agreement, "the University will pay an estimated $8 million in construction costs for the new building. . . . The company will pay the University a guaranteed income of $1.3 million a year or 12 percent of the store's gross sales up to $20 million, and 14 percent of the sales above that figure." "The bookstore is the first stake in the ground saying that we want to develop the area," Fry said.[9] The transition took place in the summer of 1996; Barnes & Noble hired thirty-eight of the fifty-four employees of the old bookstore (located since 1968 at the corner of 38th Street and Locust Walk). For various reasons, however, only seventeen of these employees remained on the company's payroll by October; the University promised to extend its tuition benefit to these individuals and their families even though they were no longer Penn employees.[10]

Predictably, this contract provoked a backlash among a sizable core of faculty and students who feared that Barnes & Noble would drive out University City's independent book dealers who specialized in academic and other small-market trade books. "One can find Barnes & Noble, with their bland selection of military histories, banal self-help books, and paperback bestsellers, in any shopping mall in the country," wrote Thomas Sugrue, a Bancroft Prize-winning history professor. "But one expects better of university communities. Harvard Square is a vital shopping district because of its many independent bookstores; Telegraph Avenue in Berkeley remains a national magnet for bibliophiles because of its wonderful small book shops. University of Chicago students can spend fruitful hours perusing the stacks at Powell's or negotiating the labyrinthine aisles of the Seminary Coop. As a student in New York, my intellectual life was greatly enriched by the independent bookstores that thrived on the Upper West Side (before Barnes & Noble drove them out of business)."[11]

The sparkling-new Penn Bookstore and retail/restaurant complex opened in July 1998—a bookstore "without peer," boasted Fry. The Inn at Penn, the companion building that completed the redevelopment of the 3601 block, opened in September 1999, with "234 guest rooms as well as 26 deluxe, hospitality and conference suites."[12] (The "Superstore"/Inn at Penn complex ended planning for the Revlon Student Center on the site; more below.) "Its Boston-based designers were familiar with contextual retail infill and readily adapted Penn's color scheme [in this case, red brick and limestone tint] to clad the immense building," writes George Thomas.[13] Despite the new bookstore's pricing advantage, the area's independent book dealers, House of Our Own and Penn Book Center, managed to retain their specialized niches, the latter at a new location in the Shoppes at Penn, the retail complex at 3401 Walnut Street.

A parking lot for twenty years: the Unit 4 block bounded by Walnut, 36th, Sansom, and 37th streets, originally planned for the Graduate Center. Photo shows groundbreaking ceremony for Sansom Commons (renamed University Square), 1996. Photograph by James R. Mann, Facilities and Real Estate Services, University of Pennsylvania.

The situation of rank-and-file employees at the Faculty Club was different from that of the former bookstore's union members who were rehired by Barnes & Noble. The privately incorporated Faculty Club, whose home since 1959 was the four-story Skinner Building on the southwest corner of 36th and Walnut streets, was scheduled to close and to transfer its functions to DoubleTree Hotels, which would operate the Inn at Penn. (Hitherto the University had provided use of this building at no cost to the faculty club, paid its yearly operating costs, and covered its deficits.)[14] In an open letter to the *Daily Pennsylvanian*, Fry explained the rationale for laying off thirty-five Penn employees: "At the Inn at Penn, food and beverage service for the Faculty Club would be provided by the hotel operator, DoubleTree, using its own employees. The DoubleTree employees providing this service would

Contemporary view of University Square and Penn Bookstore, 3601 Walnut Street. Photograph by James R. Mann, Facilities and Real Estate Services, University of Pennsylvania.

be part of a much larger food and beverage operation in connection with its overall hotel operation." More pointedly, "DoubleTree, not Penn, will be the employer at the Inn at Penn. DoubleTree will run a much different business— a 250-room hotel, not simply a private club." Put another way, the University's Faculty Club contract with AFL-CIO Local 274, Hotel Employees and Restaurant Employees, which expired on 31 July 1998, was of no concern to DoubleTree. It would be "improper," Fry concluded, for Penn "to force terms and conditions of employment and a pre-determined staff on DoubleTree and its many other employers."[15] Voicing the frustration of Penn's laid-off workers, Patrick Coughlin, the president of Local 274, said, "They're taking average working people, throwing them out of their job and then telling them that they can reapply for the same job."[16] Local 274 was not a party to DoubleTree's written offer to rehire at least 70 percent of the club's full-time employees.[17] Leafleting pedestrians at the Inn at Penn in the fall of 1999, union members called the University's actions a "disgrace."[18]

In a brash, unprecedented stroke to consolidate and streamline the management and operation of the University, Rodin and Fry, despite staunch opposition from the University Council and student groups, outsourced Penn's facilities management, residential operations, and real-estate operations (University City Associates) to Trammel Crow, "a real estate property management firm" in Dallas, Texas, with no previous experience in operating campus facilities. In October 1997, Fry notified 175 managers and support staff that their positions were being transferred to Trammel Crow, and their continued employment was at the company's discretion. The ten-year agreement specified financial obligations for both Penn and Trammell Crow: Penn to pay Trammell Crow $5.2 million yearly, and Trammel Crow to pay Penn $32 million for "providing this opportunity to enter the higher education market in a leadership position" (the latter sum was never paid). Trammell Crow Higher Education Services, Inc., a new subsidiary, would be the firm's "infrastructure management services" provider.[19] In December, Fry said in an open letter that Trammell Crow would "extend offers to a minimum of 70 percent of the people interviewed," and the University would provide "interview, resume and employment counseling" to all personnel whose positions were affected by the transition.[20] Approximately 140 employees were rehired in outsourced positions.[21] Yet just two years later Fry and his senior staff downsized the agreement with Trammel Crow to return control of facilities management and residential maintenance to the University, leaving the company to continue to provide construction-management services and "property leasing, acquisitions and dispositions."[22] Fry called the new contract "a mid-course adjustment"; Rodin called it rectifying an unsatisfactory arrangement: "We need to take responsibility for maintenance. Despite the fact that it is not our core strength, it is indeed our core responsibility. And when we don't see it going as well as we would like . . . the only default is to take it back ourselves." "For the past 21 months, many Trammell Crow employees have voiced displeasure with the management, calling it inefficient and dysfunctional, and few students or faculty have seen any improvement in facilities services," reported the *Daily Pennsylvanian*.[23] Ironically, the University found itself rehiring the same facilities managers it had laid off only two years before. Finally, in the late summer of 2002, by mutual consent, Penn and Trammell Crow terminated the contract that

(Top) View south on 36th Street from Sansom Street during the era of subway-surface construction, 1952. The truck in the background, at Walnut Street, faces the Penn campus. The West Philadelphia Title and Trust Company is on the left. Photo courtesy of PhillyHistory.org, a project of the Philadelphia Department of Records.

(Bottom) Contemporary view along 36th Street, showing University Square, completed in the late 1990s; creating a tree-lined café ambience near the corner of 36th and Walnut. Photograph by Michael M. Koehler. Collections of the University Archives and Records Center.

outsourced Penn's capital projects and real-estate management. Fry's only reported comment was, "I think together, there are some things that we have not achieved, but I'll leave it at that." Undoubtedly, the significant delays in major campus construction projects (see below) fueled the University's disenchantment with Trammell Crow.[24]

Trammel Crow illustrated the Rodin-Fry hegemony. Decisions of major import to the operation of the campus and its functioning as a "community of scholars" flowed downward from College Hall to the faculty, with only the pretense of consultation. Trammel Crow was a fait accompli by the time the leadership of the Faculty Senate was "consulted." When the University Council, the highest ranking advisory body to the president, called on the trustees to "withhold approval" of the Trammel Crow contract, the Council's resolution was ignored. The Council's Ad Hoc Committee on Consultation, appointed by Rodin and the Senate chair, in 1998, lacked any teeth to dissuade Rodin from maneuvering around the faculty.[25] LeBoy scoffs at the pretense of faculty consultation:

> So while Judy always paid attention to the requirements of faculty consultation, faculty consultation suddenly took on a very different meaning than what it had meant before. Consultation meant not that the ideas are generated by the faculty, but that you come up with an idea, make a decision, and present it briefly to a faculty group and hear their comments. Not that you're going to change your mind, but at least you have consulted and heard any concerns . . . the academic planning and budget committee became pretty much a show and tell. You never knew the agenda before the meeting and you would come in and the provost or the provost staff would have invited somebody in to make a presentation either about a part of the University or a proposal and then you were allowed perhaps five or ten minutes to discuss it. And that was it. And that was faculty consultation. And that's the way it exists today. That's what I mean by corporatization.[26]

The College Hall and Franklin Building nabobs benefited from the fact that the Faculty Senate stood at its lowest ebb of influence among the standing faculty in its forty-five-year history, a casualty of faculty apathy. Reflecting the organization's diminished stature, two of its chairpersons were "professors of lesser distinction." Low-status leadership made the Senate an easy mark for a corporatizing administration.[27]

In his 2003 book *Universities in the Marketplace*, former Harvard University president Derek Bok sketches out the proliferation of commercial activities on the nation's campuses after 1980. "What made commercialization so much more prevalent in American universities after 1980," he observes, "was the rapid growth of opportunities to supply education, expert advice, and scientific knowledge in return for handsome sums of money. During the first half of the twentieth century, the chances to profit from such activities were not nearly so abundant." Bok restricts his use of the term *commercialization* "to refer to efforts within the university to make a profit from teaching, research, and other campus activities." Many of the universal commercial indicators Bok cites have been prevalent at Penn since the 1980s: for example, corporate sponsorship of medical research (see below); licensing revenues and patent activity;[28] education for profit—notably, the Wharton School's Executive MBA program, which has been wildly profitable both for the program and the professors who teach in it; and top-dollar external consulting, which is bolstered by the University's lax ("don't ask, don't tell") policy on the amount of off-campus consulting the faculty are allowed to do in an academic year (the annual reporting form is vague and remarkably easy to fudge). Finally, and increasingly under Rodin, there was the overheated competition for national rankings in such publications as *U.S. News & World Report* (more below).

Missing in Bok's analysis are the commercial real estate transactions that involve universities; in Penn's case, Rodin's West Philadelphia Initiatives and her administration's wheeling and dealing in commercial properties on Walnut Street. Commercialization operated within a corporatized administrative culture that Rodin and her leadership team aggressively promoted. Corporate lingo—terms like *CEO*, *bottom line*, and *branding*—has been ubiquitous at Penn since the mid-1990s.[29] The spring 2002 meeting of the board of trustees marked the apex of commercialization. At this meeting, Federal Judge Marjorie Rendell (soon to be the state's First Lady when Ed Rendell was elected governor of Pennsylvania later that year) presented the report of the external affairs committee on "branding Penn." Research studies commissioned by the University showed that "Penn lacked a consistent visual brand identity." Put another way, the general public had a hard time distinguishing Penn from Penn State. "A new logo and webpage redesign" were called for. To the trustees' evident satisfaction, the firm Deutsch Advertising created the logo "Penn" as the webpage's new masthead, with the University of Pennsylvania appearing in a subdued, lower-font size below the masthead. The new webpage went online in the fall of 2002, with the schools and programs working simultaneously "to develop consistent sub-logos." For example, the Graduate School of Education and the School of Design branded themselves as "Penn GSE" and "Penn Design."[30]

∎

Often cited in articles on the subject in the *Chronicle of Higher Education*, Penn was recognized as a national leader in the commercialization of higher education. According to *Chronicle* reports, Rodin was the nation's top-paid university president in fiscal years 1998, 1999, and 2001.[31] In FY 2001, she received $808,201 from Penn ($690,450 in salary and performance bonuses; $117,616 in benefits); her total pay for membership on corporation boards that year was about $248,600. In FY 2003, her total compensation at Penn was $892,213, and her annual pay for board memberships was as much as $403,900. While the salaries of Penn's full professors increased 23.2 percent between 1998–99 and 2002–3, her salary increased 36.3 percent—hardly a pauperization of Penn professors, but an imbalance nevertheless that reflected a corporatized valuation of the Penn presidency.[32] From the trustees' perspective, keeping Penn, an institution of great "size and complexity," in the top tier of the higher education marketplace required nothing less than a hard-edged leader of Judith Rodin's ilk, a star commodity recruited from a highly selective talent pool.[33]

The same logic applied to John Fry's compensation as executive vice president. According to the University's tax declaration to the Internal Review Service for 2001, Fry was paid a salary of $763,464, compared to $534,000 for Provost Robert Barchi, the University's chief academic officer.[34] While neither Rodin nor Fry earned anything close to what Goldman Sachs executives were making, their salaries bespeak the trustees' endorsement of Rodin's commitment to manage Penn in the style of a high-flying, for-profit corporation.[35] The logic held that top performers like Rodin and Fry justified their lucrative compensation packages by giving Penn a competitive edge in the higher education marketplace.

As we have seen, Rodin and Fry's corporate approach was disruptive and provoked a great deal of anxiety and rancor on the main campus. Yet in the end it involved only a minimal number of layoffs, if only because the Trammell Crow deal backfired. The situation in the Penn Health System was radically different. Unlike restructuring on the main campus, which was a proactive measure to strengthen Penn's competitiveness vis-à-vis peer institutions, restructuring in the hospital and medical school complex was driven by a devastating financial crisis that prompted hundreds of layoffs. The crisis pitted Rodin in a bitter power struggle with William Kelley, who was CEO of the Penn Health System, a formal entity established in 1993, which included the Medical Center (HUP; the Medical School, where Kelley was dean; and the Clinical Practices of the University of Pennsylvania—a consolidation effected in 1986), three other Penn-owned hospitals, and the Clinical Care Associates, a regional network of primary care providers.[36]

■ **Rodin and Kelley in the Arena: Crisis in the Penn Health System**

Uniformly described by his colleagues as brilliant, visionary, and judicious, yet also narcissistic, imperious, and not particularly likable, William Kelley tried to manage the byzantine Penn Health System as a personal fiefdom. He produced fat surpluses at HUP in the early- to mid-'90s, and spent freely to purchase clinical practices and three hospitals (Presbyterian, Pennsylvania, and Phoenixville hospitals), recruited star faculty and clinicians, hired a raft of new staff, and erected two gigantic research buildings: the ten-story Stellar-Chance Laboratories (1994) on Curie Boulevard and the fourteen-story Biomedical Research Building II/III (1999), "the house that Kelley built," across the street. "During the 1990s, the Kelley years," writes John Kastor, "the amount of research space in the University of Pennsylvania school of medicine almost doubled, from 482,000 to 874,000 net square feet, and this figure did not include the laboratories of the department of pediatrics based at the Children's Hospital." Between 1989 and 1999, Kelley raised Penn's medical-research revenues from $102 million to $304 million, and achieved a second-place ranking in 1998 and 1999 behind Johns Hopkins in total National Institutes of Health (NIH) receipts.[37]

Yet after 1997, HUP started to lose a great deal of money. The precipitants were reduced Blue Cross payments to doctors and federal cutbacks in Medicare payments mandated by the Balanced Budget Act of 1997. In combination, these reductions took a heavy toll on Penn's four hospitals, which found themselves awash in uncompensated indigent care; the Penn Health System's total bill for uncompensated or undercompensated care in FY 1999 was $106 million.[38] Penn's fiscal problems were not atypical: teaching hospitals and academic medical centers nationwide sustained heavy losses in the late 1990s. Closer to home, "in the fiscal year ending June 30, 1999, nearly 60 percent of hospitals in Philadelphia, almost half of suburban hospitals in southeastern Pennsylvania, and 40 percent of hospitals throughout the state lost money." Shared misery was no consolation for Kelley: the Penn Health System lost $90 million in FY 1998 and a whopping $198 million in FY 1999. Despite these setbacks, Kelley kept spending and building, with Rodin's and the trustees' approval.[39]

Different structural arrangements at Penn would have helped Kelley in the crisis. An existing arrangement that applied to all schools was the University's practice of returning to each school 80 percent of the indirect costs charged to the federal government for each grant, while retaining 20 percent for University projects. (Indirect costs, an add-on of more than 50 percent to the final amount of a federal grant, covered such things as building-operation costs and research infrastructure.) Like all deans, Kelley groused about indirect costs, but he was appalled by other arrangements that he deemed unique to his situation and egregiously unfair, such as Rodin's order to the Medical Center to purchase several Penn-owned buildings near the hospital at what Kelley believed were wildly inflated prices. He told Kastor, "We moved close to $100 million per year, a total of $900 million, to the university during my time, most of it after Judy arrived, and this didn't include such capital expenditures as the new research buildings. Suffice it to say, she did not like it when I told her that the goose that laid the golden egg was anovulatory [no longer producing eggs]. This was after several years of more gentle verbiage. When I started pushing on this, Judy balked." Kelley complained that the Medical Center was forced to pay twice the amount that Penn's peer medical centers paid their universities; and "we were charged double what steam, telephone, and electricity cost and paid all the taxes levied against the university."[40]

Another arrangement that kept Kelley awake at night was the Medical Center's peculiar relationship with the Children's Hospital of Philadelphia (CHOP), whose buildings in the Philadelphia Center for Health Sciences (on the former grounds of the Philadelphia General Hospital) stand just south of HUP and east of the Medical Center's Clinical Research Building. "Doctors working at CHOP have Penn faculty titles, and Penn medical students obtain most of their experience in the care of children there," explains Kastor. "Because of the governance structure, however, the CEO of the University of Pennsylvania Health System and Medical Center has no more control over the operations at CHOP than do the CEOs of other teaching hospitals in Philadelphia." Especially disturbing was the drain of millions of research dollars and prestige away from the Medical School. "CHOP, not the university, controlled its research dollars which, not incidentally, is conducted in buildings built and owned by CHOP and not through the medical school. . . . Consequently, the amount of these grants is not listed in Penn's total of NIH awards but rather in a separate table of independent hospitals that NIH compiles. In the U.S. government fiscal year ending September 30, 2001 CHOP investigators generated more than $52 million in grants from the NIH." The sticking point for Kelley: with that money on its ledgers, the medical school would have vaulted over Johns Hopkins to number one in receipt of NIH awards.[41]

Kelley responded to the fiscal crisis by cutting 2,670 positions (20 percent of the total workforce), including corporate staff and medical support personnel at the four hospitals, with layoffs and unfilled positions taking effect in three phases from May 1999 to July 2000.[42] Rodin, however, did not believe that Kelley could return the system to financial solvency, and she had other reasons to fire him as well.

First, there was the scandal in 1995–96 over "alleged errors" in Medicare billings by physicians in the Clinical Practices of the University of Pennsylvania (CPUP), the administrative arm of Penn's faculty practices. From a random sample of one hundred records in 1993 and extrapolations between 1989 and 1994, federal auditors calculated that CPUP doctors had overbilled Medicare by $10 million. The faculty clinicians had signed off on services that were actually provided by HUP residents, whose training and salaries were supplemented by the Department of Health and Human Services, in effect double-billing the government. Though CPUP disavowed any fraudulent intent, Kelley agreed to a settlement that cost the University $30 million ($10 million for alleged billing errors, $20 million in fines), not to mention a great deal of embarrassing publicity.[43]

Second, there was the maelstrom in 1999–2000 over the tragic death of eighteen-year-old Jessie Gelsinger, a patient in the Medical Center's Institute for Human Gene Therapy (IHGT), whose director, James Wilson, a Kelley recruit, was investigated by the U.S. Food and Drug Administration (FDA) for violating research protocols in Gelsinger's treatment. Gelsinger had volunteered to participate in a clinical trial "to test the safety of delivering a potentially corrective gene to the livers of adult volunteers afflicted with . . . a rare genetic disorder that usually kills babies within days of their birth."[44] On 17 September 1999, four days after receiving an intravenous transfusion that carried the corrective gene, Gelsinger died of "acute-respiratory-stress syndrome and multiple-organ failure." In January 2000, following its investigation, the FDA temporarily suspended the IHGT's clinical trials, alleging a number of protocol violations: among others, that IHGT "didn't adequately document the process of informed consent for some of the patients," "failed to halt the human study and immediately notify the FDA after two previous patients developed severe toxic reactions," and "included Gelsinger in the study even though the ammonia levels [a measure of liver function] in his blood were too high to meet the eligibility criteria the day before the drug was administered." Assertively rebutting each charge, the IHGT insisted that Gelsinger's death "was simply not foreseeable based on informed medical judgment and the best scientific information available at the time."[45] "Complicating the issue further," explains Kastor, "was Wilson's relationship to a for-profit company [Genovo] that funded nearly a quarter of his work and would benefit from discoveries that were commercially applicable. Wilson and the university owned stock in the company, and Wilson held separate patents that could produce sizeable financial awards if effective therapy based on the discoveries became available." Unsurprisingly, in September 2000 the Gelsinger family filed a wrongful death suit, which was settled out of court, reportedly at great expense to the University. Rodin blamed Kelley for the IHGT mess.[46] Two years later, long after Kelley had left the Health System's administrative offices, Wilson stepped down from his directorship of the IHGT.[47]

Third, there was the personal matter of gigantic dueling egos, "the Bill-Judy thing," as one of Kastor's faculty informants put it. While the two were careful to avoid any public display of hostility, they privately loathed each other. Kelley deeply resented Rodin's intrusion into his fiefdom: "She wanted to run the medical center," he told Kastor, "unlike Sheldon Hackney and Claire Fagin." Rodin regarded Kelley as a loose cannon, and she resented his haughtiness; her reason for hiring Robert Barchi, a distinguished Penn neurologist and professor, as her second provost may have been, as Kastor speculates, "to help her handle Kelley."[48]

On 15 February 2000, Rodin fired Kelley even though he could justifiably claim that the Health System was on the verge of balancing its operating budget. Rodin was also not swayed by the medical school's third-place ranking in *U.S. News*. In the reshuffling that followed the abrupt resignation of Peter Traber, Kelley's replacement, Rodin and the University trustees created a new "umbrella governance structure" for Penn medical affairs, removing the multiple boards and byzantine lines of reporting that had encumbered the Health System. The board of this new entity, called "Penn Medicine," was chaired by a University trustee, and the chairman of the University trustees held an ex officio seat on the medical board. On paper, the new arrangement separated the medical school from the rest of the Health System, the latter to include CPUP, HUP and the other hospitals, a hospice, and the Clinical Care Associates. On 1 September 2001, Arthur Rubenstein, for sixteen years the chairman of medicine at the University of Chicago, assumed his new position as dean of the Penn medical school and executive vice president for health affairs; Robert Martin, who would report directly to Rubenstein, assumed the office of CEO of the Health System. Rodin acceded to Rubenstein's demand to be given de facto authority for all of Penn's medical operations. He was, after all, her appointee and a less flamboyant, more congenial type for Rodin than Kelley.[49]

■ Into the Top Ten: Rodin's Agenda for Excellence

The high-flying performance of Penn's medical school, under Kelley and later under Rubenstein, was paralleled in other schools at Penn. As we have seen,

Rodin pressured the deans to achieve a top-ten listing in *U.S. News*, if not some other high-profile medium. In November 1995, Rodin and her first provost, Stanley Chodorow, published the *Agenda for Excellence*, a $1.5 billion strategic plan for five-year planning and implementation in each of the University's twelve schools; its main goal was "to solidify and advance [Penn's] position as one of the world's premier teaching and research universities." More precisely, "the University will be considered among the top ten in undergraduate education"; "Penn's academic departments and programs will be considered among the top ten in the United States or will develop and implement strategies for moving toward the top tier. Penn's doctoral and professional students will be the programs of choice for the ablest graduate and professional students in the nation and in the world." Eight other goals in the *Agenda for Excellence*, including administrative restructuring and government and community relations (see both above), would support the academic mission.[50] Released in September 1996, *Six University Academic Priorities*, a supplemental document to the *Agenda*, broadly described six areas that would carry particular weight in planning: Life Sciences, Technology and Policy; American and Comprehensive Democratic and Legal Institutions; Management, Leadership, and Organization; The Humanities—Meaning in the 21st Century; The Urban Agenda; and Information, Science, Technology and Society.[51] Four months later, in January 1997, the deans released their strategic plans.[52]

The measure of excellence that counted the most in College Hall was the school or department's ranking in a *U.S. News* or National Research Council list; Rodin aspired to nothing less than surpassing Harvard in *U.S. News's* ranking of national research universities. And she succeeded wildly in dramatically improving Penn's rankings and shedding the last remnant of the University's inferiority complex.[53] During her decade in College Hall, Penn rose from twelfth to fourth in the *U.S. News* list ("the measure all university presidents love to hate"). "All the markers of academic success—rankings, faculty awards, student applications, selectivity, growth in endowment—have soared to record levels," she writes in prideful hindsight.[54] After a slippage from eleventh to thirteenth place in *U.S. News* in 1996, Penn broke into the top ten in 1997 at number seven in a tie with Dartmouth. Rodin cautioned that the rankings "should not be taken too seriously," yet in the same breath exulted, "This affirmation that Penn is among the finest institutions in America should be quite helpful as we continue to seek to attract the best and brightest students this year and in the future"; in other words, the rankings would be taken *very* seriously. The fourth-place ranking in *U.S. News*, a tie with Caltech, Duke, MIT, and Stanford, behind Princeton, Harvard, and Yale, was achieved in 2002. In 2004, just after Rodin stepped down, Penn stood alone at number four, again behind the same three Ivies. In the 2001 *U.S. News* rankings of "America's Best Graduate Schools," Penn counted four schools in the top ten: Medicine (#4), Wharton (#3), Education (#8), and Law (#10). In 2003, six schools appeared in the top ten: Wharton (#2), Nursing (#3, not ranked annually), Veterinary Medicine (#3, not ranked annually), Medicine (#3), Education (#5), and Law (#7). In 1995, the National Research Council ranked nineteen Penn graduate programs in its top ten; in 1999, ten departments in the School of Arts and Sciences achieved that distinction.[55]

The higher education authority qua University planner Robert Zemsky suggests the purpose of Rodin's embrace of *U.S. News* rankings, citing outcomes from a statistical model he and others developed at Stanford University's National Center on Post-Secondary Improvement. He writes, "The *U.S. News* rankings measure not quality—a conceit only *U.S. News* itself still promotes—but *market position*." Compelling her deans to pay close attention to the variables in the *U.S. News* survey, Rodin was able to secure Penn's market position as "a top-ten and occasionally top-five," national university. She understood pragmatically that "markets are here to stay" and competition is "a way of life in a market economy."[56] In a recent interview, Rodin remarked that as a psychologist she understood that "the perception mattered," that for all its flaws, *U.S. News* was good for Penn's "external image."[57]

Restructuring the Undergraduate Experience: The 21st Century Project

Recognizing the centrality of undergraduate education to the reputation, vitality, and fiscal well-being of a great university—and continuing Sheldon Hackney's emphasis—Rodin presided over changes that transformed the undergraduate experience at Penn. In the spring of 2004, she proudly recounted the most visible and dramatic of these changes in "the undergraduate landscape," namely, "the development of a comprehensive College House System," and the establishment of four cocurricular "hubs"—Civic House, Kelly Writers House, Weiss Tech House, and the Center for Undergraduate Research and Fellowships (CURF).[58] (Individual college houses predated Rodin's *system*; Penn's first college houses appeared in the 1970s, and six were in full operation with resident faculty masters by 1989.)[59]

In her inaugural address, delivered 21 October 1994, Rodin affirmed her administration's "forceful" commitment to redesign the undergraduate experience, to "involve not only curriculum, but new types of housing, student services and mentoring, to create a seamless experience between the classroom and the residence, from the playing field to the laboratory."[60] Several days later, she and Chodorow released a one-page report, "Implementing a 21st Century Undergraduate Education." It announced a three-year planning process that would be guided by the Provost's Council on Undergraduate Education, which included, among other members, the provost, the deans of the four undergraduate schools, the chair of the Student Committee on Undergraduate Education, and student representatives. Among other points, the report emphasized that faculty engagement, student research, and residential support of academics and cocurricular activities are central to the undergraduate experience.[61] This undergraduate component of the Agenda for Excellence was called the 21st Century Project.

A core component of the 21st Century Project was the work of the Residential Planning Committee, chaired by David Brownlee, a professor of art history. In their first report, *Choosing Community*, Brownlee's committee recommended "that undergraduate housing at the University of Pennsylvania should be organized as multi-year 'Residential Communities,' which include faculty and graduate students. The communities must attract and accommodate undergraduates throughout their years to further the central academic mission of the University." More specifically, the residential communities (the college houses) would provide on-site academic and computing support, and "space for quiet study"; credit-bearing academic seminars and "informal, non-credit academic programming offered by resident faculty and graduate students"; and "support for fitness activities (a recent and perhaps temporary service demand), social events, and communal dining." The committee proposed a total of sixteen college houses, each to house 400–500 students, each with a faculty master, residence dean, resident advisors (RAs), and information technology advisors. Students, including freshmen, would have the option to move from one house to another; they might choose to live off campus or in a fraternity or sorority and still affiliate with a college house.[62]

We have seen that in the wake of the Water Buffalo and newspaper-theft crises of 1993, the Commission on Strengthening the Community, formed during Claire Fagin's interim presidency, recommended the creation of a college house system. The Brownlee committee's 1997 *Choosing Community* report paid homage to the spirit of the earlier report by using the term "residential communities" to underscore the living-learning connections that both committees deemed essential to restoring civility to the campus. In April 1998, a "working group" led by Brownlee submitted their plan to implement a college house system to the provost and executive vice president. "The Working Group is convinced that we have the capacity to create 12 residential 'College Houses' (we adopt Penn's well-established nomenclature for these communities), encompassing all existing undergraduate residences," stated the report. Existing college houses, such as DuBois, Hill, and Ware, would require only minor changes. In the Quad, congeries of "freshmen houses" established in the Hackney era would be nested within Ware and three new college houses—Community, Spruce, and Goldberg—with dining provided in Stouffer Commons. In the Superblock, soon to be renamed Hamilton Village, each of the three high-rises would comprise a single, large college house, and all of the Superblock's houses would have assigned dining tables in the Class of 1920 Commons. Stouffer College House would comprise two dormitories—Stouffer, in the triangle at 38th and Spruce streets, and the former Mayer Hall, a superblock low-rise on Spruce. The existing Van Pelt and Modern Language houses (two adjacent low-rise dorms in the Superblock) would be combined as Gregory House. A distinctive feature of Penn's college house system was the Wheel Project, which offered "residentially based support" for academic learning (for example, mathematics, information technology, writing and library research, modern languages) and programming within each college house, including the participation of residential faculty and graduate students, and referral services to campus-wide academic programs and cocurricular activities.[63] To implement and direct this new system, which debuted in September 1998, Robert Barchi, Chodorow's successor as provost, appointed Brownlee the first director of college houses and services, with a direct reporting line to the provost.

Another core component of the 21st Century Project was "curriculum reform and innovation." Under Rodin, the four undergraduate schools instituted regular curriculum reviews and introduced new cross-school and cross-disciplinary programs. The undergraduate curriculum itself proved to be more durable. From 2000 to 2005, the undergraduate deans and curriculum committees tinkered with changing the general requirement, in the end reducing it from ten courses in seven sectors of knowledge to seven courses in seven sectors, one per sector; they added (controversially) a cultural-analysis requirement, and left intact courses required in "writing, language, quantitative data analysis, and formal reasoning and analysis."[64] To strengthen the quality of undergraduate teaching, the School of Arts and Sciences established the Center for Teaching and Learning for faculty and teaching assistants in all of Penn's schools. The University established the Center for Undergraduate Research and Fellowships (CURF), "a central clearing house for all undergraduate students interested in participating in research and/or applying for post-baccalaureate fellowships." And Penn offered the nation's largest and finest array of academically based community service (ABCS) courses.[65]

CURF was one of four new cocurricular hubs associated with the 21st Century Project. Another was Kelly Writers House. Established in 1995 and occupying a 150-year-old Victorian house at 3805 Locust Street (near the 38th

Street pedestrian bridge), the Writers House quickly emerged as an energetic hub of undergraduate collaborative writing and production; its high-profile activities included visiting writers and poets, dinners, lectures, and forums, with many events open free to the general public. A third hub, Civic House, operates a clearinghouse for community-service volunteers and social advocacy; its home is the mid-nineteenth-century rectory of St. Mary's Episcopal Church—the 1970s House of the Family, later the headquarters of the Penn Police. The fourth hub, the Weiss Tech House—originally just a cubicle in Huntsman Hall, now in spacious quarters at Levine Hall, 3330 Walnut Street—provides technical support to students interested in developing and marketing computer-software applications.[66]

The 21st Century Project was one way to accelerate Rodin-style excellence in undergraduate education. Another was the revved-up performance of the undergraduate admissions office. As reflected in the *U.S. News* rankings, undergraduate admissions at Penn were increasingly selective in the Rodin era, and the admissions office worked at a frenetic pace ordered by College Hall. From 1994 to 2004, the number of applications increased by 33 percent, from 13,739 submissions to 18,278, apparently with no diminishment of academic quality in the applicant pool.[67] In 2000, matriculated students averaged 1392 on the combined SAT. Barchi predicted that each subsequent class would be "the most selective class to get to Penn . . . for at least a year."[68]

Each year in the fall semester, when Penn's early admissions decisions were made, the undergraduate admissions office was a scene of fervid activity. In a trenchant 2001 essay for *The Atlantic*, James Fallows, the editor of *U.S. News* from 1996 to 1998, explained why early decisions, which make acceptance of an offer binding on applicants, are a sine qua non of Penn's hypercompetitiveness. To explain the attractiveness of an early decision policy to Penn's admissions officers, we quote Fallows at length:

> Suppose a college needs to enroll 2,000 students in its incoming class. Suppose it receives roughly 12,000 applications each year in the regular admissions cycle—a realistic estimate for a prestigious selective school [compare Penn's 18,000 above]. Suppose, finally, that its normal yield [matriculations] for students admitted in the regular cycle is 33 percent—that is, for each three it accepts, one will enroll. This, too, is a realistic figure for most top-tier schools. So to end up with 2,000 freshmen on registration day, a college relying purely on a regular admissions program would send "We are pleased to announce" letters to 6,000 applicants and hope that the usual 33 percent decided to enroll. A regular-only

admissions policy would thus mean that the college's selectivity rate—6,000 acceptances for 12,000 applicants—was an unselective-sounding 50 percent.

Now suppose that the college introduces an early-decision plan and admits 500 applicants, a quarter of the class, that way. Suddenly its statistics improve. It is very likely to receive at least as many total applications as before—say, 1,000 in the ED program and 11,000 regulars. But now it will have to send out only 5,000 acceptance letters—500 earlies plus 4,500 to bring in 1,500 regular students. Therefore its selectivity will improve to 42 percent from the previous 50, and its yield will be 40 percent rather than the original 33, because all those admitted early will be obliged to enroll.

Finally, suppose that the college decides to admit fully half the class early, as some selective colleges already do. It will need to send out only 4,000 offers to get 2,000 students. Its selectivity will become an impressive 33 percent and its overall yield will be 50 percent. With no change in faculty, course offerings, endowment, or characteristics of the entering class, the college will have risen noticeably in the national rankings.

This is how Penn used an aggressive early-decision policy to drive up its rankings—and not just Penn. (emphasis added)[69]

In effect, Penn, under Rodin, devoted itself to an "academic arms" race for the nation's best and brightest students. What then might be the harmful effects of such a policy? Fallows, who himself contributed to building the ratings game at *U.S. News*, cites several, one being the privileging of "professional-class" students who routinely have access to specialized school counselors, not to mention the affluent public and private schools that employ them; whose families have the discretionary income to afford the junior-year rite-of-spring college tour, not to mention SAT tutoring and all the other educational accoutrements that lots of discretionary income can buy. Another fly in the ointment is the potential harm from truncating the high school experience, effectively ending its formal educational component by the end of the junior year; and from compelling young people to make a life-altering decision at age seventeen, when they may not be developmentally ready to do so, thus hurrying adolescence and making its passage extraordinarily stressful. As one former Swarthmore admissions officer told Fallows, "A hallmark of adolescence is its changeability," especially at age seventeen. The Amherst admissions director told him, "Kids may begin the year with the idea of going to a large urban university and end up very happy to come to Amherst. . . .

An awful lot of kids are making the decision too early because they feel that they can't get in if they don't." By asserting that the exchange value, or marketability, of a high status credential (such as Penn's), as opposed to its use value, is the primary driver in professional-class decisions to send their children to top-tier colleges and universities, Fallows aligned himself with a legion of contemporary social scientists.[70]

Academically Based Community Service

An important curricular adjunct to the 21st Century Project is the panoply of elective disciplinary courses that fit the description of academically based community service courses. In Chapter 9, we briefly traced the origins and growth of the Center for Community Partnerships, which provides a University-community mediating structure (the Penn Program for Public Service), course-development grants, and resources for ABCS seminars. These problem-based courses, offered in various schools and departments, are core components of a strategy to redirect undergraduate teaching and learning in the service of active citizenship development, the integration of disciplinary knowledge, and local community revitalization. Also in Chapter 9, we described the CCP's continuing efforts to build a network of university-assisted community schools in West Philadelphia—local public education institutions transformed as integrative catalysts for neighborhood social and health services, community development, and democratic citizenship; as well as sites for interdisciplinary activity and knowledge production (for example, the Sayre High School Health Promotion and Disease Prevention Program, the Urban Nutrition Initiative). And, finally, we noted the emergence of a "Penn model" in the national discourse on service-learning, volunteerism, and youth citizenship in the 1990s.

In their analysis of collegiate youth culture in the 1990s, Arthur Levine and his associates noted the ascendancy of Generation X on the nation's campuses. This was a "new crop" of young people, born after the 1960s, who expressed a "cautious," "cynical," "perverse," or "pragmatic optimism" about the present and future. Surveying more than nine thousand college students in a representative sample, interviewing student leaders and chief campus affairs officers at twenty-eight colleges and universities, and conducting focus group sessions on these campuses, Levine's research team found pervasive evidence of a generational distrust of conventional politics, a "desire for change," and an interest in local volunteerism as a means for change—dispositions that co-existed with materialist career aims, utilitarian views of education, and penchants for binge drinking and casual sex. Representative "Xers" volunteered in ways that gave them the opportunity to see that their actions, however small, were efficacious. Hence "students have chosen to become personally involved and to focus locally, on their community, their neighborhood, and their block. Their vision is small and pragmatic; they are attempting to accomplish what they see as manageable and possible."[71]

College and university administrators responded in droves to this changing climate of student opinion by offering (in some cases mandating) service-learning courses, particularly after President Clinton endorsed national service as a theme of his first administration. In most cases, these courses had no relation to the academic curriculum, nor did they have any political or civic aim beyond "helping." More often than not, the service involved such nonpolitical activities as "tutoring and working in homeless shelters, soup kitchens, and nursing homes."[72] In the summer of 1991, as evidenced at a Campus Compact national conference at Stanford University, service-learning was still a negotiable concept—the term itself was up for grabs. In a series of weeklong debates and conversations, Ira Harkavy and several of his Penn faculty colleagues tried unsuccessfully to persuade the other conferees to recast service-learning as academically based community service, a conception that would accentuate the students' participatory role in constructive social change at the local level. They argued that the faculty would always regard conventional service-learning as a campus sideshow.

In the Rodin era, the CCP rode the whirlwind of undergraduate enthusiasm for local volunteerism, attracting large numbers of students to a growing number of courses. Recruitment of faculty for ABCS courses from across the schools and departments was a major undertaking, and for a while in the early 1990s, it seemed that the CCP was destined to be viewed, at best, by the standing faculty as a benign alien on the Penn campus. Ever the optimists (some would call them delusionary utopians), Harkavy and his colleague Lee Benson worked slowly yet persistently, cornering, cajoling, and eventually persuading numerous faculty members to see, if nothing else, the pedagogical value of ABCS. Penn presidents have funded and publicly applauded the CCP, which brings valuable publicity to the University—and more important, the deans in the School of Arts and Sciences have banged the ABCS drum. The endorsement of Richard Beeman, a prominent professor of American history and dean of the College in the Rodin era, was a breakthrough. In a spring 1998 speech, Beeman, who "had previously been openly skeptical of the value of academically based community service at a major research university," described his "personal conversion," waxing exuberant on the virtues of the learning concept: "I really cannot tell you how much I believe in the value of what is being done in those courses. They give our students a problem-oriented experience in learning, and all the research literature shows that the best learning takes place, not in studying theories and abstract forms, but in solving concrete problems. I am committed to getting first rate faculty involved in that effort as an important definition of their contribution to undergraduate education at Penn."[73]

A consummate *bon vivant* and adroit networker, Harkavy helped build a university civic engagement movement in the 1990s, motivated in part by the political leverage it gave him when dealing with Rodin. The national movement originated in the depths of the Reagan era, kindled by a small yet hardy band of young social entrepreneurs who built networks to promote active citizenship on the nation's campuses. The organizational pathfinders were the National Society for Experiential Education, the International Partnership for Service-Learning and Leadership, the National Youth Leadership Council, and the Campus Outreach Opportunity League. In 1986 Campus Compact, the largest of these networks, was formed to galvanize college presidents. By 1990, Campus Compact numbered 202 institutional members; by 1994, the total was 520.[74] Harkavy became a leading activist for what he calls "The Cause," traveling the rubber-chicken circuit, making hundreds of speeches, coauthoring books and book chapters, publishing in academic journals, and (with Lee Benson and others) developing a historically and theoretically grounded rationale for the university civic engagement movement. As a consultant, he also played a key role in creating the Office of University Partnerships in the Department of Housing and Urban Development. A national voice for the community school idea, he chaired the steering committee of the Coalition for Community Schools.

More Strategic Planning

In May 2001, a group of senior administrators led by Rodin's deputy provost, Peter Conn, confirmed the overall success of the Agenda for Excellence in a thirty-two-page, fine-print document titled *Agenda for Excellence, 1995–2000*. "Penn's progress has been remarkable over the past five years," proclaimed the working group in their cover letter to the report. "With enormous credit to the faculty, students and staff who grace this campus, our academic rankings have risen, faculty accomplishments have continued apace, student selectivity has increased, research funding has greatly expanded, administrative restructuring has moved far forward, revitalization of the West Philadelphia community has accelerated, globalization has increased and fundraising has broken records."[75] Commenting on the success of the plan, Rodin said, "I think that Penn has clearly moved into the pantheon of one of the few truly great research universities in the world. It's where we needed to be, it's where we deserved to be—but we needed some work to get there."[76]

Two years later, College Hall published the second strategic planning document of the Rodin era, *Building on Excellence: The Leadership Agenda*. This new planning document drew from the work of fourteen committees that met periodically in the fall of 2001, involving more than two hundred faculty, staff, and undergraduate and graduate students. A draft plan appeared for University-wide comment in the spring of 2002, though the final report was not available until the early fall of 2003. Section II of *Building on Excellence* designates five academic priorities, in order of appearance in the final report: the Urban Community, the Life Sciences, Technology Innovation, the Global Opportunity, and Arts, Humanities, and Society. The recommendations of the Urban Community committee reflect the ambition and general tenor of the broader report. The next step beyond the successful Urban Agenda of the 1995–2000 planning phase and the West Philadelphia Initiatives, according to this committee, is to establish Penn as "a national leader in urban scholarship," with cutting-edge expertise in public policy research and training, organized in conjunction with "an urban research program that focuses on the Philadelphia metropolitan area." Another recommendation is "to support and encourage the expansion of the Center for Community Partnerships," assigning a high priority to building an endowment for the Center's daily operations and fostering "academically based community service courses that integrate research, teaching, and service."[77]

Within the next six months, Rodin responded to the Urban Community committee's recommendation for a University-wide urban research program by establishing the Penn Institute for Urban Research (IUR), whose founding directors were Eugenie Birch, professor of city and regional planning in the School of Design, and Susan Wachter, professor of real estate and financial management in the Wharton School. Specifically, the Institute was charged to "develop and disseminate knowledge to those charged with managing the growth, problems and design of urban environments at the local, national, and international levels in the decades ahead."[78] In IUR's first decade, three areas have emerged as central foci: "innovative urban development strategies," urban sustainability in the 21st century, and urban anchor institutions. The Institute engages "faculty fellows" from Penn's twelve schools for cross-disciplinary participation in research projects, conferences, forums, and undergraduate and graduate education. The Penn IUR Faculty Forum program sponsors forums on such broadly based topics as "Immigration, Race, and Urban Inequality" and "Modeling Urban Environmental Impacts on Health, Development, and Behavior." IUR research programs include, among others, "instructional cases" in innovative urban development and case studies generated by the Penn IUR Roundtable on Anchor Institutions. In partnership with the IUR, the University of Pennsylvania Press publishes the City in the 21st Century book series; the first book in the series was *Rebuilding Urban Places After Disaster: Lessons from Hurricane Katrina* (2006). The IUR's research portfolio also includes special-issue journals and grant-funded reports.

A second component of the Urban Community agenda is an endowment for the Center for Community Partnerships. Under Amy Gutmann, the University's $4.3 billion Making History capital campaign counts as a small though critical part of that goal a $10 million endowment gift awarded to the CCP in the fall of 2007. Renamed the Barbara and Edward Netter Center for Community Partnerships in honor of the donors, the CCP, or the Netter Center, expanded its operations in the winter of 2009 to establish "its first regional training center on university-assisted community schools" at the University of Oklahoma–Tulsa, providing assistance to schools and communities in the Southwestern states. Funded by the Netter award, this regional replication initiative was the latest national outreach project sponsored by the CCP— previously, with funding from private foundations, Ira Harkavy's team had engaged twenty-two U.S. colleges and universities to adapt Penn's community schools model to their cities and localities, and trained teams from some seventy-five higher education institutions in the practice of university-assisted community schools. The award also allowed the Netter Center to hire a full-time evaluator for Penn's ABCS courses and their effects in the West Philadelphia schools.[79]

A Note on the Presence of Minority Students at Penn

In June 1993, the Ad Hoc Minority Permanence Retrospective Review Committee (a name that must have been chosen by committee) listed 111 "master documents" on the minority presence at Penn since 1969. Compiled in two bound volumes, these documents record a quarter of a century's worth of analyses and initiatives on the recruitment and retention of minority students and faculty at Penn.[80] Yet for all the committees and all the reports, the refrain across four decades remained constant: some minorities are chronically underrepresented at Penn.

In the spring of 1999, the University Council compiled yet another set of data on the subject and reported a familiar, by now unsurprising analysis. In 1998, Asian Americans, for whom Penn was the preferred Ivy League school, constituted 19.7 percent of matriculants; for the classes entering between 1986 and 1990, this group's graduation rate was 82.2 percent. Data for underrepresented minorities were much less encouraging. African Americans and

Latinos comprised 5.6 percent and 4.3 percent of undergraduate matriculants, respectively; the 1986–1990 graduation rates for these groups averaged
60.1 percent and 72.8 percent, respectively. Comparative data for Penn and
the other Ivy colleges showed Penn slightly below the average of the Ivies in
matriculating African Americans and Latinos—though at every school the
matriculation rates for these groups were below their proportion in the general population. As in previous decades, Penn's tenured and tenure-track
faculty remained disproportionately white, though with a slight increase in
minority faculty between 1988 and 1999. Perhaps the greatest disparity was
the presence of only one African American and no Latinos in the School of
Arts and Sciences' Natural Sciences grouping, which counted 116 standing faculty members (assistant, associate, full professors). Based on a careful scrutiny
of the data, the ad hoc committee speculated that "we are losing existing minority faculty from undergraduate schools approximately as fast as we are
hiring them."[81]

Six years later, in 2005, the University's Minority Equity Committee reported on the status of minority faculty at Penn. An extrapolation of the data
compiled for this report in 2003 shows Blacks/African Americans (the report's
named category) holding 3.1 percent of standing faculty positions and His-
panics/Latinos holding 2 percent. In 2002, African Americans accounted for
12.09 percent and Hispanics 9.02 percent of the U.S. population, respectively.
By comparison, Asian Americans, who composed only 2.82 percent of the U.S.
population in 2002, held 9.4 percent of standing faculty positions. "There has
been progress in the presence of minority faculty at the University," according to the report. "However, this overall progress masks differential increases
among racial/ethnic minority faculty, with much greater growth in Asians/
Pacific Islanders than in Blacks/African Americans and Hispanics/Latinos."
The authors repeat the lament and refrain of every campus minority report
since 1969: "There are clearly too few minority faculty at Penn. . . . For the sake
of both scholarship and equity, we must do better."[82]

The University did do better in other respects. Rodin's presidency was
marked by an ebbing of overt racial and ethnic tensions on the campus. Racially tinged flare-ups were limited to a few cases of alleged racial profiling
by the Penn police. As we show in the next chapter, Rodin's dramatic campus development program benefited from this climate of relative tranquility.

12

Harnwell Redux

I n Rodin's feverish decade in College Hall, Penn's campus development program figured prominently in enhancing the undergraduate experience, as well as advancing Penn's research mission and strengthening the intellectual, aesthetic, and cultural tenor of the campus. Rodin-era campus developments included gleaming new classroom and research buildings, expensive renovations and extensions, building conversions for social and cultural activities, splendid new or relandscaped campus venues, and major property acquisitions for Penn's eastward expansion toward the Schuylkill River. In lieu of a multiyear capital campaign such as Campaign for the Eighties (Meyerson) or Keeping Franklin's Promise (Hackney), funds for capital projects under Rodin derived in part from fabulously wealthy donors, in part from income drawn from Penn's burgeoning endowment in the raging bull market of the Clinton-era economy, and in part from cost-cutting in the University's operational budget.

This chapter centers primarily on the building and renovation projects commissioned under Rodin. Though fewer in number, these works bested the Harnwell-era construction projects in design, not having to rely on the architects of the Pennsylvania General State Authority. Secondarily, we consider the "clean plate" that Rodin inherited from Claire Fagin with respect to diminishing social tensions on the campus, arguing that Rodin's decade in College Hall was a period of relative campus tranquility, which allowed her to focus on the big agendas of her presidency. Last, we offer a summary and critical appraisal of Rodin's presidency, including some reasoned speculations regarding her legacy.

■ Building the 21st Century Campus

As we saw in Chapter 10, Penn, under Rodin, completed the redevelopment of its Unit 4 urban renewal blocks along Walnut Street with the opening of a new parking garage/retail building in the 3701 block and the massive University Square hotel/bookstore complex in the 3601 block. After 1998, the University began to transform its Unit 4 property along 38th Street, which for more than twenty-five years was the site of stores that housed the retail operations of displaced merchants in the unit, as well as the campus bookstore. The remaking of the urban renewal campus continued on the West Campus, another component of Unit 4, and was coupled with residential renovations in the Quad and elsewhere outside Unit 4. In a tour de force, Rodin moved the projected Revlon Student Center project from Walnut Street to a quadrangle of historic buildings that surrounded the plaza behind College Hall—a set of dramatic renovations that mark the starting point of our analysis of Rodin-era campus development.

Perelman Quadrangle: A New Student Center in the Historic Core

We have seen that the Sansom Common complex, completed in the 3601 block of Walnut Street in 1997–99, included the new Penn bookstore managed by Barnes & Noble. Under Hackney, and later Claire Fagin, the interim president from 1993 to 1994, the Penn bookstore was planned to be one of two freestanding buildings that would cover the ground of the old Unit 4 parking lot; the other, adjacent building was to be the Revlon Campus Center, which would replace century-old Houston Hall as the Penn student union, and include an auditorium, theater, and food court, among many other amenities. The business mogul Ronald O. Perelman, a 1964 Wharton alumnus, Penn trustee, and corporate raider who was the chair and CEO of McAndrew & Forbes Holding, which controlled Revlon, donated seed funds for the gigantic new center, which was estimated to cost about $65 million. Calling the Revlon Center plan "a misguided idea," the Penn art historian David Brownlee says, "It fundamentally meant abandoning our historic buildings, building a new building at the scale of a state university, centralizing all student activity in it, in many ways, I think, uncongenial to the university I would like to have."[1]

Soon after taking the reins in College Hall, Rodin called for a review of all capital projects, including the proposed Revlon Center, which had been on the drawing board for six years. Finding the Revlon concept too big, too expensive, and too detrimental to the main campus, Rodin and her senior administrators undertook a radically different plan: to renovate existing buildings and relandscape an important venue in the historic core. Among other things, this plan would restore Houston Hall to its former architectural glory and central role in student life. "Today this is a relatively quiet spot of campus," wrote the architects who would direct the restoration. "When the major undergraduate residence was the 'Men's Dorms' [the Quad] and Houston Hall

Perelman Quadrangle (above), Penn's student center in the historical core of the campus; College Hall (left), Wynn Commons (center), Houston Hall (right), Irvine Auditorium (background). Photograph by Michael M. Koehler. Collections of the University Archives and Records Center.

was its dining facility, spaces in and out of buildings in the area were thronged. In the 1960s, the Superblock, Hill House and their dining rooms broke the tight Dorms/Houston Hall configuration; slowly the student union functions of Houston Hall were eroded; its air of bonhomie evaporated; it became a place to bypass or pass quickly through, more than a point of arrival."[2]

With trustee approval, the University hired the famed Philadelphia architectural firm of Venturi, Scott Brown and Associates to design the student center, which would link four refurbished and newly equipped buildings via a central plaza—Logan Hall (first floor), Irvine Auditorium, Houston Hall, and Williams Hall (the ground floor). The new complex would be named the Perelman Quadrangle, in honor of Ron Perelman, whose donations totaled

$20 million. (Another Wharton alumnus, Steve Wynn, the chair, president, and CEO of Mirage Resorts, contributed $7.5 million for the central plaza, named the Wynn Commons.)[3]

The $87 million Perelman Quad held its grand opening in mid-September 2000, the major building renovations having been completed that summer. They included Houston Hall, "restored to its former grandeur" and "original purpose"; the stone-paved Wynn Commons, "set with shade trees and enriched with seating and heraldry"; Logan Hall, the ground floor of which featured a student art gallery, meeting rooms, and an auditorium; the Silfen Student Study Center, constructed as a steel-and-glass pavilion in the Williams Hall courtyard on the north side of the building; and Irvine Auditorium, its great hall restored to its "chromatic architectural glory," with redesigned "acoustical, lighting, and environmental conditions."[4] (Eight years later, the venerable Logan Hall, which was given that name in 1906, was renamed Claudia Cohen Hall, in honor of Ron Perelman's ex-wife, a deceased Penn alumna and New York gossip columnist, as the University's quid pro quo for Perelman's donations for the new student center—a pragmatic deal arranged on Rodin's watch that when made public provoked a firestorm of criticism about rampant commercialization at Penn.)

Hamilton Village: High-Rise Makeover and People's Park Conversion

For more than twenty-five years, Penn's concrete-and-glass high-rise dormitories had marred the landscape of the West Campus. Biddison Hier, a consulting firm hired in 1996 to explore Penn's options for redeveloping the Superblock, reported that replacing the triumvirate of unlovely, "worn out" buildings would be far costlier than undertaking major renovations. For Rodin and the trustees, the only viable option was to renovate. By the late fall of 1998, an ambitious, ten-year, $300 million plan was afoot to transform the West Campus into Hamilton Village[5] by building low-rise dormitories, renovating the three high-rises, relandscaping the Superblock, and redeveloping the commercial zone of 40th Street; the plan also included demolishing and replacing the Stouffer Triangle, and renovating the existing low-rise college houses in the Superblock, the four Quad college houses, and campus dining facilities.[6] Rodin's planners expected these transformations to lure Penn undergraduates then living off-campus in University City back to the campus, thereby freeing up more housing beyond 40th Street for families.

Penn's residential overhaul started first in the Quad, where across four summers, in 1999–2002, major structural renovations were undertaken at a cost of $75 million. The four Hackney-era college houses were reorganized into three houses (Riepe, Ware, and Fisher-Hassenfeld), in alignment with the

Contemporary view east along Walnut Street toward the intersection at 40th Street, in the Hamilton Village commercial zone, part of Judith Rodin's West Philadelphia Initiatives. In background, Rodin College House, in the West Campus, rises above the West Philadelphia branch of the Free Library of Philadelphia. Photograph by Michael M. Koehler. Collections of the University Archives and Records Center.

Quad's historic spatial configuration of three large groupings of courtyards. By the spring of 2002, the larger campus project had been scaled back, with new low-rise construction in the Superblock/Hamilton Village postponed indefinitely. In any event, Rodin's team moved forward with the renovations in the high-rises and new landscaping in the Superblock/Hamilton Village, contracting with MGA Partners to upgrade the college houses and with Lager Raabe Skafte to do the landscaping, all at a cost of $81 million. The high-rises were in terrible condition, their concrete façades porous and leaking, their heating and air-conditioning systems continuously malfunctioning. The three rehabilitations were staggered across the four summers, with two consecutive summers dedicated to each building. The interior work included infrastructural improvements, such as a sprinkler system; new heating, air conditioning, and electrical systems; refurbished student apartments; and a new main lobby and new lounges. The exterior work included, dramatically, installing a new metal and glass skin for the buildings and restoring the concrete façade with a tinted, double-glaze sealant.[7]

The first high-rise residence to complete its spectacular upgrade, at a cost of $26.5 million, was Hamilton College House, formerly High Rise North, in 2003. (Hamilton was renamed Rodin College House in 2004.) The renovations for the Harrison and Harnwell buildings were completed in 2004 and 2005, respectively. Lager Raabe Skafte's landscape design splendidly complements the new faces of the high-rises. In the area around the college houses, triangular grassy spaces are bounded by red-brick walkways. Other brick paths thread the larger spaces of Hamilton Village. A capacious brick walk faced by poplar trees and pairs of stylish park benches connects Locust Walk west of Rodin House to Walnut Street; this diagonal path bisects the grassy space of the former Penn People's Park between DuBois College House and the Federalist-style University City branch of the Free Library. Two kinds of granite curbing line the walkways. One kind is "exaggeratedly high"—"ankle breakers," says Brownlee— designed to keep people on the path; the other kind, where paths cross large fields, is "flush with the pavement," designed to allow people to "flow off the walkways."[8]

■ Unfinished Business: The 1977 Landscape Development Plan

Flush with urban renewal dollars in the 1950s and 1960s, Gaylord Harnwell built the physical campus that Rodin eventually inherited. In the 1970s, a decade of austerity, Martin Meyerson added to Harnwell's transformation by landscaping the historic core and creating College Green, passing on the remainder of the uncompleted 1977 Landscape Development Plan to his successors. In the 1980s and early 1990s, Sheldon Hackney added new buildings, new properties, and a new campus master plan that charted some of the major projects Rodin would undertake during her presidency. Two Rodin-era projects brought to fruition the remaining components of the 1977 campus plan.

The streetscaping of 38th Street between Walnut and Locust was one of these long-delayed projects. We have seen that the University initially redeveloped this block in the mid-1960s as a one-story, L-shaped building named University Plaza, which housed the University bookstore and merchants displaced by urban renewal in RDA Unit 4. This "temporary" arrangement endured for more than thirty years as the University searched for ideas and money for the site. Plans shifted back and forth until the Revlon Center proposal earmarked the 3601 block of Walnut for the new Penn bookstore.

In November 1996, Rodin announced that the Wharton School would build a colossal new classroom building with offices and space for four academic departments (Legal Studies, Marketing, Statistics, and Operations and Information Management) on the former bookstore and retail site, with construction to begin as soon as the Barnes & Noble superstore was completed.[9] The architectural plan called for an expansive, technologically advanced, 320,000-square foot building, with a massive, eight-story rotund tower rising above Walnut Street. The architectural firm was Kohn Pedersen Fox Associates of New York, with which Penn had originally contracted for the Revlon Center.[10] The architects apparently transferred their design for the façade of the abandoned Revlon Center project to the new Wharton building.[11]

Looking north on 38th Street, with Huntsman Hall of the Wharton School, landmark of the Rodin era, in the center; Steinberg-Aresty Hall at right. Photograph by Michael M. Koehler. Collections of the University Archives and Records Center.

Completed in 2002, the building's total cost of $140 million was paid largely through private donations to the Wharton School; it was named Huntsman Hall, after Jon Huntsman, a 1959 Wharton graduate and chairman of the Huntsman Corporation, a manufacturer of plastic food containers, who contributed $40 million to the project. Huntsman Hall's main entrance fronts Walnut Street; a second entrance, by far the busier, opens onto Locust Walk and a café plaza that faces the Wharton School's Steinberg-Aresty Hall. The three-story, red-brick flank of the building on 38th Street is streetscaped with trees and landscaping that recalls Sir Peter Shepheard's proposed design for a widened 38th Street in the 1977 Landscape Development Plan. Unfortunately, even with trees and landscaping on both sides of the street, 38th Street, a heavily used four-lane thoroughfare, is unlovely. And short of the unlikely event that the city builds a tunnel under it, 38th Street will remain an aesthetic liability for the University.

As we noted previously, by approving Huntsman Hall on Walnut Street, the trustees, who were apparently swayed by the huge sums of money Wharton promised to raise, violated a long-standing Unit 4 protocol that Penn would build no high-rise structure east of 38th Street between Walnut and Spruce. The stocky tower also violated one of the Principles of Campus Development enunciated by Robert Zemsky and the Office of Institutional Planning in 1992 and reaffirmed by Rodin in an address to the University Council on 13 November 1996: "Penn's buildings ought to maintain the dominant cityscape scale of the current campus, which features buildings of medium height that, in their placement, relate to the grid systems of the campus as well as the City of Philadelphia."[12]

The 1977 plan fared better with the Rodin administration's redesign of Hill Field, four blocks to the east of Huntsman Hall. Here, in the fall of 2003, the Olin Partnership completed the Women's Walk, "a curving brick walkway" lined with poplar trees, which extends Woodland Walk from College Green across the newly anointed Hill Square and provides a new campus gateway at 33rd and Chestnut streets. Arrayed along the walkway are sculpted stone benches inscribed with quotations apropos of the experience of women at Penn for the past 125 years.[13] In the fall of 2005, the School of Arts and Sciences opened a new building for the McNeil Center for Early American Studies on the 34th Street side of Hill Square, a Flemish-bond red-brick structure complementing "the High Georgian façade of the Law School's Silverman Hall," just across 34th Street.[14] In the fall of 2007, the University announced plans for a new College House on Hill Square, to be composed of three thin, low-rise residential buildings, with frontages on 33rd, 34th, and Chestnut streets; this "quad-like" formation would respect the green space of the existing field

Contemporary perspective: Shoppes at Penn (left), Hill College House (right), Women's Walk, through Hill Square (formerly Hill Field); the McNeil Center for Early American Studies is partially visible left of the walk. Photograph by James R. Mann, Facilities and Real Estate Services, University of Pennsylvania.

on both sides of the Women's Walk, retaining about 70 percent of the land for recreational purposes.[15] By 2007, Penn at last had a plan and the funds to realize the original purpose for which the Redevelopment Authority had leveled the full block of 33rd-34th-Walnut-Chestnut streets in the late 1950s— expanded campus housing.

Aside from Huntsman Hall on the West Central Campus, which was almost exclusively "a Wharton thing," the Rodin administration, in concert with the respective faculties, constructed six impressive new academic buildings on the East and South campuses, renovated other buildings for new purposes, and acquired the property the University needed for a large-scale expansion

Artist's rendering of an expansive new college house scheduled to open in Hill Square in 2015. Hill College House was completed in 1960; for more than fifty years this modernist dormitory has stood as the only residential building on the block of Walnut-Chestnut-33rd-34th streets—the former Unit 2 property earmarked for student residence halls by the Redevelopment Authority in the 1950s. The new college house, which wraps the corner of 34th and Chestnut Streets, forms a landscaped horseshoe. Courtesy of Facilities and Real Estate Services, University of Pennsylvania.

of HUP and Penn's medical research facilities. The first of these new buildings was designated Phase I of the Institute for Advanced Science and Technology (IAST), a Department of Defense-sponsored project for chemical and engineering research laboratories that the Rodin administration inherited from the Hackney era. When the project was still in Hackney's bailiwick, the historian and sociologist of science Robert Kohler raised a set of contrarian questions about the IAST, whose advocates expected that the Defense Department would ultimately provide at least $35 million of the estimated $75 million the building would cost. Kohler enumerated five areas of IAST research that were of high-priority interest to the Defense Department, so-called critical technologies: genetic engineering, new materials and catalysts, bioengineering, computer science and artificial intelligence, and ultra-fast detectors. While Kohler stipulated that IAST basic research could (in theory) result in "civilian uses" of sophisticated technologies, he argued that civilian technologies were of no interest to the Defense Department. "Will the fact that IAST research will be sponsored by the military make it more likely that resulting knowledge will be used for military rather than civilian technologies?" asked Kohler rhetorically. "Military hardware will not be made at Penn, of course. But does the separation of basic research from military applications remove responsibility from those who produce basic scientific knowledge?"[16]

The vice-provost for research, Barry Cooperman, who would later direct the IAST, staunchly defended the project on the grounds that basic research at the IAST's five centers (computer information and cognitive science, chemistry, bioengineering, scientific and technological information resources, and technology transfer) would ultimately produce beneficial civilian technologies. Cooperman noted that while Congress had authorized $20 million in Defense Department appropriations as grants to the IAST, the project would also be sponsored by the National Institutes for Health, the National Science Foundation, the Department of Energy, and private corporations and foundations. Cooperman said, "I believe that Congress made these awards within the Department of Defense Appropriations Act because of the simple consideration that supporting the scientific and technological research infrastructure at American universities is in the long-term national security interests of the United States."[17]

Military sponsorship of the IAST was not a hot-button campus issue in the 1990s—no sit-ins, no storming of the president's office, no disruptions of trustee meetings. The University's proposal to demolish Smith Hall, a historic Victorian structure, to make way for a laboratory building—a new wing of the Harrison Chemistry Building—had more visibility and prompted a small coterie of students, faculty, and historical preservationists to try to save the century-old building; their efforts harkened back to the Save Open Spaces (SOS) campaign of the mid-1960s (see Chapter 4). A two-story, flat-roofed, red-brick structure that was designed on the model of a German research laboratory and built to house the Henry C. Lea Institute for Hygiene, Smith Hall was a bellwether of laboratory-based chemistry research in the United States.[18] It was also an anchor in "a charming and historic precinct of the campus." Kohler, whose department was housed in Smith Hall, wrote, "Smith Walk below 34th Street is the only place left where one can stand and see nothing but 19th century or turn-of-the-century buildings: Furness Library, Smith Hall, Morgan-Music, Hayden Hall, and the Towne Building. It is the last place on campus where one can still experience Penn's distinctive late-Victorian urban campus. The proposed new wing to the Chemistry Building would destroy the integrity of this precinct and make it impossible for future generations to enjoy a special historical experience."[19]

Smith Hall's place in the city's historic registry meant that it could not be demolished without the authorization of the Philadelphia Historical Preservation Commission. Sheldon Hackney presented the University's case to this commission, arguing that Smith Hall was the only feasible site for the IAST. "As a historian, I, too, wish to preserve and interpret the past," Hackney told the commissioners. "As the President of a major research university, I must assure that Penn grows, that Penn meets its obligation to provide the best in teaching and research facilities for today's and tomorrow's faculty and students."[20] In fact, Smith Hall was probably doomed decades before, when the Harnwell administration ordained a new chemistry building for the corner of 34th and Spruce streets—a project that involved the demolition of the redbrick Harrison Chemistry Laboratories, a Cope and Stewardson structure. The planners knew that as the University grew, the new chemistry building would require a laboratory expansion in the direction of Smith Walk.[21]

Though the Preservation Commission sided with the University, the IAST stood in limbo for three years, delayed by the opposition's legal maneuvering and the time it took for the Air Force to complete an environmental impact study and for state and federal historic preservation agencies to ensure that the architectural design by Venturi, Scott Brown and Associates displayed "a harmony with the character of the existing buildings." These studies favored the IAST, and, with the city's certification, Smith Hall was finally razed in August 1995.[22] It took another two years to build the Vagelos Laboratories of the Institute for Advance Science and Technology, which opened in November 1997. George Thomas described it as "a brilliant essay in contextualism based on the hues of the red brick and brownstone of Furness's University Library and the red brick and terra-cotta of [Edgar V.] Seeler's Dental Hall [Hayden Hall]."[23]

Rodin's presidency contributed two other new buildings on the East Campus—notably, without controversy—both in the School of Engineering and Applied Sciences: Levine Hall, completed for the Department of Computer and Information Science in 2003; and Skirkanich Hall, initiated and funded under Rodin and completed for the Department of Bioengineering in 2006. Designed by Kieran Timberlake Associates, Levine Hall, which boasts a glimmering "transparent glass façade," is "tucked in" among the original School of Engineering's Towne Building, the School of Engineering and Applied Sciences' Graduate Research Wing, and the English Department's Fisher-Bennett Hall.[24] Skirkanich Hall, designed by the husband-and-wife team of Tod Williams and Billie Tsien, is hailed as "the city's best new building in years," evoking a sense of excitement that recalls the enthusiasm of architectural critics for Louis Kahn's design for the Alfred Newton Richards Building, completed in 1962 on Hamilton Walk. "The building's façade is composed of brick, cantilevered shingle-glass panes, and zinc panels," writes the journalist John Prendergast. "The brick is the most striking feature— not only is it *not* Penn's traditional red; it isn't even a single color. Instead the architects chose a distribution of shades, from acid yellow to moss green to black."[25] Apparently, tradition-minded trustees were placated by the use of brick in the design, irrespective of color.

Another building inaugurated under Rodin was the South Campus's Carolyn Lynch Laboratory for the Department of Biology and Penn's Genomics Institute, which was completed in 2006. Designed by the architectural firm Ellenzweig Associates, the new life sciences building faces University Avenue just north of Guardian Drive. Given the site's adjacency to Kasky Memorial Park, the tiny, densely foliated, sequestered arboretum that includes Penn's Bio Pond (formally called Carolyn Lynch Pond), conservationists initially contested the development, fearing that the building would encroach on the park. Happily, the architects built a site-sensitive, ecologically sound red-brick-and-glass structure, replete with wet laboratories, greenhouses, and facilities for animal, plant, and fish study. The Lynch Laboratory is designated as Phase I of the School of Arts and Sciences' plan for a life sciences complex extending along South University Avenue below Hamilton Walk.[26] At this writing, the historic Leidy Laboratories at the corner of Hamilton Walk and South University Avenue, a Cope and Stewardson building completed in 1911, seems assured of continued preservation.

The Rodin era's largest and most expensive new building—indeed, the largest, most expensive building in Penn's history—was the Biomedical Research Building II/III, or BRB II/III, designated as "the second and third phases of a complex that began [under Hackney] with BRB I, since renamed Stellar-Chance Laboratories." Built for $149 million, the fifteen-story edifice rises above Osler Circle in the area of the old Philadelphia General Hospital and is joined to Stellar-Chance by a passageway over Curie Avenue. BRB II/III houses Medical School departments and centers for biological research, and was the home of the now-defunct Institute for Human Gene Therapy (see Chapter 11).[27]

Beyond the previously described restorations (Irvine Auditorium, Houston Hall) and renovations (the first floor of Logan Hall, the exterior passage way of Williams Hall) that were part of the Perelman Center project, Rodin and Fry achieved a major coup by purchasing and then converting the Christian Association (CA) Building, a Collegiate Gothic structure built in 1927, into the ARCH (Arts, Research, and Culture House) Building. A privately owned, religiously oriented (though nonsectarian) student center, the CA was a gathering place for liberal-leftist activists in the 1960s and beyond; in the Hackney and Rodin eras, the CA leased some of its ample space to two restaurants, the Palladium and the Gold Standard. Its prime location at 3601 Locust Walk, just a stone's throw from College Green, made it imperative for the University to be the purchaser when the building came up for sale. In October 1997, "for sale or lease" signs appeared on the building following the CA's announcement that it could no longer maintain the structure. By November 1999, the Penn real estate office had negotiated a deal that transferred ownership of the building to the University for $2.9 million and gave the CA a twenty-five-year lease on Westminster House, a Penn property at 37th and Sansom streets, which the University renovated for the CA.[28] Apropos of its name, the ARCH Building houses student performance organizations, the Center for Undergraduate Research and Fellowships (CURF), the Pan Asian American Community House, Casa Latina, the Black Cultural Center (Umoja), and a "satellite office" of the Greenfield Intercultural Center.[29]

The diversification of Locust Walk, formally inaugurated by the Faust Committee's report in April 1990, continued under Rodin with a series of building conversions. Anchoring the east end of the 3601 block of Locust, the multiethnic ARCH Building is one example. In October 1996, the Women's Center moved to the converted, former Theta Xi fraternity house at the west end of the block; the renovation of this Victorian-era brownstone twin included administrative offices, classrooms for women's studies, and general-use seminars. A third renovation project converted the former Phi Sigma Kappa fraternity house at 3615 Locust Walk into the Graduate Student Center, which opened in September 2001, with spaces for socializing and study, program activities, and religious-group meetings and worship. A fourth renovation project, completed in the summer of 2000, was the conversion of the former Phi Gamma Delta fraternity house (more below) for the School of Arts and Sciences, to house the Penn Humanities Forum and the McNeil Center for Early American Studies, pending the latter's relocation to Hill Square in 2005.[30]

Building refurbishments under Rodin included, notably, the restoration of Logan Hall's green-serpentine-stone exterior and a partial restoration of the exterior of College Hall (the north façade's east wing and part of the west wing). Begun in 1990 under Hackney, these reconstructions, to the great consternation of the faculties, necessitated the relocation of Arts and Sciences departments to "swing space" at 3440 Market Street, in the University City Science Center; and to 3401 Walnut Street in the floors above the Shoppes at Penn. Logan Hall's restored exterior was finally completed in 1996, College Hall's partial restoration in 1997—and the academic departments returned to these buildings in short order.[31] As previously noted, Logan Hall's first-floor renovation was completed as part of the Perelman Center complex, which was inaugurated in 2000. Another historic building to undergo a major renovation was Cope and Stewardson's Lewis Hall, the Law School's first building in West Philadelphia. A two-year restoration of this North Campus building, which opened in 1900, was completed in 1998, when it was renamed Silverman Hall.[32]

Redesigns of the north façades of the Annenberg School for Communication and the Graduate School of Education gave these buildings main entrances facing Walnut Street. These redesigns, coupled with the location of Huntsman Hall's main entrance on Walnut, represent "Penn's rethinking of its relation to the main streets that run through campus"[33] and make an explicit statement that Penn now embraces its urban environment. "We opened all of the windows on Walnut Street to the street," says Rodin, "not only to the campus whenever we did a renovation, because we said 'we want the neighborhood to look into Penn, we don't want it to be cold brick walls that aren't welcoming.'"[34] At this writing, however, Penn has still not reckoned with the two-block-long north façade of the Van Pelt-Dietrich library complex, which presents a monolithic, six-story brick wall to Walnut, emblematic of an earlier campus generation's intentional isolation for scholarly repose.

In 1996, the University purchased the old Asbury Methodist Church, on the north side of Chestnut Street opposite Hill Field, between 33rd and 34th streets, with funds provided by Lady Barbara Colyton, the former wife of the celebrated *New Yorker* cartoonist Charles Addams, a member of Penn's class of 1934. The original Asbury Church dated to 1848, when the site was part of Hamilton Village; the Gothic church Penn acquired was designed in 1884 by John Ord, a Scotsman who for three years was the lead architect on Philadelphia's City Hall. The interior of the church was under conversion to studios for the Graduate School of Fine Arts when the building burned to the ground on March 9, 1997. The University leveled the site and moved the fine-arts project to the old Faculty Club building, Skinner Hall, on the southwest corner of 36th and Walnut streets, which was available for conversion after the Faculty Club's move to the second floor of the Inn at Penn. Maria C. Romanach Architects refaced the reddish-brown brick building with an elegant glass and turquoise-panel façade, and remodeled the interior to include a digital video center, a photography center, a ceramics center, and the Charles Addams Gallery—all state-of-the-art facilities. The Charles Addams Fine Arts Hall debuted in April 2001.[35]

Five other new campus buildings and a new athletic facility were built in the Rodin era. In 2000, on the West Campus, the Dental School opened the Robert C. Shattner Center, a new "gateway" building for patient care and dental education at 40th and Locust streets, whose brick and limestone façade "screens" the Leon Levy Oral Health Sciences Building (Center for Oral Health) and joins with the Tudor Gothic brick building of the Thomas W. Evans Museum and Dental Institute, which opened in 1915; the new building also houses a popular Locust Street coffee shop, giving the 4000 block of Locust a stable commercial anchor.[36] Also in 2000, the University completed Module VII, a futuristic central air conditioning plant above University Avenue and the Schuylkill River;[37] as well as a nine-hundred-seat baseball stadium, constructed at the south end of the River Fields on the site of the old Murphy Field, in the lee of the new chiller plant.[38] On the East Campus, the University Museum opened the Mainwaring Wing for collections storage and research rooms, as well as the Stoner Courtyard gardens, in the spring of 2002.[39] Opened in the fall of 2002, the David Pottruck Health and Fitness Center, a four-story attachment to an earlier gymnasium and swimming facility (formerly the Gimbel Gym) on Walnut Street, features modern fitness machines and recreation facilities, including a de rigueur climbing wall.[40] In the fall of 2003, the University dedicated Steinhardt Hall, a new building for the Hillel Foundation in the refurbished Superblock/Hamilton Village complex, on 39th Street between the Fels Institute of Government and the Alpha Tau Omega House and Sigma Chi House, the two former Drexel mansions; the new Hillel building offers facilities, meeting space, and kosher dining for Penn's six thousand Jewish students and twenty-seven Jewish organizations.[41]

A major renovation of the first floor of the Van Pelt-Dietrich Library was finished in the summer of 1998, strengthening both the aesthetics and the electronic capability of the Harnwell-era library complex. "Walls literally came down, revealing the beauty of College Green and the vibrancy of Walnut Street through the Library's floor-to-ceiling windows," Rodin exulted. "The Library now basks in a circle of natural light. Students and faculty no longer conduct research in the shadow of walls and darkened desks. Rather, sunlit study lounges ring the perimeter of the Library. Glass, wood, and chrome brighten carrels and computer research areas. Open staircases and improved lighting complete the picture." The first-floor renovation included locating all of the major library services in a single capacious space and installing an electronic classroom, multimedia seminar rooms, and computer centers, among other resources. A renovation of Van Pelt-Dietrich's ground-level Rosengarten Study Center was completed in the summer of 1999, and reopened at the same time as the opening of the Perelman Quadrangle's Silfen Student Study Center on the north side of Williams Hall.[42] In the fall of 2003, near the end of Rodin's term, the trustees approved an expensive, large-scale renovation of Bennett Hall. Located on the southeast corner of 34th and Walnut streets, this venerable College Gothic building, once the home of the College of Liberal Arts for Women, housed the English and music departments. The renovation was completed in 2005 under Amy Gutmann, and the building was renamed Fisher-Bennett Hall.[43]

Locust Walk was also a site of renovations. In November 2001, Rodin rededicated the Class of 1949 Bridge over 38th Street as the Class of 1949 Generational Bridge. Redesigned by Margie Ruddick Landscape with "light poles, inscribed pavers, and planted mesh columns"—the paver inscriptions are donor gifts honoring Penn graduates—the Generational Bridge is a "conceptual companion" to the Hill Square Women's Walk.[44] The redesigned pedestrian bridge complemented renovations on Locust Walk east of the bridge, which replaced the deteriorating bluestones of the Walk with more durable yet attractive tar-and-stone pavers. Lighting renovations included installing an allée of fifteen-foot lamps in facing pairs along the Walk from College Green to 38th Street—a festive arrangement that supported the University's broader effort to rejuvenate the area's evening foot traffic.[45]

■ A New Expansion: East Toward the River

Rodin's presidency brought to partial fruition the 1988 Campus Master Plan's vision of eastward expansion toward the Schuylkill River, a vision that was reaffirmed in the 2001 Campus Development Plan.[46] The envisaged two-pronged expansion necessitated the purchase of two large, critical swaths of land. In the case of Penn Medicine, the object of purchase was land occupied by the Commercial Museum, Convention Hall, and the three other buildings that composed the city's Civic Center; in the case of the main campus, the desiderata were the Left Bank and fourteen acres owned by the U.S. Postal Service south of Walnut Street and east of the Class of 1923 Ice Rink.

Expanding Penn Medicine

We have seen that Sheldon Hackney, to no avail, tried to acquire the Civic Center property for Penn. Obtaining a sizable piece of this 19.2-acre site opposite the HUP-CHOP hospital complex was essential for HUP's clinical-care expansion and Penn's medical research. After Rodin's arrival at Penn, negotiations with the city progressed fitfully and secretively until the breakthrough in 1998, when the Ed Rendell administration finally agreed to sell the land. Christened the Philadelphia Civic Center in 1967, the site had been originally developed as the home of the Philadelphia Commercial Museum in 1899, a Beaux-Arts building that stood adjacent to the property of the University Museum. The city completed Convention Hall, a massive Italian Renaissance–style building, in 1931. Originally named the Philadelphia Municipal Auditorium, Convention Hall hosted the 1936 Democratic National Convention and the 1948 Democratic, Republican, and Progressive national conventions. For sixty years, Convention Hall hosted Penn's annual commencement, professional basketball, hockey, concerts, political speeches, and religious events. For thirty years, the Civic Center's Grand Exhibition Hall, to the south of Convention Hall, hosted innumerable home, boat, and auto shows, and, famously, the annual Philadelphia Flower Show. The Civic Center lost its raison d'être after 1993 when the Rendell administration completed the $522 million, 1.3 million-square-foot Pennsylvania Convention Center at 1101 Arch Street in Center City. In the late fall of 1998, the City Council passed a bill that allowed Penn and CHOP to purchase the Civic Center property and the remaining buildings.[47]

Penn's plan was to establish two major facilities on the former Civic Center site: first to build a single comprehensive facility for all out-patient treatment, next to build a research facility; at the time of the purchase, the twenty-year-old Cancer Center and its 350 faculty members were spread across HUP's fifteen buildings and the Penn Tower Hotel.[48] While CHOP would build its own pediatric research facility on the site independent of the Cancer Center, CHOP and HUP would jointly develop a 2.2-acre parcel on the south end of the property as a parking garage, for which the two institutions established the nonprofit Civic Center Development Corporation to finance and manage development of the proposed facility.[49] Salvaging Convention Hall as a component of the Penn Health Center's expansion was not feasible—in the end, the Health System, as well as such agencies as the Philadelphia Industrial Development Corporation and the Preservation Alliance for Greater Philadelphia, decided that the historic building was not redeemable in light of the Health Center's goals. Claiming to speak for a wider community, an organization called the Committee to Save Convention Hall protested the demolition, which was under way in the fall of 2004, to no avail.[50] The demolition of this building and the removal of Smith Hall (see above) were the only catalysts for community protests against Rodin-era building/expansion projects.

Convention Hall and its colorful history were soon forgotten as the Penn Health System proceeded to build the Raymond and Ruth Perelman Center for Advanced Medicine. (Raymond and Ruth were the parents of Ronald Perelman, the donor for the Perelman Quadrangle.) Constructed at a cost of $305 million, the 500,000-square-foot Perelman Center was dedicated in the fall of 2008. The spacious facility, whose major architectural statement is "a soaring glass atrium," houses twelve clinical specialties for cancer treatment, cardiovascular medicine, and outpatient surgery.[51] In the winter of 2009, the Health System opened the $140 million Roberts Proton Therapy Center, a "cutting edge radiation therapy facility," a largely underground building that

Contemporary view of 34th Street as it enters the Penn Medicine complex; at right, the Children's Hospital of Philadelphia (CHOP), the Perelman Center for Advanced Medicine (background center), and the Smilow Center for Translational Research (background right) are located on lands of the former Municipal Auditorium and Civic Center. Photograph by Michael M. Koehler. Collections of the University Archives and Records Center.

connects with the Perelman Center.[52] A third building in the Penn Medicine expansion complex is the Smilow Center for Translational Research, a medical-research tower with eight "football-field-size" floors of research space for one hundred principal investigators and nine hundred staff members, which opened in the spring of 2011.[53] A veritable city of high-rise research, hospital, and outpatient facilities has arisen south of Curie Avenue, encompassing both sides of Civic Center Boulevard and 34th Street south of Spruce to University Avenue.

Eastward the Pedestrian Campus

In March 2004, the federal government approved the University's purchase of Philadelphia's central Postal Services facilities. "The agreements signed on March 26 by representatives of Penn and the Postal Service cover a site west of the Schuylkill River and east of the Penn campus between Market and South streets," reported the *Almanac*. "The University will be acquiring all of the Postal Service's holdings in the area, including the main post office building at 30th and Market streets and, to the south, its Annex building, a parking garage at 31st and Chestnut streets and a 14-acre parking lot south of Walnut Street." Calling the purchase "a significant milestone for both Penn and Phil-adelphia," an ebullient Rodin said, "It will ultimately have the effect of con-necting University City and Center City and has the potential to create a new research and technology zone, residential and recreational areas and a vari-ety of other activities."[54] The transfer of the Postal Service properties to Penn was completed in August 2007, though without the main post office build-ing, which was sold to Brandywine Realty Trust. Brandywine also obtained a long-term ground lease from Penn for the Post Office Truck Terminal An-nex facility on the east side of 30th Street, between Chestnut and Walnut. The company proposed to demolish the annex and construct Cira Centre South on the leased site—a spectacular office, retail, and residential facility towering above the Schuylkill River.[55] (At the time of this writing, Cira Cen-tre South was under construction.)

The city's ideas for the property south of Walnut Street had horrified the University. Under heavy pressure from Penn, the city scuttled a plan to build a new Phillies baseball stadium on the fourteen-acre parking lot, and later a "very far along plan" to put a Home Depot store on the site. Under Rodin, the University became "an active and visionary partner and leader" in a col-laboration that became the Schuylkill River Development Corporation, a public-private venture that included the Health System, Drexel, the City, the Army Corps of Engineers, and private developers; their aim was to redevelop "the Schuylkill riverfront from its confluence with the Delaware River to the

Aerial view looking west on Walnut Street near the Schuylkill River, 1963. The Media Line commuter rail runs below the Palaestra (center left); the High Line of the Pennsylvania Railroad bridges Walnut Street. The General Electric building (center right) was redeveloped as the Left Bank Apartments in 2000; the U.S. Postal Lands (lower left) became Penn Park in 2011. Collections of the University Archives and Records Center.

Fairmount Dam, a distance of about eight miles." While the Center City side of the river was already being redeveloped as the Schuylkill Banks Park, the West Philadelphia side was cluttered with abandoned warehouses and other decaying remnants of a bygone industrial era. "When people could envision what the Postal Lands could be—and the recognition was that only Penn had the real resources to do that and that it wanted to—then it became easy," recounts Rodin.[56]

Rodin bequeathed the undeveloped Postal Service acreage to her successor, Amy Gutmann, who seized the opportunity afforded by this pivotal acquisition to begin to implement a new master plan for the East Campus. In April

Penn Park, opened in September 2011; view is from Franklin Field north to Center City. The park is bounded by three rail lines: SEPTA's regional railway (lower left), the High Line (lower center), and Amtrak's Northeast Corridor (upper center). Photograph by Michael M. Koehler. Collections of the University Archives and Records Center.

2005, Gutmann appointed the ad hoc Campus Development Planning Committee, which included key administrators and the deans of the Medical School and the School of Design. The charge to this committee was to design, through a broadly consultative process with campus and community groups, a 25–30-year master plan that would give particular attention to the expanded East Campus. The planners focused on a swath of 42.3 acres that included the soon-to-be transferred Postal Lands and Penn's athletic fields north of the South Street Bridge. The fruit of their labor, the Penn Connects Vision Plan, projected the development of a spectacular park to replace the wasteland and to convert Penn athletic fields bordering the Postal Lands for new uses. The most formidable challenge they faced was how to integrate two major structural barriers permanently embossed on the landscape into the design for what is so far called (for lack of a donor) Penn Park. The first of these barriers, forming the west boundary of the proposed park in the lee of Franklin Field, is the SEPTA regional railway, which connects the western suburbs to 30th Street Station. The second obstacle, also on the west side, is the High Line freight railway, mounted sixty feet above ground on stone and steel pedestals.[57]

A new pedestrian bridge coupled with a walkway solves the problem of the SEPTA tracks and the High Line, effecting an integration of the old and new East Campus by means of an "over and under" extension of Locust Walk/Smith Walk. East of 33rd Street, the Walk leads through the Alvin B. Shumaker Green, a newly landscaped venue that fronts the Palaestra and Hutchinson Gymnasium, having replaced the old Lott Tennis Courts and a parking lot. Penn Park itself opened in the fall of 2011, replete with a synthetic-turf soccer field, a state-of-the-art women's softball stadium, the splendid new Lott Tennis Courts, and swaths of green space and pathways open to the public. The Park's border edges are grass terraces designed to contain periodic storm surges from the Schuylkill.[58] Complementing the Park, on the street above the tennis courts, an extravagant replacement of the South Street Bridge has removed the dangerous roadbed and refurbished the thoroughfare as a "cultural gateway" to the medical campus and University Museum.[59]

While the financial strength of the University was the major factor in all of the physical developments we have reviewed in part IV, diminished social tensions on the campus were a secondary factor. Rodin's presidency was not tied up in perpetual crisis management. After the mid-1990s, overt campus racial tensions ebbed, and gender tensions also abated. We turn in the following section to this abatement and the relatively minor social issues that irritated, rather than incapacitated, the Rodin administration.

■ **Ebbing Social Forces**

We have seen that by the summer of 1994 and the start of Rodin's presidency, the lingering matter of the *Daily Pennsylvanian* theft and the issue of judicial or disciplinary sanctions for the African American students involved in the newspaper removals had been resolved by the interim president, Claire Fagin, who decided to drop the matter after a faculty member's review, though not without issuing a stern caveat that henceforth newspaper thefts were not to be tolerated for any reason. Acting on the recommendation of the Hackney-appointed Commission on Strengthening the Community, Fagin also declared Penn's student speech code null and void, an abolishment Rodin reaffirmed

early in her presidency: henceforth student speech, however hateful or big-
oted, would not be subject to disciplinary action; henceforth, incidents such
as Water Buffalo would be mediated rather than adjudicated.

Fagin only mildly exaggerated when she asserted that her interim presidency left Rodin "a clean plate."[60] Overt racial tensions eased in the aftermath
of Water Buffalo, though segregated diversity was a problem, and unspoken
racial tensions pervaded campus politics, especially in the realm of faculty relations. Tolerance and recognition for LGBTs was growing. Gay and lesbian
couples now had access to married housing and the same University benefits
package that was available for married couples. Following the report of the
Commission on Strengthening the Community, Penn women were poised
to claim a home of their own on Locust Walk, formerly the preserve of campus fraternities. And more students than ever before were civically engaged—
undergraduate enrollments in academically based community service courses
soared in the 1990s. In this improved climate of campus civility, the issues
that Rodin faced were of a different genre and lower level of intensity than
those that wracked the Meyerson and Hackney presidencies.[61]

Coinciding with developments on other major campuses, student activism at the University included a campaign against the administration's dealings with clothing companies contracting with sweatshops in developing
countries to manufacture their products and a campaign to create a graduate-
student union. Both campaigns made strong yet civilly stated ideological claims
on the University. A large assemblage of undergraduate demonstrators, by comparison, conducted a frivolous, self-referential protest against the administration's efforts to manage alcohol abuse, a serious campus problem. Significantly,
none of these activities tied up College Hall for days and nights on end—
unlike, for example, fraternity gang rape, Louis Farrakhan, the *DP* theft, and
Water Buffalo, to mention the most serious problems of the Hackney era; or
the labor union conflicts of the Meyerson era.

GET-UP: Penn's Graduate-Student Union Movement

The Rodin administration's major campus entanglement was the Graduate
Employees Together–University of Pennsylvania (GET-UP) campaign for recognition as a union with collective bargaining rights vis-à-vis the University.
GET-UP's position was that Penn graduate students working as teaching assistants (TAs), research assistants, and lecturers were employees of a corporate enterprise that exploited their labor, the free tuition, stipend, and health
benefits they received from the University notwithstanding; as Penn employees, they argued, they were entitled to a voice in their work and a benefits package. The *New York Times* aptly stated their position as follows:

University fund-raising depends primarily on high-profile faculty publishing, so the smart money cuts the total number of professors in order to spend big on a few stars and give them enough free time to stay famous. Graduate students, serving at T.A.'s and even as lecturers, pick up the teaching slack. This makes for a great fiscal model—tenure produces high fixed costs, while disposable T.A.'s work for peanuts. But it also creates an ever-greater oversupply of Ph.D.'s competing for ever-fewer tenured jobs. Back when graduate students could reasonably see themselves as apprentices bound for glorious lecture halls, the low pay was tolerable, but when T.A.-ships look like the university's way of balancing the budget at the expense of their graduate students' futures, it feels like an outrage.[62]

The legal issue was whether graduate students at a private university have the right to unionize. (Graduate students have that right at public universities in many states, according to state laws.) The National Labor Relations Board responded affirmatively in a November 2000 decision that allowed New York University teaching assistants to form a union. Citing the NYU precedent, GET-UP petitioned the NLRB in December 2001 to authorize a graduate-student union election on the Penn campus. GET-UP narrowly defined its bargaining unit to include graduate students working as teaching assistants, research assistants, and lecturers in the humanities and social sciences, while excluding most of the professional schools and the physical, engineering, and natural sciences. The University challenged the petition in a month-long hearing held at the NLRB's regional office in Philadelphia in January 2002, insisting that Penn graduate students were not employees. At great expense, the University retained the prestigious Philadelphia law firm Ballard Spahr Andrews & Ingersoll to make its case to the NLRB.[63]

In November 2002, the regional NLRB hearing officer authorized GET-UP, which declared its affiliation with the American Federation of Teachers, to proceed with the campus election; to GET-UP's consternation, the University's attorneys appealed the regional board's decision to the NLRB in Washington. The NLRB process allowed GET-UP to hold its election, though the votes would not be counted until the NLRB ruled on the University's appeal. The election took place in March 2003, with GET-UP claiming victory based on the results of a *DP* exit poll and with College Hall grousing that the bargaining unit, which included only about one thousand graduate students, had been gerrymandered to exclude schools and departments whose graduate and professional students were unlikely to have voted for the union. For the next fourteen months, GET-UP hounded Penn officials, staged rallies, and even mustered a two-day strike of TAs, futilely trying to persuade College Hall to drop the appeal and to count the votes.[64]

National labor laws prohibited Penn administrators and faculty from questioning prounion students, but they were free to state their opinions. Their arguments challenged GET-UP's anticorporatist logic, the prounionists' claim to be exploited laborers, and the equating of Ivy League graduate students with blue-collar workers. "Ironically, the unionization drive may push the University away from being the sort of institution they want and toward the sort of institution the pro-union students fear," said education professor Stanton Wortham. "If a subset of graduate students does unionize, the University will be forced to adopt an adversarial, employer-employee relationship toward them. And thus the discourses and practices of financial gain will penetrate even further into our scholarly lives." Criminology professor Lawrence Sherman calculated the financial benefits of being a Penn doctoral student. "For those students who are paid a stipend, their compensation is best represented as an hourly rate," Sherman noted. "These students are expected to work 20 hours per week for a 15-week semester or 300 hours per semester, for 600 hours per academic year. At $15,000 per academic year, that works out to $25 per hour, not counting the value of the health benefits or tuition. If we factor in six courses per academic year at over $3,000 per course ($18,000) and about $2,000 for health insurance, the total compensation is $35,000 for 600 hours' work, or $58 per hour." Observing that the University had just spent more than $1 million for the new graduate-student center, Peter Conn, the deputy provost, told a journalist that it was nonsensical "that an Ivy League graduate student researching Edmund Spenser is to be identified with a sanitation worker." According to this view, Ivy League graduate students are among the least likely of the nation's graduate students to be disadvantaged in a hypercompetitive academic market.[65]

Graduate students were quick to retort that part-time positions paying $35,000 collectively allow research universities "to eliminate the very full-time positions" for which their teaching assistants, especially in the humanities, "are purportedly being trained." In 2001, part-timers accounted for 44.5 percent of higher education faculty nationwide (by the end of the decade, their share would be 50 percent). "To some," Jennifer Washburn observed, "joining unions is less about improving their own working conditions than about preventing the perpetuation of an unjust system that imperils the future of higher education."[66]

In July 2004, the NLRB, by a 3–2 vote along partisan lines (three Republicans versus two Democrats) in a decision involving Brown University, reversed its 2000 ruling in the NYU case (the Washington board at that time had a Democratic majority). The NLRB concluded that "NYU was wrongly decided and should be overruled"; that "the imposition of collective bargaining on graduate students would improperly intrude into the educational process and would be inconsistent with the purposes and policies of the [National Labor Relations] Act"; and that "graduate student assistants are not employees" within the purview of the Act.[67] The Washington board remanded the University's appeal to the regional NLRB director, who, handcuffed by the national board's precedent, ruled in favor of the University in August 2004.[68] At the end of the three-year struggle, Peter Conn remarked, "That debate was distracting, quite frankly."[69] At this writing, the union issue is dormant, and President Amy Gutmann has raised the stipend.

Antisweatshop Campaign

As the new century approached, members of the Progressive Activist Network at Penn raised hard questions about the working conditions of laborers in developing countries who produced the University's logo apparel. Progressive Activist Network members joined a movement on college campuses, United Students Against Sweatshops (USAS), which initiated antisweatshop demonstrations at Georgetown, Duke, and the University of Wisconsin at Madison in the winter of 1999. Antisweatshop activists demanded a "living wage" for apparel workers, safe and sanitary factory conditions, workers' rights, a trustworthy monitoring system, and disclosure of factory locations.[70]

By the fall of 1999, USAS counted more than one hundred colleges and universities in its fold. USAS charged that the Fair Labor Association (FLA), an international monitoring agency that Penn and the other Ivy League members had joined the previous winter, was beholden to the companies, uninterested in factory disclosures, inattentive to workers' rights, and generally ineffectual—a charge that was rebutted, if not persuasively, by FLA supporters. Penn USAS students called for College Hall to impose a stricter code of conduct on the manufacturers than the FLA's guidelines. Responding to this demand, Rodin announced that as of January 2000, Penn would require full disclosure of factory locations by the apparel companies doing new business with the University. USAS wanted more, namely, that Penn and other universities withdraw from the FLA and join the Worker Rights Consortium (WRC), a new organization founded by human rights and labor organizations that would impose a strict code of conduct and stringent monitoring to ensure compliance with the code.[71]

It is important to note that USAS, for all the publicity it generated in the *Daily Pennsylvanian* and for all the aggravation it caused Rodin, was a very small group on the Penn campus. No more than one hundred students signed an enormous T-shirt that covered the College Green statue of Franklin in early

February 2002, and only about twenty-five students rallied at the statue. That said, there is no denying that Rodin felt an obligation to give USAS's arguments a fair hearing. She appointed an Ad Hoc Committee on Sweatshop Labor to examine the issue and to report by the end of the month on whether Penn should remain in the FLA or join the WRC—at this time approximately 150 colleges and universities were FLA members, while only four belonged to the WRC. (Rodin's initial argument was that the newly founded WRC had no political clout.)[72]

Angered by Rodin's inaction, which they regarded as a fait accompli for the FLA, some twenty demonstrators launched a sit-in in Rodin's outer office on February 7, with thirteen spending the night in College Hall. The following day Rodin told the demonstrators that she would wait to read the ad hoc committee's report before making a final decision on FLA; meanwhile, a gathering, estimated by the *DP* as "more than 50," rallied on College Green in support of the sit-in. For the next several days, to the mounting irritation of Rodin and her staff, the sit-in continued, with as many as thirty students camped out in Rodin's reception area. The protestors demanded that the University immediately withdraw from FLA and join the fledgling WRC. And they were not polite in asserting their cause. "They have used bongo drums," Rodin complained to the student newspaper, "they have banged on my inner office, they have physically blocked the ability of people to move into the office." Regarding the University's open expression guidelines, Rodin announced, "They have exceeded the boundaries of what is appropriate at this University with regard to open expression and are in absolute, complete violation." Yet she took no action to enforce the open expression guidelines, apparently unwilling to attract more publicity to the demonstration.[73]

On the fifth day of the sit-in, the *DP* reported that twenty-eight student organizations supported the demonstration, though the relatively small size of the College Green rally that week raises doubts about the strength of this support. Indeed, the small size of rallies and vigils that winter suggested that sweatshop labor had no purchase with the overwhelming majority of Penn students. In any case, on February 14, Rodin reached an agreement with USAS that ended the sit-in. She would withdraw Penn from the FLA immediately, with the understanding that the recommendations of the Ad-Hoc Committee on Sweatshop Labor, to be submitted by February 29, and other consultations could change her mind. "At that time," Rodin informed the FLA on February 15, "based on the committee's recommendation, the materials I have read, and the conversations I have had with Penn Students Against Sweatshops and with other college and university leaders, I will decide if Penn should re-join the FLA, join the WRC, or some combination of both." Interestingly, the only significant objection raised by the ad-hoc committee involved a flaw in both monitoring organizations: neither had university representation on its governing board. Join the organization that makes that change, whether the FLA or the WRC, or both, advised the ad-hoc committee. Rodin subsequently importuned both organizations to appoint university representatives to their boards, making Penn's affiliation with either or both of them contingent on that factor. In May she appointed a Committee on Manufacturer Responsibility to "monitor the progress of the FLA and WRC" over the summer and, in the fall, to "face the membership issue head-on." This committee submitted its report to Rodin on 20 November 2000 and, on 16 December, she announced that she concurred with its recommendation "that Penn join the fifteen other universities and colleges that have become members of both the WRC and the FLA." This decision ended Penn's sweatshop-labor controversy.[74]

Binge Drinking and the Millennium Campus

"A 26-year-old University alumnus was found dead early yesterday morning behind the Phi Gamma Delta house at 3619 Locust Walk," reported the *DP* on March 22, 1999. "The cause of death was not immediately clear, though police said they suspect he fell from either a balcony or an outdoor staircase."[75] The alumnus, a graduate of the Class of 1994, had attended the fraternity's annual alumni pig-roast dinner on the evening of Saturday, March 20, a party at which the old grads imbibed "large amounts of alcohol," according to the Philadelphia Police Department report on the incident. The body of twenty-six-year-old Michael Tobin, dead from a severe skull fracture and internal injuries, was discovered the following morning at the littered base of the fraternity's rear-entrance concrete staircase. Following an investigation, the police ruled Tobin's death accidental and reported that his blood-alcohol content was .20.[76] The tragic death of an alumnus was the worst of several alcohol-related incidents involving Penn students on the night of March 20–21; a freshman was hospitalized for alcohol poisoning, and two sorority parties in Center City were broken up by the local constabulary.[77]

Binge drinking, always a concern of college presidents, was documented as a crisis on the nation's campuses in the mid-1990s. Researchers for the Harvard School of Public Health College Alcohol Study reported, with credible authority, on the prevalence and effects of college binge drinking, having surveyed more than 17,500 students at 140 accredited four-year colleges nationwide (two-thirds were public, one-third were private). The study defined binge drinking as

> five or more drinks in a row one or more times during a two-week period for men, and four or more drinks in a row one or more times

during a two-week period for women—a gender-specific modification to a national standard. Our research documents that it takes four drinks for women to run the same risk of various alcohol-related health and behavior problems as men do with five drinks. These problems include getting into arguments, getting injured, forgetting where they were or what they did, and engaging in unplanned or unprotected sex. A drink is defined as a 12-ounce can or bottle of beer, a four-ounce glass of wine, a 12-ounce bottle or can of wine cooler, or a shot of liquor taken straight or in a mixed drink.

The researchers found that "nearly half (44 percent) of all students were binge drinkers, and 19 percent were frequent binge drinkers (had binged three or more times in the previous two weeks)." Forty-seven percent of frequent binge drinkers and 14 percent of binge drinkers reported problems associated with their drinking. Along racial and gender lines, whites out-binged African Americans three to one; white males had the highest binge rate at 54 percent; African American females the lowest at 12 percent; and males out-binged females at a rate of 50 percent to 39 percent. Consistent with Penn's experience (more below), "The single strongest predictor of binge drinking was found to be fraternity or sorority residence or membership—*an astonishing 80 percent of those who live in sorority houses and 86 percent of fraternity house residents qualify as binge drinkers*" (emphasis added).[78]

The problem of binge drinking was a high priority for Rodin and Barchi more than a year before the Phi Gamma Delta tragedy. Their prompt was the Harvard study. Following discussions about campus alcohol abuse in the University Council in the fall of 1997, Rodin charged a special committee that included medical school, nursing, and social work faculty, among others, "to review the issues" and to recommend a program of preventive measures. The members issued their report in September 1998, with the caveat that they lacked "sufficient data to understand the extent of excessive drinking among Penn students—and faculty for that matter—and believe we need to supplement the statistics available from the Harvard study with more directed questions for the Penn constituency." As their main recommendation for changing the drinking culture at Penn, the committee called for reinstating Friday classes as a means of curtailing Penn's three-day weekend, which was jump-started in some campus quarters every Thursday evening—notwithstanding the fact that Friday is a day held sacrosanct for research by most faculty and graduate students. The committee also recommended that Rodin add her voice to Penn's admissions literature and on-campus statements to assert that Penn is a "social Ivy," not a "drinking school."[79] The fact that nine fraternities stood on or near Locust Walk, despite the growing diversification of the campus spine—not to mention that some twenty-five other fraternities and sororities were housed in close proximity to the campus—did not bode well for campus temperance. Indeed, it is likely that part of Penn's attractiveness to prospective students as a "hot school" (Rodin's oft-used phrase) was its inebriate sociability: Penn offered both a world-class baccalaureate and opportunities for world-class social networking, with alcohol as the indispensable lubricant.

The special committee recommended sensibly that the president appoint a "coordinator for alcohol related problems" to supervise problem drinkers at the University—"a mature professional, qualified for a faculty level appointment, with experience in the treatment of substance abuse, knowledge of the recent research advances in this field and experience in the counseling of undergraduate students." The committee also called for "accurate, ongoing, quantifiable data" on alcohol and drug use at Penn.[80]

Four days after Michael Tobin's death, Rodin and Barchi temporarily rescinded the University's policy that permitted serving alcohol at registered undergraduate parties, either on or off campus. "A death is a big deal," as one administrator grimly put it.[81] Rodin and Barchi immediately suspended Phi Gamma Delta, pending an investigation by the University and the national fraternity. On the afternoon of March 29, about one thousand students gathered on College Green between College Hall and Van Pelt. At first blush, some adult observers interpreted this as the first sign of a political reawakening of the campus, a mass protest against Bill Clinton's use of air strikes against Serbs in Kosovo, which were announced on March 24. This was not the case. More than twenty years after a student uprising was provoked by an earlier president's nonconsultative decision to cut some minor sports programs and to increase tuition, a new generation of sign-wielding students was up in arms against Rodin over a similar issue that had no political or social referents beyond their own needs. In this case, the issue was the lack of student consultation prior to the temporary ban. "If we had developed then a deep and lengthy deliberative process," responded Rodin in her reasoned mea culpa, "yet another weekend would have gone by and we didn't know what that weekend would bring."[82]

Just hours after the College Hall rally, Rodin and Barchi convened the first meeting of a hastily appointed twenty-one-member working group composed of seven administrators and professors and fifteen students, who were charged to identify options for responsible alcohol use at registered undergraduate parties.[83] The provost's working group completed its report in late April, and Rodin approved all of the forty-five recommendations, which the office of the vice provost for university life mailed out to students in August.

Highlighting the criticality of primary prevention, the report offered a number of pathways to engage students in education about the dangers of alcohol abuse. The working group recommended a total ban on hard alcohol "at all registered on-campus undergraduate events" and a personal limit of "one six-pack of beer or equivalent per person over 21 years of age"; to ensure compliance, a trained nondrinking monitor would be present at each alcohol-related event. The report reiterated the 1998 special committee's recommendation for the appointment of an alcohol coordinator, to "provide a confidential source to address all areas of concern related to alcohol and other drugs, to integrate policy and to enhance approaches to student education and treatment of alcohol-related problems." The working group also called for an expansion of nonalcohol social events.[84] The working group's report was adopted as campus policy, effective September 1999. In August, the vice provost for university life appointed an alcohol coordinator for the campus. Among other educational tools in 1999–2000, the University introduced Penn 101, a freshman seminar that included such topics as "Alcohol and Drugs in Identity Formation," the 1996 Harvard study, and "effective strategies for preventing and intervening in substance abuse behaviors." A mandatory, four-hour First Step Alcohol Education Program was established for first-time violators of the alcohol policy.[85] As the *DP* reported in the spring of 2000, the alcohol policy was "a work in progress," a project of gradual implementation and revision.[86]

In the weeks that followed Michael Tobin's death, the members of Phi Gamma Delta, Beta Chapter, which had a previous record of gaucheries, surrendered their charter to the national fraternity, dissolved the chapter, and left the house that had been Beta Chapter's home since 1913. In April 2010, the University agreed to reinstate Phi Gamma Delta after more than a decade's hiatus from the campus, restoring the chapter to the house at 3619 Locust Walk, which was occupied in recent years by the Penn Humanities Forum, among other groups; "Fiji [nickname for Phi Gamma Delta] now is not the Fiji of 10 years ago," averred the new president of Phi Gamma Delta. As for Michael Tobin, the University settled for an undisclosed amount a wrongful death suit filed by his parents, who charged that the staircase at Phi Gamma Delta was unsafe and negligently maintained; the University's unapologetic defense was that Tobin may have fallen from the balcony above the staircase.[87]

■ Surveying Rodin's Domain

Rodin's contributions included the West Philadelphia Initiatives and the creation of "a 'destination' campus," with upscale restaurants and high-end retail operations, the Sansom Common/University Square complex, and bold commercial ventures such as the Bridge cinemas, the Fresh Grocer, and the Left Bank; the Agenda for Excellence for 1995–2000, Penn's leap forward in the national rankings, and the implementation of the undergraduate 21st Century Project and the college house system and its Wheel support services; the Perelman Quadrangle and the historic-building renovations (Logan Hall, Irvine Hall) that accentuated the new student center; and a spate of new construction projects completed or under way by 2004, including the Vagelos Laboratories (IAST), the Biomedical Research Building II/III, Levine Hall of the Department of Computer and Information Science, the Mainwaring Wing of the University Museum, the Shattner Center of the Dental School, and outsized Huntsman Hall of the Wharton School.

Renovation projects completed under Rodin included three academic buildings—the Law School, the Graduate School of Education, and the Annenberg School for Communication. The residential-renovation projects were the Quad college houses and the three high-rises in Hamilton Village, formerly called the Superblock, with spectacular new landscaping in the West Campus. Other building makeovers included the conversion of the Skinner Hall Faculty Club to Addams Hall of the Department of Fine Arts, the conversion of the newly acquired Christian Association Building to the ARCH Building, and the renovation of the Carriage House as the home of the Lesbian Gay Bisexual Transgender Center. Seminal property acquisitions included the Civic Center for HUP expansion and medical-research facilities, and the Postal Lands for East Campus expansion.

At this writing, Rodin's legacy appears to be threefold: the West Philadelphia Initiatives, Penn's entry into the top tier of American research universities, and the corporatization of the University. We have emphasized particularly the West Philadelphia Initiatives. We have seen that the Initiatives were a pragmatic response to the accelerating violence and deterioration in the campus area and more generally in University City. The murders of two Penn affiliates, one a doctoral student, the other a research associate, in combination with other indicators of urban decline, signaled unequivocally to Rodin and her leadership team that Penn's future was in serious jeopardy. Like Hackney, Rodin understood that "high walls and imposing gates" would not shield the campus from the urban crisis: Penn's and Philadelphia's futures were inextricably intertwined.[88] The University's institutional self-interest, she ultimately realized, necessitated moving simultaneously on multiple fronts to stanch the crisis in University City.

In an interview she gave several years after leaving Penn to become president of the Rockefeller Foundation in New York City, Rodin said that the

West Philadelphia Initiatives "finally made Penn a real citizen of Philadelphia,"[89] a remark that ignored the foundation she had inherited from Sheldon Hackney. The University started on a path to become a real citizen of the city under Hackney, whose administration fostered a strategy of positive engagement and reconciliation with West Philadelphia, with the Center for Community Partnerships and the restructured West Philadelphia Partnership as lead agents for that strategy. Rodin's West Philadelphia Initiatives built on and expanded Hackney's approach to include social and economic sectors in University City that had been targeted for renewal four decades earlier in the planning of the West Philadelphia Corporation. Many of the ideas that actuated the Initiatives, notably a multisector approach to urban revival, including a Penn-assisted public school, existed on paper in one form or another prior to Rodin. Her major contribution was the implementation of these ideas.

The marker of Penn's citizenship in 2004 that clearly distinguished it from 1964 was transparency—the involvement of multiple constituencies in Penn's planning initiatives in West Philadelphia. Rodin's corporatized University had learned that the imposition of a fait accompli in West Philadelphia such as the University City Science Center in 1964 is no longer practically feasible or ethically desirable. Put another way, without irony or contradiction, Corporate Penn is also Citizen Penn, a quintessentially pragmatic institution.

Conclusion

In Franklin's Name

In his 1749 *Proposals Relating to the Education of Youth in Pensilvania*, Benjamin Franklin, a public servant par excellence, advocated a decidedly public purpose for the "Publick Academy in the City of Philadelphia," the precursor institution of the University of Pennsylvania. "The great Aim and End of all Learning," Franklin wrote, is to cultivate in youth "an *Inclination* join'd with an *Ability* to serve Mankind, one's Country, Friends and Family" (original emphasis).[1] In a letter he wrote shortly thereafter to Samuel Johnson, Franklin restated this point: "I think with you, that nothing is of more importance for the public weal, than to form and train up youth in wisdom and virtue. Wise and good men are, in my opinion, the *strength* of a state: much more so than riches or arms, which, under the management of Ignorance and Wickedness, often draw on destruction, instead of providing for the safety of a people."[2]

In Franklin's time, classical curricula, grounded in ancient Greek and Latin, predominated in Anglo-American colleges (including his Academy) and in the conventional wisdom on higher learning. Franklin challenged that hegemony in *Tract Relative to the English School in Philadelphia*, written in June 1789, when, as he put it, he was "the only one of the original Trustees and . . . just stepping into the Grave myself."[3] Decades earlier, in his treatise *Idea of the English School*, published in 1751, Franklin had proposed the curriculum he envisaged for the Academy. Spread out over six "classes" (presumably forms or levels), the English School curriculum, on paper at least, foreshadowed the modern liberal studies curriculum, though with a thoroughly practical bent, lacking Greek and Latin and giving exclusive priority to the English language, the study of which would emphasize "good Reading and proper Speaking." As an example of Franklin's utilitarian emphasis, witness his thoughts on the teaching of scientific studies (Franklin's term was "Natural and Mechanic History"): "The Merchant may thereby be enabled better to understand many

Commodities in Trade; the Handicraftsman to improve his Business by new Instruments, Mixtures and Materials; and frequently Hints are given of new Manufactures, or new Methods of improving Land, that may be set on foot greatly to the Advantage of a Country." Commensurate with the "great Aim and End of All Learning" that Franklin proclaimed in his 1749 *Proposals*, he wrote in *Idea of the English School* that as "Knowledge of *Duty*" (original emphasis) was the "most useful" knowledge, the Academy would cultivate duty, virtue, and piety in its pupils and students. Graduates would be disposed and qualified to "'pass thro' and execute the several Offices of civil Life, with Advantage and Reputation to themselves and Country."[4]

In January 1751, the Academy opened with two courses of study, a dual curriculum that suggested a compromise between the "Latinist" majority on the board and Franklin and his supporters. One was a classical course taught by the rector of the Academy, a Latin master, emphasizing Latin and Greek and also giving attention to English, history, geography, logic, and oratory. The other course was an "English school" taught by an English master who held no title and whose salary was one-half of the rector's. There seems to have been no mention of "natural and mechanic history" as an Academy subject, which must have been galling to Franklin the scientist. As the Academy's original trustees began to die, a new arrangement of trustees refused to honor the terms of the original plan. According to Franklin, who wrote his 1789 polemic with several decades' worth of trustees' minutes in hand, the English school had atrophied to the point of public disgrace as early as the 1760s, having abandoned any attention to "the Elegance of the English Language," "proper Pronunciation," and public speaking. "The English Part of our Scheme of Education," Franklin charged in his *Tract*, was a mockery of its "original design," the English school having been "injudiciously starved" by the trustees, whose "Favours were showered upon the Latin Part." Writing as the last living original trustee of what was now the College, Academy and Charitable School of Philadelphia—and in 1791 would become the University of Pennsylvania—Franklin, in his peroration, bitterly acknowledged the "long defeat" of his ideas.[5]

"His main ideas are . . . pretty clear," Edward Potts Cheyney noted in his 1940 *History of the University of Pennsylvania*, which included an elegant summary of Franklin's *Tract*. "He would have had an education utilitarian rather than cultural, entirely in the English language, though following the best models in that language, devoting much attention to training in thought and expression. It would include mathematics, geography, history, logic, and natural and moral philosophy. It should be an education for citizenship and should lead to mercantile and civic success and usefulness." Cheyney concluded, sardonically, "It is unfortunate that it was never tried."[6]

The practical, civic orientation of the pre–World War I Wharton School of Edmund James, Simon Nelson Patten, and Scott Nearing would, no doubt, have pleased Franklin. As we have seen, this trio of stalwart progressives understood the school's mission to be one of preparing its graduates to solve the problems of an advanced industrial society, not the least of which was corporate malfeasance. Their activist orientation to teaching and research was short lived, expunged by vindictive trustees. "Ameliorative, reformist social science" had vanished by the 1920s, not only at Penn, but in the American research university writ large, displaced by a so-called objective, value-free "science of numbers" (scientism). Paralleling this conservative tendency in academic research was the devaluing of moral education in the college curriculum, with Penn again proving the rule. Without the moral compass of a James or Patten, with a faculty that had largely absolved itself of any obligation to prepare students to become citizens, Penn was fertile soil for the "collegiate way" and the "College Joe/Betty Co-ed" campus ethos that prevailed from the 1910s to the late 1950s.

As we have seen, by the mid-1960s, in some quarters of the Penn campus, students and faculty had awoken to changing times with a newfound sense of civic purpose. An activist minority engaged in community service, participated in demonstrations, advanced curriculum reforms, and ended the practice of in loco parentis at Penn. Students targeted Penn and its surrogate the University City Science Center as embodiments of the ills of advanced capitalism. They cited the University's complicity in military research at the Science Center and, by implication, its support of the Vietnam War; they decried the displacement of working-poor blacks in RDA Unit 3, the paucity of low-income housing, and the lack of democracy in it all. With the Science Center issue settled (albeit uneasily) after the 1969 College Hall sit-in and the continued existence of the institution grudgingly accepted as a fait accompli, Penn activists, in the spring of 1970, turned their attention to Nixon's secret war in Cambodia. By this time, however, campus politics, following national trends, was fragmenting in different directions—toward identity groups on the one hand and civic/political apathy on the other.

Lacking the funds to sustain existing initiatives and besieged by rampant muggings, robberies, and thefts on or around the campus, Martin Meyerson's University turned its back on West Philadelphia in the 1970s. Penn's community relations stagnated. Among African Americans, and especially those displaced by Unit 3 and their sympathizers, bitterness against the University festered. With the demise of the Quadripartite Commission in 1971, undergraduate outreach activities such as the Community Involvement Council, prominent in the late 1960s, were retired to the dustbin; the Student

Committee on Undergraduate Education retreated from its activist engagement with the administration. A climate of nervous caution, if not fear, dissuaded students from venturing into West Philadelphia. Student activism splintered at Penn, with the radical/liberal minority taking up the cudgels of identity politics—blacks, women, lesbians and gays, for instance—and the majority taking an egocentric turn toward protecting their perceived self-interest by mobilizing en masse against tuition hikes and cuts in the athletic budget. Needless to say, protesting cuts in gymnastics, badminton, and the theater program was a very far cry from the civic and political sentiments that had galvanized the College Hall sit-in of the previous decade.

In the 1980s, Sheldon Hackney tried to set Penn's civic course aright by restructuring the West Philadelphia Corporation to represent community interests, and he laid the foundation for a civic revival at Penn in the 1990s by establishing the Center for Community Partnerships, today's Netter Center. Ira Harkavy, the former student activist who led the 1969 sit-in to its peaceful settlement, was the center's founding executive director. Harkavy and his colleague Lee Benson introduced the idea of "academically based community service" (ABCS), calling for the creation or redesign of academic courses and seminars that would make West Philadelphia issues and problems the focal point of student problem-solving initiatives, to be designed and implemented in partnership with West Philadelphia teachers, students, and community organizations. Cognizant of Penn's history, Harkavy and Benson regarded themselves unabashedly as disciples of Franklin's charge to cultivate in students dispositions and capacities for public service. They were heirs of James, Patten, and Nearing in their recognition of the enormous potential of young adults for making significant contributions to constructive social change. And they were devotees of Martin Meyerson's conception of "One University."

We have argued that the Netter Center, as a mediating structure, and the ABCS concept offer one—if not the only—promising way to realize Meyerson's vision. Netter and ABCS also provide a practical means to restore the racial trust that was long ago violated by Penn's and the RDA's insensitivity in dealing with the residents of Unit 3. Though Penn has taken significant steps to establish itself as a good institutional neighbor in West Philadelphia, it still confronts racial distrust, which is sometimes manifested in what the anthropologist John L. Jackson calls "racial paranoia," a concept that "stresses . . . fears people harbor about other groups potentially hating or mistreating them, gaining a leg up at their expense."[7] While racial paranoia manifests on both sides of the racial divide, our concern is with African American perceptions of Penn's motives, even when Penn is not involved in a particular decision, action, or trend in West Philadelphia; in other words, when Penn's "invisible hand" is suspected in "gaining a leg up at their expense." Sheldon Hackney, himself a racial conciliator, confronted this suspicion when he reasonably held the line during the Mayor's Scholarship imbroglio, fixing the number of awards at 125 for any four-year period, rather than the 125 per annum demanded by the Public Interest Law Center of Philadelphia and black organizations, politicians, and media. Hackney's ultimate vindication in the courts did little to sway these groups to trust Penn.

Racial paranoia in Jackson's meaning, undeniably, has a rational basis in the experience of poor and working-class blacks who were displaced in the name of the University City Science Center, the urban renewal brainchild of Penn and the West Philadelphia Corporation. As we have seen, the bitter memory of urban renewal ramifies across several generations of West Philadelphia blacks, its symbolism long since disproportionate to the relatively small numbers of displaced residents. It compounds the deep resentment fueled by the physical presence and trappings of an immensely privileged, predominantly white university in their midst.

Between 2005 and 2010, this racial distrust was evident in the education project of the West Philadelphia High School Community Partners, a loosely organized, often contentious biracial community group formed to obtain a new building and curricular program to replace the century-old West Philadelphia High School, long since a racially isolated, dysfunctional neo-Gothic colossus on Walnut Street just seven blocks west of the Penn campus. Built into the Community Partners' proposal for the new high school—and accepted by the School District of Philadelphia—was the agreement that the new building would be open to the old high school's historical constituency, meaning, since the 1950s at least, West Philadelphia blacks. This clause was motivated by the fear that Penn would somehow be able to channel Penn Alexander School graduates into the new high school, and Penn-affiliated parents would claim it as their own. Another theory concerned the final disposition of the old high school: Penn would sweep in to purchase the enormous building for condo development, drive up property values in the Walnut Hill neighborhood, and force tax-burdened black householders out.

One of us, Puckett, who helped draft the Community Partners' proposal, attended most of the group's monthly meetings for five years, and also had a hand in developments at the old high school, which, after a chaotic spring of arson, violence, and general disruption in 2007, adopted the Community Partners' proposal for small theme-based academies, preparatory to the move to the new high school, which took place in the fall of 2011. Each semester from the fall of 2007 to the spring of 2011, Puckett and his colleague Elaine Simon, the director of the Urban Studies Program in the School of Arts and Sciences and also a participant in the Community Partners, cotaught an ABCS seminar on Schools and Community Development, which engaged undergraduates and students and teachers at West Philadelphia High School in jointly planning and implementing the Urban Leadership Academy. For the high school students, these activities included, among other projects, neighborhood-based-survey and computer research and two published proposals, including scale-model architectural designs, for the redevelopment of vacant lots near the high school. As part of their seminar participation, Penn undergraduates assisted these projects and provided resource development for two new courses in the Urban Leadership Academy: the American City and Urban Sociology. These initiatives introduced the Penn students to "a first-hand contact with actualities" (John Dewey's apt phrase) and a set of theoretical lenses drawn from contemporary readings and focused discussions to interpret that experience. The Penn students wrote weekly reading-response essays, educational autobiographies, and collaborative papers on topics germane to the curriculum and the students they assisted.

While some elements of Puckett and Simon's experience—the instructors' involvement in community organizing around education, for example—are unusual for ABCS faculty, the linkage of an undergraduate seminar with informed, reflective citizen action is typical. The most widely implemented type of ABCS at Penn is undergraduate classes and seminars organized to provide on-site assistance to West Philadelphia public schools. Such courses involve Penn students and West Philadelphia schoolchildren or high school students collaboratively in studies or projects related to local history, literacy, lead toxicity, nutrition, primary healthcare, neighborhood planning and design, graffiti, school-based community publications, and theater performance, among other activities. A second type of ABCS casts a wider net by offering an important service to the wider West Philadelphia community. For example, since 2008, Mark Lloyd, director of the University archives and coauthor of this book, and history professor Walter Licht have cotaught an ABCS course, the West Philadelphia Community History Project, that lets undergraduate history majors coconstruct, with "members of the West Philadelphia community," a digital heritage museum of the area's history and neighborhoods, including historic photographs, maps, personal stories, and statistics. This "ever-revised and expanded resource," publicly available since the spring of 2009, also features special exhibits, a bibliography, and teacher guides. The website is sponsored by the University Archives.[8]

■

As we have seen in this book, urban campus expansion is a recurring phenomenon of American higher education, and urban universities have to continuously balance their growth with community needs and contingent circumstances. They exist in "a state of perilous equilibrium" (an apt phrase borrowed from the sociologist Willard Waller) with their cities and surrounding neighborhoods. Penn's experience with urban renewal is part of this larger history of urban universities confronting the crisis of the American city since World War II. Each urban university charts its own trajectory by trial and error in negotiating its place in the urban ecology. Penn's trajectory happens to have been a progression from alienation and drift to reconciliation and revival, with each phase shaped by a set of social contingencies (local and national) and a distinctive leadership style.

New York University and Columbia University provide recent examples of urban campus expansion. In 2006, NYU announced an ambitious twenty-five-year plan that would increase the University's total physical plant by 40 percent. According to the *New York Times*, "between 1991 and 2001, the number of students living in N.Y.U. housing tripled to 12,000 from 4,000, as the university raised its national profile. (In the early nineties, 50 percent of its students came from the metropolitan area; now that figure has declined to 10 to 15 percent.) By 2031, N.Y.U. expects its total student body to grow to 46,500 students, up from the current 41,000." Though the University contends that it has made "a concerted effort . . . to conduct an open public process that is mindful of the neighborhood context, architectural quality and residents' interests," influential critics describe it as a juggernaut "taking over more and more of the neighborhood."[9]

The *NYU 2031* plan proposes several expansions outside of the historic core in addition to redevelopment of the historic core, an area that NYU's planners have divided into seven districts: Washington Square (North, West, East, and South), Academic Superblock, Washington Square Village, and University Village Superblock. The four Washington Square districts and the Academic Superblock surrounding Washington Square Park, with only a few exceptions, are "fully utilized" and "offer no more opportunities for development." The University is enveloped by "the historic districts of Greenwich Village, SoHo, and NoHo," and further constrained by "current zoning rules [that] do not allow classrooms or faculty or student residences in some areas east of Broadway." The *NYU 2031* plan concludes, "If the University is to be able to add academic programs and residential capacity at its core, the two southern districts, or superblocks, offer the only significant opportunity."[10]

The North Block, Washington Square Village, will add two new academic buildings and new landscaping, establishing a new "park-like" academic center coordinated with the adjacent Academic Superblock. The South Block, including University Village/Silver Towers (designed by Mies van de Rohe and registered as a historic landmark), will add a fourth tower on the Bleecker Street (north) side of the block to accommodate faculty housing and a university hotel. The current supermarket site on the corner of Bleecker and La Guardia Place is to be redeveloped as "an expansive new playground," a park adjunct to the four "towers in the park." On the Mercer Street (east) side of the block, "a mixed-use building of a new type"—the Zipper Building—"will add needed student residential and academic space for NYU and will replace the current NYU Jerome S. Coles Sports and Recreation Center on Mercer Street." The South Block is also designated as the "potential site" of a public elementary school.[11]

At the other end of Manhattan, Columbia University, since 2003, has been engaged in the largest expansion in its history—a $6.3 billion plan that involves the redevelopment of seventeen contiguous acres in Manhattanville about five blocks north of the present thirty-six-acre campus. The site is bounded by Broadway on the east, Riverside Drive on the west, West 125th Street on the south, and West 133rd Street on the north. The first phase of the thirty-year campus plan includes, among other features, a science center for the study of neurodegenerative diseases and new homes for the Columbia Business School, the School of International and Public Affairs, and the School of the Arts. The plan boldly pledges mutual benefits to the University and West Harlem residents and businesses, promising "nearly 6,000 new University jobs with competitive health, educational and retirement benefits," a program of "affordable housing initiatives," "publicly accessible open spaces and improved, pedestrian-friendly streets—part of an environmentally sustainable urban design," "new commercial life, including local shopping, and dining, as well as a range of public amenities," and a "Teachers College-assisted K-8 public school," to be built in partnership with the community.[12] If the community components of this plan come to fruition, they will represent a volte-face from Columbia's folly in the 1967 "Gym Crow" episode.

Columbia's current president, Lee Bollinger, and his leadership team seem to have taken a hard lesson from that page of Columbia's history, and, more benignly, some lessons from Judith Rodin's West Philadelphia Initiatives. The Columbia plan targets the same areas for urban revival as Rodin's plan—housing, economic development, "pedestrian friendly streets," and public education. Offered as a quid pro quo to the area's community leaders, the proposal for a university-assisted K-8 elementary school in West Harlem is modeled explicitly on the Penn Alexander School in West Philadelphia. Indeed, the leaders of this initiative are the same individuals who led the planning and implementation of Penn Alexander. Teachers College's current president, Susan Fuhrman, was Penn GSE's dean for most of the Rodin era, and the college's associate vice president for school and community partnerships, Nancy Streim, was an associate dean at Penn GSE under Fuhrman. The new Columbia–West Harlem partnership school opened in 2011–12 in an existing public school at 5th Avenue and 130th Street, launching a five-year phase-in with two kindergarten classes in the first year. A permanent facility in West Harlem opened in 2012–13, with a full complement of grades to serve a total of three hundred (possibly five hundred) students by 2016.[13]

One cogent lesson of Penn's expansion over the last fifty years, beyond the urban university's social responsibility for transparency and consultation, is a pragmatic if not a moral obligation to shape campus expansion in ways that are mutually beneficial to the University and the community it affects. That consideration appears strongly in Columbia's declarations regarding its seventeen-acre expansion site in Manhattanville and the soon-to-be-actualized quid pro quo of a university-assisted community school. NYU, whose main campus is situated in a predominantly upscale district and has fewer concerns than Columbia about the compatibility of its surrounding neighborhoods, promises some aesthetic relief to Greenwich Village and the lower Fifth Avenue area by virtue of its plans for new landscaping and new park and playground development in the University Village Superblock and Washington Square Village.

If Penn has anything else to teach NYU, Columbia, and other urban universities, it is the desirability of establishing a systemic link between the university's urban agenda and its academic program, especially the undergraduate curriculum. The curricular involvement of students in the urban agenda provides opportunities for students' cognitive, civic, and moral development in ways that support the university's historic missions of teaching, research, and service. It also enhances the university's community relations and serves as a way to improve the community. In 1992, Sheldon Hackney created a university-wide structure for community partnerships that would mediate the urban agenda and recruit faculty across the university to teach ABCS courses, a strategy his successor, Judith Rodin, adopted and reinforced. The Netter Center is now fully embedded in Penn's core operations, and ABCS courses are a familiar component of the undergraduate catalogue.

■

We learn from this history that Penn's rise in the last half century to become one of the world's great research universities has been in no small way a function of the University's relationship with West Philadelphia, and that its present and future well-being is inextricably intertwined with that of its immediate geographic area. In the case of the Science Center in the mid-1960s, Penn was heavily implicated in the displacement of poor and working-class African Americans for the sake of an enterprise that fell short of being a true R & D hub. The shortfall of the Science Center added insult to the injury inflicted on displaced poor people by the unilateral decision making of Penn's surrogate, the West Philadelphia Corporation, and the RDA. Embracing the ethic of positive engagement in West Philadelphia that Sheldon Hackney introduced in the 1980s, Judith Rodin managed to achieve the 1960s WPC's goal of building a compatible neighborhood for Penn, without the insensitivity or lack of transparency that attended federally sponsored urban renewal in University City.

In her memoir, *The University and Urban Revival*, Rodin stipulated that Penn must now cast its net beyond the target area of the West Philadelphia Initiatives to help improve the quality of life in the West Philadelphia neighborhoods from which Sayre High School, West Philadelphia High School, and University City High School draw their students. The University-sponsored Disease Prevention and Health Promotion Clinic at Sayre is a laudable start. Yet Simon and Puckett's experience at West Philadelphia High School suggests that Penn still has fence-mending to do to quell racial distrust and paranoia regarding its actions, however well intentioned, constructive, and transparent they may be. Expanded and sustained, collaborative partnerships embodied in ABCS would go a long way toward resolving this dilemma, especially as a younger generation of West Philadelphia blacks encounters a more benign University than older generations experienced. As Penn now looks east of 32nd Street toward the Schuylkill River and beyond—a zone of uncontested campus expansion in which huge sums are currently being invested— the University, if for no other reason than enlightened self-interest, can ill afford not to continue its outreach in the schools and neighborhoods of West Philadelphia.

Appendix

The Urban Renewal University:
A Typology

Our typology of university involvement in urban renewal projects in the 1950s and 1960s includes four categories. Here we profile three of these types—de novo campus development, campus-core expansion, and scattered-site campus expansion. The fourth type, proxy campus expansion, is discussed in Chapter 3, where we look at a model that Penn adopted, primarily, from the University of Chicago.

■ De Novo Campus Development

In 1957, the state legislature of Illinois, projecting a tidal surge in college enrollments by the early 1970s, authorized funds to create a branch campus of the University of Illinois, whose main campus was in Urbana. Patiently and carefully weighing their options, the University trustees decided on the Harrison-Halsted area west of Chicago's Loop, a 55.8-acre area that was already on the city's drawing board for urban renewal, as the best site for the new campus, which would be named the University of Illinois at Chicago Circle. The historian Amanda Seligman describes the last stage of the complex decision-making process:

> An urban renewal clearance area on the Near West Side surfaced occasionally as a possibility during the campus discussions. The Harrison-Halsted area was a working-class, multi-ethnic district that Jane Addams's Hull House had served since the late nineteenth century. The site was close to downtown and could undergird the Loop's renewal, just as the railroad site would. During the summer of 1960, [Mayor Richard J.] Daley's staff began floating the area as a potential location for the campus, possibly as a way of putting pressure on the

railroads to cooperate with the city. In September the Department of City Planning announced that Daley formally recommended the Harrison-Halsted site to the university trustees, in case the best location, the terminals, ultimately proved unobtainable [that was indeed the case]. In February 1961 university trustees and city officials held a meeting with the mayor and concluded that getting the Garfield Park site—and the necessary replacement parkland—was impossible, despite the latest ruling from the Illinois Supreme Court. If he had to swallow the bitter pill of losing the railroad site, Daley was pleased to authorize the Harrison-Halsted location.[1]

The shift in the city's urban renewal plan from residential use to university development, which the federal Housing and Home Finance Agency approved, was fiercely resisted by the Harrison-Halsted Community Group, an Italian-led coterie of some three hundred women and their families who conducted a sit-in at city hall and sued the city in federal court—to no avail. "When construction began," Seligman writes, "most of the Hull House complex and surrounding residential areas were demolished. By 1965 the first classes started at the University of Illinois Chicago Circle campus."[2]

■ Campus-Core Expansion

As we argued in Chapter 2, Penn is the dominant example of an urban renewal university expanding contiguously from its historic core. Campus-core expansion plans at two other Philadelphia universities were also beneficiaries of urban renewal projects: the Drexel Institute of Technology (today's Drexel University) and Temple University. New York University and several other higher education institutions in New York City also illustrate this category.[3]

Drexel University

The nineteenth-century Philadelphia financier and philanthropist Anthony J. Drexel, who commanded the global banking firm of Drexel and Co. and partnered with J. P. Morgan, founded the Drexel Institute of Art, Science, and Industry in West Philadelphia. When the Institute opened in 1891 in the 3100 block of Chestnut Street, its ornate Main Building—its only building at the time—stood literally (and later figuratively) in Penn's shadow. The Main Building, designed by Joseph M. Wilson, was a grand architectural structure rivaling Penn's University Library as an academic emblem of Philadelphia's Industrial Age. Always mindful of his German-immigrant roots, Drexel built a coeducational institute to prepare working-class youths for careers in industry, business, and commerce.[4]

Over the next forty years, Drexel mounted an array of vocationally oriented programs aligned with the founder's vision; it was particularly noted for educating women in its schools of business and library science. Yet by the end of World War II, the tuition-dependent Institute faced bankruptcy, its enrollments having declined from nearly five thousand to twenty-six hundred during the war. A new president, James Creese is credited with restoring the Institute's financial stability, boosting enrollments, doubling the size of the physical plant, and garnering federal Cold War dollars for Drexel's programs.[5] The completion of Stratton Hall (biological sciences) on the corner of 32nd and Chestnut streets in 1955 inaugurated the Institute's expansion west of the historic core (the block bounded by 31st, 32nd, Chestnut, and Market streets). In 1957, Drexel acquired RDA Unit 1—the block of Chestnut, Sansom, 32nd, and 33rd streets—where it built the James Creese Student Activities Center in 1962, the Mandell Theater and McAlister Hall (humanities and social sciences) in 1973, and Handschumacher Dining Hall in 1990. RDA Unit 5, established in 1962, designated "32.2 acres bounded by 33rd Street and 34th Street and Powelton Avenue and Chestnut Street" for Drexel's expansion.[6]

Unit 5 bordered on Powelton Village, a historic neighborhood on Drexel's northern boundary, defined as the blocks between 34th and 38th streets from Lancaster Avenue to Spring Garden Street.[7] By the late spring of 1965, the Institute and the RDA were at loggerheads with an ad hoc community organization, the Powelton Civic Homeowners Association, over Drexel's plan to demolish housing in favor of new dormitories and parking facilities throughout Unit 5.[8] The Association fought, unsuccessfully, to restrict Drexel's expansion to six acres within the rectangle of Lancaster and Powelton avenues and 33rd and 34th streets, and to implement a housing conservation program in the remainder of Unit 5.[9] From the late 1960s to the mid-1970s, activists from at least five ad hoc community organizations mobilized protests against the RDA and Drexel, including sit-ins, "fence busting forays," legal actions, and bulldozer blockages—none of which significantly impeded redevelopment in Unit 5.[10] In the grip of a stressed economy in the 1970s, Drexel managed (remarkably) to complete three dormitories, five academic buildings, an athletic center, a performance arts building, and two buildings for administrative and support services. Five more buildings, including the W. W. Hagerty Library and the General Services and Parking Facility in the 3300 block of Market Street, were completed in the 1980s.[11]

It is important to note that Powelton Village was a beneficiary of urban renewal. Powelton Neighbors, a 400-500-member community organization founded in 1956, which purported to "speak for Powelton Village with authority," persuaded City Council to designate the "Powelton Village 220 Area"—an action that "made this area eligible for residential renewal by homeowners under FHA's Section 220 mortgages." Adopting a self-described "fence sitting position," Powelton Neighbors did not challenge Drexel in Unit 5, though the organization objected to the RDA's plans for urban renewal in Unit 3 (see Chapter 3).[12]

Temple University

Located in North Philadelphia, roughly four miles northeast of Penn, Philadelphia's third urban renewal campus is Temple University, which originated in 1884 as a night school for workingmen in the basement of the Grace Baptist Temple on North Broad Street.[13] The School of Medicine was founded in 1901, followed by the College of Liberal Arts in 1905; the College was chartered as Temple University in 1907.[14] For the first half of the twentieth century Temple "existed as a ribbon on Broad Street between Columbia Avenue and Norris Street," with only thirteen buildings and "physical space . . . [that] was not keeping pace with the enrollment demands already being experienced by the University."[15] Until the era of urban renewal, Temple lacked both land and funds for expansion. By the end of World War II, it also confronted severe social problems in the central section of North Philadelphia, a highly stressed district.[16]

In 1948, concurrent with its certification of the University Redevelopment Area in West Philadelphia, the City Planning Commission certified a redevelopment area for North Philadelphia that was bounded by Susquehanna Avenue on the north, Girard Avenue on the south, North Broad Street on the west, and 5th Street on the east. "Area #1, Temple," contained 480 acres, forty thousand people, and 15,100 housing units. On all sides of Temple, this urban renewal zone contained "blighted" neighborhoods of tenement buildings, some without running water, many with multiple families sharing toilets and baths. In 1950, the Planning Commission established the Southwest Temple Area, which included the blocks south of Columbia Avenue (today's Cecil B. Moore Avenue) to Girard Avenue between Broad and 9th streets and the tracks of the Reading Railroad. In 1953, the RDA and the Planning Commission designated the blocks from Susquehanna to Diamond between Broad and 12th Streets as an Institutional Development Zone and promised funding for Temple's expansion within these blocks. In 1955, Temple was included in a new planning entity, the Northwest Temple Area, which the Planning Commission designated for the blocks between Broad and the Reading Railroad from Susquehanna to Columbia—"one of the most blighted sections of

Philadelphia." In the Northwest Temple Area, Temple's institutional development zone was coupled with a 3.8-acre tract on the University's northwest flank, where the Philadelphia Housing Authority proposed the Norris Project, for low-income public housing.[17]

By the fall of 1952, Temple's total enrollment stood at nineteen thousand.[18] In 1954, the University's president, Robert Johnson, announced a ten-year master plan, with new classroom buildings designated as Temple's top development priority, followed by new dormitories.[19] The next decade would see a spate of new Temple buildings rising between Montgomery and Diamond avenues and in the block of 12th, 13th, Norris, and Berks streets.[20] In 1956 Temple purchased the century-old Monument Cemetery at 15th and Berks streets, the resting place of Temple's founder Russell Conwell, opening the door to campus expansion west of Broad Street.[21] Twenty-eight thousand bodies—in one form or another, including Conwell's—were removed from vaults in the summer of 1956 and transferred to a suburban cemetery for reburial, "a tedious and difficult job," observed the *Evening Bulletin*. Intramural athletic fields and a parking lot replaced Monument Cemetery.[22]

After 1956, the availability of General State Authority (GSA) funds for land and buildings made possible "a virtual blizzard of demolition and new construction," which prompted three street closings—Park, Norris, and Berks—in the University area.[23] By the fall of 1963, Temple, with a total enrollment of 20,689, was the nation's third largest private university, trailing only New York University and Columbia in this respect.[24] By now it was clear that by hook or crook, Temple University would fill in the physical space between Columbia Avenue on the south, Susquehanna Avenue on the north, 10th Street on the east, and 16th Street on the west. A landmark new building was the GSA-financed Paley Library, which opened in 1966, looking north toward the footprint of Berks Street between 12th and 13th streets.[25]

The years 1967–73, when Paul Anderson was president, "included the most substantial period of physical expansion in Temple's history," a time when RDA bulldozers and GSA cranes were a ubiquitous presence in the University Area. These emblems of urban renewal, however, drew the ire of the University's African American neighbors. "Pressure came first from African American community residents and leaders west of Broad Street," writes the historian James Hilty. Consequently, President Anderson halted plans for nearly $20 million of construction in the blocks from Broad Street to Eighteenth Street and from Columbia Avenue (now Cecil B. Moore Avenue) north to Diamond Street."[26]

More trouble percolated east of Broad Street. In March 1969, the Steering Committee for Black Students, "an umbrella organization for black students that regularly channeled demands to the university administration," demanded that Temple agree in writing not to undertake any expansion project without the approval of "the Black community or its representatives," to assist in the relocation of displaced community members, and to maintain a strong African American presence in the University area.[27] The locus of community protest east of Broad was the Norris Street Homes (see above), a public housing project near a development site in Temple's RDA real estate portfolio. Responding to the demands of the Steering Committee for Black Students and its community ally, the Norris Homes Council, President Anderson "declared a moratorium on Temple's expansion east of Twelfth Street, where the engineering, social sciences, and humanities buildings, along with a central steam plant, were scheduled for construction."[28] A settlement was finally reached in February 1970: "Of the twenty-two acres in dispute, the community would control twelve and a half and Temple less than ten. Temple turned back four city blocks, including one originally designated for the engineering building, for community use. The community agreed to allow Temple to proceed with constructing the social sciences and humanities buildings, and Temple agreed to limit the heights of buildings on the campus perimeter." The Temple-Community Agreement of 1970 marked a turning point in the University's community relations, the point at which "Temple and its neighbors, for the first time, openly and frankly discussed their differences."[29]

New York University

New York City, the home of New York University, was the national epicenter of urban renewal, the recipient of more federal Title I grants than any other city: $68.5 million to second-place Chicago's $30.8 million.[30] No one gave urban renewal as bad a name as the man who led New York's prodigious effort, the autocrat Robert Moses, "the power broker," the "urban renewal and highway building czar" who controlled "almost all public housing, public works projects, and highway construction."[31] An "imperious master builder,"[32] Moses aimed for nothing less than to make New York a nonpareil U.S. city for private and public housing, higher education, culture, and the arts; in brief, a city amenable to the middle class. Moses marshaled Title I funds for the benefit of five educational institutions: NYU, Fordham University (more below), the Julliard School, the Pratt Institute, and Long Island University.[33] Of these five institutions, NYU, the nation's largest private university, received the largest share of Title I funds and spurred the staunchest community resistance.

Founded in 1831 on the east side of Washington Square Park in East Greenwich Village, NYU, a private, nonsectarian institution, operated two urban campuses by the end of the nineteenth century— one at Washington Square, the other at University Heights in the Bronx. By 1949, the two campuses enrolled more than seventy thousand students.[34] NYU's Title I-sponsored, campus-core expansion in the 1950s and 1960s centered on the area around Washington Square; the University Heights campus, excluded from this big picture, was closed and sold in 1973.[35]

NYU's expansion into the Greenwich Village blocks of brownstone houses and artist colonies around Washington Square raised the hackles of residents and business owners in this bohemian quarter, many of whom joined the Save the Washington Square Committee to fight the expansion.[36] With the city's backing, NYU prevailed in the first round of the battle for Washington Square: a new law school (Vanderbilt Hall) opened in 1951. The second round of the conflict centered on the "Washington Square Southeast Title I" project, a Moses-led slum clearance initiative that qualified for federal urban renewal funds. In this project, Moses was allied closely with Henry T. Heald, NYU's chancellor from 1952 to 1956. Moses planned to redevelop a nine-block area just southeast of Washington Square, with six blocks (fourteen acres) designated for private residential development and three blocks (three acres) for NYU's use; the latter site included a building the University had acquired in 1926 for the School of Commerce (now Shimkin Hall). The residential component would be redeveloped as two superblocks for housing and a component for shopping—West 3rd to Bleeker Street, Bleeker to Houston Street. The University earmarked its new parcels for a new library and two classroom buildings. Despite a vigorous community protest and, ultimately, a lawsuit to stop the project, the Board of Estimate acquired the land in November 1954. The New York State Supreme Court's dismissal of the lawsuit cleared the way for NYU to purchase the three-acre site from the city in August 1955.[37]

Construction proceeded glacially. In 1959, the Loeb Student Center opened on Washington Square South in the block just west of the newly acquired Title I land; NYU had purchased the former property in 1949 from a private developer and had used it in the interim as a playground. More than a decade would pass before the new library was completed. The plan for the $25 million Bobst Library spurred fierce opposition from Save Our Square, a multiassociation neighborhood and citywide coalition that protested, in and out of court to no avail, the outsized monumentality of the proposed building, which overwhelmed the neighboring cityscape and "cast a vast afternoon shadow over the park."[38] The Jane Jacobs disciple Roberta Gratz, who grew up in the twelve-story apartment house that was condemned for the new library, charges that Moses "misinterpreted" the vigorous street life of her old neighborhood as "slum conditions."[39] Designed by the modernist architect

Philip Johnson and built between 1967 and 1973, the red sandstone Bobst Library rose 150 feet above the street, its interior space dominated by an imposing twelve-story atrium soaring 100-by-100 feet above a Palladian mosaic floor. The two classroom buildings, Tisch Hall (the new School of Commerce, built on the site of the demolished ANTA Washington Square Theater) and Warren Weaver Hall, opened in 1966 and 1972, respectively.[40] Ironically, in light of all the community resistance evoked by NYU's expansion, the university purchased the twenty-nine-story apartment hotel at 1 Fifth Avenue in 1966, continuing its operation as a residential hotel, avowedly "to preserve the character of the neighborhood."[41]

In 1959, two privately developed seventeen-story apartment buildings opened in the West 3rd-Bleecker Street superblock of Washington Square Village. When the developers abandoned their plan for a similar building in the Bleecker-Houston Street superblock, NYU purchased the 5.5-acre site in 1960, where it completed the three-towered University Village (designed by I. M. Pei, now Silver Towers) in 1966, earmarking the apartments for NYU faculty and, at the city's insistence, a middle-class cooperative. And in 1963, NYU, anticipating an enrollment of fifty thousand students on the Washington Square campus by 1970, purchased the two 1959 apartment buildings from the developers in the West 3rd-Bleecker superblock for graduate student housing. Thus, by 1963 NYU's real-estate portfolio included all of the property in the Washington Square Southeast Title I project. These and other additions to the portfolio, coupled with a financial crisis, led to the decision to close the Bronx campus in 1973.[42]

■ Remote-Site Campus Expansion

Under Title I auspices, Fordham University, a Catholic-affiliated institution located on eighty acres on Rose Hill in the North Bronx, acquired the blocks of 60th Street to 62nd Street between Columbus and Amsterdam avenues, at the southern end of Lincoln Square, for its Manhattan campus. Lincoln Square, described by the *New York Times* as a "barren urban waste" of "old-law tenements . . . blowsy and rundown, in silent shoulder-to-shoulder misery, full of filth and vermin,"[43] was "New York City's biggest Title I project, covering fifty-three acres as originally planned."[44] The largest share of the $205 million project was earmarked to develop Lincoln Center, a 3½-block, fourteen-acre campus for the performing arts, which included new homes for the Metropolitan Opera, the New York City Opera, the New York Philharmonic, the New York City Ballet, and the Julliard School. To clear a swath for Lincoln Center, the city demolished 188 tenement buildings and removed 1,647 families.[45]

Lincoln Square Title I combined Moses's interests in using urban renewal to stimulate the performing arts and education for the middle class. Taking advantage of Moses's offer of a two-block area in Lincoln Square just south of the Lincoln Center, Fordham planned a new campus for its schools of law, education, business, and social service, which at the time were housed in remote-site lofts in Manhattan.[46] "It would be difficult," Fordham's president Laurence J. McGinley told the *Times*, "to conceive any site more beneficial for Fordham's long-term growth and university prestige than this location side by side with the Metropolitan Opera and other performing arts and cultural groups in a spot that will become the most dramatic civic center of America."[47]

Though approved by the city in 1955, Fordham's relocation of its professional schools to the two Lincoln Square blocks was challenged in a lawsuit charging "that the university's land purchase constituted a state subsidy of religion and violated the constitutional separation of church and state." Fordham prevailed in the lawsuit in the spring of 1958, the site was razed the following summer, and new construction was under way by the spring of 1959. Voorhees, Walker, Smith & Smith designed the first campus plan (Stephen Voorhees had been Moses's chief architect for the 1939 New York World's Fair). The first building on the Lincoln Square property was the Fordham School of Law, completed in 1961 on a site formerly occupied by the Twelfth Regiment Armory. A second building, the Leon Lowenstein Center, "a 12-story multipurpose academic building on 60th Street"—home to two colleges and Fordham's graduate and professional schools—opened in 1969. Since the 1960s, the Lincoln Square campus has been developed haltingly: not until 1993 was the Manhattan campus's twenty-story dormitory completed, and at this writing, despite an enrollment of more than eight thousand students, the frontage area on Amsterdam Avenue remains undeveloped.[48]

Abbreviations

The following abbreviations are used in the notes:

CPA	City of Philadelphia Archives
CHE	*Chronicle of Higher Education*
CTC	Conwellana-Templana Collection (CTC), Special Collections Research Center, Temple University
DP	*Daily Pennsylvanian*
FFAL	Fisher Fine Arts Library, University of Pennsylvania
GPH	Gaylord P. Harnwell
GSA	General State Authority (Commonwealth of Pennsylvania)
NYT	*New York Times*
PAG	*Pennsylvania Gazette*
PEB	*Philadelphia Evening Bulletin*
PCPC	Philadelphia City Planning Commission
PI	*Philadelphia Inquirer*
PIM	*Philadelphia Inquirer Magazine*
PDN	*Philadelphia Daily News*
RDA	Redevelopment Authority, City of Philadelphia
SEPTA	Southeastern Pennsylvania Transportation Authority
TUA	Urban Archives, Special Collections Research Center, Temple University
UARC	University Archives and Records Center, University of Pennsylvania
UPA	University of Pennsylvania
UCSC	University City Science Center
VPL	Van Pelt Library, University of Pennsylvania
WPC	West Philadelphia Corporation

Notes

Preface

1. Roy F. Nichols, *A Historian's Progress* (New York: Knopf, 1968), 244–45.

Introduction

1. Trustees' Committee for the Physical Development of the University of Pennsylvania, report to the president of the University, *Minutes of the Trustees of the University of Pennsylvania*, 25 October 1948, appendix, p. 97f., UARC.

2. Edward Potts Cheyney, *History of the University of Pennsylvania, 1740–1940* (Philadelphia: University of Pennsylvania Press, 1940), 261.

3. Roger Miller and Joseph Siry, "The Emerging Suburb: West Philadelphia, 1850–1880," *Pennsylvania History* 47, no. 2 (1980): 99–146.

4. Paul Philippe Cret, Warren Powers Laird, and Olmsted Brothers, *Report to the Board of Trustees of the University of Pennsylvania upon the Future Development of Buildings and Grounds and the Conservation of Surrounding Territory*, 1913, 6–7, Fisher Fine Arts Library (FFAL).

5. E. Digby Baltzell, *Philadelphia Gentlemen* (Philadelphia: University of Pennsylvania Press, 1979), 322–23, a description applied to Provost Charles Custis Harrison.

6. E. Digby Baltzell, *Puritan Boston and Quaker Philadelphia: Two Protestant Ethics and the Spirit of Class Authority and Leadership* (New York: Free Press, 1979), 255.

7. The federal government paid $500,000 for the 9th Street campus; *Philadelphia Deed Book*, FTW.38.386, 4 April 1873.

8. The total purchase price was $82,184; *Philadelphia Deed Book*, UARC JAH.50.9, 21 May 1870.

9. Cheyney, *History of the University of Pennsylvania*, 262. Also see John Welsh Croskey, comp., *History of Blockley: A History of the Philadelphia General Hospital from Its Inception, 1731–1928* (Philadelphia: F.A. Davis Co., 1929), 64–129. By World War I the almshouse was officially the Philadelphia General Hospital, its services for the poor and mentally ill having been transferred by 1914 to newly built public institutions in the northeast of the city. Franklin Field was built in the general area of the almshouse potter's field.

10. Francis N. Thorpe, *William Pepper* (Philadelphia: J.B. Lippincott, 1904), 458; quoted in Baltzell, *Philadelphia Gentlemen*, 323.

11. Francis N. Thorpe, "The University of Pennsylvania," *Harper's Magazine*, July 1895, 285–303, quote from 292.

12. Baltzell, *Philadelphia Gentlemen*, 323–24.

13. Our main source is George E. Thomas and David B. Brownlee, *Building America's First University: An Historical and Architectural Guide to the University of Pennsylvania* (Philadelphia: University of Pennsylvania Press, 2000), chap. 4; also see Baltzell, *Philadelphia Gentlemen*, 323–24.

14. Cret, Laird, and Olmsted Brothers, *Report to the Board of Trustees of the University of Pennsylvania*, 7–8.

15. Ibid., 266, 320. For city ordinances related to Penn's expansion, see "Documents Concerning the Property of the University of Pennsylvania," n.d. [1954?], University Archives and Records Center, University of Pennsylvania (UARC UPA)4, box 47, folder "Development Program (Physical Plan–Extra Copies of Maps, Ordinances, etc.)–IV 1950–1955."

16. Roger L. Geiger, *To Advance Knowledge: The Growth of American Research Universities* (New Brunswick, N.J.: Transaction Publishers, 2004), 12.

17. Baltzell, *Philadelphia Gentlemen*, 323–24.

18. Geiger, *To Advance Knowledge*, 18–19, 31–34, 38, 39 (table 3). See also Jonathan R. Cole, *The Great American University: Its Rise to Preeminence, Its Indispensable National Role, Why It Must Be Protected* (New York: Public Affairs, 2009), 32–35, 525n48.

19. Edwin E. Slosson, *Great American Universities* (New York: Macmillan, 1910), chap. 11; quotes from 358–59.

20. Rexford G. Tugwell, *To the Lesser Heights of Morningside: A Memoir* (Philadelphia: University of Pennsylvania Press, 1982), 8–9.

21. Steven A. Sass, *The Pragmatic Imagination: A History of the Wharton School, 1881–1981* (Philadelphia: University of Pennsylvania Press, 1982), chap. 3; quote from Ira Harkavy and John Puckett, "The Role of Mediating Structures in University and Community Revitalization: The University of Pennsylvania and West Philadelphia as a Case Study," *Journal of Research and Development in Education* 25, no. 1 (Fall 1991): 14.

22. Sass, *Pragmatic Imagination*, 74–75, 78–79.

23. Ibid., 75–79.

24. Ibid., 91, 108, 114–115. Among the Wharton students inspired by Patten to enter professional social work were Edward T. Devine, later director of the New York Charity Organization and editor of *Survey* magazine (formerly *Charities and the Commons*), and Frances Perkins, who, as Franklin D. Roosevelt's secretary of labor, was the first female presidential cabinet member. Ibid., 107–8.

25. Daniel M. Fox, *The Discovery of Abundance: Simon N. Patten and the Transformation of Social Theory* (Ithaca, N.Y.: Cornell University Press, 1967), 40.

26. In 1896, Susan B. Wharton, a relative of the school's benefactor, herself a Quaker and cofounder of the Philadelphia College Settlement, proposed a study of the social conditions of blacks in Philadelphia's Seventh Ward to Provost Harrison. Wharton agreed to provide money for the work, and Harrison referred the project to Patten's protégé Samuel McCune Lindsay, the Wharton School's first full-time sociology professor. Lindsay hired DuBois, the first African American recipient of a PhD from Harvard University, to do the survey. Elliott W. Rudwick, "W. E. B. DuBois: A Study in Minority Group Leadership" (PhD diss., University of Pennsylvania, 1956), 32. Conducting a house-to-house canvas of the Seventh Ward, DuBois interviewed some five thousand people, completed the study in just fifteen months (assisted by Isabel Eaton, a white settlement worker), and reported on the harmful effects of racism, in particular employment discrimination, on the ward's black residents. Penn published *The Philadelphia Negro* in 1899 to a smattering of critical acclaim, but otherwise the book scarcely raised an eyebrow among academics. Foreshadowing his famous advocacy of

the "talented tenth," DuBois argued that the development of an indigenous black elite was the only way to improve the social conditions of blacks and to achieve a measure of equality; W. E. B. DuBois, *The Philadelphia Negro: A Social Study* (orig. ed., 1899; New York: Schocken Press, 1967), 316–18. Writing in 1944, DuBois bitterly recounted that the University of Pennsylvania had employed him only as an "assistant instructor" in sociology: "I was given no real academic standing, no office at the University, no official recognition of any kind; my name was even eventually omitted from the catalogue; I had no contact with students, and very little with members of the faculty, even in my department. With my bride of three months, I settled in one room over a cafeteria run by the College Settlement, in the worst part of the Seventh Ward. We lived there a year, in the midst of an atmosphere of dirt, drunkenness, poverty, and crime. Murder sat on our doorsteps, police were our government, and philanthropy dropped in with periodic advice"; quoted in Baltzell, "Introduction to 1967 Edition," DuBois, *Philadelphia Negro*, xix. Years later, Lindsay recounted a different version of the treatment accorded DuBois: "He is . . . quite mistaken about the attitude of the sociology department. It was quite friendly, I am sure, and as far as I know that was true of the entire Wharton school faculty"; personal communication from Samuel Lindsay, 8 September 1954, quoted in Rudwick, "DuBois," 32. The fact remains, however, that the study was not announced in the University's 1896–97 catalog and was included in the 1897–98 catalog only when the partial manuscript revealed "an extraordinary achievement"; Daniel Levering Lewis, *W. E. B. DuBois: Biography of a Race, 1868–1919* (New York: Henry Holt, 1993), 180. The weight of scholarly opinion supports DuBois's version. Steven A. Sass, in *Pragmatic Imagination*, writes faithfully to DuBois's text: "Although named assistant instructor, DuBois never had any real standing at the school. He had almost no contact with students, little with the faculty, and had neither an office nor an official listing in the catalog" (108–9). "An intentional snub," remarks Lewis in *DuBois*, 180; "second-tier status," write Michael B. Katz and Thomas J. Sugrue in "The Context of *The Philadelphia Negro*: The City, the Settlement House Movement, and the Rise of the Social Sciences," in *W.E.B. DuBois, Race, and the City: The Philadelphia Negro and Its Legacy*, ed. Katz and Sugrue (Philadelphia: University of Pennsylvania Press, 1998), 25. These issues notwithstanding, *The Philadelphia Negro* epitomized the University's Progressive Era commitment to marshalling social science data to solve real-world problems. For all the slights DuBois experienced, the University and particularly the Wharton School is rightfully credited for sponsoring and publishing his remarkable study.

27.   Sass, *Pragmatic Imagination*, 117.

28.   According to Patten, the central fact of American society was abundance. Accordingly, "the goal of social action was adjustment to the economy of abundance." The social program Patten derived from this proposition included not only social legislation for "industrial stability, regularity of employment, a minimum wage, the segregation of the physically defective, the elimination of disease germs, the prohibition of child labor, efficient schools, and a greater number of productive years in each worker's life," but also "public action on behalf of prosperity, conservation, health, culture, and efficiency." Fox, *Discovery of Abundance*, 95, 113.

29.   Tugwell, *Lesser Heights*, 40.

30.   Sass, *Pragmatic Imagination*, 118–19.

31.   Ibid., 125–26.

32.   For the origins of the collegiate way in American higher education, see Frederick Rudolph, *The American College and University: A History* (Athens: University of Georgia Press, [1962] 1990), 86–109.

33.   Julie A. Reuben, *The Making of the Modern University:Intellectual Transformation and the Marginalization of Morality* (Chicago: University of Chicago Press, 1996), 208.

34. David L. Angus and Jeffrey E. Mirel, *The Failed Promise of the American High School, 1890–1995* (New York: Teachers College Press, 1999), appendix table A.1, p. 230.

35. John R. Thelin, *A History of American Higher Education* (Baltimore: Johns Hopkins University Press, 2004), 155–56.

36. Reuben, *Modern University*, 7.

37. Ibid., 131–32.

38. "Agency History," Guide, Christian Association Records, 1857–2000, http://www.archives.upenn.edu. From 1926 to 2000, the Christian Association occupied its own landmark building at 36th and Locust streets, a beautiful late Gothic revival structure reminiscent of an English country house, home today to the Arts, Research, and Culture House; see George E. Thomas, *University of Pennsylvania: The Campus Guide* (Philadelphia: University of Pennsylvania Press, 2002), 58–59.

39. Thelin, *History*, 163. On Penn, see Andrew K. Becker and Michelle A. Woodson, "Rites of Passage: Student Traditions and Class Fights," in *A Pennsylvania Album: Undergraduate Essays on the 250th Anniversary*, ed. Richard S. Dunn and Mark F. Lloyd (Philadelphia: University of Pennsylvania, 1990), 32.

40. Ashish Shrestha and Mary D. McConaghy, "Rowbottom Origins," http://www.archives.upenn.edu; Becker and Woodson, "Rites of Passage."

41. Ashish Shrestha and Mary D. McConaghy, "Rowbottom Trends," http://www.archives.upenn.edu.

42. Ashish Shrestha and Mary D. McConaghy, "Documented Rowbottoms, 1910–1977," http://www.archives.upenn.edu.

43. Becker and Woodson, "Rites of Passage"; Cheyney, *History of the University of Pennsylvania*, 421–22, cited in "Rites of Passage," 37. The first women were admitted to Penn in 1876.

44. See Thelin, *History*, 297–99.

45. Lisa M. Silverman, "Women at Penn in the 1950s," in Dunn and Lloyd, *Pennsylvania Album*.

46. Roy F. Nichols, *A Historian's Progress* (New York: Alfred A. Knopf, 1968), 200.

47. Geiger, *To Advance Knowledge*, 112 (table 5), 276–77 (appendix D), quote from 230.

48. Baltzell, *Philadelphia Gentlemen*, 371–72.

49. Thomas and Brownlee, *Building America's First University*, 121.

50. Ibid., 103–5, 109–10.

51. *University of Pennsylvania in the War*, 1 May 1942, UARC UPP10.5, box 3; The *Army Specialized Training Program at the University of Pennsylvania*, vol. 1–2, May 1943–May 1945 (bound copies), UARC UPP10.5; John G. Terino, Jr., "In the Shadow of the Spreading Ivy: Science, Culture, and the Cold War at the University of Pennsylvania, 1950–1970" (PhD diss., University of Pennsylvania, 2001), 139–40. See also Nichols, *Historian's Progress*, 202.

52. David Goddard and Linda C. Koons, "A Profile of the University of Pennsylvania," in *Academic Transformation: Seventeen Institutions under Pressure*, ed. David Riesman and Verne A. Stadtman (New York: McGraw-Hill, 1973), 225–26.

53. Martin Meyerson and Dilys Pegler Winegrad, *Gladly Learn and Gladly Teach: Franklin and His Heirs at the University of Pennsylvania, 1740–1976* (Philadelphia: University of Pennsylvania, 1976), chaps. 2–4, 6–8, 11; "Guide to the I.S. Ravdin, 1894–1972, Papers, 1912–1972," UARC UPT50 R252.

54. Terino, "Spreading Ivy," 127–28, quotes from 132, 137–38.

55. Quote from Roger L. Geiger, *Research and Relevant Knowledge: American Research Universities Since World War II* (New Brunswick, N.J.: Transaction Publishers, 2004), xx.

56. Terino, "Spreading Ivy," 143–44, 183–84.

57. Scott McCartney, *ENIAC: The Triumphs and Tragedies of the World's First Computer* (New York: Walker, 1999), 7.

58. Nathan Engsmenger, *The Computer Boys Take Over: Computers, Programmers, and the Politics of Technical Expertise* (Cambridge, Mass.: MIT Press, 2010), 32–38, quotes from 32, 33.

59. McCartney, *ENIAC*. Also see Carl C. Chambers, interview by Jeannette P. Nichols, 13 December 1968, UARC UPP1, box 1, folder "Chambers."

60. McCartney, *ENIAC*, 133.

61. Geiger, *Research and Relevant Knowledge*, xx.

62. Thorpe, *William Pepper* (Philadelphia: J.B. Lippincott, 1904), 440; quoted in Meyerson and Winegrad, *Gladly Learn and Gladly Teach*, 207–8.

63. Cret, Laird, and Olmsted Brothers, *Report to the Board of Trustees of the University of Pennsylvania*, quotes from 12, 14; available at FFAL. "It could be argued that the great French architect Paul Philippe Cret did more to affect the physical face of Philadelphia than any other architect or planner besides William Penn," writes the architect and Philadelphia planner Harris M. Steinberg, in "Philadelphia in the Year 2059," in *Imagining Philadelphia: Edmund Bacon and the Future of the City*, ed. Scott Gabriel Knowles (Philadelphia: University of Pennsylvania Press, 2009), 118. "His remarkable legacy includes Rittenhouse Square, arguably the finest public space in America; the Benjamin Franklin Bridge, the longest bridge span of its day; the Federal Reserve Bank on Chestnut Street; the Barnes Foundation in Merion; and the gracious Rodin Museum on the Benjamin Franklin Parkway, the finest composition of building, garden, and site design in the city."

64. Tugwell, *Lesser Heights*, 10–11, 13.

65. Martin Meyerson, interview by Harold Taubin for the Penn Campus Planning History Project, 1959–1966, 11 June 1987, UARC UPJ9.4, folder "Facilities Planning A18."

66. John Irvin Shaw, "The Undergraduates," *Pennsylvania Gazette* (*PAG*), 15 November 1932, 112.

67. *Daily Pennsylvanian* (*DP*) editorial, 15 May 1937, cited in "New Campus Dawning," *PAG*, September 2006, http://www.upenn.edu/gazette.

68. Goddard and Koons, "Profile," 226.

69. Margaret Pugh O'Mara, *Cities of Knowledge: Cold War Science and the Search for the Next Silicon Valley* (Princeton, N.J.: Princeton University Press, 2005), 156–57.

70. Meyerson and Winegrad, *Gladly Learn and Gladly Teach*, 221–22.

71. "Expansion Plans Revealed," *PAG*, December 1948, 13; the full report is Trustees' Committee for the Physical Development of the University of Pennsylvania, report to the president of the University, *Minutes of Trustees*, 25 October 1948, UARC.

72. Thomas and Brownlee, *Building America's First University*, 116.

Chapter 1

1. W. E. Stevens and C. W. Ufford to Alexander Hamilton Frey, letter proposing Harnwell for consideration as president of the University of Pennsylvania, 11 December, 1952, Gaylord P. Harnwell [GPH] Papers, UARC T50H289, box 3, folder 17; in same series: GPH, interview by Walter M. Phillips, 22 October 1977, box 1, folder 9; Jonathan E. Rhoads, "Gaylord P. Harnwell (1903–1982)," box 1, folder 11; Carl C. Chambers, interview by Jeannette P. Nichols, 13 December 1968, UARC UPP1, box 1, folder "Chambers."

2. Roger L. Geiger, *Research and Relevant Knowledge: American Research Universities since World War II* (New York: Oxford University Press, 1993), 163–66; quote from 173–74.

3. Walter A. McDougall, *The Heavens and the Earth: A Political History of the Space Age* (New York: Basic Books, 1986), 6.

4. Geiger, *Research and Relevant Knowledge*, 179–85, 210; John Terino, "In the Shadow of the Spreading Ivy: Science, Culture, and the Cold War at the University of Pennsylvania, 1950–1970" (PhD diss., University of Pennsylvania, 2001), 227–28.

5. National Science Foundation, *Federal Support to Universities, Colleges, and Selected Nonprofit Institutions, Fiscal Year 1974* (Washington, D.C.: U.S. Government Printing Office, 1976), tables B–6, B–12.

6. "Statistical Summary of Achievements Under Dr. Harnwell Detailed," *Almanac* 6, no. 16 (February 1970), 4.

7. Rhoads, "Harnwell."

8. G. W. Armstrong, office manager, to William H. DuBarry, UPA executive vice president, 3 December 1946, UARC UPA4, box 29, folder "Development Program (Committee on Physical Development)—II."

9. Martin Meyerson, *The University of Pennsylvania in Its Twenty-Fourth Decade, 1970–1980*, 1981, n.p., Van Pelt Library.

10. *The Educational Survey*, 1959, UARC UPB35.4. For a summary of the five-volume survey, see *"Assaying a University,"* June 1960, http://www.archives.upenn.edu/primdocs/uplan/edsurvey1959.pdf; accessed 24 April 2008. In 1957, the chairs of the graduate arts and sciences departments of "twenty-five leading universities of the country," polled for the survey, ranked Penn eleventh overall. Hayward Keniston, *Graduate Study and Research at the University of Pennsylvania* (Philadelphia: University of Pennsylvania Press, 1959), 119.

11. Julian H. Levi, "Ground Space for the University," in *The University, the City, and Urban Renewal*, ed. Charles G. Dobbins (Washington, D.C.: American Council on Education, 1964), 9–10.

12. James T. Patterson, *Grand Expectations: The United States, 1945–1974* (New York: Oxford University Press, 1996), 77–81, 621.

13. U.S. Bureau of the Census, *Statistical Abstract of the United States*, 1950, p. 105; 1960, p. 212, 1972, p. 105. Also see Louis Menand, *The Marketplace of Ideas: Reform and Resistance in the American University* (New York: Norton, 2010), 63–73. The University reached its high-water mark of veteran enrollments in 1949, when the campus reported a total of 10,379 full-time students; that number diminished each year through 1952, with 8,491 full-time students; part-time enrollments followed the same downward trajectory. Penn did not construct any new facilities to accommodate the influx of students under the GI Bill. See *Report of the President*, UARC UPI25.1, box 1.

14. James L. Malone to David R. Goddard, enclosures, 27 January 1965, UARC UPA6.4, box 3, folder 17; *Integrated Development Plan*, May 1962, UARC UPA6.4, box 60, folder 21.

15. Meyerson, *Twenty-Fourth Decade*, n.p.

16. Edmund N. Bacon (senior land planner, Philadelphia City Planning Commission) to Raymond F. Leonard, memorandum, November 29, 1947 PCA 145.2, PCPC Files, box 14 A2914, folder "Redevelopment—University 1946–50." The referenced report, in the same folder, is James F. Dillon, Division of Land Planning, to Edmund N. Bacon, 4 June 1947.

17. Joseph S. Clark, Jr., and Dennis J. Clark, "Rally and Relapse, 1946–1968," in *Philadelphia: A 300-Year History*, ed. Russell F. Weigley (New York: Norton, 1982), 650, 694–96.

18. "The 1947 Better Philadelphia Exhibition," http://edbacon.org/bacon/betterphila.htm, accessed 23 September 2008.

19. Kirk R. Petshek, *The Challenge of Urban Reform: Policies and Programs in Philadelphia* (Philadelphia: Temple University Press, 1973), 23. See also Gregory L. Heller, "Salesman

of Ideas: The Life Experiences That Shaped Edmund Bacon," in *Imagining Philadelphia: Edmund Bacon and the Future of the City*, ed. Scott Gabriel Knowles (Philadelphia: University of Pennsylvania Press, 2010), 328–31; Jeanne R. Lowe, *Cities in a Race with Time: Progress and Poverty in America's Renewing Cities* (New York: Random House 1967), 322–24.

20. Harold Taubin, interview by Multimedia and Technology Services, 2 December 1988, transcript, UARC UPB1.9MM, box 4, folder 9; see also and cf. Scott Cohen, "Urban Renewal in West Philadelphia: An Examination of the University of Pennsylvania's Planning, Expansion, and Community Role from the Mid-1940s to the Mid-1970s" (Senior honors thesis, UPA, 1998), 6, UARC Collections.

21. The Greater Philadelphia Movement was "formed in December 1948 by Henry Batten and Robert T. McCracken"; Heller, "Salesman of Ideas," 154n55. Also see Petshek, *Challenge of Urban Reform*, 28–30; Lowe, *Cities in a Race with Time*, 324–25.

22. Dennis Clark, *The Urban Ordeal: Reform and Policy in Philadelphia, 1947–1967* (Philadelphia: Center for Philadelphia Studies, University of Pennsylvania, 1982), 3. For more on the Home Rule Charter of 1951, see Petshek, *Challenge of Urban Reform*, 34–40; Lowe, *Cities in a Race with Time*, 325–27.

23. Clark and Clark, "Rally and Relapse"; Lowe, *Cities in a Race with Time*; David W. Bartelt, "Renewing Center City Philadelphia: Whose City? Which Public's Interests?," in *Unequal Partnerships: The Political Economy of Urban Redevelopment in Postwar America*, ed. Gregory D. Squires (New Brunswick, N.J.: Rutgers University Press), 80–102; Guian McKee, "A Utopian, a Utopanist, or Whatever the Heck It Is: Edmund Bacon and the Complexity of the City," in Knowles, *Imagining Philadelphia*, 52–77. Petshek, in *Challenge of Urban Reform*, blames Bacon for the projects' neglect of the "social and economic factors in development": "Bacon never modified his personal priority, which was design" (3). McKee, in "Bacon and Complexity of City," shares this criticism, noting that Bacon's Center City projects did not contribute to solving the problem of jobs in a city undergoing deindustrialization. John F. Bauman and David Schuyler, in "Urban Politics and the Vision of a Modern City: Philadelphia and Lancaster After World War II," *Pennsylvania Magazine of History and Biography*, 132, no. 4 (2008), put it this way: "Modernistic planners, even those with humanistic inclinations like Bacon, focused on the city's physical plight. . . . Words like 'blight' and 'obsolescence' slipped easily from their tongues" (384).

24. Heller, "Salesman of Ideas"; Guian McKee, "Blue Sky Boys, Professional Citizens, and Knights-in-Shining Money: Philadelphia's Penn Center Project and the Constraints of Private Development," *Journal of Planning History* 6, no. 1 (2007): 48–80.

25. Bartelt, "Renewing Center City Philadelphia," 86–88; Petshek, *Challenge of Urban Reform*, chap. 6.

26. Cf. RDA, *Annual Report* 1959 to *Annual Report* 1965; both reports available at FFAL.

27. Philadelphia City Planning Commission (PCPC), *University Redevelopment Area Plan*, tentative draft, January 1950, UARC UPA4, box 30; Edmund Bacon, interview by Jeannette P. Nichols, 1 May 1975, UARC UPP1, box 1 folder "Bacon"; Edmund N. Bacon to Raymond F. Leonard, memorandum, November 29, 1947. Another West Philadelphia area certified by the PCPC was Mill Creek, located north and west of the University Redevelopment Area. In 1961 the project was thwarted by a disastrous collapse of the underground aqueduct that housed the creek. Gregory L. Heller, *Ed Bacon: Planning, Politics, and the Building of Modern Philadelphia* (Philadelphia: University of Pennsylvania Press, 2013), 66–68. As Heller notes, Bacon became the "exclusive figurehead" of the city's "success and renown" (10). Heller challenges this haloing of Bacon, arguing that William Rafsky, who, in various executive roles, managed the city's federal funding, played as important a role as Bacon; also see McKee,

"Complexity of the City." We find no mention of Rafsky in Penn's records nor do the West Philadelphia Corporation records at Temple Urban Archives show a salient role for Rafsky in the University Redevelopment Area.

28. Bacon to Leonard; GPH and Marion Pond, interview by Jeannette Nichols, 27 June 1975, UARC, UPP1, box 1, folder "Harnwell and Pond." For Hopkinson's extraordinary influence with city agencies to relocate the Woodland Avenue trolleys underground, see John C. Hetherston, interview by Jeannette Nichols, 12 November 1975, UARC UPP1, box 2, folder "Hetherston." The Home Rule Charter of 1951, which set in motion a reform program in city government, reestablished an earlier version of the Planning Commission as an "independent planning agency" (i.e., "above or out of politics"). As its major responsibility, the PCPC was charged with preparing a "comprehensive plan of the City showing its present and planned physical development" (called the Physical Development Plan). The source of its considerable power was the codicil, "No public way, ground, or open space, or building . . . shall be developed . . . or constructed unless recommendations of the City Planning Commission as to location and size *pursuant to the Physical Development Plan* shall have been first requested and obtained." The Redevelopment Authority was authorized under Pennsylvania's Urban Redevelopment Law of 1945 "to procure from the planning commission the designation of areas in need of redevelopment and its recommendations for such redevelopment . . . to study the recommendations of the planning commission for redevelopment of any area and to make its own additional investigations and recommendations thereon." Furthermore, "[the RDA] shall prepare a redevelopment proposal for any area certified by the planning commission to be a redevelopment area and for which the planning commission has made a redevelopment area plan [for example, the University Redevelopment Planning Area]." Walter H. Blucher, "The Philadelphia City Planning Commission: An Appraisal, August 1945," FFAL. For Bacon's own description, see Alexander Garvin, "Philadelphia's Planner: A Conversation with Edmund Bacon," *Journal of Planning History* 1, no. 1 (2002): 58–78. For the ascendant power of the PCPC under Bacon's direction and its status as a "national model," see Heller, "Salesman of Ideas"; Harris M. Steinberg, "Philadelphia in the Year 2059," in Knowles, *Imagining Philadelphia*, 134.

29. Southeastern Pennsylvania Transportation Authority (SEPTA), *The Market Street Elevated, 1907–2007: 100 Years of Continuous Service to the Community*, museum exhibit photographs and text, Philadelphia; authors' notes, 19 October 2007; Margaret S. Marsh, "The Impact of the Market Street 'El' on Northern West Philadelphia: Environmental Change and Social Transformation, 1900–1930," in *The Divided Metropolis: Social and Spatial Dimensions of Philadelphia, 1800–1975*, ed. William W. Cutler, III, and Howard Gillette, Jr. (Westport, Conn.: Greenwood Press, 1980), 174.

30. SEPTA, *Market Street Elevated*; "Unique Combination Tunnel and Bridge Planned for Schuylkill River at Market Street," *Philadelphia Evening Bulletin* (*PEB*), 8 November 1930; "3 Tunnels Cross Schuylkill," *PEB*, 21 September 1947, Urban Archives, Special Collections Research Center, Temple University (TUA).

31. PCPC, RDA, and Philadelphia Housing Authority, *Philadelphia Housing Quality Survey* (Philadelphia: PCPC, 1949), 5, UARC UPJ9.4, box 55.

32. PCPC, *University Redevelopment Plan*, 5.

33. "Subway Extension in Full Use, El Is Ready for Demolition," *PEB*, 7 November 1955, TUA; "Boon Is Predicted for W. Phila. Area with El's Removal," *PI*, 11 May 1953, TUA; "El Expected to Be Torn Down in 6 Months as 100 Workers Prepare Wrecking Jobs," *PEB*, 8 November 1955, UARC.

34. George E. Thomas and David B. Brownlee, *Building America's First University* (Philadelphia: University of Pennsylvania Press, 2000), 116–17; Terino, "Spreading Ivy," 171–73.

35. See Robert Trescher (trustee), interview by Jeannette P. Nichols, 8 April 1971, UARC UPP1, box 3, folder "Trescher"; Joseph H. Willits, interview by Nichols, 11 February 1971, UARC UPP1, box 4, folder "Willits"; William L. Day, interviews by Nichols, 22 September 1971, 17 January 1972, UARC UPP1, box 1, folder "Day"; Burns, interview by Nichols.

36. Terino, "Spreading Ivy," 171–72 (quote from 171), 199–200.

37. See Harold E. Stassen, "Four Years at Pennsylvania," *PAG*, March 1953, 8–17; "Biographical Sketch," *Guide to the Harold Stassen, 1907–2001, Papers, 1940–1957*, UARC; Nichols, *Historian's Progress*, 203; William H. DuBarry, "The Development Program of the University of Pennsylvania," speech to the West Philadelphia Realty Board, 5 April 1954, Philadelphia City Archives (PCA), 145.2 PCPC Files, box 14, A2914, folder "Redevelopment—University 1952–56"; "Penn Reveals New Plan for Expansion," *PEB*, 7 November 1948, TUA. The $32 million development campaign was only Penn's third in the first half of the twentieth century; the previous ones were 1924–26 ($8,070,000 raised) and 1937–40 ($5,400,000 raised); "A Brief Study of Capital Needs of the University of Pennsylvania," 23 January 1946, UARC UPA 4, box 29, Development Program files I.

38. Terino, "Spreading Ivy," 179–82.

39. Edmund Bacon, interview by Lydia Messmer, Memories Project, 25 May 1988, UARC UPB1.9MM, box 2, folder 13. "You can give Hopkinson the credit, more than any other single individual," averred the Penn planner John C. Hetherston; interview by Nichols.

40. G. Holmes Perkins, interview by Lydia Messmer, Memories Project, n.d. [1987], UARC UPB1.9MM, box 3, folder 39; "G. Holmes Perkins to Retire as Penn Fine Arts Dean," *PEB*, 5 February 1970, UARC; "G. Holmes Perkins, Dean & Architect" (obituary), *Almanac* 51, no. 2 (7 September 2004), http://www.upenn.edu/almanac/volumes/v51/n02/death_ghp.html, accessed 6 June 2009; Steinberg, "Philadelphia in Year 2059." Also see Christopher Kemek, in *The Transatlantic Collapse of Urban Renewal: Postwar Urbanism from New York to Berlin* (Chicago: University Press, 2011), 95–97; "Perkins Heads Fine Arts," *PEB*, 6 October 1950, UARC; Thomas and Brownlee, *Building America's First University*, 118. On Stassen's behind-the-scenes maneuvering in hiring Perkins, see Ethan Schrum, "Administering American Modernity: The Instrumental University in the Postwar United States" (PhD diss., University of Pennsylvania, 2009), 98–103.

41. Thomas and Brownlee, *Building America's First University*, 117–18; Lillian Burns, interview by Jeannette P. Nichols, 2 October 1975, UARC UPP1, box 1, folder "Burns."

42. Terino, "Spreading Ivy," 184–86.

43. Harold Stassen, interview by Jeannette P. Nichols, 18 October 1971, UARC UPP1, box 3, folder "Stassen." According to Lillian Burns, Valley Forge was nothing more than "a waltz" for the trustees to get their hands on a desirable piece of real estate, "an idle threat" in dealing with the city: "to try to dispose of the residence halls, the library . . . just doesn't make sense." Burns, interview by Nichols.

44. "Subway-Surface Tube Urged to 39th and Woodland Ave.," *PEB*, 11 January 1948, TUA.

45. Subcommittee of the Technical Advisory Committee on Local Transportation, "Proposal for Extension of Subway Surface Tunnel to Woodland Avenue at 40th Street," 10 September 1947, UARC UPA4, box 29, folder "Development Program (Committee on Physical Development)—II"; Raymond F. Leonard (PCPC Division of Land Planning) to Edmund N. Bacon, memorandum, 6 September 1946, PCA, PCPC Files, box 76 A–2974, folder "Redevelopment—University City, July-December 1962."

46. For biographical details on Hopkinson, see *Digby Baltzell, Philadelphia Gentlemen: The Making of a National Upper Class* (Philadelphia: University of Pennsylvania Press, 1979), 372–74; "Edward Hopkinson, Jr.," biographical transcript (2 pp.), 27 August 1948, *PEB* collection, TUA; "Edward Hopkinson, Jr.," *Philadelphia Inquirer Magazine*, 20 January 1963, 4–5, *PEB* collection, TUA. On Hopkinson and the Penn subway extension, Edmund Bacon, in his interview by Jeannette Nichols, remarked, "Well, because of his extraordinarily central position in the community, he was able to deal with the physical problems and the political problems all at the same time."

47. Bacon, interview by Messmer.

48. Untitled chronology of subway and subway-surface construction and street closings in the University area, 1920s–1960s, UARC UPP1, box 5, folder "Campus Expansion."

49. "Trolley Subway to 40th St. Ok'd," *PEB*, 25 January 1951, TUA; "PTC [Philadelphia Transportation Company], City Ask PUC [Public Utility Commission] Approval of Transportation Proposals," *PEB*, 7 May 1951, TUA; "Subway Construction Begun; Routes, Locations Released," *DP*, 20 March 1952, UARC; "5-Block Detour Is Asked by PTC," *PI*, 20 October 1952, TUA; quote from "Trolley Detours Being Prepared," *PI*, 22 March 1953, TUA.

50. *PTC Traveler*, 4 November 1955, *PEB* collection, TUA; quote from "Subway Service Starts on Nov. 7," *DP*, 25 October 1955, UARC.

51. Harold E. Stassen, *Four Years at Pennsylvania, September 17, 1948—January 19, 1953: A Report to the Trustees of the University of Pennsylvania*, 19 January 1953, p. 44, UARC UPI 25.1, box 2.

52. *"Re: Woodland Avenue,"* n.d. [January 1955], UARC UPA 4, box 47, folder "Development Program (Physical Plan—Redevelopment Authority)—II, 1950–1955"; in same folder: John L. Moore to GPH, 12 April 1955; John A. Bailey (acting city commissioner) to Joseph J. Lawler (secretary, Department of Highways), 18 November 1955, PCA, 145.2 PCPC, box 14 A–2914, folder "Redevelopment–University 1952–1956; "Gov. Leader Signs Bill Closing Woodland Ave. from 36th to 39th Sts.," *DP*, 14 May 1956, UARC; quote from "Section of Woodland Ave. Transferred to University," *DP*, 25 September 1957, UARC.

53. "Woodland Avenue Closed Tomorrow," *DP*, 10 January 1958, UARC; "End of an Era," *PAG*, February 1958, 8–9.

54. "Woodland Ave. Surface to Be Torn Up Today for Landscaping Work," *DP*, 13 January 1958, UARC.

55. "Campus Changes Under Way on 33rd Street," *PI*, 14 May 1950, TUA; "University Redevelopment Area," unsigned typescript, n.d. [December 1955?], PCA 145.2, PCPC Files, box 14 A–2914, folder "Redevelopment—University 1952–1956"; in same folder: John L. Moore to Donald C. Wagner (city managing director), 22 March 1956. Also see and cf. *Report on Recommended Transit, Highway and Land Use Plans in the University of Pennsylvania Area* (Philadelphia: PCPC, 1946), courtesy PCPC.

56. John L. Moore to Donald C. Wagner, 1 October 1956, PCA 145.2, PCPC Files, box 14 A–2914, folder "Redevelopment—University 1952–1956"; also see Moore to Wagner, 22 March 1956. The rudiments of this plan originated in the Planning Commission's discussions as early as the mid-1940s; see Raymond F. Leonard (PCPC Division of Land Planning) to Edmund N. Bacon, memorandum, 6 September 1946, re: "Recommended Transit, Highway and Land Use Plans in the University of Pennsylvania," PCA 145.2 PCPC Files, box 14 A2914, folder "Redevelopment—University 1946–1950."

57. Donald C. Wagner to John L. Moore, 31 August 1956, PCA 145.2, PCPC Files, box 14 A–2914, folder "Redevelopment—University 1952–1956"; in same folder: Allen T. Bonnell

(vice president, Drexel Institute of Technology) to David M. Smallwood (commissioner of streets), 24 August 1956, Moore to Wagner, 1 October 1956.

58. "In the Matter of the Redevelopment Authority of the City of Philadelphia, University Redevelopment Area 'A' Proposal No. 2 (Physics Unit, 27th Ward)," Court of Common Pleas No. 7, June term, 1951, no. 235; PCA 145.2, PCPC Files, box 14 A2914, folder "Redevelopment—University 1951."

59. Bacon, interview by Nichols. Of all the states, Pennsylvania "had the most active and the most generous urban redevelopment policy." By 1960, "the state had entered into contracts with cities amounting to nearly $13,000,000 in state grants [$101,000,000 in 2012 dollars] for urban redevelopment"; William L. Slayton, "State and Local Incentives and Techniques for Urban Renewal," *Law and Contemporary Problems* 25, no. 4: special issue on *Urban Renewal: Part I* (1960): 803.

60. "In the Matter of the Redevelopment Authority."

61. Edward Hopkinson, Jr., to City Council, 19 March 1951, PCA 145.2 PCPC Files, box 14 A2914, folder "Redevelopment—University 1951."

62. J. H. Churchman (Drinker, Biddle, and Heath Law Offices), to Philip C. Pendelton, Esq., 9 May 1949, UARC UPA 4, box 29, folder "Development Program (Committee on Physical Development—III)."

63. McKee, "Utopian," 57.

64. Philadelphia City Council resolution, 16 May 1951, PCA 145.2, PCPC Files, box 14 A2914, folder "Redevelopment—University 1951." The points of disagreement between the University and the city were minor and would be resolved in the course of Penn's westward expansion in the 1960s; see William DuBarry (executive vice president) to Edmund N. Bacon (executive director, PCPC), 25 January 1950, CPA 145.2 PCPC Files, box 14 A2914, folder "Redevelopment—University 1946–1950."

65. City Council resolution, 23 May 1952, UARC UPA 4, box 47, folder "Development Program (Physical Plan—Extra Copies of Maps, Ordinances, etc.)—V, 1950–1955; "University's History is Varied, Colorful," *DP*, 1 September 1954, UARC.

66. Quote from RDA, *Annual Report*, 1951, 17–18, FFAL; GPH, letter of certification to RDA, 3 June 1964, UARC box 13101.4: 0004, folder "Redevelopment Unit #4 1963–64."

67. Lillian G. Burns, interview by Jeannette P. Nichols, 2 October 1975, UARC, UPP1, box 1, folder "Burns." The RDA omitted the Wharton-physics projects in its budget statement for the 1951 annual report; more problematic, we were unable to find any RDA collection at either the Authority itself or the City Archives.

68. Aaron Levine (PCPC) to Allyn R. Jennings and Edmund N. Bacon, memorandum, 22 October 1951; PCA 145.2 PCPC Files, box 14 A2914, folder "Redevelopment—University 1951"; John L. Moore to GPH, 6 June 1955, UARC UPA 4, box 47, folder "Development Program (Physical Plan—General—II, 1950–1955)"; Trustees of UPA, "Redevelopment of Area 32nd, 34th, Chestnut, Walnut Streets, City of Philadelphia" [1955], UARC UPA 4, box 47, folder "Development Program (Physical Plan—Redevelopment Authority)—II, 1950–1955; in same folder: Trustees to Francis J. Meyers, RDA, 19 January 1955; *Minutes of the Trustees of the University of Pennsylvania* 26 (17 January 1956), 234, UARC; "U to Buy Two Blocks for Women's Dormitories," *PEB*, 28 February 1954, TUA; "Redevelopment Idea Was City's, Says Penn," *PI*, 7 May 1957, TUA.

69. RDA, *Annual Report* 1951, 18–20.

70. James H. Ward (PCPC) to files, memorandum, PCA 145.2 PCPC, box 14 A–2914, folder "Redevelopment—University 1952–1956."

71. Francis J. Meyers (chairman, RDA), to GPH, 7 December 1954, UARC UPA 4, box 47, folder "Development Program (Physical Plan—Redevelopment Authority–II, 1950–1953)"; Trustees of UPA to Francis J. Meyers, 19 January 1955, PCA 145.2 PCPC, box 14 A–2914, folder "Redevelopment—University 1952–1956"; in same folder: "Resolution #965: University Redevelopment Area—Selection of University of Pennsylvania as Redeveloper," n.d. [21 January 1955]. Also see Burns, interview by Nichols.

72. Richardson Dilworth to GPH, 26 September 1956, UARC UPA 4, box 99, folder "Philadelphia, City of (General)—I, 1955–1960." Dilworth and Joseph Clark had not had a cordial relationship with Harold Stassen, especially after Stassen, on the presidential campaign trail in 1949, called them "fellow travelers." Also see "Penn Closely Interlocked with Working of City," *DP*, 15 January 1954, UARC.

73. "Perkins Slated to Be Head of the Planning Board," *PEB*; interview with Edward N. Bacon, 25 May 1988, transcript, UARC UPB1.9MM, box 2, folder 13.

74. GPH, speech presented to the American Association of Urban Universities, Cincinnati, 6 November 1960, edited typescript, UARC T50H289, box 10, folder 18.

75. "City to Help University Acquire Needed Lands, Mayor Dilworth States," *DP*, 3 May 1957, UARC.

76. Quote from Francis J. Lammer (RDA) to Edmund N. Bacon (PCPC), 4 February 1955, PCA 145.2, PCPC Files, box 14 A–2914, folder "Redevelopment—University 1952–1956." For more on the plan, see in same folder, G. Holmes Perkins, School of Fine Arts, dictated statement, 11 April 1955; see also, Trustees of the University of Pennsylvania to Francis J. Meyers, 19 January 1955, UARC UPA 4, box 47, folder "Development Program (Physical Plan—Redevelopment Authority)—II, 1950–1955."

77. Burns, interview by Nichols.

78. Ibid.; Aaron Levine (PCPC) to Allyn R. Jennings and Edmund N. Bacon, memorandum, 22 October 1951, PCA 145.2, PCPC Files, box 14 A–2914, folder "Redevelopment—University 1951."

79. RDA fact sheet, n.d. [December 1956], PCA 145.2, PCPC Files, box 14 A–2914, folder "Redevelopment—University 1952–1956."

80. Adam Klarfeld, who examined the deeds for these properties, notes the paucity of litigation in the wake of the title transfers; in "Private Taking, Public Good?," 31–32, UARC.

81. "150 Neighbors Fight Building Plan of Penn," *PEB*, 27 February 1957, TUA; "Sansom Street in Rebellion," *PI*, clipping, 3 March 1957, TUA; "Penn Residents Ask Fair Price," *PEB*, clipping, 19 March 1957, TUA; "U of P Neighbors Decide to Fight Evictions After All," *PEB*, 2 April 1957, UARC T40H289, box 25, folder 9; in folder 17: "Last 3 Families Bitter Amid the Rubble," *PI*, 31 August 1958; "2 End Battle of Sansom Street," *PEB*, 28 November 1958, UARC UPT50 M726, box 2, folder 24. See also Elyse Sudow, "Displacement Demonized: Towards an Alternate Explanation for Penn's Poor Relationship with West Philadelphia" (senior honors thesis, UPA, 9 April 1999), 13–15, UARC.

82. Lillian Burns, untitled chronology of Penn campus development, from mid-1930s to 1954, UARC UPP1, box 2, folder "Burns"; "Ceremonies Tomorrow Will Begin Demolition for Women's Dorms," *DP*, 4 February 1958, UARC.

83. "2 End Battle of Sansom Street," *PEB*, 28 November 1958.

84. *Minutes of Trustees*, 13 May 1960, vol. 27, p. 305, UARC; UARC, *Mapping Penn: Land Acquisitions, 1870–2007*, http://venus.cml.upenn.edu/MappingPenn, accessed 31 August 2008; "Woodland Closing Approved by City," *DP*, 16 May 1960, UARC.

85. According to Perkins, he and trustee Sydney Martin formed a "committee of two" that selected Penn's architects in the 1950s. At the time, the University's policy was to hire only

architects who were Penn affiliates, either alumni or faculty. When Penn needed to build Hill Hall and the Alfred Newton Richards Biology Building, Perkins, a modernist, thought he would have to defer to Martin, a Beaux-Arts traditionalist—"old school," as Perkins put it. "He did superb Georgian architecture, and he did a number of fraternities on the campus, and things like that. Very nice, delicate work, but it was clearly very traditional. And I thought, 'Well we're never going to get any modern buildings on campus if we have to go along with this.' So it happened that two jobs came up at the same time, and I said to Martin, 'You're senior, why don't you pick the first one and I'll pick the other.' And I thought, 'Well we'll get some little conservative architect,' and he picks Eero Saarinen [for Hill Hall; Louis Kahn was Perkins's choice for the biology building]. You could have knocked me over. . . . I said 'Eero Saarinen is not a Penn man' . . . 'oh,' he said, 'I've looked him up. One of his partners, somewhat down the list, is a Penn graduate and that makes him eligible.'" Perkins, interview by Messmer, Memories Project, 1987.

86. "The Harnwell Administration: Physical Facilities," typescript with penciled edits, n.d. [1963], UARC T50H289, box 10, folder 16.

87. Thomas and Brownlee, *Building America's First University*, 204–6.

88. "Council Acts on Drexel Plea," *PEB*, 23 May 1957, TUA.

89. George E. Thomas, *University of Pennsylvania Campus Guide* (New York: Princeton Architectural Press, 2002), 89–90.

90. Alfred H. Williams (chair of trustees, Drexel Institute of Technology) to Charles J. Biddle, Esq., 12 June 1957, Drexel trustees executive committee, minutes (attachment), 13 June 1957, Drexel University Archives and Special Collections; Burns, interview by Nichols; Burns, chronology; "James Creese Student Center," 18 May 1973, UARC T50H289, box 9, folder 18. This was the only public fight between Drexel and Penn.

91. RDA, *Annual Report*, 1960, p. 26, table 2.

92. Bacon, interview by Nichols. Unfulfilled contracts and land-banking over a period of decades raised ethical and legal issues. In 1959, the executive director of the RDA wrote, "Such an area must be improved within a "reasonable" number of years. Reasonable has been variously defined, and most recently, this has been extended to as much as eight years in the process of full improvement, although disposition must be offered within a shorter period of time." Francis J. Lammers to GPH, 23 April 1959, UARC UPB101.4, box 2, folder "Redevelopment Authority, 1962–63." Harold Taubin, in "The University Environment," in Dobbins, *University, City, and Urban Renewal*, argued, on pragmatic grounds, that "an advance purchase of property of twenty-five years is not unreasonable"; "this would permit the establishment of a land bank which could be drawn upon as required by the institution's development plan" (28). A 1967 statement of the city's urban renewal process left the matter open-ended; RDA, *How Urban Renewal Works in Philadelphia: A Step-by Step Description of the City's Urban Renewal Procedure* (Philadelphia: RDA, 1967), 9, FFAL.

93. Thomas and Brownlee, *Building America's First University*, 72–74; "Orange Crates, Outposts Used to Store Library Books," *DP*, 8 March 1954, UARC; "Trustee's Study Criticizes Library Physical Facilities," *DP*, 18 March 1954, UARC; GPH to State Senator John H. Dent, 2 August 1957, UARC UPA4, box 99, folder "Pennsylvania, Commonwealth of (General State Authority)—VI, 1955–1960."

94. Barry Slepian, an undergraduate at Penn from 1953 to 1956, recalled having "two choices as to where to eat": the basement cafeteria of Houston Hall, "where the food wasn't very good," or the Horn and Hardart on Woodland Avenue, "where the food was *very* good." He chose the latter, which he managed readily on his two-dollar daily food budget. Interview by John Puckett, 10 March 2010.

95.   "Penn to Raze 21 Buildings on Campus Edge for New Library," *PEB*, 10 October 1956, TUA. The earliest parcel was acquired in 1891. For the Penn property maps, see UARC, *Mapping Penn*. Also see "Annual Report of the Trustees Committee on Physical Development," 2 June 1952, *Minutes of Trustees*, vol. 25, pp. 372–76.

96.   "Information on General State Authority Prepared by University's General Counsel," 4 June 1956, UARC UPA 4, box 99, folder "Pennsylvania, Commonwealth of (General State Authority)—II, 1955–1960." See in same box, GSA, *Annual Report*, 1958.

97.   George H. Turner, director of Physical Plant Planning, to E. Craig Sweeten (Development Fund director), 7 February 1958, UARC UPA 4, box 99, folder "Pennsylvania, Commonwealth of (General State Authority)—VII, 1955–1960."

98.   "Memorandum: General State Authority Legislation," 27 August 1968, UARC UPP 1, box 1, folder "Campus Expansion."

99.   "Buildings to be Torn Down in Woodland, Walnut Block," *DP*, 9 October 1956; "Site of New Library Will Be Grassed Area Instead of Parking Lot," *DP*, February 7, 1957, UARC; "Razing Progresses on Walnut Street," *DP*, 6 March 1957, UARC; "Demolition Begins on Woodland Ave.; Redevelopment Continues," *DP*, 25 March 1957, UARC.

100.   See map of "Fraternity Row," *Pennsylvania Record*, 1953, UARC.

101.   "Woodland Ave. Shoemaker Moves After 30 Yrs.," *DP*, 22 March 1957, UARC. It may be inferred from a PCPC report that Yegavian's shop was one of "approximately 20 small businesses of a marginal nature scattered along Woodland Avenue." Levine to Jennings and Bacon.

102.   Thomas, *University of Pennsylvania*, 43–44.

103.   Bacon, interview by Messmer.

104.   Untitled table, UARC UPB 101.4, box 26, folder "General State Authority 70–71." George Thomas, the historian of Penn architecture, complains about the ugliness of the GSA-funded buildings, especially Meyerson Hall: "I did a little study of this a couple of years ago to figure out how we got Meyerson Hall. It's a sad and unfortunate tale. GSA announced in one meeting that the way that they determined the good architects was whether they got work done on time and were not argumentative. And that was it!" Quoted in Samuel Hughes, "Treasures and Travesties," *PAG*, September–October 1999, 42.

105.   Sir Peter Shepheard, "The Spaces Between," http://www.upenn.edu/almanac/issues /past/Shepheard.html; accessed 13 March 2007; Center for Environmental Design, Graduate School of Fine Arts, *Landscape Development Plan* (University of Pennsylvania, 1977), UARC JPJ 9.4, box 59, folder "Facilities Planning E16"; UPA News Bureau, press release, 10 June 1977, UARC Collections; also see Thomas and Brownlee, *Building America's First University*, 52–55, 72–74; "Gazetteer," *PAG*, October 1979, 20.

106.   "The Good Citizen," *PAG*, March–April 2003, http://www.upenn.edu/gazette/0303 /giresi.html, accessed 21 December 2005.

107.   RDA, "Information for Owners and Residents: University Area," n.d. [1960], http:// www.archives.upenn.edu/primdocs/upf/upf8_5/upf8_5b25f12annenbergsch_redevlpmt .pdf, accessed 5 September 2008.

108.   UARC, *Mapping Penn*; "The Closing of the 200 Block of South McAlpin Street and Construction of the Annenberg School of Communications: Images from the Saalbach Collection," http://www.archives.upenn.edu/faids/upx/ssalbachannbrg.html, accessed 5 September 2008; Klarfeld, "Private Taking, Public Good," 33–34.

109.   Thomas, *University of Pennsylvania*, 61; Thomas and Brownlee, *Building America's First University*, 185. Also see UARC, "200 Block of South McAlpin Street."

110.   Thomas and Brownlee, *Building America's First University*, 186–87.

111. Quoted in Hughes, "Treasures and Travesties," 44.

112. "Proposals to the General State Authority for the 1959–61 Biennium," n.d. [April 1958?], UARC UPA4, box 99, folder "Pennsylvania, Commonwealth of (General State Authority)—VII, 1955–1960; in same folder: "Presentation to the General State Authority from the University of Pennsylvania for the Construction of Educational Facilities," May 1958.

113. *UARC, Mapping Penn*; quote from "Campus Maps," http://www.facilities.upenn.edu/mapsBldgs/view_map.php3?id=1.

114. Raymond C. Saalbach Collection, 1959–1971, UARC UPX125111, Album II, 36–45.

115. U.S. Bureau of the Census, Census of Housing: 1960, *Block Statistics, Philadelphia, PA*, vol. 3 (Washington, D.C.: U.S. Government Printing Office, 1961).

116. "Units #4 and #5: Information from Census per block in Units #4 and #5," n.d. [1962–63], TUA WPC Acc. 350, box 11, folder "#Unit 4 1962–63."

117. UARC, *Mapping Penn*.

Chapter 2

1. Harold Taubin, interview by Jeannette P. Nichols, 19 December 1975, UARC UPP1, box 4, folder "Taubin."

2. Alexander von Hoffman, "A Study in Contradictions: The Origins and Legacy of the Housing Act of 1949," *Housing Policy Debate* 11, no. 2 (2000): 309, 310.

3. Ashley A. Foard and Hilbert Fefferman, "Federal Urban Renewal Legislation," *Law and Contemporary Problems* 25, no. 4 (1960): 653–54; Jeanne R. Lowe, *Cities in a Race with Time: Progress and Poverty in America's Renewing Cities* (Random House: New York, 1967), 32. Also see Wilton S. Sogg and Warren Wertheimer, "Legal and Governmental Issues in Urban Renewal," in *Urban Renewal: The Record and the Controversy*, ed. James Q. Wilson (Cambridge, Mass.: MIT Press, 1966), 126–88.

4. Francis J. Lammer (RDA executive director) to Henry R. Pemberton (UPA financial vice president), 21 November 1952, UPA4, box 47, folder "Development Program (Physical Plan—Redevelopment Authority)—II, 1950–1955."

5. 83 P.L. 560; 83 Cong. Ch. 649; 68 Stat. 590 (hereafter Housing Act of 1954), Title III §301.

6. Foard and Fefferman, "Federal Urban Renewal Legislation," 656; citing 68 Stat. 623, 42 U.S.C. §1451 (1958).

7. Housing Act of 1954, Title III §311. Wendell E. Pritchett, in a seminal article, "'The Public Menace' of Blight: Urban Renewal and the Private Uses of Eminent Domain," *Yale Law & Policy Review* 21, no 1 (Winter 2003): 1–52, notes that the term *blight* first appeared in the 1920s, in the discourse of urban sociologists at the University of Chicago—the Chicago sociologists adopted a botanical term as a metaphor for urban deterioration, which they associated, primarily, with neighborhoods that were populated by poor southern blacks of the Great Migration. The terms *slum* and *blight* were used interchangeably in proposals to remake neighborhoods regarded by city planners as detrimental to their vision of the modern city. Writes Pritchett, "As the term originally described plant diseases, the evocation of blight created a vision of a plague spreading across the city, moving from one neighborhood to the next. The future of the city rested upon the effort to stop its spread" (21). At issue after World War II was the constitutionality of a municipality's use of eminent domain for private redevelopment in neighborhoods earmarked as slum or blighted; did public taking for a private purpose, however laudable, violate the Public Use Clause of the Fifth Amendment to the U.S. Constitution—"nor shall private property be taken for public use, without just compensation"? (1). In 1954, the U.S. Supreme Court, in *Berman v. Parker*, a suit that was

filed in 1952 in the District of Columbia, ruled on the issue, giving a green light to cities to exercise "broad powers of condemnation," including for the purpose of private redevelopment. The burden of displacement fell heaviest on blacks, more often than not the residents of the neighborhoods targeted for urban renewal. Pritchett argues that "racial motivations were often submerged under the labels of 'slum clearance' or 'neighborhood revitalization'" (47).

8. Francis J. Lammer to GPH, UARC UPB101.4, box 2, folder "Redevelopment Authority, 1962–63."

9. Burns, interview by Nichols.

10. House Committee on Banking and Currency, *Housing Act of 1959: Hearings before the Subcommittee on Housing*, 86th Cong., 1st Session, 28, 29, 30, 31 January; 2, 3 February 1959, quote from p. 248.

11. Ibid., 601–14, esp. 602–3.

12. Senate Committee on Banking and Currency, *Housing Act of 1959: Hearings before the Subcommittee on Various Bills to Amend the Federal Housing Laws*, 22, 23, 26, 27, 28 January 1959, pp. 501–2.

13. Burns, interview by Nichols.

14. Senate Committee on Banking and Currency, *Housing Act of 1959*, p. 503.

15. Levi cited in Kermit C. Parsons, "Universities and Cities: The Terms Between Them," *Journal of Higher Education* 34, no. 4 (April 1963): 205–16.

16. "Eisenhower Signs 3d Housing Bill; F.H.A. Rates Rise," *New York Times* (*NYT*), 24 September 1959; "Mason Acclaims New Housing Act," *NYT*, 25 September 1959.

17. B. T. Fitzpatrick, "Procedures for Campus Participation in Urban Renewal," in *The University, the City, and Urban Renewal*, ed. Charles G. Dobbins (Washington, D.C.: American Council on Education, 1964), 19.

18. Ibid.

19. Kenneth Ashworth, "Urban Renewal and the University: A Tool for Campus Expansion and Neighborhood Improvement," *Journal of Higher Education* 35, no. 9 (1964): 493–96.

20. Mark Joel Winkeller, "University Expansion in Urban Neighborhoods: An Exploratory Analysis" (PhD diss., Brandeis University, 1972), 37.

21. Burns, interview by Nichols.

22. Parsons, "Universities and Cities," 207.

23. Francis J. Lammer to GPH, 23 April 1959; GPH to Lammer, 11 May 1959, UARC UPB101.4, box 2, folder "Redevelopment Authority 1962–63"; *Minutes of the Trustees of the University of Pennsylvania* 27 (8 May 1959): 124, 127–28.

24. University Planning Office, "University of Pennsylvania Development Plan," report to the president, March 1961, p. 22, UARC UPA4, box 126; "Penn Campus Planning History Project," prologue 1AA, UARC UPJ9.4, folder "Facilities Planning A10."

25. "Housing for 1972," n.d. [1967–68], UARC UPB101.4, box 19, folder "Housing 1967–68"; in same folder, Francis M. Betts to Eugene Maier, Cedar Park Neighbors, 17 April 1968.

26. As Thomas H. Keels notes, in *Images of America: Philadelphia Graveyards and Cemeteries* (Charleston, South Carolina: Arcadia, 2003), 115, ten historic Philadelphia cemeteries were uprooted for urban redevelopment between 1945 and 1970.

27. Harold Taubin to GPH, memorandum, 16 April 1963, UARC UPB101.4, box 1, folder "Institutional Development Plan 1962–63."

28. Philip Price (Dechert, Price, and Rhodes) to John C. Hetherston, 10 June 1963, UARC UPB101.4, box 1, folder "Institutional Development Plan 1962–63."

29. Harold Taubin to John C. Hetherston, 14 June 1963, UARC UPB101.4, box 1, folder "Institutional Development Plan 1962–63."

30. UPA, *Integrated Development Plan*, 1962, UARC UPA4, box 126; *From Here to 1970: A Digest of the Integrated Development Plan, University of Pennsylvania*, March 1963, box 126, "Development—Integrated Development Plan II, 1960–1965."

31. John C. Hetherston, interview by Jeannette Nichols, 12 November 1975, "The Best Years Are Just Ahead," *PAG*, January 1965, 6–13; "$100,000 Smile," *PAG*, May 1969, 8–9.

32. RDA, *Annual Report* 1962, p. 31, FFAL.

33. RDA, *How Urban Renewal Works in Philadelphia*, 1–7; Harold Taubin, "The University Environment," in Dobbins, *University, City, and Urban Renewal*, 27n1.

34. Acreage reported in West Philadelphia Corporation (hereafter WPC), *Fifth Annual Report: University City, Philadelphia*, 1965, part 4, UARC UPA4, box 188, folder "West Philadelphia Corporation Annual Reports." Cf. "University City Unit No. 4 Urban Renewal Area," n.d., Philadelphia City Archives (PCA) 145.2, box 75A–2973, "Redevelopment—University City #4 1963–1967," which lists 63.6 total acres.

35. "University City Unit No. 4 Urban Renewal Area." In 1960, the total population of Unit 4 was 2,552. The total number of dwelling units was 1,072, of which 150 were owner-occupied; 87 (8 percent) of the units housed "non-white" occupants. See "Excerpt from 1960 Census Figures," TUA WPC Acc. 350, box 11, folder "U.C. Development #4 & #5 1961."

36. RDA, "Survey and Planning Application: University City—Unit No. 4 Urban Renewal Area," January 1962, Fisher Fine Arts Library (FFAL).

37. "City Council Rezones Penn Campus, Clearing Way for Fine Arts Building," *PEB*, 10 December 1965; quote from editorial "What Zoning for Penn?," *PEB*, 16 November 1965; TUA Collection; see also UPA, *Campus Development Plan*, April 1966, UARC UPB101.4, box 21, folder "Campus Design Study 68–69."

38. "City Council Rezones Penn Campus, Clearing Way for Fine Arts Building," *PEB*, 10 December 1965, TUA Collection.

39. Quotes from College dean Otto Springer, in John C. Hetherston, A. Leo Levin, and Dan M. McGill, "Chronology of Events Relating to Construction of the New Fine Arts Building," 26 October 1965, UARC UPA4, box 194, folder "Graduate School of Fine Arts (Development Program—Physical Plan) 1965–1970." The General Services Administration authorized funds for the new building in the fall of 1961. The site for the building, a pleasant green-space with elm trees some forty yards north of the Furness Building, was hotly contested by College students and faculty. The Save Open Spaces (SOS) campaign of 1964–65 was Penn's first experience with campus protest in the 1960s (more in Chapter 4).

40. Bacon, interview by Multimedia and Educational Technology Services.

41. Raymond F. Leonard, PCPC, to Edmund N. Bacon, memorandum, 6 September 1946, PCA 145.2 PCPC Files, box 14 A2914, folder "Redevelopment—University 1946–1950"; in same folder: Bacon to Leonard, memorandum, 29 November 1947.

42. Arthur R. Freedman (UPA Office of Planning and Design), to Victor Rebor, Southeastern Pennsylvania Transit Authority (SEPTA), 18 November 1969, UARC UPB101.4, box 24, folder "38th Street 1969–70."

43. "Campus Development Plan—1975, map dated 15 October 1965, UARC UPB101.4, box 200 folder "38th Street 67–68." Also see "Temporary Commercial Relocation I," TUA Acc. 350, box 10, folder "University (Walnut) Plaza 1966."

44. UARC, *Mapping Penn*.

45. Ibid.

46. "Preliminary Plot Plan, University of Pennsylvania Temporary Commercial Relocation," 14 April 1967, TUA Acc. 350, box 10, folder "University (Walnut) Plaza 1967–68"; in same folder: welcome notice for University Plaza Shopping Center, 38th and Walnut streets, *DP*, 18 October 1968. Also see "Relocated Businesses Are Booming," *DP*, 16 October 1968.

47. UPA News Bureau, 17 October 1968, UPP1, box 5, folder "Campus Expansion."

48. See UPA News Bureau, 10 October 1968, UPP1, box 5, folder "Campus Expansion."

49. "38th and Locust Street Pedestrian Plaza and Bridge Program," typescript draft, n.d. [1968?], UARC UPB101.4, box 20, folder "38th Street 67–68"; RDA, *Annual Report*, 1968, p. 31, FFAL.

50. Harold Taubin, "A Brief History and Compilation of Trustee Actions Concerned with the Planning and Development of the West Philadelphia Campus," September 1976, UARC UPJ9.4, box 55, Facilities Planning B5.

51. Pennsylvania Higher Education Facilities Authority, *Official Statement in Regard to $56,600.00, University of Pennsylvania Revenue Bonds of 1968*, preliminary draft, August 1968, UARC UPB101.4, box 21, folder "Higher Education 1968–69."

52. Displacement data for these blocks were not available for this study. We were unable to find a repository for RDA records, either at the Redevelopment Authority or the Philadelphia City Archives. Adam Klarfeld, "Private Taking, Public Good," apparently had access to some RDA records that were housed outside the University. We follow Klarfeld's lead in using census block data in lieu of RDA displacement data. All of the RDA records cited in our paper are housed in UARC.

53. Fran Scott, interview by John Puckett, 27 September 2008.

54. George E. Thomas and David B. Brownlee, *Building America's First University: An Historical and Architectural Guide to the University of Pennsylvania* (Philadelphia: University of Pennsylvania Press), 302–3.

55. "Fraternity Relocation," handwritten chart, n.d. [1968–69], UARC UPB101.4, box 21, folder "Fraternities 68–69." Among the demolished buildings was the elegant half-timbered, Tudor-style Illman-Carter School of the Graduate School of Education, which, with its adjoining playground, stood next door to the Walnut Street branch of the Free Library.

56. Lillian G. Burns to Henry M. Chance, III, memorandum, 27 October 1967, UARC UPB101.4, box 19, folder "Fraternities 1967–68: in folder "Fraternities 1969–70": Agreement between Trustees of the University of Pennsylvania and the Delancey Street Residents Association, 17 January 1967.

57. UPA, inventory of streets, 1882–1968.

58. HEFA, *Official Statement*.

59. George E. Thomas, *University of Pennsylvania Campus Guide* (New York: Princeton Architectural Press, 2002), 153.

60. "Redevelopment Staff Acts on Orders, Reverses Opposition to Penn Housing," *Evening Bulletin*, 28 January 1968, TUA. Also see Ann L. Strong and George E. Thomas, *The Book of the School 100 Years: The Graduate School of Fine Arts of the University of Pennsylvania* (Philadelphia: University of Pennsylvania Graduate School of Fine Arts); a photograph on p. 50 lists Perkins-Romañach as associate architects for the Superblock. In February 1968, Mayor James Tate refused to renew Perkins's appointment as Planning Commission chair).

61. Thomas, *Campus Guide*, 153–55.

62. Bacon, interview by Messmer.

63. Thomas, *Campus Guide*, 146. Late in his life, Perkins told a reporter that the decision "to go up in the air" was not driven by his commitment to modernism: "It wasn't a philosophical idea at all. It wasn't saying this was how you ought to live, or this was a better way to

live. But the fact was that if you were going to put 3,500 students on that block, that was the only way you could do it." Yochi Dreazen, "The Man Behind the Superblock," *PAG*, September–October 1999, 12–13. On Perkins in the broader context of American modernism, see Jill Pearlman, *Inventing American Modernism: Joseph Hudnut, Walter Gropius and the Bauhaus Legacy at Harvard* (Charlottesville: University of Virginia Press, 2007), 13, 51, 70, 79, 89, 103, 116, 133, 149, 153, 166, 181, 192–200, 202, 211, 227.

64. Holmes Perkins, interview by Lydia Messmer, n.d. [1988], UARC UPB1.9MM, box 4, folder 39.

65. "Street Parcels," provided by UARC.

66. Harold Taubin, interview by Lydia Messmer, 2 December 1988; VHS tape provided to authors by Taubin's daughter Amy Orr.

67. UARC, *Mapping Penn*; RDA, *Annual Report*, 1964, FFAL; quote from Lillian G. Burns to John C. Hetherston, memorandum, 13 February 1964, UARC UPB101.4, box 4, folder "Redevelopment Unit #4 1963–64."

68. UPA inventory of streets, 1882–1968, provided by UARC.

69. "Men's Dormitory Triangle—37th, 38th, Spruce, Woodland Redevelopment Agreement," 1962, UARC UPB101.4, box 4, folder "Redevelopment Authority 1963–64; "Special Report on Federal Programs," *Higher Education and National Affairs* 1, no. 2 (February 1963): 1–7, excerpted in "The University and Urban Renewal" (appendix), in Dobbins, *University, City, and Urban Renewal*, 46–52.

70. UARC, *Mapping Penn*; UPA UARC, inventory of streets, 1882–1968, available on request; Thomas, *Campus Guide*, 160–61. The first School of Veterinary Medicine was built by the Philadelphia architect Frank Furness in 1884 on Hamilton Walk behind the present-day Dormitory Quadrangle (the Quad); Thomas and Brownlee, *Building America's First University*, 320.

71. UARC, *Mapping Penn*; Thomas and Brownlee, *Building America's First University*, 314; Thomas, *Campus Guide*, 162.

72. "Five Chosen to Redevelop W. Philadelphia Site," *PEB*, 15 November 1966, TUA; I. Milton Karabell (WPC planning director) to Michael Arno (RDA project coordinator), 23 May 1966, TUA Acc. 350, box 12, folder "Unit 4—Shopping Center Parcel #5–1966–1968"; in same box: Leo Molinaro to Samuel Raymond (University City Shopping Center Association), folder "Unit #4 Parcel 15 1967–1968."

73. UARC, *Mapping Penn*; Judith Rodin, *The University and Urban Renewal: Out of the Ivory Tower and into the Streets* (Philadelphia: University of Pennsylvania Press, 2007), 184–85.

74. UARC, *Mapping Penn*; Thomas and Brownlee, *Building America's First University*, 268–71, quote from 271.

75. Thomas, *Campus Guide*, 138; "University Ousts Local Merchants," *DP*, 25 February 1965, TUA Acc. 350, box 26, folder "News Clippings–1965."

76. "Memorandum: General State Authority Legislation," 27 August 1968, UARC UPP1, box 1, folder "Campus Expansion."

77. Thomas, *Campus Guide*, 137–38.

78. "University Square: The Plan for 3401 Walnut Street," *Almanac*, 23 November, 1971, 7, clipping, UARC UPB101.4, box 26, folder "Commercial 1971–72."

79. "Executive Planning Committee on the Physical Plant," minutes, 6 October 1969, UARC UPB101.4, box 26, folder "Commercial 1971–72."

80. Lillian G. Burns to John C. Hetherston, memorandum, 21 June 1963, UARC UPB101.4, box 2, folder "Redevelopment Unit #4 1962–63." Also see "Lou Weisenthal's Properties," 13 February 1967, TUA WPC Acc. 350, box 11, folder "Units 4–5 Litigation 1967–68."

81. See Walnut Street photograph, UARC UPX12, box 36, folder 14.

82. I. Milton Karabel quoted in "Weisenthal Says His Properties Are Not Blighted," *DP*, 1 May 1968, UARC.

83. Statement from stenographic transcript of meeting held on 1 February 1967 at the RDA, UARC UPB101.4, box 18, folder "Redevelopment Unit #4 1966–67."

84. "Weisenthal Says Properties Not Blighted."

85. "Impact of Objections by Weisenthal, Pagano, and Raymond on Implementation of the Campus Development Plan," typescript draft, 2 February 1967, UARC UPB101.4, box 18, folder "Redevelopment Unit #4 1966–67."

86. RDA, "Status Report of Preliminary Objections to Declaration of Taking," n.d. [1967], UARC UPB101.4, box 18, folder "Redevelopment Authority 1966–67."

87. RDA stenographic transcript.

88. E. Craig Sweeten to Walter H. Annenberg, memorandum, 2 May 1968, UARC UPB101.4, box 19, folder "Graduate Center 1967–68."

89. Walnut Street photographs, UARC UPX12, box 36, folder 13; John C. Hetherston to Phillip Rief (professor of sociology), 1 March 1972, UARC UPB101.4, box 28, folder "Graduate Center 1971–72."

90. "Redevelopment Authority Sets April as Date for Walnut St. Demolition," *DP*, 10 February 1976, UARC Collection.

91. "Up and Down in Smokey Joe's," *DP*, 10 November 1982; "Tradition and Old Smokey Joe's Demolished by Philadelphia RDA," *DP*, 4 April 1978; "University Gives Shops Space in New Buildings," *NYT*, 15 December 1968, TUA Acc. 350, box 10, folder "University (Walnut) Plaza 1967–68."

92. See agreements in UARC UPB101.4, box 18, folder "Redevelopment Unit #4 1966–67." The documents are dated May and June 1968.

93. Titus D. Hewryk to Roosevelt Dicks (Office of Planning and Design), memorandum, 11 November 1971, UARC UPB101.4, box 28, "Commercial 1971–72." Also see Thomas and Brownlee, *Building America's First University*, 265–66.

94. Judy Wicks, *Good Morning Beautiful Business: The Unexpected Journey of an Activist Entrepreneur and Local Economy Pioneer* (White Water Junction, Vt.: Chelsea Green Publishing, 2013), 52–59.

95. Jon Caroulis, "Of Dirty Drugs and White Dogs," *PAG*, April 1997, 27–32.

96. Judy Wicks, interview by John Puckett, 23 November 2009.

Chapter 3

1. RDA, *Annual Report* 1960, FFAL.

2. James Wolfinger, *Philadelphia Divided: Race and Politics in the City of Brotherly Love* (Chapel Hill: University of North Carolina Press, 2007), 11–35.

3. Ibid., 113–73.

4. Maurice Isserman, *America Divided: The Civil War of the 1960s* (New York: Oxford University Press, 2000), 23; also see Nicholas Lemann, *The Promised Land: The Great Black Migration and How It Changed America* (New York: Vintage, 1991).

5. Wolfinger, *Philadelphia Divided*, 179–80.

6. Ibid., 202–03.

7. Matthew J. Countryman, *Up South: Civil Rights and Black Power in Philadelphia* (Philadelphia: University of Pennsylvania Press, 2005), 48–58; also see Martha Lovell, *Philadelphia's Non-White Population: Report No. 1* (Philadelphia: Commission on Human Relations), November 1961, UARC UPA 4, box 156, folder "West Phila. Corp. General 61–62."

8. Thaddeus P. Mathis, "A Critical Assessment of Black Power and Social Change in Post-Industrial Philadelphia," in *The State of Black Philadelphia*, vol. 3, ed. Charyn Tutton and Eric S. King (Philadelphia: Urban League of Philadelphia), 28 (table 3).

9. U.S. Bureau of the Census, accessed from socialexplorer.com, Philadelphia County, PA.

10. Carolyn Adams, David Bartelt, David Elesh, Ira Goldstein, Nancy Kleniewski, and William Yancy, *Philadelphia: Neighborhoods, Division and Conflict in a Postindustrial City* (Philadelphia: Temple University Press, 1999), 17 (table 1.3).

11. Wolfinger, *Philadelphia Divided*, 203.

12. Adams et al., *Philadelphia*, 31; Guian A. McKee, *The Problem of Jobs: Liberalism, Race, and Deindustrialization in Philadelphia* (Chicago: University of Chicago Press, 2008), 247.

13. Countryman, *Up South*, 48–58. By 1960 only six "Black or mixed race" families lived in Levittown, pop. sixty thousand, Bucks County, Pa., a town that was integrated violently; across the Delaware River, Levittown in Burlington County, N.J., grudgingly received its first black family in 1957; Wolfinger, *Philadelphia Divided*, 191–97; Thomas J. Sugrue, *Sweet Land of Liberty: The Forgotten Struggle for Civil Rights in the North* (New York: Random House, 2008), 220–28. For blacks' exclusion in the dwindling industrial sector, see McKee, *Problem of Jobs*, 41–82, 115–16, 132, quote from 116. In the mid-1960s economists noted the disproportionate representation of blacks among the city's unemployed: 26 percent of the labor force, yet 43 percent of the unemployed (ibid., 85). As McKee notes, Lyndon Johnson's War on Poverty produced social welfare programs for the city, but few jobs for African Americans. While Leon Sullivan's federally assisted Opportunities Industrialization Centers, a community-based job training and community development program founded in 1964 with roots in the African American church, reported having trained more than fifteen thousand blacks and placed more than nine thousand trainees in jobs by 1969, these gains could not be sustained in the face of two recessions in the 1970s and the accelerating outflow of manufacturing jobs. For more on the Opportunities Industrialization Centers, see McKee, *Problem of Jobs*, 111–210; Countryman, *Up South*, 110–17.

14. Wolfinger, *Philadelphia Divided*, 197–202. Chronically in short supply, inadequately funded, and poorly maintained, the city's public housing stock was in marked decline by the 1960s, increasingly home to black households headed by single women on welfare struggling gamely to maintain a decent standard of living. Lisa Levenstein, *A Movement Without Marches: African American Women and the Politics of Poverty in Postwar Philadelphia* (Chapel Hill: University of North Carolina Press, 2009), 98–103.

15. Philadelphia's experience was not atypical. Douglass S. Massey and Nancy Denton, in *American Apartheid: Segregation and the Making of the Underclass* (Cambridge, Mass.: Harvard University Press, 1993), 46, write that "racial segregation became a permanent structural feature of the spatial organization of American cities in the years after World War II" (46). For detailed studies of urban racial segregation in the postwar era, see Arnold R. Hirsch, *Making the Second Ghetto: Race and Housing in Chicago, 1940–1960* (Chicago: University of Chicago Press, [1983] 1988), and Thomas J. Sugrue, *The Origins of the Urban Crisis: Race and Inequality in Postwar Detroit* (Princeton, N.J.: Princeton University Press, [1996] 2005). On redlining, see Kenneth T. Jackson, *Crabgrass Frontier: The Suburbanization of the United States* (New York: Oxford University Press, 1985), 197–218; for Philadelphia area trends, see Steven Conn, *Metropolitan Philadelphia: Living with the Presence of the Past* (Philadelphia: University of Pennsylvania Press, 2006), chap. 3; on redlining of Philadelphia neighborhoods, see Buzz Bissinger, *A Prayer for the City* (New York: Random House, 1997), 203–12; on Philadelphia's segregated public schools, see Michael Clapper, "School Design, Site Selection and

the Political Geography of Race in Postwar Philadelphia," *Journal of Planning History* 5, no. 3 (2006): 241–63; U.S. Commission on Civil Rights, *Racial Isolation in the Public Schools*, vol. 1 (Washington, D.C.: U.S. Government Printing Office, 1967), 4 (table 1), 9–10 (table 3); Countryman, *Up South*, chap. 6; Levenstein, *Movement Without Marches*, chap. 4.

16. U.S. Bureau of the Census, accessed from socialexplorer.com, Philadelphia County, Pa.; Community Renewal Program, City of Philadelphia, *Technical Report 18*, 16 November 1966, pp. 7–7a. For Mantua blacks and the 1920 census, see William Wallace Weaver, "West Philadelphia: A Study of Natural Social Areas" (PhD diss., University of Pennsylvania, 1930), 138–43.

17. U.S. Bureau of the Census, accessed from socialexplorer.com, Philadelphia County, Pa. In 1964, the City Planning Commission, in the *West Philadelphia District Plan*, reported that "Negroes own 50 per cent of all the owner-occupied dwellings in the district"; the owner-occupancy rate in Mantua, however, was "less than 35 percent," the lowest category on the PCPC map (p. 27). Located approximately one mile northwest of the Penn campus, Belmont, the neighborhood on Mantua's western boundary, showed a similar demographic profile. Blacks became the dominant racial group during World War II; by 1960 they constituted 93.8 percent of Belmont's population, and by 1970, 95.6 percent; by 1970, one-third of black households reported incomes below the poverty level.

18. U.S. Bureau of the Census, accessed from socialexplorer.com, Philadelphia County, Pa.

19. Elijah Anderson, *Streetwise: Race, Class, and Change in an Urban Neighborhood* (Chicago: University of Chicago Press, 1990), chap. 1, quote from 21; U.S. Bureau of the Census, accessed from socialexplorer.com, Philadelphia County, Pa..

20. Seymour Shubin, "Memorial to a Murder," *American Weekly*, 11 June 1961, 11A–11B, TUA mounted clippings, box 308.

21. "Gang Murders Korean Student in West Philadelphia," *PEB*, 26 April 1958, TUA Collections.

22. "Killing Called 'Jungle-Like,' 11 Denied Bail," *PEB*, 30 April 1958, TUA; "Gang Murders Korean Student," *PEB*, 26 April 1958; "The Price Borum Must Pay," *PEB* editorial, 10 October 1958, TUA.

23. "Wipe Out Street Gangs" (editorial), *PI*, 29 April 1958, TUA; "Nine Indicted in Oh Killing," *PEB*, 17 May 1958, TUA.

24. Martin Meyerson, "The Future of the University of Pennsylvania Neighborhood," 30 June 1956, draft of possible points to be made to administration and trustees, UARC UPP1, box 5, folder "Campus Expansion." Apparently G. Holmes Perkins, dean of the Graduate School of Fine Arts, reconstructed Meyerson's notes into a polished second draft; Perkins to Meyerson, draft memorandum, 30 June 1956; UARC UPA 4, box 73, folder "The West Philadelphia Corporation Community Relations 1955–1960 I."

25. We would also note the University of Pittsburgh's abortive involvement in OakCorp, a multi-institutional urban development entity, formed in 1961 as part of the Pittsburgh Regional Planning Association's master plan, in which Pitt was the principal owner. Pitt's chancellor Edward Litchfield was president of the corporation; his audacious goal was nothing less than the creation of the world's largest research park in Panther Hollow, "a ravine 650 to 900 feet wide at the top and 150 to 200 feet deep, with a broad floor extending southward about a mile." The architectural design called for an exorbitantly expensive development, "the equivalent of a 150-story building on its side in the ravine, its 'roof' or upper side forming a seventy-five acre mall" that would join Pitt and the Carnegie Institute of Technology's campuses. By 1965, OakCorp and the Panther Hollow project had crashed on the shoals of

Litchfield's inability to raise the fantastic sums necessary to build his dream. Robert C. Alberts, *Pitt: The Story of the University of Pittsburgh 1787–1987* (Pittsburgh, Pa: University of Pittsburgh Press, 1986), 307–12, quote from 312.

26. Barry Bergoll, *Mastering McKim's Plan: Columbia's First Century on Morningside Heights* (New York: Miriam and Ira D. Wallach Art Gallery, Columbia University, 1997), quoting Robert A. M. Stern, Thomas Mellins, and David Fishman, *New York 1960: Architecture and Urbanism between the Second World War and the Bicentennial* (New York: Monaceli Press, 1995), 734.

27. Hilary Ballon, "Morningside-Manhattanville Title I," in *Robert Moses and the Modern City: The Transformation of New York*, ed. Hilary Ballon and Kenneth T. Jackson (New York: W.W. Norton, 2007), quote from 260; Michael H. Carriere, "Between Being and Becoming: On Architecture, Student Protest, and the Aesthetics of Liberalism in Postwar America" (PhD diss., University of Chicago, 2010), 182–92, quote from 190; Andrew S. Dolkart, *Morningside Heights: A History of Its Architecture and Development* (New York: Columbia University, 1998), 325–40, quote from 331. Also see Joel Schwartz, *The New York Approach: Robert Moses, Urban Liberals, and Redevelopment of the Inner City* (Columbus: Ohio State University Press, 1993), 185–89. A third housing project is also noteworthy: in 1961 the New York City Housing Authority completed Manhattanville Houses "on a five-block site between 129th and 133rd streets, Amsterdam Avenue and Broadway," to house people "who fell between the financial requirements of the Grant Houses and Morningside Gardens"; Ballon, "Morningside Manhattanville Title I," 260–61.

28. Carriere, "Between Being and Becoming," 192.

29. Ibid., 192–211, 365–66, quotes from 197, 202–3, 210.

30. Dolkart, *Morningside Heights*, 334; also see Robert A. McCaughey, *Stand, Columbia: A History of Columbia University in the City of New York, 1754–2004* (New York: Columbia University Press, 2003), 404–9.

31. Dolkart, *Morningside Heights*, 335. For a specific breakdown on these properties, see Carriere, "Between Being and Becoming," 210–11.

32. LaDale C. Winling, "Building the Ivory Tower: Campus Planning, University Development, and the Politics of Urban Space" (PhD diss., University of Michigan, 2010), 161–64.

33. Peter H. Rossi and Robert A. Dentler, *The Politics of Urban Renewal: The Chicago Findings* (New York: Free Press, 1961), 26.

34. Hirsch, *Second Ghetto*, chap. 5, quotes from 144, 152, 157. The SECC was a "front," a "pseudo-civic organization," wrote the urbanists Edward C. Banfield and James Q. Wilson in *City Politics* (Cambridge, Mass.: Harvard University Press, 1967), 29–30, 259–60. That public housing was excluded in the Final Plan was likely a relief to the liberals of the Hyde Park-Kenwood Community Conference. "The SECC protected the community's 'interests' as it took the 'practical' view of the situation," Hirsch writes. "The HPKCC, much less certain about its mission than its rival, appealed to the community's sense of justice and responsibility and formally articulated the liberal's theoretical acceptance of public housing. With the power to make the final decision in the hands of the former organization, however, the latter could safely represent the community's 'conscience' and breathe a surreptitious sigh of relief when overwhelmed by the forces of the 'real world'" (163–64).

35. Julia Abrahamson, *A Neighborhood Finds Itself* (New York: Biblo and Tannen [1959], 1971), 210.

36. Julian Levi, from a speech delivered at the Massachusetts Institute of Technology, 10 July 1959, quoted in Hirsch, *Second Ghetto*, 154. Privately, Levi confided that the target was

"slum and blight which will attract lower class Whites and Negroes"; memorandum cited in Winling, "Building the Ivory Tower," 163.

37.   Rossi and Dentler, *Politics of Urban Renewal*, 90–91.

38.   Abrahamson, *Neighborhood Finds Itself*, 200; Robert E. Streeter, ed., *One in Spirit: A Retrospective of the University of Chicago on the Occasion of Its Centennial*, 2nd ed. (Chicago: University of Chicago, 1991, 110–13.

39.   Donald K. Angell to GPH, memorandum, 19 November 1958, UARC UPA 4, box 73, folder "Community Relations 1955–60 I."

40.   "Meeting of West Philadelphia Medical and Educational Institutions," 10 June 1958, attachment to Lillian G. Burns to GPH, 1 December 1966, UARC UPA 4, box 188, folder "West Philadelphia Corporation (Community Relations) III 1965–1970."

41.   John L. Moore, typescript copy of statement, December 1958 (penciled date), UARC UPA 4, box 73, folder "The West Philadelphia Corporation Community Relations 1955–1960 II." Gaylord Harnwell told Senator John F. Kennedy, "We believe that we can do as distinguished a job as Chicago has in its pioneering work in this field"; in same folder: Harnwell to Kennedy, 24 September 1959.

42.   Lillian G. Burns to GPH, 2 September 1959, UARC UPA 4, box 73, folder "The West Philadelphia Corporation Community Relations 1955–1960 II."

43.   Margaret Pugh O'Mara, *Cities of Knowledge: Cold War Science and the Search for the Next Silicon Valley* (Princeton, N.J.: Princeton University Press, 2005), 157.

44.   "University City—Proposed Land Use: A Report to the West Philadelphia Development Corporation," n.d. [1959?], UARC UPA 4, box 73, folder "The West Philadelphia Corporation Community Relations 1955–1960 II."

45.   O'Mara, *Cities of Knowledge*, 156–57.

46.   Ibid., 159.

47.   Taubin, interview by Nichols; GPH, "An Environment for Learning," *Proceedings of the American Philosophical Society* 115, no. 3 (1971): 170–86; West Philadelphia Corporation, *Annual Report*, 11 October 1960, UARC UPA 4 box 152, folder "Community Relations—West Phila. Corp. Annual Reports 1960–65."

48.   GPH to Harry A. Batten, W. M. Armistead Foundation, Inc., 16 May 1961, UPA 4, box 154, folder "Community Relations–West Phila. Corp. (Financial Campaign for 1960–1961) 1960–1965."

49.   West Philadelphia Corporation By-Laws, Article I Members, Section 1.01, Classes of Membership, filed with WPC board of directors, minutes, 20 October 1960, UARC UPA 4, box 152, folder "Community Relations–West Phila. Corp. Minutes of the Annual Meetings 1960–65 I"; Ira Harkavy and John L. Puckett, "The Role of Mediating Structures in University and Community Revitalization: The University of Pennsylvania and West Philadelphia as a Case Study," *Journal of Research and Development in Education* 25, no. 1 (1991): 10–25.

50.   O'Mara, *Cities of Knowledge*, 162–63.

51.   GPH, "Environment for Learning," 172.

52.   Marketers Research Service, Inc., "A Profile of Basic Market Factors in the West Philadelphia Corporation Area," prepared for the West Philadelphia Corporation, April 1960, UARC UPA 4, box 73, folder "Community Relations West Philadelphia Corporation 1955–1960 I"; Walker & Murray Associates, map of West Philadelphia Corporation area and University City, n.d. [1961–62], UARC UPA 4, box 156, folder "West Phila. Corp. General 61–62"; see also, "Harnwell Urges Plan for 'University City,'" *DP*, 12 October 1960, UARC.

53. Quote from GPH, " Environment for Learning," 173. Also see "Outline of Remarks by Leo Molinaro," presentation to UPA board of trustees," TUA Acc. 350, box 4, folder "Mr. Molinaro 1959–61."

54. "University City: Dream to Reality," *PI*, 16 October 1960.

55. Hugh Scott, "Brainsville on the March," *PIM*, 19 July 1964, 4–5.

56. O'Mara, *Cities of Knowledge*, 158. See and cf. Department of State, Commonwealth of Pennsylvania, UCSC name registration, filed 30 August 1963, http://www.corporations .state.pan.us/corp/soskb/verify.asp. Racial politics in Unit 3 may have prompted Harnwell's decision to establish a "cooperative program" between Penn and Morgan State University, a historically black university in Baltimore, founded in 1867. The program, which received federal funding, was announced in the fall of 1965, its primary aim being "to increase the number of Morgan graduates who are accepted into Pennsylvania graduate programs and to enable Morgan faculty to pursue the Ph.D. here." It also offered some student, faculty, and cultural exchanges. See "Morgan State Affiliation Announced," *Almanac* 12, no. 1 (September 1965): 3; "Morgan State Project Renewed," *Almanac* 18, no. 36 (23 May 1972): 6; University Development Commission, *Pennsylvania: One University* (January 1973), printed as *Almanac Supplement*, 29 January 1973, quote from 18.

57. Philadelphia City Planning Commission, *University City—3: Redevelopment Area Plan*, May 1962.

58. For a summary, see GPH, "Environment for Learning," 170–86. For more details on these projects, see WPC press releases in TUA Acc. 350, folder "News Releases 1963–66."

59. GPH to John L. Moore, 15 June 1959, UARC UPA4, box 73, folder "The West Philadelphia Corporation Community Relations 1955–1960 II."

60. "Agenda: Research and Development in Greater Philadelphia," meeting held at the Union League of Philadelphia, 9 September 1959, UARC UPA4, box 73, folder "The West Philadelphia Corporation Community Relations 1955–1960 II"; in same folder: GPH to Richard W. Graves, 25 September 1959; also see in same folder: Chamber of Commerce of Greater Philadelphia, Commerce and Industry Council, "Research and Development Committee," 8 September 1959. For the PIDC, "the city's industrial development agency," see Kirk R. Petshek, *The Challenge of Urban Reform: Policies and Programs in Philadelphia* (Philadelphia: Temple University Press, 1973), 200–08.

61. Nicholas Dagen Bloom, *Merchant of Illusion: James Rouse, America's Salesman of the Businessman's Utopia* (Columbia: Ohio State University Press, 2004), 44–45, 126–179; "The American Council to Improve Our Neighborhoods," *American Journal of Public Health* 46, no. 11 (1956): 1445–46. For more on Molinaro, see Petshek, *Challenge of Urban Reform*, 245–47.

62. Molinaro, interviews by Mark Lloyd and John Puckett, 5 July 2007, 26 August 2008; WPC, *The University City Tower*, brochure, n.d. [1961], UARC UPA4, box 152, folder "Community Relations–West Phila. Corp. Brochures 1960–65." Business and civic leaders, including the mayor, composed the PIDC's thirty-member, "powerful" board; the nonprofit's administrative costs were paid by the city and the Chamber of Commerce. The PIDC was "basically an instrument of city policy" that "[worked] closely with public agencies, the other development corporations, and private property owners to further coordinated actions of mutual concern." It partnered with the Redevelopment Authority, which acquired "tracts marked for industrial use by the city's long-range plan" and sold them to the PIDC, which in turn sold or leased the properties and arranged low-interest loans with local banks for companies to build or expand their plants. Despite hundreds of dealings, the PIDC was unable to stem the

outflow of the city's manufacturing jobs. Jeanne R. Lowe, *Cities in a Race with Time: Progress and Poverty in America's Renewing Cities* (New York: Random House, 1967), 362, 365–66.

63. WPC board of directors, minutes, 21 January 1963, UPA 4, box 152, folder "Community Relations—West Phila. Corp. Board of Directors 1960–65."

64. O'Mara, *Cities of Knowledge*, 168.

65. Molinaro, interviews by Lloyd and Puckett; see and cf. O'Mara, *Cities of Knowledge*, chap. 4. Also see O'Mara, *Cities of Knowledge*, chap. 3: "From the Farm to the Valley: Stanford University and the San Francisco Peninsula"; John M. Findlay, *Magic Lands: Western Cityscapes and American Culture After 1940*, chap. 4: "Stanford Industrial Park: Downtown for Silicon Valley"; Victor J. Danilov, "Sites for Sale: 1964 Guide to Research Sites," *Industrial Research*, May 1964, 30–44.

66. "Papers Are Filed for New Science Center and Institute in West Philadelphia," *PI*, 29 October 1963, clipping, UARC UPA 4, box 153, "Community Relations—West Phila. Corp. Exec. Com. Agenda, Minutes, etc. 1960–65 X."

67. John C. Hetherston, "University City Science Center," typescript draft, 20 March 1964, UARC UPA 4, box 173, folder "University City Science Center Corporation 1963–1964."

68. GPH, "University City Science Institute," typescript draft, 1 March 1964, UPA 4, box 173, folder untitled; Mackenzie S. Carlson, *"Come to Where the Knowledge Is": A History of the University City Science Center* (Philadelphia: UPA UARC, 1999), accessed from http://www.archives.upenn.edu/histy/features/upwphil/ucsc.html, 9 September 2004; "A History of the University City Science Center," UARC UPA 4, box 173, untitled folder.

69. Rebecca S. Lowen, *Creating the Cold War University: The Transformation of Stanford* (Berkeley: University of California Press, 1997), 100.

70. Robert L. Trescher, "Confidential memorandum of Robert L. Trescher's conferences with Fred Glover of Stanford University, and Robert L. Woodcock and Carl L. Titus, with the Stanford Research Institute, on June 7, 1963," UARC UPA 4, box 173, folder "University City Science Center General 1963–1964." See also in same box, J. E. Wallace Sterling to GPH, 22 January 1964, folder "University City Science Center–Corporation (Formation of) 1963–1964."

71. "The University City Science Center," n.d. [1965], UARC.

72. First quote: John C. Hetherston to Wilfred D. Gillen, 20 September 1963; second quote: GPH to William Hagerty, 11 October 1963; letters in UARC UPA 4, box 173, folder "University City Science Center–(Formation of) 1963–1964." See also in same folder, Morris Wolf (attorney, Wolf, Block, Snorr and Solis-Cohen), "Suggested Examination of Dr. Harnwell re: University City Science Center and University City Science Institute."

73. "History of the University City Science Center," appendix 1. Hagerty made his own demands of Penn and the RDA: Drexel would not participate in the Science Center unless the blocks bounded by 34th, Warren, 36th, and Lancaster streets were "reserved for development by Drexel of the type of industrially oriented research toward which Drexel's graduate curricula and professional interests are oriented"; Hagerty to GPH, 25 October 1963, UARC UPA 4, box 173, folder "University City Science Center—Corporation (Formation of) 1963–1964."

74. Gustave G. Amsterdam to Paul J. Cupp, 23 June 1964, UARC UPA 4, box 173, folder "University City Science Center General 1963–1964."

75. Leo Molinaro to WPC board of directors, memorandum, 20 May 1963, UARC UPA 4, box 156, folder "West Phila. Corp. General 1962–63"; see also Leo Molinaro to William Yoltman, 13 February 1967, box 188, folder "Community Relations (West Philadelphia Corporation) 1965–1970."

76. Walter Palmer, interview by John Puckett, 26 September 2008, 4 April 2010. One city planner reported "consummate decay" in the quadrant bounded by Market, 34th, Ludlow, and 36th streets; James F. Dillon to Edmund N. Bacon, 4 June 1947, PCA 145.2, PCPC Files, box 14 A2914, folder "Redevelopment—University 1946–1950."

77. PCPC, *University City—3: Redevelopment Area Plan* (Philadelphia: Author, 1962), UARC UPA 4, box 156, folder "West Phila. Corp. Ex. Com. May 22, 1962."

78. U.S. Bureau of the Census, Census of Housing, 1970, *Block Statistics, Philadelphia, PA* (Washington, D.C.: U.S. Government Printing Office, 1971).

79. RDA, "University City Unit No. 3, Urban Renewal Area, Penna. R-128, Final Project Report Part I," Application for Loan and Grant, 30 November 1964, TUA Neighborhoods & Urban Renewal, Acc. 980, box 4, Application to Urban Renewal Administration, Housing and Home Finance Agency.

80. Palmer, interview by Puckett, 26 September 2008.

81. Michael Zuckerman, interview by Mark Lloyd and John Puckett, 1 February 2010.

82. Palmer, interview by Puckett.

83. "For Some the Bottom Was Tops: Memories of Old W. Phila. Neighborhood Pulls Them Back," *Daily News*, 18 November 1988. According to these sources, the annual picnic draws up to two thousand people.

84. For more on this, see David Lowenthal, *The Past Is a Foreign Country* (New York: Cambridge University Press, 1985); Maurice Halbawchs, *On Collective Memory*, ed. and trans. Lewis A. Coser (Chicago: University of Chicago Press, 1992). For community identity in a highly stressed, racially isolated neighborhood, see Sudhir Venkatesh, *Gang Leader for a Day* (Penguin: New York, 2008).

85. Mike Roepel, interview by John Puckett, 11 June 2009. For a similar statement about this "loss of position," see Pearl B. Simpson, *The Black Bottom Picnic: A Collection of Essays, Poems, and Other Musings* (Philadelphia: Author, 2005), 42–43.

86. Palmer, interview by Puckett; Countryman, *Up South*, 191.

87. See "Special Science High Schools Proposed by Aide of Kennedy," *NYT*, 14 June 1963; John Rudolph, *Scientists in the Classroom: The Cold War Reconstruction of Science Education* (New York: Palgrave, 2002).

88. Jessica Lee Oliff, "University City High School: An Experiment in Innovative Education, 1959–1972" (Senior honors thesis in history, University of Pennsylvania, 2000), 37–38, UARC Collections.

89. GPH to Allen H. Wetter (superintendent of schools, School District of Philadelphia), 28 March 1963; UPA 4, box 154, folder "Community Relations—West Phila. Corp. Science High School 1960–1965."

90. Dick Righter (chairman, West Philadelphia Schools Committee) to Leo Molinaro, 26 December 1963, UARC UPA 4, box 154, folder "Community Relations—West Phila. Corp. Science High School 1960–1965."

91. WPC, *Annual Report*, October 1961, TUA WPC Acc. 350, box 1, individual folder.

92. "300 Challenge University City in West Phila.," *PEB*, 16 February 1962, TUA.

93. "Authority Opposes Group's Plea to Raze Homes," *PI*, 23 May 1965, TUA WPC Acc. 350, box 11, folder "Unit #3 (1965) Clay Group (archives)."

94. "Claim-Staking in Brainsville," *Greater Philadelphia Bulletin*, September 1965, p. 3, TUA WPC Acc. 350, box 11, folder "U.C. #3 Boundaries 1960–1961"; [Leo Molinaro], "University City Urban Renewal Area Unit #3," 2 August 1966, TUA WPC Acc. 350, box 11, folder "Unit #3–Background." The mayoralty of James Tate, the rough-edged Irish Catholic Democratic who succeeded the "blue-blooded" Richardson Dilworth in that office, "marked the

effective end of reform in Philadelphia," writes Guian McKee, in *Problem of Jobs*, 72–73. Tate's political base included African Americans and the labor unions.

95. Theodore R. Husted (chairman, Housing Committee for West Philadelphia) to Michael von Moschzisker, Esq., 11 July 1961, TUA WPC Acc. 350, box 11, folder "University City Redevelopment Unit #3 1961."

96. "Authority Opposes Group's Plea."

97. "Claim-Staking in Brainsville."

98. [Molinaro], "University City Urban Renewal Unit #3." This source provides a detailed chronology of Clay's tango with the RDA.

99. Leo Molinaro to Myles Standish (Commerce and Industry Council executive director), 3 May 1965, TUA WPC Acc. 350, box 11, folder "Unit #3–Background."

100. "Authority Opposes Group's Plea."

101. John H. Clay to Thatcher Longstreth (Chamber of Commerce of Greater Philadelphia), 15 April 1965, TUA WPC Acc. 350, box 11, folder "Unit #3 (1965) Clay Group (archives)." Also see "University City Renewal Unit Shows Model," *PEB*, 4 March 1965, TUA.

102. Franny Robinson to Mayor James Tate, copy to LBJ, 14 September 1965, TUA WPC Acc. 350, box 11, folder "Unit #3 (1965) Clay Group (archives)."

103. Leo Molinaro to Franny Robinson, 20 September 1965, TUA WPC Acc. 350, box 11, folder "Unit #3 (1965) Clay Group (archives)"; in same folder: Leo Molinaro to Robert C. Weaver (Housing and Home Finance Agency), 11 October 1965.

104. "Group Charges Bias in Redevelopment Project," *PEB*, 1 December 1965, TUA.

105. Oliff, "University City High School," 36–48; [Molinaro], "University City Urban Renewal Unit #3";"University City Gets Land Fund of $24 Million," *PEB*, 1 May 1966, clipping, UARC UPA4, box 188, folder "West Philadelphia Corporation (Community Relations) II 1965–1970." Leo Molinaro to Doris Hamilton (33rd and Mantua Block Association), 14 October 1966, UARC UPA4, box 188, folder "Community Relations (West Philadelphia Corporation) 1965–1970."

106. Commencement program, 1966, UARC UPG7, R11. A baccalaureate degree was awarded to Judith Seitz, the future Judith Rodin.

107. Leo Molinaro to Doris Hamilton (chairperson, 33rd and Mantua Block Association), 14 October 1966, TUA WPC Acc. 350, box 11, folder "Unit #3 General Correspondence 1966."

108. The best account is Countryman, *Up South*, chap. 6; quotes are from 214, 224. Also see Henry S. Resnik, *Turning on the System: War in the Philadelphia Public Schools* (New York: Pantheon, 1970); Oliff, "University City High School," 51–63.

109. This paragraph draws heavily from Oliff, "University City High School," 72, 76–82, 91–95, quote from 93. According to Penn education professor Aase Eriksen, who organized the Free School's "small-house" program, which operated from 1970 to 1975, the school emphasized "a close working relationship between students and teachers. Inside the House, classes were small, non-graded, and grade levels were eliminated. An 'Elective Enrichment Program,' provided courses for students at banks, hospitals and other metropolitan institutions." Aase Eriksen, typescript response to questions from Jeannette Nichols, History of the University Project, 3 September 1971, UARC UPP1, box 5, folder "Campus Expansion." For more on the Free School, see clippings in same folder; Arthur A. Hyde, "Program and Curriculum Development in an Alternative Secondary School: A Descriptive Analysis" (EdD diss., University of Pennsylvania, 1974); Aase Eriksen, *Scattered Schools* (Philadelphia: University of Pennsylvania, 1971).

110. George E. Thomas, "From Our House to the 'Big House': Architectural Design as Visible Metaphor in the School Buildings of Philadelphia," *Journal of Planning History* 5, no. 3 (2006): 218–40.

111. Oliff, "University City High School," 109.

112. RDA, *The Urban Renewal Plan for University City Unit No. 3 Urban Renewal Area*, April 1965, attachment: "Relocation Report," R223–9. UARC box and folder could not be located for corrective citation.

113. *University City* 6, no. 4 (1967), WPC newsletter quoted in Petshek, *Challenge of Urban Reform*, 254. Also see "Urban Renewal Land Acquisition Begins in Redevelopment Units 3 & 4," *University City* 5, no. 3 (March 1967): 1, 6; WPC, news release, n.d. [April 1967]; RDA, re: Units 3, 4, 5, "Statement of Facts and Recommendations," 16 October 1967, UARC UPB101.4, box 18, folder "Redevelopment Unit #4 1966–67"; RDA, *Annual Report*, 1968, quote from p. 32, FFAL; WPC, *Ninth Annual Report*, 1969, UARC UPA4, box 188, folder "Annual Reports (Community Relations–West Philadelphia Corp.) 1965–1970."

114. The University was affiliated with Presbyterian Hospital, an independent community hospital founded in 1871. Less than one mile northwest of HUP, Presbyterian provided training for Penn medical students. This relationship remained unaltered until 1995, when Penn purchased Presbyterian to create the Presbyterian Medical Center of the University of Pennsylvania. John A. Kastor, *Governance of Teaching Hospitals: Turmoil at Penn and Hopkins* (Baltimore: Johns Hopkins University Press, 2004), 37–42.

115. It is important to note the role of International House, Inc., as a developer in Unit 3. International House was founded in 1910, at 3905 Spruce Street, by the Christian Association. In 1959, the Religious Society of Friends assumed sponsorship of the house, and it was moved to 15th and Cherry streets in the central city. The burgeoning of foreign students in the Delaware Valley in the 1960s prompted calls for a new International House. The Haas Community Funds provided a matching grant of $5 million, and the RDA designated a 1.3-acre parcel on the northwest corner of 37th and Walnut streets, adjacent to the Penn campus; Trustees and Officers of International House, *1970—60 Years of International House of Philadelphia* (Philadelphia: International House, 1970).

116. Karen Gaines to "all concerned," memorandum, 30 October 1968, UARC UPA4, box 214, folder "SDS versus University City Science Center–Student Affairs 1965–1970."

117. See Simpson, *Black Bottom Picnic*, 41–42.

118. UPA, "Report of the Senate Advisory Committee," 13–14; also see "Massive Craters Replace Homes of 3,000 in Area [sic] III," *DP*, 30 October 1968, UARC Collection. The Rev. Edward Sims claimed that fifty-two hundred were displaced, a figure entirely at odds with the 1960 Census of Housing; Sims, quoted in "Two Community Leaders Look at Their College," *College Management*, June 1969, 30. For a similar misreporting, see Richard Plunz, *Mantua Primer: Toward a Program for Environmental Change* (University Park: Department of Architecture, Pennsylvania State University, 1970), 14.

119. U.S. Bureau of the Census, Census of Housing, 1960, *Block Statistics, Philadelphia, PA* (Washington, D.C.: U.S. Government Printing Office, 1961); Census of Housing, 1970, *Block Statistics, Philadelphia, PA* (1971).

120. Young Great Society Architecture and Planning Center, *The Unit 3 Planning Charette: A Report to the University of Pennsylvania on University-Community Development*, 13 October 1969, UARC UPB101.4, box 24, folder "Quadripartite Commission 1969–70."

Chapter 4

1. "Penn Sit-In Disappoints Militants; Issues are Old, Tactics Mild," *PEB*, 23 February 1969, TUA.

2. Mark Rudd, *Underground: My Life with SDS and the Weathermen* (New York: William Morrow, 2009), 47. Rudd was the national media's poster child for student radicalism

in 1968. Detailed accounts of Columbia '68 are found in Jerry L. Avorn, *Up Against the Ivy Wall: A History of the Columbia Crisis* (New York: Atheneum, 1969); Roger Kahn, *The Battle for Morningside Heights: Why Students Rebel* (New York: William Morrow, 1970); Fact-Finding Commission on Columbia Disturbances, *Crisis at Columbia: Report of the Fact-Finding Commission Appointed to Investigate the Disturbances at Columbia University in April and May 1968* (New York: Random House, 1968). For an informed recent formulation, see Robert A. McCaughey's magisterial history *Stand, Columbia: A History of Columbia University in the City of New York, 1754–2004* (New York: Columbia University Press, 2007), 423–82. For a boldly interpretive study that situates the Columbia imbroglio in the contexts of American liberalism, modernist architecture, and postwar city planning, see Michael H. Carriere, "Being and Becoming: On Architecture, Student Protest, and the Aesthetics of Liberalism in Postwar America" (PhD diss., University of Chicago, 2010), esp. 358–99.

3. Fact-Finding Commission on Columbia Disturbances, *Crisis at Columbia*, 75.

4. John G. Terino, "In the Shadow of the Spreading Ivy: Science, Culture, and the Cold War at the University of Pennsylvania, 1950–1970" (PhD diss., University of Pennsylvania, 2001), 196.

5. Jonathan Goldstein, "Vietnam Research on Campus: The Summit/Spicerack Controversy at the University of Pennsylvania, 1965–67," *Peace and Change* 11, no. 2 (1986): 31.

6. Candace Bergen, "My College Months," *PAG*, May 1984, 22, excerpted from Bergen's autobiography, *Knock Wood* (New York: Simon & Schuster, 1984).

7. Paul Lyons, *The People of This Generation: The Rise and Fall of the New Left in Philadelphia* (Philadelphia: University of Pennsylvania Press, 2003), 106–7.

8. Ibid., 22–23.

9. "This Is the Way a Controversy Began . . ." *PAG*, February 1966, 13–15. SOS was probably "the first mass movement on any American campus to focus on matters of architecture and esthetics. . . . The issues raised by the SOS committee were . . . How does the campus articulate with the city? What face does it present at its entrances and borders?" Arthur M. Shapiro, letter to editor, *PAG*, November–December 1999, 6.

10. Charles H. MacNamara, "Penn's Brick Country Town" (reprint from *Philadelphia Magazine*), *PAG*, March 1967, 13–17.

11. Elyse D. Sudow, "Displacement Demonized? Towards an Alternative Explanation for Penn's Poor Relationship with West Philadelphia" (Senior honors thesis, University of Pennsylvania, 1999), 23–40.

12. Harnwell quoted in "The Year in Review," *PAG*, December 1965, 14.

13. Lyons, *People of This Generation*, 120–21.

14. Robert A. Gross, "A Student Editor Comments n the 'New Penn Student,'" *PAG*, June 1966, 26.

15. Goldstein, "Vietnam Research on Campus," quotes Krieger as saying that Spicerack scientists were involved in "developing delivery systems" for toxic chemicals and defoliants in Vietnam (32–33), though Goldstein fails to provide a source for this quote. (Goldstein is a former member of Penn SDS.) Krieger told Jeannette Nichols, "We . . . were not involved in anything to do with the Vietnam War except for one project on which we spent about two weeks out of fifteen years which had to do with defoliation. Now everybody thought we were working on the Vietnam War but we weren't." See Knut Krieger, interview by Jeannette P. Nichols, 13 June 1974, UARC UPP1, box 2, folder "Krieger."

16. Goldstein, "Vietnam Research on Campus," quote from 42; also see "A Season's Discontent over Classified Research," *PAG*, April 1967, 13–16; "Penn Trustees Vote to Abolish

'Spice Rack,'" *PEB*, 5 May 1967, TUA. For Mather, see and cf. "Militant Group Plans Attack on Science Center," *PI*, 6 October 1968, TUA.

17. Lyons, *People of This Generation*, 135. Consistent with his tendency to inflate the impact of the New Left in 1960s Philadelphia, Lyons, viewing the April 1967 action in New York, cites the participation of some 1,480 Philadelphia-area activists from fifteen organizations, including students from Penn, Temple, and Swarthmore, as evidence of a prairie fire of New Left radicalism.

18. "Protesters Sit in Recruitment Centers," *DP*, 2 November 1967, UARC.

19. "CIA, Dow to Continue Interviews," *DP*, 2 November 1967, UARC.

20. "Dow Co. Recruitment at the University Voluntarily Canceled," *DP*, 7 November 1968, UARC.

21. Gaylord P. Harnwell, "The Quiet Revolution," *PAG*, January–February 1968, 1–21; Rudd, *Underground*, 7. Students organized the Community Involvement Council in 1965 as a clearinghouse for community service volunteers; it soon merged with the Tutorial Board, another student service organization, creating two chairs: one for tutoring projects, the other for community projects. The service ranged from tutoring schoolchildren to working in a hospital emergency room, to helping out at the Youth Study Center (youth detention). In 1967, the Community Involvement Council coordinated a total of thirty-seven projects, most of which were located in West Philadelphia. See "CIC," *PAG*, September 1967, 11–17, 74–76.

22. Judith Ann Fowler, "Six Days in College Hall: 'A Strange War in Which Both Sides Won,'" *PAG*, March 1969, 8–9.

23. Ibid, 9–10. For the guidelines for protest behavior, see "The Mundheim Report on Open Expression and Demonstration on Campus," *DP*, 10 September 1968; Robert H. Mundheim, interview by Jeannette P. Nichols, 22 December 1975, UARC UPP1, box 3, "Mundheim folder."

24. "Penn Sit-In Disappoints Militants."

25. Burns, interview by Nichols.

26. Lyons, *People of This Generation*, 210–16, quoted phrase from 213.

27. Kirkpatrick Sale, *SDS* (New York: Random House, 1973), 514.

28. Walter Palmer, interview no. 2 by John Puckett, 7 April 2010; Ira Harkavy, interview no. 2 by John Puckett, 3 March 2010.

29. Harkavy quoted in Fowler, "Six Days in College Hall," 14; other quotes from 13–14.

30. "Penn Sit-In Disappoints Militants."

31. Fowler, "Six Days in College Hall," 14.

32. "A History of the University City Science Center," with appendixes 1–4, undated [November 1967?], UARC UPB101.4, box 23, folder "Science Center 68–69"; "Report of the Senate Advisory Committee on the February, 1969, 'Sit-In,' University of Pennsylvania," UARC UPA4, box 322, folder 9; Fowler, "Six Days in College Hall."

33. Gaylord P. Harnwell to Jean Paul Mather, 21 February 1969, UARC UPB101.4, box 23, folder "Science Center 68–69"; "Report of the Senate Advisory Committee," 7–8.

34. See Kelly Moore, "Political Protest and Institutional Change: The Anti-Vietnam War Movement and American Science," in *How Social Movements Matter*, ed. Marco Giugni, Doug McAdam, and Charles Tilly (Minneapolis: University of Minnesota Press, 1999), 97–118; E. David Cronon and John W. Jenkins, *The University of Wisconsin: A History, 1945–1971*, vol. 4: *Renewal to Revolution* (Madison: University of Wisconsin Press, 1999), 447–520; Cox et al., *Crisis at Columbia*, esp. 72–73.

35. The phrase "less adventuresome" was Robert Mundheim's; interview by Nichols.

36. See and cf. Lyons, *People of This Generation*, 11–13.

37. The quote is from Robert Trescher, interview by Jeannette P. Nichols, 8 April 1971, UARC UPP1, box 3, folder "Trescher." Also see in same series, William L. Day, interviews by Jeannette Nichols, 22 September 1971, 17 January 1972, box 1, folder "Day;" John A. [Jack] Russell, Jr., vice provost for student affairs, 10 September 1971, UARC UPP1, box 3, folder "Russell."

38. Michael Zuckerman, a student in the College in the late 1950s who returned to Penn as an assistant professor of history in 1965, says that before the sit-in he considered Gaylord Harnwell "just your stock academic from central casting, with no juice, no verve, and nothing to captivate the student—the anti-Judy Rodin." Zuckerman changed his opinion after the sit-in. "When things began to explode in the '60s and Penn got through those explosions much better than Columbia or Berkeley or Harvard or Cornell or all the places that had catastrophes, I said to somebody who I had thought was knowledgeable and wise in these things, 'How could this have happened with this nonentity, this absent president at the helm?' And somebody, I can't remember who, said, 'Do you think these things happen by accident? There's leadership there. And he may not be strutting and he may not be parading but he's the guy who's controlling all this.' It riveted me; it really astonished me to think that this guy might be competent. It never dawned on me that he was anything but a figurehead and a placeholder, and as I think back on it there were other changes that began in his administration that were really gutsy. . . . So I'm sure I underestimated the man enormously." Interview by Puckett and Lloyd, 1 February 2010.

39. Quoted in Fowler, "Six Days in College Hall," 14–15.

40. Quoted in Lyons, *People of This Generation*, 212, 215.

41. Jonathan R. Cole, *The Great American University: Its Rise to Preeminence, Its Indispensable National Role, Why It Must Be Protected* (New York: Public Affairs, 2009), 151.

42. "Report of the Senate Advisory Committee," 16–17.

43. Ibid., 18.

44. Russell Ackoff to Andrew Jenkins, 13 August 1969, UARC UPA 4, box 322, folder 5.

45. L. Lorenzo Graham, "Statement," n.d., UARC UPA 4, box 322, folder 5.

46. Francis M. Betts, "University of Pennsylvania Study Paper on Community Development," typescript (second draft), 26 February 1970, UARC UPA 4, box 322, folder 5.

47. Francis M. Betts, III, to Andrew Wolfe, Esq., 27 October 1970, UPA 4, box 322, folder 6; in same folder: Russell Ackoff to Martin Meyerson, memorandum, 17 September 1970.

48. William Day to Martin Meyerson, 29 October 1970, UARC UPA, box 322, folder 6; in folder 7: John W. Eckman to Edward R. Thornton, Department of Chemistry, 4 February 1971.

49. "Quadripartite Commission Temporarily 'Inactivates,'" *DP*, 27 October 1972; "1970–71," *DP*, 5 May 1971, UARC.

50. *PEB* articles, TUA: "Penn Refuses Students' Request for Flag at Half-Staff; Hauls It Down," 21 October 1969; "Penn Lowers Flag; Vets Want It Raised," 22 October 1969; "Shafer Refuses to Act in Penn Flag Dispute," 22 October 1969; "Penn to Fly Flag Again—at Full Staff," 23 October 1969; "Penn Council Orders Flag at Full Staff," 31 October 1969; "Peace Symbol Dedicated on U of P Quadrangle," 28 January 1970.

51. Berle Schwartz, "Strike!" *PAG*, May 1970, 6–10, 36–37. Also see "Nation Reacts to Intervention in Cambodia," *DP*, 4 May 1970.

52. For these developments, see Mackenzie S. Carlson, *"Come to Where the Knowledge Is": A History of the University City Science Center* (Philadelphia: UPA UARC, 1999), accessed at http://www.archives.upenn.edu/histy/features/upwphil/ucsc.html, September 9, 2004, part 4; Mary Ann Meyers to Paul F. Miller, memorandum re: "Financing for the University City Science Center's World Forum," 2 April 1985, UARC UPA 4, box 476, folder 18.

53. Peter Binzen, "Harnwell Era: Time of Dramatic Change," *PEB*, 17 May 1970, UARC UPT50H289, box 7, folder 7.

54. David Osborne, *Laboratories of Democracy* (Boston: Harvard Business School Press, 1988), quote from 274; UCSC, *Master Plan* (Philadelphia: Author, 1988), courtesy UCSC.

55. University City Science Center, *UCSC: Twenty Years at the Science Center, 1964–1984* (Philadelphia: UCSC, 1984), UARC UPA4, box 475, folder 22.

56. Ibid.; UCSC, *Annual Report* (Philadelphia: Author, 1988), UCSC, *Master Plan*; UCSC, *Corporate Monthly*, supplement, 1–23; courtesy UCSC.

57. Quote from Gaylord P. Harnwell, "The World's Problems Have Become the University's Problems," *PAG*, December 1966, 24.

58. Conclusion drawn from authors' review of UCSC board and executive committee minutes, 1963–1989; seven boxes on loan from UCSC to UARC, November 2013–May 2014. We acknowledge that a careful scrutiny of the Science Center's records for the period 1989–2014 may reveal a more optimistic portrait than the one that emerges from the first quarter century of its operations. At this writing, we did not have access to these records.

59. Margaret Pugh O'Mara, *Cities of Knowledge: Cold War Science and the Search for the Next Silicon Valley* (Princeton, N.J.: Princeton University Press, 2005), 179–80; WPC, "18th Police District Crime Prevention Project," UARC UPA4, box 256, folder 15.

60. O'Mara, *Cities of Knowledge*, 179–80.

61. Zuckerman, interview by Lloyd and Puckett.

62. Kirk R. Petshek, *The Challenge of Urban Reform: Policies and Programs in Philadelphia* (Philadelphia: Temple University Press, 1973), 253.

63. Samuel Hughes, "The West Philadelphia Story," *PAG*, November 1997, http://www.upenn.edu/gazette/1197/philly.html. For a contemporary perspective, see and cf. John Marchese, "Is West Philly the Next Center City?" *Philadelphia Magazine*, http://www.phillymag.com, posted 3 December 2010.

Chapter 5

1. UPA, *Financial Reports*, FY 1969, pp. 6–7; FY 1970, pp. 6, 17, UARC. Also see William L. Day (trustee chair), "Some Realities in University Management," *Almanac* 19, no. 17 (January 19, 1973): 2–3.

2. GPH, *Annual Report*, 1969–70, Harnwell Papers, UARC T50H289, box 6, folder 29.

3. Roger L. Geiger, *Research and Relevant Knowledge: American Universities since World War II* (New York: Oxford University Press, 1993), 202.

4. Ellen James, "Pennsylvania's Next President," *PAG*, February 1970, quoted on 8.

5. *Minutes of the Trustees of the University of Pennsylvania*, vol. 33, 5 November 1969, 31; 19 December 1969, 56; 16 January 1970, 81; UARC. Several other candidates ranked higher than Meyerson on the November list also declined further consideration by the trustees.

6. Eugenie L. Birch, "Making Urban Research Intellectually Respectable: Martin Meyerson and the Joint Center for Urban Studies of Massachusetts Institute of Technology and Harvard University 1959–1964," *Journal of Planning History* 10, no. 3 (2011): 219–38.

7. Ibid., quotes from 219, 221.

8. Michael B. Teiz, "Martin Meyerson: Builder of Institutions," *Journal of Planning History* 10, no. 3 (2011): 180–92.

9. Kenneth J. Heineman, *Campus Wars: The Peace Movement at American State Public Universities in the Vietnam Era* (New York: New York University Press, 1993), 31–35.

10. Ibid., 31, 33, 173–75.

11. Ibid., 210–217, quote from 267.

12. Martin Meyerson, *The University of Pennsylvania in Its Twenty-Fourth Decade, 1970–1980* (Philadelphia: University of Pennsylvania, 1981), n.p., VPL.

13. Ibid.

14. University Development Commission, *Pennsylvania: One University, Almanac Supplement*, 29 January 1973, 1.

15. Ibid., 2.

16. Meyerson, *University of Pennsylvania in Twenty-Fourth Decade*, n.p.

17. University Development Commission, *One University*, 18.

18. Ibid., 2; also see in same report, "Minority Statement of Robert W. Naison," 32–33.

19. William W. Brickman, *Pedagogy, Professionalism, and Policy: History of the Graduate School of Education at the University of Pennsylvania* (Philadelphia: Graduate School of Education, University of Pennsylvania, 1986), 210–12.

20. Neal Gross to John N. Hobstetter, with encl.: "The Graduate School of Education: An Overview and Some Thoughts About Its Future," 5 October 1973, UARC UPA6.4, box 53, folder 28.

21. Earling E. Boe, "Selective Excellence and Financial Exigency: What Precedent Will Be Established?," report to University Council, 19 March 1975, printed in *Almanac* 21, no. 26 (1975): 3–5; in same issue: AAUP, "Statement Concerning the Situation Affecting the Graduate School of Education," 2.

22. Brickman, *Pedagogy, Professionalism, and Policy*, 213–14.

23. Cf. James E. Davis (executive assistant to the provost), typescript copy of letter to editor of *DP*, 26 April 1978. Davis maintains that Stellar never intended to close the GSE, only to downsize it. Also see "President Meyerson: Achievements of the Seventies," *Almanac* 24, no. 28 (18 April 1978): n.p.

24. "Undergraduate Education in the Health Professions at Pennsylvania" (appendix 7), n.d., [February 1976], UARC UPA4, box 286, folder 19.

25. "85 Student Organizations Support SAMP," advertisement paid by Executive Board of University of Pennsylvania Student Occupational Therapy Association, signed 5 November 1976, *DP*, 10 November 1976, clipping, UARC UPA4, box 286, folder 12; protest letters in SAMP folders 10–18, UARC UPA4, Box 286; "Penn Trustees Move to Phase Out SAMP," *PAG*, February 1977, 10–11.

26. "Council: SAMP Vote: 37–11," *Almanac* 23, no. 12 (16 November 1976): 1; in same issue: "Resolution on SAMP," 3; "Senate on SAMP: Upgrade It," *Almanac* 23, no. 14 (7 December 1976): 1–2.

27. Vartan Gregorian, *The Road to Home: My Life and Times* (New York: Simon & Schuster, 2003), 239; "Trustees: SAMP Resolution," adopted 14 January 1977, *Almanac* 23, no. 17 (18 January 1977): 1.

28. Gregorian, *Road to Home*, 218–223, quote from 223. A 1982 merger formed the School of Arts and Sciences.

29. Meyerson, *University of Pennsylvania in Twenty-Fourth Decade*, n.p.

30. Gregorian, *Road to Home*, 226; "Program for the Eighties: $255 Million for the University of Pennsylvania," *Almanac* 22, 7 (7 October 1975): 1–3.

31. Meyerson, *University of Pennsylvania in Twenty-Fourth Decade*, n.p.

32. Sir Peter Shepheard, "The Spaces Between," *Almanac* 27, no. 7 (7 October 1980); Center for Environmental Design, Graduate School of Fine Arts, *Landscape Development Plan* (University of Pennsylvania, 1977), UARC JPJ9.4, box 59, folder "Facilities Planning E16."

33. George E. Thomas and David Brownlee, *Building America's First University: An Historical and Architectural Guide to the University of Pennsylvania* (Philadelphia: University of Pennsylvania Press, 2000), 122.

34. UPA News Bureau, press release, 10 June 1977, UARC Collections; Thomas and Brownlee, *Building America's First University*, 52–55, 72–74; "Gazetteer," *PAG*, October 1979, 20.

35. UPA, *Financial Reports*, FY 1976, p. 7, UARC.

36. UPA, *Financial Reports*, FY 1974, p. 6.

37. Meyerson, *University of Pennsylvania in Twenty-Fourth Decade*, n.p.

38. UPA, *Financial Reports*, FY 1976, p. 7.

39. Jon Strauss and John R. Curry, *Responsibility Center Management: 25 Years of Lessons Learned* (Washington, D.C.: National Association of College and University Business Officers, 2002), 2–3.

40. Gregorian, *Road to Home*, 227.

41. Martin Meyerson, "The State of the University," report to the trustees, January 1973, *Almanac Supplement*, 6 March 1973, 3.

42. Gregorian, *Road to Home*, 227.

43. Robert Zemsky, interview by Jeanette P. Nichols, 4 January 1973, UARC UPP1, box 4, folder "Zemsky."

44. Neal Gross, "Perspectives on Strengthening the Organizational Capabilities of the University of Pennsylvania: A Report of the Findings of a Small-Scale Inquiry," 22 March 1974, UARC UPA4.6, box 3, folder 9.

45. Faculty Senate Subcommittee on Students and Education Policy, "Making Penn the Undergraduate University of Choice in the 21st Century," *Almanac* 42, no. 28 (16 April 1996): 4–5. From the mid-1970s on, the home school received 10 percent, the teaching school 90 percent of an undergraduate student's tuition; that ratio was later changed to 20/80. No split arrangement existed for graduate or professional education until 2004, when a 20/80 ratio was introduced. Bonnie Gibson (vice president, budget and management analysis), personal communication, 1 July 2008.

Chapter 6

1. Robert A. Rhoads, *Freedom's Web: Student Activism in an Age of Cultural Diversity* (Baltimore: Johns Hopkins University Press, 1998), 54. In his meticulous study of the decade's collegiate culture, *When Dreams and Heroes Died: A Portrait of Today's College Student* (San Francisco: Jossey-Bass, 1980), Arthur Levine reports "an ethic of 'looking out for number one' and an almost single-minded concern with material success" (xvii).

2. John H. Pryor, Sylvia Hurtado, Victor B. Saenz, José Luis Santos, and Williams S. Korn, *The American Freshman: Forty Year Trends, 1966–2006* (Los Angeles: Cooperative Institutional Research Program, Higher Education Research Institute, University of California, Los Angeles), vii.

3. Ibid., 72.

4. Wayne Glasker, *Black Students in the Ivory Tower: African American Student Activism at the University of Pennsylvania, 1967–1990* (Amherst: University of Massachusetts Press, 2002), 3, quote from 29.

5. Glasker, *Black Students in the Ivory Tower*, 12–15, 34–36, 38–39; in sequence, quotes from 34, 36, 13

6. George A. Schlekat to Gaylord P. Harnwell and David Goddard, memorandum, 24 April 1969, UARC UPA4, box 231, folder 10; in same folder, "Admissions Committee Meeting, 30

April 1969"; West Philadelphia Community Advisory Board to Gaylord P. Harnwell, 9 May 1969.

7. Glasker, *Black Students in the Ivory Tower*, 88–91, quote from 89. See also "Black Center Organized and Council Weighs Black Studies," *Almanac* 16, no. 1 (September 1969): 1, 5.

8. Ibid., 92–95, quote from 94.

9. Ellen James, "What Kind of Orientation for Black Freshmen?" *PAG*, May 1970, 14–15; black students' "Press Statement," 16 April 1970, UARC UPA 4, box 231, folder 11.

10. "Summary of Events: Saturday, April 25, 1970," UARC UPA 4, box 231, folder 13.

11. The *DP* provided detailed reports on the progress of the trial; available in UARC and Van Pelt Library microform collections. Also see documents in UARC UPA 4, box 231, folder 13.

12. Glasker, *Black Students in the Ivory Tower*, 84–85.

13. http://dubois.house.upenn.edu/house_history.html, accessed 7 May 2008.

14. Martin Meyerson, "In Pursuit of Sharpened Goals," *PAG*, February 1972, 8–15; Margo Marshall, "Questions and Answers on Living-Learning Programs," *Almanac* 19, no. 27 (13 March 1973): 3–6.

15. "The Dorm Transformed," *PAG*, September 1999, excerpted, http://www.upenn.edu/gazette/0999/lonkevich4.html, accessed 7 May 2008. As president of SUNY Buffalo, Meyerson introduced six college houses. At Penn he embraced the idea as both a One University strategy and an efficiency measure in hard times. Martin Meyerson interview, Faculty Senate Oral History Project Records.

16. Glasker, *Black Students in the Ivory Tower*, 116, quoting from "Black Residence Center Announced," *Almanac* 18, no 27 (14 March 1972): 1.

17. Ibid., 122–28, quoting from "Black Residence Center Announced" and "University Gives Final Approval to Plan for Black Residential Center," *DP*, 7 April 1972, 1, 5.

18. See Jerome Karabel, *The Chosen: The Hidden History of Admission and Exclusion at Harvard, Yale, and Princeton* (New York: Houghton Mifflin/Mariner Books, 2006), chap. 13. Karabel writes, "For the 15 colleges that made up the Ivy League and the Seven Sisters, the number of blacks admitted more than doubled between 1967 and 1968—a remarkable increase for a single year and even higher than the rate of increase at Yale, which had mounted a vigorous effort to recruit African Americans earlier than most of its sister institutions" (638n72). In 1969–70, the Ivy League average for black freshman enrollments was 7.6 percent, with Dartmouth the highest at 10.6 percent, Cornell the lowest at 4.6 percent. Calculated from "Trinity College, 1969–70: Comparison of Black Freshmen Enrolled in Various Colleges," George A. Schlekat to GPH, attachment, 27 August 1969, UARC UPA 4, box 231, folder 10.

19. University Development Commission, *One University*, 17.

20. "Report of the Task Force on Black Presence," *Almanac* 24, no. 24 (21 March 1978): 9–19.

21. Office of Undergraduate Admissions, "Black Freshmen Enrollment, 1972–1975," 24 November 1975, UARC UPA 6.4, box 19, folder 12. Extant data for Meyerson-era graduate and professional enrollments are scarce: a report of 1973 shows only 338 blacks in the fall of 1972, 4 percent of a total of 8,638 students in these categories; calculated from "Black Presence Funding Report," typescript draft, 11 December 1973, UARC UPA 6.4, box 19, folder 10. Data for Mexican American, Puerto Rican, and other Spanish-speaking enrollments are also lacking: one report shows sixteen such matriculants in 1973, twenty-six in 1974. Office of Undergraduate Admissions, "Minority Recruitment Program: Spanish-American Summary 1973 and 1974," n.d. [1974], UARC UPA 6.4, box 3, folder 25.

22. "Task Force on Black Presence," 13; *The Affirmative Action Program of the University of Pennsylvania*, *Almanac Supplement*, 17 February 1976.

23. Minority Presence Retrospective Review Committee, *Minority Permanence at the University of Pennsylvania*, October 1992, p. 10, percentages calculated from Appendix I; http://www.archives.upenn.edu/primdocs/upf/upf8_5/upf8_5s_b159f13minoritypermrep 1992.pdf, accessed 9 May 2008.

24. Donald C. Shultis, "Safety, Security and the University," *Almanac* 18, no. 18 (11 January 1972): 4–6. Urban America in the 1970s was marked by escalating criminal violence. Rates for violent crime per 100,000 increased from 200.2 in 1965, to 365 in 1970, to 596.6 in 1980; Michael B. Katz, in *Why Don't American Cities Burn?* (Philadelphia: University of Pennsylvania Press, 2012), 92.

25. Robert H. Dyson, Jr., "Interim Report on Security Measures," 10 February 1970, UARC UPA 4, box 311, folder 4.

26. Henry J. Abraham to Martin Meyerson, 16 April 1971, UARC UPA 4, box 311, folder 7.

27. "Coeds Find Rape Is Fact of City Life," *PEB*, 8 April 1973.

28. "Women Plan College Hall Protest; Meetings, Sit-in Set for Tuesday," *DP*, 2 April 1973. By March 1973, the University's in-house count was a total of fourteen rapes and two attempted rapes; eleven Penn women and two University hospital student nurses were raped. Robert F. Coryell to Martin Meyerson and Eliot Stellar, "confidential" memorandum, 5 April 1973, UARC UPA 4.6, box 83, folder 16.

29. "Women Demand, Get Better Protection Against Rape," *PAG*, May 1973, 9–10.

30. John Prendergast, "Places: Alumni Talk About the Struggles to Establish Resources for African Americans, Women, and Sexual Minorities on Campus," *PAG,* November–December 2002, http://www.upenn.edu/gazette/1102/prendergast2.htlm, accessed 21 December 2005.

31. "Security: More Than a Warm Blanket," *Almanac* 26, no. 18 (20 December 1979): 3.

32. Committee on the Status of Women, "Women Faculty in the University of Pennsylvania: Part One," *Almanac* 17, no. 6 (13 April 1971): 4–5. In such reports the University used the term *fully-affiliated faculty* for these positions, compared to the term *standing faculty* presently in use.

33. "A Report on the University of Pennsylvania Affirmative Action Program," *Almanac Supplement*, 9 October 1973.

34. "President Meyerson: Achievements of the Seventies," *Almanac* 24, no. 28 (18 April 1978): n.p; Martin Meyerson, "State of the University: Perspectives on 1978," address to the trustees, 19 January 1979, *Almanac* 25, no. 26 (27 March 1979): 3–13.

35. Davida Hopkins Ramey, "Women Among Full-Time Faculty of the University (1973–82)," *Almanac* 29, no. 29 (19 April 1983): 2–3; "A Day with Some Involved Penn Women Who Mean Business," *PAG*, May 1989, 11–13. A women's studies program originated in the "short-lived" College of Thematic Studies in 1973, then stood on its own as a program in the College of Arts and Sciences, in the words of one of its directors, as "a kind of conscience and voice for women and feminist theory and issues of gender"; the program was granted the status of a major in the College in April of 1986, when twenty-one women held full professorships in Arts and Sciences disciplines. Marshall Ledger, "Bringing History Up to Date," *PAG*, May 1986, 16–22, quote from 22.

36. Quotes from UPA, *Financial Reports*, FY 1976, p. 7.

37. UPA, *Financial Reports*, FY 1980.

38. See and cf. Meyerson, *University of Pennsylvania in Twenty-Fourth Decade*, n.p. From 1971–72 to 1974–75, Penn's federally funded basic research increased over 40 percent, compared to 23 percent nationwide. Martin Meyerson, "The University of Pennsylvania: A Five-Year Review," *Almanac Supplement*, 16 April 1976, 7. Cf. the 3 percent increase for federally sponsored academic research, 1967–1976, reported in Hugh Davis Graham and Nancy

Diamond, *American Research Universities: Elites and Challengers in the Postwar Era* (Baltimore: Johns Hopkins University Press, 1997), 91–92.

39. Berl Schwartz, "Meanwhile, Back in the Community of Scholars," *PAG*, December 1971, 31–35; UPA News Bureau, fact sheet, 10 May 1971, UARC UPA6.4, box 85, folder 1, "On Open Expression: A Statement by President Meyerson," 14 May 1971, UARC UPA6.4, box 85, folder 7.

40. "Officials Hope for Normalcy Despite Union Workers Walkout," *DP*, 16 October 1975; "Union Strike Causes Campus Inconvenience," *DP*, 17 October 1975; "U. Obtains Injunction to Limit Union Pickets; Trash Problem Grows," *DP*, 21 October 1975; "Two Striking Workers Arrested for Weekend Acts of Vandalism," *DP*, 3 November 1975; "Library, Dining, Service Workers to Cross Picket Lines Today," *DP*, 10 November 1975; "Violent Incidents Mark Fourth Strike Weekend," *DP*, 10 November 1975; "U, Local 835 Reach Tentative Settlement," *DP*, 26 November 1975; "Sign of the Times: Solidarity Crumbles in Penn Strike," *PI*, 26 November 1975.

41. Martin Meyerson, edited typescript draft, 4 December 1977, UARC UPA4, box 308, folder 12. See also Fred Shabel to George Budd et al., memorandum, 10 August 1977, UARC UPA6.4, box 85, folder 4.

42. Gerald L. Robinson, open letter, *Almanac* 24, no. 10 (8 November 1977): 2.

43. Paul O. Gaddis to members of the Finance and Operations Committee of the trustees, memorandum, 11 August 1977, UARC UPA4, box 308, folder 12; Gerald L. Robinson to the editor, *DP*, 21 October 1977.

44. "Court Tries to Cool the Picketing at Penn," *PEB*, 18 August 1977, clipping, UARC UPA6.4, box 85, folder 4. See also Office of the Director, Department of Physical Plant, to Members of the Housekeeping Staff, 4 August 1977, UARC UPA6.4, box 85, folder 4.

45. "Senate Votes 45–2 for $17 Million Bill," *DP*, 14 December 1977; Martin Meyerson, "A Statement from the University of Pennsylvania on Labor Relations and the State Appropriation," advertisement sponsored and paid for by alumni and friends of the University of Pennsylvania, *PI*, 26 October 1977; Martin Meyerson, open letter to alumni and friends of the University, 1 November 1977, UARC UPA6.4, box 85, folder 6.

46. "Truckin' on Down Walnut Street," *PAG*, December 1977, 11.

47. "University Appropriation Voted," *Almanac* 24, no. 14 (13 December 1977): 1; UPA *Financial Reports*, FY 1978, p. 9.

48. On the "larger public" and the problem of "little publics," see Walter C. Parker, "Advanced Ideas About Democracy: Toward a Pluralist Conception of Citizenship," *Teachers College Record* 98, no. 1 (1996): 104–25.

49. See Levine, *When Dreams and Heroes Died*, prepared for the Carnegie Council on Higher Education; Rhoads, *Freedom's Web*, 54–58.

50. For the People's Park convulsion at Berkeley, see William J. McGill, *The Year of the Monkey: Revolt on Campus, 1968–1969* (New York: McGraw Hill, 1982), 154–94; W. J. Rorabaugh, *Berkeley at War: The 1960s* (New York: Oxford University Press, 1989), 155–65; Godfrey Hodgson, *America in Our Time: From World War II to Nixon; What Happened and Why* (New York: Vintage, 1976), 288–305.

51. Lori Steuer, "The Planting, Growth and Flowering of the Penn Community Park: An Epic in Ecological Activism," *Columns: The University of Pennsylvania Magazine of Current Affairs*, April 1973, 8–14. For the plat, see Penn Community Park Coalition and University of Pennsylvania, "A Proposal to the Fidelity Bank for Support of the Penn Community Park," May 1973, UARC UPA4, box 256, folder 1.

52. "'People's Park': An Unrealized Dream," *DP*, 1 July 1981.

53.   "Demonstrators Sit-in at Meyerson's Office, Sleep in College Hall," *DP*, 28 March 1972; "Rising Tuitions Spur New Campus Protests," *PEB*, 3 April 1972. The last Penn antiwar sit-in was in April 1972, when students protesting Nixon's renewed bombing of North Vietnam barricaded themselves inside College Hall for two days, then peacefully vacated the building under a court order—in sharp contrast to the violence that erupted at Berkeley, Columbia, Wisconsin, and Maryland. See "300 End Sit-In at Penn after Sheriff Reads Writ," *PEB*, 28 April 1972, clipping, UARC UPA6.4, box 83, folder 11; folder 12: "Coercion Can't be Condoned, Especially at the University," *PI*, editorial, 1 May 1972; "Protests Erupt on Campuses: Some Violence," *PEB*, 9 May 1972; folder 13: "Gas, Bombs and Fireworks Hurled in Maryland University War Protest," *PEB*, 20 April 1972; "9 College Heads Deplore Bombing," *New York Times*, 20 April 1972.

54.   "A Protest at Penn," *PI*, 3 March 1978. Levine, in *When Dreams and Heroes Died*, labels such concerns "me-oriented campus issues," which he finds were the dominant protest issues in 1978 (39–40). Levine's 1980 study was based on data compiled from four Carnegie Surveys and the annual surveys of the Laboratory for Research in Higher Education at the University of California, Los Angeles.

55.   "Comprehensive Settlement Ends Student Sit-In," *Almanac* 24, no. 23 (7 March 1978): 1, 3; Vartan Gregorian, *The Road to Home: My Life and Times* (New York: Simon & Schuster, 2003), 236–38; Glasker, *Black Students in the Ivory Tower*, 150–54.

56.   Irving Kravis, "Statement from the Faculty Senate Chairman," *Almanac* 24, no. 23 (7 March 1978): 4.

57.   Gregorian, *Road to Home*, 239–40; Martin Meyerson, "President Meyerson's Statement to Faculty," *Almanac* 24, no. 27 (11 April 1978): 1.

58.   "Relations Between Faculty and Administration Strained," *PAG*, May 1978, 10–11. Meyerson agreed that "our machinery of governance has not been working as it ought"; "Faculty Senate Votes to Establish Review Panel," *Almanac* 24, no. 30 (2 May 1978): 1–2.

59.   "Provost Stellar Announces Retirement" (Eliot Stellar to Martin Meyerson, 20 April 1978), *Almanac* 24, no. 29 (24 April 1978): 1–3; "President to Leave Post in 1980–81," *Almanac* 25, no. 3 (12 September 1978): 1; "Report of the Faculty Panel on the Administrative Functioning of the University," *Almanac* 25, no. 7 (10 October 1978): 2–4; Gregorian, *Road to Home*, 242. Paul Miller says that "after talking with several senior trustees," he counseled Meyerson, whom he regarded highly, to retire: "As I remember, that meeting was late in the 1979 academic year. Martin did not take kindly to the suggestion and it was only after several conversations with him that we came to a semblance of agreement that he would step aside"; Paul F. Miller, Jr., *Better Than Any Dream: A Personal Memoir* (Conshohocken, Pa., self published, 2006) 160.

60.   Regan, the CEO of Merrill Lynch, a Harvard graduate with strong Philadelphia ties, chaired the Penn board from 1974 to 1978. "Don was a very busy executive who, by my observation, did not put Penn at the front of his 'to do' list," recalls Miller in *Better Than Any Dream*. "A nice and able guy, [a] former marine corps officer, he always seemed to me to be still commanding his troops. He had no sense of Penn's traditions and culture, and it showed. By 1978, he was ready to leave the chairmanship. Not only was he now in New York but also he was becoming interested in working on the possibility of Ronald Reagan's running for the presidency" (158). Regan became Reagan's treasury secretary, 1981–85, and his chief of staff, 1985–87.

61.   Gregorian, *Road to Home*, 242–63, quote from 249.

62.   Gregorian, *Road to Home*, 242–63, quotes from 258–59.

63.   Institute for Corean-American Studies, "Martin Meyerson: Biographic Sketch," http://www.icasinc.org/bios/meyerson.html, accessed 28 May 2008; "Death of President Emeritus

Martin Meyerson, 1922–2007," *Almanac* 54, no. 1 (17 July 2007), http://www.upenn.edu /almanac/volumes/v54/no1/meyerson.html, accessed 28 May 2008).

64. Amy Gutmann, inaugural address, UPA, 15 October 2004, http://www.upenn.edu /secretary/inauguration/speech.html, accessed 28 May 2008.

65. "Making History: The Campaign for Penn," *Almanac Supplement*, 23 October 2007, http://www.upenn.edu/almanac/volumes/v54/no9/pdf_no9/penn_campaign.pdf, accessed 28 May 2008.

66. A community school is a "community problem-solving-institution": "Through the school's curriculum and community program [e.g., school-based or school-linked health and social services, youth development, adult education], youth and adults work together to ana- lyze the problems of the community, research and formulate solutions to those problems, and mobilize resources and support for putting solutions into action. The community school is cosmopolitan in the sense that community problems are always treated as local manifesta- tions of broader societal or global problems." Michael C. Johanek and John L. Puckett, *Leon- ard Covello and the Making of Benjamin Franklin High School: Education as if Citizenship Mattered* (Philadelphia: Temple University Press, 2007), 10–11; also see chap. 1, 8. University- assisted community schools have been a goal of Netter Center organizers since 1989.

67. Lee Benson, Ira Harkavy, and John Puckett, *Dewey's Dream: Universities and Democ- racies in an Age of Education Reform* (Philadelphia: Temple University Press, 2007), 99–103.

Chapter 7

1. Sheldon Hackney, *The Politics of Presidential Appointment: A Memoir of the Culture War* (Montgomery, Ala.: NewSouth, 2002), 39–47. For Lucy Hackney, see "On a Children's Crusade," *DP*, 24 March 1993.

2. "University of Pennsylvania Picks Hackney of Tulane as President," *NYT*, 25 October 1980; Marshall Ledger, "A President at Ease," *PAG*, December 1980, 16–19.

3. "An 'Accidental' Leader," *DP*, 21 October 1981.

4. Paul F. Miller, Jr., *Better Than Any Dream: A Personal Memoir* (Conshohocken, Pa: self published, 2005), 162.

5. Michael Zuckerman, interview by Mark Lloyd and John Puckett, 1 February 2010.

6. "Hackney's New Deal: A President Searches for Acceptance," *DP*, 10 October 1981. Also see "'Accidental' Leader." Hackney could not have been pleased when Gregorian returned to Penn in the early fall of 1983. This was Gregorian's first public appearance on the campus since becoming president of the New York City Public Library. His lecture at Van Pelt Li- brary attracted about two hundred well-wishers, among them two standing deans; "For Gre- gorian, an Emotional Homecoming," *DP*, 22 September 1983. A year later, Gregorian, now in his third year in New York, bristled at Paul Miller, the trustee chair, who refused to ex- tend Gregorian's chaired professorship in the History Department, offering him instead an adjunct appointment that Gregorian called an "insult"; "Gregorian Cuts Ties with Penn in Rift over His Status," *PAG*, October 1984, 15.

7. "1981 Marks Beginning of Hackney Era," *DP*, 30 November 1989.

8. Hackney, *Politics of Presidential Appointment*, 47.

9. Sheldon Hackney, *Journals*, 16 July 1981, UARC UPT50 H123, box 34, folder 5.

10. Roger D. Simon and Brian Alnut, "Philadelphia, 1982–2007: Toward the Postindus- trial City," *Pennsylvania Magazine of History and Biography* 131, no. 4 (2007): 395.

11. Hackney himself was burglarized in the summer of his first year at Penn, when he and Lucy resided temporarily on Sansom Street. Sheldon Hackney, *Journals*, 1 July 1981, UARC UPT50 H123, box 34, folder 5.

12. On 26 November 1989, the city recorded its 445th homicide for the year, breaking a record a set in 1974, "when widespread gang violence inflated the city's death tally"; no. 445 was "an apparent murder-suicide" in a house where "there was evidence of crack use"; "Homicides Break Philadelphia Record," *Washington Times*, 28 November 1989. Also see "Crack" (two-part series), *DP*, 12, 14 October 1988.

13. "Safety in Numbers: Eyes, Ears and Telephones," *Almanac* 27, no. 15 (9 December 1980): 1; Carol E. Tracy (chair, Council on Safety and Security), "Safety on Campus and Off," *Almanac* 28, no. 10 (10 November 1981): 4–5, quote from 5.

14. "Public Safety: John Logan," *Almanac* 29, no. 26 (29 March 1983): 2.

15. Elijah Anderson, *Streetwise: Race, Class, and Change in an Urban Community* (Chicago: University of Chicago Press, 1990), chap. 3; Elijah Anderson, *Code of the Street: Decency, Violence, and the Moral Life of the Inner City* (New York: Norton, 1999), chap. 3.

16. Anderson, *Code of the Street*, 77–78.

17. See esp. "40th St. Has Violent History," *DP*, 17 April 1989, which maps the incidents; also see John Shea, "The Night Watch," *PAG*, February 1988, 39–45.

18. See "McDonald's Violates Oral Agreement," *DP*, 5 April 1989.

19. "2 Dead, 2 Hurt After Shooting on 40th Street," *DP*, 6 September 1990; Sheldon Hackney, *Journals*, 8 September 1990, UARC UPT50 H123, box 34, folder 12.

20. Anderson, *Code of the Street*, 128.

21. "Crime Wave Hits 4000 Spruce Area," *DP*, 10 October 1989.

22. "Youths Attack Students," *DP*, 12 September 1988.

23. "Shops at Penn Looted, Vandalized by Violent Pack," *DP*, 6 October 1989.

24. "6 Students Hurt by Gang on 40th St.," *DP*, 17 April 1989.

25. One of Leung's assailants received a life sentence; the other two copped pleas for lesser sentences; "Three Teens Beat Graduate Student," *DP*, 10 October 1988; "Police Arrest Three in Grad Student Attack," *DP*, 12 October 1988; "Teen Convicted in Student Murder, Sentenced to Life," *DP*, 29 November 1989.

26. "Grad Student Murdered in Campus Dorm," *DP*, 3 December 1985; "Stump Gets Life Term for Murder of Student," *DP*, 20 November 1986; "Dorm Security Straddles Line Between Protection, Oppression," *DP*, 27 February 1989. Following the Graduate Towers murder, in addition to improved signage and lighting, the Department of Public Safety assigned monitors to conduct ID checks at the four entrances to the towers. See "Report on Campus Security," *Almanac* 32, no. 23 (18 February 1986): 6–7.

27. "Investigation Continues into Friday's Rape," *DP*, 3 December 1986; "Quad Security: An Old Issue," *DP*, 9 December 1986; "Dorm Security Straddles Line Between Protection, Oppression," *DP*, 27 February 1989.

28. "Safety and Security Information Report 1989," *Almanac Supplement*, 16 October 1990, 3; "Brown Police Chief to Head U. Police Dept.," *DP*, 17 September 1990.

29. "20 Acquaintance Rapes Reported Since September," *DP*, 18 April 1990; Sheldon Hackney, Michael Aiken, Marna C. Whittington, and Kim E. Morrisson, "Acquaintance Rape," *Almanac* 37, no. 3 (11 September 1990): 1; "Report of the [University Council] Committee on Safety and Security, 1989–90," *Almanac* 37, no. 12 (13 November 1990): 4. Also see "Acquaintance Rape and Sexual Violence Policy," *Almanac* 38, no. 10 (29 (October 1991): 2. Three campus groups worked to remedy the problem: Students Together Against Acquaintance Rape, Victim Support Services, and the Women's Center.

30. "Gazetteer," *PAG*, December 1990, 21.

31. "Report of Committee on Safety and Security."

32. See Penn Faculty and Staff for Neighborhood Issues, "Priorities for Neighborhood Revitalization: Goals for the Year 2000," *Almanac* 40, no. 9 (26 October 1993): 6–10; also see F. Gerald Adams, "Safety and Community in West Philadelphia: A Proposal," *Almanac* 41, no. 9 (25 October 1994): 3. In 1994–95, the Escort Service carried more than four hundred thousand riders; "View from the Top," *PAG*, May–June 1996, 28–33.

33. "Pomp and Protest Mark Formal Inauguration of Sheldon Hackney," *PAG*, December 1981, 12. Also see "Amid Pageantry and Protests," *Almanac* 28, no. 7 (27 October 1981): 1. Hackney received criticism in some quarters for authorizing an inauguration, Penn's first in eighty-six years. The last inauguration had been Provost Harrison's in 1895 at the Philadelphia Academy of Music, a ceremony that was part of the commencement services that year. Hackney's ceremony kicked off a month of festivities marked by thirteen symposia; his graduate mentor, the historian C. Vann Woodward, was the keynote speaker at the inauguration. See "After 86 Years, Inauguration Time Again," *Almanac* 28, no. 4 (29 September 1981): 1.

34. "Racist Phone Calls Spark Hackney Condemnation," *DP*, 27 October 1981; "DuBois Receives Bomb Threat; U Police Step Up Security Force," *DP*, 28 October 1981, UARC; "A Response to Racial Intolerance," *PAG*, November 1981, sidebar, 13.

35. "Somerville Slates Rally Against Racism," *DP*, 29 October 1981; "Campaign to Fight Racism: Administrators Issue Open Letter," *DP*, 30 October 1981; "Rally Against Racism: 'A Beginning,'" *Almanac* 28, no. 9 (3 November 1981): 1.

36. "Kappa Sigma Fraternity Suspended by University," *PAG*, April 1980, 18–19; Janis I. Somerville, "Text of the Kappa Sigma Decision," 9 November 1981, *Almanac* 23, no. 11 (17 November 1981): 3; also see "Student Agrees to 'Settlement' in Slur Incident,'" *DP*, 1 October 1981; "DuBois House Aftermath Could Affect Kappa Sigma," *DP*, 4 November 1981.

37. "Parting Shots," *PAG*, March 1982, 16.

38. "Council November 11: Racism, Harassment and Related Topics," *Almanac* 23, no. 11 (17 November 1981): 1.

39. Willis J. Stetson, "Profile of the Class of 1987," *Almanac* 30, no. 4 (20 September 1983): 3–4.

40. WEOUP executive committee, "Institutional Racism," letter to editor, *Almanac* 28, no. 13 (8 December 1981): 2.

41. "Law Prof Smith Receives Tenure on Second Try," *DP*, 9 September 1982. Hackney incurred the wrath of liberal faculty and students when he refused to intervene in the Smith case—an indication of his pragmatic commitment to faculty governance and established procedure.

42. Willis J. Stetson, Jr., "The Class of 1986: Progress on Two Major Fronts," *Almanac* 29, no. 3 (September 14, 1982): 4–5.

43. Willis J. Stetson, Jr., "From a Larger Pool, Heightened Selectivity," *Almanac* 31, no. 6 (2 October 1984): 3.

44. UPA *Annual Report*, 1985, *Almanac Supplement*, 19 November 1985, quote from 3.

45. "Report of the Committee on University Responsibility to The Trustees, with Recommendations Concerning University Policy Relating to South Africa," UARC UPA 4, box 472, folder 7; "Trustee Vote Firmly Rejects Divestment," *DP*, 25 January 1982; "Trustees Sharpen Policy on Investments Involving South Africa," *PAG*, March 1982, 12–15. Also see "The Debate over South Africa Investments: A Special Report," March 1986, 19–23.

46. Trustee Committee on University Responsibility, minutes, 17 January 1984, UARC UPA 4, box 472, folder 8; "South Africa," *Almanac* 30, no. 19 (24 January 1984): 2–3; "Campus Debates: What to Do About South Africa Stock," *PAG*, December 1985, 19–25.

47. Paul F. Miller, Jr., "A Statement on South Africa," *Almanac* 32, no. 4 (17 September 1985): 2.

48. Sheldon Hackney, "Countering Apartheid," *Almanac* 32, no. 18 (14 January 1986): 4–6; for Bishop Tutu and the President's Forum, see same issue, 1.

49. "Debate over South Africa Investments."

50. "Trustees: 18 Months to Dismantle Apartheid, Then . . ." *Almanac* 32, no. 19 (21 January 1986): 1; "Trustees Decide to Consider Divesting Stock in Eighteen Months," *PAG*, February 1986, 15–16.

51. "'Divest Now' Sit-in: Sixth Day in College Hall," *Almanac* 32, no. 20 (28 January 1986): 1; notice in *Almanac* 32, no. 1 (4 February 1986); "Coalition Ends 20-Day Sit-In," *DP*, 11 February 1986. The African American trustees Leon Higginbotham and Constance Clayton published dissenting essays in the *Almanac*.

52. "Students Erect Anti-Apartheid Shanties," *DP*, 9 April 1986; "Debate over South Africa Investments." Also see "The Rise and Fall of an African Village," *PAG*, May 1986, 15.

53. Sheldon Hackney, *Journals*, 26 April 1986, UARC UPT50 H123, box 34, folder 5.

54. "Trustees Toward Divestment," *Almanac* 34, no. 1 (14 July 1987): 1–2.

55. Reported in "Gazetteer," *PAG*, February 1989, 14.

56. "Trustees: Closing Two SAS Departments . . . Easing Sanctions on South Africa," *Almanac* 40, no. 19 (25 January 1994): 1.

57. In April 1911, the Penn trustees appointed the architects' commission led by Paul Cret to prepare the first campus master plan (see Introduction above). This appointment coincided with a lawsuit that was filed against the University by the trustees of the Commercial Museum. At issue was the legality of the city's transfer of fifty-six acres of Almshouse land, which included the Commercial Museum, to Penn in exchange for seventy-five Mayor's Scholarships. The 1913 Cret Report justified the University's claim to the fifty-six acres by providing a long-range plan for the land. In 1915, the Pennsylvania Supreme Court awarded the acreage to Penn, with the exception of the Commercial Museum and the immediately adjacent property, the site of the future Civic Center.

58. *Erika M. Drummond, et al. v. The Trustees of the University of Pennsylvania*, Philadelphia County Court of Common Pleas Trial Division, No. 3785, October Term 1991; Alison D. Keel (Ballard, Spahr Andrews & Ingersoll) to Debra Fickler (UPA associate general counsel), 3 April 1992, UARC UPA 4, box 587, folder 2.

59. Bill no. 832, *1977 City Council of Philadelphia Proceedings*, 1 August 1977, pp. 902–31.

60. *Drummond v. Trustees*; "Philadelphia Scholarships Are Focus of New Suit Against University," *PAG*, December 1991, 13–16; Sheldon Hackney, "On the Mayor's Scholarships," *Almanac*, 15 October 1991, 3; Reginald Bryant, "The Scholarship Siege," *Philadelphia Tribune Magazine*, November 1992, 9–10; "State Reps Tie U. Funding to Scholarships," *DP*, 17 February 1992.

61. Bill no. 382.

62. "1977 Mortgage Refinancing Facts," 2 March 1992, UARC UPA 4, box 587, folder 10.

63. Keel to Fickler; UPA press release, 23 February 1993. PILCOP lost its appeal in 1995 when the Pennsylvania Supreme Court refused to hear the case; "Gazetteer," *PAG*, October 1995, 28.

64. UPA press release, 23 February 1993.

65. "Report on the Mayor's Scholarship Program," 30 June 1993, UARC UPA 4, box 587, folder 3.

66. "Campus Racial Incidents Disquiet U. of Michigan," *NYT*, 9 March 1987. For the racial brouhaha at Columbia University, see "Race Divides College Campuses," *DP*, 8 April

1987. Sylvia Hurtado, in "The Campus Racial Climate: Contexts of Conflict," *Journal of Higher Education* 63, no. 5 (September–October 1992), writes, "Racial conflict was becoming commonplace on American college campuses throughout the 1980s, with more than one hundred college campuses reporting incidents of racial/ethnic harassment and violence in each of the last two years of the decade" (539).

67. "Blacks Stage Sit-in to Protest Remarks by Wharton Prof," *DP*, 14 February 1985.

68. "BSL Members in Hackney's Office," *DP*, 20 February 1985.

69. "BSL Draws 300 for Anti-Racism Vigil," *DP*, 25 February 1985; in same issue, "Protestors Determined to Win 'Battle.'"

70. "Exchanges on Racism," *Almanac* 31, no. 23 (26 February 1985): 4–5; "4/4/85: Update to Black Student League," *Almanac* 31, no. 29 (9 April 1985): 2. Also see "Wharton Panel Will Investigate Racism Charges," *DP*, 28 February 1985.

71. "Wharton Drops Dolfman for Fall Term," *DP*, 4 April 1985; in same issue: "Faculty Reaction Is Mixed on Administration's Ruling." Also see "Penn Suspends Lecturer for Remarks on Blacks," *NYT*, 5 April 1985. In its report to alumni, the *Pennsylvania Gazette* noted that Dolfman had taught without complaint for twenty-two years, and that he typically received high marks in SCUE teaching evaluations. See "Lecturer Accused of Racial Harassment Will Not Teach in Fall," *PAG*, April 1985, 18–19.

72. Hackney, *Politics of Presidential Appointment*, 166.

73. Alan Charles Kors and Harvey A. Silvergate, *The Shadow University: The Betrayal of Liberty on America's Campuses* (New York: Free Press, 1998); on Dolfman, 330–35.

74. "Dolfman to Resume Teaching," *DP*, 4 September 1986.

75. Sheldon Hackney, *Journals*, 4 July 1985, UARC UPT50 H123, box 34, folder 5.

76. Wayne Glasker, *Black Students in the Ivory Tower: African American Student Activism at the University of Pennsylvania, 1967–1990* (Amherst: University of Massachusetts Press, 2002), 162–66.

77. "Jews Will Protest Farrakhan," *DP*, 30 October 1986; "U. Blocks Safety Plan; Farrakhan May Cancel," *DP*, 31 October 1986; "Farrakhan Cancels; Jackson Speaks," *DP*, 3 November 1986; "In the Midst of Protest over His Appearance, Farrakhan Speaks Out," *PAG*, May 1988, 9–14. Hackney's refusal to countenance what he considered extremist demands from the Left drew the ire of leaders of Black Faculty, Staff and Administrators, who were particularly outraged when he rejected their demand for a Black Advocacy Center on the grounds that it was separatist. "Dealing with race relations is the part I hate worst of all," Hackney confided in a journal entry of 25 May 1988. Sheldon Hackney, *Journals*, UARC UPT50 H123, box 34, folder 9.

78. "Blacks, Jews Square Off in Verbal Battle," *DP*, 3 November 1986.

79. "BSL Continues Effort to Bring Farrakhan," *DP*, 4 November 1986.

80. "Farrakhan Spokesman Denies Racism," *DP*, 27 February 1987.

81. "Farrakhan Speaks; Hundreds Protest," *DP*, 14 April 1988. Also see "In Tense Times at Penn, Enter Farrakhan," *NYT*, 11 April 1988.

82. "Farrakhan Speaks"; "Peaceful Protest, Angry Debate at Irvine," *DP*, 14 April 1988.

83. "Pennsylvania Students Exercise Restraint on Farrakhan Visit," *NYT*, 15 April 1988.

84. "Racial Slurs Prompt Efforts to Expand Sensitivity Programs," *PAG*, December 1988, 11–13. *DP* headlines proclaimed "A Campus Divided" (semester-long series); other examples: "Despite All the Talk, Racism Still Prevalent at the University," 21 April 1988; "Black Leaders Assail Lack of Sensitivity at U.," 11 November 1988.

Chapter 8

1. See John Ehrman, *The Eighties: America in the Age of Reagan* (New Haven, Conn.: Yale University Press, 2005), 193–204.

2. See Ruth Sidel, *Battling Bias: The Struggle for Identity and Community on College Campuses* (New York: Viking, 1994), chap. 3: "Conflict Within the Ivory Tower." For the centrality of racial conflict and segregated diversity on college campuses, see "Race on Campus," *U.S. News & World Report*, 19 April 1993, 52–65. For more on fraternity transgressions, see William A. Bryan, "Contemporary Fraternity and Sorority Issues," in *Fraternities and Sororities on the Contemporary College Campus: New Directions for Student Services*, ed. Roger B. Winston, William R Netter III, and John H. Opper, Jr. (San Francisco: Jossey-Bass, 1987), 37–56.

3. Ehrman, *Eighties*, chap. 5, quotes from 197–98.

4. Quoted in M. G. Lord, "Greek Rites of Exclusion," *Nation*, 4–11 July 1987, 11. Four indicators reported for the first forty years of the national longitudinal survey of college freshmen by the Higher Education Institute at UCLA (1966–2006) indicate the high priority entering college cohorts attached to material life goals. The data show an accelerating trend for each indicator from the 1960s to the 1980s. The number of freshmen who said "developing a meaningful philosophy of life" was essential or very important declined from 85.8 percent in 1966 to 63 percent in 1976, to 44 percent in 1986. The number who said "to be able to make more money" was very important in their decision to attend college increased from 44.6 percent in 1971 (the first year for this indicator) to 49.9 percent in 1976, to 70.3 percent in 1989 (the number would peak in 1991 at 71.4 percent). The number who said "being well of financially" was essential or very important increased from 42.2 percent in 1966 to 50.2 percent in 1976 to 74.1 percent in 1987 (the peak year for this category). Finally, the number who listed business as their probable major increased from 10.9 percent in 1966 to 16.5 percent in 1976 to 25.7 percent in 1987 (the peak year for this category). Apparently, sociocentric, communal interests were not a high priority for this particular generation. John H. Pryor, Sylvia Hurtado, Victor B. Saenz, José Luis Santos, and William S. Korn, *The American Freshman: Forty Year Trends, 1966–2006* (Los Angeles: Higher Education Research Institute, UCLA, 2007), 62–63, 70–73.

5. David R. Goddard and Linda C. Koons, "A Profile of the University of Pennsylvania," in *Academic Transformations: Seventeen Institutions under Pressure*, ed. David Riesman and Verne A. Stadtman (New York: McGraw-Hill, 1973), 225–48, quote from 232.

6. Lord, "Greek Rites of Exclusion," 10–13.

7. "Findings and Recommendations on Fraternities and Sororities: A Report of the Senate Committee on Students and Educational Policy," *Almanac* 30, no. 30 (17 April 1984): 3–5.

8. "Report of the Committee to Diversity Locust Walk," *Almanac Supplement*, 17 September 1991, 2–16; also see and cf. Sheldon Hackney to Shelley Z. Green and Steven G. Poskanzer, memorandum, 16 October 1990, UARC UPA4, box 514, folder 8.

9. See "Violence by Students, from Rape to Racism, Raises College Worries," *Wall Street Journal*, 21 November 1983.

10. Julie K. Ehrhart and Bernice R. Sandler, *Campus Gang Rape: Party Games?* (Washington, D.C.: Association of American Colleges, 1985), ERIC ED 267 667.

11. Mark Bowden, "The Incident at Alpha Tau Omega," *PIM*, 11 September 1983, 18.

12. Peggy Reeves Sanday, *Fraternity Gang Rape: Sex, Brotherhood, and Privilege on Campus* (New York: New York University Press, 1990). Sanday's analysis, in which she generalizes speculatively to support her theory of male phallocentric/homoerotic behavior, was based

on accounts and reports published in the *Almanac* and its supplements, Court of Common Pleas documents, students' ethnographic reports of fraternity life, interviews with female habitués of the ATO house, and Bowden's account. As if to mock or caricature the ethical canons of anthropological research, Sanday thinly disguised Penn and ATO, even as she used the real names for some of the participants (for instance, Carol Tracy, director of the women's center; Carol Smith-Rosenberg, a feminist historian at Penn); enlisted Lois G. Forer, the Common Pleas judge who issued a ruling on the case, to write the foreword to her book; and gave a full citation for Bowden's article. Rather than acknowledge the unavoidability of disclosing the identity of the University, she argued disingenuously that "the specific location is not relevant to the subject of this book" (4). Her description of "the Walk" (25–26) is a dead giveaway.

13. Ibid., 75–77.

14. Sheldon Hackney and Thomas Ehrlich, "On the Alpha Tau Omega Fraternity," *Almanac* 30, no. 2 (6 September 1983): 3. Also see "Charter of the University Judicial System," *Almanac Supplement*, 2 December 1980; "Hackney Defends ATO Sanctions," *DP*, 29 September 1983.

15. Michael B. Katz, *Reconstructing American Education* (Cambridge, Mass.: Harvard University Press, 1987), 160.

16. Regina Austin et al., "Report to the Senate Executive Committee from the Committee to Review the Administrative Actions Pertaining to the ATO Incident," *Almanac* 30, no. 15 (13 December 1983): 3–6; also see "Faculty: U Mishandled ATO Probe," *DP*, 8 December 1983; "Probe by Faculty Puts Hackney on Defensive," *DP*, 9 December 1983; Sanday, *Fraternity Gang Rape*, 76–78.

17. "Faculty Criticizes Penn's Rape Probe," *PI*, 8 December 1983.

18. Sheldon Hackney, *Journals*, 14 December 1983, UARC UPT50 H123, box 34, folder 5.

19. Sheldon Hackney to editor, *PAG*, 12 March 1984, typescript, UARC UPA 4, box 479, folder 13.

20. Sanday, *Fraternity Gang Rape*, 79–80.

21. Ibid., 80–82; Hackney and Ehrlich, "On the Alpha Tau Omega Fraternity."

22. A. Leo Levin, "Decision and Opinion of the Hearing Examiner," *Almanac* 30, no. 22 (14 February 1984): 4–6. For a chronology of this complicated case, which involved three judges of the Court of Common pleas and a panel of three Superior Court justices before it reached Levin, see "A Chronology of the ATO Incident: Final Verdict After a One-Year Battle," *DP*, 9 February 1984. Also see "Alpha Tau Omega Suspended; Ruling Called Disappointing," *PAG*, March 1984, 9–12.

23. "Alpha Tau Omega Suspended."

24. Quoted in Sanday, *Fraternity Gang Rape*, 85–86.

25. "Case Closed," *Philadelphia Daily News* (*PDN*) 1 February 1984, reprinted in *Almanac* 30, no. 24 (28 February 1984): 2–3.

26. "Carol Tracy: The Exit of a Women's Advocate," *DP*, 20 April 1984. According to Jacqueline Wade, director of the Afro-American studies program, "Black students regularly report to me that they are subjected to verbal racial abuse when they walk down Locust Walk"; Lord, "Greek Rites of Exclusion."

27. Sheldon Hackney to Bernard C. Sherbok, 30 March 1984, UARC, UPA 4, box 479, folder 13.

28. "Charter of the University Student Judicial System," *Almanac Supplement*, 4 September 1984.

29. Janis L. Somerville, "Text of the Kappa Sigma Decision," *Almanac* 23, no. 11 (17 November 1981): 3.

30. Joan E. Prior to Sheldon Hackney, 21 September 1981; Hackney to Prior, 19 October 1981, UPA 4, box 479, folder 18.

31. "A Civil Discussion on Uncivil Behavior Around the Campus," *PAG*, October 1987, 25–26.

32. "X-ing ZBT," *PAG,* March 1988, 13. With impunity, Theta Xi staged a "junkyard party," replete with watermelons, to mimic the popular TV series *Sanford and Son*, which starred the black actors Redd Fox and Desmond Wilson. See Marshall Ledger, "Getting Off on the Right Foot," *PAG*, May 1987, 23–29.

33. *PDN*, 4 March 1988. Sanctions were imposed following an investigation by the Fraternity and Sorority Advisory Board, a body that included students, alumni, and faculty. Hackney denied that pressure from the Black Student League and other African American groups weighed in the decision by the provost's office to suspend the fraternity.

34. "Alpha Chi Rho Frat Suspended for One Year," *DP*, 22 April 1988.

35. "University Bans Beer Kegs on Campus," *PAG,* October 1988, 23–26. Also see "Fraternity Members Outraged by New University Alcohol Policy," *DP*, 8 September 1988.

36. "Kegs, Kegs, Kegs," *PAG,* November 1988, 18.

37. "Roll Out the Barrel," *PAG,* February 1989, 12.

38. "Two Castle Members Charged with Kidnapping St. A's Brother," *DP*, 14 February 1990. Delta Psi was also called St. Anthony Hall.

39. Alan Charles Kors and Harvey A. Silverglate, *The Shadow University: The Betrayal of America's Campuses* (New York: HarperCollins, 1999), 18–19. Interestingly, newspaper accounts failed to report this. It also does not appear in Kim Morrison's report to faculty and staff, "Decision and Findings in the Withdrawal of Recognition of Psi Upsilon," *Almanac* 36, no. 34 (8 May 1990): 4. Morrisson said, "I have taken note of the fact that Psi U has been on the Penn campus for 99 years and that the chapter's membership is composed of students from diverse racial, ethnic and socio-economic backgrounds. Such diversity is to be applauded; it is consistent with the University's goals and it should be the goal of *all* chapters within the Greek system. But diversity, however, exemplary, cannot be the cloak behind which to hide the egregious misconduct of this case nor should it be used as the justification for failure to take appropriate action."

40. "Penn Fraternity Members Charged with Abduction, to Get Probation" *PI*, 8 August 1990, citing Fraternity and Sorority Advisory Board report.

41. The nuances of fraternity ownership at Penn entailed a "huge book," according to the general counsel's office. Approximately stated, eleven fraternities owned their houses; the University owned seven houses with no stipulations that it lease them to fraternities; and the University had purchased eleven from national fraternities with a "reversionary" clause stipulating that if a house were not used for residential purposes, ownership would revert to the national fraternity. As the Castle became a college house, the reversionary clause did not apply. See John Shea, "The Fraternity Thing," *PAG*, May 1990, 17–27.

42. "U Charges Castle in Kidnapping," *DP*, 29 March 1990; "Board to Hear Charges Against Castle Today," *DP*, 11 April 1990; "JIO Calls for 5-Year Castle Suspension," *DP*, 13 April 1990; "Castle Charter Revoked," *DP*, 3 May 1990; "Kidnap Victim Gets $145,000 from Psi U," *DP*, 1991. At roughly the same time as the Psi Upsilon hearings, the Phi Kappa Alpha national organization suspended the Penn chapter for staging a fake robbery, ushering a sick horse into the house, and being collectively responsible for a brother's fight with a Phi Kappa Sigma member; Shea, "Fraternity Thing."

43. Quote from Shea, "Fraternity Thing," 18; also see "Group Marches to Protest Frats," *DP*, 12 April 1990.

44. Sheldon Hackney, "Diversifying Locust Walk," *Almanac* 36, no. 31 (17 April 1990): 5; Sheldon Hackney, "Charge to the Committee to Diversity Locust Walk," *Almanac* 37, no. 5 (25 September 1990): 3.

45. "Theta Xi Frat Vacates House," *DP*, 16 November 1992.

46. "Report of the President's Committee on University Life," *Almanac* 37, no. 8 (16 October 1990): 5–8.

47. "Report of Committee to Diversify Locust Walk," quotes from 9–10.

48. Sheldon Hackney, *The Politics of Presidential Appointment: A Memoir of the Culture War* (Montgomery, Ala.: NewSouth, 2002), 66–69.

49. Kors and Silverglate, *Shadow University*, chap. 1; Racial Harassment Policy," *Almanac Supplement*, 24 September 1991, pp. II–IV, UARC UPA 4, box 513, folder 55. In April 1988, the University of Michigan established one of the earliest speech codes, proscribing any action that "stigmatizes or victimizes an individual on the basis of race, ethnicity, religion, sex, sexual orientation, creed, national origin, ancestry, age, marital status, handicap, or Vietnam-era veteran status." In 1989, a Michigan federal court ordered the university to excise the speech code. Some 125 higher education institutions, including Stanford, Brown, Tufts, Berkeley, and the University of Wisconsin (twenty-six campuses), had speech codes as well. Like Michigan's, Wisconsin's code (called U.W.S. 17) did not survive a challenge in U.S. District Court (1992). Ehrman, *Eighties*, 201, 287–88n52. See also Ken Emerson, "Only Correct," *New Republic*, 18 February 1991; Kors and Silverglate, *Shadow University*, 167–69.

50. "Penn Students Protest Handling of Speech Issues," *PI*, 5 May 1993.

51. Richard Beeman, a highly respected associate dean in the School of Arts and Sciences, defended Kors's decision to involve the national media: "I genuinely believe that Alan was driven to go public, that he believes that Eden Jacobowitz was victimized, that his decision to go public had to do with the fact that here was a student-life bureaucracy—and, ultimately, a central administration—that was unresponsive to the real predicament that this innocent kid found himself in." Samuel M. Hughes, "Alan Kors as Others See Him," *PAG*, March 1994, 33.

52. Kors and Silverglate, *Shadow University*, 18.

53. Hackney, *Politics of Presidential Appointment*, 69–70.

54. Claire Fagin, interview, 25 June 2006, Faculty Senate Oral History Project Records, 2005–2008, UARC UPB 25.

55. Sheldon Hackney, "On the Controversy of April 15–16: Narrowing the Distance," *Almanac* 39, no. 3 (20 April 1993): 4. Sixteen standing faculty members of the law school, including Dean Colin Diver, signed an open letter vehemently condemning "conduct which cannot be excused or tolerated. . . . Those who disagree are, of course, entitled to protest, but not by attempting to silence those with whom they disagree. . . . Removal of the newspapers struck at the heart of the most fundamental diversity which the University should foster—diversity of thought, views and expression." "On Removal of DPs," *Almanac* 39, no. 33 (May 11, 1993): 4.

56. "Sheldon Hackney Enters Debate Over Controversial Exhibit," *PAG*, October 1989, 23–26.

57. "When a University Is Forced to Examine Its Very Soul," *PAG*, May 1993, 15–17.

58. Hackney, *Politics of Presidential Appointment*, chap. 4; Kors and Silverglate, *Shadow University*, chap. 1; newspaper clippings. UARC UPA 4, box 513, folder 55; Sheldon Hackney, *Journals*, 27 May 1993, UARC UPT 50 H123, box 34, folder 13. In his 1991 commencement address, Hackney denied that Penn was a hotbed of political correctness: "*Yes*, there is political correctness on campus. But *no*, it is not dominant, and it does not go unchallenged. Indeed,

the debate is the crucial sign that universities are open to all views. For to fulfill its mission, a university must not be captured by any orthodoxy, except a devotion to free inquiry"; *Almanac* 37, no. 35 (28 May 1991): 4–5; see also Sheldon Hackney, "Campuses Aren't Besieged by Politically Correct Storm Troopers," *Almanac* 38, no. 7 (8 October 1991): 3.

59.   "Questions for the Record by Senator Kassebaum for Sheldon Hackney, Nominee for Chairman of the National Endowment for the Humanities," in Hackney, *Politics of Presidential Appointment*, appendix 3. See also "Water Buffalo Charges Dropped," *DP*, 3 September 1993.

60.   Hackney, *Politics of Presidential Appointment*, 165–66.

61.   Lani Guinier, an outspoken African American professor and feminist in the Penn law school, whom Bill Clinton nominated to be assistant attorney general for civil rights in the fall of 1993, may have been a casualty of Water Buffalo. Responding to concerns within his own party about Guinier's advocacy of "proportionate *interest* representation" in American governance, Clinton withdrew the nomination. Colin Diver, dean of the law school, observed: "I can't help but think that somebody in that Senate, in the Democratic middle or left, must have at least subconsciously said to himself, 'Boy, if the 'water buffalo' and the D.P. confiscation could explode as they did, then imagine what the Lani Guinier hearings are going to be like." Samuel M. Hughes, "The 'Misquoted Queen' Speaks Up," *PAG*, October 1993, 33.

62.   Michael Zuckerman, interview by Mark Lloyd and John Puckett, 1 February 2010.

63.   Linda Koons interview, 24 July 2007, Faculty Senate Oral History Project Records, 2005–2008, UARC UPB 25.

64.   For other thoughtful criticisms of "PC," see campus reports in *New Republic*, 18 February 1991, 18–20; in same issue, Fred Siegel, "The Cult of Multiculturalism," 34–40; Irving Howe, "The Value of the Canon," 40–47.

65.   Ibid.

66.   Fagin, interview for Faculty Senate Oral History Project.

Chapter 9

1.   "U. to Prepay $10 Million in Wage Taxes to Aid City," *DP* 18 October 1990; "City Cash Crisis Looms as Year's End Approaches," *DP*, 5 December 1990; "University of Pennsylvania: Commitment to Philadelphia," February 1992, UARC UPA 4, box 587, folder 1.

2.   "Penn's Economic Impact: $2.5 Billion in FY '90," *Almanac* 38, no. 21 (11 February 1992): 1.

3.   See John Kastor, *Governance of Teaching Hospitals: Turmoil at Penn and Hopkins* (Baltimore: Johns Hopkins University Press, 2004), chap. 2.

4.   See Sheldon Hackney, "The University and Its Community: Past and Present," *Annals of the American Academy of Political and Social Science* 488 (1986): 135–47. See also "Hackney Has Slowly Repaired Relationship with West Philadelphia," *DP*, 26 April 1991; "Hackney Healed Community Ties," *DP*, 21 April 1993.

5.   Quoted John Shea, "The Night Watch," *PAG*, February 1988, 41.

6.   UPA, *Annual Report*, 1987–88, http:www.archives.upenn.edu/primdocs/uph/uph4_5 /1988fin_report.pdf, accessed 17 December 2009. The Hackney presidency's first planning document, from the winter of 1981–82, used similar language to describe "ties with the City" as one of the University's six strategic planning topics; Academic Planning and Budget Committee, *Six Working Papers for Strategic Planning*, in *Almanac Supplement*, 15 January 1982.

7.   Michael Zuckerman, interview by Mark Lloyd and John Puckett, 1 February 2010.

8.   Gerald Zahavi notes, in "The 'Trial of Lee Benson: Communism, White Chauvinism, and the Foundation of the 'New Political History' in the United States," *History and Theory*

42 (October 2003): 332–62, that Benson "stands out as one of the founders and most aggressive champions of a historiographical revolution that began to sweep through American universities in the late 1950s and 1960s. The 'new political history'—an attempt to apply social-science methods, concepts, and theories to American political history—is no longer 'new'; it is now seamlessly imbedded in contemporary practice and theory. But in the late 1950s and early 1960s, it constituted a major paradigm shift in the discipline. As numerous scholars have acknowledged, Benson's *Concept of Jacksonian Democracy: New York as a Test Case*—one of his several research projects focusing on nineteenth-century New York State history—was a central catalyst in that shift" (333). His keynote paper to the Organization of American Historians in 1981, "History as Advocacy," marked a turning point in his thinking and career, and it was rudely received by the OAH. "The paper was a howling success," Benson told Zahavi, "meaning that everybody in the audience howled at me, and I'm almost serious because my argument . . . was a very, very major critique of American historians on the ground that it [historical writing] was just scholastic, that we don't contribute anything to changing the world for the better, and that we had abandoned advocacy for 'value free' history, social science and the like" (360).

9. Sheldon Hackney, interview by John Puckett, 5 February 2010.

10. For details, see John Anderson and Hilary Hevenor, *Burning Down the House: MOVE and the Tragedy of Philadelphia* (New York: Norton, 1987). For the Philadelphia context of the incident, see Roger D. Simon and Brian Alnutt, "Philadelphia, 1982–2007: Toward the Postindustrial City," *Pennsylvania Magazine of History and Biography* 131, no 4 (2007): 395–444.

11. See Michael C. Johanek and John L. Puckett, *Leonard Covello and the Making of Benjamin Franklin High School: Education as if Citizenship Mattered* (Philadelphia: Temple University Press, 2007), which traces the history of the community school idea, giving particular attention to Benjamin Franklin High School in East Harlem, 1934–56. Chap. 8 locates Penn's community school initiative within this wider historical context.

12. Zuckerman, interview by Lloyd and Puckett.

13. For the theoretical foundations of Penn's approach, see Lee Benson, Ira Harkavy, and John Puckett, *Dewey's Dream* (Philadelphia: Temple University Press, 2007); Lee Benson and Ira Harkavy, "Saving the Soul of the University: What Is to Be Done?" in *The Virtual University? Knowledge, Markets, and Management*, eds. Kevin Robbins and Frank Webster (New York: Oxford University Press, 2002), 169–209; Lee Benson and Ira Harkavy, "School and Community in the Global Society," *Universities and Community Schools* 5 (1997): 16–71; Ira Harkavy, "De-Platonizing and Democratizing Education as the Basis of Service Learning," in *Academic Service-Learning: A Pedagogy of Action and Reflection*, eds. Robert A. Rhoads and Jeffrey Howard (San Francisco: Jossey-Bass, 1998), 11–19; Ira Harkavy and John L. Puckett, "Lessons from Hull House for the Contemporary Urban University," *Social Service Review* 68, no. 3 (1994): 299–321; Ira Harkavy and John L. Puckett, "Toward Effective University–Public School Partnerships: An Analysis of a Contemporary Model," *Teachers College Record* 92, no. 4 (1991): 552–81; Ira Harkavy and John L. Puckett, "The Role of Mediating Structures in University and Community Revitalization: The University of Pennsylvania and West Philadelphia as a Case Study," *Journal of Research and Development in Education* 27 (1991): 225.

14. John Puckett and Ira Harkavy, "The Action Research Tradition in the United States: Toward a Strategy for Revitalizing the Social Sciences, the University, and the American City," in *Action Research: From Practice to Writing in an International Action Research Development Program*, ed. Davydd J. Greenwood (Amsterdam: John Benjamins, 1999); Ira Harkavy,

Francis E. Johnston, and John L. Puckett, "The University of Pennsylvania's Center for Community Partnerships as an Organizational Innovation for Advancing Action Research," *Concepts and Transformations: Journal of Action Research and Organizational Renewal* 1, no. 1 (1996): 15–29. For a full description, see David J. Maurrasse, *Beyond the Campus: How Colleges and Universities Form Partnerships with Their Communities* (New York: Routledge, 2001), 29–64.

15. Lee Benson, Ira Harkavy, and John L. Puckett, "An Implementation Revolution as a Strategy to Fulfill the Democratic Promise of University-Community Partnerships: Penn-West Philadelphia as an Experiment in Progress," *Nonprofit and Voluntary Sector Quarterly* 29, no 1 (March 2000): 24–45.

16. Francis E. Johnston and R. J. Hallock, "Physical Growth, Nutritional Status and Dietary Intake of African-American Middle School Students from Philadelphia," *American Journal of Human Biology* 6 (1994): 741–47; Lee Benson and Ira Harkavy, "Leading the Way to Meaningful Partnerships," *Principal Leadership* 2, no. 1 (2001): 54–58.

17. Anne Whiston Spirn, *The West Philadelphia Landscape Plan: A Framework for Action*, Department of Landscape Architecture and Regional Planning, University of Pennsylvania, 1991–96; Spirn, *The Language of Landscape* (New Haven, Conn.: Yale University Press, 1998), 10–11, 161–63, 183–88.

18. Benson, Harkavy, and Puckett, *Dewey's Dream*, 99–103.

19. West Philadelphia Partnership 1983 Bylaws, revised 21 March 1983, UARC UPA 4, box 518, folder 14.

20. Sheldon Hackney, "The Great Aim and End of All Learning," *Almanac* 36, no. 20 (23 January 1990): 4–5.

21. Ibid.; Bob Michael (Office of Intramural Correspondence) to Claire Fagin, 4 November 1993, John Puckett's personal collection.

22. Sheldon Hackney, "From the Chair," *West Philadelphia Partnership Newsletter*, summer 1988, p. 2, UARC UPA 4, box 518, folder 3; in same box, folder 4: West Philadelphia Partnership, typescript [*Annual Report?*], n.d. [1989?].

23. Donald T. Sheehan to Martin Meyerson et al., memorandum, 3 May 1971, UARC UPA 4, box 440, folder 17.

24. "3401 Walnut Street Task Force and Committee on Physical Planning and Development," 18 November 1971, UARC UPA 4, box 440, folder 18.

25. "Penn Diverts Academic Land to High-Rise Commercial Use," *PEB*, 21 October 1973.

26. Martin Meyerson to David O. Meeker, Jr. (assistant secretary, HUD), 22 August 1974, UARC UPA 4, box 440, folder 20; Meyerson quoting Newcomer.

27. Judy Wicks, interview by John Puckett, 23 November 2009.

28. David O. Meeker, Jr. to Martin Meyerson, 13 September 1974, UARC UPA 4, box 440, folder 20.

29. Judith Wicks, interview by Puckett, 23 November 2009. By the late 1960s, Hetherston's behavior was, no doubt, influenced by his heavy drinking, which contributed to his death in 1978 at age fifty-three. Hetherston's death certificate, no. 484379, Commonwealth of Pennsylvania Department of Vital Statistics, listed congestive heart failure and alcohol abuse as the causes of death.

30. "The Story of Cy Braverman, Campus Businessman," n.d., UARC UPA 4, box 440, folder 23; "The Long and Winding Road to the Shops," *DP*, 23 February 1988.

31. Martin Meyerson to Sidney N. Repplier (director, Philadelphia Foundation), 24 December 1974, UARC UPA 4, box 440, folder 20.

32. "Long and Winding Road to Shops."

33. "The Story of Cy Braverman, Campus Businessman," undated typescript [November 1983?], UARC UPA 4, box 440, folder 23.

34. Wicks, interview by Puckett.

35. Mari M. Gursky, Esq. (Dechart Price & Rhoads) to John W. Fischer (Drinker, Biddle & Heath), 1 September 1981, UARC UPA4, box 440, folder 21; in same folder: Fischer to Gursky, 7 October 1981.

36. Wicks, interview by Puckett; Elliot C. R. Cook to Arthur Hirsch (vice president of Operational Services), 3 February 1984, UARC UPA4, box 440, folder 24.

37. Helen O'Bannon to Judith A. Wicks and Neil Schlosser, 26 October 1984, UARC UPA4, box 440, folder 24.

38. Letter from William G. Owen (secretary of the University) to Peter Abhorn, George Brown, Sheldon Hackney et al., 31 May 1984, attached statement, UPA4, box 440, folder 24.

39. Judith A. Wicks to George Brown (executive director, West Philadelphia Partnership), 16 July 1984, UARC UPA4, box 440, folder 24.

40. J. Newcomer, re Sansom Committee et al. vs. James Lynn, et al., Civil Action No. 73–1444, Eastern District of Pennsylvania, memorandum, 10 February 1983, UARC UPA4, box 440, folder 23; "Supreme Court Refuses to Hear Sansom St. Case," *DP*, 27 November 1984.

41. "Agreement of November 28, 1984 between the University of Pennsylvania and the Sansom Street Committee," UARC UPA4, box 440, folder 24; "U. Reaches Agreement [on] Sansom St. Development," *DP*, 17 January 1985.

42. Sheldon Hackney to Prof. Robert Engman et al., 10 January 1983, UARC UPA4, box 440, folder 23.

43. Wicks, interview by Puckett.

44. Judith A. Wicks to Sheldon Hackney, 8 February 1984, UARC UPA4, box 440, folder 24.

45. John Caroulis, "Of Dirty Drugs and White Dogs: The Evolution of Dining (Fine and Otherwise) at Penn," *PAG*, April 1997, 27–32, quote from 32.

46. Wicks, interview by Puckett; Caroulis, "Of Dirty Drugs and White Dogs"; "Shops at Penn Opening Set for February," *DP*, 23 September 1987; "After 20 Years," *DP*, 5 February 1988.

47. Zuckerman, interview by Lloyd and Puckett.

48. Paul F. Miller, *Better Than Any Dream: A Personal Memoir* (Conschocken, Pa.: self published, 2005), 165–66.

49. Calculated from UPA, *Financial Report*, 1981–93, www.archives.upenn.edu/primdocs /uph/uph4_5fin_reports.html; half-year average calculated for 1981, 1993.

50. UPA, *Annual Report*, 1985, *Almanac Supplement*, 19 November 1985, V. See also "Penn-DEC Agreement: $22.5 Million Leap," *Almanac* 30, no. 30 (17 April 1984): 1.

51. Kastor, *Governance of Teaching Hospitals*, 17–27, quote from 6.

52. George E. Thomas and David B. Brownlee, *Building America's First University: An Historical and Architectural Guide to the University of Pennsylvania* (Philadelphia: University of Pennsylvania Press, 2000), 195–96, 199, 258.

53. Sheldon Hackney, "On Smith Hall: Balancing Past and Future," *Almanac* 37, no. 18 (22 January 1991): 3, 7; "The Crown Jewels," *DP*, 11 October 1993; "President Sheldon Hackney: 1981–1993," *DP*, 14 May 1993.

54. "Penn Club of New York: NYC Landmark Designation," *Almanac* 56, no. 28 (6 April 2010): 1; "Gazetteer: Welcome to the Club," *PAG*, May–June 2004, http://www.upenn.edu /gazette/0504/0504gaz14.htm.

55. Hugh Davis Graham and Nancy Diamond, *The Rise of American Research Universities: Elites and Challengers in the Postwar Era* (Baltimore: Johns Hopkins University Press, 1997), table 5.3, p. 129; table 5.8, p. 137; ranking for federal R & D funds calculated from table appendix 1, p. 223; table appendix 2, p. 224; ranking for per capita publications calculated from table 6.1, p. 148; table 7.1, p. 177.

56. Between 1906 and 1982, writes Clark Kerr, "only three institutions dropped out from those ranked as the top 15—but, in each case, not by very much (Johns Hopkins, Ohio State, and Minnesota)—and only three (Illinois, UCLA, and Caltech) were added. Only two institutions (Columbia and Cornell) fell five places or more, and only three (Berkeley, Princeton, and Stanford) rose five places or more"; Clark Kerr, "The New Race to Be Harvard or Berkeley or Stanford," *Change*, May–June 1991, 8–15, esp. table 2, p. 13; quote from 10. Kerr draws on David S. Webster, "America's Highest Ranked Graduate Schools, 1925–1982," *Change*, May–June 1983, esp. table 11, p. 23. Unlike Webster, Kerr includes James McKeen Cattell's 1906 *Statistical Survey of American Men of Science*. "Rankings drive reputation," concludes the educational sociologist Michael Bastedo. As another commentator puts it: "When U.S. News asks a university president to perform the impossible task of assessing the relative merits of dozens of institutions he knows nothing about, he relies on the only source of detailed information at his disposal that assesses the relative merits of dozens of institutions he knows nothing about: *U.S. News*"; Malcolm Gladwell, "The Order of Things: What College Rankings Really Tell Us," *New Yorker*, 14 and 21 February 2011.

57. Robert Zemsky, "The Rain Man Cometh—Again," *Academy of Management Perspectives* 22, no. 1 (2008): 8. Hackney's journal entries occasionally mention Penn's negative self-image, which was of long lineage; see, for example, "Universities: Old Ben's New Penn," *Time*, 23 August 1963, http://www.time.com/time/magazine/article/9,9171,875129,00.html.

58. Zemsky, "Rain Man Cometh," 5.

59. Academic Planning and Budget Committee, *Six Working Papers for Strategic Planning*, 4–7, quote from 7.

60. *Choosing Penn's Future*, *Almanac Supplement*, 25 January 1983, 2–4.

61. Quoted in Amanda K. Klemas, "History of Institutional Planning at the University of Pennsylvania: Francis Sheldon Hackney (President 1981–1993)," http://www.archives.upenn.edu/histy/features/uplans/hackney.html, accessed 2 March 2010. This useful source includes electronic links to the major planning documents of the Hackney era.

62. *Choosing Penn's Future*, 3.

63. "Report on the Work of the Faculty Council on Undergraduate Education, 1984–85," *Almanac* 31, no. 30 (16 April 1985): 7; "Report on the Work of the Faculty Council on Undergraduate Education, 1985–86," *Almanac* 33, no. 9 (21 October 1986): 4; Michael Aiken, "Undergraduate Education at Penn: Progress and Prospects," *Almanac* 34, no. 12 (10 November 1987): 3.

64. Aiken, "Undergraduate Education at Penn," 3.

65. Thomas Ehrlich, "Planning at Penn: A Progress Report," *Almanac Supplement*, 1 May 1984, 3.

66. "The Penn Profile," *Almanac Supplement*, 14 May 1985.

67. Sheldon Hackney and Thomas Ehrlich, *Investing in Academic Excellence*, *Almanac Supplement*, 3 March 1987.

68. Hackney, interview by Puckett.

69. "'Keeping Franklin's Promise' Is the Billion-Dollar Goal," *Almanac* 36, no. 9 (17 October 1989): 1; "The 120 Million Question," *DP*, 22 September 1993.

70. "'Keeping Franklin's Promise.'"

71. Sheldon Hackney, "Higher Education: Spirals of Change," *Almanac Supplement*, 13 October 1987, 1–8.

72. "150 Endowed Chairs and Other Breakthroughs," *Almanac* 41, no. 18 (24 January 1995): 1. The second year of Keeping Franklin's Promise coincided with the ceremonies and activities surrounding Penn's 250th anniversary, which Hackney inaugurated on 16 January 1990, the University's Founder's Day (Franklin's birthday). The highlight was a "Peak Week" in mid-May that included a plenary address by former president Ronald Reagan at the Civic Center, which was punctuated by mass arrests of demonstrators outside Convention Hall; faculty-alumni exchanges, some of them led by anti-Reagan faculty activists; and an overhyped "Penultimate" event that featured country-western performers Dolly Parton and Kenny Rogers, comedian Bill Cosby, actor Ralph Archbold (Benjamin Franklin's perennial stand-in) and a chorus of unhappy ticket-bearing students yelling "nose-bleed seats" from the upper reaches of Convention Hall. See "University Launches the Celebration of Its 250th Anniversary," *PAG*, February–March 1990, 33–37; "Three Days in May," *PAG*, July 1990, 19–33, 55.

73. "A Master Plan for the Campus," *Almanac Supplement*, 10 May 1988; "Focus: Bob Zemsky and the U.'s Thirty-Year Plan," *DP*, 25 November 1991. Also see "Planning Ahead," *DP*, 25 November 1991; "Hospital Officials Contemplate $900 Move to Civic Center," *PAG*, April 1992, 15–6; "U. Phila. Negotiate Price for Civic Center," *DP*, 3 December 1992; "The University Is Looking to Buy Some Riverfront Property," *DP*, 2 April 1993; "Medical Center Plans Expansion," *DP*, 28 October 1993.

74. Sheldon Hackney, open letter, *PAG*, June 1993, 14; "Gazetteer," *PAG*, October 1993, 19–21.

75. "Gazetteer," *PAG*, October 1993, 21–23; the text of Arnold's report appears on 22–23; see also "Trustees Rebuke U. over 'DP' Ruling," *DP*, 20 September 1993.

76. Commission on Strengthening the University Community, "Final Report of the Commission on Strengthening the Community," *Almanac Supplement*, 5 April 1994, 1–16.

77. Claire Fagin, Marvin Lazerson, and Janet Hale (executive vice president), "Administrative Response to the Recommendations of the Commission on Strengthening the Community," *Almanac Supplement*, 3 May 1994.

78. Judith Rodin, "Welcome Back," *Almanac* 41, no. 17 (January 1995): 1–2. Also see Koons interview, 24 July 2004, Faculty Senate Oral History Project.

79. Sheldon Hackney, *The Politics of Presidential Appointment: A Memoir of the Culture War* (Montgomery, Ala.: NewSouth, 2002), 90–91.

80. "Student Judicial Charter Outline," *Almanac* 41, no. 19 (31 January 1995): 4–5.

81. "New Director," *PAG*, May–June 1996, 18.

82. Sheldon Hackney, "Policy Statement on Nondiscrimination," *Almanac* 29, no. 17 (18 January 1983): 2.

83. "Gazetteer," *PAG*, November 1991, 17.

84. "Gazetteer," *PAG*, March 1992, 15; "Dorms Allow Gay Couples," *DP*, 29 October 1992.

85. "Gazetteer," *PAG*, February 1993, 15.

86. John Pendergrast, "Safe Places," *PAG*, November–December 2002, http://www.upenn .edu/gazette/1102/prendergast.html; "A Home in the Carriage House," *PAG*, January–February 2001, 19; "Carriage House Dedicated as LGBT Center," *PAG*, November–December 2002, http://www.upenn.edu/gazette/1102/1102 gaz6.html.

87. "Provost Maintains Status Quo for ROTC," *DP*, 30 June 1996.

88. PFSNI, "Priorities for Neighborhood Revitalization: Goals for the Year 2000," *Almanac* 40, no. 9 (26 October 1993): 6–11; in Carolyn Burden Papers, provided to authors by Anne

Froehling (cochair PFSNI steering committee): Lynn H. Lees to Professor Andrew Postle-waite (chair, provost search committee), 30 November 1993; PFSNI steering committee to Judith Rodin, typescript draft, 9 February 1994; PFSNI committee report, April 1994.

89. PFSNI, "Priorities for Neighborhood Revitalization."

90. Ira Harkavy and Glenn Bryan to John Gould, memorandum, 22 November 1993, in authors' possession.

91. Spruce Hill Renewal Committee, *The Spruce Hill Community Renewal Plan*, 1995, http://www.sprucehillca.org, accessed 15 February 2011.

92. Ibid.

Chapter 10

1. "Judith Rodin to be Next President," *PAG*, December 1993, 13–14; quotes from John A. Kastor, *Governance of Teaching Hospitals: Turmoil at Penn and Hopkins* (Baltimore: Johns Hopkins University Press, 2004), 112–113.

2. Samuel Hughes and John Prendergast, "Rodin: A Look Back at an Extraordinary De-cade for Penn, and the President Who Led the Way," *PAG*, May 2004, http://www.upenn.edu/gazette/0504/editors1.html.

3. Judith Rodin interview, 23 April 2007, Faculty Senate Oral History Project Records, 2005–2008, UARC UPB 25.

4. "Remembering Al-Moez Alimohamed," *Almanac* 41, no. 3 (13 September 1994): 1; in same issue: Lynn Lees, for the PFSNI Steering Committee, to Judith Rodin, pp. 2–3. When the five youths were brought to trial, Rodin submitted the following letter for the prosecu-tion: "As the leader of the largest private employer in the City of Philadelphia, I would only be pretending to ensure the safety of our students, our faculty, and our staff if justice is not served on the criminals who prey on our community. . . . Today, over your robes of jurispru-dence, you will wear the mantle of educator. Give the criminals in your courtroom the les-son they deserve. Teach them, through the maximum sentence allowable by law that they cannot get away with murder. Teach them that the punishment will fit the crime." Two of the youths, tried as adults, were convicted of murder and sentenced to life in prison; the three others received lesser sentences; *Almanac* 42, no. 234 (19 March 1996): 20.

5. PFSNI press release, 7 September 1994, Carolyn Burden Papers, provided to authors by Anne Froehling (cochair of PFSNI steering committee).

6. Judith Rodin, "Partners in West Philadelphia," response to Lynn Lees, *Almanac* 41, no. 4 (20 September 1994): 3; Judith Rodin, "Increasing Our Collective Security," *Almanac* 41, no. 21 (14 February 1995):12; "Safety First," *PAG*, March 1995, 14; Tom Seamon, "Uni-versity of Pennsylvania Division of Public Safety Strategic Plan," *Almanac Supplement*, 26 March 1996; "View from the Top," *PAG*, May–June 1996, 28–33. The campus police patrol area was, and still is, the area bounded north to south by Market and Baltimore, east to west by 30th and 43rd streets. As Penn's security division is recognized by the state as "a fully fledged police department," Penn police have the power of arrest beyond this designated area; "Per-spective: Sizing up the Penn Patrol Zone," *DP*, 10 February 2009.

7. Lynn H. Lees, "PFSNI: 'Get Serious' on Safety," *Almanac* 42, no. 19 (6 February 1996): 4.

8. "Crime and Crime Again," *PAG*, November 1996, 13; "A Senior Is Wounded, and Safety Is Topic Number 1," *Almanac* 43, no. 6 (1 October 1996): 2.

9. "How Crime Hits Phila. Neighborhoods," *PI*, 24 October 1997.

10. Judith Rodin, "Eight New Steps in Campus Safety," address to students, 27 Septem-ber, *Almanac* 43, no. 6 (1 October 1996): 3; Judith Rodin, *The University and Urban Renewal:*

Out of the Ivory Tower and into the Streets (Philadelphia: University of Pennsylvania Press, 2007): x; "Crime and Crime Again"; *PI*, 1 November 1996. Just weeks before Vladimir Sled's death, the *DP* reported that senior Penn administrators had consulted with Drexel University, the Children's Hospital of Philadelphia, and the Philadelphia College of Pharmacy and Science regarding the establishment of a special services district in West Philadelphia, though at this time there was no proposal; "West Philadelphia Considers Plan to Create Special Services District," *DP*, 10 October 1996.

11. See esp. F. Gerard Adams, "Penn's Westward Planning," *Almanac* 43, no. 17 (14 January 1997): 5. A month before Sled's death, Rodin and her first provost, Stanley Chodorow, listed "the urban agenda" as the fifth of six academic priorities for their *Agenda for Excellence: A Strategic Plan for the University of Pennsylvania, Almanac Supplement*, 24 September 1996, designating academically based community service (ABCS) courses as a core component of that priority (3).

12. See Rodin, *University and Urban Revival*, 54. Endowment growth calculated from UPA, *Financial Report*, 1994–99, UARC on line.

13. Rodin, *University and Urban Revival*, 44.

14. Ibid., 42.

15. "Leaving Penn, but Not West Philadelphia," *PAG*, May 2006, http://www.upenn.edu /gazette/0506/gaz08.html.

16. Rodin, *University and Urban Revival*, 45–58, quotes from 46, 51.

17. For example, an officer of the Spruce Hill Community Association described the 3900 block of Pine Street as "a pretty messy looking block a lot of the time"; "Off-Campus Block Grapples with Mounting Trash," *DP*, 13 February 1995.

18. John Kromer and Lucy Kerman, *West Philadelphia Initiatives: A Case Study in Urban Revitalization* (Philadelphia: University of Pennsylvania, 2005), 22–23; "'Look Out Thief, Somebody's Watching You,'" *PAG*, November 2003, http://www.upenn.edu/gazette/1103 /1103gaz01.html.

19. Quotes from "The Special Services District: A Fact Sheet," *Almanac* 43, no. 36 (17 June 1997), http://www.upenn.edu/almanac/v43/n36/ucd.html; see also Kromer and Kerman, *West Philadelphia Initiatives*, 21–21; Rodin, *University and Urban Revival*, 70. The UCD is housed at 3940–42 Chestnut Street, a Penn-donated building that the University renovated for the UCD and the local station of the Philadelphia Police Department; under Rodin, it supplied twenty-five officers to the area; see "Groundbreaking: A Home for the UCD on Chestnut Street," *Almanac* 45, no. 9 (27 October 1998): 2.

20. Rodin, *University and Urban Revival*, 84–86; "Western Hospitality," *PAG* 97, September–October 1998, 20; "Penn Pulls Plug on Popular UC Brite Initiatives," *DP*, 11 September 1998.

21. "Lighting Up the Neighborhood," *Almanac* 44, no. 2 (2 September 1997): 1; "Penn Pulls Plug."

22. Kromer and Kerman, *West Philadelphia Initiatives*, 24. In 1998, Mayor Ed Rendell hired a former high-ranking New York police officer, John Timoney, as Philadelphia's police commissioner. Having implemented in Philadelphia the computerized ComStat (Comparative Statistics) program, which was pioneered in New York, and having tackled the city's drug trafficking and drug homicides through Operation Sunrise, "a multiagency drug operation," Timoney could report by the end of 2000, John Street's first year as mayor, that "crime was under control." John Timoney, *Beat Cop to Top Cop: A Tale of Three Cities* (Philadelphia: University of Pennsylvania Press, 2010), 250.

23. Kromer and Kerman, *West Philadelphia Initiatives*, 22; Rodin, *University and Urban Revival*, 72–75.

24. For ethnographic details, see Elijah Anderson, *Streetwise: Race, Class, and Change in an Urban Community* (Chicago: University of Chicago Press, 1990), 77–111. Citing FBI reports, Michael B. Katz, in *Why Don't American Cities Burn?* (Philadelphia: University of Pennsylvania Press, 2012), charts for the nation an unabated, precipitous rise in the rate of violent crimes per 100,000, "from 160.9 in 1960 to 363.5 in 1970, 596.6 in 1980, and 729.6 in 1990 before reversing direction, declining to 506.5 in 2000 and 457.5 in 2008" (38–39).

25. Eleni Zatz (director, Office of Off-Campus Living), 16 November 1993, document in authors' possession. The Spruce Hill Community Association reported a loss of 780 Penn graduate students from 1990 to 1994; *The Spruce Hill Community Renewal Plan*, 1995, http:11 /www.sprucehillca.org, accessed 2 February 2011. Standing faculty members were reluctant to live in University City, and their small numbers were diminishing—from 191 in November 1992 to 177 in April 1994, a 7 percent decline. Anne Froehling to Robert Lundgren et al., 19 April 1994, Carolyn Burden Papers.

26. Rodin, *University and Urban Revival*, 82–83; Diane-Louise Wormley, "Community Housing: A Report on the Expanded Program," *Almanac* 45, no. 23 (2 March 1999): 4.

27. Rodin, *University and Urban Revival*, 90–95.

28. Kromer and Kerman, *West Philadelphia Initiatives*, 32; Wormley, "Community Housing," 4.

29. "Converting the Former GE Building," *Almanac* 45, no. 20 (9 February 1999):1; "A Grand Opening: The Left Bank: A Revitalizing Renovation and Restoration," *Almanac* 47, no. 21 (6 February 2001): 6.

30. Rodin, *University and Urban Revival*, 81–106, 189–98, quote from 196; Kromer and Kerman, *West Philadelphia Initiatives*, quote from 32.

31. Rodin interview, Faculty Senate Oral History Project.

32. "More Major Reconstruction on 40th Street Between Chestnut and Walnut," *Almanac* 45, no. 23 (2 March 1999); also see Jon Caroulis, "Of Dirty Drugs and White Dogs," *PAG*, April 1997, 26–32.

33. See "Redford, Penn Officially Unveil Theater Project," *DP*, 5 October 1998; "The Campus, the Community and the Sundance Kid," *Almanac* 45, no. 6 (1998).

34. "Leaving Penn."

35. Rodin, *University and Urban Revival*, 120–23.

36. "Design Guidelines and Review of Campus Projects," *Almanac* 49, no. 6 (October 1, 2002): 12.

37. Rodin, *University and Urban Revival*, 121.

38. Ibid., 113.

39. Street quoted in "City Shows Support for Vending Bill," *DP*, 15 April 1998; "Penn's Influence in the City Evident During Vending Hearings," *DP*, 20 April 1998. Also see "Penn and Food Trucks Collide in a Vendor-Bender," *PAG*, October 1997, http://www.upenn.edu /gazette/1097/1097gaz1.html. For the text of the ordinance, see "Section 9–06: Sidewalk Vendors in Neighborhood Business Districts," *Almanac Between Issues*, 16 February 1998; also see "Council Makes Bill Tougher on U. City Vendors," *DP*, 17 April 1998. Among many other *DP* articles on University City vendors, see esp. "U. to Push City Council for Food Truck Regulations," 12 November 1996; "Vendors, U. Debate Ordinance at Town Mtg.," 19 May 1997; "Protests Delay Action on Vending Ordinance," 15 June 1997; "U. Seeks Fresh Start with Public on Vending Law," 3 September 1997; "Vending Proposal Sent to City Council,"

3 December 1997; "Vending Plans Scaled Back," 18 November 1997; "Vending Bill Shows Few Changes," 24 February 1988.

40. Rodin, *University and Urban Revival*, 114.

41. Ibid., 134–35.

42. Ibid., 150–52; "Partnering the Public Schools in University City," *Almanac* 45, no. 1 (14 July 1998): 8; Susan Lonkevich, "The Community's Schoolhouse," *PAG*, September–October 2000, 30–31.

43. "Community Responds to School Plan," *DP*, 9 July 1998.

44. "U.'s School Plan Questioned," *DP*, 2 October 1998; http://www.thedp.com.

45. "Planning a PreK-8 School for the Year 2001," *Almanac* 45, no. 9 (27 October 1998): 4–5; "Locals Get Input on U. School," *DP*, 4 November 1999; "From Pew Charitable Trusts: $325,000 Toward the Collaborative School," *Almanac* 45, no. 17 (19 January 1999): 1; "The Penn-Assisted PreK-8 Neighborhood School: A January 1999 Update," *Almanac* 45, no. 18 (26 January 1999): 12.

46. Cf. Rodin, *University and Urban Revival*, 149–55. John Puckett, associate dean at the GSE from 1998 to 2004, served on the educational programming committee and helped organize the school's speaker bureau.

47. Rodin, *University and Urban Revival*, 155–56; also see "No Decision Yet on Penn School," *DP*, 11 February 2000.

48. Rodin, *University and Urban Revival*, 156–57; "Penn-Assisted PreK-8 Neighborhood School: Opening Fall 2001 for Kindergarten and First Grade, *Almanac* 47, no. 24 (27 February 2001): 5; "Honoring Sadie Tanner Mossell Alexander: A Role Model for Future Generations of Students," *Almanac* 49, no. 2 (3 September 2002): 1.

49. "Residents Clamor for U. Funding," *DP*, 17 February 2000; Kromer and Kerman, *West Philadelphia Initiatives*, 47.

50. Trend charts, Philadelphia Neighborhood Information System (NIS), neighborhood-Base, http://cml.upenn.edu/nbase/nbTrendRequest.asp, accessed 8 July 2010.

51. Kroner and Kerman, *West Philadelphia Initiatives*, 48; School District of Philadelphia, "School Profile: Penn Alexander School," https://webapps.philasd.org/school_profile/view /1280, accessed 7 July 2010.

52. "University City Feeling the Impact [of] School Closings and Consolidation Threat Cast," http://PlanPhilly.com, accessed 25 October 2011; also see James H. Lytle, Ann Kreidle, and Leslie Nabors Olah, "Penn Partnership Schools Ten Year Report," University of Pennsylvania, n. d. [October 2011].

53. Rodin, *University and Urban Revival*, 179.

54. Ira Harkavy, Carol de Fries, Joann Weeks, Cory Bowman, Glenn Bryan, and Dawn Maglicco, "Strategy for Taking Penn's Local Engagement Effort from Excellence to Eminence," 9 January 2006, courtesy of Netter Center.

55. "On the Streets of Philadelphia, Crime Is Back," Reuters, 31 January 2007, http://www .reuters.com, accessed 6 July 2010.

56. $5 Million Initiative to Enhance Safety," *Almanac* 52, no. 19 (24 January 2006): 1; "Lights, Cameras, Cops," *PAG*, March 2006, http://www.upenn.edu/gazette/0306/gaz10 .html.

57. "Penn: No. 1 in Public Safety," *Almanac* 54, no. 16 (18 December 2007): 1.

Chapter 11

1. Phoebe LeBoy, interview, n.d. [2006 or 2007], Faculty Senate University Governance Oral History Project Records, 2005–2008, UARC UPB25.

2. "Executive VP: John Fry of Coopers & Lybrand," *Almanac* 41, no. 23 (28 February 1995): 1.

3. Coopers and Lybrand, "The University of Pennsylvania Administrative Restructuring Project" (December 1994), *Almanac Supplement*, 17 January 1995, 5–12; in same supplement, Stanley Chodorow and Jack Freeman, "The Case for Administrative Restructuring at Penn," 3–4; also see Judith Rodin, "The Changing University," *Almanac* 43, no. 2 (3 September 1996): 3.

4. "A Vice-President from the Business World Brings a New Bottom Line to Penn," *Chronicle of Higher Education* (*CHE*), 3 September 1999.

5. John Fry, "Restructuring at Penn: Four Basic Questions and Some Interlocking Goals," *Almanac* 42, no. 8 (17 October 1995): 5.

6. LeBoy, interview, Faculty Senate University Governance Oral History Project.

7. "Former Conrail Chairman Named Executive Vice President at University of Pennsylvania," 16 September 1981, UARC UPF8.5 "New Bureau—Subject Files, Executive Vice President, Office of, 1981"; "Former Conrail Chief Takes New College Post," *Wall Street Journal*, 12 August 1982.

8. "Senior Vice President: Helen O'Bannon," *Almanac* 30, no. 2 (6 September 1983): 1–2.

9. "Barnes and Noble to Manage New Campus Bookstore," *DP*, 30 June 1996.

10. "Rehired Book Store Staff Will Not Lose U. Benefits," *DP*, 3 October 1996.

11. Thomas J. Sugrue, "Speaking Out," *Almanac* 44, no. 11 (4 November 1997): 10.

12. Cohen, "Ivory Power," 27; "Inn at Penn Set for September Opening," *DP*, 5 August 1999.

13. George E. Thomas, *University of Pennsylvania Campus Guide* (Princeton, N.J.: Princeton Architectural Press, 2002), 135.

14. "Faculty Club Update: On the New Home in the Inn at Penn," *Almanac* 44, no. 34 (19–26 May 1998): 5.

15. John Fry, "A New Faculty Club Offer," *DP*, 27 January 1999.

16. "U. Lays Off 35 Faculty Club Employees," *DP*, 18 January 1999.

17. "Inn at Penn Says It Will Rehire Workers," *DP*, 17 March 1999.

18. "Vice-President from Business World."

19. "Outsourcing Facilities Management," *Almanac* 44, no. 8 (14 October 1997): 1–2; letter of intent signed by John Fry to William F. Concannon (Trammell Crow Corporate Services), 8 October 1997, *Almanac between Issues*, fall semester 1997, http://www.upenn.edu/almanac/between/letter.html; "U. Hands over Facilities Mgmt. to Outside Firm," *DP*, 9 October 1997.

20. John Fry, "Timeline for Trammell Crow Transition," *DP*, 3 December 1997.

21. "Report on Trammell Crow," *Almanac* 48, no. 6 (2 October 2001): 8.

22. Omar Blaik, "At Work with Trammell Crow," *DP*, 10 March 2000.

23. Quotes from "Trammell Crow's Role Drastically Reduced," *DP*, 3 March, 2000. Also see "Workers Cheer U.'s Trammell Crow Decision," *DP*, 8 March 2000; "Report of the Committee on Facilities, 1999–2000," *Almanac* 46, no. 30 (25 April 2000): 7–8.

24. See "Trammell Crow Contract Ended," *DP*, 29 August 2002.

25. "Senate Executive Committee Statement on Outsourcing," 30 October 1997, *Almanac* 44, no. 11 (4 November 1997): 5; "Trustees: 'Yes' to Trammel Crow Contract," *Almanac* 44, no 12 (11 November 1997): 1–2; "Report of the University Council Ad Hoc Committee on Consultation," 31 March 1998, *Almanac* 44, no. 29 (14 April 1998): 3–4.

26. LeBoy, interview, Faculty Senate University Governance Oral History Project.

27. Linda Koons, interviewed by Edwin Greenlee, 24 July 2007, Faculty Senate University Governance Oral History Project Records, 2005–2008, UARC UPB25. For Faculty

Senate leadership by "professors of lesser distinction" at research universities, see Derek Bok, *Universities in the Marketplace: The Commercialization of Higher Education* (Princeton, N.J.: Princeton University Press, 2003).

28. One administrative unit for strengthening Penn's market position was the Center for Technology Transfer. Before the 1980s, universities were rarely able to obtain patents on their federally funded research. That changed dramatically with the passage of the 1980 Bayh-Doyle Patent and Trademarks Amendment Act, which gave universities wide latitude "to license campus-based inventions to private companies in exchange for royalties and fees." Jennifer Washburn, *University, Inc.: The Corporate Corruption of American Higher Education* (New York: Basic Books, 2005), 70–71. Bayh-Dole increased industry's share of university research budgets from 2.6 percent in 1970 to 7.1 percent in 1997. David C. Mowery, Richard R. Nelson, Bhaven N. Sampat, and Arvids A. Ziedonis, "The Growth of Patenting and Licensing by U.S. Universities: An Assessment of the Effects of the Bayh-Dole Act of 1980," *Research Policy* 30 (2001): 99–119. In the 1980s, technology-transfer offices proliferated on the nation's research campuses, rising from only twenty-five in 1980 to 200 by 1990, to "virtually every American research university" by 2000. Penn was no exception, though, like most research universities, its returns on technology-transfer investments in the 1990s were modest; by 2000, Columbia University, the University of California system, and Stanford University were consistently the strongest performers; Mowry et al., "Growth of Patenting and Licensing"; Richard R. Nelson, "Observations on the Post-Bayh-Dole Rise of Patenting at American Universities," *Journal of Technology Transfer* 26 (2001): 13–19. In 1998, according to a *Chronicle of Higher Education* survey of licensing revenues and patent activity, Penn ranked fifteenth in licensing income ($7,246,695) among 132 reporting universities; of these institutions, however, Penn ranked seventh in total research spending ($414,356,000), leading Harvard, Yale, Columbia, and Stanford in that category. "Licensing Revenues and Patent Activity at 132 Universities, Fiscal 1998," *CHE*, 20 December 1999.

29. Citing our own observations of campus affairs; also see Bok, *Universities in the Marketplace*, 3.

30. External Affairs Committee, *Minutes of the Trustees of the University of Pennsylvania*, 21 June 2002, http://www.archives.upenn.edu/primdocs/upa/upa1_1/2000t009/20020621tr .pdf; "U. To Take on 'New Look' This Fall," *DP*, 1 August 2002.

31. Cited in "Rodin's Salary Tops Charts in Higher Ed," *DP*, 8 September 2003.

32. "Proving Presidential Worth," special report, *CHE*, 19 November 2004; also see "Corporate-Board Fees Add to Some Presidents' Pay," *CHE*, 22 November 2002.

33. "The Growing $500,000 Club," *CHE*, 22 November 2002.

34. Tax Form 990 for Penn (2001), pp. 33–36.

35. The 2001 tax form shows $46,228,452 in taxable assets, including ownership of two insurance companies (38).

36. John Kastor, *Governance of Teaching Hospitals: Turmoil at Penn and Hopkins* (Baltimore: Johns Hopkins University Press, 2004), 35n.

37. Ibid., 81–88, 35–52, 60–73, quotes from 65–66.

38. William N. Kelly, "Dr. Kelley to Trustees: The Losses to Date and the Cuts in View," *Almanac* 46, no. 9 (26 October 1999): 2.

39. "Health System's FY 1999 Losses: More Cutbacks, Restructuring Ahead," *Almanac* 46, no. 9 (26 October 1999): 1–2; Kastor, *Governance in Teaching Hospitals*, 89–91.

40. Kastor, *Governance in Teaching Hospitals*, 60–61.

41. Ibid., 52–54.

42. "Health System's FY 1999 Losses." The total number of layoffs in FY 2000 is not available in any published source. The *DP* reported a total of 965 layoffs by November 1999; "U. Health System Eliminates Positions, Cuts Employees," 27 May 1999; "Health Sys. Fires More than 500 Employees," 2 November 1999.

43. "Clinical Practices of the University of Pennsylvania Fined $30 Million," *Almanac Between Issues*, n.d., http:www.upenn.edu/almanac/between/fed.html; "Dean Kelley's Statement on the $30 Million Settlement in Medicare Costs," *Almanac* 42, no. 16 (9 January 1996): 4; "'A Very Serious Matter,'" *PAG*, February 1996, 17–18.

44. Judith Rodin, "Gene Therapy at Penn Should Go Forward," *PAG*, May 2000, http://www.upenn.edu/gazette/archives/archive99.html.

45. "Clinical Trials Put on Hold at Gene-Therapy Lab," *PAG*, March 2000, http://www.upenn.edu/gazette/0300/0300gaz1.html.

46. Kastor, *Governance in Teaching Hospitals*, 111–12; "Penn Researchers Sued in Gene Therapy Death," *Wall Street Journal*, 19 September 2000.

47. A residual effect of the IHGT affair has been a tightening of research oversight by the University's Institutional Review Board, which ensures that a researcher's protocols are, in every case, reviewed by the Institutional Review Board and that these protocols provide, in addition to other ethical assurances, guarantees of informed consent that are agreed to by the research subjects. Matters as innocent as oral history interviews are subject to these guarantees. See "Statement on Human Subject Research in the Social and Behavioral Sciences," *Almanac* 48, no. 8 (16 October 2001): 4. For Gelsinger and other examples of "conflicts of interest hazardous to our health," see Washburn, *University, Inc.*, 103–36.

48. Kastor, *Governance in Teaching Hospitals*, 112–17, quotes from 117.

49. Ibid., 122–25, 133–34, 140–43, 148–49, 153–54; Judith Rodin, "Proposal to Create Penn Medicine," *Almanac* 48, no. 12 (13 November 2001): 7; Kristi Pintar (Health System), personal communication, 11 August 2010. Also see "School of Medicine: Financial Stabilization Plan," *Almanac* 46, no. 18 (25 January 2000): 5; "EVP for UPHS and Dean of School of Medicine: Arthur Rubenstein," *Almanac* 48, no. 2 (4 September 2001): 1; "Take Penn Medicine and Hold Off on the 501(c) (3)," *PAG*, February 2002, http://www.upenn.edu/gazette/0102/0102gaz5.html.

50. *Agenda for Excellence: A Strategic Plan for the University of Pennsylvania*, *Almanac Supplement*, 21 November 1995. The total cost of the Agenda was about $1.5 billion; "Agenda for Excellence Achievements Require Massive Funding," *DP*, 3 April 1998.

51. *Six Strategic Priorities*, *Almanac Supplement*, 24 September 1996.

52. *Agenda for Excellence: The Strategic Plans of the Schools*, *Almanac Supplement*, 21 January 1997.

53. For an excellent analysis of the rankings game, see Robert Zemsky, *Making Reform Work: The Case for Transforming American Higher Education* (New Brunswick, N.J.: Rutgers University Press, 2009), chap. 5; on Penn, 78–80.

54. Judith Rodin, *The University and Urban Revival: Out of the Ivory Tower and Into the Streets*: (Philadelphia, Pa.: University of Pennsylvania Press, 2007), 183. Rodin's claim in her book that Penn was ranked sixteenth when she arrived is misleading; that number applied only to Penn's academic reputation, not its overall ranking. Indeed, the University achieved a twelfth-place *U.S. News* ranking in September 1994, two months after Rodin's arrival; in fairness to Hackney and Claire Fagin, we note that Rodin started at number twelve; see "Officials Encouraged by U. Jump in Poll," *DP*, 9 September 1994.

55. "Penn: #4 in U.S. News Rankings," *Almanac* 49, no. 4 (17 September 2002): 1; "One of Fab Four," *PAG*, November 2004, http://www.upenn.edu/gazette/1104/1104gaz06.html;

"*U.S. News* Rankings: Four Penn Schools in Top 10," *Almanac* 47, no. 28 (3 April 2001):1; "Graduate School Rankings," *Almanac* 49, no. 28 (8 April 2003): 3; "NRC Ranking: 19 Penn Graduate Programs Are in the Top Ten," *Almanac* 42, no. 4 (19 September 1995): 2–3; "A Strategic Plan for the School of Arts and Sciences," *Almanac Supplement*, 6 April 1999. In 2002, the *Chronicle of Higher Education* listed Penn at number five in federal research and development expenditures; table cited in Laura Fried, "Reputation and Prestige in American Research Universities: An Exploration of the History of Rankings and the Increasing Importance of Student Selectivity in Perceptions of Quality in Higher Education" (EdD diss., University of Pennsylvania, 2005), 42.

56. Zemsky, *Making Reform Work*, 78, 80, 81–82.

57. Judith Rodin, interview, 24 July 2007, Faculty Senate University Governance Oral History Project Records, 2005–2008, UARC UPB25.

58. Judith Rodin, "Sparks of Connection," *PAG*, May–June 2004, http://www.upenn.edu/gazette/0504/0504pres.html.

59. See *Residential Living: A Community Experience, Undergraduate Options 1989–90*, UARC UPA4, box 693, folder 3.

60. "The Inaugural Ceremony," *Almanac Supplement*, 25 October 1994, 5.

61. Judith Rodin and Stanley Chodorow, "Implementing a 21st Century Undergraduate Education," *Almanac* 41, no. 9 (25 October 1994): 3.

62. Residential Planning Committee of the 21st Century Project, *Choosing Community*, *Almanac Supplement*, 29 April 1997, 1, 2.

63. "Report of the Residential Communities Working Group," *Almanac* 44, no. 8 (14 October 1997): 4–5. Also see "The Village Known as Superblock, and How to Find All Twelve Penn College Houses," *Almanac* 45, no. 7 (13 October 1998): 4–5.

64. Susan Lonkevich, "This is Only a Test," *PAG*, February 2001, http://www.upenn.edu/gazette/0101/lonkevich.html; "A New Roadmap for Learning," *PAG*, September 2005, http://www.upenn.edu/gazette/0905/0905gaz13.html.

65. *Agenda for Excellence: 1995–2000, Almanac Supplement*, 1 May 2001, quote from 4; Center for Teaching and Learning website. Three years after CURF's inception, the University reported that eighteen Penn students had garnered ten-month Fulbright Scholarships under CURF auspices; "Secret to Scholarship Success: Applying Themselves," *PAG*, November 2003, http://www.upenn.edu/gazette/1103/1103gaz09.html.

66. Kelly Writers House, http://www.writing.upenn.edu/wh; Samuel Hughes, "Lucid Observations," *PAG*, October 1995, 26–31; Susan Frith, "The House That Writers Built," *PAG*, July 2006, http://www.upenn.edu/gazette/0706/feature1.html; Civic House, http://www.vpul.upenn.edu/civichouse; "The Hub Program Times Two: Civic House Joins Writers House on the Walk," *Almanac* 45, no. 2 (8 September 1998): 9; Weiss Tech House, http://www.tech-house.upenn.edu; "A House Built with Ideas," *PAG*, March 2004, http://www.upenn.edu/gazette/0304/0304gaz12.html.

67. Hughes and Prendergast, "Rodin: A Look Back."

68. Robert Barchi, "The State of the University, 2000–2001," *Almanac* 47, no. 8 (17 October 2000): 4.

69. James Fallows, "The Early Decision Racket," *Atlantic*, September 2001, accessed from http://www.theatlantic.com/magazine/print/2001/09/the-early-decision-racket/2280/, 15 August 2011.

70. For example, see David F. Labaree, *How to Succeed in Schooling Without Really Learning: The Credentials Race in American Education* (New Haven, Conn.: Yale University Press, 1997).

71. Arthur Levine and Jeanette S. Cureton, *When Hope and Fear Collide: A Portrait of Today's College Student* (San Francisco: Jossey-Bass, 1998), 29–33, 36.

72. Michael C. Johanek and John Puckett, "The State of Civic Education: Preparing Citizens in an Era of Accountability," in *Institutions of Democracy: The Public Schools*, ed. Susan Fuhrman and Marvin Lazerson (New York: Oxford University Press, 2005), 146.

73. "Dancing in the Arts and Shadows," *Penn Arts and Sciences*, Fall 1998, 2; quoted in Lee Benson, Ira Harkavy, and John Puckett, *Dewey's Dream: Universities and Democracies in an Age of Education Reform* (Philadelphia: Temple University Press, 2007), 98.

74. Matthew Hartley, "Idealism and Compromise and the Civic Engagement Movement," in *"To Serve a Larger Purpose": Engagement for Democracy and the Transformation of Higher Education*, ed. John Saltmarsh and Matthew Hartley (Philadelphia: Temple University Press, 2011), 27–48. Applying a historical lens, Hartley explains why this activity constitutes a "movement."

75. *Agenda for Excellence, 1995–2000*, cover letter.

76. "Assessing the Agenda," *PAG*, September 2001, http://www.upenn.edu/gazette/0901/prendergast4.html.

77. *Building on Excellence: The Leadership Agenda: A Strategic Plan for the University of Pennsylvania*, *Almanac Supplement*, 23 September 2003, quotes from 6.

78. "The Penn Urban Research Institute: Specializing in All Aspects of Urban Environment," *Almanac* 50, no. 24 (2 March 2004): 1.

79. "The Barbara and Edward Netter Center for Community Partnerships," *Almanac* 54, no. 6 (2 October 2007): 1; "Penn and OU-Tulsa Collaborate in Community Schools Effort," *Almanac* 56, no. 12 (17 November 2009): 1. For the $4.3 billion capital campaign, see John Prendergast, "Seizing the Moment," *PAG*, November 2007, http://www.upenn.edu/gazette/1107/feature1.html. The original target was $3.5 billion.

80. The report was issued a year later. See Ad Hoc Minority Permanence Retrospective Review Committee, *Minority Permanence at the University of Pennsylvania: A Retrospective Analysis, Almanac Supplement*, 10 May 1994, quote from 2.

81. Phoebe S. Leboy, for the Steering Committee of Council, "On Recruitment and Retention of Minority Faculty and Students," for discussion 24 March 1999, *Almanac* 45, no. 25 (23 March 1999): 3–6.

82. Minority Equity Committee, *Minority Equity Report*, 19 April 2005, *Almanac Supplement*, 3 May 2005, extrapolation from p. 2, table 4; quote from p. 2.

Chapter 12

1. David Brownlee, interview by John Puckett, 2 September 2010.

2. "The Perelman Quadrangle as Campus Center," from the essay by the architects on the Perelman Quadrangle, *Almanac* 41, no. 30 (25 April 1995): 3; Brownlee, interview by Puckett.

3. The *DP* covered the proposed Revlon Center and the early phase of the Perelman Quad assiduously; see esp. the following articles: "Lazerson Approves Final Design Plans for Revlon Center," 12 April 1994; "Officials to Restudy Revlon," 29 September 1994; "Rodin, Chodorow Scrap Perelman Center," 25 January 1995; "Perelman Plan: Rodin's First Capital Project," 26 January 1995; "Perelman Agrees to Fund Student Center," 20 April 1995; "Alumnus Contributes $7.5 million Towards Perelman Quadrangle," 22 June 1995. Also see "Back to the Center: A Proposed Quadrangle Linking Houston Hall and Its Neighbors," *Almanac* 41, no. 19 (31 January 1995): 1–2.

4. "Reestablishing the Historic Heart of Penn," *Almanac* 47, no. 2 (5 September 2000): calendar insert. Also see "Campus Development Plan 2000," *Almanac* 47, no. 5 (26 September 2000): 1–2.

5. Hamilton Village is named for the Hamilton family, whose Colonial estate included the property on which the city built the Blockley Almshouse in the nineteenth century. It will be recalled that ten acres were transferred to the University in 1870 to build the West Philadelphia campus. The postbellum Woodlands Cemetery bears the name of William Hamilton's neoclassical mansion, Woodlands, which still stands, partially restored, on a perch above the Schuylkill River.

6. "Penn's Ten-Year, $300 Million Plan for the West Campus," *Almanac* 45, no. 12 (17 November 1998).

7. Brownlee, interview by Puckett.

8. Ibid.

9. "U. Grants Wharton Use of Book Store Site," *DP*, 14 November 1996; "Sketches of a $120 Million Project," *Almanac* 45, no. 20 (9 February 1999): 8.

10. "Wharton Releases Building Plans," *DP*, 2 February 1999; "Huntsman Hall: Wharton's New Nerve Center," *PAG*, January 2003, http://www.upenn.edu/gazette/0103/0103gaz5 .html.

11. See and cf. Kohn Pederson Fox Revlon Center model in Samuel Hughes, "Unbuilt Penn," *PAG*, September 2002, http://www.upenn.edu/gazette/0902/hughes.html. The art historian David Brownlee confirms our observation; Brownlee, interview by Puckett. According to Brownlee, who served on the project's building committee, Kohn Pederson Fox's original modernist design for the Revlon Center was "darn good . . . strong, simple, abstract geometry" inspired by Russian constructivism. When campus planners allowed every student group and other interests each to earmark a place in the proposed center, however, the original design morphed into a bloated structure. Absent in the original plan, ground-floor retail operations were projected to offset some of the enormous costs of operating and staffing such an unwieldy building. A red-brick façade and pitched roof also were added to the design, most likely at the insistence of tradition-minded trustees. When Rodin nixed the Revlon Center, the trustees allowed Kohn Pederson Fox to transfer their final design for that project—red brick, tower, pitched roof—to the Wharton construction site.

12. "Principles for Campus Development," *Almanac* 43, no. 13 (19–26 November 1996): 5.

13. "Transforming Penn—from One End to Another, with Buildings and a New Gateway for the Campus," *Almanac* 50, no. 14 (25 November 2003): 6–7.

14. "A Home for History," *PAG*, March–April 2004, http://www.upenn.edu/gazette/0304 /0304gaz07.html; quote from Robert A. M. Stern Architects, "The McNeil Center for Early American Studies," http://www.ramsa.com/projects-search/academic/the-mcneil.html, accessed 5 May 2011.

15. "Council: State of the University: Report of the President," *Almanac* 54, no. 10 (30 October 2007): 7.

16. Robert Kohler, "Questioning the IAST," *Almanac* 39, no. 5 (29 September 1992): 2.

17. Barry S. Cooperman, "Response by Dr. Cooperman," *Almanac* 39, no. 5 (29 September 1992): 2–3.

18. Michael Lewis, "Edward Collins and Smith Hall," *Almanac* 37, no. 33 (14 May 1991): 6; George E. Thomas, *University of Pennsylvania Campus Guide* (New York: Princeton Architectural Press, 2002), 77–79.

19. Robert E. Kohler, "A Request to Reconsider Demolishing Smith Hall," *Almanac* 37, no. 18 (22 January 1991): 2.

20. Sheldon Hackney, "On Smith Hall: Balancing Past and Future," testimony presented to the Philadelphia Historical Commission, 9 January 1991, *Almanac* 37, no. 18 (22 January 1991): 3, 7.

21. Brownlee, interview by Puckett.

22. The *DP* provided extensive coverage of the IAST's plodding development; see esp. "Panel Approves Smith Razing," 15 January 1991; "Many Still Question IAST Plan," 30 March 1995, quote from the architects; "Smith Hall Razed to Make Room for IAST," 1 September 1995.

23. "Opening IAST's Vagelos Laboratories," *Almanac* 44, no. 9 (21 October 1997); Thomas, *Campus Guide*, 77.

24. John Prendergast, "A Passion for Putting Things Together," *PAG*, November 2003, http://www.upenn.edu/gazette/1103/prendergast1.html.

25. "Engineering's Rough-Hewn, High-Tech Castle," *PAG,* 7 January 2007, http://www.upenn.edu/gazette/0107/gaz02.html.

26. "A Trio of Buildings for Science Research at Penn," *Almanac* 53, no. 1 (11 July 2006): 16.

27. "Celebrating Research: PennMed's New High-Rise, New NIH Rankings to Match," *Almanac* 45, no. 32 (11 May 1999): 1, 5.

28. "Christian Association Up for Sale," *DP*, 17 October 1997; "Sold: The Christian Association Building," *Almanac* 46, no. 11 (9 November 1999): 2.

29. "Locust Walk to Come Alive Day and Night," *Almanac* 46, no. 28 (11 April 2000): 1; Samuel Hughes and John Prendergast, "Rodin: A Look Back at an Extraordinary Decade for Penn, and the President Who Led the Way," *PAG*, May 2004, http://www.upenn.edu/gazette/0504/editors1.html.

30. For a general description, see Hughes and Prendergast, "Rodin: A Look Back."

31. "Re: Departmental Moves," *Almanac* 37, no. 16 (18 December 1990): 2; "The Eminent Victorians," *Almanac* 42, no. 34 (18 June 1996): 1.

32. "University of Pennsylvania Law School Sesquicentennial History," *Almanac* 47, no. 12 (14 November 2000): 8–9.

33. Thomas, *Campus Guide*, 64–66.

34. Judith Rodin, interview by Edwin Greenlee, 23 April 2007, Faculty Senate University Governance Oral History Project Records, 2005–2008, UARC UPB25.

35. "Church to Be Named for Addams," *DP*, 13 September 1996; "What's Next for Charles Addams Hall: 'New Effort and New Plans,'" *Almanac* 43, no. 26 (18 March 1997): 24; in same issue, George E. Thomas, "Asbury Methodist Church," 24; "The Charles Addams Fine Arts Hall," *Almanac* 47, no. 28 (3 April 2001): n.p.

36. Thomas, *Campus Guide*, 81–83. Also see John Pendergrast, "Work in Progress," *PAG*, September 1999, http://www.upenn.edu/gazette/0999/prendergast.html.

37. Thomas, *Campus Guide*, 111.

38. "Construction to Begin on Baseball Field," *DP*, 22 July 1999.

39. "At Risk: An Irreplaceable Collection: The Case for the New Mainwaring Wing," *Almanac* 48, no. 32 (30 April 2002): 4–5. For the University Museum's architectural heritage, see Thomas, *Campus Guide*, 97–99.

40. "Trustees OK Plan for Gym," *DP*, 1 October 1999; "David Pottruck Health and Fitness Center," *Almanac* 49, no. 5 (24 September 2002): 12.

41. "Hillel's New Home," *Almanac* 48, no. 6 (2 October 2001): 16; "Dedication of Penn Hillel's New Home: Steinhardt Hall," *Almanac* 50, no. 10 (28 October 2003): 1.

42. Judith Rodin, "The 21st Century Library," *Almanac* 45, no. 2 (8 September 1998): 3.

43. "A New Chapter for English Department's Home," *PAG,* January–February 2004, http://www.upenn.edu/gazette/0104/0104gaz08.html.

44. Margie Ruddick Landscape, http://www.margieruddick.com/projects/generational01 .php, accessed 5 May 2011; "Transforming Penn."

45. "Locus Walk Renovations Slated to Continue Throughout the Fall," *DP*, 3 July 1996; "Locust Walk to Get New, Brighter Lights," *DP*, 13 April 1998.

46. "Campus Development Plan 2001," *Almanac* 47, no. 24 (27 February 2001): 6–8.

47. Sarah Elizabeth Zurier, "Commerce, Ceremony, Community: Philadelphia's Convention Hall in Context" (MS thesis, University of Pennsylvania, 1997); "Philadelphia's Sleeping Giant," *DP*, 12 January 2004.

48. "Single Home Should Help U.'s Cancer Center," *DP*, 3 November 1998.

49. "Trustees Updated on Civic Center," *DP*, 24 June 1999.

50. "Convention Hall Demolition: Despite Protests, Plans for New Cancer Center Proceed," *DP*, 15 February 2005.

51. "Raymond and Ruth Perelman's $25 Million Gift to Center for Advanced Medicine," *Almanac* 52, no. 14 (6 December 2005): 1; "Penn Medicine Advances Real-Time Medicine: The Ruth and Raymond Perelman Center for Advanced Medicine—Helping to Heal Patients Through Innovative Building Design," *Almanac* 55, no. 7 (7 October 2008): 4–5.

52. "Dedicating the Roberts Proton Therapy Center," *Almanac* 56, no. 24 (8 December 2009): 8.

53. "50 Million Gift from Anne and Jerome Fisher for New Translational Research Center," *Almanac* 55, no. 1 (15 July 2008): 1–2.

54. "Finalizing Penn's Purchase of U.S. Postal Service Property," *Almanac* 50, no. 28 (6 April 2004): 8.

55. "Council: 2005–2006 Year-End Report: Committee on Recreation and Intercollegiate Athletics (CRIA)," *Almanac* 53, no. 8 (17 October 2006): 3–5; "Collaborative Redevelopment of U.S. Postal Service Facilities," *Almanac* 54, no. 3 (11 September 2007): 8. As of 2011, the Internal Revenue Service acquired a twenty-year lease on the old main Post Office building, for which the Brandywine Realty Trust completed a $265 million renovation.

56. Judith Rodin, *The University and Urban Renewal: Out of the Ivory Tower and Into the Streets* (Philadelphia: University of Pennsylvania Press, 2007), 170–72; Rodin, interview by Greenlee. For the broader City and metropolitan contexts of the Schuylkill River Development Corporation, see Steven Conn, *Metropolitan Philadelphia: Living with the Presence of the Past* (Philadelphia: University of Pennsylvania Press, 2006), 159–203.

57. Penn Connects: *A Vision for the Future* (Philadelphia: University of Pennsylvania, 2006), vii.

58. Ibid., xi–xv.

59. Ibid., x–xi.

60. Claire Fagin interview, 15 June 2006, Faculty Senate Oral History Project Records, 2005–2008, UARC UPB 25.

61. Rodin, no doubt, benefited from the "relative tranquility" of the national zeitgeist during her decade in College Hall, a period the historian William L. O'Neil calls "a bubble in time." William L. O'Neil, *A Bubble in Time: America During the Interwar Years, 1989–2001* (Chicago: Ivan R. Dee, 2009). Relative tranquility aptly describes Penn after the mid-1990s. If any national event of Rodin's tenure had the potential for polarizing the campus, it was the Supreme Court's ruling in *Grutter v. Bollinger*, a lawsuit filed against the University of Michigan by a rejected white applicant charging reverse discrimination in the law school's admissions process. Regarding this case, campus opinion at Penn split along partisan political lines, though the debates were calm and civil; in stark contrast to the emotionally charged Hackney era, the ruminations of a conservative white editorialist who called affirmative ac-

tion "a program without morals" did not provoke a firestorm of black outrage at the *DP*. The ruling's affirmation of affirmative action strengthened the climate of civility. Rodin and law school dean Michael Fitts stood squarely behind Justice Sandra Day O'Connell's ruling for the majority in *Grutter* that "student body diversity is a compelling state interest that can justify the use of race in university admissions." Rodin and Fitts had signed separate amicus curiae briefs in the case, and Rodin hailed the decision as "an important victory for the principle of diversity." David Copley, "A Program Without Morals," *DP* column, 20 January 2003; "Campus Sees Partisan Divide on Affirmative Action," *DP*, 28 February 2003; "Penn Supports U. Michigan in Court Cases, *DP*, 29 February 2003; "U. Students Protest for Aff. Action in D.C.," *DP*, 2 April 2003; Judith Rodin, "Encouraging Interaction and Collaboration," *Almanac* 50, no. 2 (2 September 2003). Another potentially divisive cultural event was the media-hyped O. J. Simpson murder trial of 1995, the so-called Trial of the Century, in Los Angeles. Despite the unambiguous racial overtones of the trial, the tsunami of 24/7 media coverage, and Simpson's acquittal by a jury of nine blacks, one Hispanic, and two whites, the Simpson affair had little political traction on the Penn campus, mustering (mercifully) only one panel of professorial pundits and within days disappearing from the news and editorial pages of the *DP*. "Penn Profs Say Questions Linger After Decision," *DP*, 4 October 1995. A more overtly political event, President Clinton's decision to send troops to Bosnia in the late fall of 1995, with the weight of public opinion arrayed against him, fell largely on deaf ears at Penn, as did his authorization of U.S. air attacks on Serbian forces in Kosovo in 1999.

62. Daniel Duane, "Eggheads Unite," *NYT Magazine*, 4 May 2003.

63. Christina Collins, "GET-UP in Context," *DP*, op-ed, 2 February 2002; "Grad Group No Longer Represents Some Students," *DP*, 29 January 2002; Duane, "Eggheads Unite."

64. "Grad Students Win Right to Unionize," *DP*, 22 November 2002; "Gazetteer: NLRB Rules: Some Grad Students Are Employees," *PAG*, January–February 2003, http://www.upenn.edu/gazette/0103/index.html; "Bargaining Unit Causes Confusion, Contention," *DP*, 29 February 2003; "Poll: Most Voted Yes on Union," *DP*, 3 March 2003; "Grad Student Employees Rally at Rodin's House," *DP*, 3 October 2003; "Trustees' Fall Meeting Coverage," *Almanac* 50, no. 12 (11 November 2003); "GET-UP Strike Causes Limited Stir on Campus," *DP*, 27 February 2004; "Strike Ends with Little Disruption," *DP*, 1 March 2004; "GET-UP Strike Boosts Publicity; No Change in Admin. Response," *DP*, 4 March 2004.

65. Stanton Wortham, "A Comment on the Fish," *Almanac* 49, no. 21 (11 February 2003): 2; Lawrence Sherman, "Striking and Disrupting the University over $58 an Hour," *DP*, op-ed, 2 February 2004; Peter Conn quoted in Duane, "Eggheads Unite."

66. Jennifer Washburn, *University, Inc.: The Corporate Corruption of American Higher Education* (New York: Basic Books, 2005), 202–3, 211; Institute for Education Sciences, *Digest of Education Statistics* (Washington, D.C.: U.S. Department of Education, 2010), table 255, http://nces.ed.gov/pubsearch/pubsinfo.asp?pubid=2011015.

67. Quoted in Amy Gutmann, "Graduate Student Organizing Decision," message to the trustees, 16 July 2004, *Almanac Between Issues*, 23 July 2004, http://www.upenn.edu/almanac; also see, "Labor Board Says Graduate Students at Private Universities Have No Right to Unionize," *NYT*, 16 July 2004.

68. "NLRB Rules Against Grad Unionization at Penn," *DP*, 2 September 2004.

69. Peter Conn, quoted in "GET-UP to Continue Union Battle," *DP*, 2 September 2004; also see "U. President [Amy Gutmann] Not Likely to Recognize Grad Union," *DP*, 10 September 2004.

70. "U. Seeks Policy on Sweatshop Labor Standards," *DP*, 2 February 1999; "PAN Continues Sweatshop Campaign," *DP*, 23 September 1999.

71. "U. Accepts Code of Conduct on Sweatshop Use," *DP*, 17 March 1999; "Students Strip over Sweatshops," *DP*, 15 October 1999; "Penn Will Now Require Info on Insignia-Apparel Factory Sites," *DP*, 21 October 1999; "Two Sweatshop Groups at Odds on Monitoring," *DP*, 12 November 1999.

72. "Sweatshop Group Gives Ben New Look," *DP*, 2 February 2002; "New Sweatshop Task Force Created," *DP*, 7 February 2000.

73. "Sweatshop Group Stages Sit-In," *DP*, 8 February 2000; "Day 4 of Sweatshop Sit-In: Rodin Weary of Protestors," *DP*, 10 February 2000; Rodin quoted in "Sweatshop Protest Continues to Gather Steam," *DP*, 11 February 2000.

74. "Sweatshop Protest Continues to Gather Steam"; "Students Unsure of Sit-In's Usefulness," *DP*, 11 February 2000; "Rodin, Protestors Finally Reach Agreement," *DP*, 15 February 2000; "Protest Officially Over After 9 Days," *DP*, 16 February 2000; "Starting with a Clean Slate" (Judith Rodin to the FLA, 15 February 2000), *Almanac* 46, no. 22 (22 February 2000): 2; "Report of the Ad-Hoc Committee on Sweatshop Labor to University President Judith Rodin," *Almanac* 46, no. 24 (7 March 2000): 3; in same issue, "On Sweatshop Proposals," 2; Gregory L. Possehl, "From the Chair of the Committee on Manufacturer Responsibility" (Possehl to Rodin, 20 November 2000), letter posted at http://www.upenn.edu/almanac/v47/n16/contents.html; Judith Rodin, "Response to the Committee on Manufacturer Responsibility," *Almanac* 47, no. 16 (19 December 2000): 7.

75. "Alumnus Found Dead Outside FIJI House," *DP*, 22 March 1999.

76. "U. Cracking Down on Alcohol Abuse," *DP*, 26 March 1999.

77. "Death Prompts Close Look at Alcohol Policies," *DP*, 24 March 1999.

78. Henry Wechsler, "Alcohol and the American College Campus: A Report from the Harvard School of Public Health," *Change*, July–August 1996, 20–25, 60; quotes from 20, 22. Also see Ralph W. Hingson, "College-Age Drinking Problems," *Public Health Reports* 113, no. 1 (January–February 1998), 52–54. For a brief history of "alcohol misuse" in fraternities and efforts to quell it, see Hank Nuwer, *Wrongs of Passage: Fraternities, Sororities, Hazing, and Binge Drinking* (Bloomington: Indiana University Press, 1999), 57–66.

79. "Report of the President's Special Committee on Alcohol Abuse," *Almanac* 45, no. 3 (15 September 1998): 9–11.

80. Ibid.

81. "U. Cracking Down on Alcohol Abuse," *DP*, 26 March 1999.

82. "Rodin: Policy Involved 'Great Deal of Consultation,'" *DP*, 30 March 1999. Rodin accurately noted that students were represented on the President's Special Committee on Alcohol Abuse. Ironically, a *DP* headline of 31 March proclaimed, "Students Shed Apathy at Alcohol Policy Rally." Also see "Alcohol Ban Not Lifted for Spring Fling," *DP*, 15 April 1999.

83. "Hours after Mass Rally, Task Force Meets," *DP*, 31 March 1999.

84. "Final Report of the Working Group on Alcohol Abuse," *Almanac* 45, no. 31 (4 May 1999): 4–5.

85. "1999–2000 Alcohol Progress Report Year 1," *Almanac* 47, no. 3 (12 September 2000): 8–10.

86. "Penn's Current Alcohol Policy Remains a Work in Progress," *DP*, 24 March 2000. Also see "Approved Changes to the University Alcohol Policy—Section 2, B, #6," *Almanac* 47, no. 10 (31 October 2000): 2.

87. "Phi Gamma Delta Fraternity Update," *Almanac* 45, no. 28 (13 April 1999): 9; quote from "Fiji Receives Official Charter," *DP*, 11 April 2010; "Penn Settles Tobin Wrongful Death Suit, Does Not Admit Fault," *DP*, 28 August 2003. Tobin's death is recorded in a "chronology of deaths" attributable to fraternity incidents since 1847, in Nuwer, *Wrongs of Passage*, 237–74.

88. Ira Harkavy and John L. Puckett, "Lessons from Hull House for the Contemporary Urban University," *Social Service Review* 68, no. 3 (1994): 299–321.

89. Rodin, interview by Greenlee.

Conclusion

1. Albert H. Smyth, *The Writings of Benjamin Franklin*, vol. 2: *1722–1750* (New York: Macmillan, 1907), 396; James Campbell, *Recovering Benjamin Franklin: An Exploration of a Life of Science and Service* (Chicago: Open Court, 1999), chaps. 2.4, 5.3; John C. Van Horne, "Collective Benevolence and the Common Good in Franklin's Philanthropy," in *Reappraising Benjamin Franklin: A Bicentennial Perspective*, ed. J. A. Leo Lemay (Newark: University of Delaware Press, 1993), 425–40.

2. Benjamin Franklin to Samuel Johnson, 23 August 1750, no ms, reprinted from *The Port Folio*, n.s., 11 (1809), 115–16, Packard Humanities Institute, Papers of Benjamin Franklin, vol. 4: 1750–53, http://franklinpapers.org/franklin/framedVolumes.jsp.

3. Benjamin Franklin, *Tract Relative to the English School of Philadelphia* (June 1789), Packard Humanities Institute, Papers of Benjamin Franklin, unpub. 1778–92.

4. Benjamin Franklin, *Idea of the English School*, printed in Rev. Mr. Richard Peters, *A Sermon on Education. Wherein Some Account is given of the Academy, Established in the City of Philadelphia. Preach'd at the Opening thereof, on the Seventh Day of January, 1750–51*; Packard Humanities Institute, Papers of Benjamin Franklin, vol. 4: 1750–53.

5. Franklin, *Tract Relative to English School*.

6. Edward Potts Cheyney, *History of the University of Pennsylvania, 1740–1940* (Philadelphia: University of Pennsylvania Press, 1940), 29.

7. John L. Jackson, *Racial Paranoia: The Unintended Consequences of Political Correctness* (New York: Basic Civitas, 2008), 4.

8. West Philadelphia Community History Center, http://www.archives.upenn/histy/features/wphila/index.html.

9. "N.Y.U. Plans an Expansion of 40 Percent," *NYT*, 22 March 2010.

10. *NYU 2031: NYU in NYC*, http://www.nyu.edu/nyu2031/nyuinnyc/growth/the-plan.php, n.d., accessed 16 May 2013; quotes are from the original plan, n.d., accessed 22 August 2011.

11. Ibid., chap. 6.

12. "Columbia University in the City of New York: Manhattanville in West Harlem," http://neighbors.columbia.edu/pages/manplanning/DESIGNELEMENTS.html, accessed 29 March 2013.

13. "TCCS [Teachers College Community School] Grand Opening," *NYC Schools*, 6 February 2013, http://www.tc.edu/communityschool, accessed 16 May 2013.

Appendix

1. Amanda I. Seligman, *Block by Block: Neighborhoods and Public Policy on Chicago's West Side* (Chicago: University of Chicago Press, 2005), chap. 4: "A Chicago Campus for the University of Illinois," quote from 115–16.

2. Ibid., 116. Also see George Rosen, *Decision-Making Chicago Style: The Genesis of a University of Illinois Campus* (Urbana: University of Illinois Press, 1980), esp. chap. 6.

3. Yale University, a modest example of campus-core expansion, merits our attention for its architectural contributions to urban renewal and because it was a direct beneficiary of the redevelopment of New Haven's downtown. By the early 1950s New Haven was a "stagnant," "quietly dying" midsized city when a new Democratic mayor, Richard C. Lee, took office. By

the end of Lee's fourteen-year progressive mayoralty, New Haven, population 152,000, boasted "the largest per capita [urban renewal] program of any city in the country. Some $120,000,000 of all Title I funds—$790 for each resident—has been given or reserved for use by New Haven [compared to New York at $41.35 per capita]. Thirty per cent of the land, where half of the population lives, is under renewal treatment or planning"; Jeanne R. Lowe, *Cities in a Race with Time: Progress and Poverty in America's Renewing Cities* (New York: Random House, 1967), 406. Lee and his planning czar Edward C. Logue's most important renewal initiatives, the Oak Street and Church Street projects and the Oak Street Connector, contributed to rebuilding New Haven's decaying downtown, with the collateral effect of removing obstacles that obstructed views of Yale from the city's throughways; Michael H. Carriere, "Between Being and Becoming: On Architecture, Student Protest, and the Aesthetics of Liberalism in Postwar America" (PhD diss., University of Chicago, 2010), 216–20. These projects displaced whites and blacks alike, though blacks were three times as likely as whites to be relocated in public housing; Douglas W. Rae, *City: Urbanism and Its End* (New Haven, Conn.: Yale University Press, 2003), 334–34, 338–40. While Yale, situated just north of the downtown, acquired some urban renewal properties for its core-campus expansion, the university's primary role in urban renewal, as the historian Michael Carriere suggests in his dissertation "Between Being and Becoming," 58–74, was architectural. Not only was Yale's structural presence a vital "bulwark against blight," the striking new modernist buildings were the university's major contribution to strengthening the central city in the urban renewal era. In 1955 Yale purchased three high school buildings from the city in the adjoining Dixwell neighborhood—a deal that added $3 million to New Haven's coffers at a price that was $1.1 million above the appraisal value of the buildings and gave the city the funds to build two new high schools on other sites. This campus urban renewal project, which built Stiles and Morse colleges, "imaginary colleges" (that is, student residence halls) designed by Eero Saarinen, was also credited under Section 112 as part of New Haven's match for federally sponsored urban renewal projects; Lowe, *Cities in a Race with Time*, 424; Mandi Issacs Jackson, *Model City Blues: Urban Space and Organized Resistance in New Haven* (Philadelphia: Temple University Press, 2008), 76; Fred Powledge, *Model City: A Test of American Liberalism: One Town's Efforts to Rebuild Itself* (New York: Simon & Schuster, 1970), 68; Rae, *City*, 428–29. Other spectacular modernist structures of the 1950s and 1960s, what one magazine writer hailed as the "ivyless halls of Yale," contributed a new, if not uncontroversial, vitality to the collegiate Gothic campus: Louis Kahn's Yale Art Gallery; Philip Johnson's Geology Laboratory, Kline Biology Tower, and Kline Chemistry Laboratory; George Bunshaft's Beinecke Rare Book and Manuscript Library; Paul Rudolph's Art and Architecture Building; and Saarinen's Ingalls Rink. Contemporary scholars agreed that these monumental buildings bespoke a masculinity and virility apropos of a Cold War American research university; Carriere, "Between Being and Becoming," 58–74, esp. 68.

The Georgia Institute of Technology (Georgia Tech) illustrates campus-core expansion in a city outside the heavily urbanized Northeast Corridor and Midwest. Georgia Tech rose to regional and national prominence in the 1960s as a hub of scientific knowledge production, primarily on the strength of federal R & D funds for military research. The Institute's rise paralleled and contributed to Atlanta's remarkable postwar growth as the South's leading industrial and transportation hub. "As Georgia Tech expanded its research capacity, it expanded its campus, taking advantage of new federal funds for this purpose and building new alliances with city officials in the process," notes the historian Margaret Pugh O'Mara. Yet "while the school's surrounding neighborhood [the Hemphill Avenue area] had become an official Atlanta urban renewal project in the late 1950s, it was not until Section 112 had been authorized that Atlanta agreed to make Tech's development a top urban renewal priority." The master plan Tech presented to the city in 1964 "created a 42-acre campus and a host of modern buildings to house research laboratories, classrooms, and dormitories, and closed a number of streets and one cross-town roadway"; Margaret Pugh O'Mara, *Cities of Knowledge: Cold War Science and the Search for the Next Silicon Valley* (Princeton, N.J.: Princeton University Press, 2005), 203, 204.

4. George E. Thomas, *Drexel University: An Architectural History of the Main Building 1891–1991*, quoted, http://www.drexel.edu/univrel/main_bldg, accessed 15 July 2011; Constantine Papadakis, "Drexel University: A University with a Difference: The Unique Vision of Anthony J. Drexel," address delivered at 2001 Greater Delaware Valley meeting of the Newcomen Society of the United States, Philadelphia, 6 December 2001; accessed from http://www.drexel.edu/papadakis/newcomen/, 15 July 2011; Miriam Kotzin, *A History of Drexel University 1941–1963* (Philadelphia: Drexel University, 1983), chap. 1: "The First Fifty Years, 1891–1941."

5. Papadakis, "Drexel University."

6. West Philadelphia Corporation, *Fifth Annual Report: University City, Philadelphia*, 1965, part 3, UARC UPA 4, box 188, folder "West Philadelphia Corporation Annual Reports."

7. Lawrence J. Biond, "West Philadelphia and Powelton Historic District: Development Timeline," accessed from http://poweltonvillage.org/powelton2.html, 24 July 2011.

8. "Powelton Group Sues to Bar Dormitory," *PI*, 6 June 1965; "City Ready to Condemn near Drexel," *PEB*, 22 January 1967, TUA.

9. "Council Given Alternate Plan for Drexel," *PEB*, 14 September 1966, TUA; "Powelton Owners Ask U.S. to Halt University City Aid," *PEB*, 13 September 1967, TUA.

10. "Five Groups Give Conditions for Meeting with Drexel," *PEB,* 22 December 1969, TUA; "Drexel Dorm Will Be Built, Sit-Ins Told," *PEB*, 30 January 1970; "Sit-In Ends, Talks to Start at Drexel," *PEB*, 1 February 1970, TUA; "Powelton Group Blocks Demolition at 33rd, Race," *PEB*, 18 February 1970; "15 Halt Razing of Houses for Drexel Gym," *PEB*, 29 September 1970; "Powelton Group Seeks to Block Drexel Expansion," *PEB*, 24 January 1971, TUA; "Two Powelton Groups Sue to Stop Renewal Project," *PEB*, 14 March 1974, TUA.

11. "Drexel Buildings, 1891-present," accessed from http://archives.library.drexel.edu /buildings, 24 July 2011.

12. John Sennott (president, Powelton Neighbors), statement to Zoning and Renewal Committee of City Council, typescript draft with edits, 13 September 1966, TUA West Phila. Corp. Acc. 350, box 12, folder "Public Hearing (Unit 5) Sept. 13, 1966."

13. Nathaniel Burt and Wallace E. Davis, "The Iron Age: 1876–1905," in *Philadelphia: A 300-Year History*, ed. Russell F. Weigley (New York: W. W. Norton, 1982), 500.

14. "Temple University History," accessed from http://www.temple125years.com/history .php, 25 July 2011.

15. *Temple University Campus Planning Report*, May 1969, Conwellana-Templana Collection (CTC), Special Collections Research Center, Temple University.

16. "Temple Asks City's Help to Expand," *PI*, 29 May 1948, CTC.

17. Philadelphia City Planning Commission, *Redevelopment Areas—Temple* (Philadelphia: PCPC, 1951), FFAL; Jacqueline Steck and Albert R. Carlisle, "The Temple University Development Plan," *Economics and Business Bulletin*, June 1954, CTC, folder "Expansion Up to 1960"; James W. Hilty, *Temple University: 125 Years of Service to Philadelphia, the Nation, and the World* (Philadelphia: Temple University Press, 2010), 77; RDA, Redevelopment Proposal: Northwest Temple Redevelopment Area, Norris Project (Philadelphia: RDA, 1955), FFAL.

18. "19,000 Enrolled in Temple Classes," *PEB*, 24 September, CTC.

19. "Development Program," *Temple University Alumni Review*, January 1955, pp. 1–5, CTC, folder "Expansion Up to 1960."

20. "Trees for Temple: New Campus Taking Shape," *Philadelphia Inquirer Magazine*, 28 April 1957, 52, CTC.

21. "Temple Buys Old Cemetery," *PEB*, 23 March 1956, CTC.

22. "28,000 Graves Being Shifted from Monument Cemetery," *PEB*, 6 June 1956, CTC; Hilty, *Temple University*, 86.

23. Hilty, *Temple University*, 87.

24. "Temple Leads in Enrollment," *PEB*, 6 January 1963, CTC.

25. "Temple Unveils Plan to Double Its Campus," *PI*, 18 August, 1966, CTC; Hilty, *Temple University*, 106.

26. Hilty, *Temple University*, 108–12.

27. Ibid., 122–23.

28. Ibid., 123.

29. Hilty, *Temple University*, 123–24.

30. Kenneth T. Jackson, "Robert Moses and the Rise of New York: The Power Broker in Perspective," in *Robert Moses and the Modern City: The Transformation of New York*, ed. Hilary Ballon and Kenneth T. Jackson (New York: W. W. Norton, 2007), 67–71; in same volume: Hilary Ballon, "Robert Moses and Urban Renewal: The Title I Program," 94–115. This meticulously researched, beautifully illustrated book provides a detailed counterpoint to Robert Caro's magisterial though highly critical biography of Moses, *The Power Broker: Robert Moses and the Fall of New York* (New York: Knopf, 1974). Also see "A Town Revived, a Villain Redeemed," *NYT*, 11 February 2007.

31. Roberta Brandes Gratz, *The Battle for Gotham: New York in the Shadow of Robert Moses and Jane Jacobs* (New York: Nation Books, 2010), xxi–xxii.

32. "Town Revived, Villain Redeemed."

33. The Julliard School built its new five-story building for music, theater, and dance on Lincoln Center's expansion block of 65th-66th-Broadway-Amersterdam in 1969; Hillary Ballon, "Lincoln Square Title I," in Ballon and Jackson, *Robert Moses and the Modern City*, 279–89; "Progress Report on the New Arts Center," *NYT*, 25 May 1958. The 1953 Title I proposal for the Pratt Institute, a private art college established in the Clinton Hill section of Brooklyn in 1887, called for the development of three contiguous superblocks, the central component of which was to be a campus-core expansion for Pratt; the northern and southern superblocks were earmarked for upper-middle-class high-rise apartments. By 1958, the Institute had constructed two new dormitories and a new classroom building in the central superblock. By the early 1960s private developers built University Terrace, a group of three twenty-four-story, limited equity cooperatives in the southern superblock—Pratt Towers, Ryerson Towers, and St. James Towers. Concurrently, two sixteen-story rental-apartment buildings, Willoughby Walk, were completed in the northern superblock; Matthew Gordon Lasner, "Pratt Institute Title I," in Ballon and Jackson, *Robert Moses and the Modern City*, 274–75. The quote is from "Town Revived." Long Island University (LIU) acquired 7.5 acres for its permanent campus in a superblock in the Fort Greene Title I project, sharing the block with Brooklyn Hospital. Since its founding in 1926, LIU had operated out of rental buildings in Brooklyn. In 1952 LIU acquired the stately Brooklyn Paramount Theater to renovate as an academic building; short of funds to put new buildings on the site, the university had to wait until late 1958 to break ground for the first new building, "a 16-story residential building with dormitory rooms for students and apartments for faculty. . . . The remainder of the site was

used for parking and athletic fields and filled in with buildings only gradually"; Matthew Gordon Lasner, "Fort Greene Title I," in Ballon and Jackson, *Robert Moses and the Modern City*, 267–69.

34. Thomas J. Frusciano and Marilyn H. Pettit, *New York University and the City: An Illustrated History* (New Brunswick, N.J.: Rutgers University Press, 1997), 1–201.

35. Another component of NYU's postwar expansion was the NYU-Bellevue Medical Center, the product of the School of Medicine's merger with Bellevue Hospital in 1944. Development of the new medical center as a Kips Bay superblock was the centerpiece of a Moses Title I project in the 1950s. Moses's bulldozers leveled a swath of industrial and commercial buildings for NYU's new medical campus from East 31st to East 33rd Street between First Avenue and East River Drive; Hilary Ballon, "NYU-Bellevue Title I," in Ballon and Jackson, *Robert Moses and the Modern City*, 269–73.

36. Frusciano and Pettit, *New York University*, 203–208.

37. Hilary Ballon, "Washington Square Southeast Title I," in Ballon and Jackson, *Robert Moses and the Modern City*, 244–48, quote from 246; Frusciano and Pettit, *New York University*, 208–13; "Slum Fight Boils in Washington Sq.," *NYT*, 29 January 1954; "City Gets 9 Blocks at Washington Sq.," *NYT*, 19 November 1954. As Robert Fishman notes in "Revolt of the Urbs: Robert Moses and His Critics," in Ballon and Jackson, *Robert Moses and the Modern City*, 122–29, a related battle that did not involve NYU directly pitted a stalwart group of Greenwich Village mothers against "Moses's attempt to push a highway through Washington Square Park. Lower Fifth Avenue stopped at the park, with only a carriageway to the narrow streets to the south. Moses sought to expand the carriageway into a four-lane arterial that would continue as Fifth Avenue South past his Southeast Washington Square urban renewal project, cutting through what is now Soho and ultimately linking up with his cherished [never completed] elevated Lower Manhattan Expressway at Broome Street" (123). Here Moses suffered a major defeat, as the "park mothers" (among them Eleanor Roosevelt and Jane Jacobs) and their allies succeeded in persuading the Board of Estimate to close the park to traffic in the fall of 1958. The victory was fully sealed in the late summer of 1963 when the city created a one-way, counterclockwise traffic flow around the park and closed the northern end to the 5th Avenue buses, which had previously used the plaza at Washington Square Arch as a turnaround point; "City to Close Washington Square to All Buses," *NYT*, 31 August 1963. Fishman, in "Revolt of the Urbs," accords the park mothers' victory a sacred place in contemporary planning theory. "The work that truly brought the battle of Washington Square into the heart of planning theory was Jane Jacob's *Death and Life of Great American Cities* (1961). . . . Although *Death and Life* presented a national perspective on urban issues, it was dedicated to her family and to New York City. The struggle to save the unique built environment of the Village and its park was the leitmotif that ran through almost every chapter" (128). Jacobs offers a brief description of the park mothers' battle in *The Death and Life of Great American Cities* (New York: Modern Library, 1961), chap. 18, "Erosion of Cities or Attrition of Automobiles."

38. "Title I Developments," 244–48; Frusciano and Pettit, *New York University*, 213–16; quote from "$25-Million N.Y.U Library Is Dedicated," NYT, 17 December 1972.

39. Gratz, *Battle for Gotham*, 1–3.

40. Frusciano and Pettit, *New York University*, 213–16; "Bobst Library: An Emphasis on Space," *NYT*, 7 November 1973, which hails Bobst as "a welcome addition to the city . . . one of New York's most spectacular architectural experiences"; "NYU School of Commerce to Occupy Theater Site," *NYT*, 6 November 1966.

41. "N.Y.U. Buys Hotel in the Village," *NYT*, 21 January 1966.

42. Ballon, "Washington Square Southeast Title I," 244–48; Frusciano and Pettit, *New York University*, 241–42; "Controversial 30-Story Towers Nearing Completion in 'Village,'" *NYT*, 20 February 1966.

43. "Progress Report on New Arts Center."

44. Ballon, "Lincoln Square Title I," 279; also see "Moses Outlines City Within City for Lincoln Sq.," *NYT*, 28 May 1956.

45. "The Evolution of a Great Center," *NYT*, 23 September 1962; "Lincoln Center—the First 20 Years," *NYT*, 20 May 1979; "Lincoln Sq. Given 27 Million by U.S. to Help in Razing," *NYT*, 25 December 1957.

46. "Moses Outlines City Within City."

47. "Fordham Hails Role in Project," *NYT*, 9 December 1957.

48. Ballon, "Lincoln Square Title I," 281; "Fordham Unveils Lincoln Sq. Stone; Warren Is Speaker," *NYT*, 4 May 1960; "Razing Dates Set for Lincoln Sq.," *NYT*, 17 July 1958; "Fordham University," http:/www.fordham.edu, accessed 11 August 2011; "Mixed Grades for University's Growth Plan," *NYT*, 23 September 2007.

Index

Acknowledgments

We dedicate our book to the late emeritus Penn historian Lee Benson, who inspired us in many ways. Lee is perhaps best remembered as the pioneering American historian whose book *The Concept of Jacksonian Democracy* introduced social science theory and methods to the academic study of history. Lee was a World War II combat veteran—a platoon leader in Germany in 1945, a participant in the liberation of Dachau concentration camp, and a recipient of the Purple Heart and the Bronze Star for Valor. Remarkably, in light of the wartime horrors he experienced, Lee remained irrepressibly optimistic about the human condition and dedicated to making a better world. A visionary, Lee was also a pragmatist: no armchair leftist, he put his social theory into practice and recruited agents to apply his ideas. He took to heart Marx's admonition in the *Eleventh Thesis on Feuerbach* that social theorists have only interpreted the world; the point is to change it. Lee publicly chided his fellow academic historians for ignoring the *Eleventh Thesis*, for distancing themselves from social problems, for writing what he described as self-referential monographs that had no meaning for the wider society. His was a brave, radical stance that alienated many in his profession. Lee's heroes were practical theorists; his role models were Francis Bacon, Benjamin Franklin, John Dewey, Simon Nelson Patten, and Kurt Lewin. For the last thirty years of his life, he dedicated himself tirelessly to the creation and application of practical theories that have since contributed to making Penn the bellwether institution for an international civic engagement movement. Conversations with Lee starting some twenty-five years ago helped shape John Puckett's interest in Penn's history in West Philadelphia. Mark Lloyd came into Lee's orbit at a later point, when Lee convinced him to turn his attention to West Philadelphia in the twentieth century. In no small way, we attribute our collaboration to Lee's influence.

■

This book has taken nine years to produce. Along the way, we have acquired considerable debts we wish to acknowledge here. We single out Ira Harkavy and Mike Zuckerman for special mention. Not only did these two Penn historians share with us valuable information and insights based on their combined eighty years of experience at Penn, Ira and Mike also served as sounding boards for our interpretations of particular controversies, advised us on the organization of the manuscript, and counseled us on the politics of publishing a book about our own campus. We are indebted to University administrators Joann Mitchell and Leslie Kruhly, who endorsed Mark Lloyd's full participation in this project. For graciously providing oral histories and perspectives on Penn, we owe special thanks to Walter Palmer, David Brownlee, the late Sheldon Hackney, Leo Molinaro, Mike Roepel, Fran Scott, Barry Slepian, and Judy Wicks. We gratefully acknowledge Amy Orr, Ann Froehling, and Marty Solitrin for sharing with us Penn-related documents in their possession. Sheldon Hackney generously allowed us to draw on the journals he kept during his presidency of Penn. Rick Redding, director of community planning at the Philadelphia City Planning Commission, provided valuable documents and reports compiled by the Planning Commission in the 1950s and 1960s; Rick also shared with us his inimitable knowledge of West Philadelphia neighborhoods.

Archivists and librarians provided indispensable assistance for our research. We owe special thanks to J. M. Duffin, Nancy R. Milner, Alyssa B. Sheldon, and the late Mary D. McConaghy for their exceptional assistance with the historical collections at the University Archives and Records Center of the University of Pennsylvania. We also gratefully acknowledge the fine assistance provided by Brenda Galloway of the Special Collections Research Center at Temple University; David T. Baugh of the Philadelphia City Archives; William Keller of Penn's Fine Arts Library; and Hilda Pring, Patty Lynn, and Lee Pugh of Van Pelt Library.

We are particularly indebted to Eric Halpern, director of Penn Press, who welcomed our manuscript and shepherded it to publication. We also thank Edward Wade, our production editor; John Raymond, our copyeditor; Michael Koehler and James Mann, who contributed the contemporary photographs; and J. M. Duffin, who designed the book's spatial maps and mapped U.S. Census data for us.

We are indebted to Jennifer M. Moore and John Wallace for their superb assistance with editorial matters. We wish to thank four talented research assistants who worked with us at various stages of the project: Erin Walsh, Arjun Shankar, Kailey Spencer, and Horatio Blackman. For exceptional computer support and technical assistance, we are grateful to Zach Nachsin, Rakeem Jeter, and Kate McGuire. Special thanks to administrative staff members at Penn Graduate School of Education for their timely and gracious support: Alexis Wolfson, Kat Stein, Allison Palmer, Jane Lindahl, Diane Boyle, Joyce Cook, and Theresa Singleton. For their unstinted support and encouragement, we also thank Elaine Simon, Barry Slepian, Ruth Slepian, Ruth Moorman, and Sheldon Simon.

We gratefully acknowledge a research grant from the Spencer Foundation for our study of University Redevelopment Area Unit 3; we also thank the Penn Diversity Fund for its support. For permission to republish parts of "Penn's Great Expansion: Postwar Urban Renewal and the Alliance Between Private Universities and the Public Sector," *Pennsylvania Magazine of History and Biography* 137, no. 4 (2003), we thank PMHB's editor, Tamara Gaskell.

Lastly, we wish to acknowledge the personal support of loved ones. John Puckett thanks his wife, Karin Schaller, who helps him keep his head when all about him are losing theirs. Mark Lloyd thanks his loyal partner, Zelphia Ellerson, and his children, Kate Lloyd and Duncan Lloyd, who continually encouraged him throughout this decadelong undertaking.